A REMARKABLE S
OF THE SMALL-COLLEGE PROFESSOR
AND THE ATHLETES HE COACHED
ON SOME OF THE BEST CROSS COUNTRY
AND TRACK TEAMS IN THE NATION

The BAST BOYS

LARRY W. ARRINGTON, ED.D.

Outskirts Press, Inc.
Denver, Colorado

The Bast Boys
A Remarkable Story of the Small-College Professor and the Athletes He Coached On Some of the Best Cross Country and Track Teams in the Nation

V3.0

Outskirts Press, Inc.
http://www.outskirtspress.com

ISBN: 978-1-4327-2205-0

PRINTED IN THE UNITED STATES OF AMERICA

Dedication

I dedicate this book to Charles Homer Bast, who inspired us all to do our best. You were our teacher, coach, and friend–a gentle man who never stopped giving of yourself to others. We cherish the memories.

Preface

In the fall of 2006, I was retired and looking for new and interesting places to take nature photographs. Photography was a hobby born in that retirement. I decided to take my third trip through the American west and to visit the scenic Glacier National Park in Montana.

On the way, I was standing at a nearby RV in a park near Mount Rushmore in South Dakota, talking to a fellow traveler. My cell phone rang and on the other end was a gentleman representing Roanoke College. He told me about an upcoming ceremony honoring a former track and cross country coach at the College. A generous grant from an alumnus had updated the outdoor track facilities, and the track and surrounding areas were to be dedicated to C. Homer Bast. Homer, long retired, was a very successful professor, administrator, and coach at Roanoke for many years. His distance runners dominated State and Conference athletics for 13 years. His indoor and outdoor track teams often beat teams from much larger schools, and the outdoor program produced almost 40 straight dual- and tri-meet wins over several seasons.

In short, I was invited to be present at the dedication ceremony. I remember telling the caller that I was on a trip, that I was headed all the way to the northern reaches of Montana, and that afterwards I had scheduled trips to national parks such as Yellowstone, the Grand Teton, the five parks in Utah, and much, much more. No, I said. I just couldn't be back in Salem in time for the dedication.

So on I went toward Glacier National Park. For several days, I drove the famous Going-to-the-Sun road, through the park's pristine forests and across the rugged mountains. I stopped to enjoy the park's spectacular lakes. The area was a nature photographer's dream.

Then one night, as I sat around a small campsite fire, my mind returned to the phone call. Surely, I thought, I couldn't possibly cut my trip short to get back to Salem in the few days left before the ceremony. But then, in the soft glow of the fire, I thought about my own days at Roanoke. I entered the school as a student in the fall of 1959. I had enjoyed some success in throwing the shot and discus at a local high school, and wanted to be a part of the Maroon team I had heard so much about.

World Civilization was the first course I can remember taking. I got to class and took a seat on the front row, eager to take part in this new part of my life. The door swung open and in walked this tall, thin professor, with an overflowing brief case in his hands. He took out the book for our course and, leaning forward, looked into all of our eyes. Good morning, he said. I'm Professor Homer Bast, and I will be your teacher in this course.

Homer was an extraordinary teacher. He knew his subject well, but more importantly, his teaching style was simple and memorable. When he talked, it was like hearing your mom tell you a story before you went to bed. He seemed to make eye contact with me and everyone around me. He would lean forward to make a point. He would wrap himself around a column in front of the room, or drape himself across the lectern, and his voice would rise and fall with inflections that added interest and melody to his voice.

He also managed to give some of the most difficult tests I had ever taken. Each question, as I remember, had four or five multiple-choice answers. There was a subtle shade of difference between each answer. Although Homer made the class interesting, I had never thought of majoring in history. Many times during that semester, I would stay up most of the night with my pack of self-made flash cards, memorizing the hundreds of facts that might be on the next morning's history test.

But Homer was far more than a classroom teacher. To me and many others, he was a true friend. He wanted me to succeed. I could go to him with any question, whether it was about history or about my personal life. He would sit with me for as long as I needed him, taking time away from his official college duties. I left his office feeling good about myself. He was a very giving person. That first semester, in preparation for the coming track season, I wanted to work on changing my form in the shot put. "Come on down to the track this morning around 10:00," Homer said to me after about a week, "Let's work on some techniques that will make you a better thrower."

So, two or three times a week, until the cold days of winter prevailed, Homer and I would work together. I had never had a track coach in high school who knew anything about the shot put event, so I was eager to get Homer's advice. What I didn't know was that Homer didn't know much about the event himself. Recently, he told me that he would go back to the office after our workouts together and read a book on shot putting. He would learn enough to keep him, and me, on the right path when we met again. Here he was, a man who had given up being the track coach some three years before I arrived, and he was willing to take his time to help this kid from Roanoke City be the best he could be.

Professor Bast was known for his excellence in teaching History to thousands of Roanoke College students.

After graduating from Roanoke in 1963, I spent a few short years in teaching, coaching, and graduate work. Then I had the good fortune not only to return to Roanoke, but to take over the head track and cross country coaching position from Elwood Fox. Elwood had been the coach who succeeded Homer. Through those years of college coaching, it was good to know that Homer, a campus legend by that time, was always nearby and willing to help. After a week of working with my cross country runners during my first year as a coach, I was still trying to determine what training methods to use. I saw Homer outside the Administration Building one day and asked him how he knew how much was enough. In other words, I said, how do you know if a workout is too easy or too hard? The first thing he told me was to look at the runners' eyes. Then he explained some simple techniques to use in practices. He had been a fan of Fartlek training, a form of conditioning that put stress mainly on the aerobic energy system because of the continuous nature of the exercise. Most of Homer's Fartlek sessions with runners would vary from aerobic jogging to anaerobic sprinting. Any runner who ever had Homer as a coach knows very well what the method meant to him in preparing for his next performance. Homer also told me about adding the personal touch to my coaching. "Know the athlete. Care about him. Be a part of his life. And most of all encourage him to be the best he can be–in sports and throughout the rest of his days after college."

This was the Homer Bast we all came to love. Sitting near that campfire in Glacier, I could see him and all he meant to me in those days long ago. He was about 92 by that time, and his wife, Mary Jane, was a few years younger. They still lived in the brick house they built on Locust Street in Salem during the early 1950s. It was the house where two sons were born and raised. It was the house where hundreds of Homer's athletes visited over the years. It was the house where they still come today, almost to say "Thanks, Coach" for everything he had meant to them when they were young.

I thought to myself, how could I *not* go to the track dedication ceremony? So I left Glacier the next morning. Driving 10-12 hours a day, I arrived in Salem the day before the event was to occur. On the morning of the ceremony, I strolled out to the new facility with the red running surface and met a number of Homer's athletes who had returned from all over the country to share the moment with their coach. People from the Alumni Office brought Homer and Mary Jane over to the track by golf cart. It had been difficult during the past few years for either of them to walk very far. They were greeted personally by hundreds of individuals. Then everybody was seated for the dedication ceremony.

There were two or three speeches before Homer was asked to say a few words himself. Slowed by age, he was assisted to the podium and began to talk. It was déjà vu. This was the engaging, personable Professor Bast I had as a teacher when I was a freshman in college. This man was the icon of a successful coach, the type of person you always strived to emulate. And as he talked about the days of the 40s and 50s, and of all the wonderful athletes who had been a part of the track and cross country programs at Roanoke during those times, I thought to myself, "This is what it's all about. This is a story worth telling." And the feeling was intensified as I sat at his house that night, listening to him and others re-telling all of the old stories again and again.

At that moment, at least in my mind, I became an author. Seven months later, after researching every *Roanoke Times* and *Brackety-Ack* article on the Bast days, after finding more information from archives in places ranging from Virginia to North Carolina to Philadelphia, and after conducting oral interviews with dozens of Homer's former athletes, I began to write this book.

Many people have contributed in a positive way to my venture. First, I say thank you to Linda Miller and Nancy Logan at Roanoke College. Little did they know how long and how often I would bother them with my ongoing research in the Library Archives. We got to know each other so well that on many days, they would lock the door behind them after their days were finished, leaving me to work alone in the Archives area. And I will always be grateful to Stan Umberger, Director of the Library. He gave me private rooms in which to work and treated me as if I were a personal friend. Each day, I was helped greatly by the other librarians and clerical staff–Sara Blaha, Rebecca Heller, Hany Hosny, Jeffrey Martin, Patty Powell, and Dave Wiseman, in particular.

Another thank you goes to Kim Blair '93, Director of Development at Roanoke College, and to her co-worker, Sara Woody Jamison '06. Without Sara, I never would have been able to obtain the names, addresses, phone numbers, and even email addresses of former athletes.

I also appreciate the many individuals who sat patiently through interviews, talking about their own lives and how those lives were inextricably intertwined with Homer. I sensed that in all cases, their time spent in helping me was a labor of love–a tribute to one of the most admired persons in their lives and to the many teammates with whom they lived the track and cross country life.

But most of all, I wish to thank Homer Bast himself. He welcomed me into his home, gave me whatever information he could in more than 20 recorded sessions (about 30 hours of memories), and dug through old papers for documents and pictures I could use. He may be slowing down with age, using a cane to get around the house, but he can still tell a tale with the best of 'em. And Homer, you married well. Mary Jane was a jewel.

I hope you enjoy this book. I have loved writing it–getting to know the athletes themselves and understanding what these men and their teams accomplished so many years ago. And if the book brings back memories for you, re-pay me by doing one thing. Sit down and write Homer a letter or pick up the phone and call him. Better yet, visit him on Locust Street. It will be an experience you won't soon forget.

Chapter One

Mr. Bast Comes to Salem

It was the summer of 1946. Striding across the Roanoke College campus was a tall, articulate young man, C. Homer Bast, who had just been released from his service in the United States Navy. He was looking for a teaching position in history, and his upcoming job interview was scheduled at 11:00 a.m. with Dean Deloss Myers and the Chair of the school's history department, C. R. Brown.

Homer had taught and coached at Staunton Military Institute before his military service. He liked the school, and Staunton was where he had met his wife, Mary Jane. Both were familiar with the town and its people, but mutually decided that Staunton was not the place to continue Homer's teaching career. Mary Jane liked Virginia, and Homer did also. He had spent eight wonderful years in undergraduate and graduate work at the University of Virginia. Teaching jobs were easy to come by at all levels in those days, and he really didn't know if he wanted to stay in prep school teaching or take a college job. A couple of weeks before his trip to Roanoke College, he noticed an article in the Staunton News Leader that said "Dr. Charles Smith needs additional faculty." Dr. Smith was the long-time President at Roanoke. Homer knew a few things about the school, mainly because of the publicity the Five Smart Boys in basketball had gotten when they almost won the national championship. The Smart Boys team had won two consecutive state titles and played in the National International Tournament (the N. I. T.) finals. They also had competed against the University of Virginia while Homer was a student there.

Homer took a seat outside Dean Myers' office. Soon, the door opened and out stepped Dr. Myers, who shook Homer's hand and told him how much he had looked forward to meeting him. Deloss Myers had been a good addition to the Roanoke staff and was recognized across the campus as a thorough, competent individual. His Ph.D. was from Princeton. He knew where he wanted the school to go, and had the smarts to take it there.

The interview lasted the good part of an hour. The only problem came when Dr. Myers asked Homer his opinion of the famous historian, Dr. Arnold Toynbee. Homer, who knew little about Toynbee, fumbled for an answer. As he told his wife that night, "I thought sure that my prospects for a job at Roanoke were suddenly zero." But as Homer rose to leave after the usual pleasantries, Dean Myers looked at him and said "I want to see you again, Mr. Bast. Can you come down next week? And would you bring your wife? Mary Jane also had to pass inspection. To Homer, that would never be a problem. Mary Jane Bast was attractive, smart, and at ease in conversation. She knew instinctively how to act–and she was a tremendous hit with Dean Myers and C. R. Brown when the Basts visited the campus. As Homer later said, "I think they loved her more than they loved me."

At any rate, Homer was offered a job at Roanoke. He was told that he would have four courses of World Civilization to teach that next year, along with one course in European History. That was quite a heavy load for someone who had never taught history before. The school offered him a salary of $2,000 per year. Because Homer had some experience in teaching as a graduate student at the University of Virginia, and because he had come close to getting a Ph.D., Dr. Myers started him as an Assistant Professor and the College considered $2,000 per year to be quite a handsome sum for a beginning faculty member. Mary Jane and Homer went back to Staunton and, with little hesitation, notified Myers that Homer would take the job.

The Basts' first apartment was in the Methodist Church Sunday School Building in downtown Salem. Rev. Curry wanted someone in the building to show an adult presence to the many youths who met there. He gave Homer and Mary Jane one of two rooms on the third floor. The new tenants had to buy their own refrigerator and stove. They had neither bathtub nor shower. When Mary Jane wanted to bathe, she went over to Smith Hall. After getting permission from the Dean of Women, Nellie Mangus, she used their facilities. Homer took his showers in the gymnasium. The Basts stayed in that apartment for their entire first year.

Homer was just one of a number of new professors brought to the campus in the fall of 1946, and housing for these individuals was tight. The new staff was needed to meet the onslaught of former service men and women who were either starting their college careers, or who were coming back after one or more years in the service. Indeed, the GI Bill brought the college enrollment that fall to more than 600 students. The projected enrollment was 400 to 500. Incidentally, many of the new 18 faculty members eventually served more than 30 years at Roanoke. Besides Homer Bast, there were Fran Ramser, Elwood Fox, Zeb Hooker, Frank and Lucille Snow, and others. The College struggled to provide adequate facilities. Students faced delays in the Commons and the placement of bunk beds in their dormitories.

During the first three months of the first semester, Homer was kept busy trying to prepare for and teach his five classes. He often thought that he was struggling more than were his students. He had been away from classes in history for some time. His last class in history, in fact, had come in 1940. "I was rusty," he said, "and had to study particularly hard to prepare for each day's lesson."

In the back of his mind, having been a track runner at the University of Virginia, Homer knew that he wanted to start a track and cross country program at Roanoke. Cross country would be a brand new sport for the college, while track and field athletics had been dropped from the sports schedule after 1930. Homer learned quickly that around 1929, the school had constructed a new cinder track. But through all of the years since its construction, the facility had fallen into disrepair.

At the University of Virginia, Homer had been a good middle-distance runner. His team won the Virginia state championships from 1934 through 1937, and Homer was a member of the mile relay team which won the Southern Conference meet in 1936. While in graduate school at the University, from 1938 to 1940, he also served as Assistant Coach to Archie Mann. So it seemed natural that he would be interested in track and distance running at Roanoke.

Top Left: The new faculty members in the fall of 1946. Many of these individuals, like Homer Bast, worked at Roanoke College until they retired.
Top Right: The Sections in the year Homer Bast joined the college staff.
Bottom: The college campus in 1946. Photo courtesy of Pater Boisseau, alumnus, who took the picture.

The first thing Homer did in the late fall of 1946 was to visit Roanoke's Athletic Director, Buddy Hackman. Hackman was a tenacious competitor who had played football with some distinction at the University of Tennessee under Coach Bob Neyland and had graduated from that school in 1930. In fact, he was a member of the Flaming Sophomores at Tennessee, a fabled group of players still remembered today. Many remember Hackman as the tailback in the Neyland single wing. He also excelled on defense. He had joined the Roanoke College coaching staff in 1935 and went on to serve as Athletic Director for nearly 30 years.

"I'd like to form and coach a cross country and track team," Bast said to Buddy. I think these teams would be good for the College and for our students." After mulling over the point for a minute or two, Buddy told Homer, "If it doesn't cost me anything, I'm for it."

Homer figured that he could get an old shot and discus from another coach, and thought that Harry Hodges, who headed the Maintenance Department, might be able to build him some hurdles. Homer was careful, however, to avoid a discussion of the rebuilding of the track. At the time, he couldn't envision how much labor or money would be involved in that project.

That conversation was the first step in cementing a personal connection between the two. Buddy finally did give Homer some money for uniforms, although the athletic budget as a whole was anemic. In his second year at the college, Homer began to serve the first of many years as faculty representative to the NCAA and other athletic organizations. He and Buddy would drive to Mason-Dixon Conference meetings together. Sometimes, Buddy would talk the entire trip about his days at Tennessee. At the very least, the two became close friends.

Homer knew, however, that there was little money to put the track facility into usable condition. Thinking about the problem, Homer walked down to the athletic field one day to look more carefully at the old track. On the front side, near Market Street, one still could see the inside and outside boundary boards; however, there wasn't much left on the back side straightaway except a path where an occasional walker had been over the years. Almost all of the original cinders, all the way around the track, had either been compacted or were missing. He began to think about the people who could help restore the track.

The next day, he walked down to see some of the people in Salem who might help him restore the track. His pitch was simple. "I told them what I wanted to do," said Homer, "and I think they were interested because there was no track for high school athletes in the area. The closest tracks, in fact, were at Virginia Polytechnic Institute in Blacksburg and Virginia Military Institute in Lexington. Even the youngsters at Jefferson High School in Roanoke–a school known for excellence in athletics–didn't have a track.

So I really didn't have any problem getting their assistance. First, I told them I needed a scraper. We had to scrape the track to see what was there, of course. Salem workers brought up a big scraper (one of the big road scrapers, in fact) and found quickly where the inside and outside boards were located. They scraped the entire track and put all of the dirt/cinder mixture in various piles around the track."

Next, Homer knew he needed cinders – and lots of them. So he went down to Roanoke to visit Jack Fishwick, President of the Norfolk and Western Railroad and an alumnus of Roanoke College. Jack was a member of the same church that Home and Mary Jane attended in Salem. He also lived near the Basts in Salem. By the time Homer approached Fishwick, the two were on good enough relations that Homer and Mary Jane often visited Jack and Blair Fishwick in their home. All four were members of the Democratic Party. During the Presidential elections of 1948, the four even watched the poll results of the Truman/Dewey battle. They all went to bed thinking that Dewey had won.

At any rate, Homer didn't mince words. "I need some cinders, Jack." Fishwick asked him why. Homer told him that the cinders were needed in order to rebuild the Roanoke College track. Of course, he didn't know much about cinders – only that he needed a lot of them. Fishwick asked Homer if he wanted front-end or rear-end cinders. Bast didn't know the difference, so Fishwick explained that front-end cinders were finer in texture. So Bast asked for the front-end cinders, but then it hit him that even those so-called fine cinders might not be as fine as he needed. He went back to the College and talked to Harry Hodges again. He persuaded Harry to make him five sieves, and these sieves were placed at various points around the track.

The next day, Homer got a call from Jack. "I have 40 tons of front-end cinders for you," he told Homer. "They'll be on the siding down here in Salem by tomorrow." But how was Homer to pick up the cinders and take them to the track?

He went back to the Salem maintenance people and explained what he needed. They loaned the College a couple of trucks along with some manpower, and hauled those 40 tons of cinder (with the help of the College maintenance crew) up to the new track. The cinders were dumped into huge piles around the track.

For the next three months, Homer and several very loyal students began to sift the cinders every day that the weather allowed. Before putting those sifted cinders onto the track surface, however, Homer asked for the scrapers to return. He had to get down to the bedrock to see what kind of drainage system had been installed in 1928-29 for the original track. The scrapers soon found the upper layer of rock and a beautiful drainage system. There were small rocks on medium rocks on larger rocks. After it was determined that the drainage system probably was adequate, Homer then faced the problem of finding some clay to mix with the cinders. Somehow, the town found the clay.

They loaned the College their trucks and workers, and they brought the clay to the track area. They would load a truck with cinders, open its tailgate a bit, and as they drove the truck around the track a constant stream of cinders would fall out onto the track surface. Then they would do the same thing with the clay. After the process had been repeated several times, a heavy roller (but not so heavy as to crush the drainage system) was loaned by the town and their engineers and it was rolled around and around the oval.

All in all, there was tremendous cooperation between Norfolk and Western, the town of Salem, and Roanoke College. By the end of the 1946-47 session, with much help from students, the new track was finished. Although Homer formed a track team that first year, the College was unable to schedule meets on the track until the following year.

With this huge project on the way to completion, and in the early spring of 1947, Homer then turned his attention to bringing together the students who would make up the first varsity track squad since 1929.

Chapter Two
THE FIRST TRACK TEAM

In December of 1946, Homer and Mary Jane spent their first Christmas together in Salem. Looking back on his brief tenure at Roanoke, despite the heavy load of courses he was responsible for in the History Department, the first semester had gone by quickly. Already, he was getting a reputation on campus for being an excellent teacher. The reconstruction of the cinder track had not been easy, but it was made bearable through a mutual effort involving Homer, the school's maintenance department, the town of Salem, Norfolk and Western Railroad, and many helpful students. As the second semester approached, it was time for Homer to put together an outdoor track team for the coming season.

The student body was large (about 613 individuals showing up for the second semester) and school spirit seemed to be high, despite the absence of a long-running and successful football program. In March of 1946 a faculty committee had vetoed the return of a football team. Students were stunned. Alumni were outraged. Dr. Charles Smith, Roanoke's President, wasn't opposed to the sport itself, but he was opposed to the increasing costs of scholarships and for maintaining the sport. He said, "Considering Roanoke's financial restraints at the time . . . Roanoke could be a good college or have a good football team. We cannot do both." The *Brackety-Ack* took turns pleading with the administration and berating it. The editors felt that school spirit was the real loser. And there was the matter of a homecoming tradition.

But positive moves by the College were beginning to occur. Students pleaded for a recreational center, and the Cavern had opened in October. With the Cavern came a jukebox, soda fountain, and seating for forty. It was an immediate hit. The students' only complaint was that it was always crowded.

Campus fraternities and sororities had made a comeback during the year. The Pi Kaps obtained quarters above a store on Main Street; the Sigs reclaimed their house, while the KAs could only muster dorm space as a starter. The three sororities brought in 44 new pledges.

The 1946-47 school year had also brought the beginning of an organized athletics program for women. Coach Fran Ramser coached the inaugural basketball season and finished at 3-3-1. Men's basketball returned to its winning ways. Baseball played a full season.

With the addition of a new physical education and coaching staff that year, intramurals also became popular. New competitions included shuffleboard and co-ed soccer. Women's intramurals grew and expanded. Women had become more assertive and confident during the war and now that the men had returned, they were not inclined to resume their older positions and attitudes.

Students were also interested in the new spring sports. It would be the first spring at Roanoke College when four separate varsity sports would be offered.

To bring together his track squad, one of the first things Homer did was to talk with Bob McLelland, a student who wrote sports columns for the campus newspaper, the *Brackety-Ack*. McLelland was a talented, enthusiastic writer and he soon took a liking to Coach Bast. He often called Bast "the big guy" in his columns, and gave the track and cross country teams over the next few years some excellent publicity. Incidentally, Bast was also the faculty member who recommended McLelland for his first newspaper job with a Roanoke paper when he graduated from the College. Later in his career, McLelland was a sports writer and editor of that paper for many years.

Soon there was an article about track in the *Brackety-Ack*. It was entitled, "How About a Track Team?" After a few gushing comments about the advantages of track, the article said "All boys interested should sign up in the gym today. Two of the boys who have expressed interest are Bob Fagg and Larry Stephens. Both were track men at Jefferson High."

Next, Bast began to look for information from the track meets held during the earlier days of competition, through 1929. He reconstructed a set of school records from that era. Always one to distribute motivational materials to his athletes, he felt the old records would be invaluable in bringing out the best in his team. Here is what he found:

Homer Bast in his first days as a coach and history teacher at Roanoke.

Roanoke College Varsity
Intercollegiate Track and Field Records

1913-1929

100-Yard Dash

:10.4	Charles N. "Whitey" Wilson Roanoke College vs. Emory and Henry College Salem, Virginia April 11, 1927

220-Yard Dash

:23.2	Charles N. "Whitey" Wilson Roanoke College vs. Emory and Henry College Emory, Virginia May 9, 1928

440-Yard Dash

:53.0	Herman G. Fisher The First Annual Virginia Conference Track and Field Meet Richmond, Virginia May 12, 1928

880-Yard Run

2:08.0	Ambrose B. Hershberger Roanoke College vs. Hampden-Sydney College Hampden-Sydney, Virginia May 7, 1925

Mile Run

4:53.4	Tate Minix Roanoke College vs. Hampden-Sydney College Hampden-Sydney, Virginia April 29, 1926

Two Miles

10:51.8	Tate Minix Roanoke College vs. Hampden-Sydney College Hampden-Sydney, Virginia May 7, 1925

120-Yard High Hurdles

:18.8	Alfred M. Weikel Roanoke College vs. Emory and Henry College Salem, Virginia April 11, 1927

220-Yard Low Hurdles

:29.0	Martin L. Dellinger Roanoke College vs. Emory and Henry College Salem, Virginia April 11, 1927

Shot Put

41'2½"	Charles N. "Whitey" Wilson The First Annual State Conference Track and Field Meet Richmond, Virginia May 12, 1928

Discus

126′2"	Charles N. "Whitey" Wilson The First Annual State Conference Track and Field Meet Richmond, Virginia May 12, 1928

Javelin

158′3¼"	Charles N. "Whitey" Wilson Roanoke College vs. Emory and Henry College Salem, Virginia April 11, 1927

Broad Jump

21′4½"	Charles N. "Whitey" Wilson Roanoke College vs. Emory and Henry College Emory, Virginia May 9, 1928

High Jump

5′9"	Edwin I. Bell Roanoke College vs. Bridgewater College Salem, Virginia May 4, 1929

Pole Vault

10′3"	Steven F. Miller Roanoke College vs. Virginia Military Institute Lexington, Virginia April, 1927

On Wednesday, February 26, 1947, about 30 track hopefuls reported to the team meeting. Bast seemed quite pleased at the turnout and expressed a desire to get actual workouts underway. Soon, the coach had about two dozen athletes running through easy drills, designed so as not to bring on injuries this early in the season, and working on technique.

The *Brackety-Ack* noted: "For the first time since the era of coonskin coats–1929, to be exact–there'll be a track team at Roanoke College this spring. Two dozen hopefuls . . . slogged in tennis shoes through patches of snow, dug into the wet earth to retrieve a battered brass shot, tossed around an old javelin, and took turns leaping–or knocking down–one rickety hurdle. That was all the equipment left from 18 years ago, when the college abandoned the sport. In addition, the would-be runners had to sidestep barriers left from the more recent days when the Navy's training program erected an obstacle course on the oval cinder track."

About the middle of March, Homer's workouts became more focused. Still, the team didn't yet have enough equipment and supplies to hold a home meet. He turned to Harry Hodges again to build the hurdles and to construct both the pole vault and high jump standards. With the newness of the track surface and the fact that equipment took time to build, he made a decision to schedule all meets at away sites for that first year. Many of the team's workouts took place on grassy surfaces around the campus and, when snow prevented the use of grass, athletes would either move into Alumni Gymnasium to practice starts and high jumping, or they would use the asphalt oval surfaces that surrounded the quadrangle area between the Commons and the Administration Building.

The *Brackety-Ack* continued to support Bast's efforts, often reporting on the progress of the track program. One day in March, Homer confessed to Bob McLelland that the team might not have the depth it needed this first year. The next week, Bob wrote the following newspaper article, entitled "Trackmen Wanted." It went on to say:

> In a talk with Coach Homer Bast about prospects for the 1947 track team, we gathered that his biggest problem seems to be the lack of manpower. Bast explained that a well-manned team should enter three men in each of the 12 events. This means that there are positions on the squad for some 36 men. So far Bast has had considerably less than this number working out.
>
> The weakest events seem to be the sprints, namely the 100 and 220. To date very few boys have reported for these runs.
>
> Coach Bast seemed quite well-pleased with several of his boys. Bob Fagg, former Jefferson High School athlete, brings smiles to his coach's face with the manner in which he handles himself in the high and low

> hurdles. Bob has had quite a bit of hurdling experience and should develop into a stellar performer. Jim Doran, giant basketball center, has the makings of a good weight man. Jim has tossed the sixteen pound shot 43 odd feet and should progress rapidly with the discus. Jim Ruscick, another hardwooder, has had experience in the 440 and half mile runs as well as in the high jump. Many others have looked good, but the bad weather and lack of facilities has hindered workouts considerably.
>
> Good news for the men was received in the form of equipment. A discus and hurdles have been acquired and new materials are on the way. In announcing the manpower shortage, Bast explained that track was not a sport that required a great deal of former experience to participate. The coach stated that he would be glad to work with all hopefuls whether they have had experience or not.

All in all, the team was coming together nicely. Bast seemed satisfied with the team's progress and felt sure that it would be ready for the opening meet on April 22. Unfortunately, the team lacked the leadership and abilities of veterans, although several individuals showed promise. By the middle of March, as Homer mulled over his team roster, he mentally planned what he expected of each man. Bob Fagg had looked good, he thought. Perhaps he might run :10.2 or :10.3 by the end of the year, which would win some meets and place high in others.

He didn't know much about Jim Doran. Jim was a tall and talented center on Buddy Hackman's basketball team, and Homer had encouraged him to compete in track this year. He did know that Doran had potential as a track man. He was big and very athletic–the type of individual who could be good at many sports. Jim had enough raw talent to be the team's first decathlete-type performer, with decent speed and a lot of strength

Bast figured that Paul McCarty might easily run between 2:00 and 2:05 in the half mile race this spring, and had the potential to score some valuable points in the mile run as well.

Red Crockett, like McCarty, was another good prospect. He probably wouldn't be a conference champion distance runner this year, but he could hold his own.

He didn't know yet about Thanning Andersen. Maybe he could score some points in the hurdles.

Bill Williams, had the potential to be the College's first good pole vaulter. If he would get serious and practice his vaulting skills, he might just go 11'0" to 12'0" this year.

Maybe Jim Ruscick could score some points as well in the long jump or high jump. Only time would tell.

As for the rest–Teensey Friend, Dick Fraley, Harry Bower, and others–the coach thought, it was just too early to make predictions. He particularly liked Dick Dodd, however, and thought that he could have made a valuable contribution to the team this spring..

Finally, without knowing what to expect from his rookie team, Bast began his first season as coach with three scheduled meets: Bridgewater College, Randolph-Macon College, and Lynchburg College. Little did anyone imagine in those early days that the next ten years of both cross country and track competition would bring fame to the College and near-legendary celebrity to the coach, and that hundreds of students would become better athletes and better human beings by competing at Roanoke College.

The team met and selected their first Co-Captains–Bob Fagg and Jim Doran. As the first meet approached–a competition with Bridgewater College on April 8, 1947–Homer would never let on to others what he actually thought about his team's chances. Bridgewater had an established team with veteran leadership. Their coach was the already-famous Harry "Doc" Jopson. Dr. Jopson, like Homer Bast, was not only a superior coach, but he was equally skilled as a Professor. His field was biology, and students raved about how much they enjoyed his classes. How could this rag-tag team from Salem manage to compete with Bridgewater?

I remember . . . "Finally, after rounding up a few students who wanted to compete in a track program that first year, I called them all to practice near the first of March. By that time, we had removed some of the waste on the track–enough to show where the inside and outside rails were located. So the boys could determine how long a quarter mile was. At the least, I had a team on paper. It was a rag-tag group, reminding me of the Revolutionary forces of George Washington."

Homer Bast

April 22, 1947
Bridgewater College at Bridgewater, Virginia
Team Scores: Roanoke–64
Bridgewater–62

On the morning of April 22, in front of Alumni Gym, the team piled into its old, school-owned cars (and a student car) and left for its trip to Bridgewater. Not having the benefit of good highways (as they would years later when Interstate 81 was built), the cars wound their way up narrow U. S. 11 to the small Bridgewater campus which was some 60 miles north of Lexington.

After the vehicles were parked, Doc Jopson appeared and offered Homer a warm handshake and welcome. The Bridgewater coach had a unique, likeable personality. Although Homer and Doc had communicated before only a couple of times (by way of U. S. mail), this simple encounter would be the beginning of a life-long friendship between the two, and between their wives, and many years of intense competition between Roanoke and Bridgewater track and cross country teams while Homer was coaching.

The Roanoke athletes were led to the gym to dress for the meet and then begin their warm-ups for the afternoon events. Homer and Doc walked down to the track to see the facilities.

Field events began at 3:00 p.m., with the running to get underway at 3:30 p.m. In the field events, Roanoke athletes did well. Jim Doran won three events (broad jump–18'3¾", shot–38'8½", and discus–118'6"), and placed second in the high jump and third in the javelin. He finished with 19 points in the field events. Then he added a second place in the 100-yard dash and a win in the 220-yard dash to end the day with 27 total points. Jim, along with McCarty and Jim Ruscick, were basketball players on Coach Buddy Hackman's teams.

Other Roanoke field event men also picked up points in their events. Bill Williams won the pole vault with a height of 10'0" and took a second place in the javelin. Ruscick won the high jump by jumping 5'5", while Caroll Dahill was third in the discus. Overall, the weight men compiled 33 points, more than half the team's total for the day.

The other Co-Captain for the Maroons, Bob Fagg, also had a good day. He won the 100-yard dash in :10.8, finished third in the 220-yard dash, and took seconds in the 220-yard low hurdles and the 120-yard high hurdles. His points for the afternoon totaled 12.

Other highlights of the meet included the breaking of two school records by Paul McCarty and Thanning Andersen. Freshman McCarty, from Kearneysville, West Virginia, clocked a 2:05.8 half mile to better the old mark of 2:08.0 set by Ambrose Hershberger in 1925. That time by McCarty was excellent, Homer thought, because McCarty had never run track before coming to Roanoke. Andersen, a freshman from Richmond, cleared the 120-yard high hurdles in :18.1 and thus erased Alfred Weikel's :18.8 mark recorded in 1927.

Two additional Maroons also scored. Red Crockett took third place in the two-mile run, while Andersen was third in the 220-yard low hurdles.

At the end of the meet, Roanoke had rolled up 9 firsts, 5 seconds, and 6 thirds. Unbelievably, the final score showed Roanoke to be the winner by two points, 64 to 62. Team members learned that they were not as bad as the student body thought they might be. And Homer learned a good lesson also. During the meet, the Maroon coach's excitement was evident. In fact, at one point, he was running down the backstretch, side by side with one of his athletes, encouraging the runner to give just a bit more effort.

"You can do it," he would yell. "Run faster." After the meet, Doc Jopson explained tactfully and in a fatherly way that pacing a runner was against the rules. He said to Homer, "We just don't do that anymore." Homer was appreciative of the tip, and he was a quick learner. For the next ten years, his athletics would always hear him yelling words of encouragement–a Homer trademark–but there was no pacing them around the track.

Everyone was pleased with the results. After arriving back on the Salem campus, the news spread fast and many of the boys were congratulated by fellow students. Their win had been "sensational," said the *Brackety-Ack*.

I remember . . . "When we went up to Bridgewater to start our first season, we had virtually no money and needed shoes and equipment badly. In fact, Jim Doran hadn't even seen a shot or discus. So I asked Harry Jopson, their coach, if he had any old shot and discus to give us. And he did. I think he gave us a javelin, too, and maybe some old high jump and pole vault standards."

Homer Bast

I remember . . . "I wasn't expecting Harry Jopson even to keep a score. Harry didn't have a public address system on the track, so I never realized during the meet what the score was. We ended up beating his team by two points."

Homer Bast

I remember . . . "When we went to Bridgewater for our first meet, Homer Bast drove one car and Warren Snead, a sophomore, drove the other one. There was a kid on our team named Thanning Andersen, and when the gun went off, you almost had to punch him to get him to start the race. He was so deaf he couldn't hear the gun. Andersen won the high hurdles that day, and I was just behind him. I also ran the 100 and 220. Others on that team included Jim Doran and Jim Ruscick, both of whom were primarily basketball players. Doran was a fine athlete. He could throw the shot, discus, and javelin, broad jump, and high jump. He was one of the best coordinated people I have ever seen. I think he was about 6'3"in height. And Ruscick was like a cat. He had more spring than anyone I think I have ever seen. He was a forward on the basketball team, while Doran was their center. They both came from Muhlenberg College, arriving at Roanoke at mid-season. They hadn't even been to a class when Coach Hackman's team went up to Charlottesville and played the University of Virginia."

Bob Fagg

I remember . . . "Harry Jopson, the Bridgewater coach, was a good friend. We got to know each other the first year that I was coaching, in 1947. He is three years older than I am, and had been teaching at Bridgewater even before the war. He was from Philadelphia, but born and raised in South Carolina. His father was a physician. And he and I just seemed to get along well right away. We saw eye-to-eye on so many things. He introduced me to Dorsey Griffith, the famous track coach at Catholic, and between the three of us, when we would go to any of the meetings, we were sort of inseparable. Harry and I got to the point where we wanted our teams to be like Harvard and Yale or Princeton and Yale who went over to run Oxford and Cambridge, and the next year Oxford and Cambridge would come back for another competition. We thought about putting the Bridgewater and Roanoke teams together and find a couple of schools over in Europe and go over there and run them. Well, we never got to first base on that because we could never get the money together. But we would let our imaginations run wild. Because I had know him longer than just about anyone else in track coaching–and certainly longer than my colleagues at Roanoke College–we got along well. He was very nice to me. We became so close that he suggested one time that in order to cut expenses, we could bring our boys up there to Bridgewater and we would all get on the Bridgewater bus. And we would help them with our expenses. It was a good idea. And that bonded the Bridgewater and Roanoke people. And when we were up north at a Mason-Dixon meet, the two teams would eat out together. Mary Jane and I began to socialize more with them, and his wife and Mary Jane got along beautifully. His personality and mine were very close. I don't mean to be snobbish or anything, but he went to Haverford and Cornell, and I went to Mercersburg and the University of Virginia. And we had a lot in common as a result of that schooling that would come out over the course of the years. 'Oh, you experienced that too?' You find one of those friends once in a lifetime. And we have kept in contact over the past few years. It was a good relationship."

Homer Bast

I remember . . . "I remember Harry and his wife well. Sometimes, when Bridgewater came to Roanoke for a meet, she and I would spend some time together. We would sit together on the bleachers during the meet in the cold–and it always seemed to be cold–but Hope and I were determined to be there to support our husbands and the two teams."

Mary Jane Bast

I remember . . . "I remember Fanning Andersen for several reasons. One was the fact that he was totally deaf. Everyone beat him on the start because he couldn't hear the gun.

He was in my history class, so I put him in the front row. For anything he couldn't understand, I would put it on the board. He was a particularly-good lip reader. I had to continuously face him. If I made a mistake and turned away, I had to remember to turn around and repeat what I had said."

Homer Bast

April 28, 1947
Randolph-Macon College at Ashland, Virginia
Team Scores: Randolph-Macon–76
Roanoke–50

But it was time to turn their attention to the next meet, scheduled for just six days later. The opponent would be Randolph-Macon College. It was difficult in those days to learn much about the talent on Virginia teams. Most of the contact between coaches–and that was little–was done by mail. Homer had heard, however, that Randolph-Macon might have a few good athletes. They might be able to beat Roanoke, in fact, although this knowledge was never brought to the Roanoke team's attention. Homer was positive about future competition, as he was throughout his career. "You can do it," he would tell the boys. "You can win this meet. You can set a new personal record. You just need to think you can."

Ashland, Virginia, north of Richmond, was the home of Randolph-Macon and the trip to get there meant a drive of more than 180 miles from the Salem campus. Today's travel time between the two schools might be around three hours; however, in 1947, it took over four hours to make the trip.

The team arrived in Ashland around 1:00 p.m. and quickly dressed for the meet. Bill Williams, who surely would have won or scored in the pole vault and the javelin, did not make the trip. Unfortunately, he was in the hospital with a foot injury.

Co-Captains Bob Fagg and Jim Doran continued to lead the scoring parade for Roanoke, as they picked up 13 and 18 points, respectively. Fagg won both the 100-yard dash in :10.6 and the 120-yard high hurdles in :16.6, breaking the school record of :18.1 in that event, set by Thanning Andersen the week before. He also placed second in the 220-yard low hurdles. Doran won the shot and discus events along with the 220-yard dash and finished behind Fagg in the 100-yard dash.

Roanoke's Jim Ruscick won the high jump with a leap of 5'6½", Paul McCarty won the 880-yard run in 2:09.0, and Red Crockett finished first in the two-mile run with an effort of 11:09.0. Other Maroon scoring came from Rannie Taylor (third in the two-mile run) and Thanning Andersen (third in the 220-yard low hurdles).

Roanoke lost to Randolph-Macon by a score of 76 to 50. It was evident to Homer that, even with Bill Williams along on the trip, he couldn't have won. It was purely a case of being outnumbered. In the fourteen events, the Maroons captured six first places and tied for two more to split even with the Yellow Jackets. However, the Jackets gathered the winning points by placing second and third in most events.

I remember . . . "It was a long rip to Randolph-Macon in those days. I had my convertible at the time, and I took it on this and the other trips. Lots of the boys wanted to ride with me because we had a radio in the car."

Homer Bast

May 17, 1947
Lynchburg College at Lynchburg, Virginia
Team Scores: Roanoke–80½
Lynchburg–45½

During the next few days, Homer continued to get his team in good physical condition. They had just one more meet left–against Lynchburg College at Lynchburg–and he wanted to end the year on a positive note. The coach was satisfied with the efforts of his team during this inaugural season, and always talked positively to the athletes about their progress. He also knew that Bridgewater had already beaten Lynchburg, and that his team had beaten Bridgewater. It looked as if the Maroons would close strong. Then, according to the *Brackety-Ack*, Bob Fagg walked into Homer's office prior to the Lynchburg meet and dropped a bombshell, telling Homer that he would be leaving the team. Bast was understanding but knew what Fagg's absence would mean to the squad during the final meet and in all of the outdoor competition during the coming season. Fagg, who had attended Roanoke's Jefferson High School, had been scoring about 15 points a meet by collecting points in the 100, 220, and the low and high hurdles. "Coach," he said, "since I have been participating in track this season, my studies have taken a serious drop. It may be wise for me to devote more time to the books."

The news was all over the campus within the hour. In its next issue of the *Brackety-Ack,* Bob McLelland noted that with the loss of Fagg, the track team would have quite a day's work to defeat the Hornets. "Much comment will no doubt be passed along as to whether Fagg's action was justified or not," said the columnist. "However, this column after talking to him believes that his resignation is very sincere and comes only after a lot of thought. In other words, we believe that Fagg is doing only what he thinks best for his progress here at Roanoke."

A few days later, just before the final meet, Fagg changed his mind and practiced with the team once again. Homer, of course, was delighted. He had already released names of the probable entrants for the Lynchburg meet to the *Brackety-Ack*. The names included:

100-Yard Dash	Ralph Kennedy and Jim Doran
220-Yard Dash	Ralph Kennedy, Jim Doran, and Jack Thurman
440-Yard Dash	Rud Rosebro and Bill Myers
880-Yard Run	Paul McCarty and Maynard Turk
Mile Run	Bill Williams, Paul McCarty, and Ranny Taylor
Two-Mile Run	Red Crockett and Rannie Taylor
Pole Vault	Bill Williams and Steve Stone
Shot	Jim Doran and Carroll Dahill
Javelin	Hal Dunbar and Jim Doran
Discus	Ray Minnix, Jim Doran, and Carroll Dahill
High Jump	Jim Ruscick, Bill Williams, and Jim Doran
Broad Jump	Jim Doran and Jim Ruscick
Low Hurdles	Rud Rosebro and Thanning Andersen
High Hurdles	Rud Rosebro and Thanning Andersen

Lynchburg College sat along U. S. 460 about 67 miles from Salem. The connecting road was narrow and crooked, and it took the Salem squad about an hour and a half to make the trip.

In the field events that afternoon at the Lynchburg Municipal Stadium, Roanoke scored 22 points. Homer was pleased, also, to see that the boys set three new school records in the process. Jim Doran broke the Maroons' discus record previously set in 1928 by big Whitey Wilson, with a fine throw of 129'3". The throw also set a new stadium record, and was a school record that would stand for many years. He also set a new record in the shot put by recording a throw of 41'5", beating the old 41'2½" mark by Whitey Wilson from 1928. Bill Williams set the third record, jumping 11'0". The old record was 10'3", previously set in 1927 by Steven Miller.

The Maroons went on to win five of the eight running events. The real shocker was a time of :10.0 (a new school record) in the 100-yard dash, set by Bob Fagg. The winner of the Southern Conference meet that same day ran only :10.3. Bob's mark broke the school record of :10.4, set in 1927 by Whitey Wilson. Bob also broke the school's high hurdle mark, being timed in :15.9. The former record, set by Fagg, was :16.6 at Ashland in 1947.

Paul McCarty also broke a school record, running the mile race in 4:47.5. The old mark was 4:53.4, set by Tate Minnix in 1926.

Other Roanoke athletes who scored were Jim Doran (third place in the 100-yard dash and second place in the 220-yard dash), Rud Rosebro (third place in the 440-yard dash), Paul McCarty (first in the 880-yard run with a time of 2:07.5), Red Crockett (first in the two-mile run, finishing with a time of 11:39.1), Maynard Turk (second in the two-mile run), Randy Taylor (third in the two-mile run), Bob Fagg (second in the 220-yard low hurdles), Steve Stone (third in the pole vault), Jim Ruscick (first place in the broad jump on a leap of 20'6½"), and Jim Doran (third place in the broad jump).

I remember . . . "Let me tell you about Lynchburg. When you ran the sprints at Lynchburg, the track seemed to be eight feet lower at the finish line than it was at the start. I ran a :10.0 that day, and Homer had me at :09.9."

Bob Fagg

I remember . . . "We always thought that the Lynchburg track went downhill for the 100-yard dash. They always seemed to have fast 100 times over there. This was the day that Jim Doran set a new school record in the discus–about 129'. That record held up until around 1960, in fact. Doran was a nice guy, tall and athletic. Sometimes, we even ran him in the sprints."

Homer Bast

I remember . . . "Jim Ruscick is another of the people from that first team that I remember well. That's because he was such a character. We all called him an ambulance chaser. He wanted to go to law school, and we would ask him why. He told us that he wanted to make lots of money. So we got on him, telling him that he was going to be an ambulance chaser. He wasn't very inclined toward track, but I think he came out because of his friendship with Doran. I doubt that he or Doran had to study very hard. Basically, they were very smart boys."

Homer Bast

Homer, his athletes, and the school were pleased with the way the 1947 team had finished. Again, Bob McLelland of the *Brackey-Ack* couldn't be more complimentary. In his Sport Korner column of May 16, Bob wrote:

> We'd like to say we think Coach Homer Bast deserves a lot of credit and congrats for the fine manner in which he has rejuvenated interest in track here at RC. Despite the fact that the sport had been absent for some two decades, and he had only a handful of experienced candidates available, Coach Bast molded himself a very respectable squad. He is extremely popular with his team and his interest and knowledge in the sport has aided his team a great deal. One of the weaknesses of this year's team has been the lack of experienced distance men. Bast hopes to be prepared for this next season by forming a cross country team next fall. Such a team should supply him with some good one- and two-mile runners. After the showing his boys have made this season, we'll heartily back any track undertaking the big coach may attempt.

Indeed, Bast had seen some stellar and generally unexpected results from his squad. New school record holders were Bob Fagg in the 100-yard dash and 120-yard high hurdles, Paul McCarty in the 880-yard and mile runs, Thanning Andersen in the 120-yard high hurdles, Jim Doran in the shot and discus, and the consistent Bill Williams in the pole vault.

The team had conquered several problems. The track rebuilding was progressing, but the facility was unusable until the following year. Equipment was lacking, even though Harry Hodges of the Maintenance Department had assured Homer that the hurdles would be built by the following fall along with the high jump and pole vault standards. In addition, most of the men had only limited experience when they tried out for the team. All in all, Homer thought, it was not a bad start.

One of the problems the team didn't conquer during this first year was a dearth of publicity. The *Rawenoch* yearbook of 1947 failed to mention that Roanoke had fielded a track team. The Roanoke *Collegian* in March of 1947 gave the team one small, two-inch, single-column article, accompanied by a blurry head shot of Coach Bast in his University of Virginia track uniform. And to this day, the College Archives has no picture of that first team.

I remember . . . "In those first years, money for the cross country and track team was scarce. All of our hurdles were made by Harry Hodges in the Maintenance Department. They were the old wooden ones. In fact, he also made some or all of the jumping standards. A shot, a discus–all were donated by other schools. At V. M. I., Walt Cormack and I got to be good friends. He knew our economic circumstances. And he would slip me stuff from time to time. I was a scrounger. In those first two or three years, also, we didn't have enough money to purchase spiked shoes for the athletes. They bought their own in most cases. I think that we did buy flats for the runners in cross country. Even in the early 1950s, we were still begging for equipment and supplies. That's one reason I scheduled Clemson on our trip south for two years in a row. The Clemson coach was a Roanoke graduate and gave us everything from shoes to shots."

Homer Bast

Chapter Three

The 1947-48 Seasons

The summer had passed quickly for Homer. Most of his team went home to summer jobs and Homer was busy with the teaching of his history courses. The pay wasn't good, at about $400 per professor for teaching three hours a day for nine weeks, but summer school was important financially to the school and the Basts could use the money. Because the summer classes provided the school with much-needed income, the administration tried to offer just the right courses in many subject areas to entice students to enroll.

Homer and Mary Jane moved out of the sparse confines of the Methodist Church into one of four apartments in a building just purchased by the College. The purchase was one attempt to provide housing for faculty members, although in 1947-48 the need seemed to be greater than it was the previous year. They lived there throughout the summer. Then the College asked them to move out. Apparently, they had a man coming in to fill an important position and, since Homer was still new to the faculty, they thought he was the one to go. Don't worry, they told the Basts. We are negotiating to buy another house for apartments, located at 212 Market Street and next door to Harry Hodges' house. This purchase was delayed for a number of weeks, however, and Homer and Mary Jane had to make a decision. Finally, she moved back to Staunton to live temporarily with her family and Homer moved over to Mary Jane's sister's house in Roanoke. Finally, early in the fall, the Basts were back together in their new apartment.

In September, the student body enrollment again was more than 600. Officials tried to limit the number of incoming freshmen to 150, but more than five times that number applied for admission. That fact forced them to accept veterans first, followed by children of alumni, and then general high school graduates. These decisions meant that almost 40% of all new students for the 1947-48 session were veterans. Veterans, in addition, made up about half of the entire student body.

The school had been busy over the summer with several construction projects. The need for new physics and chemistry classroom space forced Roanoke to invest $65,000 to triple the space in Miller Hall. The College also purchased more property on High Street, near the Sections dormitories, and rented classroom space from the Methodist Church.

Homer was pleased to see that renowned historian Arnold Toynbee was scheduled to appear that fall on campus. The visit was coordinated through Dean Myers.

At the beginning of the first semester, good news came from Buddy Hackman. He told Homer that the College had been invited to join the expanding, 16-member Mason-Dixon Conference. Along with 43 representatives from other colleges, Buddy and Homer traveled to Baltimore to attend a conference meeting. The session was chaired by William McClure, Athletic Director of Gallaudet College. Besides Roanoke, Lynchburg and the University of Baltimore also were given membership, bringing the total to 16 schools. Other schools in the conference were Johns Hopkins, Loyola, Towson State Teachers, Western Maryland, Mount St. Mary's, Washington, Delaware, Gallaudet, American, Catholic, Randolph-Macon, Hampden-Sydney, and Bridgewater.

Hackman attended the group meetings dealing with basketball and baseball, while Homer sat in on the track and cross country discussions. Among other decisions made that day, the group awarded the conference track and field meet to Catholic University on May 14-15, 1948.

Cross Country

When Buddy and Homer returned to Salem, Homer was already planning for the upcoming cross country season. Somehow, because cross country running had no history at the College, he needed a way to pull together an above-average group of runners who would become dedicated to the sport. One of his first goals was to get the student body interested in distance running. He began to talk with numerous people on the campus, telling them that the only way to develop distance runners was through year-round training. He also felt that a cross country team would ensure that additional points would be added to all of the spring track meets. Admittedly, he said, cross country running can be boring and tedious because it involves running distances of from two and a half to three and a half miles. But he always pointed out that the sport offered an excellent opportunity for students to build up their endurance and even increase their speed. Like the military service motto from later in the century, "Be all you can be," he told students that cross-country running would get them into the best shape of their lives. He also said that any man could become good if he stuck with it long enough and practiced hard. Another incentive was that cross country running offered students an opportunity to win letters in spring track, because there is often a deficiency of distance runners at other schools.

"Of course," Homer said later, "my initial emphasis was on track and cross country was secondary. But I learned early the advantage of having a cross country team. So I thought to myself that I needed to put together a cross country team before any more time passed. Using Red Crockett and Paul McCarty, who came out of the baseball program, we had the makings of a distance team. Paul was a utility infielder. I said to him, 'Paul, you're not doing very well out here. Come on out and run for Roanoke. And then, lo and behold, I found ol' Bruce Davenport. I had my eye on that boy. He, Crockett, and McCarty became three of our musketeers at that particular point. They were all about the same quality as far as running went, although Davenport was a little bit better. It was the first time that McCarty or Crockett had ever run. So those boys formed a nucleus, and I recruited pretty heavily. I went around the campus. I'd look at students in all of my classes and say, well, maybe *he* could do it and maybe another one couldn't. Then I would watch people walk across the campus to see if they had an athletic stride. I'd look at kids who were out for various sports and see if they were doing any good at those sports. If they weren't, I'd try to convince them to join our teams."

The squad began its practices on Monday, September 29. The team chose Paul McCarty and Red Crockett to serve as Co-Captains of the team. Besides these two runners, others who showed up were Rud Rosebro, Bill Williams, and freshmen Drew Hierholzer, Jim Thompson, George King, Lloyd Stein, Maynard Turk, Hank Roth, Randy "Rannie" Taylor, Ed Renn, Ray Anderson, (N. V.) "Nathan" Nininger, and Wallace Lloyd. Freshman Bruce Davenport didn't join the team until about a month later. Bruce would go on to become the best runner on the team this season and for seasons to come and soon would be a major contributor to campus life with his participation in various organizations.

Bast was very well satisfied with the progress shown by members of the team in its first week of practice, even though he trained them lightly at first on grass; however, he felt (as he did before every track or cross country season from that point on) that additional athletes with talent were in the student body and just needed to be persuaded

The first cross country team in Roanoke College's history. Kneeling (L to R) are: Maynard Turk, George King, Bruce Davenport, and N. V. Nininger; Standing (L to R): Paul McCarty, Coach Bast, Dick Fraley, Rud Rosebro, Red Crockett, and Lloyd Stein.

to come out for the team. They didn't need to have been athletes in high school, and they might be competing on some other type of team at the College.

He turned to the *Brackety-Ack* for help. Bob McLelland and other student writers gave him some excellent publicity. The paper noted that, according to Professor Bast, "lots of fellows have the abilities to be track stars, but they don't take advantage of the opportunities given them. Plenty of chances are available this fall, for practices will be held daily on the athletic field at 4:00 p.m."

Coach Bast, said the *Brackety-Ack*, wanted everyone to know that there was an urgent need for more men. In fact, he said, he was a little disappointed in the turnouts at the daily practices thus far. The newspaper noted that it was desire, not necessarily talent that made a runner successful. Bob McLelland also gave Bast some advice. "Something we'd like to see," Bob wrote, "is for Coach Bast to arrange some of the meets for his cross country boys for Saturdays. If meets were held on Saturdays . . . and were correctly scheduled, it would be possible for boys to perform before greater crowds."

I remember . . . "Bruce Davenport was reluctant to come out for cross country because he thought that running would affect his studies. But I persuaded him to join the team, and once he got a taste of success, that helped. His father had been a successful miler at Virginia Tech. And I think his dad really wanted to see Bruce run. He knew that Bruce could run and still make good grades."

Homer Bast

I remember . . . "Running cross country, I was so far back that I never saw a finish line string. Homer asked us to run cross country strictly for conditioning. I think I was still smoking at the time. That wasn't very smart."

Rud Rosebro

October 16, 1947
Bridgewater College at Bridgewater, Virginia
Team Scores: None (Unofficial Meet)

The first competition of the fall, a non-scoring practice meet, was to be held on October 16 at Bridgewater College. Fortunately, the team was making good progress despite the fact that team members had been practicing in tennis shoes. Regular cross country shoes had been ordered, and were expected to be available before the first official meet. The same was true for the team uniforms.

Still, Homer came up with other ideas to get more students to practice with the team. Would anything besides his own encouraging words help build the team? Maybe, he thought, we can get another good athlete or two each year if we offer a distance running competition between dorms and fraternities. That idea brought on the formation of an intramural cross country meet–one that would be run annually in the early fall throughout his tenure as coach at Roanoke. Unfortunately, things didn't go well with the meet that first year. After putting out an invitation to compete, there were no entries. So Homer simply took his team, ran the intramural course one day in a simulated intramural race, and awarded medals to the first five finishers. Bruce Davenport took first and also had his name engraved on the new intramural cross country trophy. Co-captains Paul McCarty and Red Crockett, stars from the past track season, took second and third place respectively. Lloyd Stein, another promising freshman, was fourth, and veteran sophomore Rud Roseboro took the fifth position. In the years to come, many outstanding runners on Homer's cross country and track teams came from top finishers in this fall race.

Just after noon on October 22, the team left for Bridgewater. Rumor was that the Bridgewater team was strong this year, but the meet would be unofficial and the competition would be invaluable to members of the Roanoke team. Homer did worry that the boys might not be in tip-top shape. Continuous rain during the previous week had interrupted the team's practices.

In this meet, each team could run any number of men; however, only the first seven men on a team would affect the scoring. The first five placers for each squad would receive points corresponding to their place positions. The first man of those five who finished got one point for a win, the second place runner two points, the third place finishers three points, and so on. The objective, of course, was to accrue a lower number of points than the opposing team. The lowest possible team score would be 15 points.

Co-Captain Paul McCarty was the star of the Roanoke team this day. He and Bridgewater's Quinton Carr approached the finish line almost in a dead heat. At the very end, Carr lunged through the tape to take first place honors, while McCarty took second. Both were given a time of 12:49. Other scorers for Roanoke included Lloyd Stein, Maynard Turk, George King, and Ray Anderson. The final score–not counting in the team's win-loss record for the season–was in Bridgewater's favor, 19 to 44.

October 21, 1947
Virginia Polytechnic Institute at Blacksburg, Virginia
Team Scores: Virginia Polytechnic Institute–20
Roanoke–39

Back in Salem, the team prepared for its first-ever official cross country meet. The opponent would be Virginia Polytechnic Institute (V. P. I.), located less than an hour from the Roanoke campus. The event, scheduled for October 21 at Blacksburg, would begin at 4:45 p.m.

At about 2:00 p.m. on the afternoon of the meet, team members, their coach, and manager Joe McClaugherty left for Blacksburg. Soon after the firing of the starter's pistol, the Hokies' fine runner, Curtis Shelton, pulled into the lead, closely followed by teammates Beverly Middleton and Tom Loving. They remained in those positions over the 3.0 mile course, with Shelton winning the race with a time of 15:16.4. For Roanoke, Co-Captain Paul McCarty finished fourth in 16:14, followed by the other Co-Captain, Red Crockett in 16:26. In the 11th, 12th, and 13th scoring positions respectively were Maroon runners George King (17:46), Maynard Turk (18:23), and Rud Rosebro (time unknown).

V. P. I. won the meet, 20-39. Homer was not surprised at the final score.

October 25, 1947
Randolph-Macon College at Salem, Virginia
Team Scores: Roanoke–20
Randolph-Macon–35

Four days later, with very little chance to get in better shape, Roanoke met Randolph-Macon in the first and only home meet of the year. By this time, freshman Bruce Davenport had joined the team. It was easy to see from his first practice that he would make a real contribution.

Homer had set up a three-mile home course. Runners started on the track, then went up the narrow roadway and continued up High Street, High Street Extension, and further on in that vicinity. Then they circled back to the finish line on the campus. The finish line was located on the front straightaway of the track. Once or twice in later home meets, when Homer wanted members of the student body to support the team, he had the runners finish on the quad in the middle of the campus, in front of a crowd of students and faculty. Whether ending their runs on the quad or, more often on the track, runners often finished through a human chute of cheering onlookers.

As noted, Bruce Davenport had joined the squad by this time. He was one of Homer's recruits from the student body–a freshman with nothing in his background that pointed to good athletic skills besides the fact that his father was an excellent high school and college runner. Bruce would go on to startle everyone in these next four years with his terrific distance running ability.

Bruce and Paul McCarty ran together for most of the race. With a few hundred yards to go, Bruce sprinted ahead to win the race in front of a scattered number of fans in a time of 17:07.0. Five seconds later came Paul McCarty, followed by Red Crockett, who recorded a time of 17:38. Randolph-Macon's Randolph Jones took fourth place, but Roanoke's Lloyd Stein was fifth (18:08) and Rud Rosebro took the ninth spot (18:34).

People on campus were ecstatic, and so were Homer and his runners. Finally, all of the hard work had paid off. Now, however, the team must plan to enter its most important meet thus far–the First Annual Little Six Cross Country Championships to be held on November 8... Bridgewater was set to host the meet, and would use a course that was approximately 3.65 miles in length.

I remember . . . "Bruce Davenport was a great person. Smart as a whip. Good lines. His father had been a miler at Tech. Bruce and I became firm friends. He married a girl from Roanoke College–a great person–and they made a great team, those two. They had a nice family, and he worked for Sperry Rand over in Charlottesville for years. He was a physics/math major. And he was a really smart boy. He had a brother who came here, and he was a manager of the cross country and track teams. Bruce stayed with me all four years. But I didn't work with him during one of those years, because I was away in the Navy during the 1950-51 session. But he was a leader, and he was willing to tie with his teammates if they wanted to tie. But in the tough races–I think he won the Mason-Dixon Championships, for example–no one was going to tie him. He wanted to win the Championship outright. But those four boys were unselfish. It was one for all and all for one. It didn't make any difference to them who won the race. They generally were so far ahead that it didn't make any difference."

Homer Bast

November 8, 1947
Little Six Championships at Bridgewater, Virginia
Team Scores: 1st–Roanoke–15
2nd–Bridgewater–22
3rd–Randolph-Macon–49
4th–Hampden-Sydney–84
5th–Lynchburg–94

The Roanoke team had a chance to train for almost another couple of weeks before the date of the Little Six meet arrived. For the most part, coaches in the Little Six Conference picked Roanoke to finish second or third in the meet, with Bridgewater being the favorite to walk off with top honors. Yet, Homer had a feeling that something good would happen. The boys seemed to be rounding into excellent shape, and all had positive outlooks.

He did note one difference in scoring for the race. Only a team's first four runners, not the usual five, would receive scores. He knew he could count on high places from at least three of the runners–Bruce Davenport, Paul McCarty, and Red Crockett. If he could only get a fourth man to finish high enough in the race, perhaps the team could pull an upset.

The runners approached the line and the starter fired his gun. McCarty set the pace throughout, closely followed by Davenport. In the last 600 yards of the run, the two were leading the aggregation of about 30 contestants when the fleet-footed Crockett, who was running several yards behind them, put on a brilliant burst of speed and overtook them. The three then joined hands and crossed the finish line in a unique three-way tie, completing the 3.65-mile run in 20:37.

But Homer couldn't find his fourth-place runner. Could the boys finish one-two-three and still lose the championship? All he could see were the maroon shirts of five Bridgewater runners, who seemed to be everywhere and were running one behind the other just in back of Davenport, Crockett, and McCarty. Suddenly, there he was. Coming through the pack to finish ninth was freshman Lloyd Stein, whose time of 21:54 was almost 1:20 behind the winners. Lloyd's effort was all Roanoke needed to win the meet. The Maroons' team score was 15 points, with Bridgewater coming in second (22 points), Randolph-Macon third (49 points), Hampden-Sydney fourth (84 points), and Lynchburg fifth (94 points).

Other Maroons in the race were Rud Rosebro (15th in 22:30), George King (17th in 23:28), and finally N. V. Nininger (22nd in 25:08). Dick Fraley and Maynard Turk also competed in the meet.

The *Brackety-Ack*, even more than usual, played up the win and offered its heartiest congratulations to Coach Bast and his entire squad. Team members seemed proud of their accomplishments in this first season of competition. Coach Bast knew that just one meet separated his team from an outstanding record. The race, bringing together the squads from Roanoke and Washington and Lee, would occur just three days later at Lexington, Virginia.

November 11, 1947
Washington and Lee University at Lexington, Virginia
Team Scores: Roanoke–21
Washington and Lee–34

Not much was known about the Generals, but Homer had heard that Washington and

Lee had a fine runner, Pete Mitchell. Mitchell, the team's captain, would be running his last race on the school's 3.0-mile Liberty Hall course.

In trying to determine the meet results of this competition, this author uncovered very little. Neither the *Brackety-Ack*, the Washington and Lee campus newspaper, nor the Rockbridge County newspaper did any more than briefly mention the meet. We do know, however, that Roanoke swept the first three positions. Bruce Davenport won the race with a time of 15:37.0, followed by Paul McCarty and then Red Crockett. No times for anyone but Davenport were recorded. Although the finish positions of the other Roanoke and Washington and Lee runners cannot be located, Roanoke did win the meet, 21-34.

The season had ended, and Homer could not have been more proud of his team. They had been thumped in an early-season unofficial race with Bridgewater before losing to a strong Virginia Tech team. Then they became the strongest small college distance running team in the Commonwealth, beating Randolph-Macon and winning the Little Six Championships, and finally finishing first against the much larger team from Washington and Lee. What more could an inaugural season bring?

I remember . . . "Paul McCarty was a good boy. He didn't like track. He was just out for it because I asked him. He knew he wasn't going to be able to play any baseball. He wasn't that good. But he just loved baseball. And it is very difficult to get a person who loves baseball to come out for track. In this instance, I think he realized the writing on the wall and he was impressed by his first race. He ran 2:05. It was the first time he had ever run the 880. I thought that was excellent. So he was a regular member of the cross country team through all of those years and he was Captain of the track team. And he was an inspirational person. He really was. His major was economics. It's a very interesting story. After Paul graduated from Roanoke College, he couldn't get the kind of job he wanted. He did get a job, but in addition to that, he became a dance instructor at Arthur Murray's dance studios. And he did that for a couple of years. It was hard for a college to get economists in those days. So the college offered Paul a job here to teach basic economics. And he taught here for a couple of years. Unfortunately, he was always known as the guy who taught dancing over at Arthur Murray's studio. But Paul served us well as a runner. I realized that he didn't like the two-mile race. He just ran cross country to get in shape. But he did well in it and generally, he was a half miler. I would run him in the mile every now and then, and maybe in the quarter. As you well know, with these cross country boys, you can run them up or down. It doesn't really matter. I learned that trick from Dorsey Griffith, the coach at Catholic University. Dorsey and Harry Jopson (Bridgewater) and I became very close friends. Dorsey was a real furniture man – an antique man. He had an antique shop in that town near Frederick, Maryland, that is known for its antique shops. Dorsey was a specialist in 18th century glass. I mean, he was internationally known. And of course he was a wonderful track man in his day, as a sprinter, and although he didn't put the emphasis on cross country the way I did, he was very good with quarter milers. He thought that with quarter milers, you could run them up and down. Going back to Paul McCarty, he also became a President of a bank later in life."

Homer Bast

I remember . . . "Lloyd Stein was also on that first team. He was from New Jersey, and came down for a year or two. He became interested in some phase of the medical profession. Whether he was an X-ray technician (or something similar). I hadn't heard from him in about 50 years and one day he and his wife stopped by and rang the doorbell. He said that they were living in Chapel Hill at that particular point. 'And I was driving through,' Lloyd said, 'and I thought to myself that I hadn't been to Roanoke College for years and I'll just stop by and see my old coach.' I really didn't recognize him after all of those years. He had to introduce himself. He was fairly short. Most of that first team I had were short boys except for Crockett, who probably was about six feet tall, but slim with red hair."

Homer Bast

Indoor Track

In early January of 1948, Homer put out the word that the spring track practices would begin and that the first workouts would be conducted in the gymnasium. He wanted to enter several indoor meets; however, in the late 1940s, indoor competition was rare–almost nonexistant–in the Virginia area. Finally, he settled on the Southern Interscholastic Indoor Track Meet to be held at the University of North Carolina on February 28. He had no illusions of any team member placing in the event, since the competition included teams ranging from the University of North Carolina to Duke University to Navy and the University of Tennessee. They would see some of the top-flight collegiate talent in the country, in fact. The main purpose of the trip to Chapel Hill would be to give the Roanoke men some experience in competing against superior track and field athletes.

He told his team that only a few of them would be entered in the meet, but that he would try to place individuals in both the freshman and non-conference senior events. He would wait until the final entry deadline to decide who would make the trip. Meanwhile, he let it be known on campus that all boys interested in any phase of track and field athletics could try out for the team during the daily afternoon drills.

The excitement on campus was that Alvin Smith had just transferred to Roanoke from the University of North Carolina, beginning with the second semester. He was a bit older than his classmates, having taken six years to finish at a local high school and then spending time in the Navy. At the University of North Carolina, where he had been a student and a distance runner for five quarters–about a year and a half–he had been one of the stars of an excellent U. N. C. team. He almost transferred to Duke, but a high school friend, Gordon Highfill, finally suggested that he transfer to Roanoke. Gordon was an accomplished hurdler and a good friend from high school who had finished a year ahead of Smith. Gordon had entered Roanoke at the beginning the 1947-48 school year. Once Smith transferred to Roanoke, both Smith and Highfill were eligible to compete during the second semester in all meets except for those involving ACC/Southern Conference teams.

I remember . . . "Our first cross country team was an interesting one. Actually, I was happy that we even had a team that year–much less to have a winning team. That winter, as we did in subsequent winters, we practiced often around the quadrangle, even though there were cars parked on the asphalt in those days. We couldn't take the boys up to V. M. I. because their field house didn't exist at the time. When the weather wasn't good, we would try to use the gym to work out. But I always checked with Buddy Hackman to make sure that we weren't interfering with his basketball practices. At times, we could use the athletic field, but not often. Unfortunately, the boys were inclined to get shin splints from running on the quad for so long."

Homer Bast

February 28, 1948
Southern Interscholastic Indoor Track Meet at Chapel Hill, North Carolina
Team Scores: 1st–University of North Carolina–37½
2nd–Navy–20½
3rd–Duke University–20⅔
4th–University of Maryland–18
5th–Virginia Polytechnic Institute–11
6th–University of Florida–8⅓
7th–University of Virginia–5⅓
8th–University of Tennessee–3⅓
9th–Virginia Military Institute–3
10th–Shippenberg Teachers–3

11th–North Carolina State University–1
12th–University of South Carolina–1

Coach Bast finally decided to take just five individuals to Chapel Hill. Bruce Davenport, his top cross country man, would enter the freshman ¾-mile race. Homer thought he might have the best chance of placing. He also entered Wallace Lord, another promising freshman, in the same race. In the senior non-conference division, he decided that Gordon Highfill would run the 70-yard high hurdles. While at Duke the previous year, Highfill had made the finals in this event at the U. N. C. meet. He seemed to be in good condition. The other two entrants were Paul McCarty and Jim Ruscick. Paul was entered in the non-conference half-mile race, while Jim would perform in the broad jump. A basketball player, Jim had not had much practice time with the track team.

So on the morning of February 28, 1948, the five athletes and Homer loaded up their track gear and headed for Chapel Hill, which was about 150 miles from Salem. The trip took well over three hours to complete.

Highfill looked good warming up; unfortunately, he pulled a muscle in a trial heat and was out for the rest of the meet. Bruce Davenport finished sixth in a field of 25 men in the ¾-mile freshman race. Paul McCarty looked good in the 880, although against great competition, he failed to place. Finally, Jim Ruscick placed fifth in the broad jump with a leap of almost 20 feet. Unfortunately, the meet gave team points based only on the first three positions.

The next week, the *Brackety-Ack* said it was sorry that the team didn't score even a point, but lauded the individual efforts.

> An unknowing fan who picked up last Sunday's papers to get the results of the Southern Indoor Interscholastic track meet might thoughtlessly remark that Roanoke College's entrees made very poor showings since they failed to place in any of the events. This column does not want to offer any excuses for Coach Bast's boys because that is the last thing either the capable mentor or his charges would want. However, we would like to bring a few bare facts to light. First of all, the boys were competing against the cream of the crop of trackmen in the South, men who undoubtedly had had every advantage of practice. Roanoke College is without an indoor track, and, consequently, the boys were either forced to run around the flat gym floor or else bundle up and do a little outside work. Despite these handicaps, members of the team turned in some noteworthy performances.

There was nothing to be sad about, thought Homer. The 22-event program had brought together 450 very talented college and high school athletes, in front of a near-sellout crowd of around 2,000 spectators. Roanoke had competed against 19 good college teams and 14 college freshman groups. The boys also got to see athletes from 18 outstanding high school teams. The University of North Carolina won the meet, almost doubling the score on the Naval Academy and Duke University. Besides Roanoke, other schools represented were Washington and Lee, North Carolina State, Wake Forest, South Carolina, Davidson, Virginia Polytechnic Institute, Virginia Military Institute, Tennessee, Virginia, Emory and Henry, Georgia, Florida, Randolph-Macon, and Pennsylvania's Shippensburg Teachers College.

There were some suggestions in newspapers that Roanoke may have gone to at least one other meet during the indoor season, but the date and name of the meet were never given.

Outdoor Track

On March 1, daily drills for outdoor track got underway with Paul McCarty and Red Crockett serving as co-captains for the team.

As usual, Homer put out an invitation to all interested persons to report to the 4:00 p.m. practices. The coach could see that the team didn't have much depth, but the squad did have a few skilled athletes. Candidates for the sprint events were Bob Fagg, Ralph Kennedy, Dick Hunt, Dick Dodd, Dick Fraley, Harry Bower, and Bob Stultz. Middle distance men were Paul McCarty, Bob Graves, Jack Thurmond, Rud Rosebro, Jerry DeVeers, George King, Dick Fraley, Bob Ware, Wallace Lord, and Walter Denheiser. Distance runners were Alvin Smith, Lloyd Stein, Maynard Turk, Ranny Taylor, and Bruce Davenport.

In the weight events, interested athletes included Carroll Dahill, Roy Minnix, Harold Spraker, Eric Fisher, Carlo Calo, Bob Graves, and Fred Welcker. Pat Breslin and Bill Williams were the leading candidates for the javelin.

Jim Ruscick, Bob Fagg, and Dick Dodd would likely compete in broad jumping, while Ruscick, Williams, Lee Peery, and Bob Smith could handle high jumping. In the high and low hurdle events, entrants might be Fagg, Gordon Highfill, and Thanning Andersen. The main pole vaulter was Bill Williams, but he would have help from Stan Lerned.

Mr. Bast had scheduled eight meets for the spring season:

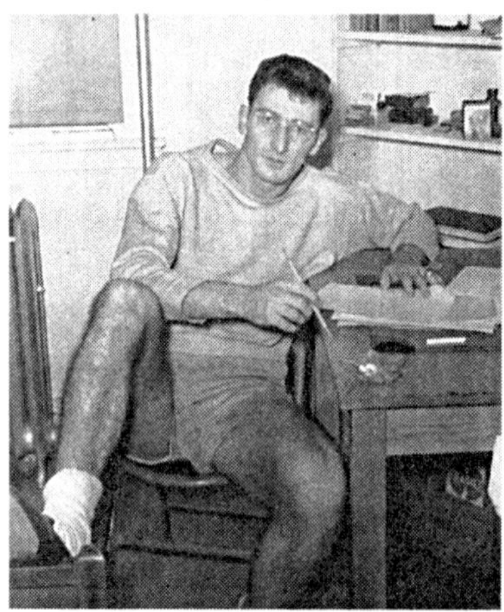

Top Left: Jim Doran, top basketball player and track man.
Top Right: First row (L to R)-Thanning Anderson, Gordon Highfill, Bob Fagg, Paul McCarty, George King, Jack Thurmond, and Dick Hunt. Second row: Carol Dahill, Jim Ruscick, Dick Fraley, Harold Spraker, Thor Whilkoren, Solly Turk, John Byerly, and Stan Larned. Third row: Roy Minnix, Rud Rosebro, Randy Taylor, Coach Bast, Lloyd Stein, Bruce Davenport, Manager Gill Robinson, Bob Stultz, Wallace Lord, and Bill Williams.
Bottom Left: Jim Ruscick, a basketball player and track star.
Bottom Right: Bob Fagg over a hurdle.

April 3, 1948	Roanoke vs. V. M. I., at Lexington
April 10, 1948	Roanoke vs. Lynchburg, at Salem
April 17, 1948	Second Annual Milligan Relays, at Johnson City, Tennessee
April 24, 1948	Roanoke vs. Randolph-Macon, at Salem
May 1, 1948	Roanoke vs. Bridgewater, at Bridgewater, Virginia

May 8, 1948 Little Six Championships, at Lynchburg, Virginia
May 14-15, 1948 Mason-Dixon Championships, at Washington, DC
May 22, 1948 Virginia AAU Track and Field Championships, at Lynchburg, Virginia

I remember . . . "We didn't even have starting blocks when I first started running track in 1948. We had to take a small shovel and dig out two places to use for our feet to sit. Maybe with blocks, we could have had faster times in the sprints. And we ran on a pretty rough cinder track. Maybe with starting blocks and a smoother track, I could have shaved off a couple of tenths of a second. Today, athletes run on all-weather tracks. It's hard to compare their times with ours. There wasn't much in the way of equipment. I remember that Bill Williams and Ray DeCosta both started out with the old bamboo vaulting poles."

Dick Fraley

April 3, 1948
Virginia Military Institute at Lynchburg, Virginia
Team Scores: Virginia Military Institute–88
Roanoke–38

Track season got underway officially on April 3 immediately after the spring vacation. The team left around 12:00 noon for Lexington, with Homer expecting perhaps the toughest competition of the year. Virginia Military Institute, under the coaching of Clarence "Pop" Strange, was thought to have the best team in the state.

Roanoke was outmanned from the start on the home team's Alumni Field. V. M. I. won 10 of the 14 events; however, the Maroons did well in a few instances. The most exciting race of the day was the 880. Paul McCarty of Roanoke uncorked a strong finish to nose out Charles Avery of the Keydets by less than a yard. McCarty's winning time was 2:07.3.

Alfred Smith, in his first race since transferring from the University of North Carolina, won the mile easily with a time of 4:48.4. The other two winners for Roanoke were Thanning Andersen, who was timed at :27.2 for a new school record in the low hurdles, and Bill Williams, who won the pole vault event with a jump of 10′5″. Williams also finished the meet as Roanoke's high scorer, totaling nine points by adding a second place in the javelin and a third place in the high jump.

Freshman Bruce Davenport showed his potential when he finished second in the two-mile race with a school record time of 10:33.0. Other second places were by Bob Fagg in the 100-yard dash, Thanning Andersen in the high hurdles, and Jim Ruscick in the broad jump. Finishing the Roanoke scoring were Dick Fraley (third in the 220-yard dash) and Rud Rosebro (third in the low hurdles).

The strong Lexington team scored 88 points for the day. Roanoke's score was only 38.

It was early in the season, however, and the 50-point defeat to a very good team simply showed Homer that more work needed to be done. He knew he didn't have the depth to beat some of the best teams around, but he was determined that his boys would end the year in good shape and with a good attitude.

I remember . . . "One day, local sports writer and former Maroon Bob McLelland told me, 'You know, you have a good distance man in school.' I asked him who that might be, and he pointed out Alvin Smith. Bob had remembered him from Jefferson High School. So, when I had my next contact with Alvin, I asked him if he were coming out for track. And he said he was. He was very loyal, and never missed a practice. It was inspirational to have Alvin on the team. The other boys knew that he was pretty darn good, and knew that he was just coasting when he was running with them."

Homer Bast

April 10, 1948
Lynchburg College at Salem, Virginia
Team Scores: Roanoke–80½
Lynchburg–45½

The next meet, Homer thought, would certainly help. Roanoke would be hosting a team from Lynchburg College on April 10, and the meet would be the first varsity track competition held on Alumni Field in Salem since late in the 1920s. The team trained hard during the week before the meet, and on April 9, Homer and some of the boys showed up to line off the lanes with lime, all the way around the track, and to mark the starting points for the 100-yard dash, for the circular races, and for the 220-yard race. It was a time-consuming job, and one that had to repeated before every home meet throughout Homer's tenure as track coach.

Fortunately for the Maroons, Lynchburg did not bring much talent in the field events. Roanoke, in fact, won four of these events, with Carroll Dahill throwing 34'3" in the shot put, Bob Graves throwing the discus 107'8", and Jim Ruscick broad jumping 20'4" and high jumping 5'7". Carlo Calo (second in the shot), Pat Breslin (third in the javelin), Rud Rosebro (second in the broad jump), and Stan Lerned (third in the pole vault) completed the field event scoring for Roanoke. Graves, Ruscick, and Evans of Lynchburg, recorded Alumni Field records.

Bast's runners gave credible, but not outstanding performances in the other events, winning six of eight events. Bob Fagg's :10.7 in the 100-yard dash and :16.8 in the high hurdles, Alvin Smith's times of :54.1 in the 440-yard dash and 2:09.0 in the 880-yard run, Paul McCarthy's 4:53.7 in the mile, and Bruce Davenport's relatively-slow 11:47.8 in the two-mile run all brought first-place points. Alumni Field running records went to Jack West of Lynchburg in the 220, McCarty in the mile, Fagg in the high hurdles, and Jean Wood of Lynchburg in the low hurdles.

Non-winning points for Roanoke were collected by Dick Dodd (100–2nd), Dick Fraley (220–2nd), Ralph Kennedy (220–3rd), Rud Rosebro (440–2nd, BJ–2nd), McCarty (880–2nd), Davenport (mile–2nd), Ranny Taylor (two miles–2nd), Thanning Andersen (LH–3rd, and HH–3rd), and Stan Lerned (PV–3rd).

Roanoke won the meet by a score of 80½ to 45½. Alvin Smith and Jim Ruscick shared high scoring honors for the Maroons with ten points each. Each would get better as the season progressed.

April 17, 1948
Milligan Relays at Johnson City, Tennessee
Team Scores: 1st–Milligan College–37¼
2nd–East Tennessee State College–36¼
3rd–Roanoke College–23½
4th–University of Tennessee–10¼
5th–Maryville College–7
6th–Mars Hill College–4
7th–Emory and Henry College–3
8th–Tusculum College–1

Next on the schedule for Bast's team was the Milligan Relays. The team almost made the trip to Johnson City, Tennessee, in 1947 to participate in the event during its inaugural year. The Milligan Relays were established to stimulate the growth of track among small colleges and high schools in this area. Roanoke would be competing with a field of fifteen other colleges from Virginia and Tennessee. Colleges that were sent invitations included the University of Tennessee freshmen, Tusculum, Emory and Henry, Carson Newman, L. M. U., East Tennessee State, Middle Tennessee State, Maryville, Tennessee Wesleyan, Mars Hill, Wofford, Appalachian, Guilford, Union, Bluefield, and Roanoke.

Homer looked over the list of Roanoke athletes, trying to decide how to get the maximum number of points from his men. It was a difficult task, of course, because almost nothing was known about the strengths of the other 15 teams. Finally, he decided to enter 11 events. They included four relays, two medleys, and five special events. In two of the relay events–the 440-yard and 880-yard relays–four men would be selected from the following: Bob Fagg, newcomers Dick Dodd and Dick Fraley, Ralph Kennedy, Dick Hunt, and Harry Bower. He would also enter Alvin Smith in the 880-yard run, along with Co-Captain Paul McCarty. Bast thought that perhaps Rud Rosebro, Jack Thurmond, Lloyd Stein, and John Byerly could score in the mile relay. If possible, he wanted to enter two teams in the distance medley. The first team, composed of some of Roanoke's outstanding runners, included Alvin Smith, Paul McCarty, Rud Roseboro, and Bob Fagg, with the second team's athletes being selected from among Bruce Davenport, Lloyd Stein, Wallace Lord, Jack Thurmond, and John Byerly.

Homer thought also that he might be able to score points in the shuttle hurdle relay race, so he entered the quartet of Bob Fagg, Rud Rosebro, Thanning Andersen, and Gordon Highfill. Fagg and Highfill, formerly of Duke University, could hold their own with most of the shuttle hurdle entrants in the meet.

Homer also wanted to give his special events athletes a chance to go up against good competition. He entered Dick Hunt in the 100-yard dash, Gordon Highfill and Thanning Andersen in the high hurdles, and Jim Ruscick in the broad and high jump. He also included Bill Williams in the pole vault.

It was a long ride for the team to get to Memorial Stadium in Johnson City. The facility was located some 180 miles from Salem, and there was no Interstate system to speed up the trip.

Bast was pleased with the way the team performed. The 480-yard shuttle hurdle team of Andersen, Rosebro, Fagg, and Highfill placed first with a time of 1:06.3. The time set a new meet and Roanoke College record.

The Maroons' distance medley relay also set a new meet and Roanoke College record, winning easily over Maryville College in 10:15.2. The team was composed of Fagg, Rosebro, McCarty, and Smith. A second team from Roanoke–Dodd, Lord, Stein, and Davenport–also competed in this event. They finished third in the race, but were not counted in the scoring.

Two other Roanoke men also won individual events. Bob Fagg became the first Maroon hurdler under Homer's coaching to break :16 seconds when he beat his teammate, Thanning Andersen, in a time of :15.9. Another member of the squad, Jim Ruscick, tied for first at 5'6" in the high jump. He also picked up a third place in the broad jump, just inches out of second.

The team was in good spirits as they returned to Salem. Homer had never expected this quality of performance, especially in mid-April. The team didn't win–in fact, its score of 23½ points placed them third behind Milligan College and East Tennessee State College–but their promise as individuals and as a team had begun to surface.

I remember . . . "I do remember the Milligan Relays that year. We won the shuttle hurdle relay. It was one of the few shuttle relay events that Homer entered during the years he was coaching. The four hurdlers for the race were Thanning Anderson, Rud Rosebro, myself, and Gordon "Specks" Highfill. Specks was a classic, really good hurdler. I ran with him in high school, in fact. After his high school graduation, he went on to a Catholic college in New Jersey, and from there to one of the services. When he came back from the service, I convinced him to come to Roanoke College. He was an excellent hurdler with great form. But he didn't do much at Roanoke because he was always beat up."

Bob Fagg

I remember . . . "The people at Milligan College sent me an announcement and said that they were hosting the Relays and wanted us to come down. I thought, that's not very far. I guess I can take the whole team. So we went down there and spent the night. They gave us quarters in the gym. I think it was an attempt to get as many teams as possible to come down. The next morning, we went out to take a look at the track. And it was one of those scooter tracks. Banked, you know. I thought, what are we going to do now. We want to get up as high as we can on this curve, and so we could come out of the curve hell bent to the inside of the track. So we tried to get the outside lane at every drawing. The banking was on all four turns. You could come down off those curves just flying, you know. I think we entered every relay event that they had. It wasn't a bad meet, actually. It was a good experience for the boys. So now they have seen a big meet. In those days, the Milligan people really wanted to attract a large number of teams. The sport wasn't really very popular in that part of the country at the time."

Homer Bast

April 24, 1948
Randolph-Macon College at Salem, Virginia
Team Scores: Roanoke–65
Randolph-Macon–61

The fourth meet of this second season of track competition featured Randolph-Macon College of Ashland. The team had beaten Roanoke by 26 points in 1947. But Homer had a feeling that things would be better this year. He had a more talented group of athletes this time around. In addition, he was pleased that the meet would be held on the Roanoke track.

That said, Bast had heard from a couple of Virginia coaches that the Randolph-Macon team still had talent. The Yellow Jackets, led by Captain Milton Drewer, Jr., hurdler and sprinter, overwhelmingly won both of their previous meets against Gallaudet and Hampden-Sydney. Their strengths probably lay in their sprinters and in several of the field events. For example, they had swept all three places against other teams in the javelin and broad jump for the past two years.

The meet got underway in the early afternoon, with first one and then the other team taking the lead. With good weather, nine separate Alumni Field records were set during the competition. Three more Roanoke College records were broken or tied.

Reliable Bob Fagg set two new track records by winning the 100-yard dash in :10.3 and the 220-yard dash in :23.2. Alvin Smith's track record came in the 880-yard run, when he was timed in a very respectable 2:03.7. Rud Rosebro ran away with the low hurdle race, winning in a field record of :27.2. A Roanoke athlete–Bob Graves–also set one other Alumni Field record when he threw the discus 106'10".

Several other track records were set by Randolph-Macon athletes. Drewer ran the high hurdles in :16.3, Bill Atkins threw the javelin 163'0", and David Garber broad jumped 20'8¾" and pole vaulted 10'6".

Several of these efforts became Roanoke College student records. They included the 220 time of :23.2 by Fagg, Smith's 880-yard run time of 2:03.7, and Rosebro's 220-yard low hurdles mark of :27.2.

Many other Maroons scored in the meet, of course. Alvin Smith placed second in the quarter mile, Paul McCarty finished third in the 880-yard run, Thanning Andersen was second in the high hurdles and third in the low hurdles, Carroll Dahill and Carlo Calo finished first and second in the shot put, respectively, Jim Ruscick was third in the broad jump and tied for first in the high jump (5'8"), and Bill Williams finished second in the pole vault. Davenport and Paul McCarty joined hands to win the mile event in 5:05.8, while Davenport and Lloyd Stein did the same to win the two-mile run in 11:39.7.

Rud Rosebro remembers the moments before he ran the low hurdles. The score was 59-58 in Roanoke's favor. The low hurdles would decide the winner of the meet. "Coach Bast rushed over," Rosebro says, "and brought the Roanoke hurdlers together. He told us that the next event–the low hurdles–was important. It would be the last event of the day, and if we could outscore the Randolph-Macon runners, we would win. But if Randolph-Macon finished first, the best we could do was to tie the meet. I didn't know if I could beat the Randolph-Macon kid, let alone imagine that I could set a new school record. Then the race started and I quickly saw that although the other team's best hurdler was faster, he couldn't get his steps down no matter how much he tried. He practically had to stop at each hurdle and jump over it. So I won the event and Thanning Anderson finished third. That gave us six more points and Randolph-Macon just three."

After the low hurdles, the official score showed Roanoke leading, 65 to 61. Homer began to gather up some of the equipment and send the boys up the hill. Then the Randolph-Macon coach came running up to Homer and said, "What about the mile relay?" Homer explained that the Maroons had no mile relay team to put on the track. "That's too bad," said the Yellow Jacket coach. "We'll run the relay ourselves and you'll have to give us the five points for the win." Of course, those points would have won the meet for Randolph-Macon. Five yards away, however, was the Roanoke Athletic Director, Buddy Hackman, who quickly intervened. Tenacious in any confrontation, and always hating to lose, Buddy and the Randolph-Macon coach argued for a solid 10 minutes. Buddy's point was that the Maroons had never run the mile relay during the entire year, and that they couldn't possibly field a team. In addition, he said, Randolph-Macon knew when the meet was first agreed upon, that the event wouldn't be run. Finally, the Jacket's coach gave up reluctantly and the relay points were not contested. Some heard him mutter that revenge would be coming in the Little Six meet about two weeks later. Mark up another win for Roanoke.

At least, that is the story told by the *Brackety-Ack*. Here is the way Homer Bast remembers it: "We knew the meet would be close. And I didn't have any boys who could run the last event of the day–the mile relay. By that time, each of the boys who might have run the event had already run in three other events. My friend, Griff Dodson, who ran with me at Virginia, was an attorney in Roanoke. I had asked him if he would come up and be an official at some of our meets. He agreed to do so. I called him prior to the meet and asked him to be the Meet Director for the Randolph-Macon meet. I told Griff that I was going to give him and the Randolph-Macon coach the order of events. The mile relay would not be listed as one of the events to be run that day. Just the events listed on the sheet would be conducted. Then I told the Randolph-Macon coach before the meet that the order of events was on the sheet, but he never glanced at the sheet and had no idea that the mile relay would not be run. As the meet progressed, he was not very pleased. He thought his team would be far ahead of Roanoke by the time the mile relay came around. It wasn't a good assumption, however. We were ahead by four points with every event run except for the non-existing mile relay. We were just a better team than he thought we'd be. So the Randolph-Macon coach was not in a good mood. Not only that, but one of his javelin throwers had a javelin go through his foot–the reason, incidentally, that the Mason-Dixon Conference dropped the javelin the next year. To sum up the situation, the Randolph-Macon coach threw a fit when he learned at the end of the meet that there would be no mile relay race. Griff explained to him, as the Meet Director, that the coach had known from the start that the mile relay would not be a part of the meet. He was given a list of events before the meet began, and it clearly showed that there would be no mile relay. In other words, Griff said that the meet was over and that Roanoke had won. The Randolph-Macon coach and his team were not happy campers."

Homer Bast

I remember . . . "I vividly recall this meet with Randolph-Macon in 1948. Notice that they don't have the mile relay results on the sheet. In his pre-meet strategy, Homer figured that we could win the meet as long as we didn't run the mile relay. So he omitted it from the schedule and the Randolph-Macon coach, although he had glanced at his copy of the schedule, didn't realize that the meet would not finish with the relay event. He even pulled one of his best quarter milers out of his regular race in order to save him for the mile relay. We just didn't have enough warm bodies for the relay. The Randolph-Macon coach raised some kind of hell. I think he even appealed the meet to the people who ran the Little Six Conference. But nothing came of the appeal and we won the meet."

Bob Fagg

May 1, 1948
Bridgewater College at Bridgewater, Virginia
Team Scores: Bridgewater–68
Roanoke–58

Back in Salem, Homer began planning for the team's next meet, in Bridgewater, with the Bridgewater College Eagles. He knew that the Bridgewater team was strong in distance events as well as in the middle distances. They had beaten Lynchburg College earlier in the spring by an overwhelming score of 100$^{3}/_{5}$ to 30$^{2}/_{5}$ and had won in a meet with Gallaudet College.

On May 1, 1948, Roanoke and Bridgewater met on Riverside Field. Literally, the track sat at the edge of a river, and almost annually the water from the stream would rise to a point where it would cover the track completely.

The Bridgewater field event men were dominant. They swept the first three places in the shot put, the javelin, and the pole vault events. Despite the fact that Jim Ruscick won both the high jump (5'0" and the broad jump (20'2½"), Bridgewater took the second and third spots in each event. In the field events alone, they outscored Roanoke 43 to 11. Bob Graves did manage to throw for third place in the discus. But Roanoke was hurt by the absence of Bill Williams, still nursing an ankle injury, who probably would have taken first or second in the pole vault as well as the javelin.

In the running events, Roanoke did pick up a few of the points lost in the field events by winning six of the nine contests. Alvin Smith won two events, the mile in 4:43.0 and the 880 (in a tie with Paul McCarty) in 2:07.0. Bob Fagg ran his usual good race in the 100, clocking :10.4, and finished second in the 220.

Rud Rosebro picked up 10 additional points for the Maroons. His times of :16.6 in the high hurdles and :27.0 in the low hurdles gave him first places in each event.

Other points went to Ralph Kennedy (second in the 440), Gordon Highfill (third in the high hurdles, Thanning Andersen (third in the low hurdles), and Bruce Davenport (second to Alvin Smith in the mile run).

Two of the Maroons set Roanoke College records. Rud Rosebro broke his own low hurdles record of :27.2, set by Thanning Andersen in 1948. Alvin Smith's 4:43.0 mile also broke a record, surpassing Paul McCarty's 4:47.5 time of 1947. The low hurdle and mile times were also track records for Riverside Field.

Bridgewater won the meet by a score of 68 to 58. Even with the overwhelming 47 points gained in the running events, to just 25 for the Eagles, Roanoke's lack of depth in the field events had been their undoing. Throughout the next few years, Maroon running increasingly became the team's strength. Field events were mostly weaker. Homer wasn't surprised, because the schools where you found success in the shot, discus, and javelin were almost always the schools which fielded football teams. Roanoke had no football team. Bridgewater did.

May 8, 1948
Little Six Championships at Lynchburg, Virginia
Team Scores: 1st–Roanoke College (R)–43
2nd–Hampden-Sydney College–35
3rd–Randolph-Macon College–34.5
4th–Bridgewater College–28
5th–Lynchburg College–21

Sitting at home that weekend after the Bridgewater loss, Homer tried his best to put the meet out of his mind. Instead, he was thinking about next weekend's first annual Little Six Championships in Lynchburg. Besides Roanoke, the other teams who had committed to the meet were Randolph-Macon, Bridgewater, Lynchburg, and Hampden-Sydney.

Over and over again, he mapped out different scenarios for how the scores might play out. He knew that Bridgewater's team would score a lot of points, and so would Randolph-Macon. But, he thought, I really liked some of the things I saw our boys doing at Bridgewater. We could have won that meet.

He did know one thing. He could bank on three good distance runners–Paul McCarty, Alvin Smith, and Bruce Davenport. Each could run multiple races and each would likely win or finish second in those races. He also knew that his hurdlers, Bob Fagg, Rud Rosebro, Thanning Andersen, and Gordon Highfill would do well in the meet despite the fact that Lynchburg's Jean Wood was favored. Fagg would place fairly high in the sprints, but it was doubtful that he could beat opponents such as Hampden-Sydney's Lynn Chewing. Randolph-Macon's Bob Evans reigned supreme in the 440.

Bill Williams would be back, having set out quite some time after an awkward fall and a twisted ankle. Still, the pole vault was one event that any of several people could win. David Garber of Randolph-Macon, Williams of Roanoke, Gene Evans of Lynchburg, and Daniel Bray of Hampden-Sydney each had a chance.

As usual, Roanoke would give up a lot of points in the shot, discus, and javelin. Williams wasn't expected to compete in the javelin because of his injury.

It was getting late at the Bast house, and finally all of the figures began to point to a win–not for Roanoke but for Bridgewater. But you never know, Homer thought. With a little luck . . . . And then he thought of a quote he had mentioned to his history class a few days before. He had told his students what Thomas Jefferson once said: "I am a great believer in luck, and I find the harder I work, the more I have of it."

So his goals for the coming week before the Little Six were clear. Make sure that the boys were in good shape. Get them mentally ready for the meet by helping them understand how good they could be with concentrated effort. And be positive and dream big. This can be a fun meet, he told them, and we can win it all.

A number of athletes accompanied the Roanoke team to Lynchburg. Bast had entered Smith, McCarty, and Davenport in the middle distance and distance runs. Accompanying them would be Randy Taylor and Lloyd Stein in the two-mile run and Wallace Lord in the 880. In the two hurdle events, entrants were Fagg, Rosebro, Highfill, and Andersen. Fagg, Dick Dodd, Dick Fraley, and Harry Bowers would handle the sprints. And Bast would choose from among Ralph Kennedy, Dick Hunt, Frank Aldred, and Jack Thurman for the quarter mile. Carlo Calo, Carroll Dahill, and Dick Graves would compete in the throwing events, while Jim Ruscick would enter the jumps. He still was unsure as to which men would make up the mile relay team. He would probably choose from among Kennedy, Fagg, McCarty, Smith, Rosebro, and Dodd.

In the first part of the meet, Bast saw his field event men score almost no points. In fact, by the end of the day, Bill Williams was the only Maroon to place in a field event, taking a tie for fourth place in the pole vault. That event gave Roanoke just 1½ points.

But in the running events, Roanoke was pouring it on all day. In fact, they won four of these nine events and placed in five.

Bob Fagg may have pulled the biggest surprise of the day. He was a definite underdog to Lynn Chewing of Hampden-Sydney. But he got a good start and stayed with Chewning until the last yard or so before the finish line. With a determined lunge toward the line, Fagg broke the tape in an outstanding time of :10.0. Fagg also finished third in the 220.

Alvin Smith, as Homer expected, was the class of the distance runners. He won two of the three events he entered, in fact. He had a winning time of 2:05.0 in the 880-yard run and tied with Bruce Davenport for first in the mile run in 4:48.3. He also picked up a second behind Davenport (whose time was 10:44.0) in the two-mile run.

The remainder of the meet points were scattered among the mile relay team (fourth), Lloyd Stein (fourth in the two-mile race), Rud Rosebro (an excellent second place finish in the low hurdles), Thanning Andersen (second in the high hurdles), and dependable Paul McCarty (second in the 880-yard run).

Although Rosebro did not win or place in the high hurdles, he remembers that he actually ran his best time qualifying for the event. "There was a fellow from Lynchburg, Jean Wood," he recalls, who was very good. I was moving along in the high hurdles qualifying heat, running very smoothly, and was in front. I glanced over my shoulder and there was Wood, just behind me in second place. Both of us would qualify for the finals if we could place in the top two finishers, so I just eased up, floating over the hurdles to save my energy. So did Wood. I won the heat; unfortunately, he came back and won the event in the finals, running :15.4. But I was so far back in the finals that I didn't even place. In fact, when Wood crossed the line, I could barely see him."

The final score gave the win to Roanoke. The team accumulated 43 points, to 35 for Hampden-Sydney, 34½ for Randolph-Macon, 28 for Bridgewater, and 21 for Lynchburg. A trophy was awarded to an excited, yelling Roanoke team. Each of the individuals placing first, second, or third also received medals.

I remember . . . "During my second year of running, we went to Lynchburg for the Little Six meet. In the qualifying heats, I would have set a record time in the 220 that would have been hard to beat for years. But I was on that flat straightaway about 20 yards ahead of everyone. And then I heard, 'Slow down. You're killing yourself.' So I slowed my pace and trotted casually across the finish line. I was burning it up that day."

Bob Fagg

May 14-15, 1948
Mason-Dixon Championships at Washington, D. C.
Team Scores: 1st–Johns Hopkins University–50 9/10
2nd–Washington College–36

3rd–Catholic University–35½
4th–Randolph-Macon College–26 7/10
5th–Roanoke College–21½
6th–Loyola University–16
7th–American University–13
8th–Hampden-Sydney College–10 7/10
9th–Lynchburg College–6½
10th–Gallaudet College–5 1/5
11th–Bridgewater College–2

On May 14 and 15, 1948, the team entered the thirteenth annual Mason-Dixon Championships, held at Catholic University in Washington. Homer was under no illusion that his boys could win this meet. Reports from other coaches seem to show without doubt that the northern Mason-Dixon teams were very strong this year. In addition, individuals on the Roanoke team had never had to endure the stress of a two-day meet, where there were qualifying events on Friday that you had to do well in before getting to the finals on Saturday. The boys may not score many points, he thought, but they all needed to see the circus that was a large meet.

Coach Bast and his team left the Salem campus on Thursday afternoon for the long drive to Washington. All were looking forward to the meet, Roanoke's first dive into Mason-Dixon Conference action, and the team seemed loose.

They awoke the next morning to an overcast sky and a slight drizzle. By the time the qualifying events were completed, the showers were steady.

Roanoke did as well as Homer thought they would in the semifinals of the running events:

120-Yard High Hurdles

First Heat:	1st -Smyth (Loyola)–:16.6; 2nd-Browning (Catholic)
Second Heat:	1st-Wood (Lynchburg)–:16.2; 2nd-Rosebro (Roanoke)

100-Yard Dash

First Heat:	1st-Chewning (Hampden-Sydney)–:10.5; 2nd-Zahringer (Catholic)
Second Heat:	1st-Nencioni (American)–:10.2; 2nd-Brunk (Loyola)
Third Heat:	1st -Rudd (Catholic)–:10.3; 2nd-Fagg (Roanoke)

440-Yard Dash

First Heat: 1st-Sterns (Johns Hopkins)–:52.9; 2nd-Groffle (Catholic)
Second Heat: 1st-Schwartz (Johns Hopkins)–:53.2; 2nd-Evans (Randolph-Macon)
Third Heat: 1st-Jackson (Catholic)–:52.2; 2nd-Brandburgh (Washington)

Note: All qualified for the finals.

220-Yard Dash

First Heat: 1st-Rudd (Catholic)–:22.6; 2nd-Schwartz (Johns Hopkins)
Second Heat: 1st-Nencioni (American)–:22.8; 2nd-Zahringer (Catholic)
Third Heat: 1st-Penso (American)–:23.1; 2nd-Hubbard (Washington)

220-Yard Low Hurdles

First Heat: 1st-Shuman (Washington)–:27.1; 2nd-Boegel (Catholic)
Second Heat: 1st-Drewer (Randolph-Macon)–:26.8; 2nd-Maskell (Loyola)
Third Heat: 1st-Smith (Loyola)–:26.7; 2nd-Rosebro (Roanoke)

880-Yard Run

First Heat: 1st-Grim (Johns Hopkins)–2:03.3; 2nd-McCarty (Roanoke)
Second Heat: 1st-Brandenberg (Washington)–2:06.7; 2nd-Jackson (CU)
Third Heat: 1st-Smith (Roanoke)–2:06.5; 2nd-Donoghue (Catholic)

As expected, Roanoke moved no one to the Saturday finals in the shot put, discus, or broad jump:

Shot Put (Qualifiers)

Blizzard (Washington)–39'10"
Dozier (Johns Hopkins)–39'5"
Hirsch (Johns Hopkins)–37'7"
Smith (Bridgewater)-37'2"

Discus (Qualifiers)

Consolo (Catholic)–131'3¼"*
Bodkin (Bridgewater)–122'9¼"
Scrivener (Randolph-Macon)–120'2¼"
Andrae (Johns Hopkins)–117'4"
Lassahn (Johns Hopkins)–116'8¾"
Blizzard (Washington)–115'6"

* Meet record. Old record of 130'10½" set by Rosenthal of Johns Hopkins in 1941.

Broad Jump

Weighart (Johns Hopkins)–20'4½"
Gaithright (Randolph-Macon)-20'1"
Moody (Catholic)–19'11⅞"
Bales (Hampden-Sydney)–19'9¼"
Garber (Randolph-Macon)-19'9"

The pre-meet favorite, Johns Hopkins, led with 10 qualifiers. Behind Hopkins were Catholic University with 9; Randolph-Macon, 8; Washington College, 7; Roanoke, 5; Loyola, 4; American University, Bridgewater, and Hampden-Sydney, 3; Gallaudet, 2; Lynchburg, 1.

The day was not kind to one person who should have made the finals, but didn't. Gene Wood of Lynchburg, whom most people thought would win the low hurdles easily on Saturday, hit the last hurdle in his trial heat and was eliminated. He had a big lead and was breezing toward the finish line when he turned for a quick look at his pursuers, struck the hurdle, and went face-down into the cinders.

Len Chewning, the excellent Hampden-Sydney sprinter, did manage to qualify for Saturday's 100-yard dash finals; however, he was eliminated Friday in the 220 semifinals by being placed in a fast heat of 220 sprinters.

Roanoke's Bob Fagg was eliminated from the high hurdles finals. Many spectators said that the judges unfairly placed him in a lower position as he crossed the line, but that he actually finished second. In addition, Thanning Andersen, another sterling hurdler, was running well in his heat of that event when he tripped and fell, failing to reach the finals.

Although another runner stepped on Alvin Smith's heel, and he had to complete the race without his shoe, he went on to win the mile run in the Mason-Dixon Meet in 4:35.7. The picture was printed in newspapers all over the country.

By Saturday morning, the weather had cleared and the day seemed destined to bring great performances. Without a doubt, the best race in which a Maroon took part was the mile run. Alvin Smith, Roanoke's spectacular miler, was expected to win. He hadn't been defeated in that event during the season. But, as he describes it, there was one hitch: "Right at the start of the race, some guy stepped on my heel and pulled the heel of my shoe down off my foot. I tried in the next few strides to get it back in place, but couldn't. So I just kicked it off and ran the rest of the race with one shoe on and the other one off." Amazingly, his first place time of 4:35.7 set a new school record, chopping more than seven second off of his own record of 4:43.0. Although he had qualified to run in the 880-yard run finals, he decided just before the race not to run.

Bill Williams was the other star of the Roanoke team. No one expected much of him because he had been unable to practice much since he turned his ankle several weeks ago. Bast was stunned when he heard that Williams had cleared 11'10" to finish in a tie for second. The winner also jumped 11'10", but placement of the first four men (one in first place and three tied for second) was based on tiebreakers.

Bob Fagg placed third for the Maroons in the 100-yard dash finals on Saturday, after running in five preliminary races on Friday. Rud Rosebro finished the scoring for the Maroons by taking fourth in the 220-yard low hurdles and fifth in the 120-yard high hurdles

At day's end, the final team scores were:

1st–Johns Hopkins University (JH)–50$^{9}/_{10}$
2nd–Washington College (W)–36

Top: Bob Fagg wins the 100 in the 1948 Randolph-Macon meet.
Bottom Left: In the Mason-Dixon Championships of 1948, L to R, Fagg (Roanoke), Chewning (Hampden-Sydney), Rudd (Catholic), and Bunk (Loyola).
Bottom Right: In the finals of the 220-yard low hurdles in the Mason-Dixon Championships of 1948, L to R, Smyth (Loyola), Rosebro (Roanoke), Maskell (Loyola), Drawer (Randolph-Macon), and Schuman (Washington). Rosebro finished fourth in the race. The winning time, by Schuman, was :26.1.

3rd–Catholic University (C)–35½
4th–Randolph-Macon College (RM)–26 7/10
5th–Roanoke College (R)–21½
6th–Loyola University (LOY)–16
7th–American University (A)–13
8th–Hampden-Sydney College (HS)–10 7/10
9th–Lynchburg College (L)–6½

10th–Gallaudet College (G)–5 1/5
11th–Bridgewater College (B)–2

I remember . . . "I have a picture of Alvin Smith running with his shoe off. That picture appeared in lots of papers. Alvin got national publicity from the photo. He lost his shoe but won the race, people said. Of course, I wasn't worried about any of the races in which Alvin ran. Sometimes, of course, he would be in one of his moods. The wind is too strong, there is too much cigarette smoke in the air, and more. At those times I would just tell him to cut out that stuff–that he could beat anyone there. I just didn't want to hear it anymore. The good thing about Alvin, however, was that he was capable of winning at any time. He had a dog-gone good kick. He could turn on that speed in the last 200 yards and blow away all of his competition."

Homer Bast

May 22, 1948
Virginia AAU Championships in Lynchburg, Virginia
Team Scores: Unknown

The final meet of the year was scheduled to be the Virginia State AAU Championships, to be held at Lynchburg, Virginia on May 22, 1948. Unfortunately, it is unclear as to whether Roanoke was represented in the event. One notation reported that Captain Paul McCarty and teammate Alvin Smith were entering the meet, with Paul running the 880 and Smith the mile; however, in no other sources are their names to be found in connection with the meet.

Homer took some time during the next few days to think about the season. He was pleased to see that, when the team met in May, Bruce Davenport and Paul McCarty were chosen to co-captain the cross country team the next year while Alvin Smith and Bill Williams were selected by the team to co-captain the track team.

Sadly, some of his steadier performers would be leaving Roanoke after the 1947-48 school year. Among others, they included all around star Bob Fagg and the dependable Jim Ruscick.

Chapter Four

THE 1948-49 SEASONS

As the campus came to life in the fall of 1948, dormitory space was at a premium because more than 630 students were being registered for classes. To create more living space, the College took over a white frame building called Hildreth Hall for a new men's dormitory, moving the Maintenance Department from that facility to a Quonset hut next door and nearer to the athletic field. In those days, you walked up a narrow, paved street from the south end of the track to the campus. Hildreth sat along this street at the top of the hill.

To the delight of students, the College also opened its new outdoor swimming pool during the summer of 1948. That pool was available to students, faculty, and alumni for some 30 years.

The athletic department saw the end of some of its problems with team transportation when Clarence Caldwell, Finance Director, purchased two new cars. The two old cars that athletes had been using had accumulated a total of a quarter million miles between them.

Caldwell told Homer to take Mary Jane, get on an airplane, and go to Detroit to pick up one of the cars. The other car would be shipped to Salem. In those days, cars had to be driven at 45 MPH the first couple hundred miles, then a couple hundred miles at 50 MPH, etc., just to break them in. Caldwell suggested that after picking up the car, Homer and Mary Jane might stop to see some sites along the way back just to get some rest and relaxation.

So Homer and Mary Jane took a plane to Detroit, stayed overnight, and went to the manufacturing plant the next morning. They picked up one of the two brand new station wagons, then drove around Detroit and went into Canada. Fran Ramser of the Physical Education Department lived in that area, at a place called Wellington, Ohio. Her father had a hotel there. The Basts surprised Fran and her family by stopping by to see them. They knocked on Fran's door after the restaurant in the hotel was closed for the day. Fran saw Homer and Mary Jane and was astonished. Fran insisted that they stay overnight in the hotel, at no charge, and immediately began to feed them. They all sat around the kitchen table and talked for several hours. Fran's father even made them pies. After a good night's sleep, Homer and Mary Jane headed for Salem.

Dr. Charles Smith (Dr. Charlie), who had been President of the school for many years, had already announced that he was retiring as of the end of the 1948-49 school year. He had been an active supporter of athletics through the years. Homer remembers that he was very much in favor of having track and cross country competition. "I think he liked track," Homer said, "because we were developing individuals. In those days, the College began to sponsor so many events in which a boy or girl could participate."

Cross Country

Needing some standard way to record cross country records from year to year, Homer decided to create a new 3.1-mile course. It was the same course that would be used for the next 10 or more years at Roanoke.

The course had its beginning on the track at Alumni Field, and from there proceeded up the paved roadway past Hildreth, across the campus, and through the East gate. Runners then turned left and proceeded up High Street to Hawthorne Avenue and along Hawthorne to Red Lane. Then the runners made a circle around the Baptist Orphanage in West Salem, and continued by the public golf course down Morton Avenue to Broad Street. The conclusion of the run was along Broad Street to the west end of Hawthorne, to Market Street, and then to the starting point on Alumni Field.

Just after the first days of classes, Coach Bast extended an invitation for any boy interested in running cross country to come to practice. About 17 individuals responded.

In the latter part of September, Homer and Buddy Hackman took a weekend off to attend the annual Mason-Dixon meeting in Washington. There, the colleges discussed plans and rules for the upcoming seasons. One of the more important questions was that of freshmen eligibility to participate in athletics against member schools. It finally was decided to keep the newcomers eligible for varsity competition. In view of the fairly large group of first year men attending Mason-Dixon schools, this move was more than acceptable to the Maroon coaches. Of course, many of the Mason-Dixon schools in those days, including Roanoke, didn't have very many students. It was essential that they be able to use freshmen on their athletic teams.

However, they also learned that because of Southern Conference rules, freshmen could not compete in meets with any of their schools. In terms of Roanoke's schedule, those rules meant that freshmen could not be used in meets with schools such as Virginia Polytechnic Institute, Washington and Lee, or Virginia Military Institute. Some of these teams, already committed to cross country and track meets for 1948-49, had to be dropped from the schedule. In some cases, as with Washington and Lee, the schools might agree to run separate freshman-versus-freshman meets in addition to the regular varsity meets.

Top Photo (L to R): Bruce Davenport, Paul McCarty, Alvin Smith,. and Red Crockett.
Bottom Left Photo (L to R): Alvin Smith and Red Crockett.
Bottom Right Photo: Bruce Davenport.

By October 1, Coach Bast had released the following cross country schedule for 1948:

October 9	Roanoke vs. Washington and Lee (Varsity) at Salem
October 9	Roanoke vs. Washington and Lee (Freshmen) at Salem
October 19	Roanoke vs. Lynchburg at Salem
October 23	Roanoke vs. Randolph-Macon at Ashland
October 28	Roanoke vs. Hampden-Sydney at Salem
November 2	Roanoke vs. Gallaudet at Washington
November 6	Little Six Championships at Bridgewater
November 22	Mason-Dixon Championships at Washington

The freshman rule did cause the cancellation of one meet. V. P. I. notified Roanoke that they would be unable to host a meet between the schools on the agreed-to date of

November 10 if Roanoke chose to compete with freshmen. By mutual agreement, the meet was never run.Training continued and Coach Bast could see that he had far more talent than he did in 1947. Just before the first meet with Washington and Lee, Homer tried for a second year to start an intramural cross country meet for students. This time, unlike in the fall of 1947, some 15 boys ran and finished the 1½ -mile course on the streets around the campus. Points were awarded to the first five finishers for each team. A team would be made up of a particular fraternity's runners or, as in future years, perhaps members of the campus dormitories or off-campus residents who hadn't pledged a fraternity. The results would count in the final intramural standings. The winner of the event would have his name permanently engraved on a trophy which would be kept in the gymnasium trophy case, and many of the runners would receive Roanoke College T-shirts.

The following individuals completed the run:

1st–White Rhyne–7:42
2nd–George Naff–7:58
3rd–Tump Lemon–8:01
4th–Bernard Dillon–8:17
5th–Alvin Stump–8:30
6th –Roy Basham–8:35
7th–William Nock–8:48
8th–James Redmond–9:00
9th–Gil Robinson–9:17
10th–Donald Cohen–9:35
11th–Jack Thurmond–9:44
12th–John Byerly–10:09
13th–Dick Fraley–11:35
14th–George Dawson and Hal Dunbar–11:44

The Sigma Chi fraternity won the team competition, with a score of 20. Kappa Alpha fraternity was second with 38 points. Pi Kappa Phi and Lambda Kappa Psi, the other fraternities on the campus, failed to field a team for the event.

The first seven, from White Rhyne to William Nock, ended up running cross country that year. Of course, one of Coach Bast's purposes in starting the intramural cross country program was to find boys with running potential and to convince them to be members of the cross country and track teams.

The intramural meet also became the vehicle for getting publicity for the cross country and track teams. Sometimes, one of the individuals from the meet would be encouraged to write for the *Brackety-Ack*. For example, Homer still remembers talking with George Naff. "I saw quickly that he wasn't very interested in running. But he was interested in writing, perhaps as a sports editor. I told him to come down to watch our practices, and we would take him on our trips. First, however, I suggested that he go to the Roanoke College library and read the New York Times to see the way sports writers wrote in that paper. He developed a pretty good style, publishing in the *Brackety-Ack*. He was a nice boy and a pretty smart guy. And we became good friends."

It was hard for Coach Bast to forecast the wins and losses for the upcoming season, but he certainly thought the team would do well. His three big-name runners were Alvin Smith, Paul McCarty, and Bruce Davenport. But he also had L. Z. "Red" Crockett, Frank Aldred, Tunstal "Tump" Lemon, Henry Roth, Maynard Turk, John Byerly, Glen Lyn, and Tommy Cartwright. Others who seemed to have talent included White "Whitey" Rhyne, Roy Basham, Alvin Stump, Sandy Worthington, Elwood Purdham, and George Naff. The manager's duties would be handled this year by Bobby Davenport, Bruce's brother.

I remember . . . White Rhyne went on to have a fine distance running career over a four-year period at Roanoke. One of his teammates remembers something that White did to help his stamina. "When I was a junior," the individual said, "White was a freshman. He sewed lead into his practice shoes. Apparently, he had read some place that all of the great runners put lead in their practice shoes so they would be light on their feet in the meets. When we were at Roanoke, there was no place we could run on level ground except for the track itself. The cross country course followed many hills and was all paved. It was bad enough running up and down those hills, but I can't imagine doing it with lead in your shoes. But I guess it worked for him."

Anonymous

I remember . . . Bruce Davenport was a superb distance runner. He and Alvin Smith were not only members of the Big Four group that received so much publicity, but they helped put Roanoke College on the map for cross country and track. Homer remembers Bruce well. "Bruce was a great person, and very, very sharp," Homer says. "His father had been a miler at Virginia Tech. Over the years, Bruce and I became very good friends. He married a wonderful girl who went to Roanoke College and they had a nice family. Bruce was a physics/math major and was active in lots of campus activities. He also had a brother who came to Roanoke. In fact, he was once the Manager of our cross country and track teams. Bruce was a leader all the way. When it came to being a part of the Big Four, he was selfless. He was willing to tie with teammates if they wanted to tie. At the same time, in meets like the Mason-Dixon Championships, he was a tenacious runner and was determined that no one else would cross the line before him."

Homer Bast

I remember . . . "We always had at least one team manager for each of our cross country, indoor track, and outdoor track teams. In 1948-49, for example, Bruce Davenport's older brother, Bobby served as manager for us. Our managers had specific tasks to perform. Their main responsibility was to the team. You had to keep their equipment straight, and it was much harder to do so with track than with cross country. I had some really good managers through the years. Generally, it was their jobs to keep the uniforms clean. On the other hand, we couldn't afford to buy all new uniforms every year. We just didn't have the money to dress all members of the team in the same uniform."

Homer Bast

I remember . . . "I think I took a class with Homer during my first semester at Roanoke College in the fall of 1948. During my two years at Roanoke, I had him for several additional classes. He inspired me, not only giving me an interest in history, but to go on into history teaching as a career."

Frank Aldred

I remember . . . "I recruited Paul McCarty from the baseball team. He finally realized that he wasn't going to play very much for Buddy Hackman. But he loved baseball. He really didn't like track when he first came out for the sport. He and I both were impressed, however, when in his first 880 race, he recorded a time of 2:05. I thought that was an excellent start. Over the years, he was an inspirational individual and a major part of our cross country and track programs. He was even elected Captain of the track team one year. His college major was economics. After he graduated from Roanoke, he couldn't find a job he liked. So he took a part-time position as a dance instructor for Arthur Murray's dance studios for a couple of years. At the same time, the College was having problems getting economists and hired Paul to teach basic economics. He taught here for a couple of years, in fact. As a runner, he served us well. I realized that he didn't like distance running very much, and despite that fact, he turned out to be a fairly good half miler. Sometimes, I even ran him in the quarter. He went on to have a fine career, ending up as President of a bank."

Homer Bast

October 9, 1948
Washington and Lee University at Salem, Virginia
Team Scores: Roanoke–20
Washington and Lee–35

Just after 3:00 p.m. on October 9, the Washington and Lee and Roanoke teams began to warm up on Alumni Field. The coaches had scheduled a freshman meet to precede the varsity competition. The freshmen would run a 2½-mile course, with the top five finishers counting in the scoring. Roanoke's entries were White Rhyne, Alvin Stump, Sandy Worthington, Bernard Dillon, Roy Basham, George Naff, and Elwood Purdham.

The winner of the race was Echols Harnsbarger of Washington and Lee, with a time of 15:10. The next three places, however, went to Roanoke freshmen. White Rhyne finished second (16:30), George Naff third (17:20), and Alvin Stump fourth (18:30). Following the fifth, sixth, and seventh runners, all from Washington and Lee, Roy Basham (19:21) and William Nock (19:34) took the eighth and ninth spots, respectively, to give the Salem team a narrow victory, 26-29.

Within a minute after the gun sounded for the varsity race, even at the east gate of the College at High Street, spectators knew that Roanoke was on its way to another win. Because much of the course could not be seen by people on campus, onlookers were unable to determine just what was happening on the course. Finally, coming down Market Street and turning onto the Alumni Field track were four Roanoke athletes–Alvin Smith, Bruce Davenport, Paul McCarty, and Red Crockett. They made a three-quarter lap trip around the backside of the track in order to finish in the middle of the straightaway near Market Street. About 100 yards from the finish line, the four runners joined hands and crossed the line together, arms held high, in a time of 19:20.0. And thus began the legend of the Big Four who, the story would go, were so good that together they could beat anyone they wanted to and with hardly a workout.

Sandy Worthington completed the scoring for Roanoke with a 10th place finish, followed by Tump Lemon and Henry Roth. The final team score was Roanoke–20, Washington and Lee–35.

October 19, 1948
Lynchburg College at Salem, Virginia
Team Scores: Roanoke–15
Lynchburg–51

Ten days later, on October 19, the Big Four triumphed again. In a meet run in Salem against Lynchburg College, Smith, Davenport, McCarty, and Crockett joined hands to finish the race in a course record 19:08. White Rhyne, just over 30 seconds back of the group, finished 5th to give Roanoke a perfect score of 15. Lynchburg's total was 51. After Rhyne, Maroons took 8 of the next 10 positions. Bernard Dillon was 7th, Alvin Stump 8th, George Naff 9th, Tump Lemon 10th, William Nock 12th, Elwood Purdham 13th, Frank Aldred 14th, and Roy Basham 15th.

By this time, the news of the fabulous four runners at Roanoke College had begun to spread. Even bus riders, according to Coach Bast, were talking about the amazing runners in Salem who couldn't be beaten. But where did the idea of holding hands originate. No one seems to know for sure; however, Alvin Smith years later thought the Big Four concept had never been new to him when he transferred to Roanoke. "We did that in high school," he said. "Our coach down at Jefferson High School, Stanley Craft, used to tell us that if we saw we were all going to finish together, there was no use in racing each other. He was the one who got me interested in holding hands as we crossed the line. Actually, we found out later that holding hands like this could have been illegal in some situations, in particular where you might have blocked a trailing runner from passing the front group."

At any rate, Coach Bast was not displeased that his runners would choose to finish together. The "Big Four" concept brought the team lots of attention. Maybe a few high school athletes would hear about it and decide that Roanoke was the place to attend college.

The team was now 2-0 for the season. Their next meet was in Ashland versus Randolph-Macon on October 23. Coach Bast had heard that Randolph-Macon already had been defeated during the fall by Washington and Lee, the University of Richmond, and Davidson; however, all of those losses had been by narrow margins.

October 23, 1948
Randolph-Macon College at Ashland, Virginia
Team Scores: Roanoke–16
Randolph-Macon–45

On the afternoon of the meet, weather conditions were miserable–so bad that it was difficult even to warm up. It was raining and the course was muddy. And there was a consistent wind. After the start of the race, as usual, Roanoke's first tier of runners moved ahead of the pack. Footing was treacherous throughout the 4.0 mile course and uniforms were soon covered with flying mud.

At the finish line, there they were again. The Big Four–Smith, McCarty, Davenport, and Crockett–crossed arm-in-arm in a time of 23:27. Francis Byrnes of Randolph-Macon finished in 5th place, some 13 seconds behind the first group, but White Rhyne, the smooth striding freshman, toured the course in 24:15 to pick up a 6th place. Roanoke also took the 9th through 13th places in the meet. Frank Aldred was 9th, Bernard Dillon 10th, Alvin Stump 11th, George Naff 12th, and Tump Lemon 13th.

The race turned out to be an easy one for the Maroons, whose final winning score was 16-45. The weather had been awful, but the victory was the team's third straight for the season.

October 28, 1948
Hampden-Sydney College at Salem, Virginia
Team Scores: Roanoke–16
Hampden-Sydney–51

On October 28, Hampden-Sydney came to town, running in their first cross country meet of the year. They didn't have a deeply talented team, but the ace of their runners–Gene Milner–was destined to become one of the state's leading distance men during the next couple of years. Coach Bast had heard through the grapevine that he was a good athlete, so he wondered if his Big Four group could finish together once again.

Bast was forced to adjust the length of the course, from 3.1 miles to 2.8 miles, because of construction on the roads in the area. Milner, Crockett, Smith, McCarty, and Davenport broke from the pack early in the race. As they came down Market Street toward the finish area, however, the four Roanoke boys sprinted ahead of Milner. They crossed the finish line hand in hand once again, with Milner just four seconds back. The Maroons also captured the 6th through 12th positions to win the meet, 16 to 51. Hampden-Sydney runners took the 13th through 17th positions.

Besides the Big Four, Roanoke men included:

6th–White Rhyne
7th–Frank Aldred
8th–Bernard Dillon
9th–George Naff
10th–Alvin Stump
11th–Tump Lemon
12th–William Nock

Homer was pleased with the team and individual efforts. Hampden-Sydney, outside of Gene Milner, had very little depth; however, Bast saw that the team responded to Milner's challenge. And he was surprised to see that Frank Aldred had moved up in the scoring. He thought Frank would be a good runner by the following year.

Bast also knew that the boys hadn't encountered a lot of opposition in any of the four meets they had run thus far. They had outscored their opponents by 67 to 182, an average of 16.7 to 45.5 in individual scores. It would be interested to see how well they would do in the Little Six and Mason-Dixon meets, both of which were coming up fast.

November 2, 1948
Gallaudet College at Washington, D. C.
Team Scores: Roanoke–15
Gallaudet–52

The next meet was with Gallaudet College in Washington on November 2. Gallaudet was a school that specialized in education for deaf and hard-of-hearing students, and the trip was a learning opportunity for Roanoke athletes. Most of them had never known anyone who used American sign language. As they warmed up for the race that afternoon, they encountered a strange feeling when they realized that there was virtually no noise around them.

The 1948 Cross Country Team:
Top Picture - Front (L to R): Bruce Davenport, George Naff, Bob Davenport, Sandy Worthington, Alvin Smith, and Henry Roth. Back (L to R): Tump Lemon, Paul McCarty, Red Crockett, White Rhyne, Bill Nock, Alvin Stump, and Roy Basham
Bottom Picture: Part of the cross country team for 1948. Kneeling (L to R) - Alvin Smith, Bruce Davenport, John Turbyfill, Paul McCarty. Standing (L to R) –Frank Aldred, White Rhyne, Red Crockett, Coach Bast

The race that afternoon wasn't very competitive. The Maroon runners pulled into a good lead early and, just as in the previous four meets, the top four Roanoke runners all moved abreast as they moved closer to the finish line. Again, the Big Four group joined hands and crossed the line together in a time of 21:19, which was the third best time ever recorded for the Gallaudet course.

Following Smith, Davenport, McCarty, and Crockett came two Maroons–White Rhyne in 5th place and Frank Aldred in 6th. The two crossed virtually in a tie, in 22:12, but the judges gave White the edge. Bernard Dillon finished in 8th place, while Alvin Stump was 10th, George Naff was 11th, and Tump Lemon was 12th.

The meet score was a lopsided 15 to 52. Coach Bast thought the boys did well, and with their fifth consecutive win, would likely have a lot of confidence going into the two big meets to come. Of course, the Gallaudet race hadn't really pushed them, but he could sense that the trip to Gallaudet would be beneficial. Gallaudet was the host of the Mason-Dixon Championships 20 days later.

Because it was late in the year, Bast had his men work out lightly for the next three days. He wanted legs to be fresh for the second annual Little Six meet, to be held on Bridgewater College's 3.6 mile course on November 6.

November 6, 1948
Little Six Championships at Bridgewater, Virginia
Team Scores: 1st–Roanoke College–25
2nd–Bridgewater College–44
3rd–Hampden-Sydney College–104
4th–Randolph–Macon College–106
5th–Lynchburg College–113

The undefeated Roanoke squad traveled to Bridgewater on the morning of the 6th. Member schools in the Little Six Conference enjoyed having their meet each year at Bridgewater. They wanted to be able to compare year-to-year times. Bridgewater was also easy to reach for most schools. Homer always enjoyed running there. He could stand on the field and get a fairly good view of the runners as they made their way around the course. They would run alongside the river and in about 200 yards or so would make a hard left turn. Then they progressed up a hill. He could see by the color of their jerseys who was in which position. Homer remembers that Harry Jopson always brought his binoculars and would tell the other coaches the positions of all the runners.

The weather was good for this time of the year, and most athletes started their warm-ups by 2:30 p.m. for the 3:30 p.m. race. All of the conference schools were present except for Emory and Henry. Little Six rules this year specified that the first five to finish would count in the scoring. Roanoke, winner of the first Little Six cross country meet in 1947, was favored to take the first place trophy again. In 1947 the trio of McCarty, Davenport, and Crockett finished in a three-way tie for first. This year, of course, they had added Alvin Smith, considered the premiere distance runner among small colleges in the Commonwealth. The full team for this year's race was composed of McCarty, Davenport, Crockett, and Smith, along with White Rhyne, Frank Aldred, Bernard Dillon, and Alvin Stump.

Pre-race gossip was that Bridgewater also had good talent this year, and might be the one team to upset Roanoke in the race. They also were unbeaten during the 1948 season, having defeated Gallaudet, Lynchburg, Catholic, and Davis and Elkins. Harry Jopson, the Bridgewater coach, seldom fielded an untalented team.

Bast had also heard about several runners, besides Gene Milner of Hampden-Sydney, who could break up the Big Four style of finish. Bridgewater had good runners in Raymond Sellers, Paul Crizer, Warren Bowman, and Dick Jarrells. Lynchburg would be running Grant Hudson, while Francis Byrnes would carry the hopes of Randolph-Macon.

The race began, and Bruce Davenport for Roanoke quickly moved into the lead, followed by the other top runners on the team. Bast lost track of the athletes for a few minutes, but toward the end of the run, he could see Bruce, Red Crockett, and Alvin Smith close in together and, hand in hand, win the top award in a time of 20:27.8, a record time for the Bridgewater course. But where was Paul McCarty? It turned out that Paul was forced to drop out. After running for nearly three miles, he lost his strength and had to leave the race because of exhaustion. At the time, however, he was running at the head of the field with his three teammates. Had he been able to stay in the race, he undoubtedly would have finished with them in a quadruple tie.

Hampden-Sydney's Milner finished in fourth place, with Byrnes (Randolph-Macon), Jarrels (Bridgewater), and Crouse (Bridgewater) close behind–all within five seconds of each other. Other Roanoke runners figuring in the score were White Rhyne (8th), Frank Aldred (11th), Bernard Dillon (15th), and Tump Lemon (23rd).

Bridgewater was second in team scoring with a total of 44 points, behind Roanoke's low of 25, when their runners took 6th, 7th, 9th, 10th, and 12th places. With 104 points, Hampden-Sydney was 3rd. Randolph-Macon finished 4th (106) and Lynchburg was 5th (113).

The race established Roanoke as one of the outstanding distance teams in the state. It also sent a message to the other Mason-Dixon teams. Roanoke was loaded and on the way for another title.

I remember . . . "I'll tell you another story about Homer. On one of those trips we took down the valley, I think it was after a meet on November 6, 1948, we were talking about the election returns for the presidential race between Thomas Dewey and Harry Truman. Everyone in the car, except for Homer, thought that Dewey would win. But Homer told us that he had voted for Harry, and he thought Truman would pull this one out. After that trip, I always believed everything Homer said."

White Rhyne

November 22, 1948
Mason-Dixon Championships at Washington, D. C.
Team Scores: 1st–Roanoke College–37
2nd–Loyola College–75
3rd–Bridgewater College–78
4th–Washington College–90
5th–Johns Hopkins University–131
6th–Catholic University–163
7th–Hampden-Sydney College–191
8th–Randolph-Macon College–197
9th–Gallaudet College–204
10th–Mount St. Mary's College–289

The Mason-Dixon Championships were set for 3:45 p.m. on November 22, at Gallaudet College in Washington. The date gave Coach Bast plenty of time to get the boys ready. The meet would bring to an end an already-successful season for members of the Maroon team. They had won all five of their dual meets. They beat Washington and Lee 20 to 35, Lynchburg 15 to 45, Randolph-Macon 16-45, Hampden-Sydney 16-51, and finished by defeating Gallaudet in the final dual meet 15 to 52. They also won the Little Six title easily with 25 points.

Thirteen Mason-Dixon schools entered the meet. Roanoke, Loyola, Bridgewater, Johns Hopkins, Mount St. Mary's, Hampden-Sydney, Randolph-Macon, Gallaudet, Catholic, and Washington all sent full teams. Western Maryland, American, and Towson would be represented by one or two runners each. Roanoke and Loyola were the team favorites based on existing records. Johns Hopkins and Bridgewater were the bets to pull an upset.

In the afternoon of the 21st, ten Roanoke team members, Coach Bast, and Manager Bobby Davenport piled in the two almost-new college cars for the trip to Washington. Not all of the athletes could compete, however. Mason-Dixon Conference rules allowed each team to enter up to eight men and provided that the first five runners from each team would score for their school.

Runners on the morning of October 22 found a 3¾-mile wind and rain swept Gallaudet course. The gun sounded and more than 70 men left the starting line. Several Maroon runners grouped toward the front of this mass of runners, but one of the opposing runners simply took off. He was George Rodney of Loyola, who had been the national interscholastic cross country champion in the fall of 1947. The talented runner moved in front and quickly separated himself from the rest of the pack. Finishing 1st, he was timed in 20:33, which set a new conference record for the course. The record erased the mark of 21:06, set by Chester Hackett of Catholic in 1946.

Roanoke was led by their best runner, Alvin Smith, who ran an excellent race and finished in second place with a time of 21:05, only 30 seconds behind the winner. Bruce Davenport and Red Crockett followed closely behind Smith to finish third and fourth, respectively. Paul McCarty took 11th place in 21:43, with White Rhyne finishing 17th with a time of 22:27. Non-scoring members of the team were Bernard Dillon (27th) and George Naff (44th).

After the last rain-soaked man had finished the race, officials announced the order of finish:

1st–Roanoke College (R)–37
2nd–Loyola College (L)–75
3rd–Bridgewater College (B)–78
4th–Washington College (W)–90
5th–Johns Hopkins University (JH)–131
6th–Catholic University (C)–163
7th–Hampden-Sydney College (HS)–191
8th–Randolph-Macon College (RM)–197
9th–Gallaudet College (G)–204
10th–Mount St. Mary's College (MSM)–289

All of the participants and their coaches then moved to Chapel Hall at Gallaudet, not far from the track, for the awards program. Coach Bast was called forward, congratulated, and given the Gallaudet Pharmacy Championship Trophy. Then the top fifteen runners in the meet were awarded medals. For Roanoke the medals went to Alvin Smith, Bruce Davenport, Red Crockett, and Paul McCarty. The trophy would go permanently into the Alumni Gymnasium trophy case.

The team arrived back to Salem and there were a few loud, celebratory horn blasts while the cars circled the quadrangle in the middle of the campus. Word quickly spread that team members had taken the Mason-Dixon championship. The next day, runners could go nowhere on campus without hearing the congratulations of students and faculty.

A few days later, Bob McLelland wrote a Sport Korner column in the *Brackety-Ack* entitled "A Cheer for Bast's Boys." It was a tribute to the team and its coach.

> Last week, the Roanoke College cross country team lived up to all expectations and captured the annual Mason-Dixon meet held in Washington. This was a very fitting climax for an all victorious season. In two years of competition, the thinclads have captured all three of the major meets they have entered (the Little Six meet in 1947 and 1948 and the 1948 Mason-Dixon). This is quite a record for such a new sport and a lot of credit goes to their capable coach, Homer Bast. This gentleman introduced the sport here and has shown to one and all that he means to follow through with whatever he starts and make a success of it. Yes, the charges of Bast have brought a lot of fame to the campus with their outstanding feats and the entire RC family is proud of them.

What a year! The team gave Roanoke College its first undefeated athletic team since Coach "Pinky" Spruhan's basketball team had a perfect record in 1916.

I remember . . . "We began to get good publicity for cross country–not only in the local papers but from individuals on the campus. The student body really got into cross country and track. In cross country, they would gather near the finish line and when the first runner appeared, they would say 'here they come, here they come.' They particularly liked the times the boys came across the line hand-in-hand. The runners would come down Market Street, turn left onto the track, go around the back side of the track, and finish in the middle of the front side. Students and some faculty would line both sides of the finish line to cheer them on."

Homer Bast

I remember . . . "I thought that Frank Aldred had potential. I told him that if he really wanted to be a good runner, he should run during the summers. I said, 'Don't kill yourself, but get out every day you can.' So he did the summer workouts and the difference in his running from one year to the next was astounding. He was running right with the 'big boys' that next year."

Homer Bast

Indoor Track

Training for the indoor track season began in January of 1949. Still, without excessive travel there were not many meets available to enter each winter. But Coach Bast expected to have a fairly good team–at least in comparison with other Virginia small colleges.

January 15, 1949
Evening Star Games at Washington, D. C.

Mason-Dixon Sprint Medley Relay:	1st–Roanoke College (Crockett, Dodd, Tramposch, and Smith)–3:47.7
	2nd–Washington College (Brandenberg, Hubbard, Twilly, and Bowie)
	3rd–Randolph-Macon College (Evans, Dreever, Sheridan, and Woods)

The first of the two indoor meets Coach Bast wanted to enter was the Washington Star newspaper's Evening Star Games at the Armory in Washington. That meet would be run on January 15, 1949.

The Games were run for the first time in 1948. Coaches from throughout the country were startled to see the excellent results. Many scoffed at the fast times in the Armory, wondering why those times were faster than they were in their own arenas. The first year, for example, produced an 80-yard dash in eight seconds flat and a mile in 4:13.7. Part of the meet's success certainly had to do with the track itself. Although it was a flat track with no banked curves, it was a fast track because it contained eight laps to the mile. Madison Square Garden featured 11 laps to the mile, and the Philadelphia Garden 12. Also, the track had been painted with a non-slip substance that some runners seemed to prefer to tracks where spikes were required. And the Armory also gave the dash men the only 100-yard straightaway available in east coast indoor meets.

Another reason athletes enjoyed competing at the Armory was the facility's superior ventilation system. As one coach noted, "When the evening wanes, it isn't necessary to bring the boys home through the tobacco smoke with radar."

This winter's entries included athletes from 37 colleges, seven independent clubs, six prep schools, and the Quantico Marines. Olympic heroes such as Bob Mathias, national champions, and world record holders were expected to compete. Seven events were added to the program – six relays and the pole vault. In the vault it was necessary to canvas the East to obtain standards that would extend upward to at least 14 feet 6 inches, a height likely to be reached by Richard (Boo) Morcum or Bob Richards, the 1-2 qualifiers for the American Olympic team.

The 1949 meet would include five additional relays, giving 13 in all, and the baton-passing events would be climaxed by the Capital Invitation relay at 11:00 p.m.–the last event on the program. The Capital Mile would find Texas A&M, champion of the Southwest Conference, a slight favorite over a Seton Hall team that set the fastest times run in the East in 10 years last season.

The Maroons' goal was to enter and win the special Mason-Dixon Conference Sprint Medley Relay. Only members of the Mason-Dixon Conference, of course, could run in this event. The seven-squad race featured four runners per team. The runner who started the relay ran 440 yards and handed the baton to the next runner, who sprinted 220 yards to hand off to the third relay member, who ran the same distance. The runner on the anchor leg would then finish with an 880-yard run.

The Roanoke team thoroughly enjoyed the meet. Before their own sprint medley race, individuals marveled at the display of world-renowned athletes, occasionally jotting down on their programs the lanes and times for particular individuals. Finally, it was their time to warm up.

At the gun, Red Crockett sprinted from the starting line and fell in toward the front of the six other runners. He held on throughout the quarter mile and handed the baton to Dick Dodd. At that point, the team was in third place. Dick held his own and passed off to Walt Tramposch. Walt steadily gained on the leaders during his own 220.

The anchor man for Roanoke, running 880 yards, was Alvin Smith. Alvin, one of the best distance men in the Mason-Dixon Conference, came from fifteen yards behind to finish going away at least ten yards ahead of his nearest opponent, Larry Brandenburg of Washington College. The official time for Roanoke's team was 3:47.7. The boys were elated, and so was their coach.

At the awards ceremony, team members were given medals to commemorate their win. The Evening Star Newspaper took the team's picture as the Du Four trophy was being presented by a meet committee member Edward Rosenbloom. That large photo, along with pictures of many of the meet's exceptional athletes in action, appeared in the Evening Star the next day. Incidentally, you can find the Du Four trophy even today in a display case in the Roanoke College gymnasium.

Another interesting fact was that the wife of one of Roanoke's physics professors, Charles Raynor, happened to be in her Washington hotel room on the night of the meet and was shocked to look over at the TV at the moment the race was being run. There was the Roanoke team, running and winning the sprint medley race. It was likely the first time any Roanoke team's performance, in any sport, had been featured live on TV.

On the way back to Salem, the team detoured to Staunton, Virginia, and enjoyed the hospitality of Mary Jane Bast's mother. Mary Jane had come up to Staunton from Salem to help her mom prepare the boys' food, including sandwiches, cookies, coffee, drinks, and more. During those early years of cross country, but seldom during indoor and outdoor track because of the large number of athletes traveling with the track squads, many of Homer's teams stopped in Staunton to socialize and grab a bite to eat.

Eating well on an athletic trip, however, was a rare treat for team members. Alvin Smith recently remarked that the school seldom gave Homer any money for food while they were on trips. "Especially for dual meets," he said, "we'd always try to get to the meet after we had gotten a meal at the College, and try to return to the campus before we needed another one.

A few days later, after students took their first-semester exams, Coach Bast received the bad news. Red Crockett had run into academic difficulties and was ineligible to compete in track during the remainder of the 1948-49 session. Red was capable of running several events for Bast, from the 440-yard dash to the two-mile run, and had been one of the people on the team on which the coach could depend.

The blow of losing Red, however, was somewhat offset by the return to school of Bill Williams. Bill had not been at Roanoke all during the fall semester. Bill's specialty was the pole vault, in which he had jumped well over 11' and could bring in another two to five points in dual meets. He also was at home in field events ranging from the high jump to the javelin, and if needed he could run the sprints.

I remember . . . "Most people don't know about the hospitality that Homer's wife and family extended to the teams. When we would go up to Washington for a meet, such as the Evening Star Games, we'd start back to Salem. Then Homer would take a short detour to Mary Jane's parents' house in Staunton. There, ready for a hungry team, were all types of food and drinks. Often, Mary Jane would go up to Staunton from Salem to help her mother prepare the food. They'd be there waiting for us. even at midnight when we finished the meets late. We'd stop and have sandwiches, cookies, coffee, and such. Then, after a reasonable period of time, we'd come on back to the campus. Sometimes, we'd get home at three or four o'clock in the morning."

Alvin Smith

February 14, 1949
Virginia Indoor Championships at Charlottesville, Virginia
Team Scores: 1st–Virginia Polytechnic Institute–41
2nd–University of Virginia–25
3rd–Virginia Military Institute–16
4th–Washington and Lee University–10

5th–College of William and Mary–4
6th–University of Richmond–3
Randolph-Macon College–0
Bridgewater College–0
Roanoke College–0

The second meet of the 1949 indoor season came on February 14. The event, the second annual Virginia Indoor Championship Games, was held in the cramped confines of the University of Virginia's gymnasium. It was a night-time meet and all of the running events except for the sprints were conducted on a narrow balcony track above the basketball court. The track had extremely tight turns and event times were slower than usual.

Today, we don't know much about Roanoke's participation in the meet. For example, there is no record of which Maroons even made the trip. We do know, however, that Dick Fraley went to Charlottesville to compete, but the decision was made at the last minute to hold him out. He was still suffering from a pulled muscle.

We also know that Harry Bower entered the 50-yard dash; unfortunately, he was placed in one of the fastest trial heats and finished third to Sterling Wingo of Virginia Polytechnic and Wilbur Harrison of Virginia Military Institute. They both finished one-two, respectively, in the finals of the 50-yard dash and Harrison also won the 440-yard dash.

From Roanoke's perspective, the interesting race of the meet was the mile run. Archie Hahn, long-time coach of the University of Virginia track team, told the Maroons' Alvin Smith that he could not compete in the mile run. There was a rule in the Southern Conference that any athlete who had competed at a Southern Conference school, and then transferred to a non-conference school, must wait a specified time before being eligible to run officially against a conference team. Smith, of course, had taken courses at the University of North Carolina (a Southern Conference member) before transferring to Roanoke for the 1948 outdoor track season. Coach Bast suggested to Hahn that perhaps Smith could be allowed to run in the race unofficially with no team points being involved. Hahn agreed, probably to appease Bast, who had been a former track athlete at the University of Virginia.

Not only did Smith run the race, but he beat the official first-place winner, Bev Middleton of Virginia Polytechnic Institute, in the process. Smith's time was 4:42.0, while Middleton was given a time of 4:44.0.

No other Roanoke athlete scored in the meet, which was won by Virginia Polytechnic Institute. Randolph-Macon College, Bridgewater College, and Roanoke College finished last, each with no points.

I remember . . . "I think the University of Virginia's indoor track was 12 laps to the mile–three laps to the quarter. It was about 150 yards around the thing. The way they ran the quarter was to put three guys on one side and three on the other. So runners had no idea where they were in the race. Going back a few years, I ran my first race there as an intercollegiate runner. I was a freshman and I had the best time in the quarter mile for the freshmen. I think we ran against Washington and Lee. Not knowing how to run on the track, I figured that you had to run up to the top on the curves and then cut down. Now a big old guy like me, at 6'2" just couldn't handle the curves. But the young, short guys could. I worked myself to death on those three laps. I really put out. I think I got second or third place. I was sick for 48 hours, with the dry heaves, because I ran so hard. That was the first and only time that I really put out in a race. From then on, I was never going to get sick again."

Homer Bast

February 26, 1949
Southern Conference Games at Chapel Hill, North Carolina
Team Scores (Non-Conference Division):
1st–Georgia Tech–36
2nd–Tennessee–20
3rd–Virginia–14
4th–Florida–10
5th–Georgia–8
6th–Louisiana State–5
7th–Roanoke–2

The Roanoke team's next competition came in the Southern Conference Indoor Track Meet in Chapel Hill on Saturday, February 26. The meet featured many events open only to Southern Conference teams; however, they also offered non-conference or open events, races for freshmen, and even a series of high school events.

Coach Bast took the following athletes to Chapel Hill: Alvin Smith, Paul McCarty, Bruce Davenport, White Rhyne, Walter Tramposch, Harry Bower, and Dick Dodd. Bast entered Smith in the non-conference 880 and mile events. In other non-conference events, he placed Bower and Dodd in the 60-yard dash and McCarty in the 880-yard run and the mile. Freshmen from Roanoke who competed were White Rhyne (three-quarter mile) and Walter Tramposch (freshman 60).

The meet was a showcase for southern talent. Freshman sensation Bill Albans won five separate events–broad jump, high jump, 60-yard dash, 70-yard high hurdles, and the 70-yard low hurdles–to lead the University of North Carolina to victory in the conference division. His high jump of 6'4⅛", and his time of :07.6 in the low hurdles, both set new meet records. In winning the meet for the 10th time in its 14-year history, Bob Fetzer's U. N. C. team rolled up 52 points, 25 of them by Albans. Favored Maryland was second with 33, followed by Duke, 25; VPI, 9; South Carolina, 4; North Carolina State and V. M. I., 3; Wake Forest, 2; and Davidson, 1.

In the non-conference division consisting of 11 schools, Georgia Tech took top honors with 36 points, easily beating runner-up Tennessee's score of 20. Other non-conference schools included Virginia, 14; Florida, 10; Georgia, 8; LSU; and Roanoke, 2.

Roanoke's two points came from Alvin Smith's third place finish in the 880-yard run. None of the other Roanoke runners managed to score.

Outdoor Track

Soon after the team returned from the Southern Conference indoor meet, the athletes began their training for the upcoming outdoor season. The team this spring was captained by Alvin Smith and Bill Williams.

In early March of 1949, workmen began to make general repairs to the college track. They turned over the running surface several times in order to loosen the old cinders and packed clay underneath. The base was then rolled and prepared for the application of new cinders which had been on hand since fall. Coach Bast was promised that the track would be ready by the first outdoor meet in early April.

Nine meets had been scheduled:

April 2	Lynchburg, Away
April 8	Gallaudet, Home
April 23	Milligan Relays at Johnson City, Tennessee
April 25	Bridgewater, Home
April 29	Hampden-Sydney, Home
May 2	Randolph-Macon, Away
May 7	Little Six Championships at Lynchburg, Virginia
May 13-14	Mason-Dixon Championships at Baltimore, Maryland
May 28	Virginia State AAU Championships at Lynchburg, Virginia

Bast could tell after a few weeks of training that this might be a building year. Not many lettermen were back. He would have Bruce Davenport, Paul McCarty, and Alvin Smith, of course, and each could run two or three events if needed. Other good distance runners were White Rhyne and Frank Aldred, both above-average runners who had shown their talents earlier in the year. He also had Bill Williams, primarily in the pole vault, and Carroll Dahill in the weight events.

Several newcomers showed up for one or more practices for the weight events, including Bill Comer, Paul Barker, Mike Sebo, John Byerly, R. K. Walsh, R. L. Jones, Roland Sontag, George Dawson, and Jack Thurmond. Bill Williams, Hal Dunbar, and John Hash also said they would like to give the javelin a try.

In the pole vault, dependable Bill Williams was back. The team's new vaulter, however, was Ray DeCosta. Bast didn't know what to expect from this fairly short and well-built guy, but he would soon find out. In this year and during the next three, DeCosta would become the school's finest vaulter and would rival the best that much larger schools had to offer.

In the broad jump, Deric Pepler showed some early interest, and Bast knew that Williams could always be called on to enter this event also. The high jump aspirants early on were Williams, Hash, and perhaps Ed Harless.

Bast's sprinters would come from the group of Harry Bower, Dick Dodd, Dick Fraley, and Teensy Friend. Unfortunately, none of them could run fast enough in the short sprints to win consistently.

The March workouts did show some good efforts by several others. They included Wallace Lord, Walt Tramposch, Roy Basham, Doug Frith, Jim Slaybaugh, Robert Walsh, and John Byerly.

I remember . . . "In taking care of the cinder track, we would put a bit of clay or cinders in the low spots on occasion. On those curves near the creek, the track might go underwater with a sustained rain. If we had a meet coming up, we'd put gasoline on the water and burn it off. At least, this made it better than it was before. For the meets of this outdoor season, including the first one with Lynchburg, I got Miles Masters to install a public address system. And I got many of the faculty to come down to be judges. Everyone turned out, it seemed, including a lot of students. We had the old metal stands on the Market Street side of the track, and they might be half full. One thing we tried to do in all of our home meets was to run them off on time. I had gotten so disgusted with attending high school meets that would start at 2:00 in the afternoon and end up at 6:00 at night. They were just awful. I told the coaches that you just don't run a meet that is not on time. Sometimes when we entertained a college in a dual meet, I would have Coach Buzzard of Andrew Lewis High School, or one of the other coaches, come up and also run a high school meet at the same time. And we would run them off on time. People came to the meets because they knew they wouldn't have to stay there all day."

Homer Bast

April 2, 1949
Lynchburg College at Lynchburg, Virginia
Team Scores: Roanoke–81
Lynchburg–45

The beginning of the outdoor season seemed to come too soon. On April 2, 1949, the team took the two school cars and a couple of student cars to Lynchburg for the first dual meet. Coach Bast and others had ranked the two teams as being equally strong. Lynchburg's power seemed to be in the field events, while Roanoke had some of the best distance men around the state.

As expected, Lynchburg did well in the field events, winning four of the six events and sweeping all three of the places in the broad jump and high jump. But Roanoke did win the shot put event on R. K. Walsh's throw of 38'1½ " and took the first two places in the pole vault. As expected, Bill Williams vaulted 11'0". The surprise was newcomer Ray DeCosta, who matched Williams' jump to take home a tie for first.

In the running events, Bruce Davenport signaled his potential by winning the two-mile race and setting a new Roanoke and Lynchburg track record of 10:08.1. That school record broke the record he set in 1948 in the V. M. I. meet in Lexington. The time was just a few seconds away from the Mason-Dixon Conference record for the event, set by Corbett of Catholic University. Bast was impressed. The time was pretty good, he thought, for a diminutive, stocky runner from nearby Roanoke who had never competed in a track meet before coming to Roanoke. Bruce also cruised to a three-way tie with Paul McCarty and Frank Aldred in the mile run and picked up a total of eight points for the day.

The other distance star, Alvin Smith, didn't have as impressive day as Davenport in terms of setting records; however, he did win the 440-yard dash in :54.7, tied for first in the 880-yard run with teammates Paul McCarty and White Rhyne, and ran second to Davenport in the two-mile event.

Roanoke also picked up valuable points in the 100- and 220-yard dashes. In the 100, Harry Bower cruised to victory in :10.3 seconds, followed closely in second place by Dick Fraley. In the 220, Fraley showed a lot of improvement when he left everybody behind in running an excellent :23.3. He was followed across the finish line by Roanoke's Walt Tramposch.

A few other Maroons also added points to the team total. Doug Frith placed second in the high hurdles and third in the lows. Teensy Friend won his low-hurdles event with a time of :28.2. Frank Aldred finished third in the two-mile race. Carroll Dahill had a third in the shot put, John Byerly a third in the discus, Bill Williams a second in the javelin, and Bob White a third in that event.

With wins in 9 of the 14 events, Roanoke beat Lynchburg by a score of 81 to 45. Coach Bast didn't expect the differences in scores to be that great.

April 8, 1949
Galladuet College at Salem, Virginia
Team Scores: Roanoke–98⅓
Gallaudet–27⅔

Another easy meet followed. Roanoke hosted Gallaudet College of Washington on April 8. Gallaudet had lost to American University in their only meet of the year, 71½ to 54½. The most Coach Bast knew about the team was that they seemed to have some strength in the high jump, hurdles, high jump, shot put, and perhaps the 220 and 440.

Roanoke athletes captured first place in 10 of 14 events sweeping first, second, and third place in the 880, mile, and two-mile runs and the broad jump.

Ray DeCosta clearly was the star of the day. He pole vaulted 12'0" to break both the school record and the Alumni Field record for the event. DeCosta also won the broad jump, leaping 19'½ ".

As usual, Roanoke was dominating in the middle distance and distance runs. Paul McCarty won the 880-yard run in 2:09.1, followed by Bruce Davenport. Alvin Smith and Frank Aldred had an easy time in the mile, finishing in a tie in a slow 5:02.1. Then Smith (10:34.5), Davenport, and Aldred finished one, two, three in the two-mile race.

The Maroons were also strong in the shorter races. Harry Bower, for example, won the 100-yard dash in :10.5, with Dick Fraley close behind. Fraley ran another good 220, winning in a time of :23.9. Walt Tramposch finished second in that race. Tramposch picked up a win in the quarter-mile with a time of :55.8. Roy Basham was second.

Roanoke won four of the six field events. Besides DeCosta's fine vault and long jump wins, firsts were taken by John Byerly in the discus (102'0") and John Hash in the high jump (5'8"). The scoring was completed by Doug Frith (second in both the high and low hurdles), Jim Slaybaugh (third in the high hurdles), Walt Tramposch (third in the low hurdles), R. K. Walsh (second in both the shot put and discus events), Paul Barker (third in the shot put), Bill Williams (second in the javelin, high jump, and pole vault), and Deric Pepler (third in the broad jump).

I remember . . . "At times, we didn't have very many people watching the home meets. I have a picture of me during one meet when we were competing against Gallaudet. I came in first or second and I guess one of my fraternity brothers had his camera there. He took a shot of me crossing the line. In the background, the stands held about two people."

Walter Tramposch

April 23, 1949
Milligan Relays at Johnson City, Tennessee
Team Scores: 1st–Tie: Wofford (W) and Maryville–56
3rd–Roanoke–41
4th–East Tennessee State–29½
5th–University of Tennessee Freshmen–17
6th–Milligan–6
7th–Mars Hill–3
8th–Emory and Henry–1½
9th–Tusculum–1

On Saturday, April 23, some of the Roanoke team traveled to Johnson City, Tennessee, for the third annual Milligan Relays. The meet had a record field to compete for trophies in 10 relay events and 11 special events. At 11:00 a.m., Milligan College hosted a luncheon in its dining hall in honor of officials and contestants. At 1:00 p.m., before a large crowd of enthusiastic track fans at wind-swept Memorial Stadium, the Roanoke men walked away with record-breaking performances in the sprint medley and distance medley relays. The excellent distance medley relay team of Frank Aldred, Paul McCarty, Alvin Smith, and Bruce Davenport overcame the rain-drenched cinder track to post a time of 10:16.8, a second or so slower than the time they posted at the Relays the year before. Later, three members of that team–Aldred, McCarty, and Smith–joined with Walt Tramposch to win the sprint medley relay by some 100 yards. Their time of 3:53.0, as was the time for the distance medley time, was each a meet record.

Roanoke also had some outstanding individual performances. Bruce Davenport and Alvin Smith crossed the finish line together in the mile run, winning the event in a time of 4:48.0, also a meet record. Bill Williams also set a new meet record by pole vaulting 11'8" to tie for first place. In third was Maroon freshman Ray DeCosta.

Roanoke's 440-yard relay team (Harry Bower, Dick Fraley, Dick Dodd, and Walt Tramposch) should have won their event; however, because of an error with the staggering system, they ended up running about 25 yards further than they should have. Wofford won the race in :47.0, with Roanoke trailing in third. An hour later, Fraley, Dodd, and Tramposch teamed with Frank Aldred to take third in the 880-yard relay. R. K. Walsh took a third place in the shot put, while John Hash picked up a third in the high jump.

As they did in the 1948 Milligan Relays, Roanoke finished in third place overall, based on a team score of 41 points. Wofford and Maryville tied for first with scores of 56. Other scores included East Tennessee State, 29½; University of Tennessee Freshmen, 17; Milligan College, 6; Mars Hill College, 3; Emory and Henry College, 1½; and Tusculum College, 1. Kingsport High School edged Johnson City High School and Virginia High School of Bristol to capture the high school championship.

Along with the light banter in his college car as the team returned to Salem that night, Coach Bast thought about the three meets the team had already run. Two were blowouts in terms of team scores, and the boys did a credible job in the Milligan meet. But, he thought, there are some tough times ahead. He knew that he had some talented athletes on the team, but his lack of depth in a number of events would surely hurt the team down the line. And it did.

April 25, 1949
Bridgewater College at Salem, Virginia
Team Scores: Bridgewater–72
Roanoke–54

Bridgewater was the next challenge. The meet was held in Salem on April 25. It would be the first mismatch of the season for Roanoke. Actually, the meet was enjoyable to watch. Fans got to see athletes from both teams setting seven new Alumni Field records and tying another.

Bridgewater's well-rounded team had power in both field and track events. In this particular meet, they scored heavily in the field events, hurdles, and dashes to hand the Maroons their first dual meet defeat of the year, 72 to 54. The Eagles won first places in 9 of 14 events.

Roanoke's Bruce Davenport just missed setting another two-mile record. Running his usual good race, he won the two-mile race in a time of 10:12.8, a full 60 yards ahead of his teammate, Alvin Smith, who came in second. Smith had already won the 880, just in front of Paul McCarty, and had teamed with Davenport and McCarty in producing a three-way tie for first place in the mile. Their time was 4:39.7.

Probably the most exciting race of the day was the 440-yard dash. Frank Aldred and Bridgewater's Harold Garner staged a classic side-by-side battle coming down the final straightaway. At the last moment, Frank lunged for the tape to beat Garner by inches, recording an excellent time of :53.9.

Ray DeCosta was sensational as usual. Back in top form, he vaulted 12'0" to win the event. Teammate Bill Williams cleared 11'6" to take second place.

There were no other Roanoke winners; however, the team did score a number of second place finishes not mentioned before: Harry Bower, 100-yard dash; R. K. Walsh, discus; and Hal Dunbar, javelin. Third place honors for Roanoke went to: Dick Fraley, 220-yard dash; Walt Tramposch, 440-yard dash; Doug Frith, high hurdles; Teensy Friend, low hurdles; R. K. Walsh, shot put; Ed Harless, broad jump; and John Hash, high jump.

Homer was disappointed, but a realist. He knew that he went into the day with a limited number of truly talented athletes. On the running side, there was Alvin Smith, Bruce Davenport, Paul McCarty, and Frank Aldred. They were the people he could depend on to score against any team. In the field events, the horses were Ray DeCosta and Bill Williams, both in the pole vault. And that was it, except for boys like Harry Bower, Dick Fraley, Walt Tramposch, Teensy Friend, and others. Those individuals tried hard, and were terrific to work with, but admittedly they were never likely to win an event against a team as strong as Bridgewater. The coach's dream had yet to be realized. He wanted to have two and three potential winners in every single event; unfortunately, he would have to wait for several years for that dream to materialize. But when it did, in the 1950s, Roanoke would be the talk of the state, going on an incredible dual meet winning streak and monopolizing every one of the teams from Virginia and the Mason-Dixon Conference. Just be patient, he told himself. Things will turn out O. K.

But first, life would get no easier. A strong Hampden-Sydney team was coming to town.

April 29, 1949
Hampden-Sydney College at Salem, Virginia
Team Scores: Hampden-Sydney–66
Roanoke–60

Like the Eagles of Bridgewater, Hampden-Sydney appeared to have a decent team. Coach Bast, however, thought that if his boys put in good efforts, the Maroons might have a slight edge. The main opposition would come from Gene Milener, a very good distance man, and Lynn Chewning. Chewning was a famed Little All America football star for the Tigers and could win the 100 and 220 against almost any team around. In addition, Hampden-Sydney had Bob Lacy, who had dominated both of the hurdle races this year, Richard Hassold in the 440-yard dash, and Henry Coghill, Jr., and Irvin Baldwin in the 880.

The meet on Alumni Field got underway at 1:30 p.m. Throughout the long afternoon, it was difficult to determine which team would win. Lynn Chewning of Hampden-Sydney easily won both sprints, in times of :10.0 for the 100 and :23.1 for the 220. Both were Alumni Field records.

Hassold won the quarter-mile race with a time of :54.3, but Alvin Smith and Bruce

Davenport tied for the win in the 880 with a time of 2:06.1. Lacy, as expected, easily won both hurdles, while Alvin Smith and Bruce Davenport again won the mile, crossing the finish line together, in a field record time of 4:36.0. The two also tied for first in the two-mile run.

In the field events, Roanoke's R. K. Walsh won the shot, Hal Dunbar the javelin, and Ray DeCosta the pole vault. His vault of 12'0" tied his own Alumni Field record.

With all other events completed, it appeared that the results of the broad jump would provide the winning margin. Without the broad jump results being recorded, Roanoke led Hampden-Sydney, 59 to 58. During the athletes' last jumps, practically the entire crowd of onlookers and athletes from both teams moved to the broad jump area to encourage the jumpers. Unfortunately, the event ended with Hampden-Sydney grabbing both first and second places. Those eight points put the Tigers in front with a winning margin of 66 to 60.

The Roanoke team had suffered its second loss of the year. But you can't lose 8 of 14 events and expect to win any dual meet. And the losses would continue to mount.

May 2, 1949
Randolph-Macon College at Ashland, Virginia
Team Scores: Randolph-Macon–71⅔
Roanoke–54⅓

On May 2, the team traveled to Ashland, Virginia, for a dual meet with Randolph-Macon College. The Yellow Jackets were rumored to be loaded in the sprints and dashes.

The most outstanding performance of the meet for Roanoke was Bruce Davenport's amazing two-mile race. He crossed the line in 9:59.8, winning the event and breaking his own record of 10:08.1. A small college runner breaking through the 10:00 barrier was almost unheard of in 1949.

Other crowd pleasers for Roanoke were Ray DeCosta's fine jump of 12'0", which won the pole vault and tied his own record set just a few days before, and the usual good performance of the team's distance runners. Alvin Smith, Paul McCarty, and Frank Aldred hit the tape together in the 880-yard run. Smith, McCarty, and Bruce Davenport did the same in the mile run.

Only R. K. Walsh and John Hash won another event. Walsh put the shot 38'5½", while Hash tied for the top spot in the high jump, clearing 5'8". Others who scored were Dick Dodd, third in the 100 and second in the 220; Walt Tramposch, second in the 440; Doug Frith, second in the high hurdles and third in the lows; Alvin Smith, second behind Davenport in the fast two-mile race; Carroll Dahill, third in the shot; Bill Williams, a tie for third in the high jump and a tie for second in the pole vault.

In the end, Randolph-Macon took top honors in nine total events and swept all three places in the discus, javelin, and broad jump.

The final score was Randolph-Macon, 71⅔, and Roanoke, 54⅓. Roanoke now had lost three straight meets, two of them by large margins.

Three meets remained on the schedule. On May 7, the Little Six Championships would be held in Lynchburg. Then came the 14th annual Mason-Dixon Championships at Johns Hopkins on May 13-14. And finally, selected members of the team would be going to the Virginia AAU meet in Lynchburg on May 28.

May 7, 1949
Little Six Championships at Lynchburg, Virginia
Team Scores: 1st–Bridgewater College–50 3/5
2nd–Roanoke College–38 3/5
3rd–Randolph-Macon College–29 1/5
4th–Hampden-Sydney College–28½
5th–Lynchburg College–15 1/5

Coach Bast and his team drove to Lynchburg on May 6 to defend their Little Six crown. Trial heats and other preliminaries were scheduled to be run off that day, with the final events slated for the next afternoon. Other schools in the meet included Lynchburg, Randolph-Macon, Hampden-Sydney, and the pre-meet favorite, Bridgewater.

Bridgewater had looked strong all season, with several decisive victories. It look like a sure thing that they would win the Championships this time around. The nod for second place likely went to Randolph-Macon, who had beaten Roanoke recently, and then came the Maroons. Most realized, however, that the power Roanoke showed all year in its middle distance and distance runners, plus a pole-vaulting two-some that just might go one-two in that event, could well propel the team to another win.

Coach Bast decided in the week before the Little Six meet that Alvin Smith and Bruce Davenport would each run in three events–the 880, mile, and two-mile. In addition, he put Paul McCarty in both the mile and two-mile runs. Frank Aldred, who had shown remarkable progress throughout the season, would enter the 880.

On Saturday morning, officials and athletes could sense that the weather that day would be highly unfavorable to good performances. Sure enough, just after the early events began on Saturday, a driving rain came quickly, accompanied by an electrical storm. Especially toward the latter part of the afternoon, the rain had a decided effect on both field and track events.

Remarkably, the meet would bring three new Little Six records and even a Roanoke College record. Roanoke's Ray DeCosta, despite a wet, slippery pole and unsure footing, broke the meet record in the pole vault by clearing 12'4". The old meet record was 12'3", originally set by John Griek of Randolph-Macon in 1938. DeCosta's height also broke the Roanoke College record of 12'0", which was set by himself on four separate occasions during the past season.

Other records were also broken. Bodkin of Bridgewater threw the discus 133'¼", ¾" better than the former record. Randolph-Macon's Emory Evans ran the 440-yard dash in excellent time of :52.4 to beat another record.

Alvin Smith ran several good times for Roanoke. He had double wins in the mile and two-mile events, sharing both firsts with teammates Paul McCarty and Bruce Davenport. Then he added a victory in the 880-yard run, with Davenport very close behind.

Roanoke's other points came from Paul McCarty (second in the 440), the mile relay team anchored by Smith (third), R. K. Walsh (third in the shot put), and Bill Williams (tie for third in the pole vault).

Near the end of the meet, it was clear that Bridgewater would take first place in team points. But Randolph-Macon and Roanoke were almost tied for the second spot. With the later performances of Smith, Davenport, and McCarty, however, they not only kept their Roanoke team within striking distance, but in fact, the scoring in their events moved the team in front of Randolph-Macon.

Favorite Bridgewater compiled a point total of $50\frac{3}{5}$ to win the meet. Roanoke was second with $38\frac{3}{5}$, Randolph-Macon had $29\frac{1}{5}$, Hampden-Sydney scored 28½, and Lynchburg finished in sixth place with $15\frac{1}{5}$ points.

May 13-14, 1949
Mason-Dixon Championships at Baltimore, Maryland
Team Scores: 1st–Washington College–57⅓
2nd–Catholic University–48½
3rd–Johns Hopkins University–37
4th–Roanoke College–23⅓
5th–Randolph–Macon College–21½
6th–Bridgewater College–18
7th–Loyola University–11½
8th–Lynchburg College–5½
9th–Gallaudet College–2
10th–American University–⅓
11th–Towson State Teachers College–0
12th–University of Baltimore–0

Roanoke's next meet, the 14th annual Mason-Dixon Championship, was hosted by

Johns Hopkins University in Baltimore. This meet, as it had been before, was conducted over a two-day period at Homewood Field. On Friday, May 13, individuals in most of the running events and some of the field events were given chances to qualify for the finals the next day. Preliminary qualifying began on Friday at 2:00 p.m., with the finals being scheduled for Saturday at 1:00 p.m.

Homer Bast remembers the facilities. The field, enclosed by a fence, normally was used by the Hopkins lacrosse team. The school annually had one of the nation's best lacrosse programs. The lacrosse field had a track around it, although Homer thought the Roanoke track may have been better.

Roanoke's entrants included only those who might place in the meet, or who could benefit from running, jumping, or throwing against top competitors. In the 100-yard dash on Friday, a sprinter had to run twice to qualify for Saturday. In the third heat of five (from which three would move to the semifinals), Harry Bower of Roanoke finished second to Zahringer of Catholic. In the semifinals, there were two heats, with three from each heat qualifying to move on to Saturday's finals. Unfortunately, Harry finished fourth in his race. His teammate, Walt Tramposch, also failed to qualify. A similar heat system was used for the 220, but neither Harry nor Walt qualified. The same came true in the 440-yard dash.

In the first heat of the qualifying races in the 880, Roanoke's Alvin Smith ran perhaps his best race of the year, winning his heat in 2:00.7, a new school record. In the process, he beat the race favorite, Catholic University's Dan Doyle. Paul McCarty failed to reach the finals from his heat.

No Roanoke men qualified for the high- or low-hurdle finals, the javelin, or the discus. The sixth-place qualifier in the broad jump finished with a jump which was just a bit over 20'3". Sixth place in the javelin was 155'½ " while in the discus it was 117'1". John Hash did not make the finals in the high jump, although Bill Williams did. Roanoke's R. K. Walsh moved on to the finals in the shot put. His 38'4¾" throw gave him the fifth of six places going into Saturday.

Washington College, the team to beat in the Championships, qualified 17 men in the preliminaries. Catholic moved 13 men into Saturday's competition, while Johns Hopkins qualified 10. Following Johns Hopkins, Bridgewater placed 7, Randolph-Macon 5, Roanoke and Loyola 3 each, and Gallaudet 1. American University, Towson Teachers, and Baltimore moved no one to the finals.

Saturday turned out to have wonderful weather. The sky was blue and the sun shined all day long. And the Roanoke boys did well.

Ray DeCosta and Bill Williams were the class acts in the pole vault. Bill easily cleared 11'6" but when the bar was raised to 12'0" he was unable to clear that height and settled for second place. Almost 60 years later, Williams remembers this meet well.

"They never gave me track shoes before this year. I did have a pair of running shoes of my own, which had long spikes on the front sole. It was on my last jump at 12'0" that I landed off balance in the pit and those long spikes ripped into my leg. I might have been better off jumping in flat-soled shoes. Coach Bast came running over to look at the injury. I loved Homer to death, but what he did next made me angry. He wouldn't let me hobble over to the medical area to get the leg bandaged. Instead, he insisted on carrying me across the field, as if I were a child. The cut required several stitches and tetanus shot from personnel in the Johns Hopkins infirmary. In addition, they insisted that I lie there for an hour while the team continued the met."

Meanwhile, DeCosta cleared 12'0" for the win, and then asked the pole vault judge to move the bar to 12'6", the current Mason-Dixon record. On his next two jumps, he failed badly to clear the bar. Then he faced his third and final try. With teammates and other onlookers urging him on, Ray began his approach down the runway. The plant of the pole was good and he soared toward the bar. The jump seemed perfect. He was over the bar and the crowd began to cheer. Then, on the way down, he nicked the crossbar and it tumbled from the standards. He was disappointed, but his first place did give Roanoke squad a valuable five points.

In the warm-ups for the mile run, Alvin Smith felt good. Maybe, he thought, I can lower the meet record of 4:24.3. It was a record that Coach Bast also felt he could get. Alvin had won this event last year in that crowd-thrilling race where his shoe was ripped off him by the foot of an opposing runner. Running with one shoe on and the other off, he had been timed in 4:35.7.

In the first 100 yards of the race, Alvin quickly moved to the front of the pack of runners. Coach Bast timed his first quarter in 60 seconds. He slowed from that pace on the second lap, of course, and Bast caught him at 2:14 for the half. Then, showing his stamina, Alvin ran an almost identical time in the second half of the race to finish in front with a time of 4:28.7, just 4.4 seconds off the meet record time. Paul McCarty finished in fourth place behind Smith.

The two-mile race was almost anticlimactic. Everyone expected Bruce Davenport to do well in the event because he had run a 9:59.8 two-mile this season. Like Alvin in the mile, he also moved to the front early, clocked by Bast at 2:22 for the first half, and maintained his lead. He finished the long run in 10:24.4, scoring an easy victory at least 25 yards ahead of Dryden of Washington College.

In the 880 on Saturday, Alvin was tired from his mile run earlier in the day, and found himself a part of a torrid pace set by the front runners. Larry Brandenburg, a slightly-built runner, came from behind to beat Dan Doyle of Catholic by three steps, with Earl Grim of Hopkins taking third, Alvin fourth, and Catholic's McKernin fifth and last. Alvin's time of 2:00.4 set a new school record, beating his time of 2:00.7 in a qualifying heat the day before. Amazingly, every one of the top five runners in the race broke the old record of 2:00.6 held by Doyle. Later, Alvin said that the second through fifth place men ran almost as one group all the way down the home stretch before separating themselves by mere inches, it seemed, at the finish line.

The meet also featured some excellent performances by many non-Roanoke athletes. The 440, for example, was a real thriller with Larry Brandenburg of Washington and Leon Schwartz of Johns Hopkins staging a stirring stretch duel. Brandenburg just lasted to win in :49.9. Schwartz's time of :50.0 also eclipsed the meet record of :50.6 he set two years before.

A new conference record in Friday's trials was set in the 120-yard high hurdles race by John Acton of Randolph-Macon. He was timed in :15.3, a tenth of a second lower than the old mark jointly held by Gibby Young and Basil Tully, both Washington College stars. He finished the race two steps ahead of Walt Smyth of Loyola.

Washington's mile relay team of Sutton, Hubbard, Twilley, and Brandenburg, the reigning Penn Relays champions in the event, also set a new meet record in this meet. On Saturday, they ran a 3:24.4 race with little competition.

Near the end of the meet, Coach Bast knew his team had no chance of winning; however, he was very pleased at how well his undermanned team had done. Roanoke had picked up 21 points on three first places by Smith in the mile, Davenport in the two-mile, and DeCosta in the pole vault, plus a second place by Williams and a fourth place by Smith. McCarty had also run well to get fourth place in the mile run. In the field events, Bill Williams managed to get a fifth place, three-way tie in the high jump.

The total of 23⅓ points pushed Roanoke into fourth place, beating fifth place Randolph-Macon (21½), sixth place Bridgewater (18), and all of the other Little Six schools.

Although they won only two firsts, Washington College's team captured first place in the meet. Qualifying at least one man in each of ten events on the 14-event program, the Shoremen scored 57⅓ points on the back of Larry Brandenburg, who turned in record-breaking performances in the 440- and 880-yard races. Second-place Catholic University finished with 48½ points on the strength of five outright titles and a share in another. Johns Hopkins, the defending champion and host college at the two-day meet, finished third with 37 points.

The meet had been a good one for Roanoke. Everyone was tired on the long trip back to Salem, but spirits were high. There was a slight feeling of revenge in their thoughts. After losing three straight dual meets (which the team would never do again under the coaching of Mr. Bast) they had beaten all of the Little Six colleges, had taken home three of the 14 first-place medals, and had set two new meet records. It was not a bad day's work.

May 28, 1949
Virginia AAU Championships at Lynchburg, Virginia
Team Scores: 1st–Quantico Marines–54¼
2nd–University of Virginia–37¼
3rd–Virginia Polytechnic Institute–29⅓
4th–Washington and Lee University–26
5th–Roanoke College–12½
6th–University of Richmond–5½
7th–George Washington High School–2
8th–Lynchburg YMCA–1
9th–Newport News Apprentice School–1

The final chance for competition came on May 28, 1949, at the Lynchburg Municipal Stadium, with the running of the 10th annual Virginia AAU Championships. The field, according to Chairman John T. Core, would be the largest in history. He had already received entry forms for 400 athletes, many of them attached to more than 30 schools and colleges.

There were several top-flight athletes in the meet. One, Bobby Jones of George Washington High School in Alexandria, was reputedly the finest scholastic distance runner ever developed in Virginia. The holder of the national high school half mile championship and the national high school indoor mile championship, Jones would be out to smash two separate records in the mile run. He wanted the senior mile record of 4:28.6, set by Cliff Muller of W&L in 1941 and the national high school record of 4:21.2 set by Lou Zamperini at Torrance, California, High School in 1933.

Jones ran the half mile in 1:57 for a new national high school record in 1948 and captured indoor mile honors in the same division for 1949 with a 4:26 mile. Reports from his coach, Tom Fitzgibbons, were that this AAU race would be Jones' last in this area for some time. On Friday, the day before the Lynchburg competition, he would be making his last scholastic appearance at the State meet in Williamsburg and reportedly planned to join Coach Don Gehrmann at the University of Wisconsin for his college education. The Alexandria runner was expected to have plenty of competition in the AAU meet, however, because Sam Lindsay of William and Mary and Alvin Smith of Roanoke had already entered the events and would run against Jones. Both were top distance runners in state college circles.

Coach Bast decided that three individuals from Roanoke would compete in the senior division of the meet–Alvin Smith, Bruce Davenport, and Ray DeCosta. Each of the three had a good chance of winning an event or taking second. On the entry form, he scheduled Alvin for the mile run, Bruce for the two-mile race, and DeCosta, of course, for the pole vault event. Not only would Smith be challenged by Bobby Jones, but Bruce would have a chance to compete against some of the state's best distance men in the two mile–Curtis Shelton of Virginia Polytechnic Institute, Blakey of the University of Virginia, Clyde Baker of William and Mary, and Sease of the University of Richmond. DeCosta would be matching jumps with Robert Bell of V. M. I. and Bob Roller of the University of Virginia. Two other Roanoke athletes also competed. Freshman distance runner White Rhyne accompanied the team, entering the Junior Division. The other Maroon entry was Richard Graves, competing in the Junior Division in the discus. Graves had been ineligible to participate in intercollegiate meets this season.

Alvin Smith entered the mile run with some confidence. He was undefeated for the year in that event and seemed to be getting stronger as the weeks went by. The gun sounded and the top runners besides Smith–Bobby Jones and Lt. Henry Hart of the Quantico Marines, both undefeated–moved toward the front. The early rabbit, Walt Mollineus of the Marines, faded fast after a lap to leave Jones and Hart as the leaders. Smith hung back in third place for the first three and a half laps, with Jones and Hart dueling side-by-side for the lead. Then, on the backstretch of the fourth and final lap, Smith made his move. He blasted past both competitors, opening up a gap of 10 yards, and kept that lead all the way down the front stretch of the track. He broke the tape to take first in an unthinkable time of 4:24.7. The time was a new meet record, beating the previous mark of 4:28.6 which was set by Cliff Miller of Washington and Lee in 1941. The time was also a new Roanoke College record, more than four seconds better than the mark he had just set in the 1949 Mason-Dixon Championships in Baltimore.

Bruce Davenport further upheld Roanoke's claim of having the best distance runners in Virginia when he put on an amazing burst of speed in the stretch to pass Winn of the University of Richmond and win going away.

The other Roanoke athlete in the meet was Ray DeCosta. First place was taken by Hunter DeButts of the University of Virginia, who cleared 12'6"; however, DeCosta did clear a height of 12'0" to share second place honors with George Brasfield of the University of Virginia.

Reports of the meet do not mention whether Rhyne placed in his junior event, nor was there any mention of Graves' performance. Coach Bast, however, remembers that Graves won the junior discus event with a throw of more than 120'.

I remember . . . "The reason I think I did well at Roanoke in pole vaulting was that as a child I had an interest in the event. In fact, I cut me a tree limb to use as a pole, and a makeshift cross bar. Then one day, a man came and saw me trying to jump. He came over and gave me some suggestions, such as when I took off, slide my bottom hand up so I could get a higher reach. Then I began to improve. You don't use that technique anymore with the new poles. I was also on gymnasium teams when I was with the New York Athletic Club after college. I competed in the rings, tumbling, and other things. I was tumbling even when I was a child. So I had a lot of background for being a vaulter. Of course, I was short, unlike many other vaulters."

Ray DeCosta

Coach Bast had begun to host an annual track meeting at his house following the season. Mary Jane would make sure the boys were well-fed, there would be lots of banter about who did what during the year, and the Coach and his captains typically said a few words to the group.

The apartment occupied by Homer and Mary Jane was located on Market Street in a house that is torn down now. Looking at Crawford Hall, one would come north past the alley to find the house, sitting directly next to the alley. The College's Maintenance Supervisor, Harry Hodges, lived in the house next door. The Basts lived in a downstairs apartment. A number of people lived above them over the years, including Professor Andrew Murphy.

This year, Homer was presented with a gift as a token of the team's appreciation for what he had done for them during the past year. Bill Williams, one of the co-captains, stepped forward to give him the gift. Alvin Smith, the other co-captain then made a short speech. He said, "Coach, we understand that all of the days in our lives–and in your life as our coach–are not sunny. So for you, for those days that are not so sunny, we give you this gift." Homer opened the gift to find an umbrella. Over the years, whether it was a simple gift like an umbrella, or fancier, like a silver tray, Coach Bast was most appreciative and generally wrote team members thank you notes for thinking of him.

Another honor went to Alvin Smith at the annual sports banquet. By a vote of the Monogram Club and the student body, he was presented a trophy as Roanoke's All-Sports Athlete of the Year.

Chapter Five

THE 1949-50 SEASONS

Coach Bast was beginning his fourth year at Roanoke. Now, in the late summer of 1949, he was still a teacher and coach. But the new President of the College, Dr. Sherman Oberly, drafted him for one more job–Admissions Director.

Oberly had replaced the very popular Charles Smith, often called Dr. Charlie. Oberly had served for some time as an Admissions Director at the University of Pennsylvania, and soon after he came to Roanoke he began to look at the figures involving student enrollment. If he could believe the predictions, the college would be getting fewer and fewer veterans over the next two or three years. The Depression also had brought on a lower birth rate in the country.

Roanoke, like many other colleges, had experienced an unprecedented period of growth beginning around the time Coach Bast joined the staff. The enrollment, particularly because of the G. I. Bill, had increased to more than 600 students. Dormitory rooms were scarce or non-existent, faculty and staff housing was almost impossible to find in Salem, and classroom space had to be found to accommodate the many new students. Now, the boom might turn to bust.

And it did. In the fall of 1949, with Coach Bast now serving as Admissions Director, student enrollment fell to 528 students. That was more than 100 fewer students than they enrolled in 1948. And the cash flow crunch began. Belt tightening was in order. A number of teachers and staff members brought in for the 1946-47, 1947-48, and 1948-49 sessions, lost their jobs or at least when they moved on their positions were never filled.

Oberly asked Bast to develop a new strategy for recruiting students to Roanoke. The strategy might include College Days for area high schools, visits to secondary schools, and more. In addition, Professor Julius Prufer was appointed Alumni Director. He was directed to rejuvenate interest among alumni with the goal of getting them to send their own children to Roanoke.

The College saw a number of significant staff changes after Oberly's arrival. Dean Myers, who had hired Homer three years before, resigned his position and English professor William Bartlett took his place. Clarence Caldwell, who would remain with the college for many years and became an avid supporter of the College's athletics program, was chosen as the school's Business Manager.

Cross Country

Cross country practice began in early September. Coach Bast, whose team had gone undefeated during the 1948 season and had won both the Little Six and Mason-Dixon Championships, welcomed back six veterans. First, there was the quartet of runners now rather famously known as the "Big Four." This group included Alvin Smith of Roanoke and Lawrence "Red" Crockett of Wytheville. Both had been selected by teammates as Co-Captains. The other two members of this group were Paul McCarty of Kearneysville, West Virginia, and Bruce Davenport of Roanoke. The other two letter winners were Frank Aldred of New Haven, West Virginia, and White Rhyne of Philadelphia, Pennsylvania.

Alvin Smith was a talented runner who had run a sub-4:25 mile in the spring of 1949 and generally dominated most of his competition. He had competed on a fine University of North Carolina team before deciding to transfer to Roanoke. When he transferred, he was 27 years old and, as he said later, ". . . maybe I was a little past my prime. I think my

Left Photo: The State A. A. U. title winners in cross country for 1949 include (L to R) Whitey Rhyne, Dick Fraley, Frank Aldred, Jim Slaybaugh, "Red" Crockett, Coach Homer Bast, Alvin Smith, John Turbyfill, Paul McCarty, Ed Cully, and Bruce Davenport.
Right Photo: Alvin Smith and Red Crockett in a practice session.

best days of running were when I was in the Navy and stationed at the University of Georgia. I ran better times then, and faster quarters. We had so many good track and cross country athletes there." But there was no doubt that, despite his age, he was a classy distance runner. And the student body appreciated his ability, voting him "Athlete of the Year" for the 1948-49 session.

L. Z. "Red" Crockett was coming back off an academic suspension the semester before, and Smith later remembered him as being not only a good runner but a colorful guy. For example, Smith said, "I don't know how he afforded the thing, but he got himself a brand new Olds 88. I rode with him to one of the meets, maybe up to Bridgewater, and that was about the most scared I was ever while in a car. That was before the Interstate was built. He wanted to see what that car could do. And he was doing 96 miles an hour with five of us in the car. I said, "Red, slow this thing down. We want to get there alive." Continuing, Smith said "He wanted to do things that were flashy. I think one of the first things he did was to order a set of seat covers made out of leopard skins. He liked flashy stuff like that on his car." But he could run. Actually, Crockett had never participated in track before he entered Roanoke College in 1946. Developing rapidly, he was a member of the 1949 indoor mile relay team, and tied for first in the Little Six Cross Country Championships in 1947 and 1948. He also finished fourth in the Mason-Dixon Championships in Washington in the fall of 1948.

McCarty, now a senior and a year or so older than most of his teammates, was also recognized as a good 880 and mile runner. "I got Paul off the baseball team," Bast said. "I told him that he wasn't going to make Hackman's baseball team. Why don't you come on out and run with us. I think you have some talent, and we could really use you." Actually, Paul was an excellent basketball player on Coach Hackman's team. He had been successful playing basketball in high school. In his senior year, the team voted him their sportsmanship award. On the Roanoke team, he was a forward and a guard. Unfortunately, during his sophomore season in basketball his basketball career was cut short when he broke his arm in an early game.

Then there was Bruce Davenport. He was small in stature, wore glasses, and was smart. He participated in and led many campus activities, and was an honors student. During the 1948-49 session, Bruce had blossomed into one of the best runners in the state. He was the first Roanoke runner, for example, to go below the 10:00 mark in the two mile. He had never had any running experience before enrolling at Roanoke; however, there was athletic talent in his family. His father had competed in track at V. P. I. and was an excellent runner. "When I saw how easily Bruce ran, I knew he would be great," Coach Bast later said. "In fact, he won the very first cross country race he entered his freshman year." Bast always thought of Davenport as being the most driven man on his team. "He was focused," the Coach said, "and seldom ran a bad race. Now there were times he laid back to run with teammates. But if he was in a big race and you counted on him, he would come through. He always ran a race to win, sometimes lagging purposefully behind his opponent throughout the event, confident of his ability to overtake him at the end of the race."

"Not far into the first practices, it was apparent that the Big Four had evolved into the Big Six. Rhyne had become a stronger runner with age and he would place much higher in meets than he did as a freshman. Coach Bast also noted how much Frank Aldred had improved. In fact, Bast said, Aldred may have been the athlete who surprised him the most during those early years. On his own, Aldred ran during the summer break, and often he ran hard. When he came back to school, according to Bast, he was in good shape. Now, Bast thought, he was better than a couple of the Big Four runners of the previous year. Still, the public remembered the 1948 cross country team, with Smith, McCarty, Crockett, and Davenport strolling home, arm-in-arm, to pick up easy wins. In some minds, they would always be the Big Four and the focus of later attention.

The team also picked up several additional runners. Some stayed out a few days and then left the team. Others, such as John Turbyfill, Doug Frith, Ed Culley, and the red-headed Jim Slaybaugh, would contribute to the team's success. In all, the *Brackety-Ack* reported in one of its early issues in 1949-50:

> Several newcomers to the squad have shown promise of becoming valuable cross country runners and with more seasoning should strengthen the team. They are Joe Baldwin, Alexandria; John Turbyfill, Salem; Ben Crumpler, formerly of Roanoke; Ed Culley, Wyckoff, NJ; Walton Mitchell, New Castle; Jim Slaybaugh, Gettysburg, PA; Doug Frith, Rocky Mount; and Berlin Wittig, Harrisonburg.

Coach Bast, as he did most years, also selected his manager for the season–Bobby Davenport. Each of his managers would take care of equipment at home and away meets, do various other jobs as asked, and even give the much-appreciated rubdowns after a hard practice session. Later in his tenure, Bast tried to get managers for cross country and track who could write well and would contribute to articles in the *Brackety-Ack* and Roanoke papers. After all, Bast thought, they had a chance to see the inside stories that went on during meets–not just who won or placed.

As usual, Bast released the list of meets. They included:

October 8	Randolph-Macon, at Salem
October 15	Lynchburg and Hampden-Sydney (Varsity), at Lynchburg

October 15	Lynchburg (Freshmen), at Lynchburg
October 21	University of Virginia, at Salem
October 28	V. M. I., at Salem
November 2	South Boston High School vs. Roanoke Freshmen (Salem)
November 5	Little Six Championships, at Bridgewater
November 12	Virginia AAU Championships, in Richmond
November 21	Mason-Dixon Championships, at Bridgewater

Washington and Lee cancelled their meet with the Maroons, leaving a season consisting of four dual/triangular meets, two freshmen competitions, and the three big meets at the end of the season. Bast was about to discover that as the success of his distance teams became more and more evident, not many larger schools wanted to run him. The same would be true with his power-packed track teams of the 1950s

As practice continued, Coach Bast once again organized the annual intramural cross-country meet. Covering the one and one-half mile course in the time of 8:32, Dick Fraley captured first place. The victory brought Fraley and his Kappa Alpha Fraternity the team championship with a low score of 15 points. Runners from the dormitories finished a close second with 16, followed by the Pi Kappa Phi and Sigma Chi fraternities with 24 and 34 points respectively.

Others finishing the running event, which opened the 1949-50 intramural program for the College, included: Doug Frith, KA; Ray DeCosta, Dorms; John Byerly, Sigs; Donn Schindler, Pi Kaps; Edward Cully, Dorms; Benton Crumpler, Dorms; Joe Baldwin, Dorms; Dick Dodd, Pi Kaps; and John Robinson, Pi Kaps.

October 8, 1949
Randolph-Macon College at Salem, Virginia
Team Scores: Roanoke–17
Randolph-Macon–42

On October 8, 1949, Roanoke hosted the meet with Randolph-Macon on its 3.1 mile course. It also would be Randolph-Macon's first competition of the year. Some thought that the visitors might have their strongest team ever. Mike Byrnes, outstanding Randolph-Macon two-mile record holder, was expected to stay with the Maroons' front four and was one of four returning veterans for the Yellow Jackets. Other squad members for the team included Emory Evans, Little Six quarter mile champion, Pat Woods, and Beano Sheridan, along with newcomers Joe Hudgins, George Resh, Bill Ayers, and Bob Haines. Coach Bast also intended to run several of his most promising freshmen. They included Ed Cully, a former miler at Staunton Military Academy; Joe Baldwin, of

Alexandria; Benton Crumpler, of Bluefield, West Virginia; John Turbyfill, of Salem; Walton Mitchell, of New Castle; and Berlin Wittig of Harrisonburg.

As the runners approached the starting line, the weather was dismal. There was a slight wind, along with a persistent mist from the softly-falling rain. After the gun fired, the star of the Randolph-Macon team, Mike Byrnes, stayed stride-by-stride with Roanoke's front runners. In the latter part of the race, however, he dropped back slightly and Roanoke's Alvin Smith, Paul McCarty, and Bruce Davenport went to the front. Joining hands as always, they crossed the finish line in 19:28.0. Ten seconds behind was Byrnes. Less than 30 seconds behind Byrnes, the other three runners of the Big Six–Frank Aldred, Red Crockett, and White Rhyne–finished the race together in a tie for fifth place. Other Roanoke finishers that we know about were Ed Culley (12th in 24:11) and Doug Frith (15th in 25:49).

The first-place time was 20 seconds slower than the course record set in 1948, but the weather had an effect on all of the runners. Going back to the 1947-48 season and Roanoke's first cross country team, Bast's squad now had won eight straight dual meets, plus two Little Six and one Mason-Dixon title.

October 15, 1949
Lynchburg College and Hampden-Sydney College at Lynchburg, Virginia
Team Scores: Roanoke–19
Lynchburg–48
Hampden-Sydney–62

On the 15th of October, a week later, the Roanoke varsity and junior varsity teams traveled to Lynchburg, Virginia. Originally, a three-school junior varsity meet was on the schedule, featuring Roanoke, Lynchburg, and Hampden-Sydney. But Hampden-Sydney declined to run, leaving the Roanoke and Lynchburg runners to compete. Following this J. V. competition, beginning at 4:00 p.m., Roanoke's varsity team would take on the varsity runners from Lynchburg and Hampden-Sydney.

Over the 2.75-mile course, Lynchburg's J. V. team took the first three places plus the 9th spot to win the meet by a score of 13 to 23. Although reports of the meet are sketchy, we do know that the following men scored for Roanoke:

4th–Dick Fraley–20:33
5th–Douglas Frith (R) and Johnny Turbyfill (R)–20:45
8th–James Slaybaugh (R)–21:07

In the varsity meet, the opposition was Hampden-Sydney and Lynchburg. Hampden-

Sydney had five veteran distance runners. Gene Milener was the number one runner for the Tigers, followed by "Mouse" Coghill, Harvey Morgan, Andy Briggs, and Bob Hassold. All of those men were back from last year's squad. Several newcomers included John Ducker, Scott Taylor, Freeman Epes, Page Henderson, Bob Steele, and Neil Wyrick. Reports were that Ducker and Taylor had shown the most promise. Hampden-Sydney had been defeated this year, losing to Washington and Lee, 26-29, in a very close race in which Milener placed second to Washington and Lee's star, Echols Hansberger. Lynchburg was led by the talented Grant Hudson, a letterman from 1948-49.

The Lynchburg course was grueling–hilly and five miles in length. Coach Bast remembers that the weather was bad and the course was muddy. Alvin Smith went to the front early and kept that lead until the latter stages of the race. Unfortunately, he then began to cramp up, and had to drop back. Davenport moved around Milener in the last quarter-mile of the race to win going away in a time of 26:26.2. The time set a new course record. About seven seconds later, Milener finished the race. He was followed by Smith, McCarty, Aldred, Crockett, and White Rhyne. All five crossed the line together, officially in third place and with a time of 27:37, to give Roanoke 19 points. Lynchburg's highly-regarded Grant Hudson, was almost 100 yards back. Ed Culley of Roanoke was 19th with a time of 33:32.

In terms of team scores, Hampden-Sydney finished second to Roanoke with 48 points. Lynchburg was third with 62. It was Roanoke's 9th straight win in dual or triangular meets.

After the meet, and before the University of Virginia contest coming up a week later, a siege of colds hit team members. Frank Aldred and Ed Culley could hardly practice, in fact, and Bast thought it best to hold Frank out of the University of Virginia meet.

October 21, 1949
University of Virginia at Salem, Virginia
Team Scores: Roanoke–15
University of Virginia–40

The University team visited Salem on October 21. Bast had changed the course to 4.0 miles in order to accommodate the Charlottesville runners who were familiar with competing on longer courses.

The Virginia coach was Archie Hahn, who wasn't very interested in cross country. According to Homer Bast, Hahn would tell his runners during practices, "Go run five miles." And that was it. He was a great person, Bast notes, but he was someone who wanted you to put out your absolute best every single solitary day. By the time his runners got to run on a weekend, they were exhausted.

Coach Bast expected the Cavaliers to have a strong team, despite the fact that they had been beaten badly the previous week at the hands of a very talented North Carolina State squad. The visitors would be bringing Stewart Walker, Henry Mason, and Henry Salhoun, considered their best athletes. Chuck Menefee, Bob Drash, and Henry Blosser were also competent runners for the Charlottesville team.

At 4:30 p.m., the race began. Surprisingly, according to Coach Bast, there was little opposition right from the start. The host team quickly went into the lead, and by the time the race finished, Alvin Smith, Bruce Davenport, Paul McCarty, Lawrence Crockett, and White Rhyne simply jogged across the finish line together, smiling and talking all the way. They were 400 yards ahead of the next runner. Their winning time was 23:45, and their score of 15 team points was perfect.

The Cavaliers then took the 6th through 12th spots, with Roanoke's Johnny Turbyfill and Ed Cully completing the race together in the 13th spot, to score a total of 40 points for the University.

October 28, 1949
Virginia Military Institute and Gallaudet College at Salem, Virginia
Team Scores: Roanoke–15
Virginia Military Institute–48
Gallaudet–67

The Roanoke team hosted another meet on October 28, featuring a triangular contest between Roanoke, Virginia Military Institute, and Gallaudet College. Neither of the visiting teams appeared to be very strong. V. M. I. had lost recently to V. P. I., 19 to 39. In that meet, the Keydets' first man finished in fourth place. Their team this season was much weaker than they would be in subsequent years. Gallaudet had also lost earlier meets, in particular one to Bridgewater College.

The race was little more than a "jog in the park" for Roanoke. At the end, Bast saw the true emergence of the Big Six. There they were, six Maroons, spread across the track in a straight line, holding hands, and finishing together in a slow time of 19:47. When Smith, Davenport, Aldred, McCarty, Crockett, and Rhyne crossed the line, the next runners were more than 40 yards back.

We don't know the names or places of many of the remaining runners. Those details never made the *Brackety-Ack*, the Roanoke newspapers, or publications in the Lexington and Washington areas. But we do know the final scores: Roanoke–15, Virginia Military Institute–48, and Gallaudet–67.

The meet had signaled the end of the varsity schedule for the year, with the Little Six, Mason-Dixon, and AAU meets to come. After three seasons of cross country competition, Coach Bast's teams had won 13 consecutive dual or triangular meets, and their combined dual/triangular meet record over the three years showed 13 wins and 2 defeats. There was no doubt going into the championship meets just which team was the one to watch.

Three days after the V. M. I./Gallaudet match up, the high school team from South Boston, Virginia, came to Salem for a meet with the Roanoke College freshmen. All we know today about the meet is that Roanoke lost by a score of 24-34 to a good South Boston team. Johnny Turbyfill of the Maroons won the 2.25-mile race in a time of 12:55, with his teammate, Ed Culley, taking third (13:13). The only two additional Maroons listed on the original scoring sheet were Doug Frith (8th in 14:15) and Jim Slaybaugh (9th in 14:29).

I remember . . . The V. M. I./Gallaudet win gave us a 4-0 record. Now that's not many meets, but I got the boys as many meets as I could. By this time, people were aware of what we had. They often wouldn't run us. We would have run anyone who wanted to run us."

Homer Bast

November 5, 1949
Little Six Championships at Bridgewater, Virginia
Team Scores: 1st–Roanoke College–27
2nd–Bridgewater College–43
3rd–Randolph-Macon College–65
4th–Hampden-Sydney College–103
5th–Lynchburg College–115

On November 5 the team went to Bridgewater College in Bridgewater, Virginia, for the annual Little Six Championships. The race would be contested over a 3.6 mile course.

Roanoke was favored to win the title for the third straight year; however, in a meet that meant so much to teams and individuals, no one expected Roanoke to walk away with a Big Four or Big Six type of finish. The school that would give the Maroons the most trouble probably was Bridgewater. The Eagles were led by an excellent runner, Merle Crouse. Both Roanoke and Bridgewater were undefeated in dual or triangular meet competition. Bridgewater had won over Gallaudet, Davis and Elkins, Lynchburg, Catholic, and the University of Virginia–all by decisive margins.

Alvin Smith felt good as he warmed up, and soon after the gun sounded he took over the lead and stayed barely in front all of the race, finishing in first place with a course-record time of 19:21. Just behind him, however, there was one terrific race going on.

Bruce Davenport of Roanoke and the Bridgewater star, Merle Crouse, brought cheers from the crowd as they drove together toward the finish line. In his customary form, Davenport dogged the Eagle runner for most of the distance before coming into the last 400 yards. Bruce then turned on his famous kick and with unbelievable speed pulled even with Crouse. But Crouse was determined not to give way. In the last two yards, Bruce lunged across the finish line one-tenth of a second ahead of Crouse. The judges gave Bruce a second-place time of 19:23.0 and Crouse a third-place time of 19:23.1.

Two other Roanoke runners–McCarty in fourth and Aldred in sixth–finished in the top ten. They were followed by Ed Culley in the 29th spot. Roanoke's other outstanding runner, Red Crockett, fail to finish. While on the course, he turned an ankle and dropped out of the race.

Roanoke won the championship trophy with a total of 27 points. Bridgewater was second with 43; Randolph-Macon third with 65; Hampden-Sydney fourth with 103; and Lynchburg fifth with 115 points.

Team members and Coach Bast celebrated the victory. Roanoke now had won three consecutive Little Six meets.

Bruce Davenport narrowly beats Merle Crouse of Bridgewater College.

November 12, 1949
Virginia AAU Championships at Richmond, Virginia
Team Scores: 1st–Roanoke College–33
2nd–College of William and Mary–68
3rd–Bridgewater College–69
4th–University of Richmond–70

But what could the Roanoke team do in the upcoming AAU meet in Richmond? The course was five miles long and the opposition was good. The race featured teams from

Roanoke, Bridgewater, William and Mary, and University of Richmond. Some of the runners would count officially for their teams, while others would run unofficially. Most thought that the Maroons faced its most serious opposition of the year.

Coach Bast entered his top six runners–Frank Aldred, Bruce Davenport, Red Crockett, White Rhyne, Paul McCarty, and Alvin Smith. Virginia Tech, most thought, would be bringing Frank Hierholzer, winner of the Big Six meet in Blacksburg the past week. Other top Tech runners would include Dave Prongay, number two man on their squad and the Captain of the team, Brad Peasley, and Curt Shelton.

William and Mary would send three outstanding runners. They were Sam Lindsey, Clyde Baker, and Bob Lawson.

Echols Hansbarger, the top Washington and Lee runner who placed second in the Big Six meet, was another capable entrant. Bill Jordan, Bill Winn, and Jeam Sease were expected to represent the University of Richmond, while Henry Hart would run for Quantico, Gene Milener for Hampden-Sydney, Mike Byrnes for Randolph-Macon, and Merle Crouse for Bridgewater.

George Rams, star distance man for Georgetown, won the race in the sparkling time of 26:52.1. Clyde Baker and Sam Lindsey of the William and Mary team finished in a tie for second. Roanoke's Bruce Davenport and Alvin Smith crossed the finish line in a tie for fourth in 27:08, just 16 seconds off the winner's time. They edged out Merle Crouse of Bridgewater who placed seventh, and in the process made a good stretch run trying to overtake the two Maroons. Paul McCarty took 8th, Frank Aldred placed 11th, and Lawrence Crockett finished 15th to account for the Maroon scoring. White Rhyne, the only other Roanoke runner in the senior event, came in 19th in the field of 34 participants.

The race had been Roanoke's best of the year. The first eight men who finished broke the previous course record.

Official results showed that Roanoke had outscored all of the other teams:

1st–Roanoke College–33
2nd–William and Mary–68
3rd–Bridgewater–69
4th–University of Richmond–70

November 21, 1949
Mason-Dixon Championships at Bridgewater, Virginia
Team Scores: 1st–Roanoke College–27
2nd–Bridgewater College–68
3rd–Washington College–72
4th–Loyola University–94

5th–Hampden-Sydney College–136
6th–Johns Hopkins University–172
7th–American University–No Score

Only one meet remained on the schedule. On the morning of November 21, Coach Bast and his team left for Bridgewater and the Mason-Dixon Championships. A win there would give the Maroons their second straight unbeaten season.

Soon after the start of the 3.75-mile race, Roanoke's Alvin Smith and Bruce Davenport moved out front to run in the top three with Bridgewater's best runner, Merle Crouse. The threesome stayed together step-by-step until, at about the beginning of the final mile, Davenport pulled ahead by a few yards over Crouse. With a dogged determination, he and Crouse closed in on the finish line. Spectators watched one of the best stretch runs in the history of the Championships, with no one able to determine the eventual winner. But one of Davenport's trademarks as a runner was his strong determination to win, which he was able to do by two strides. His time was 19:46, with Crouse running 19:47.

Alvin Smith had dropped back a bit in the final mile, but managed to finish in third place some 23 seconds behind Crouse. Only a few seconds back, Paul McCarty took fourth in front of the highly-regarded Larry Brandenburg of Washington College. The other scorers for Roanoke were Frank Aldred, who put on a stretch duel with Fillmore Dryden of Washington College to finish 8th in a time of 21:02, and Red Crockett, 11th in 21:09. Of the 45 finishers in the race, White Rhyne was 18th, Ed Cully 40th, and Johnny Turbyfill 41st.

Roanoke won the championship trophy with 27 points. As expected, Bridgewater was second with 68 points, placing five runners in the top 20. The other five teams were Washington College, third with 72; Loyola University fourth with 94; Hampden-Sydney College fifth with 136; Johns Hopkins sixth with 172; and American University. There was no score for American. They did not have five finishers.

It was Roanoke's second straight Mason-Dixon Championships win and the culmination of another unbeaten cross country season.

Everyone back in Salem was excited to hear that the team had done so well. The *Brackety-Ack* even said, "The victory firmly established the Maroons as one of the outstanding little college teams in the country, certainly one of the best in the south, and definitely the best in Virginia and Mason-Dixon circles."

The win was tempered by the fact that within days, Red Crockett dropped out of school. One of the original Big Four, he had run his last race for Roanoke.

I remember . . . "Red Crockett was a farm boy. He had a lot of courage and lots of determination. Unfortunately, he finished all of his degree at Roanoke except for a foreign language. He just couldn't master a foreign language, but neither could many other students. He was pretty irked at the College because at the time no student could take a required course at another school and transfer it to Roanoke. I knew of only one or two students who managed to get around this regulation. One was a nice youngster who finished his coursework except for French. Then he took a job as Manager of a television station in Iowa. I recommended that he go to night school out there and take as much French as possible so he was sure he could pass a French test. He did that, and I asked the faculty to allow him to come to the Salem campus and take a French competency test under the direction of one of the members of the foreign language department. He passed that test and the school gave him his college degree. By the time Crockett withdrew from college, he had about given up. Subsequently, he left southwest Virginia and got a job in a bank in North Carolina and eventually in Florida. He later became President of a bank. He was a shrewd boy and made a number of successful investments, leaving quite a sizeable estate when he died. He didn't remember Roanoke College in his will, but did come back in the 1990s when the school celebrated the Big Four runners of the 1940s with a ceremony."

Homer Bast

I remember . . . "One of Hampden-Sydney's good athletes was Gene Milener. He eventually became a very good runner, in fact. He corresponded with me regularly. I sent him workouts and that sort of thing. He just knew me from cross country. I could see that he really didn't have a regular coach. In fact, Milener actually coached his team himself. He had a good friend who ran with him. And I tried to keep up with him, too. And that friend today sits in the Virginia Legislature. When our College President, Sabina (O'Hara), went down to Richmond to visit the Legislature, she met him. And he asked her whether she knew me. And then he told her a little bit about what I had done for him, Milner, and the Hampden-Sydney team."

Homer Bast

I remember . . . "Emory and Henry wasn't fielding a cross country team. I tried to get all of the teams to do it, telling them that they would see a difference in track. But Emory and Henry was anxious about football, which would conflict with cross country seasons. Of course, during the spring, they had good field event men because of football."

Homer Bast

Indoor Track

Practice for the indoor season began in early January as usual. Occasionally, the weather cooperated, but often it was bitter cold outside or the ground was covered with snow. Coach Bast and his athletes understood that they were at a disadvantage over larger schools with indoor tracks, but if necessary limited training and stretching could be accomplished inside Alumni Gymnasium or even on the hard roadway surface that surrounded the quad in the middle of the campus. No one really complained. Everyone understood the difficulties of winter training, and life went on.

As always, Bast had few options as to which meets to enter. He didn't have the money to take the boys to places like New York City or Philadelphia to find competition. So he scheduled the team once again to enter two meets: the Washington Evening Star Games at the Armory in Washington, and the non-conference division of the Southern Conference Championships in Chapel Hill.

January 14, 1950
Evening Star Games at Washington, D. C.
Mason-Dixon Sprint Medley Relay: 1st–Washington College (Hubbard, Twilley, Brandenburg, and Howard)–3:42.6
2nd–Catholic University (McCurnin, Jackson, Killigrew, and Doyle)
3rd–Roanoke College (Aldred, Tramposch, Dodd, and Smith)

The first competition in Washington came on January 14, much too early for the team to round into shape. The third annual Evening Star Games had begun to draw some of the biggest names in track in a variety of events for Olympians, college athletes, and even high schoolers. Fans this year were assured of many thrilling finishes with the attendance of top-rated squads from schools such as Cornell, Syracuse, Georgetown, Texas A&M, and Oklahoma. The mile run promised to be one of the closest races on the card, for it matched Browning Ross, winner in 1948, and George Wade, defending champion from last year, against Don Gehrman, Big Ten champ from Wisconsin, and Alf Holmberg, the sensational Swedish ace from the University of Tennessee.

One of the events, and certainly the one Bast wanted to enter, was the Mason-Dixon Conference sprint medley relay. Roanoke had shocked the conference in 1949, winning the event with a time of 3:47.7. That team had been composed of Red Crockett, Dick Dodd, Walt Tramposch, and Alvin Smith. Crockett ran a 440, Dodd and Tramposch 220s, and Smith an 880. Smith sprinted from behind to finish some ten yards in front of Larry

Brandenburg of Washington College.

This year, with Red Crockett no longer in school, Bast substituted Frank Aldred for Crockett. Aldred would lead off with a quarter, handing off to Tramposch. The baton then went to Dodd and his 220, with Smith again anchoring with an 880.

In front of a near-capacity crowd of 5,500 in the National Guard Armory, the field and running events began. Coaches soon began to notice that something wasn't right about the fast times being recorded on the circular track. The meet was halted so the officials could make sure that the track was a full 220 yards in length. It wasn't. In fact, officials estimated that the track could be short by some 80 feet. Meet Director Dorsey Griffith, widely known and respected in track and field circles, finally determined that the error was caused by an inaccuracy in the steel tape used to lay out the radius of the curves. It had been broken and then repaired without his knowledge. The repair men took out about six feet of tape without telling anyone.

The exact distance the track was short couldn't be determined until after it was re-measured following the meet with a new tape. Griffith and official Kip Edwards offered to delay the meet while the track was re-measured; however, by consensus of the visiting track coaches, the meet continued with the track as it was. All times would be considered as unofficial pending the new measurement.

Not all times were wrong, however. The sprint races were run on a separate straightaway, so the 70 yard and 80 yard meet times would be accurate.

"This is the 57th track meet I've run," said Griffith, "and I thought everything that could happen to me already had happened. But it just seems like something new comes up every time."

In the Mason-Dixon mile sprint-medley race, Washington College held off a desperate bid by Catholic University in the final lap to win the event in 3:42.6. The time couldn't be considered a record, however, because of the track measurement problem. A bad baton pass on the third leg gave Washington a big lead and anchorman Ken Howard cruised to the tape. Roanoke's team finished third.

At the awards ceremony, the Washington College team of Milton Hubbard, James Twilley, Ken Howard, and Larry Brandenburg received their newly-designed three year possession trophy from Chairman of the games Howard P. Bailey. Gold, silver, and bronze medals were presented to members of the first, second, and third place teams, respectively.

The Roanoke team got back to Salem early the next morning. They soon were training again for the final winter meet, the Southern Conference Championships in Chapel Hill. The buzz on campus was that Bob Fagg had just gotten married to Charlotte Goodwin of Salem at St. Paul's Episcopal Church. Bob, of course, was Bast's real surprise in his first years of coaching. Fagg still was the holder of the college records in the 100-yard dash with a time of :10.0 seconds; the 220-yard dash, in :23.2; and the high hurdles, in :15.9. He was also Captain of the team in the spring of 1948.

February 25, 1950
Southern Conference Games at Chapel Hill, North Carolina
Team Scores (Non-Conference Division):

1st–Navy–27
2nd–Georgia Tech University–15¾
3rd–University of Florida–14
4th–Louisiana State University–7
5th–University of Georgia–6¾
6th–University of Tennessee, Catholic University, and Washington College–5
9th–University of Virginia–4¾
10th–Roanoke College and Newport News Apprentice–4
12th–Marshall College–¾

The second and last winter meet came on February 25 in Chapel Hill, North Carolina. Roanoke men would compete in the non-conference division of the fifteenth annual Southern Conference Indoor Games.

The North Carolina team trained in a facility called the Tin Can, which contained an old, banked wooden track that they had bought from Madison Square Garden. Alvin Smith, who had run for North Carolina a couple of years before, said he loved that old track. "It was so well banked, he noted. When they held a large indoor meet on campus, they would move the track piece by piece into the spacious Woolen Gymnasium. To run the dashes, they had to have a large crew to physically lift some of the sections out of the way to accommodate the diagonal running of the dashes. The school could run a 70-yard hurdle race, in fact, and weren't restricted to the 60-yard races that were run at other facilities. And they still would have at least 10 yards left after the last hurdle so runners could stop by hitting the mats that hung on the wall. It was a wonderful place to run."

The meet not only would provide excellent competition for the Maroons, but the boys would enjoy watching some of the finest athletes in the east and south. The results of the meet, like the one in 1949, showed that the University of North Carolina had the best conference team. The magic feet of U. N. C.'s hurdler-jumper Bill Albans set a bristling pace as North Carolina won the title for the sixth straight time. Albans, a five-event winner last year, swept three today and added a tie for second to account for 17½ of the Tarheel's 60 points. Runner-up Maryland scored 38½ points. In the non-conference division, the three top teams were Navy, Georgia Tech, and the University of Florida.

Coach Bast entered the names of five athletes, some or all of whom he thought might compete. The men were Bruce Davenport, Ray DeCosta, Dick Dodd, Paul McCarty, and Walt Tramposch. There was nothing recorded to say which, if any, of the events Dodd and Tromposch entered, although Bast's intent was for them to run the 60-yard dash. We do know, however, that DeCosta, Davenport, and McCarty were Roanoke's stars in the meet, bringing home a total of four points for the team in the non-conference division. Just a fraction of a point behind the University of Virginia in the team standing, Roanoke emerged as the second top scorer in the state.

First, sophomore DeCosta pole vaulted 12'0" to tie for second place. He barely missed clearing 12'6", the winning height, when he clipped the bar with a leg after the peak of his jump. It was the first time he had ever jumped indoors.

In addition, Davenport ran the fastest mile of his career as he nipped Trout of Navy for third place in the mile run. Running a steady race, the talented junior came from fifth position to finish in a drive to the tape. Davenport's time was 4:31.0. Paul McCarty took fifth in this race with a very respectable 4:35.0 clocking, also the fastest of his life.

Outdoor Track

Coach Bast's administrative job at Roanoke, Admissions Director, often took him out of town to visit students at secondary schools on the east coast. On a Monday in early February, therefore, team Co-Captains Paul McCarty and Frank Aldred conducted the first official workouts for the spring season without Bast. The first outdoor meet, with Randolph-Macon, was scheduled for April 1. Bast had advised his captains to start with simple conditioning exercises and jogging. When he returned, the pace of workouts would be increased and individual instruction in various events would be provided for those with no previous experience.

Alvin Smith, top distance man for Roanoke during the past two years, was unable to compete this spring because of academic difficulties primarily caused by a failing biology grade. The team would miss his guidance and outstanding performances. Bast knew that Alvin could run any race from the 880 to the two-mile, and was always able to compete as a valuable member of his relay teams. He and Bruce Davenport had set all of the team's middle-distance and distance records during the past two years. Alvin had run the 880 in 2:00.4 and the mile in 4:24.4, both school records.

Davenport was one of the best two-milers in the state, having run the three best times in school history in that event. In one of his races, in May of 1949, he broke the 10:00 mark with 9:59.8. He also had one of those rare running personalities, in that he was the one person you wanted to see in a stretch dual with an opposing runner.

Left Photo (L to R): Paul McCarty, Bruce Davenport, and Frank Aldred practice on the college track.
Right Photo: First Row (L to R): DeCosta, Bower, Davenport, Friend, Byerly, and Basham.
Second Row (L to R): R. Tramposch, Frith, Williams, Smith, Barker, and Fraley.
Third Row (L to R): McCarty, Rhyne, Slaybaugh, Aldred, Hash, W. Tramposch, and Walsh.
Fourth Row (L to R): Dunbar, Harless, Coach Bast, and Comer.

Then there was sophomore Ray DeCosta, a short, well-built athlete who would soon be known as one of the best pole vaulters in the region. He already had cleared 12'0" a number of times, had gone 12'4" once during his freshman year, and twice barely knocked the bar from the standards at 12'6". He was a talent ready to explode. Coach Bast could see no limit to what he might accomplish in his three remaining years at Roanoke. With pole vaulters, however, problems were common. Their poles–certainly not the innovative poles made from fiberglass that were later used–sometimes broke or were ill-fitted to the athlete's weight and running speed. Some approaches were uneven, plant boxes often were positioned poorly, and the pits in which the jumpers landed were little more than slightly-raised layers of wood shavings and sawdust or sometimes loose sand.

Co-Captain Paul McCarty was also returning for one more year. Always dependable, he had been one of the original Big Four runners on the cross-country team and was a consistently good runner behind Smith and Davenport. He looked like he was in good condition; in fact, he ran an excellent 4:35.0 mile indoors. And the first time he entered an 880 race, he finished in a very respectable 2:05.

Co-Captain Frank Aldred, who had transferred to Roanoke from Davidson in 1948, also was on the team. Bast marveled at how much he had grown as a runner over the past couple of years. During the past cross country season, he was a better runner than one or two of the Big Four. It would be interesting to see how his times would improve outdoors. Like McCarty, he had never run track nor cross country before entering Roanoke, so who could know how good he might become?

Veteran White Rhyne, one of the school's fabled Big Six cross country runners, was expected to do well this year in the distance events. He was a sophomore from Philadelphia.

Other veterans were also expected to help the team this year. Harry Bower was the only letterman to return in the sprints, but Dick Dodd (who was out with injuries most of last season) looked promising and Bast thought the Roanoke sprinter might win his races in several of the meets this spring.

Dick Fraley and Walter Tramposch were lettermen in the middle distances. John Turbyfill, a very promising freshman, might give the trio a run for their positions and prove quite outstanding before the year is over. Don Brown and Alvin Stump also were hopefuls in these events.

Only Doug Frith had any experience in the hurdles; however, freshman Don Fleming had obvious potential and had caught Bast's eye. Fleming, along with Turbyfill, seemed to be the most likely to succeed among the newcomers.

Robert Walsh would return in the weight events. R. K. would be the only letterman in these events for the Maroons, but Paul Barker and John Byerly were also capable of scoring points.

Bast thought the team might be weak in the high and broad jumps. But athletes such as Don Fleming and Jim Slaybaugh might be able to score points in these events.

The *Brackety-Ack* also listed several others who were training with the team in February and were expected to do well: Page Henderson, Wallace Lord, George Naff, George McCartney, Don Ettorri, Doug Ayers, Ralph Walker, Dave Maxwell, William Bradley, Dave Nickerson, Phil Davis, and Charles Mulcahey.

Here was the meet schedule for 1950:

April 1	Randolph-Macon, Home
April 5	Loyola and Gallaudet at Baltimore
April 17	Bridgewater, at Bridgewater
April 22	Milligan Relays at Johnson City, Tennessee
April 28	Emory and Henry, Home
May 3	Lynchburg, Home
May 6	Little Six Championships at Lynchburg
May 12-13	Mason-Dixon Championships at Washington
May 27	Virginia AAU Championships at Lynchburg

April 1, 1950
Randolph-Macon College at Salem, Virginia
Team Scores: Roanoke–62½
Randolph-Macon-54½

The outcome of Roanoke's first meet of the season, at home against Randolph-Macon, was a toss-up–too difficult to predict. In the spring of 1949, Bast had been very disappointed by a sizable loss to the school–Randolph-Macon, 71⅔ and Roanoke, 54⅓–in a meet held at Ashland.

The day was poor for a track meet–cold, wet, and miserable–and the team scores were close all day long. Of the 13 events, the Yellow Jackets won seven and Roanoke won the other six; however, the Maroons managed to come through with nine second places to win the meet, 62½ to 54½.

During the afternoon, Roanoke men failed to set any College records. But there were five Alumni Field records either set or tied. For Roanoke, Ray DeCosta tied his own field record in the pole vault with another 12-foot jump. The remaining field records were the result of Randolph-Macon efforts. In the 440, Emory Evans ran :52.2, breaking the record of :52.8 set in 1929 by Miles of Emory and Henry College. John Acton, Jr., the visitors' fine hurdler, tied the record of :16.3 formerly set by Milton Drewer, Jr., of Randolph-Macon in 1948. Bill Barrett, Jr., put the shot 39'5" to beat the old mark of 39'0" set in 1949. Finally, the long jump record of 20'8¾" was broken by Baylor.

Besides DeCosta, several Maroons finished first in their events. After losing the 100-yard dash to Bob Johnson of Randolph-Macon, Dick Dodd came back to win the 220 in the good time of :23.4. Paul McCarty and Bruce Davenport finished together, in the top two positions, in both the 880-yard run and the mile run. Davenport and White Rhyne also went one-two in the two-mile event. R. K. Walsh managed to win the discus throw with 113'4".

In the 440-yard dash, where Emory Evans set a new field record of :52.2, Frank Aldred ran a terrific race. According to onlookers, he finished the race barely behind the winner and likely his constant pressure on Evans pushed Evans to the new record.

Other Roanoke athletes who placed in the meet were Dick Fraley, third in the 220-yard dash; Doug Frith, second in the 120-yard high hurdles and third in the 220-yard low hurdles; Walsh, second in the shot put; Paul Barker, tie for third in the discus; Page Henderson, tie for second in the high jump; and DeCosta, second in the broad jump.

April 5, 1950
Loyola College and Gallaudet College at Baltimore, Maryland
Team Scores: Roanoke–69½

Loyola–53
Gallaudet–20½

On April 5, the team traveled to Loyola in Baltimore for a three-way meet also featuring Gallaudet. Very little was known about the strengths of Gallaudet, although Bast knew that they had fielded fairly weak teams in the past. In addition, the Maroons had not met Gallaudet during the 1949 season. Loyola, however, was said to have a number of good men in both the running and field events. This meet would be Roanoke's last before the College adjourned for the Easter vacation.

As it turned out, winning the meet was fairly easy for Roanoke. The Salem boys captured 9 of 13 first places, with wins in seven of the eight track races and two additional field events. No Roanoke College or Loyola track records were broken.

Dick Dodd, coming into his own as a sprinter, won both the 100- and 220-yard dashes by inches over Loyola's Fields. Frank Aldred ran a fine :53.4 to finish first in the quarter mile and just miss the Roanoke College record of :53.0, and Bruce Davenport easily won the two-mile race. As in the first meet, Paul McCarty and Davenport teamed up to cross the line first in both the 880 and mile runs. Doug Frith surprised the team with a win in the low hurdles, as did R. K. Walsh, who threw the discus a personal-best 122'3¼" for a victory in that event. Ray DeCosta was hampered by a short and soggy runway in the pole vault, but still won the event with a jump of 11'0".

Several other Roanoke men also scored, including Dick Fraley, fourth in the 220; White Rhyne, third in the two-mile run; Doug Frith, third in the high hurdles; Walsh, second in the shot put; Paul Barker, fourth in the discus throw; DeCosta, second in the broad jump and tied for second in the high jump; and Dave Nickerson and Charles Mulchey, who tied for fourth in the pole vault.

Roanoke finished the day with 69½ points. Loyola won its only two events when the Greyhounds' Malcolm Rose took the high jump and Jack Brunt finished first in the broad jump. Their second-place point total was 53, while Gallaudet limped home with just 20½ points.

April 17, 1950
Bridgewater College at Bridgewater, Virginia
Team Scores: Bridgewater–77
Roanoke–40

At this point, on the first day of spring break, Roanoke was a surprising 2-0 in dual and triangular meets. Back from the break on April 17, however, they traveled to Bridgewater to meet a very strong Eagles team that was favored to win the Little Six meet later in the season and possibly to take the Mason-Dixon title. Unfortunately, Doug Frith had broken a leg and was unable to make the trip. In fact, he was out of action for the remainder of the season. Harry Bower was also unavailable, at least for the next meet, after suffering an injury.

The Eagles won the meet by a score of 77 to 40, winning 8 of the 13 events. During the afternoon, however, Roanoke athletes set four new Bridgewater track records, but did not break any of the Roanoke College student records.

Track record breakers were: Bruce Davenport, running the mile in 4:31.9 (beating the top Bridgewater distance man, Merle Crouse) and then smashing the two-mile mark with a time of 10:38.7; Paul McCarty, who ran a personal-best 2:03.0 in the 880; and Ray DeCosta, who jumped 11'6" in the pole vault. When the competition was finished, Ray tried the height of 12'6", trying to set a new record of his own. Unfortunately, although he looked to have cleared this height, his hand hit and dislodged the bar on his way down.

The Bridgewater record-setter was Melvin Myers. He leaped 22'2½" to set a new field mark in the broad jump.

R. K. Walsh again threw the discus well. His fine toss of 117'½" won the event.

Roanoke men picked up several second places: Don Fleming, high hurdles; Dick Dodd, 220; and Frank Aldred, 440. Third place finishes came from Aldred, 880; Walsh, shot put; and DeCosta, high jump.

Bruce Davenport romped around the track in two events and cracked the records in both. Bruce broke the mile record when he outclassed the Bridgewater ace miler, Crouse, and turned in a time of 4:31.9. Davenport came back in the two mile to bring the existing track record for that event down to 10:38.7. Paul McCarty ran an excellent half mile and had things his own way from start to finish. He also lowered the field record to 2:03.

April 22, 1950
Milligan Relays at Johnson City, Tennessee
Team Scores: 1st–Wofford College–65½
2nd–East Tennessee State College–57½
3rd–Roanoke College–49
4th–Maryville College–43
5th–Mars Hill College–25½
6th–Emory and Henry College–19½
7th–Union University–2
8th–Milligan College–0
9th–Lincoln Memorial University–0
10th–King College–0

On April 22, the squad made the drive to Johnson City, Tennessee, to compete in the annual Milligan Relays. This was the third time that Roanoke had entered this meet. On the other two occasions, in 1948 and 1949, they had placed third.

Twenty-eight teams–10 colleges, 13 high schools, and even 5 junior highs–would be entered in 10 relay and 11 special events. The Relays were held at Memorial Stadium, which had a track that was, as one Maroon noted, rather "stony." This day, it was also muddy and slippery from a day-long rain.

Events got underway at 1:00 p.m. Experts thought that Wofford, Roanoke, Maryville, and the University of Tennessee freshmen, would compete for top honors.

The bad weather hampered the running of the meet, and the assault on any records. Ray DeCosta of Roanoke, for example, faced a slippery runway and driving rain as the pole vault began. On his first jump, he cleared 10'6". When none of the other jumpers could clear the same height, he told the judges that he would not make any more jumps; therefore, Ray was awarded the first-place trophy.

Roanoke was defending its title in the sprint medley and distance medley relays. This year, however, with the slippery, muddy condition of the track, no one could predict the winners. But in the distance relay, where the first person ran a quarter mile, the second an 880, the third a three quarter mile, and the fourth a mile, the Maroons actually set a new meet record. In this race, Paul McCarty turned in the outstanding performance of the day. Running an 880 in the third leg of the race, Bast timed him in 1:59.5, a time that made up a 20-yard deficit for the team. Paul had never run this well in an 880. Paul handed off to Bruce Davenport, giving Bruce a 10-yard lead, and at that point there was no question which team would win the race. Roanoke recorded a time of 10:14.0, which beat the Roanoke College record of 10:15.2 set in 1948 at the same meet.

The Maroons' team of Paul McCarty, Dick Fraley, Dick Dodd, and Bruce Davenport also won the sprint medley relay, setting another Roanoke College record. Actually, the team wasn't pushed, winning by 25 yards over East Tennessee State in a time of 3:43.0. That time beat the old mark of 3:53.0, set in the Milligan Relays of 1949. Once Bruce Davenport took off on his anchor half-mile run, the race was never in doubt.

Davenport came back a half hour later, splashing to victory in the open mile in a near-record time of 4:48.3. Bast considered the time to be a good one for Bruce because a driving rain fell throughout the race.

The Roanoke team of Dick Dodd, John Turbyfill, Paul McCarty, and Frank Aldred later placed second in the mile relay. The decision, many thought, was based on faulty judgments by finish line officials. As the anchor leg runners from Roanoke and Mars Hill reached the tape, the crowd was sure that Aldred was ahead by about a foot and that Roanoke would be declared the winner. Aldred had just made up a 10-yard deficit down the stretch to go ahead of the Mars Hill runner. Then, with a foot to go, the Mars Hill athlete stuck out both hands and appeared to break the tape with the hands an inch or two in front of Aldred's chest. The officials were perplexed. Who should receive the win? Finally, in a contested decision, they gave the victory to Mars Hill, but the identical time of 3:39.4 to both teams.

Bast assembled a pickup team of Walt Tramposch, Ray DeCosta, Ralph Walker, and Dick Dodd to run the 880-yard relay (4 X 220) and the team surprised everyone by finishing third behind Wofford and East Tennessee State.

There were several other Roanoke men who placed in the meet's individual events. They included Doug Frith, fifth in the high hurdles; Don Fleming, fifth in the low hurdles; and R. K. Walsh, second in the shot put and fourth in the discus. White Rhyne also ran in the mile event, Don Fleming and Joe Baldwin competed in the hurdles, and Chuck Mulcahey tried his hand at the pole vault.

The Maroons, hampered by injuries and a lack of depth, finished third in the meet with 49 points. The champion team was Wofford, with 65½ points, followed by East Tennessee State with 57½. After Roanoke came Maryville, Mars Hill, Emory and Henry, and Union. Milligan, Lincoln Memorial, and King failed to score.

At this point in the season, Roanoke had won its first two meets, and then lost to a strong Bridgewater team. In the Milligan Relays, the Maroons showed promise by scoring 49 points and finishing third. The next meet would come on April 28, when they would meet Emory and Henry in Salem. Hampden-Sydney was scheduled to take part in a triangular meet with Roanoke and Emory and Henry; however, they sent word that because of traveling difficulties they would be unable to participate. Their team bus had broken down near Lynchburg, Virginia.

April 28, 1950
Emory and Henry College at Salem, Virginia
Team Scores: Roanoke–71
Emory and Henry–51

Six days later, Emory and Henry's track team came to Salem. Roanoke took first in three of the five field events, and tied for the win in another. R. K. Walsh was a double winner, throwing 37'10' in the shot put and 119'9½" in the discus. Although his shot put distances had been only average all year, he had turned into one of the best discus throwers in the Little Six Conference.

Don Fleming, primarily a hurdler, won the broad jump. He edged the Emory and Henry jumpers by half an inch.

And finally, the results of the pole vault were a surprise. Roanoke's Ray DeCosta, unbeaten during the year, tied for first. Chick Davis of EH stayed right with the talented

Maroon vaulter and both were eliminated when the bar reached 12 feet.

Roanoke won six of the nine running events. The 100-yard dash was the most controversial of the nine races. The starter fired his pistol, but many in the crowd thought that the three Emory and Henry men in the race broke from their blocks before the gun went off. The Roanoke runners quickly stood up, thinking the other runners would be re-called; however, the starter did not call them back and Thomas Sokol of Emory and Henry went on to run a time of :10.2, followed by his two teammates.

There were two memorable races. Dick Dodd ran his fastest time ever (:23.1) in the 220-yard dash to win and set two records. His time tied the Alumni Field record, matching the mark of Lynn Chewning of Hampden-Sydney College in 1949. The time also broke the Roanoke College record of :23.2, which was set by Bob Fagg in 1948.

In the mile relay, the Roanoke team of Walt Tramposch, Dick Dodd, Bruce Davenport, and Frank Aldred ran 3:39.4 and set two records. The time was a field record as well as a College record. No time for the event had been recorded for Roanoke since track and field meets were run in the 1920s.

Frank Aldred won the 440-yard dash in :53.5 and Walt Tramposch was third in that event. John Turbyfill ran 2:13.8 in the 880 to win, with Wallace Lord just behind and taking second place. White Rhyne beat the opposition handily in the two-mile run with a time of 11:07.0 and again, Lord finished second in the race. Finally, two Maroons scored points in the hurdles. Don Fleming was second in the highs and Joe Baldwin took second place in the lows.

Roanoke won the meet, its third victory of the season, by outscoring Emory and Henry 71 to 51. Coach Bast was pleased with the progress of his team.

May 3, 1950
Lynchburg College at Salem, Virginia
Team Scores: Roanoke–64
Lynchburg–58

There was one final dual meet remaining on the schedule before the team went to the Little Six Championships in Lynchburg on May 6. On May 3, Roanoke hosted the Hornets of Lynchburg College.

Roanoke beat Lynchburg by a narrow margin of 64 to 58. The story of the day, however, was how many records the two teams would break–five for Alumni Field and two Roanoke College student records.

Dick Dodd led the record assault when he crossed the line in :22.6 in the 220-yard dash. The time was a field record, beating his own mark of :23.1 from earlier in the season, and was a Roanoke College record as well.

Bruce Davenport entered the 880-yard run, and he also broke an Alumni Field record by running 2:03.1. Alvin Smith held the former mark, :2:03.7, which he set in 1948.

Roanoke's mile relay team of Turbyfill, Dodd, McCarty, and Aldred, set their new Alumni Field mark with a time of 3:38.4. The time was a full second better than the old mark set by Tramposch, Dodd, Davenport, and Aldred earlier in the season. It was also a school record.

Paul Shelton threw the discus 125'3¾" for a new discus record for Alumni Field, while Lynchburg teammate Shirley Milam high jumped 6'2 5/16". The high jump mark was one of the best in the state for 1950.

There were five additional wins for Roanoke. Dick Dodd ran :10.3 in the 100, Frank Aldred's time was :53.0 in the 440, Bruce Davenport and Paul McCarty teamed up to tie for first in the mile, R. K. Walsh threw 38'5" in the shot put, and Ray DeCosta easily jumped 11'6" in the pole vault.

Second place finishes came from Walt Tramposch in the 440, White Rhyne in the two-mile race, Paul Barker in the shot put, and R. K. Walsh in the discus. Third place points were picked up by Dick Fraley in the 100 and 220, John Turbyfill in the quarter mile, McCarty in the 880, Wallace Lord in the two-mile run, Don Fleming in the high hurdles, Jim Slaybaugh in the low hurdles, John Byerly in the discus, and Charles Mulcahey and Dave Nickerson, who tied for the third position in the pole vault.

The first part of Roanoke's season had ended, with the team winning four dual meets and losing only to Bridgewater. Bast was positive toward his athletes, but he had done his homework, and the likelihood of winning either the Little Six or the Mason-Dixon Championships was slim.

May 6, 1950
Little Six Championships at Lynchburg, Virginia
Team Scores: 1st–Bridgewater College–50
2nd–Randolph-Macon College–33
3rd–Roanoke College–30
4th–Lynchburg College–23
5th–Hampden-Sydney College–16
6th–Emory and Henry College–2

The Little Six meet arrived just three days after the Lynchburg win. Bridgewater, Randolph-Macon, and Roanoke seemed to Bast to have the most talent among the six entering schools. Lynchburg and Hampden-Sydney would be competitive but were not expected to challenge for the trophy. Emory and Henry College would attend with its team for the first time in years, but were not likely to score very many points.

Bridgewater captured the team title in 1949 and they were the favorites this time around, having defeated Roanoke and other Little Six schools decisively during the regular season.

The team that Coach Bast took to Lynchburg consisted of the following individuals: Bruce Davenport, Paul McCarty, Ray DeCosta, Dick Dodd, Frank Aldred, R. K. Walsh, Walt Tramposch, John Turbyfill, Dick Fraley, Don Fleming, and Jim Slaybaugh. Davenport would run only the mile and two-mile races. Aldred would concentrate on the 880. Dodd, with his record 220 time of :22.6 was given a good chance in the 220-yard dash. Tramposch would run the 440, Turbyfill the mile, Fraley the dashes, Fleming and Slaybaugh the hurdles, and Tramposch, Dodd, Aldred, and McCarty the mile relay, with Davenport being an alternate.

Despite a driving rain, three athletes set records. First, big Jim Myers of Bridgewater put the shot 43'7¾" to beat the old meet record of 40'0" set by Willard Craft of Hampden-Sydney in 1938. Then Meryl Crouse of Bridgewater ran the mile in 4:33.6, setting another meet record and barely edging out Roanoke's Bruce Davenport. In the pole vault competition, Ray DeCosta tied the meet record and set a new mark for Roanoke College athletes, with a jump of 12'6". Ray tried to set a new record at 12'9" but failed to cross the bar in three tries.

Paul McCarty easily outdistanced other runners in the 880 to win that event. Frank Aldred, running the half for the first time this year, placed fourth.

Roanoke's mile relay team of Walt Tramposch, Dick Dodd, Frank Aldred, and Paul McCarty had little competition in the mile relay. Their winning time was 3:40.2, not far off the school record.

Dick Dodd just lost to winner Emory Evans of Randolph-Macon in the 220. R. K. Walsh managed to finish in third place in the discus.

Johnny Acton of Randolph-Macon and Larry Roller of Bridgewater shared individual scoring honors, each with 10 points. Team honors went to Bridgewater, whose depth showed as they collected 50 points. With its 30 points, Roanoke almost became the runner-up team. Unfortunately, they were barely beaten by Randolph-Macon, who picked up 33. Lynchburg (23) was fourth, Hampden-Sydney (16) fifth, and Emory and Henry (2) sixth and last.

May 12-13, 1950
Mason-Dixon Championships at Washington, D. C.
Team Scores: 1st–Washington College–63½
2nd–Bridgewater College–35¼
3rd–Catholic University–25½

4th–Randolph-Macon College–23
5th–American University–18
6th–Roanoke College–16
7th–Loyola College–16
8th–Lynchburg College–7
9th–Gallaudet College–5

The final meet of the season was the Mason-Dixon Championships at Catholic University in Washington. The May 12-13 meet had qualifying events on Friday, as usual, and all finals on Saturday. Twelve Conference teams would be at the meet, although Washington College was expected to defend their title from 1949.

Coach Bast, ever a realist, knew that his team this year would be entering for individual honors only. Because of the level of competition, he took only ten members of the team to the meet: Ray DeCosta, Bruce Davenport, Frank Aldred, White Rhyne, Paul McCarty, Walt Tramposch, John Turbyfill, Dick Fraley, Joe Baldwin, and Jim Slaybaugh. Dick Dodd, his best sprint man, and weight man R. K. Walsh, did not enter.

Although the Maroons could never win the meet, they did have some of the Conference's outstanding athletes. The team was fourth in the meet last year, but even that high of a finish might be impossible this time around. The Bast team had quality, but not quantity. That would be a problem in a large meet like the Mason-Dixon.

The only Roanoke winner in the meet was Ray DeCosta, who was head and shoulders above all of the pole vaulters in the meet. He easily cleared the bar at 12'0" for a win, but couldn't repeat his record-tying 12'6" that he had set in the Little Six contest.

Bruce Davenport finished second in the mile run, even though he ran the fastest outdoor mile of his career (4:31.5). Merle Crouse of Bridgewater, however, had grown stronger and stronger during the season and broke the tape in 4:29.4 just a few strides in front of Bruce. Crouse, incidentally, also won the two-mile run, a race in which White Rhyne placed fourth for Roanoke. In this race, Crouse took the lead at the halfway mark and won by 25 yards.

On Friday during qualifying heats, Davenport had won his heat of the 880 in 2:02.9. McCarty and Aldred placed second in their heats. After the grueling dual with Crouse in the mile, however, Bruce withdrew from the finals of the 880. The 880 finals were won by Larry Brandenburg, with McCarty placing fourth and Aldred fifth.

Aldred qualified for the 440-yard dash finals with a school record time of :52.6. In the finals on Saturday, however, he was unable to duplicate that performance and finished sixth.

The Roanoke mile relay team of Turbyfill, Tramposch, Aldred, and McCarty only managed a fourth place showing, but the team did set a new Roanoke College record by finishing in 3:36.2. The old mark was 3:38.4, set earlier in the 1950 season. Tramposch says that he remembers Turbyfill leading off, and then handing to McCarty. McCarty handed to him, and Aldred ran the anchor leg. When Tramposch got the baton, the Roanoke team was in last place. By the time Tramposch finished his lap, passing off to Aldred, the team had moved up to third place. Tramposch says he remembers this race well because the guys in front of him during the latter stages of the lap were beginning to run out of steam. In fact, one of these fellows audibly began to groan. Hearing this guy in such distress caused him to sprint even harder toward the finish line.

None of the other Maroons–Fraley, Baldwin, or Slaybaugh–was able to score for the team, which finished with 16 points in a tie for sixth place with Loyola. As expected, Washington College was first, followed by Bridgewater, Catholic, Randolph-Macon, and American. After Roanoke and Loyola came Lynchburg and Gallaudet.

I remember . . . "I remember the last race I ran for RC – the Mason-Dixon Championships at Catholic University in Washington. We really didn't do well, but I was able to bring the stick up. We eventually finished fourth. The runners may have been Turbyfill in leadoff, Aldred (probably fourth), myself (probably in third), and one more. I remember that I was in last place when I got the baton. By the time I finished my lap, we were in third. I remember this race because the guy in front of me (I think he was from Lynchburg), going into the latter part of our lap when we were beginning our kick, I heard this guy sort of groan in front of me and I knew he had about had it. He was fading fast. I took off after the next runner."

Walt Tramposch

On Sunday night after the Mason-Dixon meet, Coach Bast and Mary Jane hosted a dessert party at their house to honor the graduating track and cross country athletes. Mary Jane, incidentally, was pregnant with her first child. After the desserts were served, Bruce Davenport was elected cross country Captain for the coming fall and Dick Dodd and Dick Fraley were named to head the track team for 1951.

During the party, Coach Bast was presented with a Parker pen and pencil set by Frank Aldred on behalf of the two teams. Mr. Bast informed Aldred and Paul McCarty, the track Co-Captains, that he would present them with a small trophy each within a few days for their years of service with the track and cross country teams.

I remember . . . "The second year I was at Roanoke, we brought down an old Model A Ford. And we had to hide it behind the Commons. One day the Dean sent a message saying that he knew there were student cars back there. He wanted those cars gone. Alvin Smith spoke up and said that he had an empty garage we could put it in. So I did."

Walt Tramposch

Chapter Six

The 1950-51 Seasons

Near the beginning of the 1950-51 school year, Homer Bast was busy as usual, teaching summer school. In the previous school year, upon the death of Stewart Hanks, he had been appointed the College's Admissions Director. Besides his role as a teacher, his new duties would be to interview new student prospects, assemble their credentials, and present them to the Committee on Admissions. He was also expected to visit preparatory and high schools.

As usual, Homer wrote to his athletes over the summer and was looking forward to the upcoming cross country season. Although Alvin Smith and three others who were part of the Big Six of past years would not be part of the program, Bast always looked forward to his fall coaching. There was something special about cross country runners. It was hard to explain.

But he would never get a chance to coach cross country or track this year. Soon his entire life would turn upside down.

Bast and a friend, Bill Bagby, had started the Naval Reserves in Roanoke several years before. They had two units–21 and 22. Bill became the Commanding Officer because he was senior to Homer, so Homer became the Training Officer. Eventually, another group took over 22, but Homer and Bill held onto 21. Bill served his three years as Commanding Officer and at the end of his third year, he was forced to move on. After he became an inactive Reserve Officer, Homer became the Commanding Officer.

Homer hadn't taken command of the unit for more than a few weeks when he got orders to active duty. Dave Thornton was the College's Alumni Secretary, and he and Homer shared a desk in a small, crowded office. The phone rang one day, and Thornton picked up the receiver. He turned to Bast and said, "It's for you." Bast took the receiver and talked for a few minutes. As he hung up the phone, he said to Thornton, "Dave, you're now the Director of Admissions." The Navy had called him back to duty as Commanding Officer of an LST. That duty would be in Seattle, Washington, and they were requiring him to be ready to leave within a week.

Bast actually had a premonition that he would be called back to duty. International affairs were slowly boiling and suddenly there was the Vietnam situation. The Navy was interested in getting people who could take command right away, and Bast was the first Lieutenant Commander called in the entire United States.

Homer was granted a leave of absence from the College. Within days, he had to report to Richmond to get a physical exam and then return to Salem to pick up his orders. He never understood why his assignment was in Seattle. "This is an example," he said, "of all the dumb stuff they did in those days. They would take an officer on the west coast and send him all the way to the eastern United States. And someone like me would be sent to the west coast. It made no sense at all. It was just typical Navy stuff. And this happened again and again."

Mary Jane had just given birth about a month before to Michael, the Bast's first child. All the responsibility for raising Michael was in Mary Jane's hands now, and would be for some time; therefore, they closed up their apartment on Market Street and Mary Jane went back to Staunton to be with her parents. It was apparent soon that the move was a good one. Her mother and father were able to help her, and she now had someone who was experienced in raising a baby.

Meanwhile, the College was figuring a way to keep the cross country and track programs going while Homer was gone. They finally asked Alvin Smith to be interim coach. He was academically ineligible that year and out of school. He agreed to coach the team and began his preparations for the fall season. Homer had laid out some plans for Alvin before he left. The meet schedule was complete, and over the next few months he would offer much advice by mail. Alvin admitted that he was no coach, but he thought he could keep things together until Homer could return.

Cross Country

So here was the Roanoke cross country team. They had a temporary coach and had lost four of the famous Big Six runners that had given them two straight undefeated seasons. Smith did have Captain Bruce Davenport and White Rhyne, but could the other men step up to help produce a successful season?

Besides Bruce and White, the Maroons would be forced to rely on Bennie Irvin, a freshman from Roanoke who eventually would be an excellent runner for the College, along with Wallace Lord, John Turbyfill, Kelly Perdue, Bill Davis, Vernon Body, and Phil Davis. In early October, prior to the first meet, Irvin won the annual intramural cross country meet, pacing the day students to an overall victory against the fraternities and dormitories. His time of 7:40.2 over the 1.5-mile course set a new record. The old mark had been set by White Rhyne two years before at 7:42.0.

Left Picture: Some of the 1950 cross country team members. Front Row (L to R): John Turbyfill, Bruce Davenport, and Bennie Irvin. Back Row (L to R): Kelly Perdue, Phil Davis, Wallace Lord, and White Rhyne.
Right Picture: Bruce Davenport and Bennie Irvin in a practice session.

October 14, 1950
Hampden-Sydney College at Hampden-Sydney, Virginia
Team Scores: Roanoke–27
Hampden-Sydney–28

The team's first competition, with Hampden-Sydney, came on October 14, 1950. It was the last meet Homer coached before leaving for his obligation to the Navy. Lynchburg College was supposed to have been one of the teams in a triangular meet; however, at the last minute they declined to run. Homer and Alvin took 10 runners to Hampden-Sydney, including Rhyne, Turbyfill, Irvin, Davenport, Phil Davis, Kelly Perdue, Vernon Body, Wallace Lord, Chuck Marshall, and Jimmy Farmer. Also on the trip was Manager Bobby Davenport.

The main threat to the Roanoke team would be the home team's Gene Milener, one of the best runners in the Little Six Conference. Hampden-Sydney already had one meet under their belt. They had beaten the University of Richmond decisively just a few days before. Those results shocked many because Richmond had been ranked second in the state during the 1940 season.

Milener gave the Roanoke men a real race. He ran so well, in fact, that his time of 23:01.8 on the 4.1-mile course, knocked about 39 seconds from the existing record. It was an easy win.

Following Milener across the line, however, were three Roanoke runners. Bruce Davenport, White Rhyne, and Bennie Irvin pulled their version of the Big Four and finished together in a time of 25:02.

Hampden-Sydney took the next three places, but Kelly Perdue finished eighth, despite the fact that he had been ill and bedridden for the past week. Then Bill Davis crossed the line in tenth place. Roanoke's Wallace Lord was eleventh and Johnny Turbyfill was thirteenth. The final team scores gave a one-point win to Roanoke, 27 to 28.

In a matter of days, Coach Bast was with the Navy on the west coast and, psychologically, not doing well. He was Commanding Officer of a ship, one that had been decommissioned and in mothballs before he arrived. He was responsible for seeing that it came out of mothballs and for getting it in shape to use. An LST usually was commanded by a Lieutenant. He was a Lieutenant Commander and should not have been commanding that ship. Soon they relieved him of that command and sent him to Alaska as Operations Officer.

There he was, in Adak, Alaska, a small community in Alaska's Aleutian Islands. It was located halfway between Seattle and Japan, 1,300 miles southwest of Anchorage, 1400 miles from Magadan in Eastern Russia, and close to the natural resources of the Kamchatka Peninsula and Sakhalin Island. He was in charge of all of the Naval operations for the Aleutian Islands region. Basically, he sat at a desk answering phone calls and directing ships to do things like search and rescue.

The fear on behalf of the Navy was that the Russians might come down and take over. Actually, they could have done so, and perhaps easily. There was really no defense system in place there.

He did get one chance to see Mary Jane and Michael. When Coach Bast got orders to leave the LST and go to Alaska, Mary Jane flew out with Michael to visit for just a few days. Homer went down to the Seattle-Tacoma airport to meet them. As he was walking through the downtown area, he heard a newspaper boy on the street yelling, "Extra, extra. Read about the air crash." He discovered that the airplane was from the same company as the one Mary Jane and Michael were on. In those days, planes couldn't get over the mountains and had to fly through some of the passes. The particular plane written about in the newspaper had crashed, killing everyone on board.

Homer, of course, was frantic. Maybe the crashed plane was Mary Jane's. For an hour, he tried to get the details, especially the flight number of the downed plane. Finally, he learned that Mary Jane and Michael were on another incoming airplane. It was an awful experience in a terrible year for Homer and Mary Jane.

Mary Jane was able to stay only a very short time. They lived during that time with

Gordon Highfill and his wife. Highfill had been a hurdler for Homer. When he came to Roanoke College, he had just pulled a muscle. It was a bad pull, and this athlete with beautiful form was never the same. It was Highfill who convinced Alvin Smith to transfer to Roanoke.

Before graduating, Highfill dropped out of college and entered a school on the west coast. His wife was homesick and wanted to go home. Highfill graduated from that school as an engineer, and then got a job with Boeing, where he worked for the rest of his career.

After Mary Jane and Michael flew back to Staunton, Homer was depressed. There he was, in a far-away place, thinking of his wife and child constantly, and surviving in what he considered an almost meaningless job. The nights were long. Temperatures sometimes dropped to 10 degrees Fahrenheit or below. Snowfall averaged over 40 inches per year. There was no place to go and every day seemed like an eternity.

October 21, 1950
Davis and Elkins College at Salem, Virginia
Team Scores: Roanoke–21
Davis and Elkins–38

In Salem, Coach Smith and his team were preparing for the second competition of the fall, an October 21 meet in Salem with Davis and Elkins College from Randolph County in West Virginia. It would be Roanoke's lone home meet of the year. On the surface, it seemed as if Roanoke would have little trouble winning the meet. Davis and Elkins already had lost two meets.

The Roanoke course was the same as the one set up by Coach Bast in 1948. The length of the course was 3.1 miles and the course record was 19:08.0, a time set by Bruce Davenport, Paul McCarty, Alvin Smith, and Red Crockett on Thursday, October 19, 1948.

When the race began at 3:00 p.m., Bruce Davenport went to the front as expected. He was followed for a time by Johnny Lynch of Davis and Elkins. By the end of the race, however, Lynch had fallen back considerably and managed to hold on to pick up a second place some 25 seconds behind Davenport's 19:45.7. Seconds later, Maroon runners White Rhyne, Bennie Irvin, and Kelly Perdue took the third, fourth, and fifth places, respectively. Vernon Body finished Roanoke's scoring by crossing the line eighth. Phil Davis placed ninth and Johnny Turbyfill was tenth.

By taking four of the top five spots, Roanoke won the meet 21 to 38. Combined with the two previous unbeaten seasons, the Roanoke team seemed to be destined for a successful fall.

The next day, an article in the *Brackety-Ack* congratulated Bruce Davenport not on his running but on the many other things he had accomplished as a student on the campus. Bruce had just been selected to be a member of the prestigious "Who's Who in American Colleges and Universities." The paper noted that Bruce had been President of Blue Key, Captain of the cross country team, President of the Honor Council, and Secretary of the Monogram Club. During the 1949-50 school year, he was Vice President of the student body and a member of the Honor Council.

October 28, 1950
University of Virginia and Hampden-Sydney College at Charlottesville, Virginia
Team Scores: Roanoke–32
Hampden-Sydney–34
University of Virginia–60

About a week later, the team traveled to Charlottesville for a triangular meet with the University of Virginia and Hampden-Sydney. The University seemed to be weak that year, because they had lost two meets, one against Georgetown University and the other against Bridgewater. On the other hand, both of those squads–Georgetown and Bridgewater–had very talented runners. Hampden-Sydney was the same school that Roanoke had beaten by a single point not long ago and could beat the Maroons if some of their men ran good times.

Gene Milener of Hampden-Sydney along with Roanoke's Bruce Davenport and Bennie Irvin ran the 3.9-mile Observatory Hill course together for about half the race. Milener then pulled ahead to win in a time of 20:59. Davenport and Irvin took second by crossing together in 21:36. A Virginia man took fourth, followed by two Tigers. Roanoke then won the meet when Bennie Irvin placed seventh, Kelly Perdue ninth and Vernon Body eleventh. About a minute in back of Body came Phil Davis in fifthteenth place, followed 30 seconds later by Johnny Turbyfill, who crossed the line sixteenth.

The excellent finishes by Irvin, Perdue, and Body gave Roanoke the win. The score was Roanoke, 32, Hampden-Sydney, 34, and the University of Virginia, 60. Unfortunately, Turbyfill had competed in his last cross country race. His doctor ordered him to drop running altogether until the spring track season.

November 4, 1950
Little Six Championships at Bridgewater, Virginia
Team Scores: 1st–Bridgewater College–27
2nd–Roanoke College–60; Hampden-Sydney College–60
4th–Lynchburg College–73

Again, the team resumed their training, pointing toward the Little Six Championships on November 4. They would be running on the Bridgewater course where Coach Smith had placed first in the Little Six meet the previous year. Everyone expected Bruce Davenport to do well. But strong bids for first would also come from Merle Crouse of Bridgewater, Gene Milener of Hampden-Sydney, and Johnny Krebs from Lynchburg. Krebs was a very capable freshman runner for the Hornets.

The four-team meet featured Roanoke, Bridgewater, Lynchburg, and Hampden-Sydney. Randolph-Macon and Emory and Henry did not participate.

Left Photo (L to R): White Rhyne talks with fellow runners Phil Davis and Win McConchie.
Right Photo (L to R): John Turbyfill, Bruce Davenport, Frank Aldred, and Paul McCarty

The race was run under very unfavorable conditions. Inclement weather prevailed most of the day, and when the gun sounded for the start, rain was pouring down. The course was a mess, with mud and water everywhere. Times would be slow.

Bridgewater was the pre-meet favorite, and the race soon showed why. Merle Crouse, now a junior at Bridgewater, took charge early. He had finished the race in 1949 in third place, but his improvement over the past year was impressive. Close behind was Gene Milener of Hampden-Sydney. The Maroons' Bruce Davenport ran his usual steady and dogged race.

Six of the first 18 runners to cross the finish line were from Bridgewater, giving them a team-leading score of 27 points. Crouse's time was 19:51.6. Hampden-Sydney placed five men in the top 20, with Milener finishing in second place some nine seconds in back of Crouse, to tie Roanoke for second place on a score of 60.

For Roanoke, Davenport was third in 20:27, while White Rhyne (8th), Bennie Irvin (12th), Vernon Body (16th), and Kelly Perdue (21st) completed the scoring. Phil Davis was 25th and Wallace Lord placed 26th in the field of 29 runners.

One publication noted that there was a junior varsity race that day and that each team entered runners. Unfortunately, there are no records today showing names and how well each team did.

It was the first race–dual, triangular, or championship–that Roanoke had lost for the past two and one-half seasons. Yet, the team's record was better than most predicted.

November 18, 1950
Mason-Dixon Championships at Washington, D. C.
Team Scores: 1st–Bridgewater College–38
2nd–Loyola University–77
3rd–Roanoke College–91
4th–Hampden-Sydney College–103
5th–Johns Hopkins University–143
6th–Catholic University–172
7th–Lynchburg College–175
8th–Washington College–180
9th–Gallaudet College–246
10th–Towson State College–257

After two weeks off following the Little Six meet, Roanoke went to Gallaudet College in Washington to run in the Mason-Dixon Championships. Maroon runners were White Rhyne, Bennie Irvin, Bruce Davenport, Vernon Body, Kelly Perdue, and Phil Davis. Like John Turbyfill, Wally Lord had been forced to drop out for the remainder of the season because of poor health.

The rugged four-mile Gallaudet course was in perfect shape, while the weather was ideal for running. Most thought that the day's times would be fast. Almost 80 runners were entered, with each of the top 15 finishers receiving a Mason-Dixon medal. The team favorite was Bridgewater, based on their wins during the past season. Besides Roanoke, their stiffest competition might come from Hampden-Sydney, Loyola, Johns Hopkins, and Washington. Roanoke's Bruce Davenport was the defending champion, but there were questions as to whether he could beat Merle Crouse of Bridgewater, Gene Milener of Hampden-Sydney, Fred Grim of Johns Hopkins, or Phil Dryden of Washington. Grim and Dryden were both seniors, and had looked better in 1950 than ever before.

Once the race began, there was no doubt about the team trophy. Bridgewater's Crouse moved out with the front group, including Davenport, Grim, and Milener, and following behind, all in the top 15, were the Eagles' next four runners.

Crouse won the race with a course-record time of 19:46. Although the other times for the race were not recorded, Bruce Davenport in second and Earl Grim of Hopkins, third, also broke the old record. Gene Milener of Hampden-Sydney was fourth.

Bridgewater took home the team trophy with a score of 38 points. Loyola was second, with 77, and Roanoke finished third with 91 points. Besides Davenport's second-place finish, Roanoke's White Rhyne (9th), Bennie Irvin (18th), Kelly Perdue (26th), and Phil Davis (40th) also contributed to the team score.

November 22, 1950
Virginia Military Institute at Lexington, Virginia
Team Scores: Virginia Military Institute–27
Roanoke–30

Only one meet remained. Roanoke would travel to Lexington to meet the powerful Virginia Military Institute on November 22. For only the second time in three years, the Maroons were the underdogs in a dual meet. V. M. I. had just won the Big Six cross country meet, with Bill Massie winning the event and two Keydet sophomores finishing second and third.

In 1949, Roanoke had beaten V. M. I. 15-45, with six men finishing in a tie for first place. This year, however, the Lexington team was much improved. Their dual-meet record was 2-1, with their single loss being to Bridgewater by a very small margin.

Bruce Davenport looked like his former self, taking the lead early and setting a course record of 23:54 in finishing first over V. M. I.'s very hilly 4.2 mile course. Bill Massie was second, 37 seconds behind Davenport, and James McLane of the host school was third. For Roanoke, White Rhyne and Bennie Irvin crossed the line together in a fine 25:18 to capture fourth place. The eighth place was taken by Kelly Perdue. Phil Davis finished Roanoke's scoring in twelfth place, with Vernon Body taking thirteenth.

Roanoke almost pulled out a very unexpected win. But V. M. I., with five of the first nine runners, squeaked out a 27-30 victory. Although the Roanoke team had run well, the defeat was the first the Maroons had suffered in dual-meet competition since they had lost to Virginia Polytechnic Institute in 1947.

The *Brackety-Ack* wondered in one of its late season columns why the cross country team had done so poorly toward the end of the year. In reality, the team had performed well. It is very difficult to lose four of your six top runners and still compete at the same level as before. Mostly, the team needed depth. Several of the newcomers had run well, including freshman Bennie Irvin, but the Maroons really needed just one more star.

Indoor Track

Before he left for his duty with the Navy, Coach Bast had lined up three indoor meets for the Roanoke team:

January 13	Evening Star Games in Washington, DC
February 19	Little Six Championships in Lexington, VA
February 24	Southern Conference Games in Chapel Hill, NC

January 13, 1951
Fourth Annual Evening Star Games at Washington, D. C.
Mason-Dixon Sprint Medley Relay: Roanoke did not place.

The Evening Star Games, staged in the National Guard Armory in Washington, always drew stellar track and field performers from all over the nation. The focus this winter was on the mile run.

In the mile, Don Gehrmann extended his streak of mile wins to 33 in a row, passing Sweden's Ingvar Bengtsson on the last curve to win by less than a foot in 4:16.6. Some 5,000 Armory fans watched this great miler from Wisconsin run :58.8 on his last quarter.

Roanoke's single goal was to compete in the annual Mason-Dixon One-Mile Sprint Medley Relay. Their team consisted of Bruce Davenport, Evan Clay, Bennie Irvin, and Tom Bieselin. Roanoke's Frank Aldred, Walt Tramposch, Dick Dodd, and Alvin Smith had finished third in this race in 1950, but the College had won the race with Red Crockett, Dodd, Tramposch, and Smith in 1949.

The results from the race are sketchy. Irvin led off with a 440, handing off to Clay for his 220 leg. After Clay handed the baton to Bieselin for a second 220, somehow Bieselin and a Bridgewater runner tangled and both fell, knocking both teams out of contention. A notation by Bruce Davenport in his copy of the meet program showed the team winner to be Hampden-Sydney, with a time of 3:50.0. In second was the team from Catholic University, followed in third by Washington College.

February 19, 1951
Little Six Championships at Lexington, Virginia
Team Scores: None for the First Year Only

About five weeks later, with more winter training under their belts, the Roanoke men entered the first annual Little Six Indoor Championships, held in the new field house at Virginia Military Institute. The meet was held in conjunction with the Big

Six Championships.

For this first year only, just six events were held by Little Six Conference schools. No team score was kept at the request of the coaches because of the absence of two conference members.

The Little Six events included the 60-yard dash, the 70-yard high hurdles, the 70-yard low hurdles, the mile run, the mile relay, and the shot put. Although outstanding pole vaulter Ray DeCosta accompanied the team to the meet, there was no official pole vault event for the Little Six teams. He vaulted unofficially in the Big Six event, clearing 12' (a measured height of 11'10½") to tie for first place.

Bridgewater and Hampden-Sydney each took a first place in three events. Bridgewater's Wayne Spangler won the 60-yard dash in :06.4, Melvin Myers was the winner of the 70-yard low hurdles in :08.2, and Merle Crouse took the mile title in 4:31.1. Richard Hassold of Hampden-Sydney won the 70-yard high hurdles with a time of :09.7. Teammate Arthur Garst, Jr., won the shot put with a toss of 37'5" and the Hampden-Sydney mile relay won that event.

The only runners who placed for Roanoke were Bennie Irvin, who was fourth in the mile run, and Paul Barker, who recorded a third place in the shot put. Irvin finished in front of Bruce Davenport, whom the *Brackety-Ack* referred to as being "noticeably out of shape."

February 24, 1951
Southern Conference Games at Chapel Hill, North Carolina
Team Scores: Unknown

The indoor season finally ended for Roanoke with the participation of Bennie Irvin and Ray DeCosta in the Southern Conference Indoor Games in Chapel Hill. Bennie would be entering the freshman three-quarter mile event, while Ray was to participate in the non-conference pole vault competition.

Unfortunately, the *Brackety-Ack* and *Roanoke Times* failed to report the results of Roanoke's two entries. And, although there was a full accounting of the meet in the Raleigh newspaper, no mention of the Roanoke athletes could be found. One could assume that the two Maroons did not make the trip to Chapel Hill at all.

Outdoor Track

Coach Bast's duty in Alaska had not gone well. Depressed and tired, constantly wanting to be at home with Mary Jane and Michael, it was no surprise that his health began to suffer. In fact, he had been in and out of the hospital. "Frankly," he recently said, "I was a nervous wreck."

In Salem, Alvin Smith was preparing for the spring track season. Training for the opening meet with Randolph-Macon on April 3, he was building the team around nine lettermen. In truth, the squad lacked the depth needed to beat most of that year's opponents. Athletes such as Paul McCarty, Frank Aldred, and of course, Smith himself, were now gone. John Turbyfill was unable to participate this year because of poor health, and Paul Barker, who threw the shot, was on scholastic probation and was unavailable.

Co-Captains Richard Fraley and Dick Dodd would handle the 100 and 220. Fraley had earned three letters in track while Dodd held two. Bruce Davenport and White Rhyne were back for the distance events. Smith also had Ray DeCosta, a Little Six and Mason-Dixon winner in the pole vault. Surely, he would beat his personal-best vault of 12'6". And occasionally he could bring in points in the broad jump and even the high jump.

Don Fleming was also a broad jumper, as well as a fine hurdler. R. K. Walsh was returning in the shot and discus events. Since many of the other Little Six schools lost their weight men, Walsh should score quite a few points this year. Other returning members of the team included Doug Frith, high hurdles, and Joe Baldwin, low hurdles.

Smith's newcomers included Tom Bieselin, Bennie Irvin, Wally Lord, and Chuck Mulcahey. Others listed by the *Brackety-Ack* as being interested in competing were Munsey Wheby, Doug Ayers, Bill Bradley, Ben Crumpler, John Willett, and Bob Hillegas.

Left Picture: Ray DeCosta, one of the best small-college pole vaulters in the United States.
Right Picture: R. K. Walsh throwing the shot.

April 3, 1951
Randolph-Macon College at Ashland, Virginia
Team Scores: Roanoke–65
Randolph-Macon–56

The first meet of the spring season was held in Ashland, Virginia, with Randolph-Macon College. The Yellow Jackets supposedly had good field event men, but very little ability to score points in running events.

The meet was held under poor weather conditions. A strong, cold wind accounted for many of the slow times and poor field event performances. Under these conditions, Ray DeCosta amazingly cleared 12'6" to win the pole vault. Had the day been warmer and the takeoff area less slippery, most thought, he may have gone over 13'. The winning height tied his own Roanoke College record, which he had set in 1950 in the Little Six Championships.

White Rhyne and Bennie Irvin showed good form for this time of the season despite the weather. Each ran and won two races. White and Irvin tied for first in the two-mile run (5:12.8) and the two-mile race (13:35.5).

Bruce Davenport also won two races. In the 440-yard dash, he finished first in a slow time of :58.1. Then he tied for first with Wally Lord and White Rhyne in the 880. They had a time of 2:27.0 in a race with little competition.

Roanoke also won the mile relay. The team of Dick Fraley, Irvin, Dick Dodd, and Davenport had a 3:50.4 clocking.

Others scoring for the Maroons included Fraley, who was second in the 100 and 220, Dodd (third in the 220), Doug Ayers, returning after an ankle injury (second in the 440), Don Fleming (second in the high hurdles, Tom Bieslin (third in the high hurdles, Joe Baldwin (second in the low hurdles), Doug Frith (third in the low hurdles), and R. K. Walsh (a tie for first place in the shot put and second in the discus).

Randolph-Macon accumulated most of their points in the field events, where DeCosta and Walsh brought the team its only points. The Yellow Jackets even swept the broad jump and high jump events. But the Roanoke runners made the difference. The meet score was 65-56 in Roanoke's favor.

April 7, 1951
Lynchburg College at Lynchburg, Virginia
Team Scores: Lynchburg–69
Roanoke–53

The upcoming meet on April 7, at Lynchburg, might just bring a different result. Strong in the sprints, hurdles, and field events, Lynchburg would be tough to beat.

The Hornets took the lead in the first event, the shot put, and the Roanoke team could never narrow the gap any closer than five points throughout the remainder of the meet. Ray DeCosta, however, gave another outstanding performance. He had to overcome two obstacles–the wind and his nose. Twice, just as he was in the middle of his run toward the pit, the wind blew the crossbar off the uprights. When the bar was raised to 12'9", DeCosta was the only vaulter still jumping. He hit his runway marks perfectly on the first attempt. He did a beautiful handstand on the pole and jackknifed over the bar with inches to spare. But he tipped the bar off the pegs with his nose on the way down. Then he failed to clear the bar on his second jump, missing badly. On his third and final attempt, he went up and over the bar for a new Roanoke College record.

Roanoke managed to win only three running events. Bruce Davenport had a time of 2:10.0 in the 880, White Rhyne ran the two-mile race in 10:43.0, and the mile relay team of Wally Lord, Tom Bieselin, Doug Ayers, and Bruce Davenport won their event with a time of 3:52.0. And they won only two of the five field events. Besides DeCosta's victory in the pole vault, R. K. Walsh placed first in the discus with an excellent throw of 121'0".

Roanoke's other points came from Dick Dodd (second in the 100 and third in the 220), Tom Bieselin (second in the 220), Doug Ayers (second in the 440), Bennie Irvin (third in both the mile and two-mile runs), Don Fleming (second in the high hurdles), Doug Frith (third in both the high and low hurdles), Walsh (second in the shot put), Dick Burton (tie for first in the high jump), and Chuck Mulcahey (third in the pole vault).

Paced by Bobby Parrish's 18 points, Lynchburg won the meet 69 to 53. They took eight first places and tied with the Maroons for another.

April 20, 1951
Milligan Relays at Johnson City, Tennessee
Team Scores: 1st–Clemson College–87
2nd–East Tennessee State College–54
3rd–Maryville College–22
4th–William Jennings Bryan University–18
5th–Roanoke College–12
6th–Lees-McRae State College–10
7th–David Lipscomb College–6
8th–Milligan College–0

Only five members of the team went to Johnson City, Tennessee, for the annual Milligan Relays. That meet, held on April 21, would feature the best group of athletes in the history of the Relays.

During the meet, four of the five Roanoke men in the meet managed to score points. Ray DeCosta set a new meet record as he vaulted 12 feet to take a first place. The former record had been set in 1949, when Roanoke's Bill Williams tied for first with a jump of 11'8" Bennie Irvin nabbed a second in the mile as the first three milers cracked the 4:49.0 mark set by Bruce Davenport two years ago. White Rhyne took a fourth in the mile run to complete the individual Roanoke College scoring. The sprint medley team–Irvin in the 440, DeCosta and Bieselin in 220s, and Rhyne in the 880–finished in third place.

In the meet, participants broke or tied ten separate records. Big Bob Hudson and his Clemson College teammates shattered five Milligan Relays records and piled up 87 points to capture the coveted Relays Trophy. East Tennessee State College athletes were little opposition for the Tigers, but did finish in second place with 54 points. After Maryville's 22 points, and the 18-point fourth place by William Jennings Bryan University, Roanoke was fifth with 12 points for the meet.

Hudson put on a one-man show. A Tiger nominee for football's 1950 All-American team, the 215 pound athlete placed first in three events–the 100, shot, and discus. In taking first place in the shot put and discus, Hudson racked up meet records. Hudson bettered the old shot put record of 42'6¾" by heaving the shot 46'11½" to top the mark set by University of Tennessee's Horwood in 1949.

Big Bob came back to add 12' to the meet's discus record with a throw of 136'2". Hudson's time in winning the 100-yard dash was :10.1.

April 28, 1951
Hampden-Sydney College at Salem, Virginia
Team Scores: Hampden-Sydney–72
Roanoke–50

Roanoke's next competition was supposed to be a triangular meet at home on April 28 between Roanoke, American University, and Hampden-Sydney. When American failed to make the trip, the Maroons and Hampden-Sydney held a dual meet.

Doug Divers was the big point getter for the Tigers. He collected 18 points on the basis of three firsts and a second. Divers led the field in the high and low hurdles, as well as the broad jump, and was second in the pole vault. His :15.9 in the high hurdles set a new Alumni Field record.

Dick Dodd led the Maroons with firsts in the 100 and 220, while Bennie Irvin won the 880 in 2:06.6 and Ray DeCosta, as usual, took honors in the pole vault. His vault of 12'0" tied the Alumni Field record that he set in 1950. The Roanoke mile relay team of Tom Bieselin, White Rhyne, Doug Ayers, and Bruce Davenport came in first by running a time of 3:43.8. Roanoke did not win another event.

Other Roanoke men did score, however. They included Dick Fraley (third in the 100), Tom Bieselin (second in the 220), Bruce Davenport (second in the 440 and third in the 880), Doug Ayers (third in the 440), White Rhyne (second in the mile and second in the two-mile race), Bennie Irvin (third in the mile run), Doug Frith (second in both hurdles), R. K. Walsh (third in the shot), Don Fleming (third in the broad jump), and Dick Burton (third in the high jump).

Hampden-Sydney won the meet convincingly with a score of 72 points. Roanoke had 50.

This meet was the last dual or triangular meet of the season. The only meets left on the schedule were the Little Six, the Mason-Dixon, and possibly the Virginia AAU.

May 4, 1951
Little Six Championships at Lynchburg, Virginia
Team Scores: 1st–Bridgewater–45
2nd–Hampden-Sydney College–34
3rd–Randolph-Macon College–31½
4th–Lynchburg College–30½
5th–Roanoke College–12

Coach Smith took only a few men to Lynchburg for the Little Six. Most of them were tired, and for the first time since Coach Bast brought the program back to life in the spring of 1946, the season had brought little success. Four of their best distance runners from the past were now gone. Others were discouraged or simply distracted.

Ray DeCosta's pole vaulting, however, was one of the bright spots on the team. In the Little Six meet, he cleared the bar at 12'9" to set a new Roanoke College and meet record. He already had a 12'9" jump one other time in 1951. His attempts at 13'0" failed.

In all, Roanoke could pick up only 12 total points. Besides DeCosta's fine vault, Dick Fraley held on for a fourth in the 100, Dick Dodd took fourth in the 220, White Rhyne ran third in the two-mile race, and Doug Frith finished fourth in the high hurdles. The Maroons' mile relay team, composed of Doug Ayers, Tom Bieselin, Wally Lord, and Bruce Davenport, placed third in that event for the only other points.

Merle Crouse of Bridgewater was becoming one of the all-time best distance runners in the Little Six and Mason-Dixon Conferences for Bridgewater. On this day, he set two meet records, running the mile in 4:28.0 and the two-mile race in 9:58.4.

Bridgewater easily won the meet with a total of 45 points. They were followed by Hampden-Sydney (second with 34), Randolph-Macon (third with 31½), Lynchburg (fourth with 30½), and then Roanoke, who placed fifth and last. It was the lowest point total and the worst finish for a Roanoke team since 1946.

May 11-12, 1951
Mason-Dixon Championships at Washington, D. C.
Team Scores: 1st–Catholic University–44
2nd–Bridgewater College–40½
3rd–Washington College–32
4th–Johns Hopkins University–22
5th–Lynchburg College–18
6th–Randolph-Macon College–11

7th–American University–10
8th–Gallaudet College–10
9th–Roanoke College–8
10th–Hampden-Sydney College–7
11th–Loyola University–5½
12th–Towson College–2

And the Mason-Dixon meet would be no easier. It was held at Catholic University in Washington, D. C., on May 11-12, 1951. Twelve Conference schools entered teams.

Some thought that Bridgewater should be the favorite, although Washington College and Catholic University could upset the Eagles. Roanoke was given almost no chance to finish in the top half of the 12 schools.

For the first time in the years Roanoke entered the Mason-Dixon meet, only one Maroon won an event. Ray DeCosta jumped 12'6" to tie the meet record set by the famous Rev. Bob Richards, the Olympian, who at the time the mark originally was set was competing for Bridgewater College.

Athletes set several additional meet records. Merle Crouse, from Bridgewater, ran personal-best times of 4:23.6 in the mile and 9:43.3 in the two-mile race. Ed Moffatt of Catholic University threw the discus 135'5⅜", breaking the old record of 131'3¼" set by Sal Consolo of Catholic three years earlier. Mel Myers of Bridgewater ran a :25.5 in a low hurdle qualifying heat. Grimm of Johns Hopkins set a new mark in the 880 with a time of 1:56.9.

Roanoke could manage to score only eight points in the meet. DeCosta received five of those eight by winning the pole vault. The other three came from White Rhyne's third place in the two-mile run.

The meet championship came down to the final event, the mile relay, with Bridgewater and Catholic almost tied for the top score. Catholic's excellent team of McCurnin, Sefcik, Gaffney, and J. Field won the race with a time of 3:30.3, while Bridgewater could finish no higher than fourth.

The final team score showed Catholic first with 44 points, narrowly beating Bridgewater, which had 40½. Washington was third, Johns Hopkins fourth, Lynchburg fifth, Randolph-Macon sixth, American and Gallaudet tied for seventh, and Roanoke ninth of the 12 schools. Below Roanoke were Hampden-Sydney, Loyola, and Towson.

May 26, 1951
Virginia AAU Championships at Lynchburg, Virginia
Team Scores: 1st–University of Virginia–50½
2nd–University of Richmond–23½

3rd–Bridgewater College–16
4th–Lexington Athletic Club–14
5th–Norfolk Sports Club–13
6th–Lynchburg College–6
7th–Roanoke College–5
8th–Randolph-Macon College–2
9th–Long Hall Athletic Club–2
10th–Peninsula Sports Club–1
11th–Richmond-Henrico Track Club–No Score

By the time the Virginia AAU Championships rolled around, on May 26, Smith had decided to take only two athletes to the meet. Bennie Irvin would compete in one of the distance events, while Ray DeCosta could have his last crack at the 13' height in the pole vault.

Bennie was unable to place in the meet; however, DeCosta won the pole vault on a jump of 12'6" to give Roanoke its only five points of the day. The afternoon was filled with good performances, however.

Merle Crouse of Bridgewater concentrated on just the two-mile run and crossed the finish line in a terrific time of 9:33.3. Miller of the University of Virginia not only tossed the shot 49'9¼", but he also won the discus with a throw of 146'3¼". Mel Myers, from Bridgewater, won the broad jump and came within ¼" of jumping 22'. There was a 6'3¾" high jump and a :51.5 quarter mile.

Alvin Smith had done a creditable job in coaching the team. Alvin never thought of himself as a coach, but he did know that he could take care of some of the paperwork involved. And he could make arrangements for the team trips. Homer frequently corresponded by mail with Alvin during the year. He offered training advice and sometimes would suggest ways Alvin might use a particular runner by seeing if he could run some race that he normally wouldn't run. In turn, Alvin would send Homer newspaper clippings detailing the meet results.

Smith had little real talent on the team, and some of the men who should have done well weren't performing up to their usual standards. Smith was mostly a caretaker to make sure the cross country and track programs would survive until Coach Bast returned. Bast was always appreciative that Alvin had agreed to take the job.

Chapter Seven

THE 1951-52 SEASONS

During the summer of 1951, Homer was released from his duties with the Navy and was sent back to Salem. As soon as he returned, despite the fact that he already had 12 years of service with the Navy, he resigned his position in the Reserves. He knew that every time there was a problem in the world, the Navy would be calling him back. So despite the fact that he would be missing a good retirement pension by eight years, Mary Jane and Homer came to a mutual decision that he should get out of the Navy altogether.

His experiences over the past year had been very stressful. With much to do and little time to get it done, and being away from home and family, he had been relieved from duty and placed in the Naval Hospital in Norfolk for three months. During his stay in the hospital, they occasionally would give him a weekend pass to visit Mary Jane in Staunton. When he was released from the hospital, he stayed in Staunton for a few weeks.

One of the first things Homer did was to visit the College to see Dr. Sherman Oberly, the new President, and to check on his teaching and coaching status for the coming year. The College had seen a severe drop in student enrollment as the G. I. Bill was running out and students were being drafted in larger numbers. Desperate for money, Oberly and his staff were laying off faculty members and cutting expenses in any way possible. Even telephones were being removed on campus to save money.

Oberly told Bast that there was no job for him at Roanoke. Of course, not giving a veteran his job back was against the law, so Bast had some leverage. In addition, a lot of the faculty came together and suggested to Oberly that he must give Bast some type of job.

The situation worked itself out. Homer was re-hired and given the track and cross country coaching jobs and two classes in World Civilization. Dr. Brown also asked Homer to teach a U. S. History course, along with one in European History. That was three preparations. After that point, however, he and Dr. Oberly got along well with no hard feelings. In fact, Bast later served as Chairman of Oberly's inauguration.

The Roanoke College faculty at the beginning of the 1951-52 school year, after Homer Bast returned from his military service.

I remember . . . "We built our house on Locust Avenue in 1951 after I returned from the service. Mary Jane and I are still living in it as of 2008. When we arrived in Salem, we really had no place to live. They had put someone else in that rental house on Market Street. So for a while, Mary Jane just stayed in Staunton with her family. That way, she had some assistance with Michael. They kept me over at the school, in a room over the Commons. At that time, it was difficult to find any place to live in Salem. Now Mary Jane and I had bought the lot on Locust two or three years before. We let the contract on this house and built the middle section. Because we had beautiful weather, we had the house under roof in no time.

We moved into the house in April of 1952. Mary Jane came down from Staunton. But one of our problems was that we had very little furniture. We did have a refrigerator and a stove, along with a sofa and a bed. We also had a beautiful rug, 18' by 20'. By spring, we moved in. And Michael was still a little tot. It was hot, really hot, that summer. I remember that Al Bowman was on the Board. He and I grew to love one another. Just as we sat down for supper, he would call us. He wanted to talk about things like the stock market. He had very poor eyesight, and depended on Mary Jane to take his dictation for him. He didn't want anyone down at the bank to know about his personal affairs. So Mary Jane took his dictation and wrote his letters, etc. She would go over to his house two or three times a week for this, and they became good friends. He didn't mind telling her anything about his private life, because he knew she wouldn't pass it along. He was dealing in cattle at the time, and would tell her about the value, how much milk they would produce, for example. He was the banker who loaned us the money for the house. It was the best investment we ever made. Later, in about 1964, we built the room on the right, facing the house, and constructed the other room a bit later. Eventually, we moved Mary Jane's mother and father down here into our house. They had the bedroom where Mary Jane is now. They stayed with us until they both died. He died first, in his sleep. He was over 70 at the time. She died because they put in a pacemaker. She picked up a hospital infection. It was the infection that killed her. This was in the very early days of pacemakers. She suffered a great deal before dying. He had a service station in Staunton and made pretty good money from it. But because the town made the street one-way, he was beyond 65 and ready to retire from a business not making that much money anymore."

Homer Bast

Cross Country

Homer returned to find a cross country team that might not have much talent. The *Brackety-Ack* in September offered the names of several newcomers who were interested in distance running, including Ronnie Dillon, Chip Vail, Ed Sharpe, and Walt Barton; however, either these individuals never trained with the team or, if they did run, they did not figure in the scoring for any meet. The best of his runners this fall would be White Rhyne, the final Big Six athlete from Bast's successful early teams, Phil Davis, Alvin Stump, Winn McConchie, Charles Spraker, Les Noel, S. L. Spangler, and Bill Davis. Davis was a veteran of the past season along with Rhyne. The best-looking freshmen were Noel and McConchie. Each year, of course, Bast organized and ran an intramural meet. This fall, Les won the meet in an excellent time of 9:10.0. McConchie finished just four seconds back.

Overall, the team was inexperienced and Bast soon realized that it was a rebuilding year. He was right, as the results of the first meet showed.

Left Photo, 1951 Cross Country Team
First Row (L to R): Phil Davis, Robert Davis, White Rhyne, Les Noel, and Alvin Stump.
Second Row: S. I. Spangler, Jr., Charles Spraker, Edward Sharpe, III, and Win McConchie.
Right Photo (L to R): Alvin Stump, Win McConchie, Phil Davis, and Earl Johnston.

I remember . . . "When I came back from my year off, I quickly found that we didn't have a very strong team. We had White Rhyne, who was not a star, but he ran his hardest for us. He would almost foam at the mouth trying to win. He was our leader. We had Alvin Stump, who was from the Baptist Children's Home. He hated that environment. The head of the Baptist Home was not interested in Alvin going to Roanoke College. He wanted him to go to the University of Richmond. But Alvin didn't want to go to Richmond. He wanted to attend Roanoke College and live on our campus–away from the dormitory situation at the Home. So at Roanoke, he was happy when he made the team. And I thought that Alvin would be a good runner. He ended up living on campus for part of the time he was here. But the head of the Home kept a tight rein on Alvin. After all, they were supporting him. Alvin still, even today, hates that Home. He is in South Carolina now, in a retirement home. But he lives in Lynchburg. He rotates between the two places. He was a representative for a drug company. Apparently during his career he made quite a bit of money. His relations with the College were up and down over the years, although today he is very supportive."

Homer Bast

October 12, 1951
Lynchburg College at Salem, Virginia
Team Scores: Lynchburg–19
Roanoke–43

On October 12, Lynchburg College's team came to Salem. The visitors' John Krebs had little difficulty winning the race, although White Rhyne did finish about 13 seconds behind the leader. Lynchburg runners took the third through sixth places before Phil Davis crossed the finish line in eighth place and Alvin Stump took the ninth spot. Winn McConchie was eleventh and Charles Spraker thirteenth. Roanoke's score was a bit higher than it should have been, because during the race, freshman Les Noel was forced to drop out.

The score was Lynchburg, 19, and Roanoke, 43. It looked like it could be a tough season.

October 16, 1951
Hampden-Sydney College at Hampden-Sydney, Virginia
Team Scores: Hampden-Sydney–21
Roanoke–41

On October 16, Bast, Captain Rhyne, and the rest of the team drove to Hampden-Sydney, Virginia, for a meet with the Tigers. On the 4.0-mile course, Hampden-Sydney took the first, third, sixth, seventh, and twelfth places to win the meet with 21 points. Roanoke finished with 41.

Again, White Rhyne was the best runner for Roanoke. He finished in second place, but was nearly two minutes in back of Hampden-Sydney's top runner, Gene Milener. Milener, whose winning time was 22:47.6, had been his team's best athlete for the past several seasons. Other Maroons who scored included Phil Davis (fifth), Winn McConchie (tenth), Alvin Stump (eleventh), and S. L. Spangler (thirteenth).

November 3, 1951
Little Six Championships at Bridgewater, Virginia
Team Scores: Bridgewater College–35
Hampden-Sydney College–50
Lynchburg College–65
Roanoke College–102
Randolph-Macon College–Incomplete Scoring

After two consecutive losses, Coach Bast's team had to look forward to the always-competitive Little Six Championships on the third of November at Bridgewater College. Running against Roanoke would be Lynchburg, Hampden-Sydney, Randolph-Macon, and Bridgewater. Emory and Henry, the other member of the Little Six Conference, did not field a cross country team.

Leading runners for the meet were Merle Crouse, the fabulous distance star from Bridgewater, Gene Milener of Hampden-Sydney, John Krebs of Lynchburg, and Roanoke's White Rhyne. For Roanoke, Bast planned to enter Rhyne, Phil Davis, Winn McConchie, Les Noel, Alvin Stump, Bob Davis, and S. L. Spangler. Unfortunately, Bast was notified that Charlie Spraker might be out of running for the remainder of the season with a bad foot.

Crouse ran his usual good race, finishing about 20 seconds in front of Milener with a time of 19:48.6. His teammates then wrapped up the team championship by picking up the third, ninth, tenth, and twelfth positions. Hampden-Sydney was second (2nd, 6th, 7th, 17th, and 18th), Lynchburg third (5th, 8th, 11th, 20th, and 21st), with Roanoke finishing fourth (14th, 16th, 19th, 23rd, and 30th). For Roanoke, the scorers included Rhyne (14th in 21:47), Winn McConchie (16th in 21:53.5), Phil Davis (19th in 22:13), Les Noel (23rd in 22:38), and finally S. L. Spangler (30th in 24:25).

November 9, 1951
Davis and Elkins College at Elkins, West Virginia
Team Scores: Roanoke–24
Davis and Elkins–31

A few days later, the Roanoke team finally had success. They drove to the Davis and Elkins campus in West Virginia on November 9 to meet a team that had not had much distance running success in recent years.

Roanoke captured five of the first eight places to win the 4.3-mile race, 24 to 31. Davis and Elkins runner Gene Lynch, however, crossed the finish line first in bitterly-cold weather. White Rhyne of Roanoke was second, with Les Noel just a few seconds behind. After Bill Snodgrass took fourth for the host team, Winn McConchie and Phil Davis captured fifth and sixth respectively for Roanoke. Frank Barber of Davis and Elkins was seventh, but Alvin Stump grabbed the eighth spot for the Maroons. Bill Davis was thirteenth.

November 13, 1951
Washington and Lee University at Salem, Virginia
Team Scores: Roanoke–20
Washington and Lee–35

Roanoke now was 1-2 in dual meets, but would pick up another win when they met Washington and Lee in Salem on November 13. White Rhyne (20:22) and Les Noel (20:46) were the first to cross the line. Then, after Bill Diggs of Washington and Lee came in third with a time of 21:11, Winn McConchie finished fourth (21:14), Phil Davis sixth (21:16), and Alvin Stump seventh (21:58) to complete Roanoke's scoring. At the end of the pack of runners were S. L. Spangler (twelfth), Charles Spraker (returning after the foot injury, getting thirteenth place), and Bill Davis (fourteenth). Roanoke won the meet, 20-35, to even their dual-meet record at 2-2.

It obviously was a down year for Roanoke's cross country team. As a result, there had been few comments, positive or negative, about the team in the *Brackety-Ack*; however, writer Ray DeCosta did note some displeasure at how the student body was supporting the distance runners.

> While the recent cross country meet is fresh on our minds, it might be interesting to point out an appalling statistical fact concerning the student attendance at the race. Of the 360 enrollees at Roanoke College, eighteen appeared to witness the meet, leaving 95 percent of the student body without enough enthusiasm, or interest in their schoolmates, to drag themselves out to cheer for the team.

November 17, 1951
Mason-Dixon Championships at Washington, D. C.
Team Scores: 1st–Bridgewater College–46
2nd–Hampden-Sydney College–78
3rd–Johns Hopkins University–100
4th–Lynchburg College–105
5th–Towson State College–125
6th–Roanoke College–135
7th–Loyola College–163
8th–Catholic University–167
9th–Washington College–263

There was only one remaining meet–the Mason-Dixon Championships at Gallaudet College on November 17. Homer had no illusions about how Roanoke would fare. His teams had won this meet twice before, but this year he knew he couldn't come close to repeating those victories. In fact, he would be happy to stay in the top half of all the teams in the race.

Eleven schools entered the meet, although two of them–Gallaudet and Randolph-Macon–did not have the required minimum of five runners. Their remaining runners could compete in the meet, but essentially were unofficial entrants who could not influence the scoring for the other teams.

Mercifully, the race was completed in less than 20 minutes. Don Manger of Johns Hopkins surprised the crowd by beating Merle Crouse of Bridgewater. Manger's first-place time was 19:47. But Bridgewater then took the fifth, eighth, sixteenth, and seventeenth places to win the meet with 46 points. They also had won the meet in 1950. After Bridgewater, in order, came Hampden-Sydney, Johns Hopkins, Lynchburg, Towson State, Roanoke, Loyola, Catholic, and Washington.

Roanoke's position was sixth of nine teams. The individuals and positions in the race were Rhyne (13th), Noel (19th), Phil Davis (30th), McConchie (34th), Stump (39th), Spangler (61st), Bill Davis (66th), and Spraker (67th).

Roanoke's team this year perhaps was the weakest that Bast would ever coach. Lots of the veterans had finished their eligibility, Bennie Irvin from the previous year had not run at all, and in all fairness, the squad had its share of real and imaginary injuries. As a reporter for the *Brackety-Ack* noted in a column after talking with the coach:

> It seems of all the teams Bast has ever coached, there has never been one with quite so many aches and pains. He said that every day there was another man with either a bad cold or else a case of shin splints. Then too, he said, the boys seem to have weak arches and so he has had a few cases where the team could hardly afford to meet anyone because there weren't enough men who could stand on their feet. One of the primary reasons he said for the team's poor showing has been the result of poor student interest, but he closed with "As long as I still have Stump and McConchie around to keep me wondering what their next complaint will be, I guess I'll stay here until the season is over."

It was about this time that Coach Bast decided that he had to recruit some decent athletes in order to survive. Everyone else in the Little Six and Mason-Dixon Conference seemed to be looking for better talent. Bast, being Admissions Director, did have some contacts locally with teachers, administrators, and students, but how could he get to know the coaches and athletes in places like New Jersey and New York?

So he made up his mind that he was going to write five letters a day, five days a week. Basically, it was the same letter each time. He took the *New York Times* from the Roanoke College library and looked carefully at the schools that seemed to have the best track and cross country teams. Then he wrote the coach of track at each of those schools. He stated clearly in these letters that he didn't want any big-time athletes. As he said, "I just want some of the little boys–perhaps boys who have been out a year or so, for example, and have a little experience."

Those contacts, at least 25 a week, meant a lot of work for Homer. Each one was hand written, and there were no secretaries around to type or mail the letters for him. Gradually, over the next few years, all of this work paid off. Showing up on campus in a short time would be individuals like Howard Meincke, one of the school's two best all-time distance runners, and Dick Goodlake, an outstanding middle-distance and distance runner for the College. None of those athletes were stars in high school. But their coaches saw the potential in them and recommended them to Bast. Often, Bast would then write these individuals, telling them about the advantages of a small school and selling them on the idea that Roanoke should be the place they went to college. If they wrote him back, he'd personally send another letter. And on and on it went, with much success.

The letter-writing campaign went on throughout the rest of Homer's coaching career. He does remember, however, that writing letters began as an impersonal process. He didn't know anything about the boy to whom he was writing except for the fact that he was in track or cross country. Once, he got the name of a potential track athlete from one of the coaches in a New Jersey high school. He was about a :16.0 hurdler. Homer wrote to him, and the athlete wrote back, eventually expressing a real interest in coming to Roanoke. And Homer, of course, wrote back to say that Roanoke was very interested in having him run for the track team. Then, the boy wrote Homer, saying he was black. Homer had to write back to tell him that at that particular time, Roanoke did not enroll black students. It was a hard thing for Homer to do, because he didn't believe in segregation. Ironically, the boy went on to attend a North Carolina black school, and later made the U. S. Olympic team in the hurdles.

Speaking of segregation policies, we should note that Coach Harry Jopson of Bridgewater was the first conference coach in the southern division of the Mason-Dixon to have a black student on his team–long before Roanoke accepted its first African American, Frankie Allen, in the late 1960s. He turned out to be an excellent basketball player for the Maroons. Harry's track man went on to be a good sprinter and broad jumper and was a likeable guy who had a lot of white friends. He graduated and has been very successful in his career.

In the Roanoke area, public school districts seldom let black and white students compete with each other. For example, the old and fully-black Addison High School could not participate in the local City-County meet. In the Mason-Dixon Conference, Catholic University did have a black athlete but for a while, the conference was against allowing students like him compete. Eventually, because of the northern schools like Towson and Gallaudet (who had a number of black students), the policy against integration was dropped.

Homer managed to find some students because of his close contact with the Roanoke student body. Each year, he taught at least one section of the required freshman course, World Civilizations. Many of the freshmen at the College came through these classes. He got to know his students well and sometimes found traits that would make his cross country and track teams better. There was a time also when he would visit the dormitories at night, putting his young son, Michael, to bed and then going over to talk casually with students in their rooms. Soon, he was known even by students not on his teams as a straight-talking, personable, and knowledgeable member of the faculty. Sometimes, he became a father figure.

I remember . . . "White Rhyne and I became very close, in cross country in particular. He was at Roanoke during the year I was called back to active duty. And he sort of kept things going a little bit. He was on the 1948 and the 1949 teams. So he had some experience. And he became friends with Les Noel. And he and Les were good together. Unlike White, Les had come up the hard way, in the school of hard knocks. He had almost no money while he was at Roanoke. Whitey took to Les and Les took to Whitey. I can remember them when we went on trips, to the Citadel for example. They sat on the back seat of one of the station wagons and Les, White, and I would have a three-way conversation. It was very enlightening. Les Noel knew nothing about anything in his freshman year. After all, he was from the hills of Buena Vista. I don't know where he got the money to come to school. I think the church may have helped him out. Any time I could possibly give him anything, I would. I gave him an overcoat one time. He was so grateful for that coat. I saw him walking around the campus with just a little thin coat on. I said, 'Les, don't you have an overcoat?' The answer was no, so I got out an old overcoat that I had worn at Staunton Military Academy, and gave it to him. It was nice and warm, with a big collar. He wore it the entire time he was at Roanoke. Now, to finish what were discussing about Whitey, we were very good friends while we were in school together. He wasn't a star by any means, but you could count on old Whitey to get that fifth place, which was so important to the team. In cross country, as you know, you needed that man. You were always looking for that fifth man, wherever he was. I tried to keep it so that there was only one minute difference between the first man and the fifth man. Sometimes, that was difficult to do."

Homer Bast

I remember . . . I definitely remember the first time I saw Les Noel run. With just one look, you could see the ability in that boy. You knew right away that he was going to succeed. While his legs were strong, however, he wasn't used to competitive running. He had never run on a track or cross country team. He was a slight boy, about 135 pounds or so, and was well-proportioned and had good legs. As his coach, there wasn't much I could do for him–except to get him to relax. I got him to smile while he ran and it seemed to work. His opposition started calling him 'Smiling Noel.' He worked hard. He came from a small rural high school some five miles from the main road, and probably had never written a paper before arriving at Roanoke College. When he got to Roanoke, I thought to myself that I should place him in my freshman history class so I could watch his progress. I would ask him if he were prepared for the next day's test. And sometimes I would go by at night to his dorm to see if he had any questions. His relationships with his classmates and teammates were very good. I think he was a member of the Kappa Alpha fraternity. Les was one of those individuals who just showed up at the College. I never knew he was coming and would never have guessed that he would do so well before he graduated. He turned out to be golden–one of the top distance runners in the history of the school."

Homer Bast

Indoor Track

Alvin Stump, one of Homer's cross country men in the fall, also was a columnist for the *Brackety-Ack*. With encouragement and advice from his coach, Alvin wrote an article in early February, encouraging students to join the indoor and outdoor track teams. In the article, entitled "All Men Interested in Track Wanted," he said:

> Mr. Bast is issuing a call for all men who are in any way interested in track. In order to participate, a man must start now getting into shape. The first meet of the season is only three weeks away. This is an indoor meet for members of the Little Six schools of Virginia and will be held February 18 at V. M. I.
>
> There may be many who have never participated in this sport before, but this is no reason why you can't start now. Some of the best have waited until they entered college to start, but found they surprised themselves once they had done so. Bruce Davenport, class of 1951, is one of the best examples. While at Roanoke College, he was a member of the famed Big Four and excelled in all the distance runs.
>
> There are many advantages from participating in this sport. Every person who invests in an enterprise expects to get more from it than he puts into it. This is certainly true of track. Here's a logical question: What can I gain from this sport which will be advantageous to me?
>
> First, there's the regularity of a schedule. In college, you must plan some sort of schedule to live and study by. If we run, we must practice

every day. This necessitates the planning of regular sleeping and eating hours. To get in good physical shape, we must plan to practice, study, eat, sleep, and to set aside time for recreation.

Second, there is self dependence. This is a good value which track has to offer. You have only yourself to depend upon whether you are running or throwing the discus. Track offers more opportunities for stardom since you are more on your own, but to be a star, you must work and work hard.

Third, we have social acquaintances. It's another place where track offers a great advantage. Practice sessions are not too long but they do last long enough so that in between your running you are able to really meet your teammates. When you go on a trip, you are able to know them even better. Since track meets do not require your presence in every event, you are able to travel around and meet the men who represent the opposition.

Fourth, you will get in good physical condition. Most agree that we never do feel better than when we are in the best of condition. Participation in track will develop this for us.

Another valuable lesson: It's not whether you won or lost, but how you played the game.

Our prospects for the coming year look very bright indeed, but we do need more men. Mr. Bast will meet anyone interested in the gym every afternoon at 4:00. There are many events in track, so don't say you won't be of value to the team. Come on out and try, maybe like Bruce did, and no one will be more surprised than yourself at what you can do.

February 18, 1952
Little Six Championships at Lexington, Virginia
Team Scores: 1st–Bridgewater College–49½
2nd–Hampden-Sydney College–38½
3rd–Randolph-Macon College–17
4th–Roanoke College–11
5th–Lynchburg College–5

On February 18, 1952, the Little Six Conference Championships were held in the field house at Virginia Military Institute. An abbreviated, six-event meet for Little Six schools was held in 1951; however, coaches had decided not to award any team points for that year only. This year, like the last, the Little Six and Big Six indoor championships would be held at the same time and in the same facility.

The field house at V. M. I., site of the meet, was one of the finest indoor facilities in the region in those days. Not only was the building (nicknamed "the Pit") home to the school's basketball team, with a basketball floor located off-center inside the track, but it also featured a 220-yard running track plus areas for the shot put, high jump, and pole vault.

Besides White Rhyne, Roanoke entered several capable athletes. Two of them were Ray DeCosta and freshman George Gearhart. DeCosta was the region's premiere pole vaulter, having cleared 12'9" twice in the previous year. He was a consistently good jumper, and most thought he would surely clear 13' by spring. Perhaps he could go even higher. Gearhart, from Salem, was small in stature but very fast. During the remainder of his college career, he would set numerous indoor and outdoor sprint records. He also could score points in the high jump and long jump events.

Based on five points for first, three points for second, two for third, and one for fourth place, Roanoke scored only 11 points in the meet. Those points came from DeCosta's win in the pole vault (12'½"), from the mile relay team's fourth place finish, Gearhart's third in both the 60-yard dash and the high jump, and R. K. Walsh's fourth in the shot put.

Bridgewater won the meet trophy with 49½ points, followed by Hampden-Sydney (38½), Randolph-Macon (17), Roanoke (11), and Lynchburg (5). Almost none of the times, heights, and distances were outstanding in themselves, although Jack Wilson of Randolph-Macon did clear 6'0" in the high jump.

March 1, 1952
Southern Conference Games at Chapel Hill, North Carolina
Team Scores (Non-Conference Division):
1st–University of Alabama–36
2nd–Georgia Tech University–16½
3rd–Marshall University–9
4th–University of Virginia–9
5th–Bridgewater College–8
6th–University of Georgia–7
7th–University of Kentucky–6
8th–Roanoke College and University of Florida–5
10th–Hampden-Sydney College and Florida State University–3
11th–Catholic University–2½

On March 1, 1952, the team made its annual pilgrimage to the Southern Conference Games held at Chapel Hill. According to reports, only three members of the team entered the meet–Ray DeCosta, in the non-conference pole vault; Doug Frith, in the 70-yard non-conference high hurdles; and Les Noel, in the freshman three-quarter mile run.

DeCosta, performing well as usual, won his event with a personal-best 13'3", which was a new indoor Roanoke College record. His former College record, 12'0", was set in 1950.

Frith failed to score in the high hurdles and apparently, Noel didn't either in his race. The *Brackety-Ack* reported that Noel finished fourth in that race; however, the official results from the Raleigh newspaper shows another individual in that position.

Overall, Maryland won its first Southern Conference indoor track championship, outscoring Duke in a closely contested meet, 37¼ to 31¾. The University of North Carolina, winner for the previous seven years, finished third with 19¾ points.

Maryland grabbed four firsts and tied for another. After the final tally was in, the jubilant Terps hauled Coach Jim Kehoe onto their shoulders and carried him around the Woolen Gymnasium track.

Alabama won the non-conference division honors with 36 points to runner-up Georgia Tech's 16½. Roanoke finished in eighth, tied with the University of Florida, with eight points.

January 12, 1952
Evening Star Games at Washington, D. C.
Team Scores: None

Some of the best athletes in the world were on display in the Evening Star Games in Washington. A record-capacity crowd of 5,500 watched, for example, as Don Laz from the University of Illinois won the pole vault. Beating other great vaulters such as Don Gehrmann, Dick Attlesey, and the Rev. Bob Richards, he cleared 15'3". Laz, Richards, and Don Cooper were the only men besides the famous Cornelius Warmerdam ever to top 15' in this event. The Laz win ended Richards' unbeaten streak at 51 meets. For this meet, Richards could manage only a second-place finish with 14'8".

There were many other outstanding performances in the meet. For example, Don Gehrmann won the mile in 4:14, while Horace Ashenfelter set a meet record of 9:05 in the Acacia Invitation Two-Mile Race.

We are not certain that Roanoke entered a team in the Mason-Dixon One-Mile Sprint Medley Relay. These were the only results given in the *Washington Star* newspaper:

1st–Bridgewater College (Glick, Spangler, Garber, and Crouse)–
3:45.4; 2nd–Catholic University (Lee, Field, Ariente, Sefcik);
3rd–Hampden-Sydney (Hassold, Briggs, Milener, and Dunn)

In addition, we do know that the Evening Star Games officials invited a small number of athletes from across the nation to participate in the pole vault event, including Ray DeCosta. DeCosta soared over the bar at a height of 13'0" to place fourth. Each of the top three finishers had jumped 15' or better in their careers.

Outdoor Track

Homer's 1952 track team was an interesting collection of athletes, all of whom, he said, were wonderful to coach. Some 17 of the students who showed up for the first practices would carry the team through the season.

The "old men" of the squad were certainly White Rhyne and Ray DeCosta. Both were seniors.

White was a native of Philadelphia. He arrived at Roanoke the year after the Big Four runners gained their fame, and he and Frank Aldred soon became part of the Big Six. In each of the Big Four and Big Six seasons, the cross country team had gone undefeated and had won Little Six and Mason-Dixon titles. White may not have been the top point-getter among the Big Six, but he was a very good distance runner and had made significant contributions to his team during the past three years.

DeCosta, now Captain of the 1952 outdoor team, attended high school in Yonkers, New York. He did have some pole vaulting experience before coming to Roanoke, but it was Roanoke where he blossomed into one of the best vaulters in the south. During the early weeks of his freshman year, he and teammate Bill Williams jumped about the same heights. Then, Ray's strength and technique took hold and his heights began to climb. He had just won the Southern Conference games pole vault title with a jump of 13'3", and had cleared 12'9" outdoors in 1951. He was the one person on the team who could be counted on to win an event, and perennially was the Little Six and Mason-Dixon champion.

Bast always thought that DeCosta did so well because of his hard work. "Ray is a perfectionist," Bast once said. "He believes in hard work and refuses to quit until he has reached the goals he has set for himself. Grim determination and hard work are the secrets for his success."

Teammate Earl Johnston remembered DeCosta as the best athlete on the team.

> He worked with weights a lot. I'm not sure that Mr. Bast preferred that he use weights, but he was built like a bodybuilder. He was definitely ahead of his time. He was focused on his event. I remember him as a good technician. Besides strength, he had good form and knew what he was doing. He probably had more technique and strength than he had speed. I

> was high jumping in those days, and Ray and I were both landing in sawdust. That type of landing surface really hindered us because you couldn't get enough reps in training. You simply couldn't take the pounding that would be caused by lots of jumps. It was hard to develop a good technique. In addition, the approaches were also not very good when Ray and I were jumping. Sometimes, it was like we were jumping from loose gravel. Each school's jumping surface had its own personality. Sometimes the long jump and pole vaulting run-ups were just dirt paths.

School publications mentioned a number of people who might join the spring team. They included Fred Pearl, Benny Caudill, Charles Vail, Dick Burton, S. L. Spangler, Charles Spraker, and Mac Minnick. But 18 athletes would end up scoring for the Maroons in 1952. These men were Boyd Carr, George Gearhart, DeCosta, Alvin Stump, Rhyne, Les Noel, Doug Frith, Don Fleming, R. K. Walsh, Paul Barker, Earl Johnston, Karl Kummer, Winn McConchie, Mike Michaels, and Phil Davis.

Of the latter group, there were several newcomers to the team who would end up being very good athletes. Perhaps the most significant were Boyd Carr, George Gearhart, Les Noel, and Earl Johnston.

Boyd Carr grew up in Roanoke and had attended Fork Union Military Academy. No one in his family had ever gone to college. His father had lofty career goals for Boyd, wanting him to be a doctor, lawyer, or engineer. Although he could see the economic advantages of going to college, he didn't want his son to attend just any school. Boyd finally decided to come to Roanoke, thinking perhaps that he might transfer to V. P. I. in a couple of year. The soccer team needed a goalie that year, and soon Boyd was their man. No one knew at the time that he could run track, so all through the fall and winter, no one approached him about running in the spring. He didn't even know about the team's indoor season. But there he was, in the spring, practicing with Homer and the other members of the team. He would become not only a good high and low hurdler, but an excellent dash man and jumper.

George Gearhart was from Salem, having attended Andrew Lewis High School. The school did not have a track team until George's junior year. As he admitted, he had little technique and his times weren't exceptional in the dashes. He did some high jumping for the team, ending up clearing 5'8". He never thought about going to college, but one day Homer saw him practicing on the College track and began talking to George and another runner about attending Roanoke the following year. Finally, after clearing up some financial worries, he did enroll. According to Gearhart, he never worked so hard in his

Freshman Boyd Carr became one of the team's most versatile athletes, running the hurdles and competing in several field events.

life. He was trying to work at a part-time job, go to classes, and participate in track. But Homer was able to teach him how to come out of the starting blocks–a definite weakness–and reduce the tension in his upper body when he ran. Gearhart would go on to be one of the school's best sprinters and a pretty good high jumper.

Les Noel grew up, almost on his own, near the small, rural town of Beuna Vista, Virginia. Determined to do well in life, Homer Bast notes, Noel often ran five miles or so from where he was staying to catch a school bus. He came to Roanoke with little money but with a lot of running talent–despite the fact that he had never competed in track or crosss country.

Left Photo: Star sprinter George Gearhart as a freshman.
Right Photo: Coach Bast and the best pole vaulter in the Mason-Dixon Conference, Ray DeCosta.

Earl Johnston was a good friend and high school classmate of George Gearhart. He never competed in high school track until his senior year, and he admitted that he wasn't very good at either high jumping or the hurdles. His first choice of colleges had been V. M. I., but finally a good friend of the family talked him into going to Roanoke. It was a decision he never regretted. He would be one of Homer's more productive athletes, an individual who could be counted on to score points in either the hurdles or the high jump.

I remember . . . "George Gearhart was at Roanoke College for his first year. He was a fine boy. He worked for Kroger's to make enough money to pay for college. I knew he would be a bit weak academically. In high school, he really didn't take an academic program. He took subjects like bookkeeping. That didn't mean much to the College. As long as they had adequate scores, we'd take them. We were in need of students. We were downsizing rapidly. George was interested in running in college. I really didn't have any speedsters. I had watched his progress in the local paper. And I knew him from his work at Kroger's. At one point, he wasn't even going to college. Kroger had offered him a full-time job. So during that summer, I went down to the Kroger store every day. I tried to explain to him the advantages of going to college. I told him we needed him on our track team. He came to school at Roanoke College, spent a year, and then was drafted into the service. He said he was going to run for those two years in the service. He was much better when he came back to RC."

Homer Bast

April 5, 1952
Randolph-Macon College at Salem, Virginia
Team Scores: Roanoke–85
Randolph-Macon–36

The season began with a meet on April 5 when Randolph-Macon came to Salem. It was a good day for the Maroons, with athletes setting three Roanoke College and Alumni Field records. Both teams were hindered by the high winds.

Boyd Carr won the 100-yard dash in :10.6, followed closely by George Gearhart. Boyd went on to break the College record by winning the 220-yard low hurdles in :26.6. Later in life, Boyd remembered the race. The night before the race, he and weight man Paul Barker had double-dated. Unfortunately, he didn't get home until 2:30 a.m. Tired and sleepy, he hitch-hiked to the campus the next morning and friend Don Fleming put him to bed in the Kappa Alpha fraternity house. The house was quiet because residents were in class. When he woke up, he saw that Rud Rosebro was visiting the fraternity house. Rosebro was a former student and track man who still held the school record at :27.0, which he had set in 1948. He and Don Fleming were talking, and Rud asked "Do you think anyone will ever break my record?" Don pointed to Boyd and said simply, "Meet Boyd Carr." And a few hours later, the prophecy came true. That one race, Carr said, "Made me somebody on campus."

White Rhyne and Les Noel crossed the line together to win both the mile and two mile events. Doug Frith won the high hurdles in :16.8, with Don Fleming right on his heels and Carr finishing third.

R. K. Walsh easily won the shot and finished second in the discus. Paul Barker won the discus, and Walsh was second. Earl Johnson and Mike Michaels tied for first in the high jump.

Ray DeCosta finally cleared 13 feet outdoors in the pole vault, jumping 13'0" to break the Alumni Field and College records. He held both marks.

Others who scored for the Maroons included DeCosta (third in the 220), Win McConchie (third in the 440), Alvin Stump (third in the 880), the Roanoke mile relay team (first), Carr (third in the high hurdles), Fleming (third in the broad jump), and Karl Kummer (second in the pole vault).

Coach Bast's team took 12 of the 14 events to win the meet 85 to 36. It looked like the start to a successful season.

I remember . . . "This story is about what we had to tell Doug Frith. Don Fleming and I decided that we would have a tie in the high hurdles. So I slowed up a bit, and Doug Frith came up parallel to me. At the end, I eased off a bit and Frith won. I think he was very pleased with himself. Unfortunately, Don and I had to tell him what we had done."

Boyd Carr

April 9, 1952
Clemson University at Clemson, South Carolina
Team Scores: Clemson–98⅔
Roanoke–28⅓

Just a few days later, while the rest of the student body was home enjoying the spring vacation, the track team journeyed to South Carolina to meet two Southern Conference opponents, Clemson and the Citadel. Bast had no illusions of winning the meets, but they would provide excellent competition and allow the team to relax and enjoy the sunshine. These types of spring-break trips, which he scheduled for the remainder of his coaching career at Roanoke, also served as inducements to get students on campus to join the team.

Actually, Bast may have had another reason for making the trip. The coach of Clemson was a Roanoke College alumnus. Bast couldn't afford to purchase very much equipment, and the Clemson coach gave Bast lots of items he could use–from a shot and discus to batons and even running shoes. He was glad to see someone from Roanoke, and he made sure that the boys had a good time. In addition, Clemson provided the team's food during the stopover, and the athletes thoroughly enjoyed the food and accompanying music during meals.

Roanoke, competing against a much more experienced and talented Clemson team, won only 2 of the 14 events. They were hurt by the fact that Boyd Carr, who couldn't get free from his job in Roanoke City, was unable to make the trip to compete at Clemson. He did fly down on Piedmont Airlines to meet the Citadel.

Dependable White Rhyne won the two-mile run with ease, recording a time of 10:33.3, and placed second in the mile run. And Ray DeCosta won the pole vault on a jump of 12'6". Otherwise, the Roanoke points were all from seconds and thirds. DeCosta, for example, picked up a third place in the broad jump, while George Gearhart tied with two Clemson jumpers to take second in the high jump and finished second in each of the short sprint races. The only others scoring were Winn McConchie, third in the 880; and Doug Frith, second in the high hurdles and third in the lows.

The win was rather lopsided in favor of Clemson, 98⅔ to 28⅓, but the results were about what Bast expected. Perhaps with Boyd Carr joining the team for the Citadel Meet, the team might pick up a few more points.

I remember . . . "I felt that the boys needed as much competition as they could get. And I thought that extended trips like that would meld the team. At that time, the coach at Clemson was a Roanoke College graduate. I wrote him and he gave us lodging, food, and $125 in expenses. Then he saw that some of our boys needed shoes. He told me to send some of the boys who needed equipment down to the equipment room and the fellow would give them what they needed. So they gave us a number of pairs of shoes. Then we had a meet with them and the boys did the best they could, which really wasn't very good. Clemson had a pretty good team that year. The coach was doing me and RC a favor. At the time, he was a pretty loyal RC alumnus. He also gave us some old equipment like a shot and discus. We went back to Clemson the next year; however, I couldn't travel with the team that much because Mary Jane was pregnant with Stephen."

Homer Bast

April 12, 1952
The Citadel at Charleston, South Carolina

Team Scores: The Citadel–67½
Roanoke–53½

He was right. The Citadel did beat Roanoke, but not until the latter stages of the meet did they pull away to win by a score of 67½ to 53½.

This time, Roanoke won five events. The best effort was given by Boyd Carr, who ran the 220-yard low hurdles in a school record time of :26.3, breaking the record he had set just a few days before on the Salem track. Les Noel and White Rhyne tied for first in the mile and two-mile races, and Ray DeCosta won first place in the pole vault on a jump of 12'0". And Doug Frith ran a time of :16.8 to take first in the high hurdles. He also was third in the lows.

Sprinter George Gearhart placed second in each of the 100- and 220-yard dashes, with Carr in third for both races. Alvin Stump took a third place in the 880-yard run, just in back of Winn McConchie, who finished second. Don Fleming was second in the highs and also second in the broad jump, R. K. Walsh took a second in the shot put, and finally, Gearhart finished tied for third in the high jump.

I remember . . . "The College actually flew me down for the Citadel meet. I couldn't make the Clemson meet because I had to work. The one-way ticket probably cost the school about $20 in those days. I competed against the Citadel and then drove back with the team."

Boyd Carr

April 19, 1952
Lynchburg College at Salem, Virginia
Team Scores: Roanoke–82
Lynchburg–40

Seven days later, the Maroons hosted the team from Lynchburg College. George Gearhart was a double winner for Roanoke, running a :10.2 in the 100 and a :23.5 in the 220. He also won the high jump at 5'6" to finish with 15 points for the day. Boyd Carr also won two events. In a "planned three-way finish" Don Fleming, Doug Frith, and Boyd tied for first in the high hurdles. Then Carr won the 220-yard low hurdles with a time of :26.5.

R. K. Walsh was first in the shot put, and Ray DeCosta cleared 12'6" to win the pole vault. Ray also finished second in both the broad jump and high jump. In the high jump, he and Earl Johnston tied for the first-place points. White Rhyne ran 4:52.0 to win the mile, and then he and Les Noel tied for first in the two mile. Alvin Stump, who grew up at the Baptist Children's Home near the College, also won the 880 race in 2:11.2. It was the first win of his career.

Earl Johnston picked up a third place in the 440, Phil Davis a third in the 880, Paul Barker a third in each of the throwing events, and Fleming a third in the broad jump.

The Maroons easily outscored the Hornets, winning 82-40. It was Roanoke's second dual-meet victory for the year. They had yet to be defeated, and the next competition with Davis and Elkins of West Virginia was sure to provide another win.

I remember . . . "I thought Alvin Stump was going to be a pretty good runner. He and I had a very good relationship. He was brought up at the Baptist Home, not too far from the College. After graduation, he went on to work for a drug company as a salesman and did quite well. Today, he is a generous contributor to Coach Pincus' cross country and track programs and the two of them have developed a close friendship. Over the years, he has also given a lot of money to the school. He gave the school a $25,000 scholarship in honor of Buck Murphy, one other faculty member, and me. He's very loyal to Roanoke College."

Homer Bast

April 29, 1952
Davis and Elkins College at Salem, Virginia
Team Scores: Roanoke 89 ⅔
Davis and Elkins–32⅓

The Davis and Elkins meet was held on a soggy track, leading most to believe that there would be no records in the running events. Instead, there were Alumni Field records and Roanoke College student records set in both the 100-yard dash and the high hurdles. In addition, Ray DeCosta again jumped 13 feet to tie the Alumni Field record as well as the student record.

Boyd Carr again was outstanding. He began by erasing the student record in the 100-yard dash, running a :10.0. That time also tied the existing Alumni Field record. Later in life, he said, "Let's just say that I got a good start." Then he won the 120-yard high hurdles and the 220-yard low hurdles. His time of :15.7 in the highs set both an Alumni Field and school record, and he nearly broke records in the 220. His total of 15 points was high for the meet.

Top Left: Boyd Carr broad jumping.
Top Right: Don Fleming in the high hurdles.
Bottom Left: Richard Burton clears the high jump bar.
Bottom Right: Paul Barker and R. K. Walsh practice for the shot put event.

Ray DeCosta set the other records. He cleared the bar at 13'0" for a win in the pole vault. It was a height good enough to claim the Alumni Field record and tie for the Roanoke College student record.

But, with Roanoke winning 12 of the 14 events on their way to an 89⅔ to 32⅓ team victory, there were plenty of other Roanoke first places. George Gearhart won the 220

(:23.2) and the high jump (5'4"), Earl Johnston the 440 (:55.5), White Rhyne (mile and two-mile runs), the mile relay team, R. K. Walsh (shot put), and Don Fleming (broad jump, tying with Davis and Elkins' Bill Illig).

Several Maroons placed second or third in their events. Included were Earl Johnston (220); Phil Davis (440), Alvin Stump (880), Les Noel (mile, along with a tie for first with Rhyne in the two-mile race), Doug Frith (high hurdles) Don Fleming (high hurdles), Paul Barker (shot put and discus), R. K. Walsh (shot put and discus), Johnston (high jump), and Fleming (high jump).

Only three meets remained for Roanoke. The Little Six meet, to be held in Lynchburg, was scheduled for May 2. The Mason-Dixon meet would come on May 9-10, followed by an unusual late-season dual meet with Hampden-Sydney on May 17.

May 2, 1952
Little Six Championships at Lynchburg, Virginia
Team Scores: 1st–Bridgewater College–65
2nd–Hampden-Sydney College–36½
3rd–Roanoke College–32½
4th–Lynchburg College–15
5th–Randolph-Macon College–5

Despite the fact that Roanoke had picked up some good athletes, and that there were several top performers scattered on teams throughout the Conference, Bridgewater College was again favored to win the Little Six meet. They won the meet in 1950 and successfully defended their title in 1951.

The Eagles set the pace from the start. Wayne Spangler got a great start in the 100 and smashed the meet record with a time of :09.6. The time was one of the best in any southern college or university in 1952. A few strides behind were Boyd Carr, second, followed by George Gearhart in third. Spangler also won the 220-yard dash with a time of :22.0. Gearhart was second.

There were two other records set during the afternoon. Melvin "Shifty" Myers of Bridgewater broke the 1948 record of Lynchburg's Gene Wood when he ran the low hurdles in a fast :24.3. Boyd Carr was a few steps behind in second place. In the pole vault, with a personal-best jump of 13'6", Ray DeCosta broke both his own meet record of 12'9" and his Roanoke student record of 13'0". Actually, noted the *Brackety-Ack*, Ray sincerely thought he could go over 14' in the meet. And he almost did. During his first jump at 13'6", reports were that he not only cleared the bar with ease, but that he had over six inches to spare. Even though he missed at subsequent jumps at higher heights, when he finished the crowd gave him a big ovation. They realized that he had not only set a new record for the meet, but that they were watching the premiere pole vaulter in Virginia.

Besides DeCosta, Roanoke's only winner was White Rhyne. White was timed in 10:25.0, which was eight seconds better than he ever had run before.

Les Noel ran third in the two-mile race. The mile relay team of Stump, McConchie, Davis, and Johnston placed fourth. Don Fleming finished the high hurdles in third place. R. K. Walsh scored twice by finishing third in the shot put and third in the discus. Paul Barker threw the discus for a fourth place. And Gearhart tied for third place in the high jump.

I remember . . . "Wayne Spangler of Bridgewater was sensational, running a time of :09.6 in the 100-yard dash. And that probably was a legitimate time. He was a local boy, you know. He went to Andrew Lewis High School. He was a Brethren and Bridgewater was a Brethren school. That was the reason he went there. I never tried to recruit a Brethren boy. I knew they would end up at Bridgewater."

Homer Bast

May 9-10, 1952
Mason-Dixon Championships at Baltimore, Maryland
Team Scores: 1st–Bridgewater College–$58^7/_{10}$
2nd–Washington College–$32^1/_5$
3rd–Johns Hopkins University–28½
4th–Catholic University–28½
5th–Loyola University–$15^7/_{10}$
6th–Roanoke College–$13^1/_5$
7th–Hampden-Sydney College–$10^1/_5$
8th–Western Maryland College–9
9th–Gallaudet College–7
10th–Lynchburg College–4

The Mason-Dixon Championships on May 9 were even more competitive. Only Ray DeCosta for Roanoke could win an event. He pole vaulted 12'6" to finish first. This height tied the meet record originally set by the Rev. Bob Richards, the famous Olympian, when he was jumping for Bridgewater in 1945. It was also a height cleared by DeCosta in 1951.

George Gearhart (fourth in the 220 and a tie for third in the high jump), Boyd Carr (fourth in the high hurdles), and Les Noel (third in the two-mile) also scored to give

Roanoke a final point total of 13. The team finished in sixth place. Carr actually turned in the best qualifying time in the high hurdles on Friday, but was forced to settle for fourth place in Saturday's finals, crossing the line in a blanket finish with several runners. Both Gearhart and Carr qualified for the semifinals of the 100-yard dash; however, each passed up the chance to run the 100 on Saturday to concentrate on his specialty.

Final team scores for the meet were:

1st–Bridgewater College (B)–58 7/10
2nd–Washington College (W)–32 1/5
3rd–Johns Hopkins University (JH)–28½
4th–Catholic University (C)–28½
5th–Loyola University (LOY)–15 7/10
6th–Roanoke College (R)–13 1/5
7th–Hampden-Sydney College (HS)–10 1/5
8th–Western Maryland College (WM)–9
9th–Gallaudet College (G)–7
10th–Lynchburg College (L)–4

The results were very much as Coach Bast had figured. Roanoke could beat most of the Little Six schools, but still were not competitive enough to stay with the northern teams. They would be a much-improved team the next year, and dominate in the Conference afterwards.

I remember . . . "Ray DeCosta was a big-time performer. He was chasing the pole vaulting records set by the Reverend Bob Richards, known as the Vaulting Vicar. Richards went to Bridgewater and then on to Illinois before he became the Olympic pole vault gold medalist in 1952 and 1956. He was on his way to breaking Richards' record in the 1952 Mason-Dixon meet. Unfortunately, the plant box was too shallow and he just couldn't do it. He did jump 12'6" that day to win the event, but most people thought he could go 13'6" under the right conditions."

Boyd Carr

May 17, 1952
Hampden-Sydney College at Salem, Virginia
Team Scores: Hampden-Sydney–74
Roanoke–48

The home meet with Hampden-Sydney on May 17 would close out the season for Roanoke. Some thought it would be a close meet because the Maroons had beaten Hampden-Sydney by only three points in the Mason-Dixon meet. Bast, however, had seen the comparative times, heights, and distances of the two teams and thought Roanoke might not be able to win the meet. As usual, he was correct. Hampden-Sydney won 9 of the 14 events to outscore Roanoke, 74 to 48.

Two Roanoke men did very well, however. Boyd Carr, after finishing second to George Gearhart in the 100 and 220, and finishing third in the high hurdles, tied his own Roanoke College record in the low hurdles with a time of :26.3. And Ray DeCosta, in the last meet of his successful college career, cleared 13'3". He not only won the event, but set a new Alumni Field record.

Other Roanoke participants who picked up points were Earl Johnson (third in the quarter-mile); Les Noel (second in the mile and third in the 880); White Rhyne (first in the two-mile run); R. K. Walsh (second in the shot put and third in the discus); and Don Fleming (tie for second in the high jump with Johnston, Gearhart, and Joe Rushbook of Hampden-Sydney).

I remember . . . "Ray DeCosta was the class of Virginia schools, and was respected as a great vaulter all over the east coast. Ray worked with weights a lot. I'm not sure that Mr. Bast preferred that Ray use weights. But at the same time, he was the best track man on our squad. He was built like a body builder. He was focused on his event, practiced his skills a lot, and I remember him as a good technician. Besides his strength, he had good form and knew what he was doing. He probably had more technique and strength than he had speed. I know what he was going through, trying to land from 13' in the air into a pit of sawdust. I was high jumping in those days, so I know what a sawdust pit does to your body. Landing in sawdust hampered us because you just couldn't get in enough repetitions in practice. You couldn't take the pounding that would be caused by taking lots of jumps." Johnston also noted that high jumpers were doing the Eastern Roll when he was in college. "Then, on the national scene came the Western Roll, followed by the flop. The flop wasn't popular, of course, until the landing surface improved and became much softer."

Earl Johnston

I remember . . . "I couldn't get with it in the early part of the race. I am on the outside, and way behind in the 220. George Gearhart and the two Hampden-Sydney guys all came by me. Guess I just wasn't that interested in putting out more effort. But there were a couple of people sitting in the stands, cheering for me. One of them was this little girl who worked in the library, and she had been nice to me. I said to myself, 'Boyd. You can't be seen losing like this. You're going to have to pick it up to make the finish close.' So I increased my speed and I notice that these Hampden-Sydney boys were beginning to wobble. And I am saying, 'Hey, maybe. Who knows? Why not?' So I kept on and caught them at the line and finished in second place. I realized later that I had a talent for writing poetry and telling stories. I wrote this poem when Homer retired. John Summers wanted us to write letters to him and send $100. But I had just lost my job, so I sent the poem and no money."

Dear Homer,

john Summers writes that
you are to retire soon &
asks that i send money &
some letter to warm your heart
so i have & here it is.

this is the story about a 220 yard race
that was run at roanoke college in salem, VA
between hampden-sydney college & us
george gearhart was our sprinter & me
plus these two fellows from H. S.

george was a strong runner but
the pressure of competion sometimes
became his biggest opponent &
he would come around before a race
& tell me how he was doing

if he had things going well
he would say
but when his insides were raw
he would moan
i could tell kinda how hard
i would
have to work by visiting a little
with george
before the race we were
to run in

today was warm & george was ready
& i knew if i could just help him
get started he would be unbeatable
so i did what i could which was
to give him the inside lane
around the turn.

the other two gentlemen took 2 & 3
& i camped out there ahead of all three
in what was not the most used
part of the cinders rocks gravel mud & grass
however this was for me because
george was ready

they shot us off & i began to fritter away
that huge lead i had as first george
came galloping by & then my competitors
i was like doing 55 on the interstate
& everyone else homeward bound

i was so far behind that when i came
to the straight stretch and saw this
little girl from rocky mount sitting
with another girl in the sun all alone
i was embarassed to be this far
out of the race

i had spent some time in the library
with this person & even though she
was spoken for i still had fantasies
& here i had my name in the papers
& there she was watching me dissolve

i felt so bad that i decided to pick it up
a little anyway
so as not to look like i wasn't even trying
at least i could try and make it close
& so i did put a little something into it

as i came down the straight a way
the noise of the crowd got my attention
& i said as some of the people began
to notice me that i know i am out of it
but don't you see i am trying to make it close

neatness counts & after the race i can claim
a bad lane or carburator trouble but
for now i am just passing through without
making any statement & i'll be lost
in the general chaos of competition

& then one of those visions came to me
that educators have a fear of because
they lose control & probably can't handle
unless they change so they practice
only what they preach
& hold tight

i saw george gearhart down the track
heading for the finish line way out
in front of these two fellows from H. S.
& they were faltering
they were beginning to get a little
rubber legged

i said now what do you suppose
those two are doing in this race
trying to make a show of it & george
done run off ahead the way he did
& them struggling with each other

so i say put a little more pressure on them
& see how they squirm now
my own discomfort has been transferred
to these competitors up ahead of me
& i did & the crowd must be more agreeable

as i found i could torment these two runners
i began to notice that
the distance between us was diminishing
& i had another vision
one that track coaches have late at night

i saw the possibility of winning this race
of course george was already finishing
but of the last three runners only one
was going to get second place
& sinner that i was it may be me

i let the shaft all the way out
& as my two tormented competitors snatched
at things impeding them & sought
sanctuary with honor among demons
i passes them both at the finish line

george got 5 points & i got 3
H. S. got 1 & i don't remember which
one got that one & didn't care because
something had happened that day
that had been hard for me to get
from a textbook

we picked up 7 points on H. S. & they
had a hard row to catch us in the meet
their coach complimented me on a nice run
& i thought he was teasing & i asked him
about what it was exactly he had seen

all of this has to do with getting
second place when first place
is usually the thing people remember
as being the important thing in life
& little girls on the side are left out

& there i was that day caught

between george gearhart and his
super machine running act
& a pretty little girl from rocky mount
& those two fellows from H. S. i never knew

ps
dear homer, since i composed this letter
& poem I have been fired
& no longer have a job
which is what being fired means
it also means a new race & a new lane
of my own which is
the same thing that is facing you
clean white paper as o hector lee would say
is usually ruled

here is looking for a clean start
run the turns & float the straightaways
& a creditable finish

© boyd carr 1979

Chapter Eight

THE 1952-53 SEASONS

Cross Country

Homer began the cross country season with a mixture of veterans and freshmen. It was one of those teams that might come around for him in the latter part of the season, but for now all you can hope for is that the boys get in good condition.

Sophomore Les Noel was back. In his first year, he certainly contributed to the team scoring; however, little did Homer know that during this year and the next two, Les would become one of the best distance men in Virginia or Mason-Dixon circles. Bennie Irvin, who showed promise in his freshman year under Coach Alvin Smith, but who was not on the team in 1951-52, also returned.

The 1952 cross country team.
First Row (L to R): Winn McConchie, Lessely Noel, John Summers, Bennie Irvin
Second Row (L To R): Coach Bast, S. L. Spangler, Bob Tutoni, Dave Hubble, Asst. Coach Paul McCarty

The team chose Phil Davis as its Captain. He had been on the cross country team since the 1950-51 season. Also returning were veterans Winn McConchie and S. L. Spangler. Three freshmen would score for the Maroons during the coming season. They included John Summers, Dave Hubble, and Bob Tutoni. Summers grew up in New Jersey and came to Roanoke primarily to run the 440-yard dash outdoors; however, Homer talked him into trying cross country, saying that distance running would make him a much better quarter miler.

The *Brackety-Ack* listed others who were expected to train with the team. They were Leon Knowles, Bruce Homer, Terry Grant, John Varsa, Tom Cole, and Bob Davis.

October 17, 1952
Lynchburg College at Lynchburg, Virginia
Team Scores: Lynchburg–24
Roanoke–31

On October 17, 1952, Roanoke faced its first test when the team traveled to Lynchburg, Virginia, to meet the Lynchburg College Hornets. According to the *Brackety-Ack*, the course was run on two ovals, with a total distance of 4.3 miles. Les Noel of Roanoke took the lead as soon as the race began, followed closely by Lynchburg's Carl Gillespie. Gillespie stayed just a few steps behind Noel for the distance of the first oval. Then Noel began to pull away, winning in a new course-record time of 24:22. Gillispie crossed the line in second almost a minute behind Noel.

Bennie Irvin finished third in 26:31; however, the Hornets' Tom Snavely, Tom Clayton, Pat Thomas, and Don Freeman came across the line together in 27:18 to secure the win for their team. For Roanoke, Winn McConchie and Phil Davis tied for eighth. John Summers was tenth, Bob Tutoni was thirteenth, Dave Hubble was fifteenth, and S. L. Spangler finished in sixteenth place.

The team score was Lynchburg, 24, and Roanoke, 31. Roanoke was 0-1 for the season.

October 25, 1952
Virginia AAU Championships at Richmond, Virginia
Team Scores: 1st–University of Richmond (UR)–41
2nd–Bridgewater College (B)–55
3rd–Lynchburg College (L)–83
4th–Roanoke College (R)–No Team Score

The Virginia AAU Championships were run on October 25. Roanoke did not enter an entire team of five runners, but reports indicate that Les Noel and Bennie Irvin did participate and ran well. Both won medals for finishing in the top 15.

Lt. Warren Druetzler, a member of the 1952 Olympic team, won the individual championship after Jordon of the University of Richmond set the pace for some three and one-half miles. The weather was perfect for running, and most were sure that a new course record would be set. Jordon covered the first mile in 4:44, but Druetzler finally passed him in the last mile of the four-mile course and won with a time of 21:13. That time was 30 seconds better than the old mark of 21:43.

Noel and Irvin, running well within themselves, took the fourth and eleventh positions, respectively, in the field of 32 runners. The University of Richmond, with 41 points, won the team trophy. They were followed by Bridgewater College, 55, and Lynchburg College, 83. Without five runners, Roanoke did not score.

October 31, 1952
Hampden-Sydney College at Hampden-Sydney, Virginia
Team Scores: Roanoke–24
Hampden-Sydney–31

The Maroons' second dual meet was with Hampden-Sydney, who had beaten Roanoke in 1951. They ran on a 3.6-mile course.

Les Noel and Bennie Irvin led throughout the race. Les then pulled ahead and won the race in 20:15, with Bennie finishing in second place 16 seconds back. Hampden-Sydney picked up the next three positions, however, before John Summers, Winn McConchie, and Phil Davis won the meet for Roanoke. John finished sixth, and Winn and Phil tied for seventh. Dave Hubble (twelfth) and Bob Tutoni (thirteenth) followed.

The team scores were Roanoke, 24, and Hampden-Sydney, 31. The victory evened the dual meet record of the season at one win and one loss.

Homer had two fairly good runners at the top, but limited support below. It was the type of team he could build on, but also the type which might have lots of trouble in the larger races such as the upcoming Little Six and Mason-Dixon Championships.

November 7, 1952
Washington and Lee University at Lexington, Virginia
Team Scores: Washington and Lee–25
Roanoke–33

First, however, the team had one more dual meet–with Washington and Lee in Lexington. Roanoke had beaten the Generals 20 to 35 in 1951.

Again, Les Noel and Bennie Irvin finished in the first and second positions, respectively. Noel's time was 20:44, and Irvin ran a respectable 20:58. Unfortunately, Washington and Lee packed five of their individuals in the third through eighth spots to take the team win, 25 to 33. Phil Davis (ninth), Bob Tutoni (tenth), John Summers (eleventh), Winn McConchie (twelfth), and Dave Hubble (thirteenth) also finished for Roanoke.

The team now had a 1-2 dual-meet record. Both Noel and Irvin had done well, but none of the other runners on the team were as successful. For the Little Six and Mason-Dixon meets, therefore, Homer decided to take only a partial team of three runners–Noel, Irvin, and Tutoni.

November 14, 1952
Little Six Championships at Bridgewater, Virginia
Team Scores: 1st–Bridgewater College–25
2nd–Lynchburg College–41
3rd–Hampden-Sydney College–67
Roanoke College–No Score (Less Than Full Team)

At the Little Six Championships at Bridgewater on November 14, Bridgewater College won the meet for the third consecutive time. Even without Merle Crouse, who had been the best runner in the Conference while at Bridgewater, the Eagles' top five runners finished in the first eleven spots. Lynchburg runners were second, with 41 points, while Hampden-Sydney scored 67 for third place. Roanoke, of course, entered less than a full team and received no points.

On the other hand, Les Noel ran an excellent race and won the first-place medal with a time of 20:17.4 on the 3.7-mile course. Bennie Irvin also finished well, in the fifth position, with Bob Tutoni crossing the line in the seventeenth position.

I remember . . . "In 1952-53, the cross country season was very disappointing to me. In fact, I was so disappointed in the team that before the Mason-Dixon race, I told them that we were not going. We're not going to go up there and get humiliated. If you can't do better than this, well let's just stay home. And boy, did the word get around that I had disbanded the cross country team. And I'll tell you, I took it. But they soon got over it, for the next year we were right back and had a pretty good group. I wasn't going to take any stuff from them. I was out there working hard and by golly they were going to work as hard as I was."

Homer Bast

November 22, 1952
Mason-Dixon Championships at Washington, D. C.

Team Scores: 1st–Bridgewater College–54
2nd–Johns Hopkins University–67
3rd–Towson State College–96
4th–Washington College–115
5th–Catholic University–122
6th–Gallaudet College–133
7th–Lynchburg College–153
8th–Hampden-Sydney College–195
Loyola College–Incomplete Score
Roanoke College–Incomplete Score

The same three runners went to the Mason-Dixon Conference meet. Held on a 3.75-mile course at Gallaudet College in Washington, the meet would feature 95 runners from 10 schools.

Noel might have won this meet if it hadn't been for the fact that he was sick for much of the past week. In a weakened condition, and without any recent training, he managed to finish in eleventh place with a time of 22:06. Irvin was timed in 21:34 for sixth place. Both won medals for placing in the top 15 runners. Bob Tutoni finished down the list with a time of 23:31

Again, the strong Bridgewater team won the championship trophy with 67 points, beating Towson State, 96; Washington College, 115; Catholic University, 122; Gallaudet College, 133; Lynchburg College, 153; and Hampden-Sydney, 195. Loyola, like Roanoke, received no points because they entered fewer than five runners.

Indoor Track

January 10, 1953
Evening Star Games at Washington, D. C.
Mason-Dixon Sprint Medley Relay: 1st–Catholic University (Lee, Schmidt, Favo, and Arienti)–3:50.4
2nd–Roanoke College (Carr, Moore, Summers, and Irvin)
3rd–Bridgewater College

The first meet of the indoor season was the Evening Star Games in Washington. In the Mason-Dixon Sprint Relay, Bast entered the team of John Summers, Kearny, New Jersey; Boyd Carr, Roanoke; Don Moore, Radford; and Bennie Irvin, Roanoke. Summers would run the lead-off 440, Carr and Moore would continue with 220s, and Irvin would run the anchoring 880. Roanoke College won this event in 1949, running Lawrence Crockett, Dick Dodd, Walt Tramposch, and Alvin Smith. Their time was 3:47.7. The team finished third in 1950 and did not enter teams in 1951 or 1952.

There was some thought of entering not only the sprint medley, but the mile relay handicap race and the open two-mile relay. At the last minute, however, Homer dropped the idea of entering these events, deciding that the sprint medley would give Roanoke the best chance of winning.

In the sprint medley, Bast expected the main opposition to come from Towson Teachers, Bridgewater, Johns Hopkins, and Catholic. Bridgewater, with a good half miler, was a good choice to finish first.

The race was run in two sections. The first section was won by Catholic University and the second by Bridgewater College. Roanoke ran in the first section, coming in second. Roanoke had a better time than did Bridgewater, so the Maroons were given second place overall. Catholic's winning time with the team of Sam Lee, Fred Favo, Larry Schmidt, and Tom Arienti was a comparatively slow 3:50.4.

The Evening Star Games had always presented Roanoke with a chance to compete with some of the best athletes on the east coast. By this time, in fact the Games were on par with almost any large meet in the nation.

Incidentally, this was the meet in which Ray DeCosta had done so well in the pole vault the previous year. He had been invited to compete again in 1953; however, he was in the service and was unable to attend.

January 24, 1953
Virginia Military Institute at Lexington, Virginia
Team Scores: Virginia Military Institute–72½
Roanoke–31½

On January 24, 1953, Roanoke met the strong Virginia Military Institute team in the Keydets' field house in Lexington. It would be the first time since Bast came to the college in 1946 that a dual meet involving Roanoke had been held during an indoor season. In the January 23 edition of the *Brackety-Ack*, the newspaper said that the following athletes were expected to compete:

60	Boyd Carr and Don Moore
440	Pete Lawson, Jack Fleshman, John Summers, and Earl Johnston
880	Winn McConchie
Mile	Bennie Irvin and Les Noel
Two Mile	Bennie Irvin, Les Noel, and Richard Hansel

Shot	Bill Lund, Robert Hock, Donald Morel, and Dan Posluszny
HJ	Don Fleming and Earl Johnston
BJ	Boyd Carr, Don Moore, and Jack Fleshman
PV	John Varsa and Benny Caudill
HH	Boyd Carr and Don Fleming
LH	Boyd Carr and Charlie Britsch

The V. M. I. team was led by the talented Johnny Mapp. He was capable of winning any of four or five events.

The young Roanoke team was totally outclassed by the Keydets, who won 10 of the 12 events on that afternoon's schedule. Mapp himself topped two state indoor track records and tied another. His record-breaking performances came in the high hurdles, the low hurdles, and the broad jump.

In his first attempt in the broad jump, Mapp went 21'2" to beat the mark held by Frank Spencer of V. M. I. at 20'11". In the low hurdles, he covered the 70 yards in :07.7 to break his own mark by one tenth of a second. And in the high hurdles, he tied the time of :08.9 originally set by Devand Latham of the University of Virginia.

Mapp also took a first for the Keydets in the high jump (5'5") and finished the meet as the high scorer with 20 points. Other Keydet records in the mile and half mile were bettered by V. M. I.'s Ben Angle, who had a mile time of 4:42.0 and an 880 time of 2:05.5.

Two Roanoke men also took first places. Boyd Carr won the 60-yard dash in :06.5 and Les Noel won the two-mile run in 10:42.2. Both were Roanoke College indoor records.

Others who placed for Roanoke included Don Moore, tie for third in the 60 and second in the broad jump; John Summers, second in the quarter mile; Bennie Irvin, second in the 880; Les Noel, second in the mile run; Boyd Carr, second in both the high and low hurdles; Don Fleming, third in the high hurdles; Boyd Carr, second in the low hurdles; and Bill Lund, third in the shot put.

At the end of the meet, there was more than a 40-point difference in the team scores. Paced by Johnny Mapp, the Keydets took a 72½ to 31½ victory.

February 7, 1953
Virginia Military Institute Winter Relays at Lexington, Virginia
Team Scores: Non-Scoring Meet

The second annual Winter Relays brought together 11 colleges and universities, from Roanoke and Bridgewater to Duke and North Carolina State. No team scores were kept.

There is not much known today about Roanoke's participation in the meet; however, the meet results do show that the Maroon team of Earl Johnston, John Summers, Bennie

Irvine, and Les Noel finished second to Catholic University in the Mason-Dixon Distance Relay. No additional Roanoke athletes appear to have placed in any of the other events, although the distance medley may have been the only competition for the Maroons. The *Brackety-Ack*, which was good about reporting on the track team's fortunes, had no comments at all about the results of the meet. Neither did local newspapers.

Maryland's excellent team captured firsts in five events. In four of the events they won, the Terps set new records. Duke and host V. M. I. each took two first places, with one event each going to North Carolina State, Virginia Tech, and Catholic.

Duke's Durham Lawshe was the individual star of the meet. Weighing only 185 pounds, he threw the shot 48'10", a new Relays record and several feet ahead of his nearest competitor.

Another outstanding performance was given by Otey Garrison, who anchored North Carolina State's winning team in the distance medley relay and almost pulled the Wolfpack runners to victory in the four-mile relay. He was voted the outstanding competitor in track events.

February 14, 1953
Little Six Championships at Lexington, Virginia
Team Scores: 1st–Roanoke College–70
2nd–Bridgewater College–39
3rd–Hampden-Sydney College–10
4th–Lynchburg College–5
5th–Randolph-Macon College–2

The Little Six Indoor meet, scheduled for February 14 at the V. M. I. field house in Lexington, was held simultaneously with the Virginia Big Six Conference Championships. For the first time in several years, Roanoke was favored to win the team trophy. Except for top sprinter Wayne Spangler, the defending team winner Bridgewater College had graduated most of its star athletes. Of course, last year's freshman sprinter sensation for Roanoke, George Gearhart, had been drafted into military service and his points would be missed.

The resurgent Maroon team broke four Little Six Indoor Track Meet records and tied a fifth. Les Noel established a record in the two mile run of 10 minutes 39.9 seconds. John Summers broke a record in the 440 with a time of :54.4. The old record was set by Henry Coghill, Jr., of Hampden-Sydney, with a time of 57.9 seconds in 1952. Freshman Bill Lund also broke the shot put record with a distance of 41'9". The old mark of 38'10" was set by Bussard of Bridgewater in 1952. Roanoke's mile relay team of Earl Johnston, Pete Lawson, Boyd Carr, and John Summers won with a new record of 3:47.9. The old mark of 3:50 by Hampden-Sydney was set in 1952. Boyd Carr tied the 70 low hurdle record (:08.2) set by Mel Myers of Bridgewater in 1951.

Dave Foltz, freshman star on the basketball team, was hampered by the flu. Still, he competed and won the high jump at 5'6", and came in second behind Bill Lund in the shot. Don Moore, who was entered in the 60 and broad jump with no practice, placed third in the 60 and first in the broad jump with an effort of 20'1½".

Several other Roanoke men placed in their events. Earl Johnston placed second in the high jump behind Foltz and John Varsa was fourth in the pole vault. Pete Lawson finished fourth in the 440, Les Noel and Bennie Irvin tied for first in the mile run in a non-record time of 5:02.0, and Winn McConchie was fourth in that event. Bennie Irvin was second to Noel in the two-mile run, Boyd Carr was second in the high hurdles, first in the low hurdles with a time of :08.2, and fourth in the broad jump. Don Fleming was second in the low hurdles.

The Maroons broke eight Roanoke College records during the meet, including:

John Summers	440-Yard Dash–:54.4
John Summers	880-Yard Run–2:08.3
Les Noel	Two-Mile Run–10:39.9
Boyd Carr	70-Yard Low Hurdles–:08.2
Earl Johnston, Pete Lawson, Boyd Carr, and John Summers	Mile Relay–3:47.9
Bill Lund	Shot Put–41'9"
Don Moore	Broad Jump–20'1½"
Dave Foltz	High Jump–5'6"

Charlie Britsch injured his knee while going over a hurdle and was expected to be lost for several weeks. Freshman Don Verleur sprained ligaments in running the 60.

Roanoke College ousted Bridgewater as champion, scoring a total of 70 points to only 39 for the runner-up Eagles. Hampden-Sydney was a distant third with 10 points, while Lynchburg had 5 and Randolph-Macon 4.

February 28, 1953
Southern Conference Games at Chapel Hill, North Carolina
Team Scores (Non-Conference Division): None

On February 28 the winter schedule finished with the Southern Conference Games at Chapel Hill. Roanoke entered six athletes in the non-conference division of the meet. Four of them came back with medals.

Bill Lund took first in the shot, with a throw of 40'9¾". In the mile, Bennie Irvin took third and Les Noel took fourth, while Boyd Carr was third in the low hurdles.

In the larger and more competitive conference division, Duke's star-studded track team dethroned Maryland to win its first Southern Conference indoor championship in 15 years.

Coach Bob Chambers' surprising Blue Devils grabbed the lead at the very start of the day-long program and nursed it through the 12-event schedule to emerge with 34⅚ points to 27⅔ points for runner-up North Carolina and 18⅔ for Maryland. Duke's total was the lowest for a winning team in 19 years.

Virginia Military Institute, Virginia Polytechnic Institute, and North Carolina State all had individual winners.

Pacing Duke to its long-awaited triumph were sophomore Joel Shankle of Level Cross, NC, John Tate, and Durham Lawshe.

Outdoor Track

For some reason, there was a good feeling on campus about Roanoke's chances for the spring track season. The team was fairly young, of course. But of the nine athletes expected to carry most of the load, only one was a senior. One was a junior, three were sophomores, and four were freshmen. Even their coach, generally reserved in his predictions, was optimistic. "We could have a good year," Bast said, "although we will be lacking in depth. If some of the youngsters come through, we might be up there in the Mason-Dixon Conference. The boys have a great deal of potential. If they work hard, they could turn in some fine showings." Unfortunately, only one of the spring meets was at home.

For the College team, the outdoor season began during the spring break. Bast had scheduled meets with two southern schools–Clemson University on April 1 and Davidson College on April 4. Both had good track squads.

Don Fleming, senior from Bayside, New York, was elected Captain of the 1953 Maroon track team.

April 1, 1953
Clemson University at Clemson, South Carolina
Team Scores: Clemson–90⅓
Roanoke–39⅔

For Roanoke, the injury and sick lists were growing. The injury that would probably hurt the Maroons most was a pulled muscle in the leg of sprinter and broad jumper Don Moore. He wasn't expected to compete on the southern swing. Ailing from spring colds were Bennie Irvin and Boyd Carr.

The 1953 track team.
First Row (L to R): Boyd Carr, Don Fleming, Don Moore, Dave Foltz, John Varsa, Winn McConchie
Second Row (L to R): Bennie Irvin, Earl Johnston, Les Noel, John Summers, Bob Cline, Don Verleur
Third Row: Coach Homer Bast, Bill Lund, Don Morel, Dan Posluszny, and Pete Lawson.

Clemson spoiled Roanoke's first meet by soundly defeating the Maroons, 90⅓ to 39⅔. The Tigers took 10 first places, 9 seconds, and a tie for first in the pole vault to win easily. Clemson football captain Dreher Gaskin was high point man in the meet with a first in the shot and second in discus and high jump.

For the Roanoke team, John Summers, freshman from Kearney, New Jersey, did set a new Roanoke College record. The star quarter miler, who indoors had set a school record in this event, ran the 440 in :52.2, knocking a tenth of a second off the old record set in 1950 by Frank Aldred.

Roanoke also took first places in the 880, mile, and two-mile runs. In the 880, Bennie Irvin was timed in 2:09.2 for the win. Les Noel and Irvin tied for top honors in the mile run with 4:52.0. Noel also won the two-mile race with little competition, crossing the line in 11:04.3.

Boyd Carr picked up seven team points by placing second in the high hurdles and low hurdles, and third in the broad jump. Earl Johnston and Dave Foltz tied for third in the high jump. Foltz also placed third in the 220-yard dash. Bill Lund, freshman weight man, finished second in the shot put, Don Fleming was third in the high hurdles, and Pete Lawson picked up a third place in the 880.

I remember . . . "The Clemson coach, an alumnus of Roanoke, would always give me $150 or so to run them. And I could expect to bring back some equipment. I think he just enjoyed talking to me. Of course, Clemson was all football in those days. If you walked into that lobby of the gym, you would see a big, silver Orange Bowl trophy there."

Homer Bast

April 4, 1953
Davidson College at Davidson, North Carolina
Team Scores: Davidson–87
Roanoke–44

This meet looked a bit like the one with Clemson. Davidson walked off with first places in 8 of the 12 events to beat the Maroons 87 to 44. But there were some excellent results from several Roanoke men.

Sophomore Boyd Carr broke two of his own Roanoke College records. In the high hurdles, he won with a time of :15.6. That time beat the former record of :15.7. In the low hurdles, he ran a time of :25.6, which easily beat the :26.3 mark he had set as a freshman in 1952.

Freshman Bill Lund broke the outdoor school record for the shot put. His winning throw was 41'8", while the old mark of 41'5" was set by Jim Doran in his only year of competition in 1947.

Bennie Irvin tied for the win in the mile run, and was second the 880. Les Noel also won, taking the two-mile race in 10:45.0.

Roanoke's John Summers finished second behind a winning :51.4 time in the 440, and was third in the 880. Senior Don Fleming was third in the high hurdles, Lund was second in the javelin, Don Moore was third in the broad jump, Dave Foltz was third in the high jump, and Don Middleton tied for second in the pole vault.

At this point in the season, the Roanoke team was 0-2. It would have been easy to dismiss them as having little talent; however, the reader should mark the date of April 4, 1955. This defeat, to Davidson, was the last dual- or triangular-meet loss for the Maroons through the end of the 1956-57 season. During this period, with the annual addition of new stars and the development of those already on the teams, Roanoke became a perennial power in the Little Six and Mason-Dixon Conferences. Those close to the team later called the succession of wins of 1952-53 through 1956-57 "the streak." That streak would continue unblemished until powerhouse Florida State beat Roanoke in the first meet of 1957-58.

I remember . . . "This was the year that Stephen was born. So after the Clemson meet, I sent the team on down to Davidson. Mary Jane was ready to give birth and I needed to be in Salem. I flew home. I told the athletes why I was leaving and that I wanted them to behave. I told them that they were old enough to know the difference between right and wrong. I wanted them to be a model group, and apparently they were. I believe that they stayed at Clemson overnight and then probably stayed at Davidson the next night. It had taken us a long time to make the trip down and back. It seemed like we went through every one of those small, industrial towns in North and South Carolina. I think it was remarkable that we got there and back. At any rate, the team left, and I left. Very few schools of our size were making that kind of trip. And it was very hard for me to pick up small college meets on the way south. The Roanoke Athletic Department couldn't put in very much money for these trips. Buddy Hackman may have given us $1 per athlete per day for food. And even in those days, you really couldn't get much food for a dollar. I would give the boys their buck and they would go to the cheapest place they could find to eat. I said, 'I'm sorry. I just don't have any more money.' Sometimes we were lucky and would find a White Castle, where the dollar went a long way. I believe their small burgers were five cents each."

Homer Bast

I remember . . . "When we scheduled Davidson, I knew how good they were. But I wanted to take the trip and, as you know, to do so you really had to have two meets to make it worthwhile. It was difficult. Davidson gave us some money. And they provided the meals we needed. And I believe that they gave us an overnight stay."

Homer Bast

April 11, 1953
Randolph-Macon College at Ashland, Virginia
Team Scores: Roanoke–84½
Randolph-Macon–37½

The Randolph-Macon meet marked the beginning of basketball star Dave Foltz's career as one of the best track and field athletes in Virginia. Foltz won the 100 in :10.7, the discus with a throw of 105'4", and the high jump when he cleared 5'8". He also finished second in the 220 and third in the discus for a point total of 19 for the day.

Boyd Carr won the high hurdles in :16.0 and ran on the winning mile relay team with Earl Johnston, Bennie Irvin, and John Summers. John Summers won the 440 (:55.3) and the 880 (2:12.0), Bennie Irvin placed first in the mile run with 5:12.0, and Les Noel finished first in the two-mile run with 10:35.6.

Bill Lund continued to throw well, picking up a first in the shot with 41'6" and placing second to Foltz in the discus. And Don Moore won the 220 in :24.4.

Others who scored were Don Verleur, second in the 100; Earl Johnston, second in the 440 and a tie for third in the high jump; Winn McConchie, second in the mile run; Don Fleming, second in the high hurdles, second in the low hurdles, and third in the broad jump; Charlie Britsch, third in the low hurdles; Don Morel, third in the discus; and Don

Middleton, third in the pole vault.

There was little competition from the Randolph-Macon team, likely one of the main reasons that no Roanoke College records were broken during the afternoon. The final score was Roanoke College, 84½, and Randolph-Macon, 37½.

I remember . . . "After the Randolph-Macon meet at Ashland, which had been a rainy, muddy affair, I remember driving back that night. I still had my convertible. There was thunder, lightning, and rain all the way back. It was a really messy drive home."

Homer Bast

April 17, 1953
Washington and Lee University at Lexington, Virginia
Team Scores: Roanoke–75
Washington and Lee–47

Roanoke's fourth meet of the season came on April 17, 1953, at Washington and Lee. The Generals were said to have a good team this year, yet Bast was skeptical because they had been beaten badly by Virginia Polytechnic Institute just a few days before the Roanoke meet. The Roanoke-W & L meet was run at the same time as the V. M. I.-William and Mary meet.

As it turned out, Roanoke won or shared nine first places in beating Washington and Lee with ease, 75-47. The only bright spot for Washington and Lee was when pole vaulter Walt Diggs easily won his specialty, but missed barely in an attempt at 12'9". Had he made that height, he would have set a new school record.

For the Maroons, Boyd Carr was high point man with 13 points. He won the broad jump (20'2¾") and the 220-yard low hurdles (:26.0), and also placed second in the high hurdles.

John Summers also was a double winner. He won the 440-yard dash in :52.8 and teamed with Bennie Irvin to place first in the 880-yard run.

Left Photo (L to R): Bill Lund, Dave Foltz, and Earl Johnston.
Right Photo (L to R): Don Moore and Boyd Carr.

Les Noel continued to run well. With little competition, he and Bennie Irvin tied for first place in the mile (5:05.6), and then Noel won the two mile in 10:28.2.

Other winners included Don Moore, who ran the 100-yard dash in :10.4; Don Verleur, with a :23.6 in the 220-yard dash; Bill Lund, who threw the shot 40'11½"; and Dave Foltz, whose only win was in the high jump, where he tied with Tom Fieldson of W & L at 5'10". That jump was a new Roanoke College record, beating the old mark of 5'9" set in 1929 by Ed Bell. The mile relay team of Winn McConchie, Pete Lawson, Earl Johnston, and John Summers also won their event in a time of 3:40.2.

Roanoke athletes took three seconds and six thirds to complete the scoring. Earl Johnston (440), Boyd Carr (high hurdles), and Bennie Irvin (two miles) all had seconds. Verleur (100), Moore (220), Lawson (44), Charlie Britsch (low hurdles), and Foltz (shot put and discus) all took third places.

April 25, 1953
Hampden-Sydney at Salem, Virginia
Team Scores: Roanoke–83
Hampden-Sydney–34

On April 25, Roanoke met Hampden-Sydney in Salem. As usual, it seemed, the Maroons were plagued with injuries. John Summers had a bad cold. Hurdler Don Fleming, Captain of the team, would not be competing because of a pulled muscle. Don Moore had a bad heel.

To promote the College in the surrounding area, Bast and school officials had arranged for a day-long celebration called "Meet the Roanoke College Family." Throughout the day, local high school students and their parents were invited to see the college facilities and roam through numerous science exhibits. If they desired, they could sit in on college classes. Included in the day's activities were exhibition tennis matches on the College courts; athletic and recreation activities for girls; swimming for everyone; and a box lunch in the gym at noon.

From 10:00 until 11:00 in the morning, the College had arranged an exhibition tennis match between Frank Snow, faculty member of the school, and Charlie Turner, Director of the Salem Recreation Department. Both were well-known senior players in the area.

In the afternoon, running simultaneously with the meet featuring Roanoke and Hampden-Sydney, Bast had arranged for the first-ever track meet featuring the four major high schools located near the college. Those schools were Jefferson, William Fleming, Andrew Lewis, and William Byrd.

Many local track athletes had used the school's track facilities over the past several years. Sometimes, their coaches would bring them to the campus to practice. At other times, individual high school athletes would come to the facility to practice on their own. In all cases, Bast welcomed them even when his own team was practicing. Some said that he often coached them himself, showing them the proper form or just explaining the art of training. Helping high schoolers, and simply having them on the campus, was a good recruiting tool.

This high school meet, eventually called the City-County Championships, was continued for several years with Bast as the Meet Director. Its presence stimulated interest in track and field athletics throughout the western part of Virginia. The meet eventually was turned over to the local Cosmopolitan Club, who provided the manpower and hard work it took to put on a first-class meet from year to year.

It was the type of circus on the field that afternoon that few had ever seen. Athletes were everywhere. Action was continuous, and the combined event drew the largest number of spectators for any home track meet in the history of the college.

In the high school portion of the meet, Jefferson came roaring back in the final two events of the afternoon to edge William Fleming 63⅓ to 56⅚. Andrew Lewis of Salem finished third with 20⅚. William Byrd of Vinton failed to score.

In the college meet, Roanoke had little problem beating Hampden-Sydney. In fact, the score was 83-34. Much of that success came from the four first places taken by sophomore Boyd Carr. Carr, who grew up within 10 miles of the College, won the 100-yard dash (:10.6), the high hurdles (:16.0), the low hurdles (:25.5) and the broad jump (20'1½"). His low hurdle time set a new school record, beating the :25.6 mark Carr had set earlier in the season. Carr himself finished the meet with 20 points. The high hurdle time and place were significant because Carr's main opponent was Doug Divers. Divers was the reigning Little Six indoor champion for the high hurdles.

Freshman Bill Lund again proved to be a good competitor in the weight events. He easily broke the Alumni Field record of 40'7½", set in 1952, with a throw of 42'10½". This distance was also a Roanoke College record, beating the 41'8" throw he had made in 1953. He had not been known for his discus throwing, but he won that event also with a distance of 116'7¼".

Earl Johnston and Don Fleming, hurdlers for the 1953 outdoor track team.

Another double winner was Les Noel, the Maroons' dependable and talented distance runner. He easily won the two-mile race with a time of 10:48.0 after he teamed with Bennie Irvin for victory in the mile run with 4:51.2.

John Summers continued to improve in the 440. He won the event in an Alumni Field and Roanoke College record time of :52.2. Irvin also won the 880-yard race in a respectable 2:05.0.

Dave Foltz was not at his best, but he did manage to pick up a second in the high jump, a third in the 100, and seconds in both the shot and discus. Don Moore took seconds in the 100 and 220, Earl Johnston finished behind Summers in the 440, Summers was second to Irvin in the 880, Charlie Britsch finished third in the low hurdles, Winn McConchie was third in the two-mile run, and Don Middleton was third in the pole vault.

April 30, 1953
Norfolk Division of William and Mary at Norfolk, Virginia
Team Scores: Roanoke–73
Norfolk William and Mary–49

The April 30 meet in Norfolk between Roanoke and the Norfolk Division of William and Mary, later called Old Dominion, marked the first time the two schools had met in any sport. Sadly, the weather failed to cooperate with a rainstorm and strong winds hurting all of the athletes throughout the afternoon. Had it not been for strong tail winds, in fact, two Roanoke College records would have been broken. Don Moore was timed in :22.4 in the 220, and Boyd Carr ran a :25.0 in the low hurdles. Neither made the record books.

The wind didn't seem to bother the home team's Van Story. He won three first places, tied for a fourth win, and even took one third place. But his 20 points did little to brunt the constant scoring of the Roanoke team, who won all of the events that the Norfolk star didn't.

Bennie Irvin and John Summers tied for first in the 880 with 2:14.9. Noel and Irvin crossed the finish line together in the mile run for a win, and Noel took the two-mile race himself. All of their times were sub-par; however, the wind was a major factor in all circular runs.

John Summers placed first in the 440. His time was a respectable :52.6.

Boyd Carr was a multiple winner again, as he placed first in the 100-yard dash (:10.4) and the low hurdles, and also had a second in the high hurdles. Dave Foltz threw the discus 109'3" for his win. Bill Lund won the shot with a throw of 41'¾" and was third in the discus.

Don Verleur finished behind Carr in the 100 and behind Moore in the 220. Earl

Johnston was second in the 440, Don Fleming was third in the broad jump, and Don Middleton finished in a tie for second in the pole vault. Winn McConchie was third in the two-mile race. And Don Middleton tied for second place in the pole vault.

The Roanoke team of Don Moore, Pete Lawson, Earl Johnson, and John Summers cruised through their race. Their time was 3:44.0.

Bast was coaching a well-balanced team. It may have been his best team since he came to Roanoke, in fact. Scrap Chandler, coach of the Norfolk team, said after the meet, "Roanoke College has one of the best small college teams I've ever seen."

I remember . . . "We already had the meet won and I wanted to go over to the broad jump and try some more jumps. But Don Fleming and I were good friends, and I knew that he really wanted to place in the event. I couldn't take a chance that I might knock him out of a place, so I just watched him take his last jumps."

Boyd Carr

I remember . . . "In track, Don Moore was a pretty good runner. He was from the New River Valley. I had seen him in high school, and I may have convinced him to come to Roanoke to run. We needed someone to take George Gearhart's place when George went into the service. Moore stepped into that role nicely. He ran the 100 and 220, and occasionally broad jumped."

Homer Bast

May 4, 1953
Lynchburg College at Lynchburg, Virginia
Team Scores: Roanoke–72
Lynchburg–50

The Roanoke-Lynchburg meet was held on May 4, 1953. The Maroons had beaten Lynchburg in 1952, but had lost to them–53 to 69–in Lynchburg in 1951. Coach Bast thought the scores of this year's meet might be close, but he was encouraged by hearing that Lynchburg had only a 1-3 record this season.

Of the 14 events on that day's card, Roanoke won 8 and Lynchburg 6. The real differences were in the numbers of second and third place finishes that Roanoke gained.

The Hornets' small sprinter, hurdler, and jumper, Clayton, took scoring honors for the day. His 16 points came from wins in the 100 and 220, and seconds in the broad jump and low hurdles.

Boyd Carr, the Maroons' best all-around performer, was close on Clayton's heels in terms of points. He won the broad jump along with both hurdle events for a total of 15 points.

Bennie Irvin and Les Noel remained undefeated. Irvin won the 880 in 2:05.8, then tied with Les Noel for top honors in the mile. Noel won the two-mile run.

John Summers, a smooth-striding freshman who was getting stronger as the weeks passed, was timed with a :52.1 in the quarter mile. That time beat his own Roanoke College record of :52.2.

Freshman Bill Lund took first place in the shot put. He also finished second in the discus.

Second places were taken by Don Verleur (100 and 220); Summers (880), Earl Johnston (high hurdles and high jump); Dave Foltz (shot); and Lund (discus). Thirds went to: Don Moore (100 and 220); Johnston (440); Charlie Britsch (low hurdles); Foltz (discus), Don Fleming (broad jump); and Johnston and Foltz (high jump).

The victory gave Roanoke a 5-2 season record. Better yet, it was the Maroons' fifth straight win. The streak was on.

May 8, 1953
Little Six Championships at Lynchburg, Virginia
Team Scores: 1st–Roanoke College–53
2nd–Bridgewater College–46⅓
3rd–Hampden-Sydney College–24$\frac{5}{6}$
4th–Lynchburg College–20½
5th–Randolph-Macon College–8⅓

It was May 8, just three days after the Lynchburg meet. Sitting at his kitchen table that morning with his note pad, Coach Bast was trying every way possible to predict the score of today's Little Six meet in Lynchburg. The only thing he could determine for certain, however, was the meet would come down to a showdown with Bridgewater. The two teams had not met during the 1953 season, but they had competed against some common opponents. Roanoke had beaten Lynchburg and Randolph-Macon, but so had Bridgewater. The only problem was that Bridgewater's margins of victory were greater in both cases. The Maroons' win-loss record was 5 and 2. Bridgewater's was 4 and 1.

Adding to Bast's problems was that several individuals on the Roanoke team were injured. Don Moore had a stone bruise on his heel. Don Fleming had a pulled muscle in his leg. Bill Lund had a bad back. And Dave Foltz was hurt. He would make the trip, but might enter only one or two events. Foltz especially would be quite a loss since he usually could win, place, or show in several different events.

He might as well toss a quarter in the air, he thought. "I suppose we won't know until tonight which team will win."

During most of the afternoon, the Roanoke and Bridgewater scores were virtually even. First, one would pull ahead, and then the other.

Several athletes were spectacular in their performances. Wayne Spangler, the terrific sprinter from Bridgewater, was timed at :09.9 in the 100. Later, he came back in the 220 with a time of :21.5, a meet record. John Summers closed fast in the 440, winning in a Roanoke College record time of :52.0. Summers also placed third in the 880. Bennie Irvin ran his best 880 of the year, finishing first for Roanoke in 2:03.2, and Les Noel was well ahead in the mile, winning in 4:37.6. Teammate Bill Lund upset the field to win the shot put with a throw of 42'4½", his second-best effort of the year.

Other Maroons who added to the team score were Don Verleur, third in the 100 and fourth in the 220; Don Moore, fourth in the 100; Irvin, third in the mile run; Lund, second in the discus; and the injured Dave Foltz, who entered only the high jump and finished in a tie for second.

And then there was Roanoke's rising star, Boyd Carr. After finishing second to Doug Divers of Hampden-Sydney in the high hurdles, Carr won the low hurdles in a school record time of :24.9 and placed second in the broad jump. His point total for the day was 11, the best of any competitor in the meet.

As the meet neared its conclusion, the Maroons gained a slender lead going into the mile relay. For the first three runners, the race was strictly between Roanoke and Bridgewater. For Roanoke, Pete Lawson began the race and ran about a :55 split. He handed off to Bennie Irvin, who was timed at around :54 for his lap. Earl Johnston then ran another :55 lap. On the handoff to begin the anchor leg, the Bridgewater runner had a 10-yard lead. John Summers, the team's number one quarter miler, took the baton from Johnston and began a steady gain. On the final turn, Summers passed his opponent and, according to spectators, yelled "I got'cha!" He pulled away down the stretch to win by 10 yards, being timed in about :51.5. The Roanoke team's time was 3:36.2, which tied the school record from 1950 held by John Turbyfill, Walt Tramposch, Frank Aldred, and Paul McCarty.

I remember . . . "I remember Bill Lund. He was a Lutheran and his folks wanted him to attend a Lutheran college. He was a pretty good thrower in high school, despite the fact that he had only one good eye. He was only with us for two years. He was a good boy. I may have helped him a little bit. He did improve while he was at Roanoke, and even won the Little Eight shot put one year. And he managed to place in most meets. He wasn't a very big boy. Not like Bob Palm, for example. I understand that when he got to Tech, he was not on their track team."

Homer Bast

I remember . . . "John Summers was a good runner. We were at the Little Six Championships in 1953, and we were coming down to the end and needed some points. The mile relay and the broad jump, I think, were the only scores not in. I was in the broad jump. So I said to John, 'You win the mile relay, and I'll win the broad jump. And we'll take care of business.' So John's team won the relay, with John making up a pretty good distance. Coming home toward the tape, John could be heard saying 'I gotcha, I gotcha.' Then I had to do my part and win the broad jump. This event was a fun experience for me, because I never knew what was going to happen next. I got off a pretty good jump for me and got second place. And we won the meet. Divers for Hampden-Sydney broke his vaulting pole. The local press said that if he hadn't broken the pole, he would have been the meet's top scorer, and Hampden-Sydney would have beaten us. Of course, that wasn't true and Homer and some of the boys took exception with those remarks. But at the same time, we all realized that this was a home-town press. John and I went out one night and painted 'Little Six Indoor and Outdoor Champions' on a prominent wall."

Boyd Carr

May 15-16, 1953
Mason-Dixon Championships at Washington, D. C.
Team Scores: 1st–Catholic University–41½
2nd–Johns Hopkins University–40
3rd–Roanoke College–29
4th–Bridgewater College–23¼
5th–Loyola University–21¾
6th–Hampden-Sydney College–13½
7th–Towson College–8¾
8th–Western Maryland College–8
9th–Randolph-Macon College–7½
10th–Gallaudet College–6
11th–Lynchburg College–5
12th–Washington College–2
13th–Mount St. Mary's College–¾

Most coaches in the Conference thought Roanoke was the favorite to win this year's Mason-Dixon Championships at Catholic University in Washington. Only Loyola, Johns Hopkins, Catholic, or Bridgewater had a chance to beat them. Bill McElroy, coach of the Loyola team, agreed. "Roanoke is definitely the favorite," he said. "One of the other four may sneak in first but it isn't likely. Roanoke figures to get from 40 to 48 points."

Catholic University had won the meet 6 times in the past 17 years and even that school's coach, Dorsey Griffith, picked Roanoke to win. "Roanoke figures to win by anywhere from 4 to 10 points on the basis of its performance to date," he said. "As for our own team, Catholic will be minus its top men in six events, all of them lost by injuries in previous meets this year. Now, we'll be lucky to get third."

After all, most thought, Roanoke would be bringing a real mixture of veterans and freshmen. Upperclassmen included Boyd Carr, dangerous in the sprints, hurdles, and even the broad jump; Don Fleming, another fine hurdler; miler Winn McConchie; distance stars Bennie Irvin and Les Noel; and versatile Earl Johnston, who could score points in the high jump, 440, hurdles, or relays. Among the freshmen, John Summers was the one who might even win either the 440 or 880.

Johns Hopkins, however, probably had the top-billed individual in Don Manger. The talented junior was defending champion in both the mile and half mile. Last year, he broke the mile record with a time of 4:21.3 and hadn't been defeated in that event since.

The only other returning title holder from 1952 was Johnny Benzing. The Loyola star high jumped more than six feet last year.

Bridgewater won the 1952 meet with 58⁷⁄₁₀ points, 26½ more than runner-up Washington. Mel Myers was Bridgewater's workhorse in that meet, but graduated at the end of the year and would be missed badly in 1953.

As usual, the Mason-Dixon Championships were scheduled to cover two days. On Friday, May 15, many athletes would have to qualify in heats for the finals the next day. According to the *Brackety-Ack*, here are Roanoke's entries in Friday's heats:

220-Yard Dash	Don Verleur and Don Moore
440-Yard Dash	John Summers
880-Yard Run	Bennie Irvin and John Summers
High Hurdles	Boyd Carr and Earl Johnston
Low Hurdles	Boyd Carr
Shot Put	Bill Lund
Discus	Bill Lund
High Jump	Earl Johnston
Broad Jump	Boyd Carr

Generally speaking at these two day meets, one could predict the top two or three teams who would be in contention for the championship by the number of men they qualify on Friday afternoon. Here are the semi-final summaries:

Shot Put	1st–Lund (Roanoke)–42'⅜"; 2nd–McComas (Loyola); 3rd–Pedric (Johns Hopkins); 4th–Amundsen (Gallaudet); 5th–McInerney (Mount St. Mary's); 6th–Duhl (Western Maryland); 7th–Pollock (Mount St. Mary's)
Broad Jump	1st–Cheatwood (Bridgewater)–22'0"; 2nd–Jackson (Hampden-Sydney); 3rd–Ware (Washington); 4th–Thompson (Johns Hopkins); 5th–Della Ratta (Catholic); 6th–Woods (Randolph-Macon)
Discus	1st–Duhl (Western Maryland)–118'10"; 2nd–Poist (Johns Hopkins); 3rd–Burke (Gallaudet); 4th–Hill (Lynchburg); 5th–Amato (Catholic); 6th–Pollock (Mount St. Mary's)
120-Yard HH (First Heat)	1st–Divers (Hampden-Sydney)–:15.9; 2nd–Carr (Roanoke)
120-Yard HH (Second Heat)	1st–Mason (Bridgewater)–:15.8; 2nd–Halvin (Johns Hopkins); 3rd–Johnston (Roanoke)
440-Yard Dash (First Heat)	1st–Favo (Catholic)–:53.5; 2nd–Heatwole (Bridgewater); 3rd–Eichelberger (Washington)
440-Yard Dash (Second Heat)	1st–G. Field (Loyola)–:53.5; 2nd–Martin (Johns (Hopkins); 3rd–R. Bix (Western Maryland)
440-Yard Dash (Third Heat)	1st–Arienti (Catholic)–:53.8; 2nd–Summers (Roanoke); 3rd–Pallace (Loyola)
100-Yard Dash (First Heat)	1st–Heck (Johns Hopkins)–:10.1; 2nd–S. Lee (Catholic); 3rd–Clark (Western Maryland)

100-Yard Dash (Second Heat)	1st–Spangler (Bridgewater)–:10.1; 2nd–Clayton (Lynchburg); 3rd–Peacock (Gallaudet)
220-Yard LH (First Heat)	1st–Thompson (Johns Hopkins)–:25.9; 2nd–S. Lee (Catholic); 3rd–Clarke (Western Maryland)
220-Yard LH (Second Heat)	1st–Carr (Roanoke)–:25.2; 2nd–Hockworth (Loyola); 3rd–Farrell (Catholic)
880-Yard Run (First Heat)	1st–Manger (Johns Hopkins)–2:01.5; 2nd–Will (Bridgewater)
880-Yard Run (Second Heat)	1st–Schmid (Catholic)–2:01.5; 2nd–Summers (Roanoke)
880-Yard Run (Third Heat)	1st–Colburn (Loyola)–2:04.3; 2nd–Irvin (Roanoke)
220-Yard Dash (First Heat)	1st–Favo (Catholic)–:22.1; 2nd–Spangler (B); 3rd–Clarke (Western Maryland)
220-Yard Dash (Second Heat)	1st–S. Lee (Catholic)–:22.8; 2nd–Heck (Johns Hopkins); 3rd–Seild (Loyola)

For Roanoke, Boyd Carr qualified in both the low and high hurdles for Saturday's finals. Bill Lund would throw the shot, Earl Johnston would run the high hurdles, John Summers would compete in both the 440 and 880, and Bennie Irvin would run in the 880 finals. One of Roanoke's problems, however, was that both Catholic and Johns Hopkins would be sending many more individuals to the finals.

By Saturday afternoon, therefore, Roanoke's hopes for a victory in the meet had faded. Boyd Carr did his best to help, winning both the high and low hurdles. His time of :15.6 in the high hurdles tied his own Roanoke College record. In the low hurdles, he first set a meet record of :25.2 in the qualifying heats, then ran :25.0 in the finals to set another meet record. His 10 points tied him for the meet's high scorer with Don Manger of Johns Hopkins and Fred Favo of Catholic.

Bill Lund came very close to winning the shot put. McComas of Loyola beat him by less than two inches to win the title and leave Lund in second place.

Top Left: The high hurdles race in the 1953 Mason-Dixon Championships.
Top Right: Les Noel and Bennie Irvin (white shirts) in the two-mile race of the 1953 Mason-Dixon Championships.
Bottom: The two-mile race in the 1953 Mason-Dixon Championships.

Freshman John Summers placed second, just three steps behind favored Al Favo of Catholic, in the 440-yard dash. Although his time was not recorded, Summers likely ran his best quarter mile of the year in that race. Summers also ran for a fifth place in the 880.

Les Noel, whom many thought might win the two-mile race, placed second to Keith Wilson of Towson and third in the mile. Teammate Bennie Irvin was fifth in the mile run.

The only other Roanoke points came from a fifth place finish in the mile relay. That race was won by Catholic in a decent 3:30.7.

Catholic University won the team title with 41½ points, narrowly beating Johns Hopkins University's 40. Roanoke followed in third place with 29 points. Bridgewater was fourth with 23¼ and Loyola was fifth.

I remember . . . "This is perhaps the high point of my athletic career at Roanoke. It was a really messy day. I was over trying to broad jump, but couldn't get my act together. And Homer was getting after me, wanting me to quit my jumping. He wanted me to get prepared for my races, and thought I might hurt myself in the broad jump. He was always after me to stop broad jumping and come on over to run the 220 or something. And I would say, 'Coach, just one more jump.' The second day of competition was pretty muddy. The night before, there was a prize fight on television. And there was a professional baseball game we could go to. So most of the team stayed and watched the fight, while the rest of us went to the ball game. I think we watched the Washington Senators play the St. Louis Browns. Sachel Paige was playing that night. We sat way out in the bleachers. Homer and I sat together, with the other athletes at another spot. Homer pulled out his pencil and paper and said, 'Let's dope out tomorrow's scoring.' I thought that was high-class stuff, doping out the meet with your coach. I said, 'Well, Coach, I am going to win the high and low hurdles. So just put down 10 points for Roanoke.' He did, and I did. That's about as good as it got."

Boyd Carr

I remember . . . "Well, I thought that Boyd Carr was a terrific athlete. And it was one of the greatest disappointments in my coaching career that he left for the University of Virginia. He not only left us flat in the various events in which he competed, but Boyd had natural speed and you could put the hurdles out there and teach him to hurdle. I don't know how much he originally knew about hurdling. But Boyd was the leading scorer in so many of the meets he was in before leaving. He was an individual who would practice hard and would do anything you wanted him to do. All I can remember is that all of a sudden Boyd Carr–a man I really depended on to be our high scorer–just leaves us. Think of all the vacancies that you had to fill. It was a terrible loss. But I understood what he wanted to do, so there were no hard feelings. To my knowledge, he was a far better hurdler when he left here than when he arrived. And I presume, although I never saw him run, he ran the hurdles when he went to Virginia. He was not the first high hurdler on their team. But he placed in a lot of the meets."

Homer Bast

I remember . . . "Doug Divers of Hampden-Sydney and I became good friends. In the 1953 Mason-Dixon meet, I won the high and low hurdles, while Doug had come in third in the pole vault, second in the high hurdles, and fifth in the lows. He and I went swimming in the gym pool. I got to see the 'other side' of my competition. How you act and how you respond are always important."

Boyd Carr

I remember . . . "I remember some of the instructions that I gave to Boyd Carr, and later to Dave Foltz, about hurdling. I would tell them that those last two hurdles were crucial to their success. I don't care how good you are, that's where you win or lose the race. If you don't pick the trailing foot up, it's going to get caught. And I would say that before every single low hurdle event. Don't forget the last two hurdles."

Homer Bast

May 23, 1953
Virginia AAU Championships at Lexington, Virginia
Team Scores: 1st–Quantico Marines–57⅓
2nd–Virginia Military Institute–56⅔
3rd–Bridgewater College–10
4th–University of Richmond–8
5th–Norfolk Sports Club–7
6th–Roanoke College–6
7th–Handley High School–3

The annual AAU meet featured such good competition that Bast decided to send only a handful of athletes to this year's meet in Lexington. In the junior division, he entered John Summers in the 440, Bill Lund in the shot put, Earl Johnston in the high hurdles, and Don Verleur in the 220.

In the senior division, Roanoke's participants were Boyd Carr (high and low hurdles) and Les Noel (mile and two miles). Carr would be running against the south's top hurdler, V. M. I.'s Johnny Mapp. Mapp held the second best time in the country for the low hurdles and was the Southern Conference champion. Noel's main competition would come from Dave Schaffer of V. P. I. and Joe porter of the University of Richmond. Shaffer was the Big Six mile- and two-mile champion and held the Southern Conference mile crown.

The Quantico Marines and V. M. I. almost made a dual meet out of the Championships. Quantico won by a mere two-thirds of a point, the closest margin in the meet's history. V. M. I.'s Johnny Mapp, as expected, was a one-man track show and the senior division's outstanding performer. He scored two firsts, two seconds, and ran the first leg on the winning mile relay team for 18½ points, high for the meet. In the low hurdles, Mapp ran :24.6, breaking the old meet record of :24.7 originally set by Wilson of the Norfolk Navy in 1942.

In the junior division, Jim Frazer's discus throw of 134'7¼" broke the old mark of 133'8½" set by Lucas of Blacksburg High School.

For Roanoke's senior entries, Boyd Carr finished fourth in the high hurdles and was just a step in back of Mapp in the low hurdles. Les Noel was third in the two-mile run.

No report was provided concerning the junior competitors except for a notice that this division had been the closest in the seven years the meet had been held. The Norfolk Sports Club had 42 points to 38 for the Richmond Sports Club and 37½ for the Downtown Athletic Club. The Portsmouth Sports Club scored 22, V. M. I. 5½, Roanoke College and the University of Richmond, 5 each, Waynesboro High School 3, and Culpepper High School 2.

I remember . . . "My daddy saw me run against the talented Johnny Mapp of Virginia Military Institute in the AAU meet. I finished fourth to Mapp's second in the high hurdles. Then Mapp ran a :24.6 to win the low hurdles, and I was just behind him in a time of about :25.0. Homer told my dad that it was extremely hard to run :25.0."

Boyd Carr

I remember . . . "It was about this time, at the end of the 1952-53 session, that I almost left Roanoke College. Virginia Tech offered me a job. I learned that there would be a track position open at Tech the following year. That was because Lou Honesty was getting ready to leave Tech and go to the University of Virginia. I knew Buddy Snead of Snead Lumber Company in Salem. Both he and his brother, George, were Tech graduates and had some influence with the school. I asked if there was any chance that I could be interviewed for the job. Buddy said, 'Certainly. I will call Tech's Athletic Director tomorrow.' So I went up to Blacksburg and they interviewed me. I wanted to do track and cross country, but I didn't want to be just a coach. I was a historian. I had done all of my work except for the oral exam for my Ph.D. in history. I wanted to be known primarily as a teacher and not just as a coach. Tech went out of their way to try to hire me. They gave me two sections of history to teach, along with the track and cross country jobs. This was a full-time position at more pay than I was getting at Roanoke. And there was the prestige of being at a large school. So I was faced with a real problem. Looking back on the situation, I don't think Mary Jane wanted to go up to Blacksburg. That was a cow college, as far as she was concerned. While she was in college, she had gone to some of the Tech dances. And she just didn't warm up to Tech. She loved Salem. She fit in with all of the people in the town and she was part of close-knit groups. She had her gardening club, her book club, and all of that sort of stuff. And she had given birth to both children while in Salem, Her sister was nearby, and her mother was fairly close, in Staunton. I finally asked Mary Jane, 'Do you want to go or don't you?' She said the decision was up to me. So I talked to Perry Kendig. He didn't advise me one way or another. And I wasn't getting any advice or help from Roanoke College. I began to think that they might want me gone. I didn't know what my status was at the time. So I ended up going to Clarence Caldwell's office. I said, 'You've got to help me out here.' So I told him the story. He said, 'There is one thing that we can do. We can match Tech's salary. The rest is up to you.' I told him thanks, but asked him if he had any specific advice for me. He didn't. It would be my decision and mine only. So I decided right then and there that I would stay at Roanoke until I retired. So I thanked Buddy Snead for everything he had done, thanked the Tech Athletic Director and their Chairman of the History Department for everything, and told Mary Jane that we would be staying in Salem."

Homer Bast

Chapter Nine

THE 1953-54 SEASONS

Cross Country

Coach Bast found himself with only a few lettermen as he met the cross country team for the first time. Veterans included Les Noel, of Buena Vista, Virginia, who was making a name for himself as an excellent distance runner, and senior Bennie Irvin of Roanoke. Irvin, not quite as good a runner as Noel, nevertheless brought the cross-country and track teams a lot of points during the past year. And there was sophomore John Summers of Kearny, New Jersey. Summers' was on the team last year, but he never thought of himself as a cross country runner. He ran because Coach Bast told him that his work to build stamina would be useful during track season. His passions were the 440-yard dash and the 880-yard run. During the spring season of 1952-53, he had lowered the school 440 record several times. Additions to the team included Phil Shaw, Bruce Fariss, Jack Kaylor, Dick Rader, David Brumbaugh, Jack Herring, David Moore, and Lenny Eppard. Of this group, Shaw and Fariss would become the most well-known and accomplished runners during the next few years.

I remember . . . "When I first got to the college and began to think about what sports I wanted to play, I went on down to the soccer field one day to practice with the team. We kicked the ball around some, and then we began some drills to bounce the ball off our heads. And that hurt. Coach Fox would look at me and say, 'Well, you're not hitting it right.' I'd say that it seemed right to me. But if I kept on doing that, I would end up with brain damage. I can find something better to do. With that, I went to Homer Bast and said that I wanted to be one of his cross country guys."

Bruce Fariss

I remember . . . "Bruce Fariss had never run cross country or track before he came to

Roanoke. I must say that he was the most awkward-looking runner that you had ever seen in your life. At least in his freshman year. I told him that he probably wouldn't do very much that first year. I let him know that all I wanted him to do was to come on out there and run. I guaranteed him that by his senior year, he would be scoring enough points to get his letter. And that was fine by Bruce. He was a plugger and stuck in there and held out to the bitter end. You could count on him for points along the way. Like many others on the team, he wasn't a big fellow at all."

Homer Bast

I remember . . . "I remember Bennie Irvin. He was the team's comedian. He worked for Valley Cadillac all during his years of school. He would leave school and go to work selling Oldsmobiles and Cadillacs."

Les Noel

October 9, 1953
Lynchburg College at Salem, Virginia
Team Scores: Lynchburg–25
Roanoke–30

Going into the first meet, on October 9, 1953, it seemed like every man on Roanoke's small squad was ailing in one form or another. For example, Bennie Irvin was hampered by a bad cold. John Summers had a back problem and a blistered foot. Bruce Fariss had an over-stretched tendon in his heel.

Lynchburg would not be Coach Bast's choice for opening the season. With his own team crippled by colds and injuries, Bast saw Lynchburg as having potentially one of the strongest teams in the state as well as in the Mason-Dixon Conference. Most coaches said that Lynchburg and V. M. I. were the teams to beat in Virginia, while Johns Hopkins was favored to win the Mason-Dixon meet.

The meet between Roanoke and Lynchburg began at 4:00 p.m. Les Noel, Captain of the Maroons team and the defending Little Six champion, took the lead early.

Bast had re-routed the course, leaving a hilly run of some 3.0 miles. He would change the course at least once more before the end of his coaching career at Roanoke.

Noel coasted across the finish line, pretty much by himself, in a time of 15:28.5. Almost a minute behind were Lynchburg's Carl Gillespie and Preston Wilson, crossing together in 16:21.

The other Roanoke runners just couldn't pack it tight enough to bring a win. Bennie

Irvin finished in fourth place, with 16:50; Richard Rader was sixth in 17:31; David Moore was ninth, with 17:57; Phil Shaw came in tenth with a time of 18:12; Jack Kaylor crossed in the twelfth spot, with a time of 18:38; and Jack Herring was 16th and last on a time of 19:17.

Lynchburg won the meet, but only by five points. The score was 25 to 30. Without the injuries, and with Bruce Fariss and John Summers running, perhaps Roanoke would have won. At any rate, Bast's team was now 0-1 and facing a team from nearby Ferrum Junior college.

On October 10, 1953, the day after the Lynchburg meet. Bast conducted the campus' annual intramural meet. The meet was run on the same 1.5-mile course that many athletes before them had used. Three of the previous intramural cross country winners were still in college. They included John Summers, from 1952; Les Noel, 1951; and Benny Irvin, 1950. Besides these three, other intramural winners who had gone on to outstanding careers with Bast's cross country teams, included Richard Fraley, White Rhyne, and Bruce Davenport.

The current course record of 9:10 was set by Les Noel in 1951. In this year's race, however, Richard Rader and Phil Shaw finished together in a new record time of 9:04. Running third was Jack Kaylor. In team competition, the dormitory team was first, Sigma Chi second, and Kappa Alpha third.

October 13, 1953
Ferrum Junior College at Salem, Virginia
Team Scores: Roanoke–15
Ferrum–55

The race with Ferrum wasn't very competitive. All eight of the Roanoke men finished before the first runner from Ferrum.

Les Noel set a new course record of 15:22 in placing first. The threesome of Bennie Irvin, Phil Shaw, and Bruce Fariss finished second in 17:10; Dave Moore was fifth, Richard Rader sixth, and Jack Kaylor and Dave Brumbaugh tied for seventh place. Ed Mawyer of Ferrum was that school's top runner, finishing in ninth place with a time of 19:01.

The team score was heavily in favor of Roanoke, 15-55.

I remember . . . "I remember this race, the first one I ran at Roanoke. Bennie Irvin was a senior and he picked me up along the way and paced me for a good part of the course. We finished together, along with Phil Shaw. After that, Bennie and I paced each other in a lot of our meets, although sometimes we didn't finish together. I always thought that Bennie, the 'old guy' on the team, was taking care of us."

Bruce Fariss

October 17, 1953
University of Virginia and Virginia Military Institute at Charlottesville, Virginia
Team Scores: Virginia Military Institute–28
Roanoke–37
University of Virginia–77

Sophomore John Summers, freshman Jack Herring, and freshman Bruce Fariss were still on the injury list as the Maroons traveled to Charlottesville to run a triangular meet against the University of Virginia and Virginia Military Institute. The event would begin at 11:00 a.m. and was part of the University's home coming festivities.

Virginia wasn't expected to offer much competition; however, V. M. I. had a good team. They were defending Big Six champions and already had defeated Richmond 15-55 and William and Mary 17-33. The star of the seasoned and veteran-led V. M. I. squad was Ben Angle, nationally-known half-miler, who had beaten Les Noel last January when he ran a 4:40 mile indoors.

In this race, however, Les was by far the better runner. He ran the 3.7 miles in a course record time of 18:59, a full one minute in front of Angle. After Jerry Tonkin of V. M. I. placed third, two more Roanoke men scored. Bennie Irvin was fourth and Bruce Fariss fifth. Unfortunately, V. M. I. took six out of the next seven places to win the meet. The final score was V. M. I., 28; Roanoke College, 37; and the University of Virginia, 77.

After Noel, Irvin, and Fariss, Roanoke runners and their places were: John Summers and Phil Shaw, 13th; David Moore, 15th; and David Brumbaugh, 17th.

October 24, 1953
Virginia AAU Championships at Richmond, Virginia
Team Scores: 1st–Quantico Marines–24
2nd–Virginia Military Institute–70
3rd–Roanoke College–115
4th–Bridgewater College–128
5th–University of Virginia–168
6th–University of Richmond–17

The always-strong Quantico Marines ran to an easy victory in the Virginia AAU

Championships held on the University of Richmond's 4.2 mile course. Of the winners, John Slayton of Ohio was the first of the 60 contenders to finish the course. His time of 21:21 was eight seconds off the meet record, but far behind the course record of 20:43.

Although the University of Richmond team was the defending champion, the Marines finished five men among the first nine, an effort giving them 24 points. V. M. I. was second with 70, with Roanoke College placing third on 115 points.

The race was a true duel between Stayton and Roanoke's team Captain, Les Noel. Running with the Marine through much of the race, Noel took the lead in the stretch and seemed to have the race won. But Stayton finally passed him in the last 20 yards. Another Quantico runner, Art Garcia, matched strides with Stayton and Noel for almost four miles; however, he faltered in the final quarter mile and finished third.

John O'Connor of the Marines' squad was fourth, while Bill Jordon, Captain of the 1952 University of Richmond team and now a graduate student at U. N. C., was fifth. Jordan, running ahead of durable Alvin Smith of Roanoke City, a former star at Roanoke College, finished sixth in the race. The *Brackety-Ack* noted, "This shows that an old man with 18 years of running experience can still beat the young 'uns."

Other Maroons who placed in the competition included Bruce Fariss (21st), Phil Shaw (25th), Bennie Irvin (26th), John Summers (41st), and David Moore (46th).

October 30, 1953
Hampden-Sydney College at Salem, Virginia
Team Scores: Roanoke–16
Hampden-Sydney–46

The Hampden-Sydney meet in Salem on October 30 wouldn't offer the Maroons much competition. It was an easy decision, therefore, to allow Les Noel some rest time and run only the other members of the team.

As expected, the Maroon team took a nice, pleasurable stroll around the 3.1-mile course to take six of the top seven places, and seven of the top nine to finish with an almost perfect score of 16 to 46. Bennie Irvin and Bruce Fariss finished together with a winning time of 16:31 and some 30 seconds later the duo of John Summers and Phil Shaw did the same for third place. The Tigers' Dave Brown took the fifth spot. Finishing the romp for Roanoke were Dave Moore, 6th; Richard Rader, 7th; and Lenny Eppard, 9th.

November 7, 1954
Washington and Lee University at Salem, Virginia
Team Scores: Roanoke–25
Washington and Lee–30

Les Noel had broken the course record in each of his two meets at Roanoke. On October 9, in the Lynchburg College meet, he had set the first record by finishing in a time of 15:28.5. He followed that record with another, running 15:22.0, in the Ferrum Junior College meet four days later. But today, November 7, no one thought those marks would be in jeopardy. During the morning hours, the thermometer read 32°F. A slight breeze made the day seem even colder.

Despite the miserable conditions, Noel and other members of the team ran well. Noel won the race in 15:29, just seven seconds off his course record. Bennie Irvin and Bruce Fariss crossed the line together for third place, while Phil Shaw finished 7th, John Summers 10th, Lenny Eppard 11th, Richard Rader 12th, and David Moore 13th.

The team scores were a bit closer than most people thought they would be. Roanoke hung on to take a 25 to 30 victory.

November 13, 1953
Little Six Championships at Bridgewater, Virginia
Team Scores: 1st–Roanoke College–37
2nd–Bridgewater College–38
3rd–Lynchburg College–50
4th–Randolph-Macon College–126

Four schools entered teams in this year's Little Six Meet–Bridgewater, Lynchburg, Randolph-Macon, and Roanoke. Hampden-Sydney and Emory and Henry brought no runners. But it was Bridgewater who would provide the biggest obstacle to a team win for Roanoke. Lynchburg might play a role since they beat Roanoke in an early-season meet; however, Roanoke had improved greatly throughout the year.

All of the coaches knew of Les Noel. He had become one of the best runners in the mid-Atlantic region of the country. Most of the coaches conceded him the individual title. But for Homer Bast, Noel wasn't at all the problem. He knew that he had three other runners–Bennie Irvin, Bruce Fariss, and Phil Shaw–who could make good showings in the meet. But could they find a fifth runner who would pull them through? Could it be John Summers, Dick Rader, or perhaps Lenny Eppard? One of them had to stay close to the front runners for Roanoke to take home a team title.

Of course, if you were one of those persons who just went with your feelings, it was Roanoke's time to win again. When the meet was first held in 1947, the Maroons won three straight titles. Then along came Bridgewater to grab first places in 1950, 1951, and 1952. "Perhaps it's Roanoke turn to begin winning again," Bast joked with a *Brackety-Ack* columnist a couple of days before the big Friday race.

The gun sounded and the top ten runners quickly separated themselves from the pack.

Les Noel, Bruce Fariss, and Bennie Irvin then took charge. Coach Bast moved to various spots, trying to see the outer fringes of the race where the title was being decided. As the large group of runners began the final trek toward the finish line, there at the front were Noel, followed in about 15 seconds by Irvin and Fariss. Noel broke the tape in a new course record of 17:52.8. Running extremely well–sensing the importance of their finish positions–Fariss and Irvin crossed the line together to take second and third places.

Bast felt a bit better, with his team having taken first, second, and third in the meet. But where were the other two runners he needed for the win? By this time, he was positioned near the finish line, his stop watch in hand, and recording times and places. Suddenly, he realized what was happening. Fourth place went to Lynchburg. Then came two Bridgewater men, another from Lynchburg, and three more from Bridgewater. Bridgewater had brought in their top five runners within the top ten places. His spirits rose slightly as Phil Shaw came down the stretch and finished in 12th place. Then there was a long line of Lynchburg and Bridgewater runners. Suddenly, there he was. Richard Rader sprinted past Frank Wood of Randolph-Macon to place 19th in the meet. It was Richard Rader, an unlikely hero, who handed his coach and teammates the team trophy. Final scores were Roanoke, 37; Bridgewater, 38; Lynchburg, 50; and Randolph-Macon, 126. Incidentally, John Summers was 22nd in the race and Lenny Eppard 24th.

November 21, 1953
Mason-Dixon Championships at Washington, D. C.
Team Scores: 1st–Johns Hopkins University–81
2nd–Bridgewater College–83
3rd–Roanoke College–86
4th–Washington College–88
5th–Towson State College–115
6th–Gallaudet College–128
7th–Catholic University–155
8th–Lynchburg College–204
9th–Loyola College–239
10th–Randolph-Macon College–266

Coach Bast was an optimist to his runners, but a realist to himself. Here he was, going into the season's toughest competition with three of the Conference's best runners on his own team. In fact, one of them, Les Noel, was a favorite to take individual honors in the race. The Maroons had won the Little Six meet, but barely. He needed one or two more good efforts to ensure a victory here in what always seemed to be the toughest meet of the year.

Gallaudet College hosted the Championships on November 21 in Washington. Don Manger of Johns Hopkins, who had won the individual title in 1951 and 1952, moved to the front in the latter part of the race to win with a time of 15:55.2. About nine seconds behind Manger came Roanoke's Les Noel and Robin DeLaBarre of Johns Hopkins. Both sprinted toward the finish line. At the last second, DeLaBarre lunged forward and beat Noel by a tenth of a second for second place. Bennie Irvin ran his usual good race to finish fifth in 16:15 and Bruce Fariss took the 11th spot. For Roanoke, Phil Shaw was 27th, Richard Rader was 40th, and Lenny Eppart was 59th.

The team championship went to Johns Hopkins, with a total score of 81. Bridgewater, whose first runner could take only 14th place, nevertheless grouped 7 runners between the 14th and 21st places to take second with 83 points. Roanoke was third with 85 and Washington College took fourth with 88. It was the closest finish by teams in the history of the meet. Only 7 points separated the first from the fourth squad.

From Roanoke's perspective, it was a case of "so close, yet so far away." One more outstanding runner and the team would be back on top. So Coach Bast continued to write his five letters a day. He talked to high school coaches, visited high school and prep meets when he could, and talked to a lot of young men about continuing their education at Roanoke College. And it all worked. Paralleling the success of his spring track teams, whose amazing streak of wins would continue throughout the next few seasons, his cross country teams by 1954 became unbeatable in the state and in the Mason-Dixon Conference. A cross country team led by Coach Bast would not lose the Mason-Dixon Championships trophy until 1960.

Indoor Track

In January of 1954, just after the Christmas break, a group of 21 athletes met Coach Bast in the gymnasium to kick off practices for the indoor season. Spirits were high, because it was apparent that this year would bring the most active indoor program in Roanoke College track history. The defending Little Six champions were scheduled to compete almost on successive Saturdays beginning January 23rd at the Evening Star Games in Washington, the V. M. I. Relays, the Little Seven Championships, the first annual Mason-Dixon Conference Indoor Championships, and the 175th Regiment Armory Games in Baltimore.

Although Dave Foltz and Don Moore were playing basketball during this indoor season, Coach Bast's team had a lot of veterans and several promising newcomers. John Summers, sophomore from Kearny, New Jersey, was back to run the 440 and 880 for the Maroons. He was recognized as the finest quarter miler in the Conference.

A bright spot for the winter might be the mile relay team, which could be the best in the College's history. Besides Summers, the relay team could be pulled from Richard Rader, local boy from Troutville; Don Verleur, 1953 letter winner from Hawthorne, New Jersey; Jim Wallwork, a good-looking freshman runner from Tenafly, New Jersey; Captain Bennie Irvin, the team's number two distance runner and a senior; and Earl Johnston, a junior from Salem. Johnston had scored points in several events, but likely for this year's indoor and outdoor seasons, he would concentrate on the high and low hurdles. Verleur was not able to work out daily in January or February, but should be ready by the outdoor season.

Then, of course, there was Les Noel, junior from Buena Vista, Virginia. He was one of the finest distance men in the area. He would join two freshmen–Phil Shaw of East Irvington, New York, and Bruce Fariss of Alisonia, Virginia–to give Roanoke perhaps the best combination of distance men in the Conference.

Bill Lund, who had thrown very well last spring and was the indoor and outdoor Little Six shot put champion, gave the team sure points in almost every meet. Other points would come from freshmen Jim Wallwork, from Tenafly, New Jersey, Dick Seed of Philadelphia, and Allen Ide, of Arlington, Virginia. All three would be major contributors by the outdoor season and especially during the remainder of their college careers.

Boosting the fortunes of Roanoke's field events was Jay Jackson, a Little Six and Mason-Dixon broad jump champion, who had just transferred as a third-year student from Hampden-Sydney College. A native of Roanoke, Jay was ineligible for Little Six or Mason-Dixon competition this year, but in other meets his certain points in the high jump and broad jump would help immensely.

Others who trained for the indoor season were Chris Rittman, an excellent middle-distance and distance man who also could be used on the mile relay team; John Varsa, who would score consistently in the pole vault outdoors; Wylie Barrow of Chevy Chase, Maryland, in the shot put and discus; Jim Cabler; Ray Lucas; Gene Grabowski; Buck Woolwine; Don Dewitt; David McCredy; and Tom Butts.

January 23, 1954
Evening Star Games at Washington, D. C.
Mason-Dixon Sprint Medley Relay:

Over 5,000 fans saw a circus of track activities in a meet that brought together the best athletes from across the world. We do not know from the information printed in the *Evening Star* whether Roanoke entered a team in the Mason-Dixon One-Mile Sprint Medley Relay. The *Brackety-Ack* also failed to report on the meet. In the Sprint Medley Relay, these teams placed in the top three:

1st–Catholic University (Flynn, Powderly, Libert, and Favo)–3:48.1;
2nd–Bridgewater College; 3rd–Towson State Teacher's College

If Roanoke athletes were present, they were able to watch some outstanding performers. Don Laz, the noted pole vaulter, was beaten at 14'8" by Jerry Welborn of Ohio State. In the two-mile race, Horace Ashenfelter ran the first mile of his race in 4:31.5. After falling back in the pack, he took command again with two laps to go. Ashenfelter ran 9:02.9, a new meet record. Michael Agostini, unattached, set a new meet record by running the 100-yard dash in :09.6. And in the mile run, Leonard Truex, unattached, won the mile in 4:13.4 for another new meet record.

January 30, 1954
Virginia Military Institute Winter Relays at Lexington, Virginia
Team Scores: None

The Winter Relays were held on January 30, 1954. The meet always featured an eclectic group of small and large schools, from Roanoke and Bridgewater to the University of Virginia and Duke University.

Coach Bast entered athletes in several events. Newspapers such as the *Roanoke Times* and the *Brackety-Ack* failed to report on the meet results; therefore, all we do know today is that Roanoke relay teams placed in three events. First, the foursome of Jim Wallwork, Earl Johnston, Richard Rader, and John Summers placed fourth in the 880-yard relay (4 X 220 yards). First place in that event went to the University of Maryland in a time of 1:35.2. Second was V. M. I., while third was V. P. I. Roanoke's time was unlisted.

In the four-mile relay, Roanoke's team finished in second place behind the University of Maryland. Maryland's time was 19:05.2. We do not know a time for Roanoke, or the names of Maroon participants.

Finally, Roanoke's team of John Summers, Jim Rittman, Bennie Irvin, and Les Noel won the Mason-Dixon Conference Distance Medley Relay in a time of 11:23.2. Catholic University was second, Towson State third, and Bridgewater College fourth.

February 13, 1954
Little Seven Championships at Lexington, Virginia
Team Scores: 1st–Roanoke College–63
2nd–Bridgewater College–32
3rd–Lynchburg College–13
4th–Randolph-Macon College–12
5th–Hampden-Sydney College–10

The V. M. I. field house was a busy place this weekend. On February 12, 1954, the facility was the venue for the Group I high school championships, with athletes attending from throughout the state. On the next day, Saturday, the field house was the host to the largest track and field indoor meet in the state's history. The Saturday events featured two meets–the Big Six and Little Seven Championships–running simultaneously. Joining these athletes were freshmen of the Big Six schools.

V. M. I. was the favorite to capture team honors in the Big Six meet, where 109 men were entered in the varsity competition. In the Little Seven meet, five schools were competing with a total of 64 entrants. Roanoke was the coaches' favorite to take the trophy in their division; however, Bridgewater was a perennial Little Seven power and could dethrone the Maroons.

For Roanoke, Bill Lund would certainly place in the shot put, but only a miracle would allow him to repeat as the winner in that event. Hampden-Sydney was bringing a rising new star, Jim Frazer, who was the state's leading interscholastic shot putter in 1953.

Roanoke also would have difficulty in winning either hurdle event, even though the school had entered Earl Johnston. Johnston, Bill Miller of Bridgewater, and Bill Trapnell of Hampden-Sydney were the three hurdlers to watch. Miller bettered the Little Seven record in the high hurdles in a dual meet with V. M. I. a few weeks before, and many considered him the frontrunner.

In the mile relay, in addition, the Maroons would enter Jim Wallwork, Chris Rittman, Richard Rader and John Summers, but they might have serious competition from Lynchburg and Bridgewater. Roanoke would be trying to better the current 3:47.9 record.

It was apparent from the first event that Roanoke now had the best indoor team in the Little Seven. In a show of depth, the team captured its second consecutive Little Seven indoor track and field meet. The team scores were Roanoke, 63; Bridgewater, 32; Lynchburg, 13; Randolph-Macon, 12; and Hampden-Sydney, 10.

Les Noel picked up 10 points with wins in the mile and two-mile runs. After running a 4:43.9 mile, Les set a new Little Seven and Roanoke College indoor two mile mark with an excellent 10:22.0 effort. Noel shared high point honors for the meet with Jack Nuttycombe of Randolph-Macon, who was first in the 60-yard dash and broad jump.

Earl Johnston of Roanoke was the second highest scorer with 9 points. He won the 70-yard low hurdles in :08.4, then took a second in the high hurdles, and tied for third in the high jump.

John Summers tied his 1953 quarter-mile record for the meet by running :54.4. That time also tied his Roanoke College indoor record. Summers went on to gain a third in the 880 and to anchor the mile relay team's Little Seven and Roanoke College indoor records. His teammates for the mile relay were Richard Rader, Jim Wallwork, and Chris Rittman.

In the high jump, freshman Richard Seed showed his talents by jumping 5'9" to set a new Roanoke College record. The old mark was 5'6", set by Dave Foltz in 1953.

Jay Jackson, the ineligible transfer student from Hampden-Sydney, unofficially jumped 5'10" in the high jump and broad jumped almost 21'0". Jim Wallwork placed in every event in which he participated to pick up 6¼ points. He placed third in the high hurdles, third in the low hurdles, and finished the evening with a good second leg on the mile relay team.

Phil Shaw and Bruce Fariss each showed improvements. Fariss placed third in the mile and second in the two-mile, while Shaw took a third place in the two-mile.

Probably the most thrilling event of the night was the 880-yard run. Captain Bennie Irvin and Bridgewater's Paige Will matched strides for the last 220 yards of the race. As they came out of the tunnel and onto the short straightaway, Irvin stumbled and broke his stride. The stumble was just enough to allow Will to win by a couple of inches. The judges gave each of the runners the identical time of 2:05.1. With his narrow victory, Will was designated the Little Seven indoor record holder.

In the broad jump, Jim Cabler was Roanoke's only entry; however, he placed fourth in his first varsity meet. John Varsa participated in the pole vault for the Maroons, but failed to place.

V. M. I. won the Big Six meet with 73 points, winning 7 of 13 events. Virginia Tech was second with 29, Virginia had 18½, Richmond 7, William and Mary 4½, and Washington and Lee 0.

V. M. I.'s highly-touted athlete, Johnny Mapp, smashed one record, tied two others, and collected a personal total of 18 points. Altogether, five records were broken and three were tied in the Big Six meet, something that had veteran track observers shaking their heads.

February 19, 1954
Mason-Dixon Championships at Lexington, Virginia
Team Scores: 1st–Roanoke College–52½
2nd–Catholic University–27½2
3rd–Bridgewater College–21½
4th–Hampden-Sydney College–20½
5th–Johns Hopkins University–10

There seemed little doubt by now that the Roanoke team was the best in the Little Seven and Mason-Dixon Conferences. In the Mason-Dixon meet on February 19, in fact, the Maroons almost doubled the score on second-place Catholic University. The scores were Roanoke, 52½; Catholic, 27½; Bridgewater, 21½; Hampden-Sydney, 20½; and Johns Hopkins, 10. The Maroons won 6 of the 12 first places and scored points in every event except the pole vault and broad jump.

Earl Johnson had one of his best days as a track man at Roanoke. He won both the high and low hurdles, breaking the Roanoke College record in the lows, tied for second in the high jump, and ran on the second place mile relay team. His total for the night was 13¼ points.

The other double winner for Roanoke was Les Noel. He jogged through a fairly slow mile win, and then picked it up a bit to win the two-mile in 10:29.4.

John Summers almost upset the highly-favored Fred Favo in the 440. Favo tied the field house record with a winning time of :52.8, but Summers was only a couple of steps behind, recording his own Roanoke College indoor track record of :53.6.

Dick Seed, the remarkable freshman, scored an unusual first in the high jump. He cleared the bar at 5'10" despite the fact that his height was only 5'7".

Bennie Irvin got his revenge in the 880. Will Paige of Bridgewater had beaten him by inches in the Little Seven race, but this time Irvin won in a time of 2:07.4. Irvin also placed second in the mile run.

Jim Wallwork, one of Coach Bast's talented freshmen, ran in four events and placed in all four. He was fourth in the 60-yard dash, fourth in the 440-yard dash, fourth in the low hurdles, and ran on the second place mile relay team.

Bill Lund improved considerably in the shot put according to one report. Unfortunately for Lund, the meet was the Conference debut of winning thrower Jim Frazer of Hampden-Sydney. In the next three years, Frazer would go on to put the shot over 50'.

Several other Maroons contributed to the scoring. Chris Rittman placed third in the mile run and fourth in the two-mile. Phil Shaw was third in the two-mile run.

John Varsa suffered a spike wound while pole vaulting, removing him from further competition. Wiley Barrow threw the shot, but failed to place.

March 5, 1954
Fifth Regiment Armory Games at Baltimore, Maryland
Team Scores: None

Roanoke's final meet of the indoor season came in Baltimore on March 5, 1954, at the Fifth Regiment Armory Games. The meet was one of the indoor showcases for athletes, attracting world-class competitors such as Horace Ashenfelter and Mike Agostini. During his career, Ashenfelter, captured 17 national titles in events as varied as the two-mile run and cross-country races. In the 1952 Olympics, he had thrilled the free world by his unexpected victory over Vladimir Kazantsev in the Olympic steeplechase, setting a world-record mark. Because Ashenfelter was an FBI agent at the time, his win was played up in the press as the Cold War clash won by America. Ashenfelter won the Sullivan Award as the outstanding amateur athlete of 1952.

Then there were athletes like Mike Agostino, who ran a :06.1 this night to equal the world record in the 60-yard dash. Later in 1954, at the fifth British Empire Games, Agostini (from Trinidad, but a student at Villanova in Pennsylvania) whipped Australia's Hector Hogan (co-world-record holder in the 100-yard dash, tying the Games record with a :09.6 sprint.

Coach Bast entered teams in two relay events. In the Mason-Dixon Sprint Relay, the team of John Summers, Earl Johnston, Jim Wallwork, and Bennie Irvin beat the teams from Towson State Teachers College and Johns Hopkins in a new meet record time of 3:44.2. That time also set a new Roanoke College indoor record.

Then Summers and Irvin teamed with Les Noel and Chris Rittman to run the two-mile relay. Baltimore Olympics Club won the race in 8:08.5, but Roanoke was second, just a half of a second behind. The University of Maryland team finished in third place.

I remember . . . "In the Fifth Regiment Relays that year, we ran the two-mile relay. It was a flat floor to run on. I think there were 12 or 13 laps to the mile. We put together a pretty good two-mile team. But up there, we were running against very good competition. Les Noel anchored the team. I might have run John Summers as the anchor man, but John objected mentally to running anything past the quarter. He was a quarter miler in his own mind. He wasn't fast enough to run the 220. And not enough stamina to run the half mile. He was a well-developed boy when he came down here, with good muscles."

Homer Bast

Outdoor Track

The consecutive winning streak for the outdoor team was now at five. Very early in the spring of 1953, Roanoke had been beaten by Davidson while on a trip during their spring break. From that point forward, the team had won their next five dual meets. And it looked as if they might be undefeated during the 1954 season. The *Brackety-Ack* was happy (as reflected by all of the complimentary articles about the team and team members), the athletes were optimistic, and even their coach managed a few extra smiles. But what was there not to be happy about? All of those empty spots in the team roster were filling nicely. Just look at the list of athletes Coach Bast would have on the team this year. All of his indoor team would be competing outdoors. Dave Foltz, a possible winner in several events, would be available after basketball season, along with the talented Don Moore.

The 1954 track team.
First Row (L to R): Bennie Irvin (Captain) and Homer Bast (Head Coach).
Second Row (L to R): Earl Johnston, Chris Rittman, Bill Lund, Richard Rader, Jay Jackson, and J. Cabler.
Third Row (L to R): John Varsa, Jim Wallwork, John Summers, Don Moore, Lessely Noel, and Phil Shaw.

The total list showed the following possible entrants:

Dashes	Don Moore, Dave Foltz, and Richard Rader
440	John Summers, Don Moore, Richard Rader, Jim Wallwork, Al Ide, and Chris Rittman
880	John Summers, Bennie Irvin, Les Noel, and Chris Rittman
Mile	Bennie Irvin, Phil Shaw, and Les Noel
Two Miles	Bennie Irvin, Phil Shaw, and Les Noel

Hurdles	Earl Johnston, Russell Smiley, Dave Foltz, and Jim Wallwork
Shot Put	Bill Lund, Wylie Barrow, and Dave Foltz
Discus	Bill Lund, Dave Foltz, and Wylie Barrow
Broad Jump	Don Moore, Jim Cabler, Jay Jackson (ineligible except for non-conference meets)
High Jump	Dick Seed, Dave Foltz, Earl Johnston, Jay Jackson, and Morris Smiley, Jr.
Pole Vault	John Varsa and David Moore

Practice began officially on March 15. Within days, the annual onslaught of physical ailments could be seen throughout the squad. John Summers, Don Moore, and Jim Wallwork were nursing leg injuries. Les Noel was just regaining his form after a severe cold had limited his practices.

At the same time, Chris Rittman, the promising freshman, and senior Bennie Irvin both looked like they would be in good shape for the season opener on the third of April.

April 3, 1954
Elon College at Salem, Virginia
Team Scores: Roanoke–102½
Elon–24½

It was the first Saturday in April of 1954. The weather was cool but pleasant. And the Elon College track team was in Salem for a meet with Roanoke.

The difference between the teams was significant. Roanoke was filling in the weak spots, building to become a dominant team. Elon had only a few star athletes on its entire team.

In front of a sizeable home crowd, Roanoke won 14 of the 15 events on the day's card. Elon did manage a win in the pole vault, but the Maroons had not had a good vaulter since the days of Ray DeCosta, whose jumps of 13' to 13'6" gave him an almost legendary status throughout the state.

Bill Lund, Roanoke's weight man, won the shot, discus, and javelin events. In the javelin, his throw measured 165'2", a new Alumni Field and Roanoke College record.

Another Alumni Field and Roanoke College record was set by the very talented Jay Jackson. He broad jumped 21'4¾" to win that event. Until this year, Jackson had been one of the field event stars on Hampden-Sydney's track teams; however, Jackson transferred to Roanoke at the beginning of the 1953-54 session. He was ineligible to compete against either Little Seven or Mason-Dixon teams this year, but could participate in meets like this one, against non-conference schools.

Jackson and Roanoke's Dick Seed tied for a win in the high jump, clearing 5'8". The remainder of the scoring in the field events went to Richard Rader, third in the shot; big Dave Foltz, second in the discus and third in the high jump; Wylie Barrow, second in the javelin; Don Moore, second in the broad jump; and John Varsa, second in the pole vault.

In the running events, Don Moore won the 100-yard dash in an excellent time of :10.1. The Alumni Field and Roanoke College records were :10.0. Richard Rader and Jim Wallwork were close behind in the second and third spots, respectively. Moore also won the 220-yard dash in :23.6, with Rader taking third.

Bennie Irvin and Chris Rittman tied for a win in the 880-yard run. With little effort, they had a time of 2:13.5. And John Summers, even with his leg problems, won the 440-yard dash with an easy :53.6, followed across the line by Irvin.

Chris Rittman easily won the mile run. Phil Shaw was second. In the other distance race, the two-mile run, Les Noel was the only entrant, jogging the eight laps in 10:54.7.

The mile relay team showed signs of getting a school record before the end of the season. Richard Rader, Jim Wallwork, Chris Rittman, and John Summers posted an excellent early-season time of 3:38.8.

In the high hurdles, Earl Johnston won with a time of :16.2. He then finished second in the low hurdles. But the story of Dave Foltz and the hurdles is an interesting one. Although he was a sophomore at Roanoke, Dave had never run the hurdles until this first meet with Elon, when he won the low hurdles and finished third in the highs. A superior basketball player on the Roanoke team, Coach Bast had convinced him in the spring of 1953 to "come on out for track and try a few of the events." This spring, Bast was convinced that the hurdles could be one of Foltz's best events.

Bast had always enjoyed coaching the hurdles. When he was a student at Mercersburg Academy, his coach there had tried to make a hurdler of him. "But they weren't very successful," said Bast recently. "I just feared the hurdles." Figuring that Foltz and the hurdlers following him would have the same fears, Bast devised a training tactic to get rid of the fear of hitting a hurdle and falling. He set up two hurdles, side by side, with about 30" of space between them. He had Harry Hodges, the Maintenance Director, make him some very thin strips of wood that were each about 36" in length. He taped these strips between the two hurdles and had Foltz train by going across the strip. "If he hit the strip, he would just break the wood," said Bast. "But he wouldn't hit his knee or fall or get cinder burns. And it worked. As Dave became more at ease in clearing the hurdles, he would begin to ask questions about his form. For example, he wanted to know whether he should go over the hurdle with one hand first, or use two hands. He had good natural ability, and I certainly didn't want to confuse him. So when he would ask how I wanted him to run the hurdles, I'd simply say 'as fast as you can.' " Bast would answer other questions the same way. If Foltz would ask how to run the low hurdles, Bast again would say, "Run them as fast as you can. Don't think about your form."

Whatever Bast did for Foltz, it must have worked. By the end of the 1954 season, he was a good hurdler. By the end of his senior year, he would set numerous records in both the high and low hurdles and dominate the events in the Little Seven and Mason-Dixon Conferences.

I remember . . . "I remember the first race that Dave Foltz ever ran. He went over those hurdles so smoothly that it looked like he had been doing it for years. He had a two-hand approach over the hurdles."

Homer Bast

April 10, 1954
Norfolk Division of William and Mary at Salem, Virginia
Team Scores: Roanoke College (R)–94 1/6
Norfolk Division of William and Mary (NWM)–24 5/6

The Norfolk Division of William and Mary, later to be re-named Old Dominion University, was a school just beginning its athletics program. In 1954, there was no way it could compete successfully with a track team like Roanoke's–one destined to get better and better over the remainder of the decade.

The visitors had few quality athletes, and were handicapped even more when early in the meet their star, Jerry Van Story, pulled a leg muscle. His only points came in the broad jump with a third-place finish.

For Roanoke, there were a number of double winners. Don Moore won the 100 in :10.4, then took the 220 in :23.6. Bill Lund again won the shot put and discus events with respectable throws. Jay Jackson almost set a record in the long jump (21'2¼") and he and Chris Rittman each jumped 6'0" for a win in the high jump. Incidentally, it was the first time any Roanoke athlete had cleared six feet in that event.

Other double winners for the Maroons included Les Noel, Bennie Irvin, and Chris Rittman. Noel tied with Irvin in taking first place in the mile run, then tied with Phil Shaw to win the two-mile run. Rittman was co-winner of the 880, with Irvin, and tied with John Summers to win the 440. Rittman's 12 points (from the 440, 880, and high jump) tied Foltz for high points of the day. Foltz tied for a win in the high hurdles, won the low hurdles outright, and finished second to Lund in the discus.

The only other winner for Roanoke was Earl Johnston. He tied for the high hurdles win in :16.2.

The other Maroons who scored points were Dick Rader, seconds in the 100 and 220 and third in the shot put; John Varsa, third in the pole vault; Al Ide, third places in the 100 and 220; Dick Seed, third in the high jump; Jim Wallwork, third in the quarter mile; Moore, second in the broad jump; and Johnston, second in the low hurdles.

The meet score was Roanoke, 94 1/6 Norfolk Division of William and Mary, 24 5/6. Roanoke had swept all three places in the 220, 440, and high jump.

April 13, 1954
Washington College at Chestertown, Maryland
Team Scores: Roanoke–81
Washington–36

Coach Bast planned a spring break trip again this year. The team traveled to Chestertown, Maryland, for a meet with Washington College on April 13. Then they met George Washington University in Washington, D. C. on April 15. After that competition, many of the athletes went home for a few days. A few returned to the campus, where classes resumed on Wednesday, April 21.

The Washington College meet was a bit more competitive than the meets with Elon and Norfolk W & M. Still, the winning margin was large–81 points for Roanoke and 36 for Washington. The Maroons captured eight first places and tied for one other.

Dave Foltz, improving greatly in the hurdles, won the highs in :15.4 and the lows with a time of :25.8. He also surprised by winning the discus throw with 117'7½", and tied for third in the high jump. His 16 points were high for the meet. As his skills in the sport increased, he would lead the meet scoring many more times before graduating.

Bill Lund won the shot put as usual, and finished in third place in the discus. John Summers floated through an easy 440, still protecting his pulled hamstring muscle. Bennie Irvin and Chris Rittman won the 880 in 2:06.8. Rittman also teamed with Noel to win the mile run. Dick Seed cleared 5'7" in the high jump for first place. And David Moore took the pole vault win with 10'0".

Richard Rader finished third in each of the shorter sprints, Al Ide tied for first in the 220 in :23.6, and Don Moore was beaten narrowly by Young of Washington, who finished first in the 100.

Jim Wallwork was third in the 440 while Earl Johnston just trailed Foltz in each of the hurdle event. Others who scored for the Maroons were Phil Shaw, second in the two-mile run; Rader, second in the shot; Wylie Barrow, third in the shot and second in the discus; Al Ide, second in the broad jump; Johnston, tie for third in the high jump; and John Varsa, third in the pole vault.

The Roanoke mile relay team also won. The team of Jim Wallwork, Bennie Irvin, Chris Rittman, and John Summers had little competition and turned in a time of 3:48.0.

Summers was clocked in his anchor role as running a :52.3 quarter.

I remember . . . "David Moore was a pole vaulter primarily–a home-made pole vaulter. He came down to the field every day and practiced, working on his form. I went home every night and read about pole vaulting so I could help him with his form. David was a good boy. He went into the Navy after Roanoke College and stayed in as a career man. He rose to the rank of Commander. He's retired now. He was from Salem and had some tough times in his early life. I believe his parents committed suicide. And they left four boys who were adopted or stayed with two or more families. All four of the boys went to college, and all four turned out to be wonderful people. I think he probably jumped around 11', but you have to remember that he had no experience in pole vaulting before coming to the College."

Homer Bast

I remember . . . When we went to Washington College, I wrote asking for the meet and asked if they could put us up. They put us up in a hotel. There was one hotel in town. One of the reasons I wanted to stay up there was that my father was still living at that particular time. And he had not married again, so he was living by himself. I had very few opportunities to go home to see him. So I thought that if I could get a meet with Washington College, I'd let the boys stay in the hotel with a pledge that they would behave, and I was going to spend the night with my father. That was only about 30+ miles away. So I went down there, had breakfast with my father, and brought my father to Chestertown. I put him in the stands in a comfortable place where he could see everything and I said I will see you at the end of the meet. I thought the meet would take about an hour and 50 minutes; unfortunately, the Washington officials weren't particularly interested in running the meet on time. The Washington track program was up one year and down the next. That was the first time my dad had seen me as coach of the team. After the meet, I drove my father home and returned the 36 miles to Chestertown. By that time, the boys were ready to go back to Salem. They had already eaten, so we took off. It was a good trip for us. I think the boys enjoyed it."

Homer Bast

April 15, 1954
George Washington University at Washington, D. C.
Team Scores: Roanoke–88
George Washington–38

Just like the first meet of the spring break, Roanoke had no problems with George Washington, beating the Colonials by 50 points–88 to 38. Many of the Maroon runners, throwers, and jumpers did well.

John Summers, solidly built but with that smooth, enviable stride, won both the 220 and the 440. His :23.0 timing in the 220 was his best of a four-year career. In the quarter, his preferred race, he was timed in :52.3.

Bill Lund was back in good form, winning the shot (41'3"), discus (120'0"), and javelin (156'2") for a total of 15 points. All of the distances were close to personal bests.

Transfer Jay Jackson, eligible to compete because George Washington wasn't in Roanoke's conference, also won multiple events. He broad jumped 20'2" without much effort, then tied for first in the high jump at 5'10".

Chris Rittman and Les Noel also had double wins. Rittman tied with Bennie Irvin for a first in the 880 and tied with Noel in the mile. Noel, besides winning the mile with Rittman, also won the two-mile run outright with a 10:50.

Dick Seed, whose favorite event at the time was the high jump, placed third in that event. Al Ide was second in the broad jump and Jim Cabler placed third. Jim Wallwork didn't win an event during the afternoon, but picked up third places in the 100, the high hurdles, and the low hurdles. Dave Foltz, still learning the hurdles, finished second in the highs and won the lows with a time of :26.0. He also picked up a second place in the discus behind Lund.

Bennie Irvin was second in the 440, while Phil Shaw was third in the mile run and second in the two-mile race. And Wylie Barrow was third in both the javelin and discus.

April 23, 1954
Penn Relays at Philadelphia, Pennsylvania
Mason-Dixon Mile Relay: 1st–Catholic University–3:28.6
2nd–Roanoke College (Rittman, Irvin, Summers, and Wallwork)–3:30.0
3rd-Unknown
4th–Unknown

On April 23, 1954, the Penn Relays were held in Philadelphia. Having attended the Relays himself while in school, Coach Bast was eager to have his team experience the atmosphere of one of the most important meets in the country. So he sent his mile relay team to run in the Mason-Dixon Mile Relay event. The team consisted of Chris Rittman, freshman; Bennie Irvin, senior; John Summers, sophomore; and Jim Wallwork, freshman. The team's main competition in the race came from Catholic University in Washington.

The two teams stayed close until the final lap, when Catholic pulled away slightly down the stretch. The Cardinals' time was an excellent 3:28.6. Just behind by two steps was the Roanoke team, which set a new school record time of 3:30.0. The old record was 3:36.2, set by Summers, Irvin, Pete Lawson, and Earl Johnston in 1953.

As soon as the medal ceremonies were finished, the group left Philadelphia and drove all night to get back to Salem on Saturday morning. Maybe they would have something left to get the team some points in Saturday afternoon's meet at home against Randolph-Macon College.

April 24, 1954
Randolph-Macon College at Salem, Virginia
Team Scores: Roanoke–82
Randolph-Macon–40

The Randolph-Macon/Roanoke meet was held concurrent with the second annual City/County high school meet. There were lots of athletes on the field and much to see by the large crowd of spectators.

Several of the Maroons remained unbeaten for the year in their events. They included Bill Lund of Lynchburg; Dave Foltz of Narrows; John Summers of Kearny, New Jersey; Les Noel of Buena Vista; and Captain Bennie Irvin of Roanoke.

Charlie Nuttycombe of Randolph-Macon was the real star of his team. He was a sprinter with extraordinary talent. In the meet with Roanoke, he ran :10.0 in the 100 and an easy :22.5 in the 220. The 100-yard dash time tied an Alumni Field record first set in 1949 and tied the year before by Boyd Carr. The 220-yard dash time was also a field record, wiping out the fine :22.6 mark set by Dick Dodd in 1950. Don Moore was second for the Maroons in both sprints. Nuttycombe, also a jumper, wasn't finished. He broad jumped 21'8¾" to break another field record originally set by Jay Jackson earlier in the season. Nuttycombe tied with Dave Foltz of the Maroons with the most points for the meet.

Still learning the hurdles, Foltz seemed to be getting better day by day. He led teammate Earl Johnston across the line in the high hurdles, winning in a time of :15.7, then beat Johnston again by winning the low hurdles in :25.5. His third win came in the discus. He didn't always do well in this event, but today the muscular, agile Foltz threw the discus 114'2½".

John Summers, tired from his overnight drive from Philadelphia, had no trouble winning the 440 in :53.2. Dick Seed tied for a win in the high jump, clearing 5'8¼", Les Noel and Chris Rittman tied to win the 880, Noel and Bennie Irvin tied for first place in the mile, David Moore jumped 10'0" in a three-way tie in the pole vault, and Bill Lund won the shot put and finished second in the discus. Others from Roanoke also scored, including:

Johnston, third in the high jump; Al Ide, second in the broad jump and third in the 220; Jim Cabler, third in the broad jump; Richard Rader, third in the shot put and second in the 440; Richard Hansel, third in the two-mile run; and Phil Shaw, second in the two-mile.

The team of Rader, Ide, Irvin, and Noel wasn't pushed in the mile relay. They won with a slow time of 3:41.8.

I remember . . . "The Randolph Macon meet was at Roanoke. It was run with the City-County meet. We had a real crowd there. By that time, Bob McLelland took a real interest in this. The *Roanoke Times and World News* was helping us to promote the annual meet. We had a pretty good time. I told the high school coaches that the meet would be run absolutely on time. If a boy wasn't at the starting line, we'd start without them. They generally listened to me. I had a little authority in those days, and after all they were running on our track."

Homer Bast

April 30, 1954
Hampden-Sydney College at Hampden-Sydney, Virginia
Team Scores: Roanoke–78⅔
Hampden-Sydney–43⅓

There were few people who thought that Hampden-Sydney could beat the resurgent Roanoke team on April 30; however, like the Maroons, they were undefeated for the season and had some athletes who could compete with the best in Virginia. One of those men was Jim Frazer, the very talented shot putter and discus thrower.

Frazer won those events, as expected, in the Roanoke meet. His shot put distance was 48'7" and he threw the discus 139'6½". Roanoke's Bill Lund managed to place second in the shot and Dave Foltz was third in the discus.

Foltz also won both hurdle races. His time in the highs was :15.9. But in the low hurdles, which he seemed to like better, he set a new Roanoke College record of :24.7. The only other Maroon to break the 25-seconds mark was Boyd Carr, in 1953. Earl Johnston was second in each race.

Another win for Foltz came in the high jump, where he and Dick Seed both cleared the bar at 5'10". With three first places–in the low- and high-hurdle races and in the high jump–and a third in the discus, Foltz picked up a total of 15 points for the afternoon.

Another Roanoke athlete with a terrific day was Don Moore. Moore won both the 100 and 220 races. His 100 time of :10.1 was just one-tenth of a second off the Roanoke College record. In the 220, he was timed in :22.7, the second-best 220 time of his career.

Bennie Irvin and Chris Rittman won the 880 in the fast time of 2:01.8. No Roanoke men had run that fast since Alvin Smith, who recorded times in 1949 of 2:00.4 and 2:00.7.

John Summers and Richard Rader tied for first in the 440-yard run. Their time of :53.2 wasn't exceptional, but there was little competition. Summers also finished third in the 220.

There was also little competition in the mile. Les Noel, Chris Rittman, and Bennie Irvin simply jogged their way to a three-way tie and a time of 4:49. Noel came back to win the two-mile race with ease, with Richard Hansel taking third.

The mile relay team of Rader, Irvin, Rittman, and Summers, easily won their event in a time of 3:34.6. They were 4.6 seconds over the 3:30.0 the team ran at the Penn Relays.

David Moore and John Varsa tied for second in the pole vault, and Don Moore was third in the broad jump.

The team score was Roanoke 78⅔ and Hampden-Sydney 43⅓. Roanoke won all but three of the events, giving Roanoke 6 wins in a row and 11 consecutive dual-meet victories over a two-year period.

May 4, 1954
Lynchburg College at Lynchburg, Virginia
Team Scores: Roanoke–84½
Lynchburg–37½

On the fourth of May, Roanoke's team went to Lynchburg to meet the Hornets. As much as anything, the meet was a tune-up for the upcoming Little Seven Championships four days later. The Maroons beat Lynchburg 84½ to 37½ and in the process members of the team broke three Roanoke College records.

In the field events, Bill Lund continued to throw consistently well. His first place effort of 43'1½" broke his own record of 42'10½".

In the hurdles, after winning the highs in :15.9, blond-haired Dave Foltz ran :24.1, clipping an amazing four tenths of a second off the record he had just set against Hampden-Sydney.

The other record was set by sophomore sensation John Summers. He won the quarter in a time of :51.9, taking a tenth of a second off the record he set as a freshman.

Don Moore could place only third in his 100-yard dash race, won by Lynchburg's Dick Jarrett in a fast :10.0; however, Moore came back strong in the 220, running a quick :22.9 to win that race. He also placed third in the broad jump.

Chris Rittman ran another good 880 race, finishing for a win in 2:02.8 just in front of Les Noel. Dick Seed nosed out Earl Johnston for second in the high hurdles, but Johnston was second in the lows.

Roanoke runners swept the three places in the mile run. Chris Rittman (4:37.3) was followed across the line by Bennie Irvin and then Les Noel.

Irvin and Phil Shaw finished side-by-side to win the two-mile race. Their time was 10:54.

Both Seed and Johnston cleared 6'0" to win the high jump. It was unheard of at the time that one team would have four six-foot high jumpers–but Roanoke now did. Earl Johnston and Dick Seed had cleared 6'0", while Chris Rittman and Jay Jackson jumped 6'1" on April 10, 1954.

Foltz was third in the discus, Al Ide second in the broad jump, Don Moore third in the broad jump, while Foltz took third in the discus and gained a tie for third in the high jump. David Moore tied for second in the pole vault.

I remember . . . "This was Dick Seed's first year. I don't think he did anything but the high jump at first. He was an outstanding soccer player and was Captain of the soccer team for a couple of years. I just couldn't see him competing only in soccer. I can't remember how I got him out for track, but I don't think he was reluctant to join the team. He was a smart boy–a chemistry major. He came from a good high school, so academics were no problem for him. He actually did not need to study a great deal. He knew how long to study to get a good grade. But he was a good boy. I really liked him. He is very articulate. He comes by every time he gets to Salem and brings his wife. I loved her. I think she was in my class. I knew Dick's parents. They came down to see him often and one time they brought me a puzzle. I think it was a picture of Dick going over a hurdle or some such thing. I had that puzzle for years. Dick gave his captain's sweater to the college to put on display. They gave me a white sweater at the dedication. I thought that I would bundle that up sometime and send it to Dick. And say that this was a replacement for the one he gave Roanoke. I don't deserve the white sweater. And I really should give it to one of the boys."

Homer Bast

May 8, 1954
Little Seven Championships at Hampden-Sydney, Virginia
Team Scores: 1st–Roanoke College–$68^{17}/_{28}$
2nd–Hampden-Sydney College–$30^{3}/_{7}$
3rd–Randolph-Macon College–20
4th–Bridgewater College–$18^{1}/_{28}$
5th–Lynchburg College–$14^{3}/_{7}$

6th–Emory and Henry College–1½

Last year, at Lynchburg, Roanoke barely won the Little Six Championships by six points. Since that point, the Maroons had been undefeated. They scored 605 points in their seven dual meet wins to just 240 for the opposition. According to Coach Bast, it was the best squad he had coached in his years at Roanoke. Another plus was that Roanoke was primarily a sophomore team, with its Captain, Bennie Irvin, being the only senior.

Some thought that Hampden-Sydney might be the only team who could beat Roanoke in the Little Seven meet. They had won four of their five outdoor meets during the current year, with the Roanoke meet being their only loss. Certainly, they had the meet's premier weight man, Jim Frazer. Frazer, the ex-St. Christopher's star, already had shattered his own school's records in the shot and discus, and was certain to win the events at the Little Seven meet on May 8.

The Tigers, who were rebuilding under their new coach, Bob Thalman, also had a good-looking sprinter, Mickey Moore, a fast hurdler, Bill Trapnell, and a fine pole vaulter, Bill French. As a whole, however, the team was likely a year or two away from its full potential.

Bridgewater might offer a surprise or two in the meet. Half miler Paige Will, who grew up in Bridgewater, could beat anyone on a good day. And Bill Miller was a good hurdler for the Eagles. Bridgewater had some depth, as they always did, and had beaten Lynchburg, Western Maryland, and Juniata in dual meets. But the rest of the teams–Randolph-Macon, Lynchburg, and Emory and Henry–didn't appear to have the depth nor individual performers necessary to match the Roanoke team.

Randolph-Macon's best athlete was Charlie Nuttycombe. He was one of the best sprinters and broad jumpers in the history of the Conference.

The meet was held on the brand new Hampden-Sydney track. The sky had beautiful cumulus clouds and the sun was shining. It was a perfect spring day for a track meet.

There were very few upsets. Both short sprints went to Charlie Nuttycombe, who was timed at :10.2 in the 100 and :22.0 in the 220. Don Moore was able to place third in the 220, followed closely by Al Ide. Nuttycombe also won the broad jump with a leap of 21'6¼". Don Moore was second.

Dave Foltz, becoming more confident in his abilities as a hurdler, won both the highs (:15.7) and lows (:24.5). He also placed second in the discus. Behind Foltz in the low hurdles, Earl Johnston placed second. In the high hurdles, Johnston was third.

Both the shot put and discus wins went to Jim Frazer of Hampden-Sydney. The well-built freshman put the shot 47'6" and threw the discus 134'6¾". Both were meet records. Roanoke's Bill Lund placed second in the shot.

Bennie Irvin and Chris Rittman tied for first in the 880. Their time was 2:03.1.

Unfortunately, Rittman was disqualified by the judges. The disqualification moved John Summers into second place behind Irvin. Summers already had won the 440 in an excellent time of :51.6.

There was a three-way tie in the mile run, with Roanoke's Irvin, Les Noel, and Rittman clasping hands coming across the finish line. In the two-mile run, Les Noel easily won that event in 10:22.7. Phil Shaw was second.

Roanoke's mile relay team of Don Moore, Jack Summers, Dick Rader, and Chris Rittman broke the old meet record by 2.8 seconds in winning the race. Their time was 3:31.2.

The high jump, most thought, would be won by a Roanoke athlete; however, Sam Bland of Randolph-Macon outlasted his fellow jumpers to clear 6'0" for the win. Dick Seed placed second, with Earl Johnston and Dave Foltz in a seven-way tie for third.

In the pole vault, Dave Moore tied for third place. It was not a bad effort for someone who had been pole vaulting for just two or three months.

Roanoke, with its overwhelming strength in the middle- and long-distance races, easily won the meet with 68 17/28 points by winning 7 of the 14 events. Hampden-Sydney took the second spot, 38 points behind Roanoke, while third place went to Randolph-Macon with 20 points. Bridgewater was fourth, followed by Lynchburg and Emory and Henry, a late entry.

May 11, 1954
Washington and Lee University at Lexington, Virginia
Team Scores: Roanoke–91
Washington and Lee–31

The meet with Washington and Lee in Lexington would be Roanoke's eighth of the season. It was May 11, 1954, but the weather was cloudy, windy, and cool. Because of those conditions, almost none of the times, heights, or distances were very good.

Jay Jackson, however, did set a new Roanoke College record in the long jump when his winning jump was measured at 21'8½". He had set the former record himself, going 21'4¾" earlier in the spring.

To summarize the remainder of the meet, Don Moore won both the 100 and 220, becoming the only double winner of the day. Dave Foltz won the low hurdles and Coach Bast even got him to run the 440, where he finished second behind Richard Rader's :52.4. John Summers won the 440 as usual, and Chris Rittman, Bennie Irvin, and Phil Shaw tied in winning the mile run. Les Noel placed first in the two-mile race with a very slow time of 10:50. Bill Lund won the shot put and placed second in the discus. Dick Seed was first in the high jump, clearing 5'9". And a number of other Maroons also placed second or third.

All in all, the team was tired from a long dual-meet season and, just days before, the Little Seven Championships. With the Mason-Dixon meet to run in three days, and with the sure knowledge that the team could beat Washington and Lee, everyone seemed to take it easy. There was no reason to push for a record and come up with a pulled hamstring or other injury.

Roanoke won by a score of 91 to 31. With a sigh of relief, it was time to mentally prepare for the Mason-Dixon Championships at Lynchburg on the 14th.

May 14-15, 1954
Mason-Dixon Championships at Lynchburg, Virginia
Team Scores: 1st–Roanoke College–61 9/14
2nd–Hampden-Sydney College–29 9/14
3rd–Johns Hopkins University–29
4th–Catholic University–23
5th–Bridgewater College–15 13/14
6th–Towson State College–14 1/7
7th–Randolph-Macon College–11 1/7
8th–Lynchburg College–9½
9th–Loyola University–8½
10th–Gallaudet College–5
11th–Mount St. Mary's College–2½
12th–American University–0

On Friday, May 14, the two-day Mason-Dixon meet began with various events holding qualifying trials in order to narrow down the field that would move to the finals the next day. Catholic University was the defending champion, having won by a slim margin of 1½ points in 1953. Roanoke and Johns Hopkins were the two schools picked by coaches to prevent Catholic from winning again.

This 19th annual meet was unusual because of where it was run. Its appearance in Lynchburg marked the first time the schools had visited Virginia to decide the track championship.

Besides Roanoke, Catholic, and Johns Hopkins, coaches predicted that Towson State Teachers might make it a four-way race to the finish. Gallaudet, Western Maryland, Washington, American, and Loyola had sent word that they wouldn't be entering full teams.

Although the Bridgewater team had the advantage of numbers, entering 21 athletes, they were not expected to win or even to be close to the top when the meet was over.

Host Lynchburg College entered 20, Towson 18, Roanoke 16, Catholic 15, Hampden-Sydney 15, Johns Hopkins 15, and Randolph-Macon 10.

With the right weather conditions, there were several meet records that might be broken. They included a :49.9 quarter mile, a 45'10" shot put, a 135'5" discus throw, and perhaps the 12'6" pole vault record. But the weather failed to cooperate.

During the qualifying events on Friday, there were steady rains. As a result, the track became muddy and slow. Conditions were so bad, in fact, that qualifying efforts in the discus and high jump were postponed until Saturday.

In Friday's rainy preliminaries, Roanoke qualified 12 men while 8 were qualified by Catholic University. Hampden-Sydney and Johns Hopkins each qualified 7 men.

The weather the next morning was no better. The skies appeared to be clearing during the opening field events, but rain began falling again during the first running events and continued throughout the meet.

So muddy did the track become that the judges were forced to group the six runners in the finals of the 100-yard dash into five lanes in order to run the race. The result was one of the strangest finishes in the history of the event.

John Libert of Catholic was in the outside lane and after the race, was not included in the placings when the judges wrote down the first through fifth finishers. They awarded first place to Al Heck of Johns Hopkins, with second going to Hofler of Towson, third to Dick Jarrett of Lynchburg, fourth to Charlie Nuttycombe of Randolph-Macon, and fifth to Bryars of Towson.

Coach Dorsey Griffith, the widely-respected coach at Catholic, was livid. He said it was obvious that Libert had placed no worse than fourth. According to the judges, he was sixth and last. Of course, there was no way for the judges to change their decisions, as no cameras in those days were ever placed at the finish line. Griffith was vindicated the next morning, however, when a newspaper photo taken parallel to the finish line showed Libert bunched with the second and third men about two yards from the finish line. It also showed that Charlie Nuttycombe, the excellent Hampden-Sydney sprinter whom the judges placed in the fourth place, was at least three yards behind and Bryars of Towson did not even show up in the photo.

The meet continued under some of the worst weather conditions possible. A steady rain beat down all afternoon and temperatures, even in May, were in the high 40s. As the meet wore on, the track became muddier and almost all of the running times were slow.

Roanoke's Dave Foltz, even under these conditions, won the day's scoring honors with 11 points. He won both hurdle events and was third in the discus. Don Manger of Johns Hopkins, Jim Frazer of Hampden-Sydney, and Fred Favo of Catholic all had 10 points.

Les Noel placed first in the two-mile run in 10:36.5, not a bad time for such a muddy track. Dick Rader placed fourth in the 220; John Summers was third in the 440 and third in the 880; Bennie Irvin was fourth in the 880; Chris Rittman was fifth in the 880; Dick Seed and Earl Johnson were second and third, respectively, in the high hurdles; and Johnston was third in the low hurdles.

In addition, although Don Manger took the win in the mile run, Roanoke runners finished in the next three spots. Les Noel was second, Bennie Irvin third, and Chris Rittman fourth. Dependable Les Noel finished on top in the two-mile run.

The only other Roanoke men who scored were Bill Lund, fifth in the shot; Al Ide, third in the broad jump; and Earl Johnston, a tie for fifth in the high jump. Dick Seed, despite the slippery run-up area, tied with Benzing of Loyola in winning the high jump at 5'10".

In the entire meet, only two new records were set. While the rain diminished briefly for the shot put and discus on Saturday, Jim Frazer of Hampden-Sydney set both records with a shot put of 47'6" and a discus throw of 142'$\frac{3}{4}$".

Here were the meet results at the end of the day on Saturday: Roanoke–$61\frac{9}{14}$; Hampden-Sydney–$29\frac{9}{14}$; Johns Hopkins–29; Catholic–23; Bridgewater–$15\frac{13}{14}$; Towson State–$14\frac{1}{7}$; Randolph-Macon–$11\frac{1}{7}$; Lynchburg–$9\frac{1}{2}$; Loyola–$8\frac{1}{2}$; Gallaudet–5; Mount St. Mary's–$2\frac{1}{2}$; and American–0.

The Roanoke team quickly left the rain-soaked field and had their own celebration in the locker room. "Men," said Coach Bast, "you did it and I'm proud of you. I can see right now that this championship is only the first of many for you in the coming seasons." The room erupted with noise, with athletes hugging and laughing and passing around the team trophy. Roanoke would not lose another Mason-Dixon Championship Meet until 1959, long after Homer had given up track coaching.

After a rainy day at the 1954 Mason-Dixon Championships, the team gathered in the locker room to celebrate their win.
Front Row (L to R): Dave Foltz, Coach Bast, and Bennie Irvine.
Second Row (L to R): David Moore, Allen Ide, Phil Shaw, Lessely Noel, and John Summers.
Third Row (L to R): John Varsa, Earl Johnston, Manager Lou Sutphin, Bill Lund, Richard Rader, Jim Wallwork, Chris Rittman, and Dick Seed.

May 22, 1954
Virginia AAU Championships at Lexington, Virginia
Team Scores: 1st–Quantico Marines–60½
2nd–Virginia Military Institute–54½
3rd–Roanoke College–10½
4th–Richmond Sports Club–10
5th–Hampden-Sydney College–6
6th–University of Virginia–5
7th–Washington and Lee University–5
8th–Norfolk Sports Club–5
9th–Lynchburg College–4
10th–Fort Eustice–4
11th–Fort Lee–3

The AAU Championships on May 19 were anticlimactic for Roanoke. After all, the team had just won eight straight dual meets, the Little Seven Championships, and the Mason-Dixon Championships. So Coach Bast took only those who said they wanted to compete in one more meet. The caliber of competition, as usual, was excellent.

No Maroon won any of the 16 events, but a few did place. The team was paced by Les Noel and Dave Foltz, who placed second in the two-mile run and the low hurdles, respectively. Teammates Dick Seed and Jay Jackson tied for third in the high jump, while John Summers came in third in the 440 and Jackson was fourth in the broad jump.

The meet also had a junior division, in which two of the Maroon runners competed for the *Roanoke Times and World-News* Sports Club. Dick Rader placed second in the 440 and Earl Johnston was second in the low hurdles. Their efforts helped the Roanoke Times and World-News Sports Club to place third behind the Norfolk Sports Club and the Charlottesville Downtown Athletic Club.

In the meet's senior division, Quantico won team honors with 60½ points, followed by Virginia Military Institute, who had 54½ points. Roanoke finished third with 10½. After Roanoke came the Richmond Sports Club, 10; Hampden-Sydney, 6; Virginia, Washington and Lee, Norfolk Sports Club, and Bridgewater, 5 each; Lynchburg College, 4; Roanoke Times-World News, 3½; Ft. Lee and Randolph-Macon, 3 each; Ft. Eustis, 2; and unattached competitors, a total of 3.

I remember . . . "Well, I used to baby-sit for Michael and Stephen when I was in college. And I liked Mary Jane a lot. I always thought of her as a party girl. Everybody enjoyed being with her. I can remember many a Friday or Saturday night being over there looking after Michael and Stephen. At the time, I was going with the campus May Queen,

Corina Henderson, and we spent a lot of time with them. You got to know the family and you got to know more about what they thought. It was like a Leave It to Beaver episode. You'd sit there and say, isn't this great. You always felt like you meant something to Homer–that you were important. Maybe you weren't very important to him as one of the parts that went into making up the whole. One year, I was running against one of the best runners in the south, at Clemson. I knew that Homer knew how good the guy was, but I don't know if he knew that I knew. I would ask Homer, 'How good is this guy?' He would say, 'Don't worry. You can beat him.' He would never let you doubt yourself. So you went out there thinking, 'Coach thinks I can win.' As I said before, I had two coaches who meant so much to me–one in high school and one in college. Each coach approached life differently. But both were the two greatest men I have ever known other than my dad. They could do so much for you, because they always thought that you had something you could give back."

John Summers

I remember . . . "There were a number of track and cross country athletes over the years who never competed in those sports in high school. The one of these people who really surprised me with their abilities was probably Dave Foltz. The only track experience he had at Narrows High School, as I remember, was in the discus throw. I knew that he would be a good track man, because he was a natural athlete. Dave was a great jumper in basketball. So I thought that we could make a good high jumper out of him. And then I thought about the pole vault. But he really didn't want to vault. He was pretty heavy, and in those days we had a terrible time with poles that would snap on you. And I certainly didn't want to see him get hurt. So we didn't really do much with the pole vault; however, we did work on the high jump, the broad jump, the hurdles, and more. I saw him as a decathlon man. He had tremendous power. When he turned it on, it was sort of like an after-burner. And surprisingly, he had a lot of stamina. He actually developed more rapidly than I thought. For example, he had those hurdles mastered within a year's time. He was good enough that I let him use the two-arm extension in front of him when he went over the hurdle. And he mastered that. And it didn't take him long before he could clear the hurdles so well that he could have knocked a coin off. I never heard complaints from Dave about sore knees or legs, or anything of the sort. He even competed one year with a cracked bone in his left arm. I have pictures of that."

Homer Bast

Chapter Ten

THE 1954-55 SEASONS

Cross Country

Always one for catchy slogans, Coach Bast's motto for the team this year was "Win one more in '54." Actually, despite the loss of a couple of good runners, winning probably wasn't going to be very difficult. Gone were Bennie Irvin, who graduated as one of the best of the Maroon middle- and long-distance men, and there was a good chance that Bruce Fariss would not run at all this year. Bast was depending on Fariss to place in his top five each meet; however, Bruce was thinking about not competing because of a heart condition.

The two main returning lettermen were Les Noel, Captain of this year's cross country team, and Phil Shaw of Irvington, New Jersey. Noel, now a senior, grew up in the small town of Buena Vista, Virginia, about 55 miles northeast of Salem and had never run on a track or cross country team before entering Roanoke College. At this stage in his career, Noel ranked among the best distance men in the state. Shaw, a sophomore, ran well in the fall of 1953, but would become a much better competitor in the next three years.

To better the previous year's record, which included a win in the Little Seven meet and thirds in both the Mason-Dixon and AAU meets, Bast would have to find several other good runners. He did have Chris Rittman, who entered school in 1953-54, at the beginning of the second semester, and earned his letter in track. He had a chance of doing well in cross country. Lenny Eppard and Dick Hansel were also back and should do well, along with Winn McConchie, who seemed to be rounding into good shape.

The rest of the team would be freshmen. The *Brackety-Ack*, as it always did at the beginning of a season, assessed the newcomers as follows:

> One of the most promising candidates is Ronnie Garst, who lettered as a half miler last spring at Jefferson High. The other hopefuls are Dick Goodlake, Garden City, New York; John McLaren, Kearny, New Jersey;

Bob Cross, Alexandria, Virginia; and Bill Cerelli, West New York, New Jersey.

From this list of hopefuls, several would be important contributors to the team. Dick Goodlake was an excellent runner, even as a freshman, and would push Les Noel to be even better than he would have been without team competition. Ronnie Garst would score for the team many times over the season and so would McLaren, Cross, and Cerelli.

I remember . . . "Les Noel was a unique character. He was a running machine. I roomed with him for one year, and that was an education. He was a fun guy to have around. Sometimes, he would look at you and say, "Let's go out and run." Then he would proceed to run you in the ground. You'd come back and you'd be exhausted, but Les would be in the shower singing and getting ready to go out on the night. He basically was raised in a taxicab stand. He answered the telephone and would call the drivers telling them where to meet their customers. He made his money hustling people in the pool hall. Les had a real gift of gab. He could talk himself in and out of anything. He was a nice-looking guy, and carried himself well. People just liked him. People on the team liked him. People at the school liked him. He was about 5'8" or maybe 5'9" tall. He was not a big guy, but he could solid run. Dick Goodlake was also a good runner, but was not as consistent as Les. Noel would give you the best performance that he could in every race."

Bruce Fariss

I remember . . . "When Les ran, he had pretty good form. But there were certain things that I felt we should work on. He would screw his face up so that he was just tied up. And I said, "Lessely, what we are going to have to do is to learn to smile while you run." And so help me, if he didn't work on that smiling so that the boys he would compete against began to call him 'smiley.' And it relaxed him all over. Everyone would say, 'Who is this guy. He's already run two miles and he's smiling.' But he was good. He really was. And he was a good competitor. If you needed points in an event, Leslie would run it for you."

Homer Bast

October 8, 1954
Randolph-Macon College at Salem, Virginia
Team Scores: Roanoke–15
Randolph-Macon–49

On October 8, 1954, the Maroons hosted Randolph-Macon College. It wasn't much of a race, with Roanoke winning by a score of 15 to 49. But Les Noel did set a course record of 16:13.0 on the restructured 3.1-mile course. Surprisingly, he was shadowed most of the way by freshman Dick Goodlake, who finished in second place only 14 seconds back of Noel.

Roanoke also took the third through fifth places with Phil Shaw and Chris Rittman crossing together in third, with a time of 17:28, and freshman John McLaren taking fifth place in 18:00. The other three who scored for Roanoke were Bill Cerelli (eighth, 20:00) and Lenny Eppard and Bob Cross (tie for ninth, 20:38).

October 15, 1954
University of Virginia at Salem, Virginia
Team Scores: None (Meet Cancelled Because of Weather)

Coach Bast was looking forward to the meet with the University of Virginia on October 15. Virginia was the school where he had completed his undergraduate and graduate work a few years before. And he was proud that his teams had never been defeated by the Cavaliers since he had begun his coaching.

Unfortunately, hurricane Hazel began to form in the Atlantic on October 5 and finally made landfall at the North Carolina/South Carolina border on the morning of October 15. The storm quickly passed over Raleigh, North Carolina, as a strong Category 3 storm. Its rapid forward speed allowed hurricane conditions to spread farther inland than any other storm in recorded history. Wind gusts over 100 mph were recorded as far as upstate New York, where Hazel still carried Category 2-force winds.

The storm brought 600-1,200 direct fatalities, $381,000,000 in damage (about $3 billion in today's money), and an end to the Roanoke College/University of Virginia cross country meet of 1954. The meet was not re-scheduled.

October 23, 1954
Virginia AAU Championships at Richmond, Virginia
Team Scores: None (Meet Cancelled)

The annual AAU Championships were supposed to be held in Richmond on October 23. Unfortunately, a few days prior to the meet, Coach Bast was notified that the meet was being cancelled for 1954 because of a lack of interest.

October 24, 1954
Virginia Polytechnic Institute at Salem, Virginia

Team Scores: Roanoke–21
Virginia Polytechnic Institute–36

Coach Bast didn't know what to expect from the Virginia Polytechnic Institute team, who came to Salem to run on October 26. The last time the two cross country teams had met was on October 21, 1947. V. P. I. won the meet, 20-39, in the very first season that the Maroons fielded a team. By rights, with the huge size advantage, they should have a good team.

Tech had won its only meet to date–a triangular victory over Washington and Lee and Lynchburg College. Tech's leading runners were Bobby Wingfield, a William Fleming High School graduate from Roanoke, and Bill Catlett.

Actually, Bast also didn't know about his own squad this early in the season. Although it was almost November, the team had participated in only one meet thus far. The coach's wish was that only one minute would separate the first- from the fifth-place time for the team. His team just wasn't running that well right now.

Les Noel, Dick Goodlake, and Chris Rittman went to the front early in the race. Near the end, coming down Market Street, Noel and Goodlake pulled ahead and seemed to run stride for stride toward the loop on the track and the finish line. Finally, Noel pulled ahead by a couple of steps and won the race in a new course record time of 16:03. Goodlake, just a freshman, finished a couple of steps back for second place. Both broke Noel's course record of 16:13, set in the Randolph-Macon meet a few weeks before. Rittman, running by himself, took third about 40 seconds later.

After V. P. I. took the next three places, Bruce Fariss (who decided to run despite his medical condition) finished seventh and Phil Shaw and John McLaren tied for eighth in a time of 17:31. Other Maroons who scored against V. P. I. included Bill Cerelli (thirteenth, 18:39); Dick Hansel (sixteenth, 18:55); Bob Cross (seventeenth, 19:28); Ronnie Garst (eighteenth, 19:49); Lenny Eppard (twentieth, 20:12); and Winn McConchie (twenty-first, 20:38).

The final score of the meet was 21-36 in Roanoke's favor. Oddly enough, the two teams would meet again in a dual meet at the end of the season.

October 29, 1954
Hampden-Sydney College at Hampden-Sydney, Virginia
Team Scores: Roanoke–18
Hampden-Sydney–44

Roanoke's next win, by a score of 18-44, came at Hampden-Sydney, Virginia, on October 29, 1954. Les Noel, improving each week, led the field all the way, winning in a time of 15:39.5. Dick Goodlake was second, about 20 seconds back, while Phil Shaw (fourth), Chris Rittman (fifth), and John McLaren (sixth) completed the scoring. Bruce Fariss was eighth, Bill Cerelli was tenth, and Bob Cross finished in the eleventh spot.

Thus far in the 1954 season, no team had come close to beating Roanoke. The dual-meet record was 3-0.

November 2, 1954
Washington and Lee University at Lexington, Virginia
Team Scores: Roanoke–27
Washington and Lee–28

If Roanoke was going to lose a cross country meet this year, it would be to Washington and Lee. The Generals had one of their best-ever teams, and already had beaten Virginia Polytechnic Institute, Lynchburg College, and Hampden-Sydney College. Only Bridgewater College, Roanoke's major rival in the Little Seven Conference, had managed to beat them.

Washington and Lee also had one of the finest freshman runners ever seen in the area. Bill Barry, from Chicago, had won first place for his team in every one of their meets. But was he a better runner than the Maroons' own Les Noel?

On the cold and windy day, with a wet course, Barry covered the long 4.5-mile course in 21:06. Noel trailed in second place some 40 seconds behind. In fairness, Noel failed to run as well as he had in 1952, when his time of 20:44 set the course record. In this meet, Barry's 21:06 was a school record on that course. When running this course, athletes had to go over and under fences, etc.

Another problem for the Maroons was that at the last moment, the team decided not to wear spikes. On the wet, slippery course, it was difficult for them to get traction.

Third place was taken by Dick Goodlake, who finished the race with a time of 21:51, about 10 yards behind Noel. After W & L took the fourth place, the outcome of the meet was still in doubt. Then down the stretch came Roanoke's Bruce Fariss and the Generals' Chick Duffy. It was a wild race for the finish line, with Fariss barely holding off Duffy by a single second for fifth place. Little did Bruce realize at that point that he had won the meet for Roanoke, for Chris Rittman crossed the line 29 seconds later to give Roanoke a narrow 27-28 win. John McLaren finished tenth and Phil Shaw was twelfth.

The Bast team had, indeed, won one more in '54. This meet might have saved a perfect season for the Maroons.

November 5, 1954
Lynchburg College at Lynchburg, Virginia

Team Scores: Roanoke–19
Lynchburg–42

Coach Bast still didn't have a team that could finish its fifth man within a minute of its first, but it was obviously a pretty good group of athletes. At this stage in the season, they had won four straight dual meets. Only the Lynchburg and Virginia Polytechnic Institute meets were left. Roanoke had beaten V. P. I. earlier in the fall, but the Blacksburg team wanted another meet and Bast accommodated them.

The Lynchburg meet was held in Lynchburg on November 5, 1954. Each of the first three Roanoke runners broke the existing course record. Les Noel won the meet, finishing in a time of 15:29. Ten seconds back, in second, was Dick Goodlake, and in third was the rapidly-improving Chris Rittman, whose time was 16:03. Lynchburg's top runner, Herman Atwood, held the old course record.

After two Lynchburg runners took fourth and fifth, four Maroons took the next four spots. John McLaren and Phil Shaw jogged across the line together for sixth place. Bruce Fariss was eighth and Bill Cerelli ninth. Bob Cross, in addition, was timed in 19:00 for twelfth place.

Roanoke won the meet, 19-42. It was their fifth straight win.

November 12, 1954
Little Seven Championships at Bridgewater, Virginia
Team Scores: 1st–Roanoke College–22
2nd–Bridgewater College–43
3rd–Lynchburg College–94
4th–Hampden-Sydney College–103
5th–Randolph-Macon College–115

Roanoke had met and defeated three of the four other teams in the Little Seven meet this year. They had no regular-season meet with Bridgewater, whose coach, Dr. Harry Jopson, always seemed to have a surprise or two for opponents.

The meet was held at Bridgewater, Virginia, on November 12. In the latter stages of the race, Les Noel and Roanoke freshman Dick Goodlake moved to the front of the pack, followed by a group of runners some 30 seconds behind. Noel outkicked Goodlake to win the race in a time of 17:33.9. Goodlake finished in second place in 17:42.

After Herman Atwood of Lynchburg and Roy Cunningham of Bridgewater crossed the finish line in the third and fourth positions, respectively, Roanoke's Chris Rittman took fifth in 18:28 and Bruce Fariss sixth in 18:40.

These Roanoke College cross country runners (L to R) competed for their fifth Little Seven meet championship Friday (Nov. 12) at Bridgewater College: Chris Rittman, Bob Cross, John McLaren, Bill Cerelli, Bruce Fariss, Phil Shaw, Captain Les Noel, and Dick Goodlake.

Noel's efforts gave him a new course record, beating the old record of 17:58 that he had set two years before. Also breaking the record was Dick Goodlake.

John McLaren was Roanoke's fifth man. He finished eighth in 18:50. Bill Cerelli was fourteenth and Bob Cross was twenty-seventh.

The Maroons, winning their fifth championship in eight years of competition, finished with a low score of 22 points. Bridgewater was second with 43 points, Lynchburg third with 94, Hampden-Sydney fourth with 103, and Randolph-Macon fifth with 115. Roanoke won the Little Seven title in 1947, 1948, 1949, and 1953, and had done it again in 1954.

November 20, 1954
Mason-Dixon Championships at Washington, D. C.
Team Scores: 1st–Roanoke College–59
2nd–Bridgewater College–68
3rd–Catholic University–93
4th–Johns Hopkins University–115
5th–Washington College–140

6th–Towson State College–150
7th–Gallaudet College–173
8th–Lynchburg College–181
9th–Randolph–Macon College–249
10th–Loyola College–255

Gallaudet College in Washington hosted the 1954 Mason-Dixon Conference Championships on November 20. The meet was held on a 3.1-mile, hilly, and wet course.

It was an interesting race, first for the battle for top individual honors, and second for the amazing comeback by one particular runner. Early in the race, Dick Goodlake, Roanoke's outstanding freshman runner, took over the lead. In back of Goodlake were Lou Buckley of Washington College, their team Captain, and Les Noel of Roanoke. Noel had been the pre-meet favorite to win the race.

Goodlake led the field for more than two miles. Then Noel took over the pace at about the two and one-half mile mark and lengthened his lead to 25 yards by the time he had run another quarter of a mile. Nearing the three-mile marker, however, Noel and Lou Buckley were running side by side. In the last 25 yards, the Washington College runner pulled ahead for the win. Noel finished the race just four seconds back. Buckley's time of 16:11 probably wasn't a bad time considering the damp, slow paths they were following.

The top individual story came from Steve Kugel of Gallaudet. The 19-year-old deaf student was in last place, 20 yards behind the pack, at the halfway point in the race. The crowd marveled as he began to pick off his opponents one by one, passing each with his eyes focused on the front runners. By the time he got within a couple of minutes of the finish line, he could see Roanoke's Dick Goodlake, who was following Noel for a sure third place. Instead, Kugel finally passed Goodlake to take the third spot. Some in the crowd thought that if he had been able to run another 50-100 yards, he might have won the race.

Besides Noel's third place and Goodlake's fourth, Roanoke also got scoring points from Chris Rittman (12th), Bruce Fariss (14th), and John McLaren (27th). The other Maroon runners were Bill Cerelli (30th) and Phil Shaw (46th).

Roanoke won the meet with a low score of 59 points, breaking a three-year monopoly on the title by Johns Hopkins University. It also represented the first conference championship for the Salem team since the meets in 1948 and 1949. Bridgewater was second and Catholic third.

Another interesting story from the meet involved Dick Goodlake. Coach Bast came very close to leaving him in Salem because the freshman had come down with a whopper of a cold. In addition, John McLaren finished the meet despite the fact that he had a side ache for most of the race.

I remember . . . "The meet was held at Gallaudet College in Washington, D. C. I held the lead for the first two miles of the race. As we neared the finish line, Steve Kugel of Gallaudet, who was deaf, ran just a few steps behind me. He seemed to squeal when he ran, and the sound just drove me nuts. I think Les Noel may have been in third place, but he soon took over the lead. Lou Buckley of Washington College passed Les in the final 25 yards to win the race. Noel was right behind. Then came Kugel, me, and in fifth, Herman Atwood of Lynchburg. The course was very slow."

Dick Goodlake

November 22, 1954
Virginia Polytechnic Institute at Blacksburg, Virginia
Team Scores: Roanoke–17
Virginia Polytechnic Institute–41

The final dual meet of the season was run in Blacksburg. Although Roanoke had beaten V. P. I. with ease early in the season, V. P. I. needed one more meet and Roanoke agreed to add them to the schedule for a second time.

Roanoke won again, this time by an even more convincing 17-41 score on the 4.1-mile course. The Maroons, in fact, took five of the top six places in the meet.

Les Noel, who had been beaten only twice during the season, won again. His time of 22:03 was 30 seconds better than the time by Dick Goodlake and 48 seconds faster than third place finisher Chris Rittman. Bobby Wingfield of V. P. I. managed to pick up a fourth, but Phil Shaw and Bruce Fariss strolled across the line side by side in 23:33 to take the fifth and sixth positions. John McLaren was ninth and Bill Cerelli finished in the eleventh spot.

This win gave Roanoke a dual-meet record of 6-0, with additional victories in the Little Seven and Mason-Dixon meets.

I remember . . . "We took Les Noel to the track once, and we used a different runner every quarter while Les ran his mile. He just ran us into the ground. He was a running machine. There was no end to him. And then following Les was Howard Meincke. He was really good. As I look back at my time at Roanoke, there were three outstanding runners. They were Les Noel, Howard Meincke, and Dick Goodlake. Those three came to the college with natural talent. But the people I admired the most were people like Lenny Eppard, Bill Cerelli, etc. They were there and they knew they weren't going to finish toward the top. They were always there and they always struggled to get there. I used to think, how do these guys do this when they know they are not ever going to place very high?"

Bruce Fariss

Indoor Track

Most members of Coach Bast's strong team of 1954 returned for the current season. The most notable individuals who had graduated or were gone for other reasons were Bill Lund, the weight man who transferred to V. P. I.; Don Moore; Richard Rader; and the excellent distance runner Bennie Irvin. Experienced quarter miler John Summers was hurt and might see limited action until the outdoors season.

On the other hand, the Maroons picked up several new track men who were destined to do well for several years. Two of these individuals were from the same high school, Jefferson, in Roanoke. Bruce Johnston would become a superb hurdler and in his final year of competition a record-breaking 100-yard dash man as well. Howard Light, who almost attended another college on a football scholarship, became one of the top quarter miler and relay men in the history of the college.

After Don Moore decided not to enroll for another year, the sprints would be turned over to George Gearhart, returning to school this year after serving for two years in the military. Before he graduated, he would become the school's finest, most consistent runner in the 100, 220, and relays.

Two seniors, distance runner Les Noel and jumper Jay Jackson, were Co-Captains.

January 15, 1955
Virginia Military Institute at Lexington, Virginia
Team Scores: Virginia Military Institute–61
Roanoke–43

The Keydets of V. M. I. were Southern Conference Champions with an impressive array of veterans. Few people thought that Roanoke could beat them in a head-to-head contest. Even the Maroons' fine group of distance runners might not be able to compete against this team. V. M. I., after all, placed 16th among the nation's cross country teams this past fall. It was one of those meets, however, that Coach Bast wanted to run, especially because he had a number of first-year men on the squad who needed good competition.

Top Left: Lessely Noel wins the Little Seven Championships one-mile run in 4:37.6. He also won the two-mile race that night in 10:37.7, as his team took home the first-place trophy.
Top Right: In the indoor meet with V. M. I., Dick Seed (in the wall lane) and Earl Johnston (second from the right) run the high hurdles. Seed finished in second place with a time of :09.4 seconds, losing by one tenth of a second. Johnston was fourth in :09.7.
Bottom Left: Lessely Noel (left) fights for position in the two-mile run.
Bottom Right: Front Row (L to R): John Varsa, Les Noel, Coach Homer Bast, Captain Bennie Irvin, and James Wallwork. Second Row (L to R): John Summers, David Moore, Phil Shaw, James Cabler, and Bill Lund. Third Row (L to R): Chris Rittman, Earl Johnston, Richard Rader, and Jay Jackson.

V. M. I. beat Roanoke 61-43, but according to the V. M. I. campus newspaper, the score was much closer than they had expected. The only place where Roanoke showed a real weakness was in the shot put, as expected with Bill Lund gone, and V. M. I. swept those three places. The host school also finished one-two in only a single event, the low hurdles. Roanoke won two firsts and the mile relay, along with seconds in 8 of the 11 events.

Ben Angel of V. M. I., winner of the quarter and half mile runs, and Carter Valentine, top man in the high and low hurdles for V. M. I., were high scorers. Pacing Roanoke were Les Noel, who won the mile in 4:38.7 and placed second in the two mile, and Jay Jackson, top high jumper and number two man in the broad jump.

Dick Seed and Jackson both set or tied new Roanoke College indoor records. Seed was timed in :09.4 when he finished second to V. M. I.'s Carter Valentine in the high hurdles. The former record by a Maroon was Earl Johnston's :09.4 set in 1954. Jackson broad jumped 20'11½" to finish in second place, and won the high jump with 5'8½".

Many other Roanoke men scored in the meet. David Moore cleared 11'0" in the pole vault, with Don Wilkie placing third with 10'6". Roanoke finally had two pole vaulters who could score well in upcoming months, easing Coach Bast's concerns.

In the 60-yard dash, George Gearhart missed tying the school record by a tenth of a second, running :06.6 to finish second. In the other sprint event, the 440-yard dash, freshman Howard Light took second place and, with very little practice, ran a :54.7.

The mile relay team won with a time of 3:49.0; however, the lack of training time also showed in the split times for all of the runners–Ronald Garst, Jim Wallwork, John McLaren, and John Summers.

Phil Shaw and Chris Rittman finished second and third in the 880-yard run. Phil also finished third in the mile run. Bruce Johnston took a third in the low hurdles and Cliff Shaw went 20'4" in the broad jump for third, just behind Jackson. Seed tied for second in the high jump.

January 22, 1955
Evening Star Games at Washington, D. C.

Mason-Dixon Sprint Medley Relay	1st–Catholic University (Groschan, Powderly, Flynn, and Favo)–3:45.1; 2nd–Roanoke College (Rittman, Ide, Gearhart, and Noel)–3:51.5; 3rd–Bridgewater College (Will, McGarrel, Hylton, and Smith); 4th–Towson State College; 5th–Gallaudet College
Two-Mile Invitational Relay	1st–Providence College–8:12.0 2nd–St. Joseph's University

3rd–Roanoke College (Rittman, Shaw, Summers, and Noel–8:22.0); 4th–Unknown; 5th–Unknown

Coach Bast sent two relay teams to Washington to compete in the Evening Star Games on January 22. Chris Rittman, Al Ide, George Gearhart, and Les Noel would run in the Mason-Dixon Conference Sprint Medley Relay, and the team of Rittman, Phil Shaw, John Summers, and Les Noel would try its hand at the Two-Mile Invitational Relay. Because of a bad cold, Mr. Bast could not accompany his runners.

The Maroons finished second in the sprint medley relay even though Allen Ide, their number two runner, had the baton knocked out of his hand as Chris Rittman finished his leadoff 440 and tried to give the baton to him. Ide, a junior from Alexandria, scooped up the baton and took off. He handed off to George Gearhart, who then gave the baton to Les Noel. With Noel running a terrific 2:02.0 half-mile on the anchor leg, the Maroons hit the tape in second place behind Catholic University's team. Bridgewater was third, Towson fourth, and Gallaudet fifth. Catholic was timed in 3:45.3, with Roanoke a few steps behind in 3:51.2. Most observers thought that without the dropped baton, Roanoke might have won the race.

In the two-mile invitational relay, Noel ran another fine anchor lap (2:04.0) to bring his teammates in third behind Providence and St. Joseph's. Providence's winning time was 8:12.0, just 10 seconds in front of Roanoke.

In other competition, Rev. Bob Richards set a new meet record in the pole vault, clearing 15'4". It was the 61st time that he cleared 15'. Richards, a former Bridgewater College jumper in his undergraduate days, came close twice to making 15'6".

In addition, Charles Holding of the Armed Forces raised the meet high jump mark to 6'7⅝", and Gunnar Nielson of Denmark held back until the last lap, and then beat Wes Santee of Kansas in the mile. Nielson ran 4:09.5, which was a new meet record, erasing the 4:13.4 mark set last year by Len Truex. Santee was the American outdoor record holder in the mile run.

February 5, 1955
Virginia Military Institute Winter Relays at Lexington, Virginia
Team Scores: None

The Winter Relays brought together entries from 14 schools. Most were schools larger than Roanoke from the Atlantic Coast and Southern Conferences, and many had the indoor facilities they needed to train through inclement weather.

Coach Bast this year was aiming for a first in the Mason-Dixon Distance Medley Relay, the only event on the card exclusively for Mason-Dixon Conference teams. The distance medley relay covers a distance of two and one-half miles. Howard Light would run the 440 leg, followed by Chris Rittman, another freshman, in the 880. Sophomore Phil Shaw then would run the three-quarter mile leg, with Les Noel closing with the anchor mile. Last year, Roanoke set a record for this race with a time of 11:23.2. This same group of runners would enter the two-mile relay.

Bast also entered runners in the shuttle hurdle relay. Jim Wallwork, Bruce Johnston, Earl Johnston, and Dick Seed would carry the Roanoke banner in this race. Maryland held the meet record.

The 880 relay (four 220-yard legs) would have George Gearhart, Allen Ide, Wallwork, and Bruce Johnston running for Roanoke. The Maroons placed fourth in last year's event. Maryland's time of 1:35.2 was the record.

For the first time, Roanoke also would enter the mile relay. The team consisted of George Gearhart, Allen Ide, John McLaren, and Dick Goodlake, each of whom would run 440 yards. Maryland held the record at 3:32.4.

In the four-mile relay, Coach Bast would be running Bruce Fariss, Shaw, Rittman, and Noel. Maryland held the record in this event with a time of 19:05.2.

Finally, in the running events, McLaren, Gearhart, Ide, and Goodlake would compete in the sprint medley. V. M. I. held the record here with a time of 3:43.1.

In the individual events, the high jump and pole vault would have Roanoke competitors. Dick Seed and Jay Jackson were trying for the record jump of 6 feet 2 inches. Ben Schwartz of Maryland held the record pole vault, 13'4¾", and Roanoke's David Moore and Don Wilkie would enter this event.

Just the number of entries for Roanoke gives one a hint of the increasing strength of the team. For the first time, Bast would be entering men in almost every event.

In the shuttle hurdle relay, Roanoke's team of Jim Wallwork, Dick Seed, Bruce Johnston, and Earl Johnston ran very well to finish in third place behind winner Duke University and second-place V. M. I. No Roanoke time was recorded.

Roanoke did win the Mason-Dixon Conference Distance Medley in 11:18.1, running Light, Rittman, Shaw, and Noel, and in the process set both a meet record and the Roanoke College indoor record. The former meet and Roanoke College record of 11:23.2 was set by Roanoke's John Summers, Chris Rittman, Bennie Irvin, and Les Noel in the Winter Relays of 1954.

In the two-mile relay (4 X 880), the Maroon team of Howard Light, Chris Rittman, Phil Shaw, and Les Noel finished in third place behind the University of Maryland and V. M. I. Officials did not publish the third-place time.

In the field events, only high jumper Dick Seed managed to place. He finished in third behind a winning jump of 6'0".

February 12, 1955

Little Seven Championships at Lexington, Virginia
Team Scores: 1st–Roanoke College–67
2nd–Lynchburg College–20
3rd–Bridgewater–16
4th–Hampden-Sydney College–14
5th–Randolph-Macon College–12

The Little Seven Championships were held on February 13 in the V. M. I. field house in Lexington. The Big Six and Little Seven indoor meets were run concurrently.

Roanoke had a team that was stronger than the one which had won last year's Little Seven meet. In fact, the Maroons won six of the twelve events on the schedule and outscored all four of the other teams combined. The final scores were Roanoke, 67; Lynchburg, 20; Bridgewater, 16; Hampden-Sydney, 14; and Randolph-Macon, 12.

Athletes set seven separate meet records. Included were three by Roanoke men. Phil Shaw set one of the records in the 880, running 2:04.6. The time also was a Roanoke College indoor record, beating the mark set by Bennie Irvin last year. Dick Seed won the high hurdles in :09.2 for another meet and Roanoke College record. Both former records were :09.4. Seed also won the high jump, clearing the bar at 5'11". His height was a Roanoke College record, beating the old mark of 5'10" that he had set in February of 1954.

Les Noel, dominant as always, won both the mile (4:37.6) and two-mile (10:37.7) events. The mile relay team– Jim Wallwork, Allen Ide, Howard Light, and George Gearhart–took it easy and still won their event in 3:45.5. The time was only 1.1 seconds over their existing Roanoke College record.

The only other Roanoke winner was Bruce Johnston. Bruce won the low hurdles in :08.4.

A number of individuals picked up second-, third-, or fourth-place points. Don Wilkie was second in the pole vault, followed by David Moore in third. Neither had a chance of catching winner Taylor Goode of Lynchburg, who was creeping up on the records of Roanoke's Ray DeCosta from the early 1950s. Goode jumped 12'6".

George Gearhart was second in the 60-yard dash, narrowly beaten by a tenth of a second at the finish. The second, third, and fourth places in the 440-yard dash were taken, respectively, by Chris Rittman, Howard Light, and Allen Ide. Although Jay Jackson broad jumped 20'6½" for a second-place finish, he was unable to overtake Randolph-Macon's Charlie Nuttycombe, who set a new meet record of 21'8" in winning. Allen Ide also jumped well, taking fourth with 20'¼".

Chris Rittman finished fourth in the 880 and John McLaren was third. Phil Shaw was second in the mile run. Dick Goodlake barely trailed Les Noel in the two-mile run to take second, and in the same race Bruce Fariss was fourth. Bruce Johnston was third in the high hurdles, while Bob Nilson threw for a third in the shot.

February 19, 1955
Mason-Dixon Championships at Lexington, Virginia
Team Scores: 1st–Roanoke College–53 1/6
2nd–Lynchburg College–24 5/6
3rd–Catholic University–17
4th–Bridgewater College–15
5th–Randolph-Macon College–9½
6th–Hampden-Sydney College–8
7th–Towson State College–4½

Team depth made Roanoke at least a slight favorite to retain its Mason-Dixon title on February 19. The meet was held at the V. M. I. field house in Lexington, in conjunction with the annual Southern Conference meet. Time trials began at 2:30 in the afternoon, with finals in most events being held at night.

Coach Bast, however, was worried about the physical condition of his squad. Injuries and colds had hampered practices during the week before the meet.

Bruce Johnston, the outstanding freshman hurdler, had a pulled muscle and there was a good chance he might not compete. David Moore, who had done well recently in the pole vault, had a sprained ankle.

Colds were spreading throughout the team. So far, they had slowed freshman Howard Light, sophomore Jim Wallwork, and freshman Dick Goodlake.

As in the Little Seven meet, Roanoke's depth won the meet. In fact, the Maroons placed in every event. In this meet, Roanoke scored 53 1/6 points to 24 5/6 for Lynchburg, 17 for Catholic, 15 for Bridgewater, 9½ for Randolph-Macon, 8 for Hampden-Sydney, and 4½ for last-place Towson State. Nine meet records were broken, one Roanoke College record was set, and another Roanoke record was tied.

Roanoke's Dick Seed was dominant in his two events. He won the high hurdles in :09.2 seconds, beating the meet record of :09.4 set last year by Maroon Earl Johnston. The time also tied the Roanoke College indoor mark set by Seed earlier in 1955. Seed then tied with Jay Jackson and Lynchburg's Taylor Goode to win the high jump at 5'8½".

Roanoke had no other double winners, but both Les Noel, in the mile run, and Bruce Johnston, in the low hurdles, won their events. Noel's time of 4:38.5 was a new meet record. Johnston's :08.2 timing also gave him a meet record.

Freshman Don Wilkie continued to impress in the pole vault, taking second place in back of Taylor Goode of Lynchburg. Jay Jackson was second by inches in the broad jump, with Allen Ide placing third and Cliff Shaw fourth.

The 60-yard dash was interesting, as all four of the front runners had times within .2 seconds of each other. George Gearhart of Roanoke was fourth with a time of :06.6. The winning time by Lynchburg's Dick Jarrett was: 06.4.

Fred Favo of Catholic University was favored to take both the 440 and the 880. He did win the quarter-mile race in :52.3, a meet record, with Howard Light of Roanoke in third place. But he was upset in the 880 by Paige Will of Bridgewater, who was timed in 2:04.0, another meet record. Phil Shaw was third, a few steps behind Favo. Shaw was timed in 2:08.6.

In the mile run, Roanoke took two places in addition to Noel's win. Phil Shaw was second and Chris Rittman was third. Only Bruce Fariss, in fourth place, was able to pick up points in the two-mile run.

Catholic University set a new meet record in the mile relay, with Roanoke just behind in second. Unfortunately, the records don't show the names of those who ran on the Maroon team.

In the high hurdles, Bruce Johnson was second and Earl Johnston finished in fourth place. In the low hurdles, Earl was also fourth.

Bob Nilson was fourth in the shot put.

February 26, 1955
Atlantic Coast Conference Games at Chapel Hill, North Carolina
Team Scores (Non-Conference Division): 1st–Virginia Military Institute–22⅓
2nd–Naval Academy–21
3rd–University of Florida–15
4th–University of Georgia–12½
5th–Georgia Tech University–10
6th–University of Alabama–7⅓
7th–Florida State University–5⅝
8th–Presbyterian College–4
9th–Davidson College–3½
10th–College of William and Mary–2
11th–Virginia Polytechnic Institute–2
12th–Roanoke College–1½

The Atlantic Coast Conference Indoor Games were held on February 26, 1955, at the University of North Carolina. Coach Bast's runners set or tied five Roanoke College indoor records in the meet's non-conference division.

George Gearhart ran :06.5 in both the trials and finals of the 60-yard dash. He tied

Boyd Carr's record, set in 1953.

Dick Seed finished fourth in the 70-yard high hurdles. His time of :09.1 was a new record. Although he didn't place, Bruce Johnston also set a school record :07.9 in the low hurdles.

Les Noel didn't place in the mile run, but his time of 4:30.5 set a new record. Phil Shaw finished about 14 seconds in back of Noel.

Four Maroons entered the 880-yard run. Phil Shaw failed to place, but ran a school-record 2:03.5 to beat his own record of 2:04.6 which he set earlier in the year. In the trials John Summers was timed in 2:08.5 and Richard Lewis ran a 2:04.6.

Seed also placed fourth in the high jump. Unfortunately, the height he cleared was not recorded.

I remember . . . "If you looked at me carefully, you would see that my left hand was limp. I was born that way. I learned somewhere along the way that my mother carried me in an abnormal way before my birth. That stopped the proper development of my left hand. But I turned out to be right-handed, so the problem wasn't that serious for me in athletics or in daily life. I even learned how to play a guitar. I just turned it around backwards. There was a fellow on the track team at Salem's Andrew Lewis High School who had the same problem. I saw that he was a pretty good athlete, and I thought I could also be a good track man despite the hand."

Bruce Johnston

Outdoor Track

The streak was now at 12 meets. During the past two seasons, Coach Bast's outdoor track and field teams had won an impressive 12 consecutive dual or triangular meets. In addition, they won two Little Seven and one Mason-Dixon Championship. It was hard to believe going into the spring of 1955 that this team would not be even stronger than before. They now were capable of scoring points in each event.

Almost everyone was back from the 1954 team or from the undefeated cross country squad from this past fall. The distance men were led by Les Noel. But the team also had Phil Shaw, Dick Goodlake, Bruce Fariss, Bill Cerelli, and John McLaren. No team the Maroons would run had a distance crew like this one.

The 1955 outdoor track team.
Front Row (L to R): James Wallwork, Cliff Shaw, Bill Cerelli, Dick Goodlake, Hank Hershey, Phil Shaw, Co-Captain Lessely Noel, Chris Rittman, and George Gearhart.
Second Row (L to R): Co-Captain Jay Jackson, Dick Seed, Dave Foltz, Bruce Johnston, Howard Light, John McLaren, Don Wilkie, Jack Summers, Bruce Fariss, and Fred Baker.

In the middle distances, Bast could rely on veteran John Summers, freshman Howard Light of Roanoke, Al Ide, and Jim Wallwork. The dashes, once thought to be the team's weak spot, had freshman Bruce Johnston, Dave Foltz, Wallwork, Ide, and George Gearhart. Gearhart had been a team member in 1951-52, but Uncle Sam called him to serve in the military during 1952-53 and 1953-54. His times during his freshman year weren't spectacular. But for this and the next two years of his eligibility, he not only would win consistently in the 100 and 220 races, but he would set numerous meet and school records.

Foltz, freshman Bruce Johnston from Roanoke, and Dick Seed were supposed to be the stars in the high and low hurdles. The multi-talented Foltz joined the track team from basketball, where he had become one of the finest players in the state. Dick Seed was an excellent hurdler, and getting better. Johnston could become one of the team's best athletes.

In the high jump, a number of individuals would make this another strong event for the Maroons. Dick Seed and Jay Jackson were both six footers, but Bast could also rely on Foltz, Goodlake, and even Gearhart if he needed the points.

The track team's star, Dave Foltz, talks with Homer Bast during the 1955 outdoor track season.

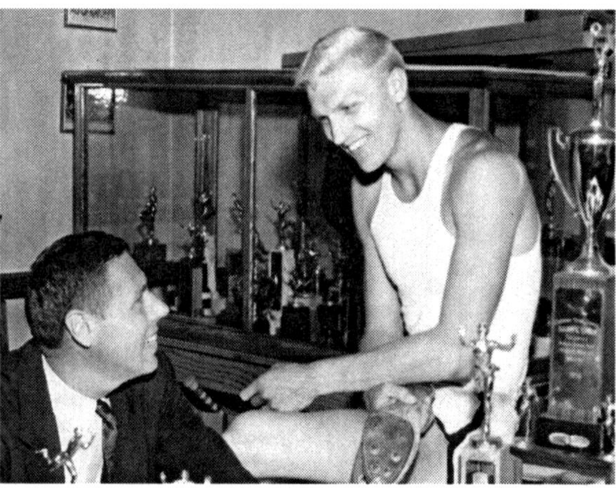

Jay Jackson was likely the best of the broad jumpers, but Foltz, Ide, and Cliff Shaw would also compete. This event may or may not produce many points this season.

Two athletes in the pole vault would score points, although neither of them likely would vault more than 11 feet. But David Moore and Don Wilkie had surprised many in 1954, and might again this spring.

In the shot put and discus, participants included Foltz, Bob Nilson, Bill Goldsby, and Bob Upton. The discus might be a bit stronger than the shot.

I remember . . . "I remember Dave Foltz more than anyone else, especially when I was a freshman. We had Foltz, Dick Seed, and myself in the hurdles. Foltz was a big, strong, blond-headed fellow. I learned from him how to properly cross those hurdles. I didn't have a lot of coaching in the hurdles in high school. Our coach then was pretty much happy if we showed up and won a few races."

Bruce Johnston

I remember . . . "When I got to Roanoke, I had no idea that I would participate in any sport. I was probably influenced to try for the team by my roommate, Wylie Barrow. He threw the shot for Homer. I was 6'1" tall and weighed about 195 pounds. And Wylie was about the same size. One day during my second year, a couple of us were walking down near the track. Wylie was over there throwing the shot. I asked him to let me see what that felt like. So I threw the shot and it went further than where Wylie was throwing it. So someone said, wait a minute. Let's go get the coach. So Homer came over and watched me throw the shot for a couple of minutes and suggested that I come down and see what I could do. I agreed, and he worked with me a little, and I got somewhat better. It never occurred to me during my first year that I could do anything to help the team. I had never seen a shot put in my life."

Bob Nilson

I remember . . . "When we went home for a break, Homer would tell me to take a shot home and work on the event. I remember showing the shot to my friends, who didn't have a clue about what it was. Homer always told me that the wrist flick was one of the most important part of the shot put event. I never really mastered that move, however.

Bob Nilson

I remember . . . "In my first years at Roanoke, Dave Foltz was still there. He was an interesting individual. He played his own game. He lived in the basement of the gym. He was a nice guy, but he was sometimes a loner. I wouldn't classify him as cocky or arrogant, but he did have a lot of confidence. He was just a good athlete."

Cliff Shaw

I remember . . . "In the 1954-55 season, Dave Foltz was becoming more enthusiastic about track day by day. By the time he graduated, I think he enjoyed track more than basketball. When he went into the Marines, I believe that he ran track but didn't play basketball at all. He was on a Marine team, I'm pretty sure. Many members of our teams in the 1950s went into the Marines. I was friendly with the Marine recruiter here. We had a lot in common because we had served in the war. I would tell him about individuals on our teams that I thought would make pretty good Marines, and he'd go recruit them. Now Dick Emberger stayed in the Marines because he thought his time there would get him to the Olympics."

Homer Bast

I remember . . . "I can't tell you about many of the athletes on the team, even the outstanding ones. We had our little niche, and many of the others were in another fraternity, so I didn't get to know them well. I do remember a few guys on the team, however. Dave Moore, for example, was a pole vaulter. He loved the event, even from his first days at the college. He worked really, really hard at it. He did a lot of chin-ups, trying to build up his arms. He wanted to be good at pole vaulting and was always trying to build his arm strength. David was a brother Sig and a nice fellow."

Bob Nilson

April 2, 1955
Bridgewater College at Salem, Virginia
Team Scores: Roanoke–89
Bridgewater–33

Of all the teams who had given Roanoke trouble over the past few years, Bridgewater was number one. Dr. Harry Jopson was well known and respected in his position as Bridgewater's coach. His teams were always well-prepared and deep in talent. Since Bast rejuvenated the track program in 1946-47, here is his record in dual meets with Bridgewater:

Date	**Location**	**Roanoke**	**Bridgewater**
April 22, 1947	Bridgewater, VA	64	62
May 1, 1948	Bridgewater, VA	58	69
April 25, 1949	Salem, VA	54	72
April 17, 1950	Bridgewater, VA	40	77

This particular meet, in Salem, was just the fifth meeting of the schools. Bridgewater held a 3-1 lead in wins.

Roanoke began the day by winning four of the five field events. Bob Nilson won the shot put with a throw of almost 41'. Then Dave Foltz took second, and Wylie Barrow third, in the discus. The Maroons swept all three places in the broad jump. Jay Jackson won with 20'1½", with Al Ide taking second and Cliff Shaw placing third.

Jackson and George Gearhart tied with two Bridgewater men for first in the high jump. All four went 5'8". David Moore and Don Wilkie tied for first in the pole vault, jumping 11'0.

There were two Alumni Field records set. The first was by Paige Will of Bridgewater. He ran the quarter in :51.4, breaking John Summers' record from 1953. Summers, in second, and Howard Light, in third, pushed Will to the record time.

The other field record came from the Roanoke mile relay team of Jim Wallwork, Les Noel, John McLaren, and Howard Light. Their winning time was 3:38.2.

George Gearhart won both the 100 and the 220 for the Maroons. The Eagles were swept in each event. Dave Foltz was second in the 100 and Al Ide third. In the 220, Ide finished second and John Summers was third.

Will came back to win the 880 in a slow time of 2:06.0. Second place in the event went to Chris Rittman and third to Phil Shaw.

Roanoke hurdlers almost swept both events. In the highs, Dick Seed ran :16.1 for a win, followed in second by Foltz and in third, with a tie, by Bruce Johnston. In the low hurdles, Foltz won in :25.9 and Johnston was second.

A surprise came in the mile run, where Roanoke's Chris Rittman won the event a tenth of a second ahead of Les Noel. It was the first time that Rittman had beaten Noel. Third place went to Bob Miller of Roanoke. In the two-mile run, freshman Dick Goodlake was timed in 10:31.6 for a win.

As expected, Roanoke's deep and balanced team won the meet. The score was 89-33.

April 13, 1955
East Tennessee State University at Salem, Virginia
Team Scores: Roanoke–81½
East Tennessee State–49½

In the early morning hours of April 13, 1955, Coach Bast lay awake in his second-floor bedroom, hearing the steady rain that struck the roof. If he listened closely, he could hear the trickles from tiny streams running through the sloping yard. All night long, the rain would ease up slightly at times before returning with intensity once again. Occasionally, he could hear distant thunder rumbles. At dawn, he could see through the front windows that this day would not be a good one for a track meet.

He took an umbrella and his briefcase and walked over to the campus. It was a walk he made each morning. He stopped to look at the condition of the track. Mostly, it was under water. The high jump and pole vault areas were in terrible shape, each holding water mixed throughout the sawdust. The shot put and discus circles were slick and filled with water. There were no concrete throwing circles in those days. "These are nasty conditions for a meet," he said to himself before heading off to teach his first history class of the morning.

Throughout the morning, Coach Bast had some lingering questions. East Tennessee State was a large school, with excellent athletic programs, located just south of Bristol, Tennessee. How would the day's terrible weather conditions affect the outcome of the meet? Would the rain stop?

The meet began at a time when there were no downpours, but there were was a persistent, drizzling rain falling. Soon, the heavy rain reappeared and lasted through most of the meet.

Amazingly, two Alumni Field records were set that day. First, Dave Foltz set a field record in the 120-yard high hurdles. His time of :15.6 beat his own mark of :15.7 set last year. The second record came from Les Noel. Like a little kid jumping in puddles to amuse himself, Les ran through seemingly one continuous puddle all the way around the track to win the mile run in 4:30.6. The old record had been set in 1949 when Bruce Davenport and Alvin Smith tied in a time of 4:36.0.

The rain also made little difference to other Roanoke athletes. George Gearhart won both short sprints. His :10.1 in the 100 was an excellent time considering the weather. He also ran a respectable :23.1 in the 220.

Top Photo: The outdoor meet with East Tennessee State University was run in the rain, with puddles of water almost completely around the track. This photograph shows Bruce Fariss leading Les Noel in the two-mile run. Noel went on to win the race, and Fariss was third, as Roanoke beat E. T. S. U. easily by more than 30 points.
Bottom Photo: George Gearhart wins versus Washington College.

John Summers (first), Howard Light (second), and Chris Rittman (third) swept the 440. Summers had a time of :53.2, while Light and Rittman were not more than a couple of steps behind.

The Maroons also took the first three spots in the 880. John McLaren ran 2:07.3 for first place. Summers and Rittman finished second and third, respectively.

Bruce Johnston won the low hurdles in :26.1, with Foltz second. Dick Seed placed second in the highs.

Noel, besides his record-breaking mile run, also won the two-mile race in 10:41.0. Bruce Fariss was third in that event.

Dick Goodlake, John McLaren, Howard Light, and George Gearhart easily won the mile relay. The time was 3:43.5.

In the pole vault, Roanoke's Don Wilkie and David Moore tied for third place. Jay Jackson and Dick Seed tied for first with an East Tennessee athlete in the high jump, but because of the slippery approach and poor landing area, the height was only 5'6".

Only Wylie Barrow could place in the javelin throw. He picked up a third.

And in the shot put and discus events, with slippery rings full of water, Bob Nilson won the shot and Dave Foltz won the discus. Foltz also took third in the shot, and Bob Upton was third in the discus.

The score was Roanoke, 81½, and East Tennessee State University, 49½. Dave Foltz of Roanoke was high scorer with 14 points. George Gearhart was second with 11¼ points, Les Noel third with 10 points, and John Summers had 8. Bob Bowman was top man for the visitors with 11¼ points.

April 16, 1955
Washington College at Salem, Virginia
Team Scores: Roanoke–99
Washington–18

If the 13th was a lousy day for a track meet, the 16th was one of those days track athletes look forward to seeing. The skies were blue, with few clouds and mostly sunshine. When there was a slight breeze, it seemed to favor the runners.

Unfortunately for Washington, Roanoke's classy team won firsts in all 14 events. In fact, the Maroons so dominated the meet that Washington was able to get only two seconds and ten thirds in the meet. In addition, Roanoke men tied or broke five Alumni Field records and tied two Roanoke College records as well, on their way to winning the third meet of the year, 99 to 18.

Let's begin with the individuals involved with new records. The first was George Gearhart. He won the 100-yard dash in :10.0. That time tied the Alumni Field record, set in 1949, 1952, and 1954. It also tied a Roanoke College record. Bob Fagg had run a :10.0 in 1947 and 1948, and Boyd Carr did the same in 1952. Gearhart came back in the 220-yard dash to win and tie the record of :22.6 originally set by Dick Dodd in 1950.

Chris Rittman set another Alumni Field record when he placed first in the 880-yard run. His excellent time of 2:01.8 beat the old record of 2:03.1 that Bruce Davenport had set five years before.

Dave Foltz continued to improve and impress in the hurdles. His winning high hurdles time was :15.2, which set new Alumni Field and Roanoke College records. The field record of :15.6 was set by Foltz earlier in the season. He also held the Roanoke College record of :15.4, which he set the previous year. When he won the 220-yard low hurdles in a time of :25.2, he erased the Alumni Field record set by Shook of Bridgewater in 1949.

The Maroons' potent mile relay team of Howard Light, George Gearhart, Chris Rittman, and John Summers set the other field record. Their 3:31.1 broke the old record of 3:38.2 originally set in 1955 by Jim Wallwork, Les Noel, John McLaren, and Howard Light.

Other winners, but not record setters, were: John Summers, 440 in :52.5; Les Noel, mile in 4:32.3; Dick Goodlake, two-mile run in 10:24.4; Bob Nilson, shot put, 41'10¼"; Dave Foltz, discus, 120'5½"; Jay Jackson, broad jump, 21'3¾", and the high jump, 5'8"; and David Moore and Don Wilkie, who tied for first in the pole vault with 11'0".

In the photograph on the left, George Gearhart passes the baton to Chris Rittman. Each helped teammates Howard Light and John Summers set a new Alumni Field record of 3:31.1mile relay record Gearhart also won both the 100-yard dash and the 220-yard dash in outstanding times. Rittman set a new Alumni Field record by winning the 880 in 2:01.8. Roanoke won the meet by a score of 99 to 18. The photograph on the right shows big, talented Dave Foltz. In the Washington meet, he won both hurdles and the discus, and placed third in the shot put. In the high hurdles, he set an Alumni Field and Roanoke College record. He also set a field record while winning the low hurdles.

Additional scoring for Roanoke came from: Al Ide, 100, third place, and 220, second; Howard Light, 440, second; Don Moore, 880, second; John McLaren, 880, third; Dick Seed, high hurdles, second; Bruce Johnston, low hurdles, second; Phil Shaw, mile, second; Bruce Fariss, two-mile run, second; Foltz, shot put, third; Bob Upton, discus, second; Cliff Shaw, broad jump, second; Seed, high jump, tie for second with George Gearhart; and David Moore and Don Wilkie, pole vault, tie for first.

April 23, 1955
Randolph-Macon College at Ashland, Virginia
Team Scores: Roanoke-101
Randolph-Macon–21

This year's spring break trip included competition with three schools–Randolph-

Macon, Norfolk Division of William and Mary; and Newport News Apprentice School. Randolph-Macon, whom the Maroons visited on April 23, did not have a very strong team. The one shining light on their squad was Charlie Nuttycombe, one of the finest sprinters and jumpers in the history of Virginia small colleges. In fact, Nuttycombe picked up his team's only two first places on this humid, warm, sunny day with a slight cross wind.

In the 100-yard dash, Nuttycombe led Roanoke's George Gearhart throughout much of the race. Unexpectedly, however, Nuttycombe fell, allowing Gearhart to place first in :10.4. Al Ide was third. Nuttycombe did win the 220-yard dash, however, followed by Ide in second and Howard Light in third.

Roanoke swept the pole vault for the first time in history. Don Wilkie and David Moore won the event with jumps of 10'6". Even Dick Goodlake, pole vaulting for the first time, managed to place third.

Bob Nilson won the shot, followed in second by Dave Foltz. In the discus, Foltz won the event with what was for him an excellent throw of 123'2". Bob Nilson was second.

Nuttycombe, the state's best broad jumper, took first in that event with a measurement of 22'5½". Jay Jackson was second with almost 21 feet, and Cliff Shaw was just four inches behind Jackson in third.

Dick Seed won the high jump with 5'9", with Gearhart and Jackson tying for second.

Les Noel did not run the mile and two-mile races, but did win the 880 in a time of 2:02.5. John Summers was second.

Howard Light ran :53.1 to win the 440. John McLaren was seven-tenths of a second behind.

Dick Goodlake was the mile run winner, in 4:39.3, and Chris Rittman finished second. The two-mile run went to Bruce Fariss and Phil Shaw, who tied in a very slow time of 11:22.4.

The mile relay won in a relaxed 3:40.1 time. The team was composed of John McLaren, Al Ide, Chris Rittman, and John Summers.

And finally, Bruce Johnston won both of his hurdle races. After a :16.4 in the highs, he ran the lows in :25.8. Seed was second in the high hurdles, while Foltz was second in the lows.

The meet score was in Roanoke's favor, 101 to 21. The Maroons had now won four straight meets this season, and it appeared that numbers five and six were on their way in the next few days.

I remember . . . "Do you remember the small white house that was near one end of the track? It was called Hildreth Hall. That's where I lived for the years I was at Roanoke. Chris Rittman also lived there and we roomed together. It was a popular place, as I remember, and lots of the guys from the Sections would come over. We had one guy,

Bud Brown, who had been in the military. He came back to college and lived in Hildreth. He brought in these big metal tins, like the army used for saltines, etc. He showed us how to make beer using the tins. So we put the ingredients together and Bud had a big sea locker. We put the containers of beer in the sea locker, locked it, and shoved it in the back of Bud's closet. It was O. K. for about a week. Then the beer started to get ripe so that every time a person walked down the hall, they could smell the beer. So we had a meeting and decided that, with the pressure building, the last thing we needed was for Homer to walk in and smell the beer. So the Sigma Chi fraternity was having a party that weekend. We poured the beer into bottles and took them to the fraternity house to be consumed there. That stuff was so green that it was all we could do to drink it."

Allen Ide

April 25, 1955
Norfolk Division of William and Mary at Norfolk, Virginia
Team Scores: Roanoke–90⅔
Norfolk Division of William and Mary–31⅓

The meet with the Norfolk Division of William and Mary was held at Foreman Field in Norfolk on April 25. The track was slow and sloppy, with a hard rain coming down just prior to the meet. There were a few good performances, but like the Randolph-Macon meet, no records were set. The competition wasn't as challenging as it needed to be for record times, heights, and distances.

Roanoke captured all nine first places in the running events, and two of the five field events, to win the meet 90⅔ to 31⅓. One highlight of the meet was the distance running of Phil Shaw, Les Noel, and Chris Rittman. The threesome tied for a win in the 880 and for another win in the mile. Noel also won the two-mile race with Bruce Fariss following in second.

Dave Foltz ran the 100, and won in a time of :10.3, with George Gearhart a half-step behind. Then Gearhart won the 220, with Al Ide nine-tenths of a second behind in third.

Bruce Johnston won the high hurdles ahead of Dick Seed. Foltz placed first in the low hurdles, a half second ahead of Johnston.

The mile relay team–John McLaren, Phil Shaw, Al Ide, and Howard Light–won its event in a respectable time of 3:37.9.

The Braves' Gerald Tiedemann threw the shot 46'7" for a win. He would go on in later years to throw well over 50'.

Bob Nilson won the discus with a throw of 126'1¼", almost a school record, with Foltz placing second. Jay Jackson was second in the broad jump, jumping 20'7" and losing first place by one inch.

Dick Seed, Jackson, and Foltz tied for the win in the high jump, clearing 5'8", while David Moore and Don Wilkie tied for a third place in the pole vault.

April 26, 1955
Newport News Apprentice School at Newport News, Virginia
Team Scores: Roanoke–83⅙
Newport News Apprentice–38⅚

On the next day following the Norfolk Division meet, Roanoke met the team from Newport News Apprentice School. It was a cool and damp day, with a very heavy track.

Again, the Maroons had a much better team and won the meet 83⅙ to 38⅚, leaving Apprentice with a 1-4 record for the season. It was Roanoke's sixth win without a loss.

There were no Roanoke College records set during the meet, although the team won or tied for first in 11 of the 14 events. George Gearhart won both the 100 and 220. Bruce Johnston placed second in the 100 and Dave Foltz was third in the 220. In the 440, John Summers placed first in :52.5, with Al Ide third.

Foltz also won the discus with one of his best throws, 122'½", with Bob Upton placing third with 111'0". Foltz also placed second in the shot.

Jay Jackson was first in the broad jump with 19'9½". Cliff Shaw was third, just 4½" behind.

In the 880, Phil Shaw won easily with a time of 2:04.3. John McLaren was second.

Dick Seed and Jackson won the high jump. Foltz and Gearhart tied for third.

David Moore jumped 10'6" for a tie for first place in the pole vault, while Don Wilkie tied for third place.

Bruce Johnston and Dick Seed each scored eight points in the hurdles. The high hurdles were won by Seed in :16.6, with Johnston second. In the low hurdles, Johnston won in :26.6, with Seed a step behind.

Phil Shaw and Chris Rittman tied for the win in the mile, and Bruce Fariss finished second in the two-mile run.

Newport News Apprentice won the mile relay in a good time of 3:33.7, the shot put on a throw of 41'2½", and the two-mile run with a time of 10:33.8. Both the two-mile time and the shot put distance were new Apprentice field records.

April 30, 1955
Hampden-Sydney College at Salem, Virginia
Team Scores: Roanoke–79½
Hampden-Sydney–42½

Four days after the spring break trip, the Roanoke team was back in Salem to face Hampden-Sydney on Alumni Field. The meet was held at the same time as the local City-County High School Championships. There was some wind, but basically it was a sunny day–ideal for a track meet.

Two of the Roanoke freshmen in particular were interested in the results of the high school meet. Bruce Johnston held the city-county record in both hurdles, while Howard Light was the record holder in the 440. Neither of their records was broken.

Ten of the 14 college events were won by Roanoke athletes. Five Alumni Field records were set–four of them by Roanoke–and another field record was tied by Hampden-Sydney.

For Hampden-Sydney, the best team Roanoke had met during the season, Jim Frazer won the shot put event with 42'6" and set a new Alumni Field record in the discus on a toss of 133'4". Charles Holt tied George Gearhart's Alumni Field 220 record of :22.6, and David Brown ran a :52.5 440 to win that event.

Roanoke record setters included Phil Shaw, who ran an excellent 2:01.5 to break the field record that teammate and second-place runner Chris Rittman had set just a couple of weeks before. Another Maroon record came in the low hurdles, with Dave Foltz running a time of :24.5. That time beat his old record of :25.2. Foltz also won the high hurdles in a non-record time of :15.6.

In the two-mile race, Les Noel shocked even his coach when he posted a time of 10:08.9. That time beat the 10:12.8 Alumni Field record set in 1949 by Roanoke's Bruce Davenport. It was a surprising effort because Noel was favoring a pulled tendon. Reportedly, one of his feet was heavily bandaged.

The officials were right. Several bystanders disagreed with the judges when they ruled that Roanoke College's George Gearhart won this 100-yard dash in the Hampden-Sydney meet. But this picture taken at the finish tape shows Gearhart ahead by inches, with Hampden-Sydney's Holt second. The Maroons won the dual meet by a margin of 37 points.

The other field record by Roanoke was by the mile relay team of Howard Light, John Summers, George Gearhart, and Chris Rittman. Their winning time of 3:31.0 beat the mark of 3:31.1 this team set earlier in the season.

Many others on the Maroon team also scored points, including Gearhart, tie for second in the 220; Summers, second in the 440; Light, third in the 440; Rittman, second in the 880; Dick Seed, second in the high hurdles and third in the low hurdles; Bruce Johnston, third in the high hurdles and second in the low hurdles; Phil Shaw and Rittman, winners of the mile run; Bruce Fariss, second in the two-mile run; Foltz, third in the discus; Jay Jackson, winner of the high jump; David Moore, winner of the pole vault; and Don Wilkie, third in the pole vault.

Roanoke beat Hampden-Sydney 79½ to 42½, the narrowest of winning margins of the 1954-55 season. The win was Roanoke's seventh in a row.

May 3, 1955
Lynchburg College at Salem, Virginia
Team Scores: Roanoke–74 1/6
Lynchburg–47 5/6

May 3, 1955, was a beautiful day. It was warm on Alumni Field, the wind was minimal, and the track was fast.

Lynchburg, like Hampden-Sydney, had one of their best teams. By far, however, Roanoke had the most depth. On this afternoon, the Maroons won nine of the 14 events and scored most of the points in the second and third places. They also swept both hurdle races for a total of 18 points.

The stars of this meet were Dave Foltz, George Gearhart, and John Summers. Foltz scored 20 points by winning the 120-yard high hurdles in :15.5 and the 220-yard low hurdles in :25.0. He also won the shot put with a throw of 40'4½" and the discus with 119'½". It was only one of several times in his college career that he would score at least 20 points.

Gearhart tied the Alumni Field and Roanoke College records for the 100-yard dash. His time of :10.0 tied the field record set by Gearhart and three others. The College record tied the marks set by Bob Fagg in 1947 and 1948, Boyd Carr in 1952, and Gearhart himself earlier in 1955. Gearhart also won the 220-yard dash in :23.1 for 10 points.

Summers, with his smooth, almost effortless glide, won the 440-yard dash in a time of :51.8. This time knocked a tenth of a second off the old Roanoke College record which he set in the spring of 1954.

Not many of the other times, heights, or distances by Roanoke athletes were close to record-breaking. Chris Rittman won the 880 in 2:04.8; Cliff Shaw won the broad jump with 19'10½"; and Dick Seed tied for first with Taylor Goode of Lynchburg in the high jump, clearing the bar at 5'8".

Other Roanoke points came from Al Ide, who tied for third in the 100 and picked up a third in the 220; Bruce Johnston, second in both hurdle events; Seed, third in each hurdle event; Phil Shaw, second in the mile run; Chris Rittman, third in the mile run; Bruce Fariss, second in the two-mile race; Bob Nilson, third in the discus; Jay Jackson, second in the broad jump and third in the high jump; and Don Wilkie and David Moore, tie for second in the pole vault.

Roanoke won the meet, $74\frac{1}{6}$ to $47\frac{5}{6}$. The win was Roanoke's eighth during the current season.

May 6, 1955
Little Seven Championships at Hampden-Sydney, Virginia
Team Scores: 1st–Roanoke College–55
2nd–Hampden-Sydney College–39
3rd–Bridgewater College–26
4th–Lynchburg College–19
5th–Randolph-Macon College–15
6th–Emory and Henry College–0

The Little Seven meet this year was held at Hampden-Sydney. Everyone seemed to think that Roanoke was the heavy favorite to win; however, Coach Bast had some doubts. "In other years," he admitted, "we always seemed to lack something–maybe a high jumper, maybe a shot putter. This year, we have a man for every event. We have the depth." But for the Little Seven Championships this year, the Maroons had four important injuries.

Distance star Les Noel had a pulled tendon, and likely would be running only the two-mile race. Also ailing was Co-Captain Jay Jackson, who transferred from Hampden-Sydney last year, along with freshman quarter miler Howard Light and his second-best distance runner, freshman Dick Goodlake. "What was a very fine team," Bast said, "is now a very mediocre team."

Roanoke's opposition was Bridgewater, Emory and Henry, Hampden-Sydney, Lynchburg, and Randolph-Macon. Emory and Henry, however, was sending only a few members of its team. Richmond Professional Institute, the only other member of the Little Seven Conference, did not field a track team.

The strongest of the competing schools likely would be Hampden-Sydney, Lynchburg, and Bridgewater. The host Tiger team had a 6-2 record and possibly could sweep the shot put with big Jim Frazer, Jim Wiley, and Tom Lee. Frazer consistently threw over 48' during the season.

Bridgewater may have a winner in the sprints, Paige Will, and Lynchburg was figured to win the pole vault with Taylor Goode.

Randolph-Macon, although not expected to challenge Roanoke for the title, may have had the best all-around athlete in Charlie Nuttycombe. Nuttycombe was so talented that he could win the 100, 220, broad jump, and even the low hurdles.

No one, however, took Roanoke lightly. They were favorites for a reason. They had potential blue-ribbon winners such as Dave Foltz. He was undefeated in the high hurdles this year and had lost only to teammate Bruce Johnston, in the low hurdles during the spring. Roanoke also had individuals such as ex-service man George Gearhart, who just ran :10.0 in the 100, a crack mile relay team, Phil Shaw, Dick Goodlake, Howard Light, John Summers, Dick Seed, and Chris Rittman. Any of these men could win with a good effort.

Bast knew what he needed the most. Perhaps the rest of the first places would be divided among the other four teams and Roanoke could grab most of the seconds, thirds, and fourths to win.

Nevertheless, Coach Bast showed up at Hampden-Sydney with a point-heavy 38-man squad. The number of athletes alone should have been a tip-off about the popularity of the sport at the Salem school. The College at the time had an enrollment of about 450 students. Bast, of course, was the one primarily responsible for the interest shown in the sport. He was constantly hunting talent in the school dormitories, instructing and even recruiting area high school students who worked out on the track almost every day, and writing letters to those high school students in Virginia and elsewhere. In his spare moments, he also served as the College's Registrar and as an associate professor in history.

Charlie Nuttycombe of Randolph-Macon and Jim Frazer of Hampden-Sydney were very impressive. The multi-talented Nuttycombe won the 100, tied for the win in the 220 in :22.2, and placed first in the long jump with 21'4". Frazer, the freshman weight man, won the shot put with a toss of 48'½" and threw the discus 138'10⅞". Frazer's marks both broke the meet records.

You wouldn't have known that Les Noel was running with an injury. In the two-mile event, he kept an even pace around the eight laps to finish first in 10:16.9

After a second place in the 100, just a stride behind Nuttycombe, George Gearhart was timed at :22.4 in finishing third in the 220. The time was a new Roanoke College record, beating Dick Dodd's mark of :22.6 in 1950 and his own time of :22.6 from the current season.

The terrific crew of Roanoke hurdlers, however, put the meet out of reach. Dave Foltz

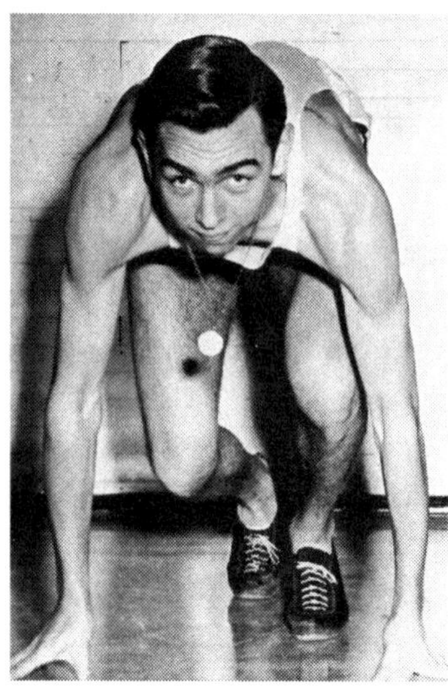

Two of the top three hurdlers Homer Bast ever coached were Dave Foltz (left) and Bruce Johnston (right).

won both events–the highs in :16.0 and the lows in :24.4, just three-tenths of a second off his own Roanoke College record. In the high hurdles, Dick Seed was second and Bruce Johnston third. Johnston was second in the low hurdles, with Seed finishing in fourth place.

The Maroons won no other event; however, they did have a number of second-, third-, and fourth-place finishes. Seconds went to Gearhart in the 100; Dick Goodlake in the 880; Phil Shaw in the mile; and Foltz, Jay Jackson, and Seed in the high jump. Third place finishers were Shaw in the 880; Chris Rittman in the mile; the Roanoke mile relay team; Bob Nilson in the discus; and Don Wilkie and David Moore in the pole vault. Wilkie and Moore flipped for the third place medal. Moore won the flip and to this day, he keeps that medal to remind him that it was the only one he ever won in track. Finally, the Maroons took three fourth places. Included were Al Ide in the 220; Howard Light in the 440; and Cliff Shaw in the broad jump.

Roanoke won the meet by a margin of 16 points. They had 55, Hampden-Sydney 39, Bridgewater 26, Lynchburg 19, and Randolph-Macon 15. Emory and Henry, with a partial team, failed to score.

May 9, 1955
Washington and Lee University at Lexington, Virginia
Team Scores: Roanoke–77½
Washington and Lee–53½

The final dual meet of the year came on May 9, 1955, when the Roanoke squad traveled to Lexington to compete against Washington and Lee. The Generals has a fairly good team, but Roanoke was favored to win.

Washington and Lee swept the javelin, an event in which Roanoke athletes seldom competed, and took first and second in the discus. Otherwise, the meet belonged to Roanoke.

Dave Foltz put on his usual show, winning the high hurdles in :15.3 and the low hurdles with a time of :25.0. Then he took second in the shot put, second in the discus, and second in the high jump. At the end of the meet, he had 19 points.

After placing third in the 100, just behind second-place finisher Bruce Johnston, George Gearhart came back later to win the 220 in :23.2. Al Ide was close behind in second.

John Summers was back on form. After failing to place in the Little Seven meet, he won the 440-yard dash. His time of :51.8 was a new Roanoke College record. Howard Light finished close behind.

In the 880, Chris Rittman ran another good race. He crossed the line in 2:02.4.

Dick Seed was third in the high hurdles and third in the high jump. The mile relay team of Gearhart, Rittman, Light, and Ide won in 3:34.2.

In the field events, Bob Nilson placed third in the shot, Seed was third in the high jump, Don Wilkie tied for first in the pole vault, and David Moore tied for third in that event.

With its balanced team, Roanoke won the meet, 77½ to 53½. For the 1954-55 outdoor season, the team had won nine consecutive meets. Looking back two years, when Davidson College beat them, the Roanoke squad had won 21 consecutive dual/triangular meets without a loss.

May 13-14, 1955
Mason-Dixon Championships at Washington, D. C.
Team Scores: 1st–Roanoke College–$62\frac{1}{10}$
2nd–Hampden-Sydney College–32
3rd–Catholic University–23
4th–Bridgewater College–$22\frac{1}{5}$
5th–Johns Hopkins University–$16\frac{14}{15}$
6th–Lynchburg College–10
7th–Randolph-Macon College–$7\frac{3}{5}$
8th–Western Maryland College–7
9th–Towson State College–6⅔
10th–Washington College–6
11th–Loyola University–6
12th–American University–5½
13th–Gallaudet College–5
14th–Mount St. Mary's College–0

For the 20th annual Mason-Dixon meet, held over a two-day period, 14 schools entered teams. The meet was run at Catholic University in Washington.

Roanoke was heavily favored to take the champion's trophy, although three of their top runners were hurt. Co-Captain Les Noel still could feel the pain in his right foot. Jay Jackson, the other Co-Captain, had hip problems. And freshman quarter-miler Howard Light had a chest injury.

Despite a steady rain, the trials and semifinals on Friday ran smoothly. Roanoke, as expected, led the field by qualifying 14 men for the next day's finals. Hampden-Sydney qualified eight.

Here were the finalists and the best times, heights, or distances from Friday's competition:

880 Yards	1st–Will (Bridgewater)–2:04.3; 2nd–Goodlake (Roanoke); 3rd–Shaw (Roanoke); 4th–Sutherland (Johns Hopkins); 5th–Rittman (Roanoke); 6th–Messersmith (Catholic)
220 Yards	1st–Favo (Catholic)–:23.0; 2nd–Holt (Hampden-Sydney); 3rd–Moore (Hampden-Sydney); 4th–Nuttycombe (Randolph-Macon)
220-Yard LH	1st–Foltz (Roanoke)–:26.2; 2nd–Seed (Roanoke); 3rd–Vaeth (Loyola); 4th–Johnston (Roanoke); 5th–Hylton (Bridgewater)
100 Yards	1st–Holt (Hampden-Sydney)–:10.5; 2nd–Hufler (Towson State); 3rd–Gearhart (Roanoke); 4th–Nuttycombe (Randolph-Macon); 5th–Favo (CU)
120-Yard HH	1st–Foltz (Roanoke)–:16.5; 2nd–Johnston (Roanoke); 3rd–Seed (Roanoke); 4th–Hort (Western Maryland); 5th–Wampler (B)
Broad Jump	1st–Nuttycombe (Randolph-Macon)–20'11¼"; 2nd–Flynn (Catholic); 3rd–Jackson (Roanoke); 4th–Gold (Hampden-Sydney); 5th–Rushbrooke (Hampden-Sydney); 6th–Wright (Johns Hopkins)
Discus	1st–Frazer (Hampden-Sydney)–137'11⅛"; 2nd–Pence (Bridgewater); 3rd–Love (Johns Hopkins); 4th–Foltz (Roanoke); 5th–Wiley (Hampden-Sydney); 6th–Baklar (Johns Hopkins)

Shot	1st–Frazer (Hampden-Sydney)–44'7"; 2nd–Wiley (Hampden-Sydney); 3rd–McCullough (Loyola); 4th–Itzkof (American); 5th–Love (Johns Hopkins); 6th–Foltz (Roanoke)
440 Yards	1st–Favo (Catholic)–:49.5; 2nd–Brown (Hampden-Sydney); 3rd–Overby (Hampden-Sydney); 4th–Butler (Western Maryland); 5th–Will (Bridgewater); 6th–Groschan (Catholic)

Dave Foltz of Roanoke qualified in four events–high hurdles, low hurdles, and even the shot put and discus. Dick Seed and Bruce Johnston joined him in qualifying for both hurdles. The Maroons also moved three individuals to the finals in the 880, when Dick Goodlake, Phil Shaw, and Chris Rittman all placed among the top six. Although not mentioned in the official listing for the 220 above, George Gearhart went to Saturday's finals based on his 220 race and on his third place in the 100. Jay Jackson qualified in the broad jump. Trials were not held on Saturday in the pole vault, high jump, mile, two-mile, or the mile relay.

Three meet records were set during the two days of competition. Fred Favo of Catholic ran a :49.5 quarter-mile in the trials, beating the mark of :49.9 set in 1949 by Larry Brandenburg of Washington College. Unfortunately, he was able only to place second in Saturday's finals. Catholic's outstanding mile relay team, clearly the best team on the track Saturday, won their race in 3:25.8. The time beat the old record of 3:27.4 set by Washington College. In the pole vault, Taylor Goode of Lynchburg jumped 13'0". The height finally erased the mark of 12'6" shared by two great vaulters. One was Ray DeCosta of Roanoke and the other was the Rev. Bob Richards, who vaulted at Bridgewater and then went on to become an Olympic champion.

Roanoke had two of the three top scorers for the meet. Dick Seed finished with 10½ points, while Dave Foltz had 10.

In terms of team scoring, Roanoke picked up a total of 24 points in the hurdles alone. Foltz won both hurdle races, running :15.6 in the highs and :25.5 in the lows. Bruce Johnston and Dick Seed placed second and third in each event, respectively.

Maroons also got a one-two-four finish in the mile run. Dick Goodlake was first with a 4:36.2. Les Noel was just behind Goodlake in second. And Phil Shaw took fourth.

In the high jump, Dick Seed was at the top of his game, winning the event with a jump of 6'0". It was the first time since May of 1954 that he had jumped that high.

George Gearhart, just a sophomore, ran well against some of the best sprinters in the Conference. He placed second in both the 100- and 220-yard dashes.

Roanoke also did well in the middle distance races. Chris Rittman finished third in the 880. Trailing Rittman in fifth place was Phil Shaw.

Other scoring for Roanoke came from Foltz, who finished fourth in the discus; Jackson, fifth in the broad jump and a tie for fourth in the high jump; and Don Wilkie, who jumped well in the pole vault by finishing an unexpected third.

By the end of the day on Saturday, Roanoke men had accumulated $62^{1}/_{10}$ points, which almost doubled the score of 32 points for second-place Hampden-Sydney. Third was Catholic (23), fourth place went to Bridgewater ($22^{1}/_{5}$), and fifth was taken by Johns Hopkins ($16^{14}/_{15}$).

The win meant that Roanoke was Mason-Dixon champions for the 1954-55 session in cross country, indoor track, and outdoor track.

I remember . . . "This was the meet when George Gearhart, myself, one person I can't remember, and John Summers ran the mile relay. At the three-quarters point in the race, Roanoke had a tremendous lead. Unfortunately, the anchor man for Catholic University was the unbelievably-talented Fred Favo. Favo, when pushed, easily could run a 48-second quarter. We must have had a 30-yard lead when our anchor man, John Summers, took the baton. John was an outstanding 440 man in his own right. As soon as Favo got the baton, he took off after John, catching and passing him before John could reach the backstretch. The Catholic team went on to win the race in 3:25.8, setting a new Mason-Dixon record."

Howard Light

I remember . . . "Dick Goodlake ran with such ease. Coming into the homestretch of the Mason-Dixon meet his freshman year, I stood at the beginning of the home stretch yelling, 'Go, Dick. Go.' I think I scared him to death so much that he turned it on. I had gotten so mad at him because he was just cruising along. And after I yelled at him, he actually won the event. He had a good kick and could run a pretty good quarter mile. We even ran him in the mile relay occasionally."

Homer Bast

May 21, 1955
Virginia AAU Championships at Lexington, Virginia
Team Scores: 1st–Virginia Military Institute–65½
2nd–Downtown Athletic Club of Charlottesville–25
3rd–Norfolk Sports Club–24
4th–Quantico Marines–22½
5th–Miller School–6

6th–Roanoke College–5
7th–Lynchburg College–4
8th–Bridgewater College–2
9th–Washington and Lee University–1

For the State AAU meet on May 21 in Lexington, Coach Bast entered only two men–Les Noel and Dave Foltz. In the meet, won by V. M. I. with 65½ points, Roanoke still finished in sixth place with 5 points.

Noel ran the mile and placed second. Foltz placed third in the high hurdles. Neither of their times was recorded.

Dash man and hurdler, Johnny Mapp, running unattached this year, picked up individual scoring honors with wins in the 100 and 220. Mapp, who was a scoring sensation through his last year at V. M. I., was now a medical student at the University of Virginia.

I remember . . . "And there was George Gearhart. I'll never forget the time that we had a guy who came to do an assembly of some kind. We all had to go down to the Salem Theater. The guy was a hypnotist. He was bringing people up on the stage and hypnotizing them. And then he would wake them up. I think that one of the guys he brought up was George. Or maybe George was just sitting in the audience. At any rate, after the performance, everyone got up to leave and there was George–just sitting there. So we called the guy down from the stage and told him that George was still out. He was hypnotized and couldn't wake up. It took the guy a long time to bring George out. That was the funniest thing. And finally, George came out of the Salem Theater and he was just ga-ga."

John Summers

Chapter Eleven

The 1955-56 Seasons

Cross Country

During early training for the coming cross-country season, Coach Bast suspected that he might not be able to match last year's undefeated season, not to mention the championship titles for the Little Seven and Mason-Dixon Conferences. In addition, he had lost to graduation one of the best distance runners in the history of the College, Les Noel. He had no seniors on the squad and so far knew little about the abilities of some of the new athletes.

The *Brackety-Ack*, as it usually did, listed about 15 men who were showing up at practices. By the first meet, however, six of them–juniors Alfred Base, Larry Carlson, and Phil Duvall, along with freshmen Lynwood Thomas, Bruce Briggs, and Howard Brodsky–had dropped off the team altogether.

That left Bast with a nine-man roster. At the end of the track season last year, the returning team members had elected Bruce Fariss of Allisonia, Virginia, and Phil Shaw of Irvington, New York, as their Co-Captains. Both were juniors. Before coming to Roanoke, Shaw had very little track experience in high school. Fariss, who had no experience at all in running high school track, couldn't participate in track during the past outdoor season because of an illness. The other lettermen were sophomores Dick Goodlake of Garden City, New York, and Bill Cerelli of West New York, New York. Junior George Grove of Strasburg had not lettered at Roanoke, but would become a good runner for the team this year.

What Bast didn't know was that he had four of the best freshman runners ever to enroll at Roanoke. The four included Howard Meincke of Milltown, New York; Warren Light of Baldwin, New York; Richard Lewis of Carnford, New Jersey; and Pete Wise from Absecon, New Jersey.

The 1955 cross country team.
First Row (L to R): Phil Shaw, Coach Bast, and Bruce Fariss.
Second Row (L to R): Dick Goodlake, Bill Cerelli, Dick Lewis, and Howard Meincke.
Third Row (L to R): George Grove, Pete Wise, Don D'Agostino, and Warren Light.

October 1, 1955
The University of Tennessee at Knoxville, Tennessee
Team Scores: University of Tennessee–27
Roanoke–29

Roanoke opened its 1955 season against the University of Tennessee in Knoxville on Saturday, October 1. The meet, also Tennessee's opener, would be an event coupled with the Tennessee-Duke football game. Even with a young squad, Bast thought he might have at least a good chance of beating the Volunteers. On the other hand, Tennessee had been the runner-up team in the potent Southeastern Conference the year before.

Early in the race, Dick Goodlake led the rest of the runners through about the $1\frac{1}{2}$-mile mark on the fairly-short, 2.7-mile course. At that point, says an article in the *Brackety-Ack*, Dick was stricken with a stomach cramp which felt worse with every step. When the cramp hit, he was leading the race by a comfortable margin. Homer today swears that Dick took a wrong turn because he hadn't been listening well when Tennessee showed the team the course before the race. He says that Dick simply took the wrong turn and couldn't reverse himself in time to help his team win the race. According to Homer, it was a race that Dick should have won.

On the other hand, Bruce Fariss–just behind Goodlake in the race–gives the correct version of the story. Bruce said, "Dick had cramps and stopped running, I came up to him and threatened him with his life if he didn't start to run again." Bruce then continued the race and was leading until the last half mile, when Howard Meincke overtook Bruce and went on to win by some 70 yards. Meincke's winning time was 13:46. Bruce finished second, only 14 seconds behind.

Four Tennessee runners then took the third through sixth places before Goodlake managed to cross the line in 14:50 and Warren Light took the eighth position with a time of 14:58. Phil Shaw was eleventh and George Grove twelfth.

The team scores were University of Tennessee, 27, and Roanoke, 29. Goodlake's stomach cramps were the deciding factor. Had he stayed in the top three, a likely scenario, Roanoke would have taken the first, second, third, eighth, and eleventh places to win the meet, 25 to 31.

I remember . . . "This was the meet that finished during the halftime of one of their football games. I was in pretty good shape at that time, but with about a half mile to go, I had one of those major stitches. It practically crippled me. We lost by a couple of points, and I took the loss badly. I thought it was my stitch that had been at fault. At the time of the stitch, I wasn't leading the race. But I was up front in about the third spot."

Warren Light

I remember . . . "At the Tennessee meet, we ran during the half time of their football game. There were about 90,000 to 100,000 people in the stands. After we finished the race in front of the fans, we were allowed to sit on the bench near the football players for the rest of the game."

Homer Bast

October 7, 1955
Randolph-Macon at Ashland, Virginia
Team Scores: Roanoke–20
Randolph-Macon–36

On October 7, Roanoke met Randolph-Macon College in Ashland. This is the meet Coach Bast still remembers as a comedy of errors. Randolph-Macon wasn't supposed to give Roanoke much of a fight.

And they wouldn't have, if four of Roanoke's top runners–Dick Goodlake, Howard Meincke, Bruce Fariss, and Warren Light–hadn't all taken a wrong course turn.

The mistake allowed Phil Shaw to win the race in a time of 18:02, with Dick Lewis unofficially finishing five seconds later. Bill Cerelli took the official second place spot, followed by Pete Wise. George Grove came across the line in fifth place. Shaw later said that he couldn't believe his eyes when he came down the stretch that the finish line string hadn't been broken. He had been so far behind during the race that he never noticed that his four teammates had taken the wrong turn.

Goodlake, Meincke, Fariss, and Light all got back on the right path, and finished in ninth, tenth, twelfth, and thirteenth place, respectively.

I remember . . . "I was running with a buddy and we come to the end, where you were to run toward the finish line on the track. And there was this ribbon across the track. We knew something was funny, because there were several Roanoke runners who should have been in front of us. What happened was that they got lost. So Phil Shaw won, Dick Lewis was second, and I finished third. But our team was so strong that it didn't really matter. We still beat Randolph-Macon badly. When I saw that tape, I said to myself, 'What the hell is going on here?' I knew that I had run the correct course."

Bill Cerelli

I remember . . . "There was a cross country meet where Howard Meincke and others got lost. I was so far behind that I didn't see the group make the wrong turn, so I ended up winning the meet."

Phil Shaw

I remember . . . "We came to a fork in the road and when there was nobody around in front of you, we just went the wrong direction. We ran and ran, and didn't see anyone. We said to each other, something is wrong with this. So we turned around and went back, and took the other fork. We gave Phil Shaw a chance to win, and for Bill Cerelli to come in second. That was especially good for Bill. Bill was a skinny guy who only ran cross country. He looked like he was going to die every time he ran. But he always managed to stick in there. I would think, "Look at this guy. He is really struggling. But he is sticking with it."

Bruce Fariss

October 14, 1955
Washington and Lee at Salem, Virginia
Team Scores: Roanoke–17
Washington and Lee–42

Washington and Lee visited Salem seven days later. Before their first meet of the year, the Maroons had only 10 days of practice, and then competed against a strong University of Tennessee team. The next week was the wrong-turn fiasco at Randolph-Maxon. So Coach Bast still couldn't tell the exact strength of his team. Now, however, the men had trained sufficiently and Bast was eager to find out just how good they might be.

To be honest, Homer suspected that the Lexington school didn't have anywhere close to the talent of his Roanoke team. In fact, Washington and Lee was still looking for its first win after close defeats in two triangular meets. Pacing the visitors would be Mike Barry and Bill Armstrong.

Despite the wet home course, freshman Howard Meincke gave a hint of good things to come when he surged to the front and won the meet with a time of 16:14, just 10 seconds shy of Les Noel's course record. Dick Goodlake, as he did last year when he seemed to stay close to Noel each week, finished in second with a time of 16:23. Bruce Fariss was third in 16:45 and Phil Shaw took fourth in 17:03. After John Duffey and John Armstrong of W & L crossed the line, Warren Light finished the Roanoke scoring by taking seventh place.

Other Maroons were Bill Cerelli, in eighth; Dick Lewis, in tenth; and Pete Wise, in thirteenth. The final score of the meet was 17 to 42 in Roanoke's favor.

October 20, 1955
Virginia Polytechnic Institute at Blacksburg, Virginia
Team Scores: Virginia Polytechnic Institute–28
Roanoke–29

Sometimes as a cross country coach, you can only stand back and watch what happens. That was the case in the V. P. I. meet. Homer's young and inexperienced squad was meeting a team from a school that was much larger and should have superior talent.

The Roanoke team left the Salem campus and took the road for a short distance to compete in Blacksburg. V. P. I.'s course–about 4.2 miles in length–would be a challenge. Howard Meincke was the pace setter, covering the distance in 22:48 for a win. He was 23 seconds ahead of Tech's Charles Catlett. Then came Bruce Fariss of Roanoke, Bob Wingfield of Tech, Phil Shaw of Roanoke, Herb Huffman of Tech, and Terry Drew of Tech, who finished in seventh place. Unfortunately, the Maroons could not place a fifth man high enough to win the meet. The score was V. P. I., 28, and Roanoke, 29. Bill Cerelli finished in eighth place, Pete Wise in twelfth, and Dick Lewis was thirteenth.

Coach Bast took the loss in stride. He knew he had the makings of a good team–one certainly good enough to win the Little Seven and Mason-Dixon Championships–but again he needed to keep the time span between first and fifth place to 1:00 or less. In today's meet, the span stretched to 2:11.5. Look at how close some of the runners were to their opponents from Tech, he thought. Cerelli was just a second behind seventh place, for example. And Wise and Lewis weren't far out of eleventh place.

October 24, 1955
University of Virginia at Charlottesville, Virginia
Team Scores: Roanoke–21
University of Virginia–39

The team record now was 2-2, with both losses so close that Roanoke easily could be 4-0. On October 24, Bast's team traveled to Charlottesville to meet the University of Virginia on their 3.9-mile course.

The coach had a good feeling about this one. His teams had met the University squads several times over the past few years, and Roanoke had never lost to them.

Today's star was sophomore Dick Goodlake. He covered the distance in 20:42. Not only was that time just eight seconds off the course record, but the record had been set earlier in the season by U. N. C.'s famous distance runner, Jim Beatty. Beatty is perhaps best remembered as the first person to break the four-minute mile barrier on an indoor track when he ran 3:58.9 on February 10, 1962, in Los Angeles.

Goodlake was three seconds ahead of Virginia's John Farrier and five seconds in front of teammate Bruce Fariss. Except for the meet when he took the wrong turn, Howard Meincke failed to win. Instead, he crossed in fourth place with a time of 21:10. Phil Shaw was sixth, Dick Lewis was seventh, Bill Cerelli was eighth, and Pete Wise finished in tenth place.

Roanoke won the meet, 21 to 39. And Coach Bast felt good about their efforts.

October 28, 1955
Hampden-Sydney at Salem, Virginia
Team Scores: Roanoke–17
Hampden-Sydney–46

On October 28, Roanoke hosted the cross country team from Hampden-Sydney. Howard Meincke finished well out in front with a time of 16:14. It was the same time he recorded in the only other home meet, against Washington and Lee, and again he couldn't erase the course record time of 16:04.

Well behind Meincke were Bruce Fariss and Dick Goodlake, who tied for second in a time of 16:53. Roanoke's Phil Shaw was fifth and Dick Lewis was sixth to finish the scoring. Bill Cerelli, in seventh, was just three seconds behind Lewis, and Pete Wise in eighth place ran an 18:14.

Roanoke captured the first, second, third, fifth, and sixth places for a total of 17 points. Hampden-Sydney was able only to place fourth (Bunting Brown), ninth, tenth, eleventh, and twelfth for 46 points.

The win was Roanoke's fourth against two losses.

November 4, 1955
Lynchburg College at Salem, Virginia
Team Scores: Roanoke–20
Lynchburg–43

Roanoke's third home meet came on May 4, 1955. Their opponent, Lynchburg College, had beaten Hampden-Sydney during the season, but had lost to the Bridgewater and V. P. I. teams. Herman Attwood, a cross country veteran, paced the Lynchburg squad. A freshman, Peter Little, was almost as talented.

Warren Light, a fine freshman prospect, was still out of the lineup with a severe pull in his side. His problems, along with those of George Grove, out with a similar injury, had handicapped the squad throughout the season. On the other hand, Bast had complimented Bill Cerelli for his efforts. He had scored some valuable points for the team during the past few meets.

Roanoke had few problems defeating Lynchburg. The score was 20 to 43. Although the day was cold and the wind blustery, Howard Meincke covered the 3.1-mile course in a personal-best of 16:07. Lynchburg's Atwood was second.

Then the Roanoke team took the next three positions. Dick Goodlake finished just 14 seconds behind Meincke in taking third place, while Phil Shaw finished fourth and Warren Light, running for the first time since the Washington and Lee meet, took fifth. Bruce Fariss was Roanoke's fifth man across the line, placing seventh. Bill Cerelli and Dick Lewis tied for the eighth spot, and Pete Wise finished eleventh.

November 11, 1955
The Little Eight Championships at Bridgewater, Virginia
Team Scores: 1st–Roanoke College-33
2nd–Bridgewater College–55
3rd–Lynchburg College–95
4th–Norfolk William and Mary College–95
5h–Randolph-Macon College–120
6th–Hampden-Sydney College–128

Roanoke and Bridgewater were the co-favorites to win the Little Eight Championships on Friday afternoon, May 11. The meet was held on Bridgewater's 3.1-mile course. The Maroons had won the title five times–in 1947, 1948, 1949, 1953, and 1954. Bridgewater took team honors in 1950, 1951, and 1952.

This year, Roanoke went into the meet with a 5-2 overall record. The team's only two losses were by a total of three points when they ran the University of Tennessee and Virginia Polytechnic Institute. Bridgewater was unbeaten in dual meets.

Norfolk Division of William Mary competed as a conference member for the first time and there was some concern that they might surprise Roanoke or Bridgewater. The other teams in the meet were Hampden-Sydney, Randolph-Macon, and Lynchburg. Emory and Henry and Richmond Professional Institute, other members of the conference, did not enter teams.

Howard Meincke, one of two or three favorites in the race, was the star for Roanoke College. A freshman, he covered the 3.25 mile course in the record time of 17:33. The old record of 17:33.9 was set last year by Roanoke's Les Noel.

Roanoke's Dick Goodlake finished second, about 50 yards in back of Meincke. Trailing Goodlake were Herman Atwood of Lynchburg; Baxter Berryhill of Norfolk Division of William and Mary, Dick Little of Lynchburg, Jim Lohr of Bridgewater, and Ronnie Drumwright of Norfolk Division of William and Mary.

Roanoke's next three runners, Bruce Fariss in eighth place, Phil Shaw in ninth, and finally, Bill Cerelli in thirteenth, brought Roanoke the meet's low winning score of 33 points. Warren Light was fourteenth and Pete Wise came in twenty-second.

In team scoring, Bridgewater had 55 points for second place; Lynchburg had 95 for third; Norfolk Division of William and Mary took fourth with 95; Randolph-Macon was fifth with 120, and Hampden-Sydney brought up the rear with 128 points.

The first five finishers in the meet were awarded Little Eight medals.

November 19, 1955
Mason-Dixon Championships at Bridgewater, Virginia
Team Scores: 1st–Roanoke College-26
2nd–Bridgewater College–57
3rd–Catholic University –91
4th–Johns Hopkins University–142
5th–Gallaudet College–167
6th–Hampden-Sydney College–183
7th–Loyola College–212
8th–Towson State College–212
9th–Washington College–231

10th–Mount St. Mary's College–247
11th–American University–Incomplete Score

The only competition remaining this fall for the Roanoke team was the Mason-Dixon Championships. This year, the race was to be held at Bridgewater on the same 3.1-mile course used just a week before during the Little Eight meet. The starting time was 2:00 p.m.

Roanoke was the favorite in the 11-team field to win the fourteenth annual Conference meet. But it would be difficult to predict the individual winner. The 1954 race was won by Lou Buckley of Washington College over a heavy track in a fairly good time of 16:11.

One of the highest-rated competitors was Steve Kugel of Gallaudet. He finished third last year with an amazing comeback effort, and this year had broken several course records. Roanoke's Howard Meincke, just a freshman, had looked good all season and won the Little Eight title over the Bridgewater course last week. His teammate, Dick Goodlake, took fourth place last year, but during 1954 had lost a bit of his effectiveness because of calcium deposits. Dick Messersmith of Catholic, Ned Billeb of Loyola, and Herman Atwood of Lynchburg each had a chance of winning.

In terms of team competition, the host Bridgewater team might be the best-balanced team and able to challenge Roanoke for top honors. Yet, they lacked an outstanding runner who could compete at the front of the pack. At the same time, they were unbeaten in five straight regular-season meets.

Catholic, featuring three excellent runners in Messersmith, Nelson, and Madison, lost only one of seven meets. The single loss was to Bridgewater by a slim 28-31 margin. And even Towson State could push the top teams for the trophy, but theirs definitely was a dark horse role.

Coach Bast, looking for his fourth Mason-Dixon cross country crown, took seven men to the meet. They were Howard Meincke, Dick Lewis, Bill Cerelli, Phil Shaw, Dick Goodlake, Bruce Fariss, and Warren Light.

On the morning of the meet, Coach Harry Jopson had to make a decision about the course. Generally, the course began on a macadam road, and then wound its way over a dirt road and a grass surface to a finish on cinders at Riverside Field. Unfortunately, the weather for the race was more suitable for skiing than for running. Because of the snow, the race was changed so that the athletes ran over an all-macadam course totaling, the best Bridgewater officials could tell, about 2.5 to 3.0 miles in length.

The gun sounded and 81 runners left the starting line. Gallaudet's Steve Kugel was first across the finish line in a time of 13:57.7, but Roanoke runners came home second, third, fourth, and seventh to assure the Maroons of another crown. In second place was

Howard Meincke, only 15.3 seconds behind Kugel. Third place was taken by Dick Goodlake in 14:20, with Phil Shaw grabbing the fourth spot in a time of 14:29. All they needed to win now was to bring two more runners across in decent positions. Bruce Fariss and Warren Light placed seventh and tenth in the race, just a few seconds in back of Shaw, and the Maroons had taken its fourth Mason-Dixon title since Bast had begun the cross-country program in 1947-48.

Bridgewater, as expected, placed second in the meet with 57 points. Catholic was third, Johns Hopkins fourth, Gallaudet fifth, and Hampden-Sydney sixth.

And Coach Bast was happy. Finally, the time span between his first and fifth runner was just 26 seconds. In addition, the team had finished its dual-meet season with a 5-2 record and the possibility of finishing with no losses at all, and had won both the Little Eight and Mason-Dixon crowns to finish the season.

Indoor Track

Beginning in 1952, Roanoke won the first- and second-annual Mason-Dixon Championships and took first place in all three Little Six, Little Seven, or Little Eight Conference meets. This year's team would be stacked even more than before with quality athletes. For the state and Mason-Dixon teams, competing against Roanoke was like staring down the barrel of a loaded gun. There was so much talent already on the Maroon squad, with more to come, that a repeat of the two indoor championships was not only likely, but expected.

Here are some of the athletes Bast was able to call upon during the season:

60	George Gearhart Jim Nichols Bruce Johnston
440	John Summers Dick Lewis Al Ide George Gearhart Howard Light John Summers
880	Dick Lewis Phil Shaw John Summers

Mile/Two Mile	Howard Meincke Johnnie Blanton Bruce Fariss Dick Goodlake Phil Shaw
Hurdles	Bruce Johnston Dick Seed Jim Driscoll
Jumps	George Gearhart Jim Nichols Bill Schreiner Dick Seed Don Wilkie Frank Vest Jim Driscoll
Throws	Palm, Bob Jim Driscoll

January 21, 1956
Evening Star Games at Washington, D. C.

Intercollegiate Class B Mile Relay	1st–Montclair State Teachers College (Harrell, Scofield, Lavach, and Rame)–3:38.2; 2nd–Roanoke College (Shaw, Meincke, Goodlake, and Lewis); 3rd-Virginia Military Institute
A. A. U. One-Mile Handicap Relay	Section One: 1st–Baltimore Olympics Club, 12 Yards (Jimeson, Voight, Waggner, Fleming)–3:34.3; 2nd–Roanoke College, 12 Yards (Shaw, Summers, Meincke, and Gearhart); 3rd–Oriole Track Club, 15 Yards; 4th–Baltimore CC, 20 Yards Section Two: 1st–New York Pioneer Athletic Club, No Yards (Bright, Jones, Majocco, and Pearman)–3:24.2 (new meet record);

	2nd–Sjamejam CC. 6 Yards; 3rd–Maryland Frosh, 10 Yards; 4th–Stevens Trade School, 12 Yards
	Section Three: 1st–Winston-Salem Teachers Frosh, No Yards (Mack, Johnson, Horne, and Conoway)–3:30.8; 2nd–Seton Hall, No Yards; 3rd–Morgan State, No Yards; 4th–Virginia State Frosh, No Yards
Mason-Dixon One-Mile Sprint Medley Relay	1st–Roanoke College (Summers, Ide, Gearhart, and Lewis)–3:46.5; 2nd–Catholic University; 3rd–Towson State Teacher's College

For the large, prestigious Evening Star Games in Washington, Coach Bast entered teams in the Mason-Dixon Conference Sprint Medley Relay, the Intercollegiate Class "B" One-Mile Relay, and the A. A. U. One-Mile Handicap Relay.

In the sprint medley race, the Roanoke team of John Summers, Al Ide, George Gearhart, and Dick Lewis won the event with a time of 3:46.5. They beat second-place Catholic University, who had defeated the Maroons in the 1955 sprint medley relay.

Phil Shaw, Howard Meincke, Dick Goodlake, and Dick Lewis combined for second place in the Intercollegiate Class "B" Mile Relay. Montclair State Teachers College just nipped Roanoke for that title. No time for the race was recorded.

Roanoke also placed second in the A. A. U. One-Mile Handicap Relay. The Baltimore Olympic Club won the race with a time of 3:34.3. The Roanoke team consisted of Phil Shaw, John Summers, Howard Meincke, and George Gearhart.

The highlight events of the day included the sprints. The new sensation Dave Sime of Duke University made a clean sweep of the sprint series. The 19-year-old sophomore from Fair Lawn, New Jersey, was a favorite of the gallery of more than 5,000. Sime set a new American indoor record for the 100-yard dash with at time of :09.5, after winning both the 70- and 80-yard races. He had a time of :07.0 in the 70, good for a meet record, and an :08.0 in the 80. A 6'2", 180-pound, crew cut runner attended Duke on a baseball scholarship. When he came to the University, he had never participated in track.

Rev. Bob Richards again won the pole vault. Horace Ashenfelter was the winner of the two-mile race, and Tom Courtney took first in the Touchdown Club 1,000-yard run.

February 4, 1956
Virginia Military Institute Winter Relays at Lexington, Virginia

Team Scores: None

By this time, in its fifth year, the V. M. I. Winter Relays attracted some of the best track teams in the east–the University of North Carolina, Georgetown University, Duke, and others. It was the type of meet where Roanoke would have the chance to compete with some great athletes. If they brought back any medals, Bast thought, then all the better.

Maryland and the University of North Carolina put on displays of strength to capture four first place medals each and tie for another. The Tarheels' amazing distance runner, Jim Beatty, was voted the outstanding runner of the meet. Teammate Charley Yarborough won the trophy as the best field performer. In the two-mile event, Beatty was timed in 9:36.5, which was almost unheard of in winter track in those days. He beat the old Relays record by more than 42 seconds. Dave Pitkethly, the very talented V. M. I. sophomore, was second. The first four runners all beat the former record.

The Maroons were entered in several relay events. The event they most wanted to win was the Mason-Dixon distance medley relay (440, 880, three-fourths mile, and mile legs). Roanoke held the record for that event, set in 1955 by Howard Light, Chris Rittman, Phil Shaw, and Les Noel.

It was an excellent race, matching Roanoke against a strong Catholic University team. Roanoke broke the record in the event, only to have Catholic beat them by a couple of seconds. The Catholic time was almost four seconds better than the record that Roanoke had set in 1955. Running for Roanoke were John Summers, Dick Lewis, Howard Meincke, and Phil Shaw.

Howard Light, George Gearhart, Al Ide, and Dick Lewis also entered the sprint medley relay (440, 220, 220, and 880). Although their time was not recorded, the team finished second to Georgetown and ahead of good teams from V. M. I. and the University of Maryland. The *Brackety-Ack* noted that the team ran well, and that they were beaten narrowly by the winning team from Georgetown, who were timed in 3:46.3. In the recent Evening Star Games in Washington, Roanoke had run a 3:47.2 for first place.

In the four-mile relay, where each individual runs one mile, Roanoke's entries were Warren Light, Bruce Fariss, Dick Goodlake, and Howard Meincke. They placed fourth in this event, behind outstanding teams from U. N. C., Maryland, and North Carolina State.

Coach Bast even entered a team in the shuttle relays. The team was composed of four of these five athletes: Jim O'Mahony, George Gearhart, Jim Nichols, Bruce Johnston, and Bill Driscoll. The exact names of the participants are unknown. The team failed to place.

A similar situation occurred in the 880 relay (4 X 220). The *Brackety-Ack* reported before the meet that Bast would choose his team from among Al Ide, George Gearhart, Jim Nichols, Bruce Johnston, and Bill Driscoll. Again, this team did not place in the top four.

Several Maroons also entered individual field events. Bob Palm threw the shot. Dick Seed, Bill Driscoll, and Dick Stauffer high jumped. And Don Wilkie, Bill Schreiner, and Frank Vest pole vaulted. None of these individuals placed.

February 11, 1956
Little Eight Championships at Lexington, Virginia
Team Scores: 1st–Roanoke College–72
2nd–Norfolk Division of William and Mary–22
3rd–Lynchburg College–14
4th–Randolph-Macon College–11
5th–Hampden-Sydney College–9
6th–Bridgewater College–1

Roanoke was favored to win its third straight Little Eight indoor games, held in Lexington at the V. M. I. field house on February 11. As usual this meet and the Big Six meet with larger state schools would be run concurrently. If the Maroons were to be pushed for team honors, the competition likely would come from Lynchburg College or the Norfolk Division of William and Mary, a first-time entrant in the meet.

Team depth was the factor that almost guaranteed a Roanoke win. Other teams, such as Lynchburg, Norfolk Division of William and Mary, Bridgewater, and Randolph-Macon, all had outstanding individuals who could win their events.

Going into the meet, here is how most of the coaches picked the winners of the Little Eight contest:

60-Yard Dash	Dick Jarrett (Lynchburg) – Defending Champion George Gearhart (Roanoke) Charlie Nuttycombe (Randolph-Macon) Charles Holt (Hampden-Sydney)
440-Yard Dash	Dick Lewis (Roanoke) Howard Light (Roanoke) John Summers (Roanoke) Allen Ide (Roanoke) Bunting Brown (Hampden-Sydney) Pete Grandel (Bridgewater)
880-Yard Run	Phil Shaw (Roanoke)–Record Holder from the 1955 Meet Dave Brown (Hampden-Sydney)

	Ronnie Drumwright (Norfolk Division of William and Mary) John Summers (Roanoke) Dick Lewis (Roanoke)
Mile Run	Herman Atwood (Lynchburg)–Conference Outdoor Champion Dick Goodlake (Roanoke) Baxter Berryhill (Norfolk Division of William and Mary)
Two-Mile Run	Herman Atwood (Lynchburg) Baxter Berryhill (Norfolk Division of William and Mary) Howard Meincke (Roanoke)
Hurdles	Dick Seed (Roanoke) Bruce Johnston (Roanoke) Bill Armstrong (Randolph-Macon) Cowleck (Lynchburg) Charlie Nuttycombe (Randolph-Macon)
Mile Relay	Roanoke (Ide, H. Light, Wise, and Gearhart)
Shot Put	Jim Frazer (Hampden-Sydney)–Defending Champion Bob Palm (Roanoke)
Pole Vault	Taylor Goode (Lynchburg)–Defending Champion
High Jump	Dick Seed (Roanoke)–Defending Champion Richard Bland (Randolph-Macon) Taylor Goode (Lynchburg)
Broad Jump	Charlie Nuttycombe (Randolph-Macon)–Defending Champion

In the Big Six meet, most thought that Coach Walt Cormack would be hard put to keep V. M. I.'s strangle-hold on the crown. This year, there would be powerful challenges by Virginia Tech, Virginia, and William and Mary.

But what a meet it was for Roanoke! Maroon athletes won every single running event, and one of the four field events. It was also a day of record-breaking for the meet.

George Gearhart, fast becoming the Conference's top sprinter, won the 60-yard dash. His time was :6.3, which tied the Little Eight indoor record and set a new Roanoke

College mark as well.

Then Dick Lewis set a new 440 record, running a :53.8. The time beat the old record of :54.0 set by Paige Will of Bridgewater in 1955.

In the 880-yard run, Lewis won again. His time was a respectable 2:05.2, although he did not get the meet record. The mile was won by Roanoke's Dick Goodlake in 4:42.6.

During the two-mile race, Howard Meincke ran a good, steady race to win. His time was 10:42.6.

Roanoke, favored in the mile relay, came through to win the race in a meet record time of 3:43.4. On that team were Al Ide, Pete Wise, Howard Light, and George Gearhart.

In the hurdles, Roanoke runners picked up first and second places in the highs and first and fourth in the lows. Bruce Johnston was at his best, winning the high hurdles in :09.1 and the low hurdles in :08.0. The :09.1 was not only a meet record, but a Roanoke College record as well. The :08.0 knocked two-tenths of a second off the old mark.

The only field event which Roanoke won was the high jump. Dick Seed and Dick Stauffer tied for first place on jumps of 5'11¼".

Roanoke took second, third, and fourth places in 9 of 11 events, excluding the mile relay which they won. These places were awarded to Jim Nichols, third in the 60; Howard Light, second in the 440; Al Ide, third in the 440; John Summers, third in the 880; Phil Shaw, fourth in the 880 and third in the mile run; Bruce Fariss, third in the two-mile run; Dick Seed, second in the high hurdles and fourth in the low hurdles; Bob Palm, second in the shot put; Don Wilkie, third in the pole vault; and Bill Schreiner, fourth in the pole vault.

Roanoke won the meet with a total of 72 points, more than all of the points from the other five teams combined. Norfolk Division of William and Mary, in their inaugural appearance, placed second with 22 points. Lynchburg was third with 14; Randolph-Macon was fourth with 11; Hampden-Sydney scored 9 for fifth place; and Bridgewater, which usually had a strong team indoors, could score only 1 point for sixth place.

February 18, 1956
Mason-Dixon Championships at Lexington, Virginia
Team Scores: 1st–Roanoke College–60½
2nd–Lynchburg College–25¾
3rd–Catholic University–22
4th–Randolph-Macon College–10¾
5th–Bridgewater–10
6th–Towson State Teachers College–0

The Mason-Dixon contest was run at the same time as the Southern Conference meet at the V. M. I. field house. After the dominating performance by Roanoke in the Little Eight meet, coaches in the Mason-Dixon conference knew what was coming. No one believed that the Maroons would have any real trouble winning this meet.

Strength in depth paid off for V. P. I., especially in the last half of the program, and the Gobblers captured the Southern Conference championship with a total of 41 points. In the Mason-Dixon meet, Roanoke made a shambles of almost every event, rolling up an unheard-of 60½ points to take first place as a team. Lynchburg shocked many by taking second with 25¾ points, just ahead of Catholic (22 points, third place); Randolph-Macon (10¾, fourth place); Bridgewater (10 points, fifth place); and Towson State Teachers (no points, last place).

Six Maroons won first places. Of these six, three established new records for events in this three-year-old meet. Roanoke placed at least one man in every event, clearly establishing Roanoke as the best of the smaller area colleges.

In the field events, Roanoke athletes won, or tied for the win, in two of the four events. Bob Palm won the shot put with a throw of 41'4¼". Dick Seed and Dick Stauffer tied for first in the high jump with a height of 5'10", which tied Seed's Mason-Dixon record from 1954. In addition, Jimmy Nichols took fourth place in the broad jump, Don Wilkie took second in the pole vault, and Frank Vest was third in the pole vault.

In the high hurdles, Maroon athletes took three of the four places. Bruce Johnson was nipped at the tape and had to settle for second, while Dick Seed was third and Bill Driscoll was fourth. In the low hurdles, Johnson came back to win in :08.0, another Conference record, beating his own mark of :08.2 which he set in 1954. In that race, Dick Seed took fourth place.

In the 60-yard dash, George Gearhart's time wasn't as low as it was in the Little Eight meet, but he managed to place third. John Summers was second in the 440-yard dash, just ahead of Howard Light.

Dick Lewis, just a freshman, was outstanding in the 880. He ran away with the race, being timed in 2:01.7. The time was a meet record, beating the 2:04.0 by Paige Will of Bridgewater in 1955, and a Roanoke College record. The College record of 2:03.5 had been set by Phil Shaw in 1955. This year, Shaw was third in the race.

In the mile run, Dick Goodlake ran a 4:39.0 to win. Johnnie Blanton was fourth.

Howard Meincke, as expected, won the two-mile run in an excellent time of 10:19.8. The time was a new meet record, beating the mark of 10:22.0 set by Roanoke's Les Noel in 1954. It also set a new Roanoke College record. Bruce Fariss was second in the race and Warren Light was fourth.

The Roanoke mile relay team placed second to a good Catholic foursome.

February 24, 1956
Atlantic Coast Conference Indoor Games at Raleigh, North Carolina
Team Scores (Non-Conference Division):
1st–University of Florida–29
2nd–Naval Academy–16½
3rd–College of William and Mary–14
4th–Virginia Military Institute–10
5th–Georgia Tech University–8
6th–Virginia Polytechnic Institute–6½
7th–Roanoke College–4
8th–Presbyterian College–3
9th–Davidson University–3
10th–Norfolk Division of William and Mary–1

Coach Bast sent just a few team members to the Atlantic Coast Conference Indoor Games, an annual affair in Chapel Hill, North Carolina. This year, the meet was held on February 24.

Competing in the non-conference division, Roanoke scored four points. Dick Lewis was third in the 880 and Dick Seed tied for second in the high jump. Lewis' time and Seed's high jump height were not recorded.

Outdoor Track

The consecutive winning streak for the Roanoke outdoor track teams, beginning after the Davidson loss in 1952-53, had risen to 21. That streak included four wins in 1952-53, eight in 1953-54, and another nine in 1954-55. With seven dual meets scheduled for this year, the team could finish with 28 straight wins over four seasons.

In addition to regular-season triumphs, Roanoke had won the Little Eight title three consecutive seasons and the Mason-Dixon crown the past two years. Coach Bast had a team for the coming season which was deep in both talent and desire, with a wonderful blend of veterans and freshmen.

It was the type of squad which most coaches long to see and seldom do. In an interview with the *Brackety-Ack*, Bast said that he expected his 1956 track team to be just as strong as his championship squad of 1955. "If we don't do as well," he said, "I will be greatly disappointed." Bast went on to say that he had the best freshman material that the school had seen in recent years. The freshmen included Jimmy Nichols, a dash man and broad jumper from Roanoke; Bill Driscoll, husky and strong, who would help in the discus and other events; Dick Lewis and Pete Wise, exceptional middle distance men;

Howard Meincke, who could become Roanoke's best-ever distance runner; and Bob Palm, a big and strong weight man.

He also noted that he had a group of proven veterans who should be even better this spring. The team had lost two fine stars via graduation–Les Noel, veteran distance runner, and Jay Jackson, primarily a high jumper and broad jumper. The two were talented leaders who would be missed. On the other hand, two of the returning veterans were Dave Foltz and John Summers, selected by their teammates to be this year's Co-Captains. Both were seniors.

Foltz was from the small, rural community called Narrows, not too far from Salem. He had never competed in track before coming to Roanoke to play basketball. When Coach Bast saw him play during his freshman year, he saw Foltz's agility and will to win and invited him to come out for track–which the blond athlete did reluctantly.

As a senior, Foltz was recognized as the finest athlete ever to participate in track at the college. Since the beginning of his sophomore year at Roanoke, his best events were the high and low hurdles. He held the school record in the high hurdles, first set in 1954 with a time of :15.4 and then broken the next year with a :15.2. In the low hurdles, his own school record was :24.1, set in 1954. But the multi-talented Foltz could also gain points, and often did, in the sprints, the high jump, in the shot put and discus events, and most anything else Bast needed for him to do during a meet–except, perhaps, for the pole vault. The Coach had tried to introduce Foltz to that event early in his track career, mainly because he saw him as a future decathlete; however, it was one event to which Foltz never warmed. As this spring season opened, Foltz had accumulated the most points in track than any other athlete in Roanoke's history. Couple this fact with his winter sport of basketball, in which he also was high scorer, and one could see that this senior had enormous talent. Said one of his teammates, "When he came toward you, especially when he ran the high hurdles, Dave had that intense look on his face. His rhythm was even and you could see his desire to win the race. And his breathing sounded like a locomotive." He could have been the high scorer on any team in the Conference, and probably the high scorer on 95% of the small college teams in the nation.

The other Co-Captain was John Summers. Sometimes called Jack, the Kearny, New Jersey, runner was Mr. 440 on the team. Beginning in 1953, his freshman year, he set a series of seven school records in that event. He also ran the 880, and enjoyed that event as much as he liked the quarter mile. He was also a very good mile relay runner. He first helped break the school record in the mile relay in the Little Six Championships his freshman year but also ran on the record-setting team of 1954. This year, it looked like he had the teammates to set many more relay records.

Another veteran of the team, Bruce Johnston, was a sophomore from Roanoke, Virginia. The ex-Jefferson High School star set school records for the hurdles during the indoor season and was expected to push and perhaps even beat Foltz this spring.

Another Jefferson High School grad, also a sophomore, was Howard Light. Although prone to injuries, he had the ability to be the best quarter-miler on the team. He and Johnston were liked by almost everyone on campus, including the Coach. "They were two of the finest athletes I ever coached," said Bast. "Just wonderful boys who would do anything you asked them to do."

Another important member of the team was George Gearhart, an enormously-talented sprinter and mile relay runner. In 1955, he had set the school record in the 100-yard dash by running :10.0. In fact, he ran that time twice that year. He was also quite a competitor in the 220. In 1955 he was timed at :22.6 twice to set a new school record, then ran :22.4 in the Little Seven Championships.

Two other polished veterans were Dick Goodlake, an outstanding distance runner slated to set new school and Alumni Field records, and Dick Seed, who would become a fine hurdler and already was one of the best high jumpers around. Add them to Allen Ide, who was excellent in the dashes and broad jump; David Moore, pole vault specialist; Cliff Shaw, a very capable broad jumper; Jim Wallwork, a journeyman in the hurdles and dashes; Johnnie Blanton, a good distance man; and Don Wilkie, who joined David Moore to give strength to the pole vault event. And there was also Phil Shaw, a junior letterman who was a terrific middle-distance and distance man. He had set the Alumni Field record for the 880 at 2:01.5 during the 1955 season.

In terms of freshmen, there were several men who would help the team this year. One was Bob Palm, who set the school record for the shot put during the indoor season.

The school's number one cross country runner in the fall of 1955, Howard Meincke was expected to do well in the mile and two mile. He had the potential to become Roanoke's all-time best distance runner.

Another freshman, Jim Nichols, came from Roanoke's Jefferson High School. Coach Bast saw him as a top dash and broad jump candidate.

First year men Dick Lewis, Dick Stauffer, Frank Vest, Warren Light, Bill Driscoll, and Pete Wise were also set to play important roles for the Maroons. Lewis, it was obvious, could make mincemeat out of the current 880 records. Stauffer was a fairly good high jumper. Vest was a good-looking pole vaulter, and so was Bill Schreiner. Light looked as if he could score lots of points in the distance races before he graduated. Driscoll was a decent shot putter, but would likely make his name as a discus thrower. He also could run the hurdles. And Wise seemed to be the type of hungry, talented runner who be one of the finest athletes on the team in the next two or three years.

I remember . . . "Well, I liked to throw the discus and may have been better at the event in high school than in college. In high school, I threw it 146'6". At the time, that was close to being the state high school record. I had some practice throws of around 160'. But in those days, I was skinny as a rail. Even at Roanoke, I weighed around 165 pounds or so. I was 6'2" tall. I found that the difference in weight between a high school and college discus made a great deal of difference to me. If I could have been about 50 pounds heavier, it might have been a different story."

Jim Driscoll

I remember . . . "Well, Homer told me to go out and watch people jump. I knew nothing about the pole vault. I had seen it, of course, but never thought about me actually competing in the event. And I had seen Bob Richards' picture on a box of Wheaties. Then Homer gave me one of those little books, where you could flip the pages quickly and see a figure doing something physical. In my case, it was a book showing how the pole vault was done. He told me, 'Flip through that book a hundred times a day. You've got to get that image in your mind.' And that's how I learned to jump. In my first practices, I did a lot of run-throughs, trying to get my steps right and without a bar. I would just plant the pole and swing upward. And also, Homer watched me and coached me a lot in those early weeks. As I remember, we didn't have a pole for every vaulter. I believe we shared the same pole. I remember that the pole was made of Swedish steel. I started out practicing with a bamboo pole. Then I switched to the Swedish steel pole for competition, which was absolutely inflexible."

Frank Vest

April 7, 1956
Norfolk Division of William and Mary at Salem, Virginia
Team Scores: Roanoke–90
Norfolk Division of William and Mary–32

The opening meet of the 1956 outdoor season was held on April 7, 1956. The visiting team was the Norfolk Division of William and Mary. Unfortunately, the weather that day wasn't very good for a track meet. There was a gusting wind and because of recent rains, the track in spots was filled with puddles of water. On top of all that, it was cold–the type of day when you really don't want to take off your sweats to compete. Despite the adverse conditions, Roanoke showed its team strength by placing first in 13 of the 14 events and winning the meet 90 to 32.

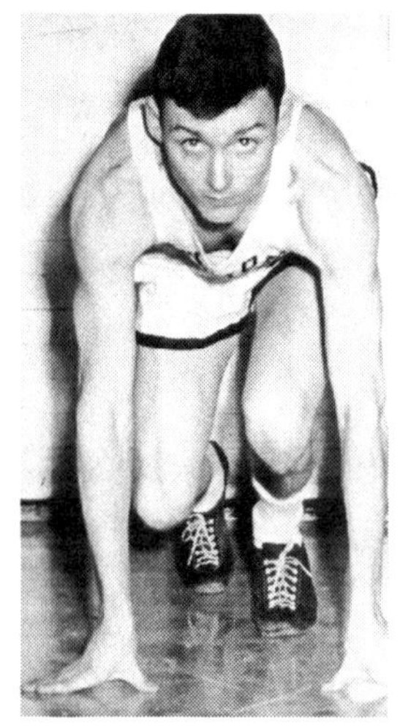

Left Photo: In the meet with Norfolk Division of William and Mary, George Gearhart (left) won both the 100- and 220-yard dashes, while Dave Foltz (right) finished second in each of the races.
Middle Photo: Dick Goodlake was an excellent runner even in 1955, his freshman year.
Right Photo: George Gearhart, a junior, was Roanoke's best sprinter.

Only one man set a record. Freshman Bob Palm threw the shot 43'10¼" to set a new Alumni Field record. The old mark of 42'10½" was set in 1953 by Bill Lund. Palm's throw also set a new school record, beating the record of 43'1½" set by Lund in 1954.

Otherwise, Maroon athletes were good but not great. In the 100, for example, George Gearhart won with a decent time of :10.1, with Jim Nichols in third with a :10.6. The 440-yard dash winner was Howard Light, running :54.0. Teammate Al Ide was second in :55, with Pete Wise running third in :55.2. Gearhart came back to win the 220, in :23.2, while Nichols was timed at :23.8 in third.

Dick Lewis coasted through a 2:07.4 880-yard race to place first. Phil Shaw was third in 2:09.

Dick Goodlake had an easy race in winning the mile run. His time was 4:35.4. Johnnie Blanton was third. Howard Meincke won the two-mile race in a slow 10:49.5, with Bruce Fariss taking third place in 11:00.0.

As expected by most everyone on the field, Dave Foltz won both hurdles. Dick Seed was third in the high hurdles and Bill Driscoll came in second well back of Foltz in the low hurdles.

Foltz scored points in the shot and discus, as he often did. He placed second in the shot, throwing a bit over 40', and third in the discus. Palm's discus throw placed him second in that event. Jim Driscoll won the discus with a throw of 120'4".

In a fairly weak event for the Maroons, the only person for Roanoke who placed in the broad jump was Jim Nichols. His jump was 19'5½", about 1½' behind the winner.

Dick Seed did well in the high jump considering the weather, winning with 5'10". Dick Stauffer was second with a 5'9" jump.

Bill Schreiner tied for the win in the pole vault with a fine 11'6" effort and Don Wilkie was third, clearing the bar a foot lower than Schreiner.

The final Roanoke win came in the mile relay. The team of Ide, Light, Lewis, and Summers was timed in 3:39.0.

April 14, 1956
Newport News Apprentice School at Salem, Virginia
Team Scores: Roanoke–114
Newport News Apprentice–12

On April 14, 1956, Roanoke hosted the track team from the Newport News Apprentice School. The home team had beaten Randolph-Macon in its only meet of the season, 85-37.

It was one of those perfect days for athletics–very little wind, some humidity, and sunny. And the records would fall.

In the shot put, Bob Palm again broke both the Alumni Field and the Roanoke College record by finishing first with a throw of 45'2". Both previous records were his own from the week before.

Two other runners also set or tied records. John Summers tied his own Roanoke College record of :51.8, set last year. Freshman Dick Lewis ran a spectacular 880, crossing the line in 1:58.7. The old Alumni Field record had been Phil Shaw's 2:01.5 from 1955. The Roanoke College record was set by one of the Big Four runners of 1949, Alvin Smith. Incidentally, just a couple of steps behind Lewis at the finish line was Johnnie Blanton, who also broke the old records with a 1:59.6.

The final record was set by the mile relay team of Al Ide, Pete Wise, Lewis, and Summers. Their time was 3:28.6, both an Alumni Field and a Roanoke College record. The old Alumni Field record was 3:31.0, set by the same four in 1955. The former College record was set in 1954 by Chris Rittman, Bennie Irvin, Summers, and Jim Wallwork.

There were several other good performances. The Maroons swept the high jump, with Dick Seed winning the event with 5'10". Dick Stauffer and Dave Foltz finished in a tie for the second spot.

The team also picked up all of the places in the broad jump, the 100, the 220, the 440, the two-mile run, and the 220-yard low hurdles. George Gearhart won the 100 in :10.2, with Dave Foltz in second on a time of :10.4 and Jim Nichols in third. Gearhart also won the 220 in :22.9, followed once again by Foltz and Nichols. At the tape during Summers' outstanding run of :51.8, Al Ide was on his shoulder just a foot behind, being timed at :51.9. Pete Wise was third, a couple of steps back. Dick Goodlake won the two-mile race in 10:05.0. Well back in second was Howard Meincke in 10:37.0, with Warren Light following in third. In the low hurdles, Bruce Johnston ran a great race, finishing first in :24.8. Dick Seed was second and Foltz third.

Others who scored in the meet included Phil Shaw, second in the mile run; Foltz, first in the high hurdles, third in the lows, second in the shot, and second in the broad jump; Dick Seed, second in both the high and low hurdles; Bill Schreiner, tie for first in the pole vault at 10'8"; and Frank Vest and Don Wilkie, who tied for third in the pole vault.

April 17, 1956
Elon College at Elon, North Carolina
Team Scores: Roanoke–116¼
Elon–13¾

On April 17, the Maroons drove to Elon, North Carolina, for a meet with Elon College. They weren't expecting much competition, mostly because in 1954 at Salem they had beaten Elon by a score of 102½ to 24½.

It was a cool, windy day with an almost constant tail breeze down the front straightway in favor of the runners. The day would bring three new Roanoke College records, wins in every event, and one special legend about Dave Foltz that almost every teammate can tell you even today. By now, there are different versions of this story, but if you talk to Coach Bast, he will give you this version.

"We went down to Elon College," says Bast. "That was in the days before Elon acquired a huge amount of money and built that new campus. They were a good football power for a small school and they had won their North Carolina conference meet in track. They thought they were pretty good. As the boys were sitting at the dining room tables prior to the start of the meet, one of the student waiters began to brag about the Elon team. Finally, Dave couldn't take the bragging any more. He reached into his pocket and pulled out his billfold, and where he ever got it I don't know, but he pulls out a $20 bill. And to some of the braggarts from Elon who were standing there, Foltz said, 'I've got $20 that says that I get more points myself today than your entire team.' They covered the bet, of course. And I will never forget that day. Foltz was hot. We came up to the final event, the mile relay, and Dave wanted to make sure that he won the bet. He knew that Roanoke was going to win the mile relay and he said 'Coach, let me run the mile relay.' I asked him if he was sure he wanted to do that. And he replied, 'Coach, I've got to run it.' And I had no idea why, knowing nothing about the bet. So I told him he could run the first leg of the relay, and the other three could make up the distance he lost. Well, he didn't lose any time at all. He was one of those guys who could run the quarter mile with a full pack and beat the entire group down there at Quantico when he was a Marine after graduation at Roanoke."

After talking with many of the athletes who were there that day, the author decided that the story was true. But was the part about the mile relay an embellishment that has gotten better over the years? During the meet, Foltz had placed third in the 100, first in the high and low hurdles, second in the shot put and discus, and third in the high jump. So as the mile relay was to begin, he already had a team-leading 17¼ points, more than enough to win his bet against Elon's final team score of 13¾. A post-meet article from the *Brackety-Ack* says that Pete Wise ran the leadoff leg of the mile relay (although Coach Bast to this day swears that Foltz ran the first leg). And the article says nothing about Foltz's bet. But let's not quibble about the facts. Dave Foltz was one of the two finest all-around track men ever to enroll at Roanoke. The other was Dick Emberger, who went on to become a decathlete in the 1964 Olympics and to place 10th in the world in that event.

Getting back to the Elon meet, three runners wiped out Roanoke College records. George Gearhart not only won the 100 in :10.1, but ran the 220 in a very fast time of :22.1. That set a record, beating the old time of :22.4 that Gearhart set the previous year. Dick Lewis also set a record by running the 440 in :51.5, knocking three-tenths of a second off the time John Summers recently ran. And finally, Dave Foltz, who won the high hurdles in :15.7, broke the Roanoke College record in the low hurdles by running :23.5. At that point, that time was the best in all Virginia colleges. Of the men coached by Bast, only Bruce Johnston, who in the same race at Elon ran second with a :23.6, and then ran another :23.6 the next year, would ever come close to that record.

Several others did well in the meet. Jim Nichols placed second in the 220 with an excellent time of :22.7. Howard Light finished in second in the quarter mile race with a good time of :52.1 and Al Ide took third, also with a :52.1.

Phil Shaw had little competition and won the 880 in 2:04.8. A few strides back was Pete Wise, with a 2:09.5.

Johnnie Blanton ran a 4:39.8 mile to win, with Phil Shaw in second. Dick Goodlake, never pushed, won the two-mile run with a 10:15.9. He was followed by Warren Light in second place and Bruce Fariss in third.

Bob Palm won the shot put, although this time without setting a record, and also finished in first place in the javelin. Jim O'Mahony was third in the javelin and also third in the broad jump. Bill Driscoll showed himself to be a good discus thrower. He won the discus on a throw of 124'10" with Bob Upton in third. Jim Nichols led the broad jumpers with a leap of 21'4½". Dick Seed, as usual, placed first in the high jump by clearing

5'10", with Dick Stauffer in second. And finally, the Roanoke pole vaulters came through with eight points. Don Wilkie won the event with a jump of 11'0" and freshman Frank Vest went 10'0" to take second-place points.

As the *Roanoke Times* said the next morning, "Like 'Ole Man River,' the Roanoke College track team keeps rolling along." This was, indeed, a flashy set of Maroons.

I remember . . . "Well, we went down to run Elon College. They were supposed to have a good track team for the conference they were in. After getting there, we went into their cafeteria to eat. There was a little black guy who was working the tables, and he said to us 'You guys have a good track team, but you're going to get beat today.' And Dave Foltz looked at him and said, 'Hell, I'll score more points myself than your whole damn team.' Near the end of the meet, we were getting ready to run the mile relay. Foltz was afraid he might not have enough points already in order to win the bet. So he went up to Homer and said, 'Coach. You've got to put me in the mile relay. I need more points.' So Coach Bast let him run a leg, the Roanoke team won the race, and Foltz collected on his bet."

George Gearhart

I remember . . . "During the Elon meet that year, we had an unusual starter. He would put you in the blocks and then, just after he said, 'Set,' he would look down the track away from the runners before firing the gun. Well, Dave saw him doing that and he told me, 'When he says set, start running.' So in the 220, when the starter said 'set,' I took off running. I was about four or five steps out of the blocks, all by myself, when I thought I'd better stop and go back–even though the man hadn't re-fired the gun to bring us back on a false start. Suddenly, everyone passed me and I had to start running again. I could have probably run 19 seconds that day if I had kept running."

George Gearhart

I remember . . . "I remember Dave Foltz well. We went to one meet, at Elon, and there was an exchange of verbiage between the two teams. Dave bet the Elon boys that he would get more points than their whole team combined. He bet them $20. And he collected his $20, too. I was there, and he definitely bet the money."

Bruce Fariss

April 21, 1956
Lynchburg College at Lynchburg, Virginia
Team Scores: Roanoke–90
Lynchburg–32

It was April 21 and three more school records were about to be set at Lynchburg College. The weather was clear and a bit cool, with a slight breeze to the runners' advantage down the straightway.

The first record was set by Bob Palm, who tossed the shot 45'9¼". The effort beat the old mark of 45'2", also held by Palm, set on April 14. Dave Foltz finished second behind Palm, while Jim Driscoll was third.

Then George Gearhart broke the other two College records, one in the 100 and the other in the 220. With the slight breeze helping, he exploded from the blocks in the 100-yard dash and by the 60-yard mark had built a commanding lead. As he crossed the finish line, everyone in the stands knew that he had run a fast race. Then the announcer told them that the time had been recorded as :09.9, a tenth of a second faster than the best time ever run by a Roanoke athlete. In 1927, big Charles "White" Wilson first set the record with a :10.4. The great Roanoke runner, Bob Fagg, broke that record twice, running :10.0 in 1947 and 1948. Boyd Carr tied Fagg's record in :1952, as did Gearhart two times during the 1955 season. The :09.9 was the best time in the Little Eight or Mason-Dixon Conferences for 1956.

Later in the meet, Gearhart ran the 220-yard dash in another record time–:21.7. The old mark was :22.1, set by Gearhart at Elon just four days ago. In this race, incidentally, Jim Nichols placed third in :22.6 and Al Ide, who came in a non-scoring fourth, ran :22.8. Three of the best 220 times in Roanoke's history had been run in a single race.

Foltz won the discus, throwing :127'9", just missing the school record by 18". The old record of 129'3" was set by Jim Doran in 1947. Jim Driscoll, usually the winner in the event, placed second with a fine throw of 126'0". And Bob Upton also threw well to take third with 125'0". It was the first time in Roanoke's track history that three Maroons threw over 120' in the same meet.

Taylor Goode, Lynchburg's one-man team who scored nearly half of his team's points, won the broad jump with 21'3½". Jim Nichols was second, just an inch behind, and Jim O'Mahony was third with 20'5½". Goode and Dick Seed tied for the win in the high jump, each clearing the bar at 5'9". Dick Stauffer placed third. In the pole vault, Goode won his third event of the day with a jump of 12'6", and Bill Schreiner of Roanoke jumped 11'0" for third.

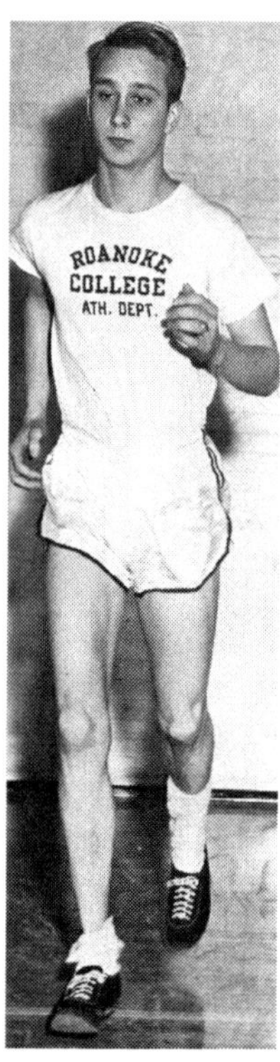

Left Photograph: George Gearhart became an excellent sprinter while at Roanoke. By his senior year, he held or shared the school record in the 100-yard dash (:09.9). He also ran a :21.7 220-yard race in 1957, again a school record.
Right Photograph: Bruce Fariss, distance runner, in a publicity shot taken in a handball cage in Alumni Gymnasium early in the outdoor season.

Roanoke swept all three places in both the 440 and 880. In the 440, John Summers won with a time of :51.9, with Howard Light in second (:52.1) and Pete Wise in third (:52.6). Dick Lewis ran well again in the 880, winning in 2:01.2. Phil Shaw was just on his heels in 2:02.0, with third place being taken by Johnnie Blanton, who ran a 2:03.0.

Maroons dominated both of the distance races. Howard Meincke beat Lynchburg's top distance man, Herman Atwood, in the mile run but had to run only a 4:33.8 to capture first place. In third was Dick Goodlake. In the two-mile race, Goodlake won with a time of 10:38.3. In a sweep of the event, Warren Light was second and Bruce Fariss third.

In the hurdles, Dave Foltz ran very well as the first three places in the highs and the lows went to Roanoke. Foltz won the high hurdles in :15.3, just nipping Bruce Johnston at the tape. The judges gave both of them the same time of :15.3. In third, Dick Seed had a :15.7.

Foltz then won the low hurdles in one of his best races of the year, running :24.0. Again, Bruce Johnston was less than a step behind in :24.2 and Jim O'Mahony finished third.

There was no mile relay race. With the score being 90 to 27 at the time the race was to begin, Coach Bast simply gave Lynchburg the win.

The final score, therefore, was Roanoke, 90, and Lynchburg, 32. It was Roanoke's fourth win of the season, with no losses.

I remember . . . "I was actually clocked by one of the officials at :09.8. But that time was on just one of the watches that were timing the 100 that day."

George Gearhart

I remember . . . "Warren Light was an average runner for us. He was big, 6 feet or over, and weighed about 175 pounds. I didn't know what event to put him in. He didn't have a great deal of speed. But he was a wonderful person and would run anything you wanted him to run. And I couldn't build very much speed or distance into him. I don't know why. He practiced faithfully, but you would never expect anything really great out of him in terms of times. On the other hand, he was very reliable. Especially in cross country. He majored in biology. He actually taught biology in high school after leaving Roanoke."

Homer Bast

April 24, 1956
Washington and Lee University at Salem, Virginia
Team Scores: Roanoke–100⅔
Washington and Lee–30⅓

Perhaps the *Brackety-Ack* columnist was correct when he said "About the only way Roanoke College's potent track team could win more meets is to schedule more opposition." The team had just won 25 straight meets and, if one looked at the huge margins of victory this year, more wins were coming.

The first chance for the Maroons to continue the streak was on April 24, 1956, when Washington and Lee's team came to Salem on a day that was cloudy and cold with gusting winds in no particular direction. Washington and Lee brought a team of average to good talent; unfortunately, they met a home team with lots of talent and momentum.

Before the afternoon was over, Roanoke had accumulated 100⅔ points to their opponent's 30⅓. Not only was the margin of victory large, but Roanoke athletes tied two Alumni Field records and broke two more, and they set one new school record.

Let's begin with the records. George Gearhart, no stranger to setting records, ran the 100-yard dash in :10.0. Although he missed the Roanoke College record of :09.9, which he had just set in the Lynchburg meet, the :10.0 tied the fastest time ever run on the College track. Jim Nichols, freshman from Roanoke, finished in second place.

Dick Goodlake ran a great two-mile. In winning the event, his time was 9:57.2. His old Alumni Field record was 10:05.0, set earlier in the season. The 9:57.2 also set the school record. Not since 1949, when the great distance star Bruce Davenport ran a 9:59.8 at Randolph-Macon, had any Roanoke runner gone under two minutes. Behind Goodlake in the race were Warren Light, in second, and Bruce Fariss.

A third Alumni Field record was tied by sophomore Bruce Johnston in the low hurdles. He won with a time of :24.5, matching the mark Dave Foltz had set in 1955. In the same race, Dick Seed was third.

And finally, there was one more Alumni Field record set by Bob Palm in the shot put. His winning throw was 45'6½". He had set the old record of 45'2" in an earlier meet. Dave Foltz placed third.

In other field events, Frank Vest and Don Wilkie tied for first in the pole vault, both going 10'6". Dick Seed won the high jump at 5'9", with Foltz and Bill Schreiner in a tie for second. As part of his 11 points in the meet, young Jim Nichols won the broad jump with 20'8½", followed by Foltz in second. Palm and Jim Driscoll were second and third, respectively, in the javelin throw. In the other event not won by Roanoke, Jim Driscoll threw very well to take third place. His distance was 126'8".

The scoring for the rest of the running events was heavily in Roanoke's favor. Gearhart won the 220 in :22.8. Jim Nichols ran :23.2 for second. Howard Light ran :51.7 in the 440, missing the track record by just three tenths of a second. John Summers was second with :51.9 and Pete Wise took third in :52.5.

In the 880, Johnnie Blanton picked up an easy win in 2:05.6. Howard Meincke placed first in the mile run with a 4:33.5. Close behind was second-place finisher Dick Lewis. Phil Shaw finished third just a couple of strides behind Lewis.

Dave Foltz and Bruce Johnston were awarded a tie in the high hurdles. Their time was :15.8. Seed finished in third place, just a tenth of a second behind.

Roanoke also won the mile relay. The time for Howard Light, George Gearhart, Dick Lewis, and anchor man John Summers was 3:32.9. Gearhart ended the day with a meet-leading 11¼ points, while Jim Nichols had 11.

April 27, 1956
Hampden-Sydney College at Hampden-Sydney, Virginia
Team Scores: Roanoke–92
Hampden-Sydney–30

There were just two dual meets left in the season when Roanoke met Hampden-Sydney College at Hampden-Sydney, Virginia. It was Roanoke's third meet in six days, and many on the team were tired.

The outstanding performance of the meet came from Howard Light. Without a strong competitor from Hampden-Sydney, the race really was between Light, John Summers, and Al Ide. As the threesome reached the half-way point, Summers was in the lead with Light a step behind and Ide two strides in back of Light. After rounding the curve and starting down the home stretch, Light pulled even with Summers and they fought each other off all the way to the finish line. At the last second, Light lunged and broke the tape in a time of :51.4 to set a new school record. Dick Lewis held the old record of :51.5. Summers, in second, tied Lewis' record.

There were three double winners in the meet–two from Roanoke and one from Hampden-Sydney. Big 220-pound Jim Frazer of Hampden-Sydney won both the shot put and discus events. He threw the shot 50'⅛" on his fourth attempt and the discus 136'2". Bob Palm finished in second place in the shot with 45'7½", only a few inches less than his own school record. The throw by Frazer made him the first representative of a Virginia college to break the 50-foot barrier. The distance was also a field and school record. In the discus, with 126'7", Roanoke's Bill Driscoll threw well once again to take third place.

Another double winner was George Gearhart. In the 100, he ran :10.1. Jim Nichols was third with a :10.3. Gearhart also won the 220 in :22.9, with John Summers taking third.

And in the hurdles, Bruce Johnson placed first in the high hurdles with a :15.5, followed by Dick Seed in :15.7. Johnston also won the low hurdles in :25.5. Again, Seed finished in second.

In the 880, Dick Lewis pulled away from Johnnie Blanton and Pete Wise in the last 100 yards to win with an excellent time of 2:00.4. In the earlier meet with Newport News Apprentice School, Lewis had set the record with a 1:58.7. Blanton's 2:01.7 brought him a second place, while Wise ran 2:03.4 for third.

Dick Goodlake took it easy in the mile run, finishing first with 4:32.2. Warren Light, who fell behind early in the race, was third.

As expected, Howard Meincke won the two-mile race. He ran 10:36.0, with Bruce Fariss finishing in third place.

The mile relay was also taken by Roanoke. Their team of Al Ide, Pete Wise, Howard Light, and Dick Lewis ran 3:32.0.

In the remainder of the field events, Jim Nichols, Dick Seed, and Bill Schreiner all won their events. Nichols was first in the broad jump with 21'4". Jim O'Mahony was second. Seed almost broke the school record in the high jump. He won with 6'¼", only three quarters of an inch less than the 6'1" set by Jay Jackson and Chris Rittman in 1954. Schreiner won the pole vault with a height of 11'0", with Don Wilkie second on a jump of 10'6".

The meet's final score was 92 to 30 in Roanoke's favor. It was the Maroons' sixth win of the season without a loss.

May 4, 1956
Bridgewater College at Bridgewater, Virginia
Team Scores: Roanoke–92⅓
Bridgewater–29⅔

On May 4, Roanoke met the Bridgewater College Eagles at Bridgewater, Virginia. It was a sunny, clear day, although it was windy.

Bridgewater came into the meet undefeated for the season. Roanoke had just won six straight dual meets in 1956, and probably would have little difficulty winning this one. This team was Coach Bast's best since he brought the program back to life in 1947. Mentally, the Maroons were as tough as old boots. Physically, there were few small colleges in the country with as much raw talent. It was the first year that Bast had been able to field a squad with at least two athletes in each event who were each capable of winning. The competition was seldom with their opponents as much as it was among members of their own team. Everyone pushed someone else on the team to become better.

This meet with Bridgewater wasn't a very difficult one for Roanoke. In fact, they won 11 of 14 events.

George Gearhart was the only double winner in the meet. He ran the 100 in :10.4. Bruce Johnston, trying his luck in the race, was third. Gearhart also won the 220 in :23.2. Al Ide finished third in that event.

John Summers failed to win the 440, but did finish second. Dick Goodlake was almost five seconds behind Summers in third place.

Phil Shaw placed second in the 880, with Dick Goodlake in third. Shaw ran 2:03.5 and Goodlake 2:10.0.

Howard Meincke won the mile with little problem, beating teammates Johnnie Blanton by three seconds and third place Dick Lewis by over eight seconds. The other distance race went to Warren Light, who ran a 10:44.0.

The Roanoke mile relay team won easily. Johnnie Blanton, Phil Shaw, Dave Foltz, and Dick Lewis–definitely not the team's usual runners–crossed the line in 3:38.7.

Roanoke took all three places in each hurdle event. Dave Foltz won the high hurdles in :15.8, followed by Bruce Johnston and Dick Seed. Johnston came back to win the low hurdles in :25.5, which was a new track record at Bridgewater. The former record of :26.1 had been set by Charlie Nuttycombe of Randolph-Macon College. Second place in the low hurdles went to Seed and third place to Foltz.

Roanoke athletes won four of the five field events. In the shot put, Bob Palm threw 45'1". Foltz placed second. Bill Driscoll continued his good year by winning the discus with a throw of 122'6½". Foltz placed second, only two inches behind Driscoll.

Jim Nichols was second in the broad jump. Dick Seed and Dick Stauffer each jumped 5'10" for first place in the high jump. Don Wilkie won the pole vault with 11'3", with Bill Schreiner second and Frank Vest in a tie for third.

Foltz, competing in five events, was high scorer for the meet with 13¼ points. Bridgewater's Pete Grandal, who won the 440 and finished second to Roanoke's George Gearhart in the 220, led the Eagles.

At the end of the meet, Roanoke led 92⅓ to 29⅔. The win put the Roanoke meet record at 7-0. The streak had reached 28. There was no evidence that results of the 1956-57 session would be any different.

I remember . . . "The worst track we ran on in those days was probably the one at Bridgewater. It was down next to a stream, which meant that it was flooded out occasionally each year. And when I ran the 220 on a curve, it was hard to see what lane I was in. It was marked, but there were so many lines."

George Gearhart

May 11-12, 1956
Mason-Dixon Championships at Baltimore, Maryland
Team Scores: 1st–Roanoke College–63
2nd–Catholic University–37
3rd–Johns Hopkins University–22
4th–Hampden-Sydney College–20½
5th–Lynchburg College–15½
6th–Randolph-Macon College–13½
7th–Loyola University–12
8th–Western Maryland College–8

9th–Bridgewater College–6½
10th–Mount St. Mary's College–4
11th–Towson State College–3
12th–Washington College–2
13th–American University–2

Frank Vest, who was a good pole vaulter for Roanoke, also wrote a column for the *Brackety-Ack*. He summed up Roanoke's preparation for the 1956 Mason-Dixon meeting with the following comment:

> "Partly because the Maroons are the reigning Mason-Dixon champions and partly because of the fact that they have a long string of consecutive victories, all the teams in the meet will be out to beat Roanoke College. There is nothing that gives an athletic team more pleasure or prestige than to knock off a previously-undefeated team, especially one with a record comparable to Roanoke's."

The 21st annual Championships were held on May 11 and 12 at Homewood Field at Johns Hopkins University in Baltimore. If Roanoke won, it would be their third straight Mason-Dixon title. It looked to Coach Bast that Catholic University would offer Roanoke it's most serious threat. Catholic had a team loaded with good runners from the dashes up to the mile. Despite the fact that Roanoke was heavily favored to win, Catholic just might spoil the day. One of the problems Roanoke had at the moment, thought Bast, was overconfidence. Roanoke had won seven straight meets during the current season, and 28 consecutive meets beginning in 1953. The victories had come so easily for the Maroons that the athletes might be coasting, mentally and physically, not realizing that the Mason-Dixon meet always brought out the best of competition.

On the first day of the meet, a Friday, officials held their usual qualifying trials so that a large number of athletes in certain events could be whittled down to no more than six for Saturday's meet. Roanoke athletes performed almost as expected, moving 15 members of the team on to the next day's finals. Johns Hopkins and Catholic each qualified nine men.

Here are summaries from Friday:

100	First Heat:	1st–Gearhart (R)–:10.5; 2nd–Wright (JH); 3rd–Bassett (A)
	Second Heat:	1st–Heck (JH)–:10.2; 2nd–Jarrett (L); 3rd–Kennedy (WM)

	Third Heat:	1st–Leibert (C)–?; 2nd–Harris (L); 3rd–Nichols (R)
	Fourth Heat:	1st–McKenna (LOY)–:10.3; 2nd–Nuttycombe (RM); 3rd–Kady (JH)
220	First Heat:	1st–McKenna (LOY)–:23.1; 2nd–Leibert (C); 3rd–Caples (JH)
	Second Heat:	1st–Nuttycombe (RM)–:23.5; 2nd–Wright (JH); 3rd–Mathews (C)
	Third Heat:	1st–Gearhart (R)–:23.5; 2nd–Heck (JH); 3rd–M. Flynn (C)
440	First Heat:	1st–Mathews (C)–:51.5; 2nd–Caples (JH)
	Second Heat:	1st–Light (R)–:52.1; 2nd–B. Flynn (C)
	Third Heat:	1st–Grandal (B)–:51.6; 2nd–Ide (R)
880	First Heat:	1st–Lewis (R)–2:01.5; 2nd–Messersmith (C)
	Second Heat:	1st–B. Flynn (C)–2:02.9; 2nd–Sutherland (JH)
	Third Heat:	1st–Madison (C)–1:59.9; 2nd–Hort (WM)
120 HH	First Heat:	1st–Johnston (R)–:16.0; 2nd–Seed (R); 3rd–Pence (B)
	Second Heat:	1st–Foltz (R)–:15.5; 2nd–Hort (WM); 3rd–Flavin (JH)
100	First Heat:	1st–McKenna (LOY)–:10.3; 2nd–Leibert (C); 3rd–Jarrett (L)
	Second Heat:	1st–Heck (JH)–:10.3; 2nd–Gearhart (R); 3rd–Nuttycombe (RM)

220	First Heat:	1st–Leibert (C)–:22.9; 2nd–Heck (JH); 3rd–Nuttycombe (RM)
	Second Heat:	1st–McKenna (LOY)–:23.1; 2nd–Caples (JH); 3rd–Mathews (C)

Shot 1st–Frazer (HS)–48'10¼"; 2nd–Wiley (HS); 3rd–Palm (R); 4th–Unknown; 5th–Unknown; 6th–Unknown

Broad Jump 1st–Nuttycombe (RM)–23'1-½"; 2nd–Tie: Nichols (R) and Goode (L); 4th–Unknown; 5th–Unknown; 6th–Unknown

Note: No other information was available.

The closest race of the day occurred in the second heat of the 880. Trailing much of the way in the early part of the race, Jack Sutherland, top distance man for Johns Hopkins, began to move into contention in the last 200 yards. Right behind Sutherland, who was in third place at the time, was Bob Flynn of Catholic. Sutherland finally took the lead 150 yards from the finish. Then, Flynn put on a strong kick and passed the Johns Hopkins star 10 yards from the finish.

Catholic's John Madison and Western Maryland's John Hort also staged a close duel in their heat of the 880. Madison finally nosed out Hort at the tape. Madison's time was 1:59.9, just three seconds from the old meet record.

As for Roanoke, they qualified men in all events with the exception of the 220, where George Gearhart fell and failed to make the finals.

Two meet records were broken on Friday. Jim Frazer of Hampden-Sydney, who had thrown the shot over 50' during the season, broke his own shot put mark of 47'6" with a throw of 48'10¼". Randolph-Macon's Charlie Nuttycombe, who had jumped 23'5" earlier in the year, leaped 23'1½". The distance eclipsed the former record of 22'9", set by Kenney Howard of Washington in 1952.

In the meet beginning Saturday afternoon, Roanoke men won six separate events. The Roanoke winners included Dick Lewis, who ran an excellent 2:00.1 in the 880; Howard Meincke, with his 4:27.1 in the mile run; Dick Goodlake, whose time in the two-mile race was 10:04.7; and Dick Seed, who tied with two others in jumping 6'½". The other two wins for the Maroons came from Dave Foltz. Foltz was sharp as a razor in the high hurdles, beating the field badly with a time of :15.1. The time was a new meet record, topping the old mark of :15.2. It was also a Roanoke College record. The old school record was :15.2, which Foltz set in 1955. Foltz also was flawless in winning the low hurdles. His time of :24.2 set a new meet record. The old Mason-Dixon record was :25.0. Unfortunately, Maroon star Bruce Johnston fell in the low hurdles finals, suffering a bad cut. Had he finished the race, Roanoke's team score would have been several points higher.

Foltz also scored with a fifth place in the discus on a throw of 125'4½", the second best mark of his career at Roanoke, and was fifth in the shot put with 42'4¾". Again, that throw was the second best of his career. In addition, Howard Light finished second in the 440, just in back of the winner, Bob Flynn of Catholic. Flynn ran :49.7. Al Ide was fourth in that race. Johnnie Blanton was fourth in the mile run and Dick Seed second in the high hurdles and third in the lows. Bob Palm scored four points in the shot put by placing second with 44'6¼". In the broad jump, Jim Nichols placed second to senior Charlie Nuttycombe, who broke the old meet record of 22'9½" when he leaped 23'1½". Nichols's jump was 21'5¼". Finally, two Maroons scored in the pole vault, won by Taylor Goode of Lynchburg in a meet record of 13'1½". Bill Schreiner and Don Wilkie tied with two others for second place.

In the mile relay, Bast asked Al Ide, Pete Wise, John Summers, and Dick Lewis to be members of the team. The competition was some of the best in the history of the meet. Catholic University, annually Roanoke's nemesis in this event, won the race with an outstanding time of 3:22.3. It was a meet record, beating the old mark of 3:25.4. But the race down the straightaway was superb, matching Catholic's Bob Flynn against Roanoke's Dick Lewis. At the finish line, Flynn led Lewis by about a yard. Roanoke's time was 3:22.6, a new Roanoke College record. The old record of 3:28.6 had been set by Al Ide, Pete Wise, Dick Lewis, and John Summers earlier in the season.

Roanoke won the trophy again with 63 points. Catholic had 37; Johns Hopkins 22; Hampden-Sydney 20½; Lynchburg 15½; Randolph-Macon 13½; and Loyola 12. The other schools, in order of finish, were Western Maryland, Bridgewater, Mount St. Mary's, Towson State, Washington, and American.

I remember . . . "Dave Foltz came up to me after he had taken a shower and he pulled open his coat. We had to wear coats and ties to meets in those days. And he had all of his Mason-Dixon medals pinned to the inside of his coat. I said, 'Dave, you are hanging a little bit on one side, aren't you?' He said, 'Yeah, I did pretty well today.' "

Homer Bast

May 16, 1956
Little Eight Championships at Hampden-Sydney, Virginia
Team Scores: 1st–Roanoke College–$94\frac{2}{5}$
2nd–Hampden-Sydney College–$34\frac{1}{2}$
3rd–Norfolk Division of William and Mary–$30\frac{7}{10}$
4th–Lynchburg College–$20\frac{1}{5}$
5th–Bridgewater College–$15\frac{1}{5}$
6th–Randolph-Macon College–14

The 1956 Little Eight meet, before a crowd of some 300 spectators, was held at Hampden-Sydney on May 16. The weather was breezy but beautiful. This was the third straight year that Hampden-Sydney hosted the meet, and the first time the Mason-Dixon Championships had preceded this meet. Besides Roanoke, five teams sent teams. They were Bridgewater, Hampden-Sydney, Lynchburg, Norfolk Division of William and Mary, and Randolph-Macon. Richmond Professional Institute, a member of the Conference, was not entered because it did not field a track team. Emory and Henry also failed to send any athletes.

Most people, of course, favored Roanoke to win the meet. Indeed, the Maroons were the big gorilla in the room. The Maroons first won the championship of the meet in 1948, just one year after Coach Bast started the modern era of track and field athletics at the College. They also won the trophy in 1953, 1954, and 1955. In addition, their streak of 28 straight wins over the past four years, combined with the overwhelming way that they won the Mason-Dixon meet, let everyone know that it would take a massive effort to dethrone them. No team in the Little Eight Conference appeared capable of such an effort.

There were some problems, however. The Mason-Dixon Conference victory could have proven costly to the Maroon team. Bruce Johnston, sophomore hurdle star from Roanoke, tripped over a high hurdle in the finals at Baltimore and cut his leg. Homer told the *Roanoke Times*, in fact, that the team might have to compete in the Little Eight meet without Johnston. "I doubt that we will be able to use him," Bast told the *Times* reporter. "It will really hurt us. Bruce has shown much improvement and beats Dave Foltz his share of the time."

Another worry for Bast was the running of George Gearhart. The junior sprinter from Salem failed to place in either the 100 or 220 at Baltimore. The Maroons would need his points in the upcoming meet.

On the other hand, the Mason-Dixon meet had given Bast reason to be happy with the showing of such athletes as Foltz, Dick Seed, Johnnie Blanton, Dick Goodlake, and Howard Meincke.

It didn't take long after the meet started to see what the results would be. Roanoke won seven of the 14 events and in the process broke four meet and school records.

Dave Foltz, in the final meet of his remarkable track career, was high scorer for Roanoke. He won the 120-yard high hurdles race in :15.6 and the low hurdles in :24.5. He also placed fourth in the shot put and third in the discus for a total of 15 points. He was followed by Charlie Nuttycombe of Randolph-Macon, who for once failed to grab a single first place but scored three seconds and a fourth for 14 points.

One of the four records by Roanoke athletes was set in the mile relay. The Roanoke team of Al Ide, Howard Light, John Summers, and Dick Lewis was timed in 3:28.4, narrowly beating a team from Norfolk Division of William and Mary. The time broke the old meet record of 3:30.7 set in 1955 by Hampden-Sydney.

Another record was set by Howard Light. His second-place time of :51.0 in the 440 broke his own Roanoke College record of :51.4.

Pete Wise set a meet record in the 880 with a time of 2:00.4. That time was four tenths of a second lower than the old record set by Paige Will of Bridgewater in 1955.

Jim Nichols, although he placed third in the broad jump, set a new Roanoke College record at 22'9". The old mark, set by Jay Jackson in 1954, was 21'8½".

Another meet record was set by Dick Goodlake. He ran a terrific 9:58.2 in winning the two-mile race.

Those scoring points but not breaking records were Gearhart, third in the 100; Jim Nichols, fourth in the 220; John Summers, third in the 440; Al Ide, fifth in the 440; Dick Lewis, who finished second and barely lost to Pete Wise in the 880; Johnnie Blanton, fifth in the 880; Howard Meincke, first place in the mile run; Phil Shaw, third in the mile; Warren Light, fourth in the two-mile run; Dick Seed, second in the high hurdles and third in the low hurdles; Bruce Johnston, second place in the low hurdles; Bob Palm, second in the shot put with a throw of 44'5"; Bill Driscoll, with a second in the discus on a throw of 125'6; Bob Upton, fourth in the discus; Jim O'Mahony, fifth in the broad jump with a best-ever distance of 21'2"; Dick Stauffer and Dick Seed, ties for third in the high jump; Don Wilkie, tie for second in the pole vault; and Frank Vest and Bill Schreiner, tie for fifth in the pole vault.

Roanoke won the meet with $94\frac{2}{5}$ points, followed by Hampden-Sydney (second, 34½); Norfolk Division of William and Mary (third, $30\frac{7}{10}$); Lynchburg (fourth, $20\frac{1}{5}$); Bridgewater (fifth, $15\frac{1}{5}$); and Randolph-Macon (sixth, 14). It was the fourth time in as many years that Coach Bast had taken the winner's trophy home to Salem.

I remember . . . "In 1956, we went down to Hampden-Sydney to run the Little Eight Championships. I was worried about running Randolph-Macon's Charlie Nuttycombe. He was a great sprinter and also talented in three or four other events. He and I were very competitive. In the 220 finals, I was running against Nuttycombe and one of my teammates, Jimmy Nichols. Just after the start of the race, Jimmy began to yell, 'Go, George, go.' Over and over again throughout the race, he kept telling me to 'Go, George, go.' Nuttycombe and I came to the finish line in a virtual dead heat. After deliberating for a couple of minutes, the judges gave me the win. Charlie told me after the race that he never was worried because he thought he could beat me. 'But,' he said, 'it was that crazy guy who was yelling behind us that bothered me.' "

George Gearhart

I remember . . . "When I arrived at Tech, after spending two years at Roanoke, I lived in the same house as Bill Lund. A woman there had a house with two bedrooms that she rented out. Bill lived in one of them and I lived in the other. He was one of my fraternity brothers at Roanoke College. He was a big, strong Swede–a lot stronger than I was. He was quite proud of his Swedish heritage. He was strong as a bull. He only had one eye, as a result of an accident as a child. He told me that when he finally graduated from college, he wanted to get up enough money to buy a good glass eye. His eye was kind of grey – not very nice looking. He was in an accident with a pair of scissors as a child."

Bob Nilson

I remember . . . "Dave Foltz lived downstairs in the gym. The story I heard was that he had a female dog living with him. And she got pregnant and had puppies. And they had Alumni Weekend, and an alumnus walked into the room to find out what was there. And there were all of these puppies crawling all over the place. Apparently, the administration was not pleased."

George Gearhart

I remember . . . "Dick Seed was just outstanding. Of course, he was a tremendous soccer player. But I got him to come out for track. I could see a little bit of high jumping talent in there. So there's where I started him. And I think he did 5'8" the first time he tried it. I don't know whether or not he participated in the high jump in high school. Now these boys in small schools are not satisfied at participating in just one event. They want to compete. And Dick Seed wanted to compete. So he decided that he wanted to hurdle. I said 'O.K. We'll learn to hurdle.' I took the fear away from him, just like we had done with earlier hurdlers, and you can see by your records the amazing improvement that he made. He wasn't all that fast, but he had pretty good form over the hurdles. And not only that, but he was a great person."

Homer Bast

I remember . . . "Jim Nichols ended up with the school record in the broad jump–about 22'9". I remember when he did that. But he didn't stay at Roanoke very long. He transferred to Virginia Tech. Yes, 22'9" was wonderful for little ol' Roanoke. Actually, I tried to make a hurdler out of him. But he wasn't interested."

Homer Bast

As of the end of the 1956 season, here were the records for the Little Eight meet:

100	:09.6	Spangler (B)	Set in 1952
220	:21.5	Spangler (B)	Set in 1953
440	:50.8	Will (B)	Set in 1955
880	2:00.4	Wise (R)	Set in 1956
Mile	4:28.0	Crouse (B)	Set in 1951
Two Miles	9:58.2	Goodlake (R)	Set in 1956
120 HH	:15.2	Keat (RM)	Set in 1937
220 LH	:24.3	Myers (B)	Set in 1952
High Jump	6'2¼"	Cipolat (L)	Set in 1939
Pole Vault	13'6"	DeCosta (R)	Set in 1952
Broad Jump	23'2½"	Harmon (NWM)	Set in 1956
Shot Put	48'½"	Frazer (HS)	Set in 1955
Discus	138'10⅞"	Frazer (HS)	Set in 1955
Mile Relay	3:28.4	Roanoke (Ide, H. Light, Summers, and Lewis)	Set in 1956

Chapter Twelve

THE 1956-57 SEASONS

Cross Country

At the end of the 1955-56 session, Coach Bast and his wife invited the team to their house for a celebration of the good work the athletes and managers had done that year. During the activities, Phil Shaw of Irvington, New Jersey, and Bruce Fariss of Allisonia, Virginia, were elected to be cross-country Captains for 1956. They also had served as Co-Captains in 1955. The group then voted for George Gearhart of Salem and Dick Seed of Philadelphia to be the indoor and outdoor track Captains. All four were seniors in 1956-57.

Shaw had lettered three years in cross country and track and was an education major. At one point, he held the college track record for the 880.

Fariss, majoring in biology, was a leader in campus activities. He placed in the top 10 in the Mason-Dixon and Little Eight meets the past three seasons. He also was Vice President of the class of 1957.

The 1956 cross country team.
First Row (L to R): Bruce Fariss, Co-Captain, Dick Goodlake, Howard Meincke, and Bill Cerelli.
Second Row (L to R): Wayne Wilson, Warren Light, Coach Homer Bast, Rhodes Messick, and Pete Wise.
Insert: Co-Captain Phil Shaw.

Dick Seed was an outstanding hurdler and high jumper. Although he hadn't been the number one hurdler on the team, because of the presence of two of the most talented hurdlers in the state–Dave Foltz and Bruce Johnston–he had gone over 6' in the high jump.

Gearhart held the school record in the 60-yard dash indoors with a :06.3, and the outdoor records in the 100 and 220. He ran :09.9 in the 100 and :21.7 in the 220, both races coming in the Lynchburg dual meet of 1956. He was the second leading scorer in outdoor track in the college's history.

The last two cross country seasons had been good ones for Bast and the team. In 1954-55, the squad had gone undefeated in dual meets. In 1955-56, the Maroons lost by two points to the University of Tennessee and one point to Virginia Polytechnic Institute–both much larger schools than Roanoke–but won the rest of their dual meets to finish with a record of five wins and two losses. In both years, they easily won the Little Seven and then Little Eight meets, as well as the championship of the Mason-Dixon Conference.

With Bruce Fariss and Phil Shaw being the only seniors on this year's cross country team, Roanoke looked as if it would again be the class of small colleges in the region. Besides these two, veteran runners included Dick Goodlake, a junior from Garden City, New York; Bill Cerelli, junior from West New York, New York; Howard Meincke, outstanding sophomore from Milltown, New York; Warren Light, sophomore from Baldwin, New York; Dick Lewis, sophomore from Cranford, New Jersey; and Pete Wise, sophomore from Absecon, New Jersey.

Three local runners were among the newcomers. They were Emory Bogle, a former Andrew Lewis distance runner from Salem; Bill Stout, who had running experience at Jefferson High School in Roanoke; and Danny Bennett, who ran for a high school in Delaware.

Others new to the team included Wayne Wilson, Paul Rosenberger, Luther Mauney, Rhodes Messick, Bob Wortmann, Fred Daley, Dick Emberger, Tom Sitton, and George Jocher, a sophomore transfer from Hofstra. Emberger never considered himself a distance runner, but Bast saw him as an outstanding all-around star in outdoor track and field events, and encouraged Emberger to run cross country in order to develop stamina and speed. Emberger would later break numerous records as a track athlete and, in 1964, become a member of the Olympic team. Jocher would see some action in meets this year, but the team would not be able to count his score because of his transfer status. From the very first practice, Coach Bast saw the potential in Jocher, who was from Bellerose, New York. What he didn't know was that Jocher would become one of the best distance runners in the area and a leader in campus activities.

I remember . . . "I wasn't an outstanding runner, but I think I was a solid, dependable runner. Bill Cerelli and I were many times at the end of the pack during practice. When we went to a meet, I would manage to pace myself and gradually make my way toward the front. Sometimes, I would be in sight of the finish line when Les Noel, Howard Meincke, or Dick Goodlake would go zipping by me. I had this urge to trip them, but never did."

Dr. Bruce Fariss

I remember . . . "I think that one of the things that we did, perhaps not every year, that was a lot of fun, was that Coach Fox would say that he wanted his soccer boys to run with us. We thoroughly enjoyed running them into the ground."

Dr. Bruce Fariss

I remember . . . "One little thing about Howard Meincke. He always ran with a pair of colored socks. They were red, and he ran in them all the time. We got to a meet once and he couldn't find his socks. And he said that he wasn't going to do well because he didn't have the socks. We told him that it was all in his head. But as it turned out, he didn't run very well at all. He wouldn't even wash the socks during the season. After the meet, his socks showed up and he was O. K. He was so focused before a race that you couldn't talk to him. He was a great runner."

Dr. Bruce Fariss

September 29, 1956
Mount St. Mary's College at Emmitsburg, Maryland
Team Scores: Roanoke–21
Mount St. Mary's–40

Roanoke was heading to Emmitsburg, Maryland, to meet a fairly good Mount St. Mary's team. The two schools' soccer teams were playing the same day in Emmitsburg.

Some of the better Maroon runners had various ailments that had curtailed their training program. At the last minute, Coach Bast asked Dick Lewis, Dick Goodlake, Pete Wise, and Bill Cerelli to stay in Salem and get some rest. These four were some of the best runners from the 1955 season.

The meet, won by Roanoke 21 to 40, was run on a humid, cloudy, and cold day. The Mount St. Mary's course was 3.7 miles in length.

No complete set of results for the meet were saved; however, we do know that super-sophomore Howard Meincke finished first in 19:00.4, a new course record. George Jocher, running unofficially, finished second to Meincke. In the official second place slot was Mount's Jim Murphy with a 19:38.0. Freshman Wayne Wilson of Roanoke surprised even his coach when he finished third in 20:01.0. Bruce Fariss was fourth in 20:17. Beyond that point, we know only that Roanoke took 8 of the first 12 spots, with Warren Light being in the eleventh position. Light's old problem, a side stitch, hit him hard during the race, but he was able to finish. We also know that Don Bennett and Emory Bogle were among the top ten runners.

October 5, 1956
Virginia Polytechnic Institute at Salem, Virginia
Team Scores: Roanoke–23
Virginia Polytechnic Institute–38

V. P. I. was the last team, and only one of two, to beat Roanoke during the past season. This year they came to Salem on October 5, 1956, to compete on a 3.1 mile course first established for the 1954 season. In 1954, Les Noel set the record with a time of 16:13.0, and then broke it about three weeks later when he ran 16:03.0. Howard Meincke seemed destined to lower that record more than one time during the current season.

Salem had experienced several days of rain up to and including the morning of the meet. But the slick course was just fine for Meincke. He went to the front early and finished in a new record time of 16:01.0. Just behind by nine seconds was Dick Goodlake. George Jocher, running unofficially, finished in 16:27.

Bruce Fariss finished in the fifth position, running 16:59, with Wayne Wilson, Warren Light, Pete Wise, Dick Lewis, and Phil Shaw placing in the seventh through eleventh spots, respectively. Others for Roanoke included Rhodes Messick, fourteenth; Danny Bennett, fifteenth; Bill Cerelli, sixteenth; Emory Bogle, seventeenth; Bob Wortmann, twenty-second; and Luther Mauney, twenty-third.

Roanoke won the meet by a score of 23 to 38. It was a strong showing, with just 1:09 separating their first and fifth runners.

October 13, 1956
Washington and Lee University at Lexington, Virginia
Team Scores: Roanoke–15
Washington and Lee–49

The Washington and Lee meet took place on October 13 in Lexington on a 4.0-mile course. Some Maroons remembered the course well. Two years before, Roanoke beat the Generals by a single point on a very wet, slippery course in Lexington. The problem was that the Maroons wore flat-sole shoes instead of spikes, a decision that almost ruined a perfect season.

The first five finishers in the meet were from Roanoke. Howard Meincke again led the Maroons across the finish line. It was his third straight individual victory of the season. His time of 20:40.0 was just six seconds behind the course record, which was set the previous week by Southern Conference cross country champion Dave Pithkepley of V. M. I.

Dick Goodlake was second in 21:04.5. Bruce Fariss placed third in 21:53, Phil Shaw was fourth in 22:17, and Warren Light ran 22:31 for fifth place. W & L's Captain, John Arnold, ran sixth as his team's first man.

Other Roanoke runners were Rhodes Messick, eighth in 22:45; Emory Bogle, ninth in 22:48; Dick Lewis, tenth in 22:58; Danny Bennett, eleventh in 23:01; and Pete Wise, fourteenth in 23:25. Freshman Wayne Wilson had to drop out because of a dislocated toe.

Roanoke won by a score of 15 to 49. It was their third win for the year.

I remember . . . . "I remember this meet well. We held the race during a Washington and Lee homecoming football game. They started the race during the game and we went out into the fields and dodged some cows and jumped some fences. Then we finished the race by entering the football stadium at halftime. The whole stadium was packed with football fans."

Warren Light

October 25, 1956
Hampden-Sydney College at Hampden-Sydney, Virginia
Team Scores: Roanoke–15
Hampden-Sydney–45

Coach Bast had scheduled two meets–with Hampden-Sydney and West Virginia State–just two days apart. Neither of those teams was very strong; in fact, Bast calculated that both could be beaten with perfect scores. So he divided his team approximately in half, with one group competing against Hampden-Sydney and the other staying in Salem for the West Virginia State meet. This arrangement allowed the runners more rest time and gave some who normally would not be in the top five to have their own sense of achievement.

The Hampden-Sydney College meet at Hampden-Sydney was run on a 3.0-mile course on October 25. Dick Goodlake set a new course record with a time of 15:39.5. The record, set in 1954, was held by former Roanoke runner Les Noel. Warren Light was second, Phil Shaw third, Danny Bennett fourth, Rhodes Messick fifth, and Emory Bogle sixth. Hampden-Sydney's first man finished in seventh place.

The score was Roanoke, 15, Hampden-Sydney, 45. So far, Bast's plan was working.

October 27, 1956
West Virginia State College at Salem, Virginia
Team Scores: Roanoke–16
West Virginia State–43

The other half of the team also did well, running against West Virginia State College in Salem on October 27. For the second time in a row on his own course, Howard Meincke set a new record. His time of 15:30.5 was more than 30 seconds faster than the record he set during the season against Virginia Polytechnic Institute.

George Jocher finished well behind Meincke in second place, but his score wasn't counted. Dick Lewis was officially second, running 17:03, and five seconds later Bruce Fariss crossed the finish line. Pete Wise was fourth and Bill Cerelli was sixth.

Others who finished were Dick Emberger, ninth in 18:38; Tom Sitton, eleventh in 19:04; and Bob Wortmann, twelfth in 19:45.

Roanoke won, 16 to 43. It was the Maroons' fifth win of the season with no losses.

November 1, 1956
Lynchburg College at Lynchburg, Virginia
Team Scores: Roanoke–18
Lynchburg–48

Roanoke captured its sixth win by beating Lynchburg College 18 to 48. The race was run on November 1 in Lynchburg over a slippery 3.1-mile course. Part of the Maroons' team took the day off, including Howard Meincke, Bruce Fariss, and Warren Light.

The race was won by Dick Goodlake, who was timed at 17:28.4. Phil Shaw was second, less than 30 seconds behind. Fourth place went to Danny Bennett, fifth to Dick Lewis, sixth to Rhodes Messick, seventh to Emory Bogle, eighth to Pete Wise, and tenth to Bill Cerelli.

I remember . . . "One time we ran three meets in about one week. And Homer said, 'You bring your books.' And you went to the professors and said that we would be out of class. Can you let me know what homework we are going to have? I was in Organic Chemistry at the time, and I went to Dr. Robey to ask him about homework and the fact that we would be gone. And he said that it was our problem. I said, 'Sir, what can I do?' And he said, 'You catch up the best you can.' And that's what he meant."

Bruce Fariss

I remember . . . "One of my fraternity brothers was Keith Haley, who became a dentist and is my own dentist today. He and I went to Bridgewater one summer and took Organic Chemistry up there. This was still the time when I was aiming toward dental school. I really took the course up there because the teacher of the course at Roanoke was Dr. Robey. He was very hard to get a good grade from."

Jay Jackson

November 5, 1956
The University of Virginia Freshmen at Salem, Virginia
Team Scores: Roanoke–19
University of Virginia–39

Coach Bast had so many freshmen on the team that he scheduled both a freshman and a varsity meet with the University of Virginia. Both meets were at Salem on November 5.

The Maroons had little problem beating the University of Virginia freshmen, 19 to 39. In fact, they took the first through third places, fifth, and eighth for their points.

Rhodes Messick took top honors, covering the 3.1 miles in 17:07. He was followed closely by Danny Bennett, in second place, and then by Emory Bogle in third.

Dick Emberger was fifth, Tom Sitton eighth, Bob Wortmann ninth, and Luther Mauney eleventh.

November 5, 1956
The University of Virginia Varsity at Salem, Virginia
Team Scores: Roanoke–24
University of Virginia–32

This meet would be the last for Roanoke before the Little Eight and Mason-Dixon Championships. The Cavaliers had never beaten Roanoke in cross country. A win here would bring Coach Bast his fourth unbeaten season in the ten years he had coached the sport. On the other hand, all of the talk about the win and about the successful season had

Bast worried. The University in 1956, before the Roanoke meet, had a very respectable 6-2 record in Atlantic Coast Conference competition.

There were two remarkable performances in the meet. First, Howard Meincke finished in first place with a new course record of 15:27. Then, just six seconds later, Dick Goodlake crossed the line.

The Cavaliers took the next three places, but three Maroons sewed up the win. Warren Light was sixth, Dick Lewis was seventh, and Bruce Fariss finished eighth. Those places gave Roanoke 24 points. The University of Virginia could total only 32.

The other two runners for Roanoke were Bill Cerelli, who finished in tenth place, and Pete Wise, who took the twelfth spot.

November 8, 1956
Little Eight Championships at Bridgewater, Virginia
Team Scores: 1st–Roanoke College–37
2nd–Bridgewater College–44
3rd–Norfolk William and Mary College–77
4th–Lynchburg College–117
5th–Randolph-Macon College–136
6th–Hampden-Sydney College–147

The injury list for Roanoke grew during the week before the Little Eight meet. A late decision by Coach Bast left several runners on the sidelines. Dick Goodlake, who had done so well against the University of Virginia and came within six seconds of beating Howard Meincke in that race, had a neck injury and wouldn't compete. Bill Cerelli, another valuable member of the team, was sidelined with a cold. Freshman Wayne Wilson, a very promising freshman, had been lost to the season because of a foot injury.

Phil Shaw would run in the Little Eight meet, but had been hampered by a pulled groin muscle aggravated in the previous meet. Warren Light would also run, but all year he had competed with side stitches. Even Howard Meincke, obviously the best runner in the field, might not be at full strength because of a bad ankle.

Undefeated Roanoke was heavily favored to clinch its fourth consecutive triumph, with Bridgewater being the dark-horse team. Meincke was expected to be challenged by Baxter Berryhill and Ronnie Drumwright, both of Norfolk William and Mary; Joe Renfro of Lynchburg, Bob Packard of Randolph-Macon, and the Bridgewater threesome of Bert Lohr, Bob Kline, and Bev Good.

Howard Meincke turned on the afterburners about half way into the Bridgewater course and won going away with a time of 16:42.9, beating his own record time of 16:53 set in 1955. Berryhill was second for Norfolk William and Mary, but Warren Light put on a nice surge to finish third in 17:32.9. It was an effort that possible saved Roanoke from a loss.

Then came a man from Lynchburg, another from Norfolk William and Mary, and three straight men from Bridgewater College. Bast was beginning to wonder whether the loss of several individuals might result in a team loss. But Phil Shaw crossed the line in ninth place, Dick Lewis finished in tenth, and the Maroons needed only one more person, not too far back, to win the meet.

After three more Bridgewater men finished, the Eagles had taken the sixth, seventh, eighth, eleventh, and twelfth places for a total of 44 points. As Bast strained to see where his other men were located on the course, Bruce Fariss, Roanoke's fifth man, finished strong in a time of 18:30 to give Roanoke 37 points and the win.

The third-place team was Norfolk Division of William and Mary, with 77 points; Lynchburg had 117; Randolph-Macon 136; and Hampden-Sydney 147. The seven-point margin between Roanoke and second-place Bridgewater was the smallest between the two top teams in several years of the Little Eight meet. In retrospect, however, the addition of Dick Goodlake to the race for Roanoke might have reduced the Maroons' score by another five to ten points.

The other Roanoke men were Rhodes Messick, fifteenth place; Danny Bennett, seventeenth place; and Emory Bogle, who finished in the twenty-third spot.

Meincke and Light, having finished in the top five, took home medals. The team had won its fourth straight team trophy.

November 17, 1956
Mason-Dixon Championships at Washington, D. C.
Team Scores: 1st–Roanoke College–52
2nd–Bridgewater College–65
3rd–Loyola College–119
4th–Catholic University–121
5th–Johns Hopkins University–143
6th–Washington College–148
7th–Gallaudet College–176
8th–American University–191
9th–Mount St. Mary's College–214
10th–Lynchburg College–231

Ask five coaches who would finish first, second, and third in this meet, and you would get five different answers. The meet, held at Gallaudet College in Washington on a 3.2-mile course, was scheduled for Saturday, November 17. The Maroons faced their stiffest challenge from Catholic University, with Bridgewater capable of upsetting either Roanoke or Catholic.

In the Little Eight meet, Roanoke had managed to beat Bridgewater for the first-place trophy; however, the margin of victory was just seven points. Catholic was undefeated for the season, and in one of its meets, had beaten Bridgewater decisively, 24-32; therefore, most thought the competition between Roanoke, Catholic, and Bridgewater to be a toss-up.

Individually, the meet offered at least six great runners. They included the Little Eight champion, Roanoke's Howard Meincke. He was undefeated in 1954. Teammate Dick Goodlake was almost as good. Gallaudet's Steve Kugal was the defending champion and would be difficult to dethrone. Catholic had three terrific runners–John Madison, Bob Nelson, and Ed Matthews–but their fourth man was about 45 seconds behind the top three and they had struggled to bring in the fifth man with a decent time. Bridgewater's Bob Kline, Jim Lohr, and Bev Good, along with Jim Murphy of Mount St. Mary's and Ken Billeb of Loyola could each do well.

Kugal had just run in a Maryland-Duke cross country meet and placed first against some of the south's finest runners. He was slightly favored for the individual title over Meincke.

The race began on a rain-soaked course. Kugel, as expected, led throughout the first half of the race. But Meincke was his shadow, running just in back of the Gallaudet star. As Meincke began to make his presence known, he and Kugel swapped leads a couple of times. Finally, Meincke "checked out," as cross country runners say, putting on a short sprint that sent him to the lead for good. Meincke broke the tape with a time of 16:48.2, beating Kugel by 11.8 seconds.

Not too far behind Kugel was the Maroons' Goodlake, who took third in a time of 17:27.5. Warren Light, running his usual good race, finished tenth. Bruce Fariss was seventeenth, and Phil Shaw, just off the injury list, became Roanoke's fifth man when he finished in the twenty-first place. Other Maroons finishing the race were Rhodes Messick, twenty-fourth; Danny Bennett, twenty-ninth; and Dick Lewis, thirty-first.

Roanoke took home the champion's trophy with its 52 points. Surprisingly, Bridgewater finished in second place with 65 points, with unheralded Loyola sneaking into third on 119 points. Catholic, pre-meet favorite to beat Roanoke, could finish no better than fourth. Other schools were Johns Hopkins, fifth; Washington, sixth; Gallaudet, seventh; American, eighth; Mount St. Mary's, ninth; and Lynchburg, tenth.

For Roanoke, the year had been a success. They won all of seven of their dual meets and took first place in both the Little Eight and Mason-Dixon meets.

November 24, 1956
First Annual N. A. I. A. Cross-Country Championships at Omaha, Nebraska
Team Scores: 1st–South Dakota State–71
2nd–Ft. Hays State–88
3rd–Howard Payne–94
4th–Emporia State–97
5th–Moorehead State–110
6th–Oklahoma Baptist–112
7th–Roanoke College–147
8th–Kearney State–162
9th–Geneva College–172
10th–University of Omaha–212
Others: Wayne State–No Score
University of Redlands–No Score
San Diego State–No Score
Tarkio College–No Score
Pasadena College–No Score
Mankato State–No Score
Lincoln University–No Score

Several weeks into the season, Coach Bast opened his mail one morning and found that his cross country team was being congratulated on having one of the finest small college squads in the nation. Because of the team's success, the writer of the letter invited Roanoke to participate in the first National Association of Intercollegiate Athletics (N. A. I. A.) Cross-Country Championships in Omaha, Nebraska. It didn't take Bast long to accept the invitation, even though Omaha was more than 1,100 miles from Salem and might take the team 18-20 hours to get there by school car.

Only one team from the College had ever participated in a national tournament. Back in the late 1930s, the famous "Five Smart Boys" basketball team not only won consecutive state titles, but went to the finals of the National Intercollegiate Tournament at Kansas City in 1938. Now Bast's cross country team would be the second to participate nationally. The meet would bring together some of the best small college teams in the United States.

The N. A. I. A. meet would be held during Thanksgiving weekend at the University of Omaha. Bast had heard that the 4.1-mile course would be the most difficult of all the courses on which his teams had run. It was spotted with long hills of medium slopes, which gave runners no chance to rest.

Coach Homer Bast poses with the six Roanoke College runners who competed in the N. A. I. A. cross country meet at the University of Omaha.
Kneeling (L to R): Co-Captain Bruce Fariss, Bast, and Co-Captain. Phil Shaw
Standing (L to R): Warren Light, Dick Goodlake, Howard Meincke, and Dick Lewis.
Meincke, incidentally, finished fourth in the nation in this race.

The meet was run on Saturday, November 24, 1956. Bast and six Maroon runners left by the school's station wagon on Thursday late in the morning for the long trip. They would be on the road for about 10 hours per day, reaching Omaha late Friday night. After the meet on Saturday morning, they would drive all the way back to Salem so the students could attend classes on Monday morning. It was a tough, 40-hour round trip, but one the runners would never forget.

On Saturday morning in Omaha, Roanoke athletes were shocked to read the local newspaper and find that they were one of the two or three teams favored to win the championship. The publication even printed pictures of some of the Roanoke stars.

When the team reached the University of Omaha that Saturday morning, they found that snow was piled as deeply as six inches on some parts of the course. The wind was biting cold, with the recorded temperature sitting at about 27 degrees. A critical mistake was that the team did not pack any long johns or other under-clothing to help them fight off the effects of the frigid weather. They had tried to find long johns and gloves in the surrounding area Friday night, but had no luck. So here were all of the northern teams, accustomed to the cold weather, bundled up and ready to go. Roanoke runners could wear only their running shorts and lightweight jerseys with no sleeves.

Fortunately, team members were able to warm up in the school's field house. Warren Light even renewed an acquaintance with on old friend from high school, Artie Dunn of Emporia State, who also was warming up for the race. Being a high school state champion in cross country, Dunn went on to finish 9th in the race.

As the race was about to begin, the Roanoke team approached the slot on the starting line that they were assigned. Howard Meincke had the best chance of doing well in the meet, and took his place in the front row. Besides Meincke, those representing Roanoke College were the team Co-Captains and only seniors on the squad, Bruce Fariss and Phil Shaw, junior Dick Goodlake, always a top threat, and two sophomore stars, Warren Light and Dick Lewis.

The starter's gun sounded, and the 77 runners fought for position. Meincke did his best to move toward the front of the first pack of runners who literally were sprinting for position so they wouldn't find themselves trapped well back in the pack when the course narrowed. It was a grueling race for everyone. The footing was poor almost all the way around the wind-blown and snow-packed course.

Finally, the first of the runners began to cross the finish line. The race was won by Ray Manion of the University of Redlands in a time of 22:42.3. Three runners later, in fourth place, was Roanoke's Howard Meincke. His time was 23:15.

Dick Goodlake finished in 30th place among the 75 runners who completed the race. Warren Light was 39th, Bruce Fariss came across the line in 48th position, and Phil Shaw was 54th. The other Maroon was Dick Lewis, who was in 61st place.

Coach Bast was disappointed in the results. First, he honestly thought that Meincke could win the race. He certainly was the most prominent distance runner in Roanoke College history. Meincke ran with his head, Bast was fond of saying, always planning his races. On the other hand, it was the most difficult competition Meincke and the other team members had encountered, and coming home with an individual fourth place medal and a seventh-place team award, wasn't too bad. Not many teams did well in their first taste of national competition. And just getting to the meet, with 20 straight hours of driving, had been an exhausting ordeal.

After the meet, the runners didn't wait for the presentations to take place. They quickly jumped in the station wagon and left for Salem. Those with 8:00 a.m. classes that Monday morning had a tough time getting out of bed.

Incidentally, South Dakota State University won the meet with a total of 71 points. They were followed by Ft. Hays State, Howard Payne, Emporia State, Moorehead State, Oklahoma Baptist, and then Roanoke. Roanoke's total was 147 points.

I remember . . . "I finished in the 48th place in the Omaha meet. The way I saw it, however, was that given the weather–eight inches of snow and bitterly-cold temperatures–I felt that I had done everything I could in that race. And I knew that Homer wasn't going to be critical of me. For that and many other reasons, he became one of my inspirations. It was an interesting trip. We packed everybody into one vehicle. On the way to Omaha, the wind blew the luggage off the roof rack. We were out in the corn fields trying to catch our clothes. And we had no long johns. We went downtown in Omaha, trying to buy heavy underwear. But we couldn't find any. So we went out to race that day in regular old underwear. We froze our butts off. Actually, it was kind of funny. We got to Omaha and these people from the colder states, like Nebraska, were rolling around in the snow, saying that it was such a warm day. And all of us were blue out there in that biting cold weather. All we wanted to know was where we could buy gloves and long underwear. Athletes on the other teams all thought we were crazy."

Bruce Fariss

I remember . . . "Another cross country meet was in Omaha, Nebraska. We got up there and it started snowing, and it was cold, and we weren't dressed for the meet. We didn't have long johns or anything."

Phil Shaw

I remember . . . "At the time, we were members of the NAIA and had a pretty good team. I went to Clarence Caldwell, the school's Business Manager, and suggested that we might do pretty well out in Omaha. So we did get some money together, and they gave us one of the college station wagons to use for the trip. We loaded up the car there just outside the Administration Building. And we had a tremendous crowd there to see us off. There were lots of good wishes, good luck, etc. So we put the whole team of six runners and myself into the car. And we were off to Omaha. We did not ride all night, because we got away a bit late. So I got one motel room. There were very few motels on the road. I think the motel was some place in Indiana. We got a fairly good night's sleep and left the next morning pretty early. After what seemed like an eternity, we finally arrived in Omaha. Again, we got one room in a reasonably-priced motel. The NAIA, of course, was not paying any of our expenses. But we had pretty good newspaper publicity out of the trip – both at home and out there. In fact, the Omaha paper made us one of the favorite teams to win the entire meet. So we got through that night. I was bound and determined that the boys would have steak. I wanted us to go to a nice restaurant and have one of the famous Omaha steaks. And that was our pre-race training meal. Once the race was finished, I was very disappointed in the results by our team. I shouldn't have been, of course. They did the best they possibly could under the circumstances. It was bitter cold. We had a full car, with little space for extras. I hadn't even thought of taking long johns, but space for extra clothing was at a premium. So we ran the race, and immediately afterwards we jumped in the car and left. We didn't stay for the ceremony or anything. We just headed home. And we drove it straight through, alternating drivers. Occasionally, we would stop for a bite to eat. By driving all night, I think we got home around mid-day on Sunday. Of course, the traffic during the night was very light. It was a trip that every one of the six boys would remember for years. I had expected too much from them. I think that under normal circumstances we would have done O.K.–certainly better than what we did in the cold weather with snow on the ground. That weather out in Omaha just knocked our boys cold. And to see that snow on the ground . . . ."

Homer Bast

Indoor Track

Official practice for the 1957 indoor season began on December 3. The date was a bit early compared to other years, but Coach Bast and team members were looking forward to the season. It was difficult for the runners to get in shape at this time of the year. There were bitter-cold afternoons and occasionally snow on the ground. Sometimes the best they could hope for was to strengthen and stretch the leg and back muscles and avoid injuries. For the jumpers and throwers, practice was possible during the winter, but the athletes often ended up in the gymnasium–coordinating their training schedules with those of men's and women's basketball.

Every sign pointed to the fact that this winter's team would be as strong as the one fielded in 1956. Bast had at least two good men in almost every event, and generally speaking, they had been on the squad before.

In the 60, the team would have veterans George Gearhart and Jimmy Nichols. Gearhart was a senior who owned the school record in that event. Nichols wasn't quite as fast, but was a solid point-getter in dual meets. Several freshmen who were at the first practices might also help. They included Jack Dempsey, Scott McKinney, Ken Connoly, and Bob Wortmann.

The 440 and 880 events appeared to have plenty of stars, such as Howard Light (currently on the injured list with a pulled muscle), Dick Lewis, Pete Wise, Phil Shaw, and Johnnie Blanton. John Summers, indoor record holder in the 440 had graduated, but Shaw set two indoor records in the 880 in 1955, and Lewis held the current record in that event–a time of 2:01.7, set in last year's Mason-Dixon Championships. Several freshmen looked good. They included Tom Sitton and Dan Bennett.

In the mile and two-mile events, the team had Howard Meincke, Phil Shaw, Johnnie Blanton, Dick Goodlake, Warren Light, and freshmen Emory Bogle and Wayne Wilson. Meincke had an outstanding cross country season, winning the Little Eight and Mason-Dixon Championships and finishing as the number four runner in the nation in the N. A. I. A. meet in Omaha. He held the indoor record in the two-mile run. Dick Goodlake was perhaps the second-best runner in this group. In fact, he and Meincke would end the indoor season this year with the first- and second-fastest two-mile times of any athletes coached by Mr. Bast.

Two superb hurdlers gave Roanoke unusual strength in the events. Bruce Johnston, from Roanoke, Virginia, was the holder of the Maroons' indoor records in both the high and low hurdles. Philadelphia-born Dick Seed once held the record in the high hurdles before Johnston took the mark lower by a tenth of a second. Three promising freshmen were Dick Emberger, Jim Hackett, and Fred Daly.

Bob Palm and Bill Driscoll gave the shot put event some strength. Palm had been an excellent outdoor thrower in 1956, and everyone expected him to get the indoor record with no problem. John Hylton, a freshman, looked like he might also help in this event.

Seed and sophomore Dick Stauffer were considered the best high jumpers on the team. They were co-holders of the school record in the event. They would be supported by Emberger and Driscoll.

Frank Vest, sophomore from Bedford, Virginia, was the only veteran in the pole vault; however, freshman Win Niles and sophomore Cliff Shaw seemed to be good prospects. Before he left Roanoke, in fact, Niles would clear more than 13' in the pole vault and come within two inches of the 1952 school record set by the fabled Roanoke jumper, Ray DeCosta.

Jim Nichols and Dempsey would be the main broad jumpers. They would end the season as the first- and second-best broad jumpers in the history of indoor track at Roanoke.

With the strength of the team, some predicted that 10 or more school records would be broken during the six scheduled indoor meets. As the season began, the records to beat were as follows:

60-Yard Dash	:06.3	George Gearhart	1956
440-Yard Dash	:53.6	John Summers	1954
880-Yard Run	2:01.7	Dick Lewis	1956
Mile Run	4:30.5	Les Noel	1955
Two-Mile Run	10:19.8	Howard Meincke	1956
70-Yard High Hurdles	:09.1	Bruce Johnston	1956
70-Yard Low Hurdles	:07.9	Bruce Johnston	1955
Shot Put	41'9"	Bill Lund	1953
Broad Jump	20'11½"	Jay Jackson	1955
High Jump	5'11¼"	Dick Seed and Dick Stauffer	1956
Pole Vault	13'3"	Ray DeCosta	1952
Mile Relay	3:44.4	Rader, Wallwork, Rittman, and Summers	1954
Distance Medley Relay	11:16.6	Summers, Lewis, Meincke, and P. Shaw	1956
Two-Mile Relay	8:09.0	Irvin, Noel, Rittman, and Noel	1954
Sprint Medley Relay	3:41.5	Summers, Ide, Gearhart, and Lewis	1956

I remember . . . "I missed almost all of the indoor season that year after injuring my Achilles tendon. I remember going down to old Dr. Smiley. He was the College's official doctor for some years. I walked into the examining room and he asked what was wrong. I told him that I thought I had pulled my Achilles tendon. After a cursory glance of about three seconds, he said 'Yep. That's what you did.' "

Howard Light

I remember . . . "We tried to run outside during the winter, but the weather was often a problem. We had a maintenance man tell us one day that we were crazy being out in sub-freezing weather with just towels around our necks. And you had to run where there was no snow. When the basketball team wasn't using Alumni gymnasium, of course, we could run a little in there. We would get in the cages at the north end of the gym floor, and run through the cage door toward the other end of the gym. And they couldn't afford more than to give you one pair of shoes per year. That was better than in high school, however, when we had to buy our own. When we went on track trips, we would use college cars. They called one of them 'the hearse.' It was an old black Dodge."

George Gearhart

January 26, 1957
Evening Star Games at Washington, D. C.
Team Scores: None

The Evening Star Games, held on January 26, 1957, was such a large and competitive meet that Coach Bast decided to take only ten men: seniors George Gearhart and Phil Shaw; junior Dick Goodlake; sophomores Pete Wise, Howard Meincke, Dick Lewis, and Warren Light; and freshmen Jack Dempsey, Tom Sitton, and Danny Bennett. This group would be entering four events. The first, and the one the team always wanted to win more than any other, was the Mason-Dixon Conference Sprint Medley Relay. They also would enter the Class "C" Intercollegiate Mile Relay, the Ellery N. Clark Memorial Two-Mile Relay, and the 880-yard run.

In the Mason-Dixon Sprint Medley Relay, Roanoke entered the team of Wise, running the 440; Sitton and Gearhart, each running a 220; and Meincke, who would finish with an 880 leg. Catholic University generally gave Roanoke the most problems in this race. Today, there is little information on how the race progressed, but we do know that the Roanoke team won with a time of 3:42.4. The school record was 3:41.5.

Wise, Sitton, Lewis, and Bennett ran as a team in the mile relay event. LaSalle University won the race going away, running 3:23.3. That time was one of the best in the nation at that point in the season. Roanoke did take second place, but with a time of 3:40.0, which left the anchor man well behind his counterpart from LaSalle. On the other hand, the 3:40.0 was a new school indoor record for Roanoke. The old record of 3:44.4 had been set in 1954.

Meincke, Goodlake, Warren Light, and Shaw each ran an 880 leg in the two mile relay. Unfortunately, the team did not place. Neither did the athletes (unspecified in news reports) who were in the 880-yard run.

January 30, 1957
Virginia Military Institute at Lexington, Virginia
Team Scores: Roanoke–55⅔
Virginia Military Institute–48⅓

It was bound to happen. There was this Virginia Military Institute track team with a great field house and top-flight athletes–a school with a rich tradition in their indoor track program. They were good and they knew it. Down the road about 50 miles sat a small college called Roanoke. The school had an indoor team that many thought was the best around. And they were getting a lot of publicity. But the V. M. I. fans looked at Roanoke with disdain. The proud Keydets and their supporters could never see themselves losing to a Little Eight school.

In the local Roanoke newspaper, a V. M. I. fan even challenged the Maroons to put up or shut up. "We believe that Roanoke College does have a real good team," the gentleman said, "but we think that we have a good team also since we beat such schools as Georgia Tech, Florida State, and Alabama in the nonconference meet in North Carolina. I guess the only way to tell the better team is to have a meet together sometime in the future."

That meet would occur on the 30th of January. The pre-meet hype was heavy. Each team had great individual performers. One of the meet highlights, for example, would be Roanoke's Howard Meincke versus V. M. I.'s Dave Pitkethly. Both runners ranked as the best all-time distance runners at their schools.

Four field events–shot, broad jump, high jump, and pole vault–led off the meet. In the shot put, Bob Palm of Roanoke placed first with a throw of 43'8", with two V. M. I. men in second and third. The win was unexpected because football schools like V. M. I. seemed to have good shot put men on their team every year.

In the broad jump, the Maroons got two other surprises. First, Jack Dempsey set a new school record with a winning jump of 22'6¼". It would be the best distance Dempsey would ever record in his indoor career. Second, Jim Nichols jumped 21'6½" for third place.

Roanoke also scored big in the high jump. John Machen of V. M. I. won the event with a jump of 6'2". But Maroon Harry Clegg cleared 6'1" for second place. Clegg, from Philadelphia, entered Roanoke College for the spring semester just two days before the meet. His 6'1"jump was a new indoor record for Roanoke. Dick Emberger and Dick Seed each picked up ⅓ of a point by jumping 5'10" and tying a Keydet jumper for third place.

In the mile run, Meincke lost to Pitkethly, with Meincke running 4:35.0 to Pitkethly's winning time of 4:30.6. And in the other distance race, Pitkethly won the two-mile run in 9:48.8, with Dick Goodlake about 26 seconds behind in second.

Gearhart couldn't match the winning :06.3 in the 60-yard dash, but he did get second-place points. In the 440, Tom Sitton showed his talents by winning in :53.3, another school record. Dick Lewis grabbed third-place honors.

Meincke and Wise finished second and third, respectively, in the 880. Meincke's time was 2:02.2. Wise's time was 2:05.0.

Bruce Johnston ran an excellent :09.1 in winning the high hurdles. That time tied his own school record, set in 1956. Freshman Dick Emberger placed second in :09.4.

Johnston and McCloud of V. M. I. hit the tape together in the low hurdles. Judges gave the narrow win to McCloud, putting Johnston in second place. Both were given identical times of :07.8, another school indoor record for Roanoke.

The pole vault still was in progress when most of the fans realized how close the meet scores were getting to be. The team scores at this point were 44⅔ for Roanoke and 45⅓ for V. M. I. Many of the spectators and lots of athletes were grouped around the pole vault pit to see what would happen. Down the runway came freshman Win Niles. He hit his marks and his plant was perfect. The pole bent and up and up he went, clearing the bar at 13'1". The 13'1" height was 10" higher than he had ever jumped. Here, perhaps, was the successor to Roanoke's legendary Ray DeCosta. Frank Vest had been eliminated at a lower height, but still placed third.

Now, with only the mile relay to go, Roanoke had re-taken the lead. The team score was 50⅔ to 48⅓. Since points were awarded only to the winner in a mile relay, the team winning that race–the last event of the long afternoon–would win the meet.

Roanoke's mile relay team would be George Gearhart, Dick Goodlake, Dick Lewis, and Tom Sitton on the anchor leg. With just three minutes to go before the race began, in the middle of eight nervous runners, Coach Bast met with his relay team. Over 50 years later, leadoff man George Gearhart remembered the moment as if it happened yesterday.

Talking about Bast and the mile relay event, Gearhart said: "He was more than just a coach. He was a father figure to me. And he could get you to do things whether or not you wanted to do them. V. M. I. had a tremendous track team. But near the end of the meet, and before we finished the meet with the mile relay, Roanoke was just slightly in front in terms of the team score. If V. M. I. had won the relay, we would have lost the entire meet. Homer came up to me just before the race and said, 'George, I want you to be the leadoff man for this race.' And I said, 'No. No, I can't do that.' I think I was remembering another time when I had been the leadoff man–with what I thought had been disastrous results. And Coach Bast looked right at me and said calmly, 'O. K. Then we will just lose the meet.' And he turned and walked away. And I thought to myself, 'Oh, my gosh. I can't let the team down like that.' So I ran over to him and agreed to run the first leg. Homer said, 'Good. Here's what I want you to do. You can beat any of their guys at the start and on the straight-aways. And they won't pass you on the curve. When you get to a straightaway, you just sprint. Then coast the curve, keeping the V. M. I. man behind you.' So that's what I did. I gave our guys the lead after the first 440, and the team went on to win the relay and the track meet. To V. M. I., that was quite an upset."

Roanoke won the meet, 55⅔ to 48⅓. Once again, Roanoke's depth told the story. Roanoke College and V. M. I. each had six first places, but Roanoke took seven of the possible eleven seconds, plus five thirds, and that made the difference.

I remember . . . "School was out because of winter break. It started to snow early on the morning of the meet. The depth of the snow grew steadily during the day. I was in Bedford with a mountain between me and Lexington. Roanoke College had a powerhouse of a team, and I didn't think my absence from the meet would make much difference. There wasn't any question that we were going to win that meet. It was a no-brainer. I called Mr. Bast and told him that I was in Bedford with 15" of snow on the ground. I said that at best, I was going to get a point or half a point during the meet. I told him that he didn't need me. But he said, 'Frank, we are right on the brink. I have been adding up the points and we need all the help we can get. You've got to come back. You've got to come.' So I got in a car with my little brother, who later would be a Cadet at V. M. I., and we drove to Lexington via Roanoke, because we couldn't go over the mountain. By that time, there was 20" of snow on the ground. We got there, and I think I tied for third in the pole vault."

Frank Vest

I remember . . . "I remember the Roanoke/V. M. I. indoor meet during the 1956-57 season. I think that was the meet when I made a jump early on and the sawdust flew up and got in my eyes. I ended up rubbing my eyes and couldn't see. I had to go sit and they washed my eyes out. It was on the first jump, and somehow I landed wrong and the dust came up. I remember them washing them out, and the medical guy there trying to get the sawdust out."

Cliff Shaw

I remember . . . "The most famous meet during the indoor season was the one with Virginia Military Institute in Lexington. V. M. I.'s Coach Walt Cormack and I were pretty good friends. He was like us – not being able to find any good competition with the big teams, because most teams weren't doing very much during the indoor track season. Of course, he may have been able to schedule a team like Navy, but I think that Walt was like us–on a limited budget for these indoor meets. Today, I have no idea how or why our meet came into existence. George Gearhart's version of the last race, the mile relay, was pretty accurate. George hated the quarter mile. I had told him that he could be a great quarter miler. And we are going to run you in some 440s. That day, I gave him a chance. I knew he was going to get out front, because by that time he had a quick start, just like Boyd Carr had several years before. Incidentally, I took a very loyal V. M. I. alumnus over to the meet with the team. He had been a guard on V. M. I.'s football team. I had invited him to go with us, saying that the meet should be very interesting, and he agreed. V. M. I. gave us a training meal and he stayed around for the entire time. I don't know who he was rooting for during that last race, but . . . . By the way, Win Niles was instrumental in our winning that meet. He won the pole vault, an event we *never* expected to win. When Win Niles came down to Roanoke College and I saw him practice for the first time, I knew that he had real talent. Apparently, he had been a good high school jumper. I don't know what happened to him after that year. He just disappeared."

Homer Bast

February 2, 1957
Virginia Military Institute Winter Relays at Lexington, Virginia
Team Scores:None

Three days later, the Roanoke team returned to the Lexington field house to compete in the annual Winter Relays. This affair had grown to be one of the top five indoor meets of the season for mid-Atlantic teams. Roanoke and Gallaudet were the only small colleges represented among the 12 schools that entered teams.

The University of Maryland, dominating the meet for the fourth year in a row, won four of the nine relays on the 18-event program and added firsts in two individual events. Except for Maryland, no college won more than one relay. William and Mary, Virginia Military Institute, Georgetown, Navy, and Roanoke won one event each.

That win for Roanoke was in the distance medley relay. The team of Pete Wise, Tom Sitton, Dick Goodlake, and Howard Meincke beat larger teams such as Maryland, V. M. I., Georgetown, the University of North Carolina, and William and Mary to finish first in a time of 10:50.0. The mark tied the meet record set by Carolina in 1955. It also broke the Roanoke College indoor record by almost 27 seconds.

A new indoor record for Roanoke also was set by the 880-yard relay team of Jim Nichols, Dick Engel, George Gearhart, and Jack Dempsey. They ran 1:38.8 in a heat with William and Mary and North Carolina State. The final placements were judged by the times within the different heats, however, and in the final standing, Roanoke was fifth.

In the sprint medley relay, the quartet of Dick Lewis, Tom Sitton, George Gearhart, and Howard Meincke won their individual heat with a time of 3:44.8. They missed the school record by 3.3 seconds, but finished fourth in back of Maryland, North Carolina, and V. M. I. Their time, 3:44.8, beat the efforts of major schools such as Duke and Navy, and was just 2.1 seconds greater than Maryland's winning time.

Roanoke also placed fourth in the four-mile relay with the team of Phil Shaw, Johnnie Blanton, Emory Bogle, and Wayne Wilson. Their time of 20:22.0 set a new school record.

Harry Clegg, barely in school for a week, did well again in the high jump. The freshman jumped 6'0" but managed to place only fifth because of the quality of the competition.

I remember . . . "Another thing I learned came at the V. M. I. field house, where you had to go under the stands. Those Marines would push you and they would spike you in the tunnel when no one could see you. Sometimes you would come out of there with a bloody leg. They were bad. And on the cross country courses, they would push you down over the bank. Their intent was to win. It didn't matter how they did it. You quickly learned that when you were up against a Marine, you didn't run beside him. You sprinted on ahead as quickly as you could."

Bruce Fariss

February 9, 1957
Little Eight Championships at Lexington, Virginia
Team Scores: 1st–Roanoke–71½
2nd–Norfolk Division of William and Mary–40½
3rd–Lynchburg–10
4th–Hampden-Sydney–6
5th–Randolph-Macon–1

As in recent years, the Little Eight Championships was being run concurrently with the Big Six meet. In the Big Six competition, Virginia Polytechnic Institute was defending its title against a field that was so evenly matched that four other teams were given a chance to win.

William and Mary, possessing the state's premiere sprinter in Walt Fillman, was regarded as the most likely to win if the Tech men didn't. But V. M. I., Virginia, and even Richmond also appeared to have an opportunity to post the best score.

In the Little Eight meet, Roanoke's team was heavily favored to take home another championship trophy. In this meet last year, Roanoke had collected more points than all of the other Little Eight teams combined. They were expected to do so again in 1957. The Maroons' domination of the meet in 1956 was so complete that the Maroons won nine of the 12 events, setting four records in the process. In defending a sterling record of four straight crowns, Coach Bast was fielding a team that had stellar talent and lots of depth.

The team most likely to give Roanoke problems was Norfolk Division of William and Mary. In the shot put, they had Jerry Tiedemann, a prodigious thrower who promised to be even better than the 50-footer, Jim Frazer, of Hampden-Sydney. Norfolk also had several individual stars, such as Ronnie Drumwright and Baxter Berryhill in the middle and longer distance events, along with a 23-foot broad jumper, Kenny Harmon. After those individuals, unfortunately, there was little depth.

Competition began at 3:00 p.m., with trial heats in all races of less than a half mile and finals in the broad jump. Finals in the other field events were to begin at 7:00 p.m., with finals in the running events starting at 7:30 p.m.

An unbelievable 11 new Little Eight records were broken or tied by the time the meet was finished. Roanoke College athletes broke or tied nine more of their own school records.

In the first event to be completed, Jim Nichols broad jumped 22'3" to win the event; however, two other Roanoke men also placed. Jack Dempsey was second and Cliff Shaw took third. Nichols' distance tied the Little Eight indoor record, set by Harmon of Norfolk William and Mary in 1956.

Other field events were just as interesting. In the shot put, Bob Palm was able to take third place, but his throw of 45'¾" set a new Roanoke College record. Gerald Tiedemann won the shot, throwing 48'9½" and setting a new meet record. Harry Clegg came through again for Roanoke, winning the high jump with a new meet and Roanoke College record of 6'1⅛". Freshman Dick Emberger tied for second by jumping 5'10¼". And in the pole vault, few people predicted what happened there. Taylor Goode of Lynchburg had been the number one pole vaulter in the area for two or three years. Tonight, however, Win Niles of Roanoke and Goode stayed close all night and the two finally tied for first with 12'9", another meet record.

In the high hurdles, Bruce Johnston was upset for first place by Thomas of Norfolk William and Mary, who set a new record with :08.9. Johnston's time was :09.1, which tied his own school record. Johnston came back to win the low hurdle race, running a :07.8. The time set a new Little Eight record and tied his own Roanoke record set in 1957.

The mile and two-mile titles were taken by Roanoke. Howard Meincke placed first in the mile with a time of 4:36.8, with Phil Shaw running third. Dick Goodlake won the two-mile run. His 10:12.0 was a meet record and tied a Roanoke College record. Warren Light was second in the two-mile race.

Drumwright of Norfolk William and Mary won the 880-yard run, just nipping Pete Wise at the tape and beating Howard Meincke, who was third. Drumwright's 2:03.8 was a meet record.

The 60-yard dash went to Roanoke's George Gearhart. He tied his own school record and also tied the Little Eight record.

Young Tom Sitton powered through the tape in the 440 in a time of :53.1, a meet and school record. Dick Lewis was second with :53.9 and Pete Wise finished third in :54.8.

And finally, the Roanoke mile relay team of Gearhart, Goodlake, Lewis, and Sitton also broke the meet and school records with their winning time of 3:34.4. The old Little Eight record was 3:34.3, while the school record of 3:40.0 had been set earlier in the year by Hackett, Bennett, Howard Light, and Lewis.

Roanoke easily finished the meet with top honors, totaling 71½ points and almost doubling the score on the nearest pursuer. After Roanoke came Norfolk Division of William and Mary, with 40½ points; Lynchburg, with 10; Hampden-Sydney, with 6; and Randolph-Macon, with 1. It was Roanoke's fifth title in a row.

V. M. I., which ruled the Big Six meet for three years until dethroned by V. P. I. last year, built up a 10-point advantage in the first eight events, then held on to win with a total of 35 points. William and Mary was second with 31 and V. P. I., the defending champion, third with 27½. Trailing were Virginia, 21; Richmond, 17½; and Washington and Lee, 0.

There was no doubt that Roanoke was the track power in Virginia. On the same night as V. M. I. won the Big Six title, Roanoke won the Little Eight crown. But Roanoke had beaten the Keydets just two weeks ago.

February 16, 1957
Mason-Dixon Championships at Lexington, Virginia
Team Scores: 1st–Roanoke–81
2nd–Hampden-Sydney–15
3rd–Lynchburg–10⅓
4th–Mount St. Mary's–10
5th–Randolph-Macon–7⅓
6th–Gallaudet–5⅓
7th–Western Maryland–2

The Mason-Dixon indoor meet this year was a bit strange. The only teams to participate, besides Roanoke, were Gallaudet, Hampden-Sydney, Lynchburg, Mount St. Mary's, Randolph-Macon, and Western Maryland. Loyola and Johns Hopkins did not send teams, while usually powerful Catholic University withdrew because of a segregation rule which involved a member of their team.

From Roanoke's viewpoint, the competition would be less intense than it was in the Little Eight meet the week before. There would be a number of outstanding athletes at the meet–Jim Frazer of Hampden-Sydney in the shot put, Steve Kugal of Gallaudet in the distance runs, and Taylor Goode of Lynchburg in the pole vault, for example–but no one team had the depth to ruin the Maroons' bid for a fifth straight indoor title. In most events, the battle was not for first place but more for second, third, and fourth.

Roanoke was almost at full strength, except for Dick Seed and Howard Meincke. Both of them had ankle injuries. The injury would keep Seed from high jumping or running the hurdles. And the sore ankle would hobble Meincke in his mile and two-mile races.

Homer Bast likely was the only coach in the field house who wore a smile throughout the meet. Before a sizeable crowd, the Maroons won ten of the 12 events and in the process set four new meet records and tied another. School records also fell. They broke four of these records and tied a fifth.

This meet was fun to watch. In every event, it seemed, there were outstanding performances. One of the first events to finish was the shot put. Jim Frazer of Hampden-Sydney, based on the fact that he was the only 50-footer in the meet, was favored to win that event. And he did, throwing 46'11" to break the meet record. Roanoke's Bob Palm placed second and also broke the meet and school records. His throw of 46'6" was better than the school record of 45'¾" which he set at the Little Eight meet the previous week.

Another interesting event was the broad jump, where Roanoke swept the first three places. Jim Nichols set a new Mason-Dixon record of 22'9⅞" with his winning jump. The distance also was a Roanoke College record, breaking the mark of 22'6¼" owned by Jack Dempsey. Second-place Dempsey jumped 22'3", also breaking the meet record, and Cliff Shaw was third. Nichols' jump, incidentally, was just ⅛" off the field house record of 22'10".

The pole vault also was a crowd pleaser. Taylor Goode, who for years had been the best vaulter in the conference and certainly the best since Roanoke's Ray DeCosta in the early 1950s, traded jumps all night with Win Niles, the freshman from Roanoke College. Niles and Goode had tied for first place in the Little Eight meet. Finally, Niles failed to make his final jump and Goode cleared the bar at 13'0" for the win. Another Maroon, Frank Vest, finished third.

In the only other field event, Roanoke's Dick Stauffer and Dick Emberger tied with Sam Bland of Randolph-Macon for first place. All three cleared 5'9¾". After setting a new school record of 6'1⅛" last week, Harry Clegg settled for a fourth-place tie.

George Gearhart ran :06.4 in the 60-yard dash to win, setting a new meet record. Jim Nichols was third.

Roanoke's Dick Goodlake, in a rare appearance in a mile race, finished with a strong 4:32.3 effort to place first. The time was a new Roanoke College record, better than the 4:38.5 time run by Les Noel in 1955, and also was a meet record. He took the lead at the beginning of the race and was never pushed. Howard Meincke, even with his ankle problem, finished second behind Goodlake.

Meincke then ran in the two-mile race, beating his old rival Steve Kugel for first place with a time of 10:09.0. The time was a Mason-Dixon record, and also broke the school mark of 10:12.0 set by Dick Goodlake earlier in the season. Warren Light took third place.

Tom Sitton made the crowd yell when he won the 440 in :52.7. He made the effort look easy. His :52.7 mark was a new College record, erasing the :53.1 time that Sitton had set in 1957. Dick Lewis was second.

In the 880, Pete Wise reached the first turn in front of the pack and was never challenged. His winning time was 2:02.2. Phil Shaw was third in the race.

Bruce Johnston had little problem winning the high hurdles. The smooth junior ran a :09.2, just a tenth of a second behind his own school record. Harry Clegg finished in fourth place.

In the low hurdles, he tied his own school record by winning in a time of :07.8. Roanoke picked up three more points when Bill Driscoll placed third and Dick Emberger fourth.

In the end, the powerful Roanoke team won 10 of the 12 events and had been responsible for 9 of 10 Mason-Dixon or Roanoke College records. Their winning team score was 81, more than five times the score of the second-place team, Hampden-Sydney. Lynchburg was third with 10⅓; Mount St. Mary's was fourth with 10; Randolph-Macon took fifth place with 7⅓; Gallaudet was sixth with 5⅓; and Western Maryland last with 2 points.

February 23, 1957
Atlantic Coast Conference Indoor Games at Raleigh, North Carolina
Team Scores (Non-Conference Division): 1st–Florida State–50
2nd–University of Georgia–23
3rd–Davidson–22
T4th–East Carolina–5
T4th–Roanoke–5
6th–Presbyterian–1

The Atlantic Coast Conference Games were held in Raleigh at the State Fair Arena. This meet succeeded indoor games at Chapel Hill–games which were staged there for approximately 28 years. For the first two seasons as the A. C. C. meet, the event remained at the University of North Carolina. It was moved to Raleigh last year.

The Maryland Terps were favored for the Conference title. Coach Jim Kehoe's team had done well at the recent V. M. I. relays and overall the team was very strong. It was a meet that featured several outstanding athletes. U. N. C., for example, was entering the famous runner, Jim Beatty. He had won the mile and two-mile runs in this meet for the past two years and in 1962, he would become the first person to break the four-minute barrier on an indoor track. The conference division also spotlighted the running of Dave Sime. At one point in his career, the Duke star held nine world records in track and field. His record in the 220-yard dash stood for 10 years–from 1956-66. After injuries kept him from competing in the 1956 Olympics, he won a silver medal in the 1960 games in Rome. Years later, he was selected "Best Athlete Ever to Attend Duke."

As usual, the meet featured events only for conference members, some for non-conference teams, and a division for freshmen. Roanoke would be competing with a small number of individuals in the non-conference division.

Roanoke's George Gearhart, Pete Wise, Dick Lewis, and Tom Sitton entered the non-conference mile relay event. They finished second behind Florida State's winning 3:35.3, with Davidson in third and the University of Georgia placing fourth.

The only other Maroon in the meet that we know of was Harry Clegg. He tied for second place in the non-conference high jump, although his height was not noted.

I remember . . . "We had one meet indoors in the 1956-57 season, in North Carolina. We ran in the Cow Palace, as they called it, at the State Fair Arena in Raleigh. It was the Atlantic Coast Conference Indoor Games. I finished tied for fourth in the non-conference division. We competed in a large, brick, oval building. Through the middle of that oval, it was open and they had their 60-yard dash starting at one brick wall and ending at another brick wall. I remember watching the great sprinter, Duke's Dave Sime, run. In the 60, he would finish three yards ahead. He was a tall guy. I remember him being about 6'5", although I could be wrong. That was very unusual for a sprinter. At the time, he was the fastest man I had ever seen."

Allen Ide

February 23, 1957
Virginia AAU Championships at Richmond, Virginia
Team Scores: 1st–College of William and Mary–44⅚
2nd–Virginia Military Institute–44⅓
3rd–Norfolk Division of William and Mary–13
4th–University of Richmond–12½
5th–Mount St. Mary's College–7
6th–Hampden-Sydney College–3
7th–Randolph-Macon College–3
8th–Washington and Lee University–2

Roanoke's sole participant in this meet in Richmond was Dick Emberger, who entered the high jump competition but failed to place. The winning jump was 6'2¼", a mark set by Storm of William and Mary.

The meet was won by William and Mary's Southern Conference championship team, which surged from behind in the final events to overtake V. M. I. The winning margin was one-half point.

All of the events were run in the indoor arena except for the shot put, which was held outdoors and won by big Gerald Tiedemann of Norfolk William and Mary. Tiedemann, a burly 220-pounder with a crew cut, threw the shot 51'½"–about five feet better than the Big Six Conference record and almost three feet better than his own Little Eight Conference record.

I remember . . . "Well, long after I graduated from Roanoke College, when I went to Charlotte as Rector, I became good friends with Bruce and Mary Rhinehart. We were great buddies and still are, as a matter of fact. About eight or nine years later, Bruce and I were talking. We had never talked much about our college athletic careers. He had been a superb athlete–a great high school football player. He went on to the University of Virginia, where he was too small to play football. We got to talking about track and it turned out that he was talking about a meet in Lexington where all of the Virginia Colleges got together in a winter meet. It turned out that he and I both tied for third place in the pole vault in that meet. There was only one third place medal, so he and I flipped a coin to see who would take home the medal. I won. In 1982, I gave that medal to him and told him that I wanted it back in 25 years. And I just got it back. I have written a letter to his grandson, telling him that in 25 years from now, he would need to send the medal to one of my grandsons."

Frank Vest

Outdoor Track

What can you say about a team like Roanoke that has so much talent that virtually no opponent thinks the Maroons can be beaten? Look at this list of Roanoke College outdoor record holders in individual events. Those names in italics were competing on the 1957 team.

100-Yard Dash	00:09.9	*George Gearhart*	April 21, 1956
220-Yard Dash	00:21.7	*George Gearhart*	April 21, 1956
440-Yard Dash	00:51.0	*Howard Light*	May 16, 1956
880-Yard Run	01:58.7	*Dick Lewis*	April 14, 1956
Mile Run	04:24.4	Alvin Smith	May 28, 1949
Two-Mile Run	09:57.2	*Dick Goodlake*	April 24, 2956
120-Yard High Hurdles	00:15.1	Dave Foltz	May 11-12, 1956
220-Yard Low Hurdles	00:23.5	Dave Foltz	April 17, 1956
Shot Put	45'9¼"	*Bob Palm*	April 21, 1956

Discus	129'3"	Jim Doran	May 17, 1947
Javelin	165'2"	Bill Lund	April 3, 1954
Broad Jump	22'9"	*Jim Nichols*	May 16, 1956
High Jump	6'1"	Jay Jackson and Chris Rittman	April 10, 1954
Pole Vault	13'6"	Ray DeCosta	May 2, 1952

Left Photo: Phil Shaw participated in several events for Roanoke. He was a 2:01.5 half miler and a 4:34.0 miler.
Right Photo: Richard Lewis was one of the school's best athletes in the 440-yard dash and in the 880-yard run. Before he graduated, he had run :50.7 in the quarter and had recorded a 1:58.5 (and two other sub-2:00.0 times), second only to the great Howard Meincke.

Since very early in the 1953 season, Roanoke had never lost a dual meet. Going into this season, the consecutive winning streak was sitting at 28. During the current season, they would face nine more teams for a potential streak of 37. Few people would have bet against them reaching that number. In addition, the Maroons had won the last four Little Eight meets and were champions of the Mason-Dixon Conference for the past three years.

Dave Foltz graduated in 1956. A terrific athlete in several events, he had scored more than 450 points during his four years of competition in outdoor track and field. The team also had lost John Summers, a Co-Captain with Foltz, who was a key player in the 440 and mile relay, along with another good runner, Allen Ide. These losses, however, were more than offset by the number of experienced veterans who were returning, along with a good-looking crop of freshmen.

To a talented collection of veterans, Bast was adding individuals who, in some cases, would become some of the school's best all-time athletes: Jack Dempsey, Dick Emberger, Ashton Lough, Scott McKinney, Win Niles, Tom Sitton, Wayne Wilson, Harry Clegg, Dick Engel, and John Hylton.

The only injured athletes at the beginning of the year were Jimmy Nichols, Jack Dempsey, and Dan Bennett. Nichols, Roanoke's great broad jumper who had reached 22'9¾" indoors, was slowed a bit by a leg injury received in basketball. Dempsey also jumped over 22' indoors, but likewise was hampered by a leg injury. Freshman Bennett re-injured a muscle and likely would be lost to the team for the entire season.

I remember . . . "None of the Big Six teams really wanted to run us by this time. William and Mary was the only big school who agreed to run us, but we couldn't get enough additional meets on the trip to Williamsburg for us to go down there. With our limited budget, you just couldn't go that far for one meet."

George Gearhart

I remember . . . "Someone told me not long ago that the discussion in our big meets–in particular the Little Eight and Mason-Dixon Championships–was not who was going to win, but who would be second."

Bruce Fariss

March 30, 1957
Newport News Apprentice School at Newport News, Virginia
Team Scores: Roanoke–87⅔
Newport News Apprentice–34⅓

The team's first meet came early, on March 30, during a trip to Newport News and a meet with Newport News Apprentice School. Five of Coach Bast's top performers stayed behind in Salem because of academic commitments, but even so, the strong Maroon team won 10 of 14 events and scored in them all. On this windy day, each team set one record as Roanoke won easily 87⅔ to 34⅓.

In the next-to-last event of the day, the Roanoke team of Scott McKinney, Dick Engel, Howard Light, and Dick Lewis won the seldom-run three-fifths mile relay in a time of 2:18.4. The time beat the old 2:19.2 record set in 1947 by Catholic University and was a track and Roanoke College record.

The Apprentice School record came in the 220-yard low hurdles. Without the presence of Bruce Johnston, Kenny Selfe of the host team ran the hurdles in :27.0 to erase the :27.1 track record set in 1949. For Roanoke, Harry Clegg was second.

In the high hurdles, Dick Seed placed first. His time was not recorded. Again, Clegg was second. Freshman Dick Emberger was third in the same time, :16.6, as Clegg's.

The two-mile run turned out to be an interesting race. Roanoke's Wayne Wilson took an early lead, but Bob Cooke of the Shipbuilders kept pace immediately behind him. Just before the half-way point, Cooke passed Wilson only to relinquish the lead on the succeeding lap. With less than four laps to go, Cooke made one more bid. He passed Wilson for the second time and then pulled away for about a 50-yard victory. His winning time of 10:38.0 was just five seconds off Buck Bucklin's track mark set in 1955. It was Cooke's third of the season, after winning a mile/two-mile double against Randolph-Macon College the previous Wednesday.

In the mile run, Warren Light and Johnnie Blanton won together and easily in a time of 4:44.4. Cooke trailed, placing third.

George Gearhart had little trouble winning the 100-yard dash in :10.4, with Scott McKinney placing third in :10.7. In the 220, Jack Dempsey won in :23.6 and McKinney was second.

The Maroons took first and second places in both the 440 and 880. Howard Light coasted through a good, early-season time of :53.0 in the quarter mile, followed by freshman Dick Engel, who ran :54.4. In the half-mile race, Dick Lewis and Phil Shaw crossed the line together in first place, running 2:05.0.

Roanoke athletes won three of the five field events. Bill Driscoll, who threw consistently well, finished in first in the discus with a toss of 124'5". Ashton Lough was third with 118'0". Cliff Shaw and Jack Dempsey tied for first in the broad jump with 19'5" efforts, while Dick Stauffer, Harry Clegg, and Dick Emberger cleared 5'9" to win the high jump.

Others who scored in the field events were John Hylton, second in the shot put, and Frank Vest and Dick Emberger, who tied for second in the pole vault.

The win was Roanoke's first of the season, with no losses. Newport News Apprentice School, after beating Randolph-Macon earlier, now was 1-1.

I remember . . . "We went to Norfolk to run track meets for a couple of days and we checked into the motel. I was with Bruce Johnston and a couple of the other guys. We began to laugh because we were thinking about the rest of the students back in Salem who had to take their exams. Then Coach Bast walked in and said, 'I know you want to take these exams while you are here. You wouldn't want to miss them.' So there we were, on the road at track meets, taking our exams."

Howard Light

April 1, 1957
Norfolk Division of William and Mary at Norfolk, Virginia
Team Scores: Roanoke–79½
Norfolk William and Mary–42½

On December 1, Roanoke visited the usually-strong team from Norfolk Division of William and Mary. The meet, held on a windy, cloudy, and cool afternoon, had three double-winners–George Gearhart and Howard Meincke from Roanoke and Gerald Tiedemann of Norfolk Division.

Gearhart ran very well. After a :10.1 first place time in the 100, with Jack Dempsey tied for third, he tied his own Roanoke College record with a winning :21.7 in the 220. Dempsey also finished third in that race.

Howard Meincke, running the best of his college career, placed first in both the mile and two-mile races. In the mile, he won with a time of 4:25.0, just six tenths of a second off the school record 4:24.4 set in 1949 by Alvin Smith. Dick Goodlake was just half a second behind Meincke. Meincke also ran 10:03.0 in the two mile for a win, with Warren Light just behind in 10:04.6.

The final double came from big Gerald Tiedemann of Norfolk William and Mary. In the shot put, he finished first with a prodigious throw of 51'4¾". Bob Palm of Roanoke, responding to the challenge, set a new school record of 46'0" and finished second. Tiedemann came back to win the discus with 125'3". Bill Driscoll was third.

Another school record was tied in the 440 when Dick Lewis placed first with a :51.0. That time tied the mark that Howard Light set during 1956. Tom Sitton was close behind, running :51.3 for second, and Dick Engel placed third in :52.6.

Phil Shaw was unable to win the 880, but did finish second in :2:02.6 with Dick Lewis following for third.

Dick Seed, with :15.9, won the high hurdles. Dick Emberger ran :16.1 to finish second, while Harry Clegg finished the sweep with his :16.4. Bruce Johnston won the low hurdles in :24.7, although Dick Seed was close behind in :25.5.

Gladys Ulrich and Bob Palm, the track team's best shot putter and school record holder in that event, study in Bittle Memorial Library.

Dick Stauffer and Dick Seed won the high jump with 5'10", Jack Dempsey and Cliff Shaw finished second and third, respectively, in the broad jump, and Frank Vest took a third place in the pole vault.

Roanoke won the meet, 79½ to 42½.

I remember . . . "Dick Stauffer was a one-arm boy. He could run the hurdles and also high jump for us. He was just interested in track, and did everything I asked him to do. I know I shouldn't have felt this way, but with his arm, I was sometimes afraid that he would hurt himself. He was from Philadelphia and became a pretty good athlete."

Homer Bast

April 5, 1957
West Virginia Wesleyan at Salem, Virginia
Team Scores: None (Meet Cancelled)

Maroon fans likely missed a good track meet when the April 5 contest with West Virginia Wesleyan was cancelled on the morning of the event. The Maroons were favored to win the meet, as they usually were; however, they may have been pressed in many events.

The weather forecaster called for heavy rain, severe hail storms, and even tornadoes to hit the area in the early afternoon. In fact, a small tornado swirled out of dark clouds near Big Stone Gap at about that time, doing thousands of dollars of damage to homes and buildings in that section of Wise County.

But another tornado then struck about a mile south of Big Stone Gap at 1:15 p.m. And even another one hit the Ramsey section of Norton around 2:30 p.m.

With rain falling in the Salem area off and on all day, Coach Bast had no choice but to call off the meet. It was not re-scheduled.

April 12, 1957
East Tennessee State University at Johnson City, Tennessee
Team Scores: Roanoke–81
East Tennessee State–41

On the afternoon of April 12, 1957, the Maroons encountered one of their strongest opponents of the season when they ran East Tennessee State at Johnson City. The host team was the defending Tennessee state champion and at the end of the 1955-56 season, several of their star runners had performed well in the N. A. I. A. championships held in

Los Angeles. East Tennessee State did win 6 of the 14 events, more than any other team had won during the long dual meet winning streak, but Roanoke's depth brought them far more second and third places.

Dick Seed was Roanoke's top scorer for the day with 11 points. He won the high hurdles and placed second in the high jump and low hurdles.

In the high hurdles, Seed and Bruce Johnston were each given times of :15.7, but Seed was declared the winner. The positions were reversed in the low hurdles, with Johnston winning in :25.4 and Seed finishing second.

The 100 and 220 were won by East Tennessee State's Bill Cassell. His time in the 100 was :10.0 and he ran the 220 in :21.5. Each was a field record. George Gearhart was second in both races, while Tom Sitton was third each time.

Another field record was set by Dick Goodlake, who ran an excellent two-mile time of 10:02.8 to win. Warren Light was third.

The other distance event, the mile run, was won by Kent Osbourne of East Tennessee State in 4:30.0. It was a surprising win over Howard Meincke, who ran only 4:36.7. Warren Light was third in 4:48.5.

Roanoke swept the 440 and 880 races. In the 440, Dick Lewis finished first in a time of :52.0, with Howard Light placing second and Dick Engel third. Pete Wise won the 880 in 2:01.4. Phil Shaw placed second in 2:02.0, with Dick Lewis in third place.

East Tennessee State won three of the five field events. Roanoke's two first places came from Bob Palm and Win Niles. Palm was first in the shot put on a throw of 44'10½". Freshman Win Niles, who pole vaulted well indoors, took first in that event with 12'0". Frank Vest finished in second place on a good jump of 11'6".

In the field events not won by Roanoke, Bill Driscoll was second in the discus with 122'0"; Jack Dempsey jumped 20'4" for second in the broad jump, with Jimmy Nichols in third; Dick Seed was second with 5'10" in the high jump. Dick Stauffer was third.

The meet score was Roanoke, 81, and East Tennessee State, 41. The Maroons were now 3-0 for the season.

I remember . . . "I remember the trip down to East Tennessee State University. One of their sprinters was Ollan Cassell, who went on to be an outstanding athlete on an Olympic team. Later, he became Executive Director of The Athletics Congress, the governing body for track and field in the United States. We ran on a track where, I think, they also ran cars."

Dick Engel

I remember . . . "I'll tell you a little story about Bob Palm. He used to have a German

Shepherd, which he kept in the dorm. One day, he brought the dog to the pool. And he gave the dog a bath in the pool. Fran Ramser walked into the pool area the day after that, and there were all of these soap bubbles. She wasn't very happy."

Dick Emberger

April 18, 1957
Adelphi College at Garden City, New York
Team Scores: Roanoke–119
Adelphia–16

The meet with Adelphi College on April 18 was the first of three during Roanoke's spring break. The second was a triangular meet on April 20 between Queens College and Brooklyn Polytechnic College, while the third competition was with Hofstra College on April 22.

It was difficult for Roanoke or any small college to finance trips like this. For this trip and the previous trips east and south, Coach Bast would follow the same procedures. Long before the trip, he would write letters to many of the colleges and universities in the area in which they were headed. He would explain that Roanoke was trying to set up a schedule for their spring break and ask if it were possible to have a meet with that school. He would explain that the trip was being made on a shoestring, and any guarantee they could throw into the pot would be appreciated. Generally, he was successful. Not many wrote him a check for any amount of money, although some did. Clemson gave him $100, for example. Most of them did give the team room and board.

Except for some meals along the road, some of which were paid for by Coach Bast himself and some paid for out of the students' pockets, that was the only money they had except for a meager amount from the College's Athletic Department budget. On this trip to New York, the schools for the most part didn't have dormitories. Or if they had dormitories, the facilities were limited. But many of the boys on the team lived in the area. So Bast asked anyone who lived near the schools on the spring break schedule to take two or three guys home with them. Frank Vest remembers, for example, that he and several others stayed at Bob Palm's home and even got a chance to see New York City. Howard Light and Bruce Johnston stayed with Phil Shaw.

Many years later, Roanoke athletes remembered this trip as being one of their favorites. They got a chance to socialize with teammates, meet their families, and get some good home-cooked food. And members of the families, such as Phil Shaw's mother and father, got to see them compete in one or more of the meets. A few, such as Howard Light and Bruce Johnston, had hardly been away from home and they were able to see some of the sites in the area.

Coach Bast would simply ask, "Who's going where? Just keep me informed." One would raise his hand and say, "We'll take three guys. Another would take two. And that's how the team was housed. Bast would say to them, "O. K. Our next meet is at such and such a time at such and such a place. You've got enough local boys to get you to the meet." On the northern trip, they had five automobiles and Bast distributed them among all of the boys. This arrangement led to some interesting moments. As Bast said, "You would get to the meet and there would be no one. So you cooled your heels and, gradually, one by one, here would come the athletes. They were usually there in time to warm up. Pretty soon, everyone would show up and we would warm up and then beat the tar out of them."

That was the way, in general, that Bast was able to take his spring trips. But as the team got better over the years, it became more and more difficult to schedule the number of schools needed. A team's reputation travels many miles, and opposing teams just didn't want to get beat as badly as they knew they would in a competition with Roanoke.

The first meet, with Adelphi, was little more than a workout for the Maroons. The team set no school records, but there were some good performances. Howard Meincke, for example, won the 880-yard race in 1:59.6, just nine tenths of a second off the record. Pete Wise finished in second place with a time of 2:02.0.

Roanoke runners swept four events. Dick Lewis ran an excellent :51.5 for first place in the 440, followed by Howard Light and Dick Engel. In the mile run, Phil Shaw won in 4:34.0, in front of second place Warren Light and third-place Johnnie Blanton. George Jocher, ineligible but present on the trip, unofficially won the event in 4:31.5.

Both hurdle events were also sweeps. Bruce Johnston, the only double winner for Roanoke, won the highs in :16.0 and the lows in :25.2. Dick Seed was second in the high hurdles and Dick Emberger third. In the low hurdles, Emberger was second and speedy Dick Engel finished third.

George Gearhart was second in the 100, losing to a fast :09.9 by Bob Baratta. Tom Sitton was less than a step behind Gearhart. In the 220, Sitton was second and Gearhart third.

Roanoke won five of the six field events. Win Niles cleared 12'0" again in the pole vault to win, with Frank Vest jumping 11'6". Emberger and Dick Seed tied for first place in the high jump at 5'10", and Jack Dempsey (21'1⅞") and Cliff Shaw (21'1") finished one-two in the broad jump. Bob Upton was second in the discus at 119'0" just in front of Bob Palm's 116'6". Palm won the shot put on a throw of 43'5", with John Hylton placing second and Bob Upton third.

Left Photo: Freshman Dick Emberger went on in his career to clear over 6 feet 5 inches in the high jump. After graduating from Roanoke in 1960, he became the 10th best decathlete in the world after competing in the 1964 Olympics.
Right Photo: Frank Vest had never pole vaulted before being talked into trying the event by Homer Bast. His best jump at Roanoke during the three years he competed in track was 11 feet 6 inches.

The teams also competed in the hammer and javelin events. Although Roanoke men had never thrown the hammer, and had seen the javelin an average of every other year, they swept the first three positions in the hammer and took the first two in the javelin. In the hammer, Bill Driscoll muscled the ball 90'0" to take first place. Palm was second and Hylton third. Palm also won the javelin on a throw of 157'8". Emberger was second.

The score of the first meet was Adelphi, 16, Roanoke, 119. It was the most points a Bast-led team had ever scored, and left the Maroons 4-0 for the season.

I remember . . . "I also remember that during the outdoor season that year, our spring trip was up to the New York area. It was the first and only time I have been in that part of the country. As usual, we had to take cars. And I and some others stayed at Phil Shaw's home out on the Hudson. Now the meets we ran – there wasn't much to them. It was cool up there. And also, I think, it was Easter weekend. Or close to it. We spent some time in New York City, looking up at the skyscrapers. We went up on the Empire State Building. I can't remember exactly, but someone told me that we also went to see the Yankees play. It was a memorable trip. I remember that when we left to come back to Salem, one of the guy's (maybe Dick Goodlake's) mother had prepared a meal for us. She put the meal in bags for us – whoever was in the car I rode in. She made us rye bread, ham, and Swiss cheese sandwiches. That I remember well. I was just an old country boy, and had never eaten anything like that before. It was *good.* One good thing about those trips was that you got to know your teammates well – something that was difficult if you were a day student and just saw them at practice."

Bruce Johnston

I remember . . . "That northern trip was interesting in many ways. For example, I think that it was the first time that Howard Light and Bruce Johnston had ever been out of the local area. Of course, we slaughtered the schools we met on that trip. I remember that Bill Driscoll was on the team that year, and went with us on the northern spring break trip. At Adelphi, we had to throw the hammer. Adelphi wouldn't take it out of their schedule of events. Bill said, 'Sure, I'll throw it.' And he won the event with a throw of 90'. I think it was the only time while I was coaching that any of our boys had to throw the hammer."

Homer Bast

April 20, 1957
Queens College and Brooklyn Polytechnic College at Queens, New York
Team Scores: 1st–Roanoke–108
2nd–Queens–22
3rd–Brooklyn Polytechnic–2

At Queens, New York, on the 20th, Roanoke met Queens and Brooklyn Polytechnic in a triangular meet. It was an interesting, although not especially pleasant meet. The day was cool and damp. A cross wind made some events difficult. There were no marked lanes and the hurdles were set up incorrectly. There was no broad jump pit. And in place of a mile relay, there was only a 4-by-350 race. In Coach Bast's words, "It was a long, weary meet."

Bruce Johnston was one of the two top performers for the Maroons, winning both the high and low hurdles. He ran a :15.5 in the highs and :26.8 in the lows. Dick Seed was second in the highs and lows, and Dick Emberger placed fourth in the low hurdles.

Howard Meincke also won two events. He ran 4:32.7 in the mile and an excellent 10:02.4 in the two-mile race. Johnnie Blanton placed third in the mile, and Warren Light ran a good time of 10:07.2 for second in the two-mile event.

George Gearhart ran a fast :10.0 in the 100-yard dash, just missing his school record of :09.9. Dick Engel was a step behind. In the 220, Engel placed first in :23.2, with Jack

Dempsey second and Howard Light, in an event he didn't generally run, finished in third.

Tom Sitton was first in the 440, with a time of :51.2, followed by Dick Lewis (:52.0) and Light (:52.2). The 880 went to Dick Goodlake, whose time of 2:00.8 missed the school record by 2.1 seconds. Pete Wise was second and Phil Shaw third.

The special four-lap relay, with each runner covering 350 yards, was won by Roanoke. The team of Dick Engel, Pete Wise, Dick Lewis, and Tom Sitton covered the shortened distance in 2:40.0.

Roanoke athletes also won four of the six field events. Bob Palm placed first in the shot put with a good throw of 45'3" with John Hylton in third place. Bob Upton did very well in the discus, winning the event with his best-ever throw of 123'1". Bill Driscoll was second at 120'7" and Palm finished third.

Palm also placed second in the javelin, throwing 150'8". Driscoll was second in the hammer throw, with Upton a few feet behind.

In the high jump, Dick Emberger and Dick Seed cleared the bar at 6'0" to tie for the win. And in the pole vault, Frank Vest and Win Niles tied for first at 10'6". Emberger placed fourth.

Roanoke won the meet with 108 points, to 22 for Queens College and just 2 for Brooklyn Polytechnic College. The team was now 5-0 for the season, with one more meet left on the northern trip.

April 22, 1957
Hofstra College at Hempstead, New York
Team Scores: Roanoke–101
Hofstra–34

The final meet of the trip was held in Hempstead, New York, on a cool, windy, clear day. According to Coach Bast's notes, the wind was behind runners except in the high hurdles. The 220 race was run on a straightaway.

Again, the home team didn't provide very strong competition and Roanoke won the meet by a score of 101 to 34. Of the 15 events, Roanoke men placed first in 13 of them.

There was one outstanding performance, however. Howard Meincke, followed closely by the ineligible George Jocher, stunned his teammates and the crowd when he crossed the line in the two-mile race in 9:44.6, 12.6 seconds below the old Roanoke College record of 9:57.2 and 14 seconds better than the field record. Dick Goodlake had set the school record in 1956. Jocher finished the race in a terrific time of 9:56.0–also below the old record had the mark counted.

George Gearhart won both the 100 and 220. In the 100, he ran :10.0 and almost matched the :09.9 he had recorded as a school record in 1956. Jack Dempsey was second

Action pictures of (L to R) Dick Lewis, George Gearhart, and Howard Light.

and Jimmy Nichols third. In the 220, Gearhart ran :22.0 on the straight track. Again Dempsey placed second and Nichols third.

Bruce Johnston, now carrying the load in the hurdles along with Dick Seed since the graduation of Dave Foltz, set a new field record when he placed first in the lows with :24.3. Dick Seed placed second. Dick Seed won the high hurdles with a time of :16.2. Johnston was second.

In the mile, winner Warren Light was cheered by a "hometown crowd" as he won the race in 4:31.6. He was a former runner from nearby Baldwin High School. Dick Goodlake finished second in 4:35.0, with Phil Shaw placing third in 4:57.0.

Five of the seven field events were won by Roanoke men. Bob Palm threw 41'8" for a win in the shot put, with John Hylton finishing third. Bill Driscoll placed first in the discus on a throw of 123'0", with Palm in third. Driscoll also was third in the hammer.

The broad jump winner was Jimmy Nichols, who jumped 21'4". Cliff Shaw placed second with almost 21' and Jack Dempsey was third.

Dick Seed cleared 5'10" for a high jump win. Dick Emberger tied for second.

Finally, Win Niles set a new field record in the pole vault with a fine vault of 12'6". Frank Vest did well also, going over 11'6" in a tie for second.

The Maroons were 3-0 on their northern trip and had won six straight dual and triangular meets during the season. And the winning streak was at 34.

After the northern trip, and after the impressive string of victories, most thought the track squad would see influx of freshman talent again next fall from the New York and New Jersey areas. The big question was what to do with them? Practically everybody would be back next year from the present squad and where would you put new talent among this star-studded group?

I remember . . . "I think that in this meet I beat Dick Goodlake in the mile for the first time. He was from Garden City, and he had some friends over to Hofstra to watch him run. And I had my friends and parents coming to see me run. At the end of the meet, Hofstra fans were fit to be tied. Here was little ol' Roanoke from Hicksville coming up here, and we just destroyed them. Our teammates referred to the event as the 'Mutt and Jeff' race. I was 6'2" tall and Dick was about 5'7" or maybe 5'8" in height. This was probably my best race of the year. Our teammates stayed at each other's houses during the trip. My mother and father never forgot our trip because we brought along our big weight men. I think those guys could down five gallons of milk in one sitting."

Warren Light

I remember . . . "On that northern trip, I don't remember the house where we stopped, but they opened the door and handed us a beer. I thought, 'We're not supposed to be doing this. We're in training.' Now there were a lot of guys on our team who were no strangers to beer. They liked to go down to a little place by the river near Salem that served beer. Many spent a lot of time down there."

Bruce Johnston

April 26, 1957
Penn Relays at Philadelphia, Pennsylvania
Mile Relay: 1st–Ohio Wesleyan
2nd–Catholic

3rd–Roanoke

It was the 63rd Annual Relay Carnival at Franklin Field in Philadelphia. They called it simply The Penn Relays. It was the Mecca of spring track competition, where every team with talent wanted to compete.

Coach Bast sent a mile relay team to the meet. It consisted of Pete Wise, Tom Sitton, Dick Engel, and Dick Lewis. The team would run its race on Friday, April 26, and then re-join Bast and other members of the team at the Mason-Dixon Relays the next day.

The mile relay race was won by a team from Ohio Wesleyan, whose time was 3:26.0. Catholic University barely beat the Roanoke team for second, and the Maroons finished in third place. No time was recorded for Roanoke or Catholic.

April 27, 1957
Mason-Dixon Relays at Washington, D. C.
Team Scores: None

After the Penn Relays, Wise, Sitton, Engel, and Lewis traveled down to American University in Washington, where they joined up with the rest of the team to run away with nearly all of the honors of the Mason-Dixon Relays. The Maroons, in fact, won six of the eight first places in the relay events and also placed first in the broad jump. In the process, they set four Roanoke College records.

One of those records was in the Sprint Medley Relay. Dick Engel, Jimmy Nichols, Bruce Johnston, and Phil Shaw ran 3:40.1 to win. The time beat the old record of 3:43.0 by almost three seconds.

Another school record was set in the 440-yard relay, when Win Niles, Jack Dempsey, Tom Sitton, and George Gearhart ran :43.9. In the two-mile relay, Sitton, Shaw, Warren Light, and Dick Goodlake easily won in another school record, 8:14.7. And in the 880-yard relay, Jimmy Nichols, Dempsey, Johnston, and Gearhart crossed the finish line in a new school record of 1:31.3, with the Roanoke team barely nipping Catholic at the tape.

Roanoke also won the distance medley and the shuttle hurdle relays, but in non-record times. The team of Pete Wise, Howard Light, Warren Light, and Howard Meincke ran an easy 11:00.0 to win the distance medley, while Harry Clegg, Dick Stauffer, Dick Emberger, and Johnston had an easy 1:07.0 win in the shuttle hurdles.

Jim Frazer of Hampden-Sydney won the shot put with a throw of 46'8" and the discus on a toss of 139'0". Bob Palm threw 43'6" for second in the shot and 119'0" to place fourth in the discus.

Jack Dempsey won the broad jump with 21'8" and Jimmy Nichols tied for third place. In the high jump, Stauffer and Emberger tied with Bridgewater's Fred Pence for first, jumping 5'11". Taylor Goode, the outstanding pole vaulter from Lynchburg College, cleared the bar at 13'0" in his event for a first. Win Niles of Roanoke was second, going 12'0".

As usual, no team scores were kept. But it was obvious that Roanoke had a decided advantage over the rest of the Little Eight and Mason-Dixon teams.

May 3, 1957
Bridgewater College at Bridgewater, Virginia
Team Scores: Roanoke–78⅓
Bridgewater–43⅔

It was May 3, 1957–a cool, clear, sunny day with a very slight breeze. At the Bridgewater track, the Eagles were set to host the strong Roanoke team.

Bridgewater had not beaten Roanoke in a dual meet for several years, and a win by the Eagles wasn't likely to happen today. Expecting few problems, therefore, Coach Bast gave some of the top squad members a rest. Doing so allowed a few of the inexperienced men to compete and perhaps to win points toward their end-of-year letter.

No school records were set for Roanoke, but they did set four field records. After winning the 100-yard dash in :10.2, with Jack Dempsey in second, George Gearhart placed first in the 220 on a time of :22.6. The :22.6 was a new field mark.

Dick Lewis set another field record with a 1:59.8 in the 880. Phil Shaw was second in 2:02.6.

The Roanoke mile relay team set the third field record. Dick Engel, Gearhart, Dick Lewis, and Tom Sitton finished with a time of 3:28.2.

The fourth record was a :25.2 in the low hurdles by Bruce Johnston. In that race, Dick Seed was second and Dick Emberger third. Johnston also won the high hurdles in :15.9. Again, Seed was second.

Sitton was first in the quarter mile in a time of :52.1. Engel finished in third place.

In the mile run, Warren Light placed first with a time of 4:40.6, with Johnnie Blanton in third place. George Jocher also ran in the race, timed in 4:33.0, but he was a transfer student and his score was not counted.

Wayne Wilson ran in the two-mile race, where Bridgewater took a rare one-two finish. Wilson was third in 11:03.0.

Bob Palm of Roanoke won the shot put, while Bob Upton placed second in the discus. Cliff Shaw placed second and Dick Emberger third in the broad jump. Dependable Dick Seed placed first in the high jump, clearing 5'10", with Dick Stauffer and Emberger tied for second.

In the pole vault, Emberger and Frank Vest finished in a tie for second place, giving a final team score of 78⅓ to 43⅔ in Roanoke's favor.

Roanoke had won seven meets in a row. One more meet, with Hampden-Sydney, would complete the dual-meet season.

May 8, 1957
Hampden-Sydney College at Salem, Virginia
Team Scores: Roanoke–93
Hampden-Sydney–28

The track was fast on this warm day in May. A slight wind blew toward the runners as they reached the straightaway before the finish line. The Maroons were at their best, setting four new marks for the Salem track in this, the last dual meet of the season and their only home competition. Three of these four marks were also school records.

Sophomore Howard Meincke set a new school record in the 880 by running 1:56.4, best time in the state during the 1957 season. Incidentally, this was the first time he had run this event. Other Roanoke record setters were George Gearhart in the 220 and Dick Lewis in the 440 and mile relay.

Hampden-Sydney won only two events. Big Jim Frazer set new field marks in winning the shot and discus.

Roanoke's Dick Seed, with 11 points, was high point man for the meet. Teammates George Gearhart and Bruce Johnston each had 10 points. Frazer also scored 10.

Dick Lewis ran a :50.7 quarter, followed closely by Howard Light, to break the old record which he shared with Light. Tom Sitton placed second in the 880 with a time of 2:00.8. He had run the 880 only twice before. Dick Goodlake ran an uncontested 10:14 in the two-mile race. Roanoke's George Jocher, a non-eligible sophomore, unofficially broke the track record with a time of 4:30 in the mile.

With a bid for their fifth consecutive Little Eight title coming on Friday, few of the Maroons competed in more than one event.

May 10, 1957
Little Eight Championships at Hampden-Sydney, Virginia
Team Scores: 1st–Roanoke College–101½
2nd–Norfolk Division of William and Mary–51
3rd–Hampden-Sydney College–25
4th–Lynchburg College–14½
5th–Bridgewater College–14
6th–Randolph-Macon College–4

On the 10th of May, the Maroons traveled to Hampden-Sydney College for the Little Eight Championships. The Little Eight meet was being held at Hampden-Sydney for the third straight year.

The battle this day was for second place. Roanoke had won the meet for the past three years and had assembled an almost-unbeatable team this time around.

It was a good day for Roanoke, for the talented team set four meet records–in the 440, mile, mile relay, and high hurdles–and captured 9 of 14 events before the meet was finished. Not only did Roanoke win the meet with 101½ points, but the Maroons came within eight points of outscoring the rest of the field combined. Norfolk Division of William and Mary, getting stronger each year, took the second spot with 51 points. Hampden-Sydney was third with 25, Lynchburg fourth with 14½, Bridgewater fifth with 14, and Randolph-Macon sixth with just 4. Two members of the Little Eight Conference, Richmond Professional Institute and Emory and Henry, did not enter teams.

The Maroons' Dick Lewis began the record assault by running a :50.7 in the quarter mile. That time erased the time of :50.8 set by Paige Will in 1955. Dependable Howard Meincke of Roanoke won the mile easily in 4:26.5 to lower the previous record by a second and a half. The Maroon mile relay team, consisting of Dick Engel, Lewis, Howard Light, and Tom Sitton, won their event in a time of 3:26.5. This mark shattered the old mark by 2.9 seconds. The other meet record was set by Bruce Johnston, who won the high hurdles in a time of :15.1, breaking the oldest record on the books. The former mark was :15.2, set in 1937.

The other meet records were set by Ronnie Drumwright and Gerald Tiedeman of Norfolk William and Mary and Jim Frazer of Hampden-Sydney. Drumwright smashed the 880 record with a time of 1:59.5, narrowly beating Roanoke's Phil Shaw, who ran an excellent 1:59.7. The sprint down the final straightaway between the two was spectacular. Big Tiedeman threw the shot 50'7¾" and Frazer tossed the discus 150'7".

Roanoke's Dick Seed was the individual high scorer in the meet with 12 points. He won the high jump at 6'0", and then placed second in the low hurdles and third in the high hurdles.

Maroons George Gearhart and Bruce Johnston, both of whom grew up in the Roanoke-Salem area, were the meet's only double winners. Gearhart won both the 100 (:10.1) and 220 (:22.0) dashes, while Johnston won the high (:15.1) and low (:24.4) hurdle events.

Several other Roanoke athletes also scored points during the day's activities. Tom Sitton finished second behind Gearhart in both the 100 and 220. Howard Light was barely second in the 440, losing to Lewis by a mere inch. The judges gave both Light and Lewis the same time of :50.7. Lewis was third in the 880, and teammate Dick Goodlake was third in the mile and won the two-mile event in 10:05.4. Freshman Dick Emberger took fourth in the high and low hurdles and tied for second in the high jump. School record holder Bob Palm threw well in the shot put, but finished third to super-star throwers Tiedeman and Frazer. Jim Nichols was beaten by less than one inch in the broad jump, finishing second to the great Kenny Harmon of Norfolk William and Mary. Dick Stauffer tied for second place in the high jump; Win Niles was second in the pole vault; and Frank Vest tied for third in the pole vault.

May 17-18, 1957
Mason-Dixon Championships at Hampden-Sydney, Virginia
Team Scores: 1st–Roanoke College–76½
2nd–Catholic University–26
3rd–Hampden-Sydney College–20
4th–Johns Hopkins University–15
5th–Bridgewater College–13½
6th–Loyola College–12
7th–Lynchburg College–11
8th–American University–10½
9th–Gallaudet College–8
10th–Washington College–7½
11th–Randolph-Macon College–7
12th–Western Maryland College–3

Roanoke College's track team was like Man O' War in terms of the Mason-Dixon Conference track teams. The team was trying for its fourth consecutive Mason-Dixon trophy. In no year since the present conference was formed had a single team managed to score four straight titles. Indeed, no team around could match the depth and talent of the Maroons.

Bruce Johnston, junior hurdler from Roanoke, led the team in scoring this season with 97 points. Dick Seed of Philadelphia and George Gearhart of Salem, Co-Captains of the team, were next with 92⅓ and 88, respectively.

The conference championships this year were held on May 17-18 at Hampden-Sydney where, the week before, the Maroons had set four new records in the Little Eight meet and scored almost twice the points of the second-place team. Catholic University was expected to offer the most competition, followed by Hampden-Sydney.

As usual, the meet was conducted over two days, with qualifying events held on Friday and finals on Saturday. Here are Friday's qualifiers, with the best times in each heat:

Shot	Frazer (HS)–48'1¾"; Wright (JH); Palm (R); Wiley (HS); Hahman (AU); Atkinson (WM)
Discus	Frazer (HS)–146'5½" (New Conference Record. Old Record 142'¾"); Wiley (HS); Harlan (RM); Driscoll (R); Pence (B); Snydor (L)
Broad Jump	C. Shaw (R)–21'6"; Stinespring (HS); Pardue (RM); Goode (L); Nichols (R); Whitlow (B)
220 Yard Dash	Libert (CU)–:22.0; Gearhart (R)–:22.3; Heck (JH); Benson (HS); Mathews (CU); McKenna (LOY)
High Hurdles	Johnston (R)–:15.3; Seed (R)–:15.6; Hort (WM); Emberger (R); Armstrong (RM); Chapman (HS)
Low Hurdles	Johnston (R)–:25.2; Caples (JH); Diashyn (WC); Hort (WM); Seed (R); Chapman (HS)
440 Yard Dash	Mathews (CU)–:50.7; Sitton (R)–:51.2; Smith (G); Engel (R); Madison (CU); Light (R)
880 Yard Run	Sherman (LOY)–2:00.5; Lewis (R)–2:02.6; Shaw (R); Ladd (AU); Madison (CU); Graves (HS)

On Saturday, the team completed one of the best seasons in College history by winning six of the fourteen events. They were so good, in fact, that they almost tripled the score of the second-place team, Catholic University. Roanoke finished with 76½ points, while Catholic had 26 and third-place Hampden-Sydney had 20.

The Roanoke team was paced by Bruce Johnston, who won two events. In the high hurdles, he placed first on a time of :15.1, which tied the old record set by Dave Foltz the previous year. Johnston also won the low hurdles with a time of :24.1, setting a new Roanoke College record and also beating the old record of :24.2 set by Foltz in 1956.

The Maroons' Dick Lewis won the 880 in a fast 1:58.5. Teammate Tom Sitton barely lost the 440, finishing a step behind Matthews of Catholic, who ran :50.0.

Win Niles vaulted 12'6" and settled for second place in the pole vault. Frank Vest finished the event in a tie for third.

Cliff Shaw won the broad jump with 21'6", with Jim Nichols in second. In the high jump, Dick Seed cleared 6'0" to take the high jump, and finished third in the low hurdles and fifth in the highs. Dick Stauffer and Dick Emberger tied for second in the high jump. Emberger also placed fourth in the high hurdles. Bob Palm finished second in the shot with one of his best throws, 45'6¾", while dependable Jim Driscoll was third in the discus on a throw of 124'2¼".

George Gearhart finished third in the 100 and second in the 220. Phil Shaw was fifth in the 880. Warren Light ran a 4:40.0 for a fifth-place finish in the mile run. The Roanoke mile relay team (Lewis, Wise, Howard Light, and Sitton) won the event in a time of 3:27.3.

A major disappointment on Saturday was the running of the usually steady and talented Howard Meincke. In the two mile run, where he was the favorite to win, he dropped out of the race early. In the mile run, he placed second to Catholic's Nelson, whose winning time was 4:29.6. Meincke, in the first part of April, already had run a time of 4:25.0.

Bruce Johnston finished the season with a total of 107 points, followed by Dick Seed with 100½ and George Gearhart with 95.

Following the last meet and perhaps after exams were finished for the second semester, several of the track athletes were among a group that participated in a "panty raid" in one of the girls' dorms. Although what happened was all in good fun, someone turned them in to the administration. In those days, the school was very strict as to the behavior of students. For example, a girl could not walk across the campus at night while wearing shorts, unless she wore something like a raincoat that extended at least to the knees. And students were never allowed to enter a dorm housing the opposite sex except for limited reasons and under supervision. Several of the participants in the panty raid were suspended from school for a semester by Dean of Men Don Sutton. Here are three versions of what happened:

Jim O'Mahony — "I remember the panty raid. Dick Lewis and Bob Palm were my roommates at the time. The girls invited the guys into the dorm. We all had been drinking during the day. I went home and fell asleep. They were just having a good time. Someone reported the two to the administration."

Dick Lewis — "Bob Palm and I started out thinking that we would leave Roanoke after two years and transfer to an engineering school. Then, he and I and several others got involved in a panty raid at the college. It came right at the end of our sophomore year. Bob and I had already been accepted to go to V. P. I. the following fall. After exams, we came back from a Kappa Alpha party and were headed back to Hildreth Hall. On the way, we cut in behind the girls' dorm. It seems like the building housed boys in one section, and girls in the other. Each had its own entrance. The girls' dorm was under curfew already, and the girls yelled out to us, hanging bras out the window, etc. We ended up getting in that dorm and partying. Nothing happened, of course, but it was just the challenge of entering the girls' dorm after midnight. By the next morning, someone had reported us to Dean Sutton's office. Now that didn't bother Bob or me. We had already been accepted to Tech. What could Roanoke do to us? I think there were four of us involved. So Bob and I took the blame for the whole incident. And we got suspended for one semester. As a result, when V. P. I. got word of the suspension, they rescinded their approval of our going there. So by the middle of the summer, we weren't laughing anymore. We had been kind of brazen about the whole thing, laughing about the fact that we were going to be in school at V. P. I. in the fall. As I remember, we had to write letters to the college apologizing for our transgressions, and we finally came back after one semester. So Bob and I forgot about engineering. I changed majors from pre-engineering to economics with a math minor. Of course, after graduation I went into the Marine Corps and never really used the degree."

Dick Goodlake: "Yes, it was the infamous panty raid. It was Bob Palm, Dick Lewis, me, Jack Herring, Phil Shaw, and others. You know, it was very funny, because ultimately I went into the Marine Corps. As I was coming out of Vietnam in 1970, I was in Japan. And I put in for a top-secret clearance. Because of that request, they did a background investigation on me. The investigation came back and this old Colonel, who was the Intelligence Officer of the First Marine Aircraft Wing, called me in and said "Major Goodlake, your background investigation is back and it looks good. You only have one discrepancy there. It says that Major Goodlake was expelled from Roanoke College for six months because he was part of a panty raid in a girls' dorm." He had a big cigar in his mouth and after a pause, he said, "Damn good Marine. Clearance approved." What was interesting about the panty raid was that there were no girls in the dormitory. It was after school was out. But at a conservative, right-wing school, in 1957, you just didn't go and have a panty raid in a girls' dorm. The raid took place at the end of 1957. I had to sit out part of 1957-58. That was when I should have graduated, but ended up graduating in 1959. I'll bet you that Phil Shaw told you that story. He never lets me forget that. Again, the guys who got a semester off from school, besides myself, were Bob Palm, Dick Lewis, Jack Herring (who subsequently became the Dean of the History Department at the University of Kentucky and one of the foremost authorities on the Vietnam War), and other Kappa Alpha members. We were at a fraternity party when we decided to do this. It was right after finals. So we got up on the roof of the dorm and shimmied down a sheet to one of the windows. We ran through the dormitory and out the entrance. To us, it was fairly harmless. But Don Sutton, in his first year at Roanoke, didn't see it that way. Maybe he was trying to make an impression. This was after the second semester and just before the summer break in 1957. My parents were very irritated over the suspension. They didn't want me to go back to Roanoke. But I did go back. I had too much invested in the school not to return."

I remember . . . "I am not surprised that Dick Emberger went on to become an Olympian. When I was at Roanoke College, Dick already showed the potential to become an all-around athlete. I used to know him pretty well. One time, John Hylton and I were kidding around in the gym, lifting weights. Dick came in and, by gosh, he had so much coordination and strength that he could clean and jerk a weight that was almost as much as John and I could lift. And I don't believe that Dick ever lifted weights on any regular basis."

Bill Driscoll

I remember . . . "Remember that I went one year at Roanoke and then joined the Navy for about two years before coming back to the College to run another three years. In my senior year, the Lynchburg coach asked Homer, 'Isn't that Gearhart boy ever going to graduate?' "

George Gearhart

I remember . . . "The person who influenced me a lot was Phil Shaw. I looked up to him. He was ahead of me in school, and we used to run a lot together. And we competed against each other. He went into the Marine Corps. I really didn't know what I wanted to do after graduation. Phil persuaded me that the Marines would be a good choice–and looking back at the situation, it was."

Dick Lewis

I remember . . . "Bill Driscoll came close so many times to setting a new school record in the discus. The old record was set in 1947 at around 129'. Bill was from the Bedford-Lynchburg area. He came to Roanoke because he was a Lutheran. Stuart Saunders, of Norfolk and Western, was his cousin. Bill was really interested in dentistry. And he studied a lot. Now as far as track was concerned, I understood the situation. And I said, Bill, when you can, come on down to the field and we will do a little practicing. Well, I really didn't see ol' Bill Driscoll very much and that's likely why he didn't get the record. He didn't really improve a great deal. But Bill was versatile. He could do a lot of things. He really wasn't in good shape at Roanoke, however. I think that in high school he may have been a pretty good hurdler as well as a discus thrower, etc. He was a fairly tall boy and may have weighed about 175 pounds. I was pleased to see him come to Roanoke. When I looked over the list of incoming students, I said to myself, we can put this boy in a lot of events. I thought he was good enough to be a decathlon man. I believe in those years you could leave after three years, if you had good grades, and enter dental school. And that's what he did. He was a good boy. He fit right in with the others."

Homer Bast

Chapter Thirteen

The 1957 Cross Country Season

Homer Bast gave up his track and field coaching responsibilities after the 1956-57 session; however, he decided to coach the cross country team for this and perhaps more seasons to come.

Cross country practice officially began on Thursday, September 12, led by acting coach and team Captain Howard Meincke. This would be a good squad and the runners knew it. Many had been practicing daily since they arrived on campus a week ago.

Returning veterans included Howard Meincke, a junior; Bill Cerelli, senior; Warren Light, junior; Pete Wise, junior; George Jocher, an excellent runner who spent last year as an ineligible transfer from Hofstra; Wayne Wilson, sophomore; Dick Emberger, sophomore; Tom Sitton, sophomore; and Scott McKinney, sophomore.

According to the *Brackety-Ack*, several freshmen had shown an interesting in competing this year. They included Bill Davis, New Brunswick, New Jersey; Russ Polochko, Perth Amboy, New Jersey; George Bopp, Katanah, New York; Jack Richards, York, Pennsylvania; John Snyder, Tenafly, New Jersey; and Chuck Stagleano, North Tarrytown, New York.

Homer admitted to friends that prospects for the year looked as good as or even better than last year, which saw the Maroons compile an unbeaten record against six schools. They also won their fifth Little Eight crown, their fourth Mason-Dixon Conference Championship, and a finished in seventh-place in the NAIA Championships in Omaha, Nebraska. In that meet, Howard Meincke placed fourth.

Roanoke College vs. Norfolk William and Mary
October 2, 1957
Norfolk, Virginia
Distance: 3.2 Miles

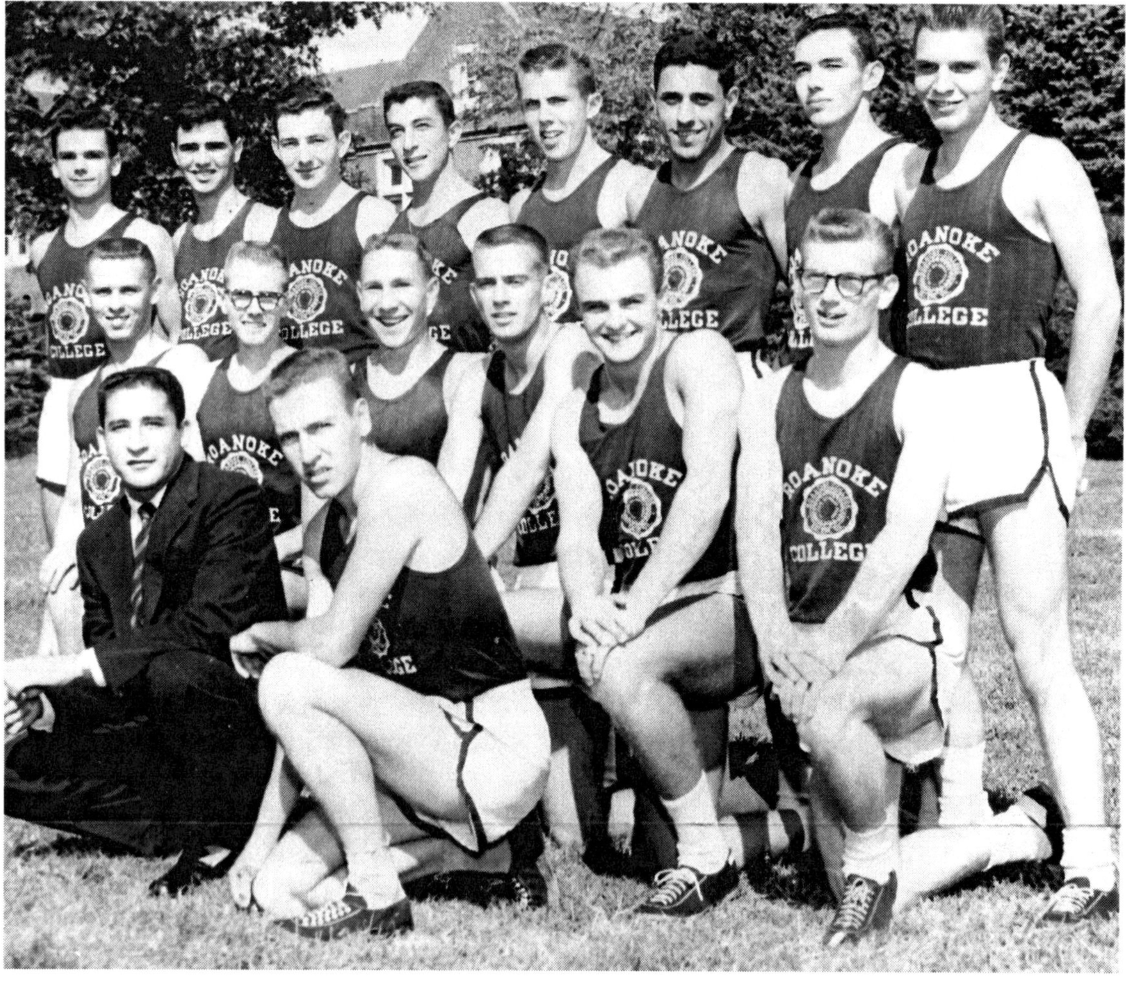

Cross country team of 1957
Front row (L to R): Manager Jose Sitton, Captain Howard Meincke.
Second row (L to R): Warren Light, Wayne Wilson, Dick Emberger, Bill Davis, Pete Wise, and George Bopp.
Third row (L to R): Scott McKinney, Ben Stafford, Bill Kelly, Tom Sitton, George Jocher, Bill Cerelli, Johnnie Blanton, and Russell Palochko.

Team Scores: Roanoke College (R)–22½
Norfolk William and Mary (N)–32½

The team continued where it left off in 1956, beating Norfolk Division of William and Mary by a score of 22½ to 32½. The Maroons took three of the first four places in this Wednesday meet in Norfolk. George Jocher was a surprising winner in 15:40.5, beating the Roanoke star, Howard Meincke. Baxter Berryhill, Norfolk's best runner, finished second, some nine seconds behind. The third and fourth spots were given to Meincke and Warren Light, respectively, with Wayne Wilson placing 6th, Pete Wise 8th, freshman George Bopp 11th, Bill Davis 12th, and Bob Miller 14th.

With Jocher, Meincke, and Light all in good form, could the team be headed for another undefeated season? Of the six remaining dual meets, only the College of William and Mary could give Roanoke a loss, and the deep Maroon team seemed certain to repeat as Little Eight and Mason-Dixon Champions.

Roanoke College Freshmen vs. Blacksburg High School
October 07, 1957
Salem, Virginia
Distance: 1.7 Miles

Team Scores: Roanoke College (R)–28
Blacksburg High School (B)–30

The next meet of the season involved only the freshmen runners from Roanoke and the talented Blacksburg High School cross country team. Roanoke hosted the meet.

Jim Miller, a Blacksburg junior, won the 1.7-mile race with a time of 8:33.5. Just 4½ seconds behind was George Bopp, who was not really a cross country runner but would become a terrific 440 man in outdoor track.

For Roanoke, Bob Miller was 5th, Russ Polochko 6th, Bill Davis 7th, Bob Fray 8th, Ben Stafford 9th, and John Richards 11th. This group helped insure a close victory for Roanoke, 28 to 30.

Roanoke College vs. University of the South at Sewanee, Tennessee (Telegraphic Meet)
October 11, 1957
Salem, Virginia and Sewanee, Tennessee
Distance: 3.0 Miles–Quarter-Mile Track
Team Scores: Roanoke College (R)–15
University of the South at Sewanee (S)–48

The Roanoke team had amazing depth this year, and Coach Bast decided to split the team and run two meets on the same day. One of the meets was with University of the South at Sewanee, Tennessee. Roanoke ran the 12-lap race on its track in Salem, while

University of the South used their track in Sewanee, about 250 miles away. The results, all based on time, were compiled as if the two teams had run competitively on the same track, and telegraphed to the other team. This is only the second time that a "telegraph meet" has been held in Virginia. Washington-Lee initiated the practice in a meet with Howard University several years back.

Howard Meincke won the meet in a time of 15:46 as the Roanoke team easily defeated University of the South, 15 to 48. Roanoke, in fact, took the first six places. Second was Warren Light. Then came Pete Wise (3rd), George Bopp (4th), Bob Miller (5th), and Bill Davis (6th). Another runner, whose name is unknown, placed 9th for Roanoke.

Roanoke College vs. Fairmont State Teachers College
October 12, 1957
Fairmont, West Virginia
Distance: 3.5 Miles

Team Scores: Roanoke College (R)–18
Fairmont State Teachers College (F)–39

In the meet with Fairmont State Teacher's College, held the following day, Roanoke competed with the other half of its team. The first four Maroons broke the old record of 21:00 for the hilly 3.5-mile course. That record had just been set a week before by a runner from West Virginia Wesleyan.

Roanoke took the top four places in winning the meet 18 to 39. In winning, George Jocher set the new course record with a time of 19:14. Wayne Wilson was second, Dick Emberger third, and John Blanton fourth.

Completing the scoring was Bill Cerelli, who placed 8th. Russ Polochko was 9th and an unknown runner from Roanoke was 10th.

Scott McKinney had to drop out of the race about mid-way. He was suffering from stomach cramps.

Roanoke College Freshmen vs. Andrew Lewis High School
October 14, 1957
Salem, Virginia
Distance: 1.7 Miles

Team Scores: Roanoke College (R)–27

Andrew Lewis High School (AL)–28

Homer held a second meet, versus local Andrew Lewis High School, for his freshman runners on October 14. Coach Raymond Buzzard of Andrew Lewis had been building an excellent cross country track and track program for his school recently, and Homer wondered whether his young team could make the meet competitive. Some of the Lewis team members, however, had the flu bug.

Eddie Eades of Lewis won the meet in a time of 8:40.9 and his teammate, Dewey Nester, placed second. Then four Roanoke runners took the third through sixth positions. Bill Davis was 3rd, George Bopp 4th, Russ Polochko 5th, and Bob Miller 6th. Ben Stafford was the fifth runner to score for Roanoke, taking the 9th spot. John Richards was 11th, with Bob Fray in the 13th position.

In a close meet, the young Maroons won by a score of 27-28.

Roanoke College vs. Lynchburg College
October 16, 1957
Salem, Virginia
Distance: 3.1 Miles

Team Scores: Roanoke College (R)–20
Lynchburg College (L)–37

Roanoke's Howard Meincke set another home course record as the team beat Lynchburg College 20 to 37 in Salem. He ran the 3.1-mile course in 15:25.5 to break by 1½ seconds the record he set last year. George Jocher was 2nd in 16:12, 20 seconds in front of Joe Renfroe of the Hornets.

Wayne Wilson, rounding into good shape, finished in the 4th position with Warren Light just behind by about 10 seconds. Dick Emberger was 8th in the race and Pete Wise 9th.

It was the fourth varsity win of the year for the undefeated Maroons and extended their winning streak to 14 meets.

Roanoke College vs. Mount St. Mary's College
October 19, 1957
Salem, Virginia
Distance: 3.1 Miles

Team Scores: Roanoke (R)–15

Mount St. Mary's College (M)–47

Just three days later, Mount St. Mary's College came to Salem for a meet. The race was held during the halftime of the homecoming soccer game.

Roanoke was at full strength, beating Mount St. Mary's easily, 15 to 47. Five runners for the home team took the first five places in the meet before visitor Jim Murphy grabbed the sixth position.

Howard Meincke, as expected, won the meet with a time of 15:42.5 on the 3.1-mile course. He led all the way. George Jocher was 2nd, Warren Light 3rd, Wayne Wilson 4th, and John Blanton 5th. Other Roanoke men were Dick Emberger, 7th; George Bopp, 9th; Bill Cerelli, 10th; Pete Wise, 11th; Bob Miller, 12th; and Bill Davis, 13th.

Roanoke College vs. College of William and Mary
October 24, 1957
Salem, Virginia
Distance: 3.1 Miles

Team Scores: College of William and Mary (WM)–27
Roanoke College (R)–31

No streak lasts forever. Until the Roanoke team met the College of William and Mary on October 24, 1957, the Maroons had won 15 straight dual meets. The last team to beat them had been Virginia Polytechnic Institute on October 20, 1955.

The Indians came to Salem as the dominant Big Six team in the Commonwealth and the current Southern Conference champion. They also were undefeated in 16 consecutive meets.

Of all the opposing runners that Howard Meincke wanted to beat, William and Mary's Bob DeTombe was number one. They had met before, with DeTombe the winner. DeTombe placed 14th in the N. C. A. A. meet last fall.

The race essentially was between these two stars. As they went out the east gate of the campus and onto High Street, Meincke took the lead. It was Meincke and then DeTombe all the way–until the final 200 yards. As they virtually sprinted around the Alumni Field track, headed for the finish line on the Market Street side of the field, DeTombe put on a tremendous kick and passed Meincke. He crossed the line in a new course record of 15:08–a record previously set by Meincke. Meincke, almost totally exhausted by the late effort, was just a step behind in 15:10 and also broke the record.

Homer watched as almost all of his men gave their best efforts of the year. In fact, George Jocher finished in the 3rd position and Warren Light took 4th. William and Mary then packed five of its runners in the 5th through 9th places before Wayne Wilson came across the line in 10th place. The records do not show who the other Roanoke runners were, nor do they indicate their positions; however, Homer knew that the team as a whole had done as well as it could. Despite the score, 27 for William and Mary and 31 for Roanoke, there was much to be said for the talented Roanoke team. "I think the boys gave all they had," Homer said just after the race. "I don't think anyone could have asked for more. They did better than they ever had before but just got beat by a stronger team."

Roanoke College vs. Hampden-Sydney
October 28, 1957
Salem, Virginia
Distance: 3.1 Miles

Team Scores: Roanoke College (R)–17
Hampden-Sydney College (HS)–47

The meet with Hampden-Sydney, postponed from earlier in the season, was held in Salem on October 28. There is some confusion here, however. One source said that only half the team ran in this race and that the other half of the squad met American University within three days of the 28th. No report of the American University meet exists, but it is possible that this scenario did play out. Team members such as Howard Meincke, Warren Light, George Bopp, and Pete Wise did not run against Hampden-Sydney and could have made up the team that went to Washington, D. C. On the other hand, against a weak opponent, Homer could have given some of his runners a day off.

Against Hampden-Sydney, junior George Jocher led the race all the way from start to finish. His winning time was 16:01.5 over the 3.1-mile course. Wayne Wilson finished second, just 11.5 seconds behind, with Dick Emberger taking the third spot. After Hampden-Sydney's Waddell placed fourth, six Roanoke men took the next six places. Bill Cerelli was 5th, with Tom Sitton placing 6th, Pete Wise 7th, Bob Miller 8th, Bill Davis 9th, and Scott McKinney 10th.

Sadly, John Blanton fractured his ankle during the race. He was running his fastest race ever when, coming downhill on Market Street and with less than a quarter of a mile to go before he finished, one of the bones in his ankle snapped. His season was finished.

The final team score wasn't very close. Roanoke won with a total of 17, with Hampden-Sydney able to score only 47.

Little Eight Conference Cross-Country Championships
November 16, 1957

Bridgewater, Virginia
Distance: 3.3 Miles

Team Scores: Roanoke College (R)–22
Bridgewater College (B)–49
Lynchburg College (L)–59
Hampden-Sydney College (HS)–104
Norfolk William and Mary (N)–No Score

There was little chance that Roanoke would fail to win its fifth straight Little Eight meet. The Maroons had lost only one meet this year, to a powerful College of William and Mary team, and were the class of Virginia small college cross country teams.

As usual, Bridgewater hosted the meet on its 3.3-mile course. After the race began, Howard Meincke soon went to the front of the pack to lead the rest of the way home. The defending Little Eight champion crossed the finish line in 16:52.4, followed by George Jocher (2nd, 17:26.7), Wayne Wilson (4th, 17:36.1), Dick Emberger (7th, 18:11.0), Warren Light (8th, 18:14.0) despite side cramps, and finally Bill Cerelli (20th, 19:01). Reports did not show the names of additional Maroon runners, if there were any.

Roanoke, as expected, won the meet with ease with 22 points. It was the lowest winning score since Roanoke scored just 22 points in winning the 1954 meet. The closest opponent, Bridgewater, could total just 49. They had been unbeaten during the dual-meet season. Lynchburg, Hampden-Sydney, and Norfolk Division of William and Mary finished in the next three spots.

Norfolk William and Mary failed to score when their star, Baxter Berryhill, had a stomach cramp during the race and was forced to drop out. Because his team entered only five men, and just four of them crossed the finish line, the team received no points. Berryhill was expected to finish in the first or second positions and with his score, the Norfolk Division may have finished in second place.

Mason-Dixon Conference Cross-Country Championships
November 23, 1957
Gallaudet College–Washington, D. C.
Distance: 2.8 Miles

Team Scores: 1st–Roanoke College (R)–42
2nd–Bridgewater College (B)–71
3rd–Johns Hopkins University (JH)–83
4th–Lynchburg College (L)–103

5th–Loyola College (LOY)–135
6th–Catholic University (C)–145
7th–Mount St. Mary's College (MSM)–164
8th–Washington College (W)–175
9th–American University (A)–181
10th–Gallaudet College (G)–262
11th–Towson State College (T)–268
Hampden-Sydney College (HS)–No Score

No one predicted a Roanoke loss in this meet. The team was headed, it seemed, toward their fourth straight Mason-Dixon title. Homer did have some concern, however, that several other teams might run well enough to challenge for first place. Homer knew that Bridgewater had some talented runners. Catholic, Loyola, and Johns Hopkins each lost only once during the regular season. Johns Hopkins edged Loyola, 27-28; Hopkins was beaten by outsider Franklin and Marshall, 27-29; and Catholic University lost only to Loyola, 23-24.

Although several runners could win the meet, the favorite was the defending champion, Roanoke's Howard Meincke. But eight of the top ten finishers from last year were entered in the meet.

It was not a good weather day for the athletes. The course was muddy and slippery due to heavy rain and snow and many of the runners in the 110-man field fell on curves and hills.

Meincke stayed with a group of front runners through the first half of the 2.8-mile race. The group picked its way carefully along the slick pathways. Then, with about 1½ miles to go, Meincke put on a quick spurt of speed and took the lead for good. He crossed the line in 15:34.7 to win the championship medal. Running a good race himself, George Jocher finished just a second behind the second-place runner, Morris Jones, from Johns Hopkins. For Roanoke, Wayne Wilson finished 11th, Warren Light was 12th and a step behind Wilson, Dick Emberger 15th, Bill Cerelli 39th, and George Bopp 44th.

With its winning team score of 42 points, Roanoke became the first team in the history of the Mason-Dixon Conference to win four straight titles. After Roanoke (1st, 42 points) came Bridgewater (2nd, 71 points), Johns Hopkins (3rd, 83 points), Lynchburg College (4th, 103 points), Loyola College, 5th, 135 points), Catholic University (6th, 145 points), Mount St. Mary's College (7th, 164 points), Washington College (8th, 175 points), American University (9th, 181 points), Gallaudet College (10th, 262 points), and Towson State College (11th, 268 points). Hampden-Sydney was scratched when only three of its runners finished the muddy race.

I remember . . . "After the Mason-Dixon meet at Gallaudet, we took the whole team over to my house. Even my high school coach, Buddy Stein, was there. We had dinner at my house in Arlington. In that meet, I finished 11th. It was one of my better meets. I still have medals like that one hanging in my office."

Dr. Wayne Wilson

Chapter Fourteen

THE 1958 CROSS COUNTRY SEASON

Coach Bast liked his 1958 cross country team. As he told a *Brackety-Ack* reporter, "If the boys make up their minds to do a good job, we could enjoy our most successful campaign. In fact, I think our squad this year could rank as the best in the history of the College."

There were 11 veterans running for the team this year. They were George Jocher, Warren Light, Howard Meincke, Dick Goodlake, Pete Wise, Bill Davis, Tom Sitton, Dick Emberger, Wayne Wilson, Bob Miller, and Johnnie Blanton. Jocher and Light were elected Co-Captains of the team for 1958.

The *Brackety-Ack* mentioned several newcomers who might help the squad. There was Eddie Eades of Salem; Warren Orndorff of Washington, D. C.; Mickey Hamaker of Arlington, Virginia; Don Ballou of Highland Park, New Jersey; John Chrismar of Fords, New Jersey; Lance Bolint of Perth Amboy, New Jersey; Jack Chicman, also of Perth Amboy; Bill Reeves of Fort Lee, New Jersey; and Ronnie Jones of Valley Stream, New York. Another prospect mentioned was Robert Stonaker, a sophomore from Princeton, New Jersey.

Before the season began, Homer published this schedule of meets for 1958:

Date	*School*	*Location*
September 27	Atlantic Christian	Home
October 4	Pfeiffer	Home
October 11	American	Home
October 18	Norfolk William and Mary	Home
October 24	Hampden-Sydney	Away
October 25	Pembroke State	Home

October 27	Mount St. Mary's	Away
October 31	Lynchburg	Away
November 1	Fairmont State	Home
November 6	College of William and Mary	Away
November 15	Little Eight Championships	Bridgewater, VA
November 17	N. C. A. A. Championships	Wheaton, IL
November 22	Mason-Dixon Championships	Bridgewater, VA

Members of the outstanding cross country team of 1958.
Kneeling (L to R): Warren Orndorff, Mickey Hamaker, Don Ballou, Ron Jones, Lance Balint, John Chismar, Joe Sitton (Manager), Dick Goodlake, Tom Sitton, Russ Palochko, Bob Rein, Bill Davis, and Dick Emberger.
Back (L to R): Eddie Eades (kneeling), Wayne Wilson, Warren Light, and George Jocher. Absent was Howard Meincke.

The toughest competition likely would come from the College of William and Mary on November 6. They supposedly had one of the strongest teams in Virginia. Should Roanoke beat William and Mary, they might have another unbeaten season.

As usual, Coach Bast organized and ran the Intramural Cross Country meet prior to the cross country season. The top 10 participants finished in this order:

Place	*Name*	*Group*	*Time*
1st	Bob Jenkins	Sigma Chi	8:33.5
2nd	Scott McKinney	Kappa Alpha	8:54.0
3rd	Bob Fray	Kappa Alpha	Unknown
4th	Ken Gerkin	Kappa Alpha	9:31.0
5th	Bob Miller	Kappa Alpha	9:43.0
6th	Brendan Cavanagh	Unknown	Unknown
7th	John Nugent	Pi Kappa Phi	9:54.2
8th	Lane Melton	Pi Kappa Phi	10:04.0
9th	Bob Armstrong	Sigma Chi	10:11.0
10th	Bart Richwine	Pi Kappa Phi	10:17.0

Bob Jenkins was recruited immediately by Homer to be a distance runner. He went on to become one of the top cross country men in the state.

Roanoke College Freshmen vs. Andrew Lewis High School
September 26, 1958
Salem, Virginia
Distance: 1.7 Miles

Team Scores: Roanoke College Freshmen (R)–26
Andrew Lewis High School (AL)–29

As he did the year before, Coach Bast agreed to run his freshmen in a meet versus Salem's Andrew Lewis High School. Lewis had lost only one meet during the past three years. That loss came at the hands of the Roanoke freshmen in 1957.

The meet was held on a warm and humid day. There was no breeze.

Mickey Hamaker of Roanoke won the meet on the 1.7-mile freshman course with a time of 8:33.0. That time was almost eight seconds faster than Salem High School's Eddie Eades time when he won the race last year. Now a Roanoke College runner, Eades placed 4th in the race. Don Ballou was 5th, Warren Orndorff was 7th, Bill Reeves was 9th,

Another photo of the 1958 cross country team.
Front Row (L to R): Warren Light, Coach Bast, and George Jocher.
Standing (L to R): Howard Meincke, Dick Emberger, Bob Jenkins, Jose Sitton (Manager), Ed Eanes, Wayne Wilson, and Dick Goodlake.

and Robert Rein was 20th.

Roanoke barely beat Andrew Lewis by a score of 26 to 29.

Roanoke College vs. Atlantic Christian College
September 27, 1958

Salem, Virginia
Distance: 3.1 Miles

Team Scores: Roanoke College (R)–15
Atlantic Christian College (AC)–45

The opening meet of the season for Roanoke came on a windy and cool day. This would be the first time the two schools–Roanoke and Atlantic Christian College of Wilson, North Carolina–had met in competition. Homer didn't know much about the team but had heard that they had been very weak in track and had no strong runners on the team. That was good news, for he also knew that Howard Meincke and Dick Goodlake would be sidelined with leg injuries and could not compete in the meet.

Roanoke swept the first six places to record a perfect score of 15, while Atlantic Christian took places from 7th to 13th for a team score of 45. The Maroons' George Jocher ran a time of 16:31 to win going away. Second place was taken by Wayne Wilson in 16:58.0. Other Roanoke runners were Eddie Eades (3rd, 17:09); Warren Light (4th, 17:20); John Blanton (5th, 17:58), and Dick Emberger (6th, 17:58).

Roanoke College vs. Pfeiffer College
October 4, 1958
Salem, Virginia
Distance: 3.1 Miles

Team Scores: Roanoke College (R)–15
Pfeiffer College (P)–50

Pfeiffer, a college in Misenheimer, North Carolina, was the Roanoke team's next opponent. The meet was run during the halftime of a soccer match between the same two schools. At race time, the runners found the weather to be warm and sunny.

George Jocher led the two teams throughout the race, finishing first in a time of 15:40.5. Running in the shadow of teammate Howard Meincke for the past two years, this meet marked the beginning of his 11 straight defeats of Meincke during the 1958 season.

After Jocher, nine other runners finished before Pfeiffer took the 11th through 16th places. Meincke was 2nd in the race, running 16:16.5. Dick Emberger finished 3rd, Eddie Eades was 4th, Johnnie Blanton was 5th, Wayne Wilson was 6th, Mickey Hamaker was 7th, Bill Reeves was 8th, Warren Orndorff was 9th, and Bill Davis took the 10th spot.

Roanoke, therefore, won with a perfect score. They beat Pfeiffer 15 to 50.

Roanoke College vs. Pembroke State College
October 8, 1958
Salem, Virginia
Distance: 3.1 Miles

Team Scores: Roanoke College (R)–16
Pembroke State College (PS)–47

Pembroke State College, a team from Pembroke, North Carolina, was the next opponent for the Maroons. The day was warm and sunny with little wind.

Again, Roanoke runners dominated the meet. In fact, they finished in the 1st through 4th places, gave up the 5th spot to a Pembroke State runner, and then took the 6th through 8th places to beat the visitors by a score of 16 to 47.

Although the race this time was much closer, George Jocher won the meet in a time of 15:51, with Howard Meincke just seven seconds behind in second. Eddie Eades ran well, finishing 3rd, with Dick Emberger just behind in fourth. Wayne Wilson placed 6th, Johnnie Blanton 7th, and Bill Davis 8th.

In 1958, four of the top cross country runners in the Little Eight and Mason-Dixon Conferences were (L to R) Dick Goodlake, Howard Meincke, George Jocher, and Warren Light.

Roanoke College vs. Hampden-Sydney College
October 13, 1958
Hampden-Sydney Virginia
Distance: 3.0 Miles

Team Scores: Roanoke College (R)–19
Hampden-Sydney College (HS)–42

Another easy meet for Roanoke came on October 13. The meet was held on the Hampden-Sydney 3.0-mile course. The weather was clear and warm.

Some of the runners took the day off. Dick Goodlake won the race in a time of 15:22.5, knocking 10 seconds off the course record. After Hampden-Sydney's runner, King Waddell, finished second, the Roanoke squad took the next six positions. Dick Emberger was 3rd, Warren Light was 4th, Wayne Wilson was 5th, Eddie Eades was 6th, and Mickey Hamaker finished in 7th place.

Roanoke College vs. Norfolk William and Mary College
October 17, 1958
Salem, Virginia
Distance: 3.1 Miles

Team Scores: Roanoke College (R)–25
Norfolk William and Mary College (NWM)–32

The Norfolk Division of William and Mary came to Salem to meet Roanoke's cross country team on October 17. The visitors had participated in only one meet this year, winning over Bridgewater by a score of 18 to 38. The meet began on this warm, sunny day at 2:00 p.m.

Coach Bast was a bit worried, because the opponents today were gaining strength each year. Norfolk William and Mary had finished within 10 points of Roanoke last year, and were reported to have a better team in 1958. Both teams had top-flight freshmen. Don Mears of the Norfolk team, for example, was the Virginia high school cross country champion in 1957.

George Jocher pulled away from the pack and won the meet with a time of 15:31.8. Freshman Don Mears of Norfolk William and Mary was second about 10 seconds back. Dick Goodlake of Roanoke, running well, took the 3rd spot. He was followed in 5th place by Howard Meincke. Eddie Eades was 7th, Warren Light was 9th, and Wayne Wilson and Dick Emberger tied for 10th.

Only seven points separated the teams at the end. Roanoke maintained its perfect dual-meet season for 1958 by winning 25 to 32.

Roanoke College vs. Fairmont State College
October 18, 1958
Salem, Virginia
Distance: 3.1 Miles

Team Scores: Roanoke College (R)–16
Fairmont State College (F)–45

Fairmont State College, from Fairmont, West Virginia, did not have the runners to challenge Roanoke's outstanding team. Coach Bast forecast not only an easy win, but perhaps a perfect score of 15 for his team.

The weather was good for racing. At the gun, it was cloudy and warm.

George Jocher and Dick Goodlake did not run in the meet. That gave Howard Meincke an opportunity to win again, as he crossed the line in a time of 16:11. In second was Bob Jenkins, winner of the intramural cross country race at the beginning of the season. Wayne Wilson finished in 3rd place, and Dick Emberger took the 4th spot. The remainder of the Maroons included Mickey Hamaker (6th), Don Ballou (7th), Bill Reeves (10th), and Pete Wise (13th).

The final score was Roanoke, 16, and Fairmont State, 45. It was Roanoke's sixth straight win.

Virginia Senior A. A. U. Cross-Country Championships
October 24, 1958
Williamsburg, Virginia
Distance: 4.0 Miles

Team Scores: 1st–Roanoke College (R)–31
2nd–College of William and Mary (WM)–38
3rd–Norfolk Division of William and Mary (NWM)–61

The Virginia State A. A. U. meet was held, we think, on October 24. Two sources of information about the meet had different dates. We do know that the meet was held at Cary Field in Williamsburg.

The varsity competition was preceded by a freshman meet, entered by three schools. The Norfolk Division of William and Mary won with a low score of 32. In second was a team of freshmen from William and Mary. Third place went to Fork Union Military Academy, with 56 points.

In the varsity competition, Roanoke's main competitor would be the College of William and Mary. They had been the only school to defeat Roanoke during the 1957 cross country season. Their star was still Bob DeTombe. Another good runner to watch was Norfolk Division of William and Mary's Baxter Berryhill and several unattached athletes.

Every man on Roanoke's team ran well this day. George Jocher finished 4th in a time of 22:06, with Howard Meincke in 6th place just seven seconds back, and Dick Goodlake, who followed Meincke across the line. Meincke ran a 22:13 and Goodlake a 22:14 over the four-mile course. In addition, Warren Light (13th, 22:56), Eddie Eades (14th, 23:04), Dick Emberger (15th, 23:14), and Wayne Wilson (18th, 24:00) all figured in the scoring.

In the official scoring, Roanoke won the meet with 31 points. The College of William and Mary was second with 38, and the Norfolk Division of William and Mary finished third with 61. It was the first time a Roanoke cross country team had won the state A. A. U. meet since the Bast-coached team won in 1949.

Roanoke College vs. Lynchburg College
October 31, 1958
Lynchburg, Virginia
Distance: 3.2 Miles

Team Scores: Roanoke College (R)–27
Lynchburg College (L)–30

Coaches around the state, and even Coach Bast, predicted an easy win for Roanoke in its October 31 meeting with Lynchburg. They were as wrong as they could be.

Left Photo: George Jocher wins a cross country race.
Right Photo: Howard Meincke (L) and George Jocher (R) finished 1-2 in most races.

On a warm, ideal day for running, the Maroons drove to Lynchburg and made their way to the athletic field. Homer walked over to say hello to the Lynchburg coach while the Salem team began to stretch. "You're late," he said to Homer. "We start the race in 20 minutes." Homer was shocked. "But we haven't seen the course," Homer noted, "None of them has ever run this course before. And besides, 20 minutes is not enough time for us to warm up." But the Lynchburg coach insisted that the race would start in 20 minutes, and that if the Roanoke team were not on the line at that time, they would forfeit the race to Lynchburg.

The gun sounded 20 minutes later, with the Roanoke team on the starting line. Whether it was a lack of warm-up time or simply being out of their pre-race routine, many of the runners on Roanoke's team did not run well.

Their two top runners, of course, were among the best in the state. They had no problems finishing in front on the 3.2-mile course. George Jocher won the race with a time of 16:49, with Howard Meincke just five seconds behind in second place.

But Lynchburg runners placed third, fourth, fifth, and sixth. It began to look as if Roanoke would lose its first meet of the year in a stunning upset. Fortunately, however, the next Lynchburg runner finished well back in 12th place.

Roanoke's Warren Light was 7th, Eddie Eases was 8th, Bob Jenkins was 9th, Wayne Wilson was 10th, and Don Ballou was 11th. A few seconds back were Bill Reeves, in 13th place, and Mick Hamaker in 14th. Roanoke won the meet by a score of 27 to 30. Only Lynchburg's fifth and final scoring runner, who placed 12th, made the difference.

Roanoke College vs. University of the South (Sewanee)
November 1, 1958
Telegraphic Meet–Each School's Quarter-Mile Track
Distance: 2.0 Miles

Team Scores: Roanoke College (R)–18
University of the South, Sewanee (S)–38

To cut travel expenses for both schools, as they had done the previous year, Roanoke and the University of the South held a telegraphic meet on November 1. This year, each team ran a total of 8 laps on its own track, and then combined the individual times to determine a winner.

Running in ideal weather conditions, Roanoke's George Jocher again placed first. His time was 10:04.4. Howard Meincke finished just two seconds behind Jocher, with Dick Goodlake taking third about 50 yards in back of Meincke.

Johnnie Blanton (5th), Tom Sitton (7th), and Don Ballou (10th) completed the Roanoke scoring. The final team score was 18 to 38 in Roanoke's favor.

Roanoke College vs. College of William and Mary
November 5, 1958
Williamsburg, Virginia
Distance: 4.0 Miles

Team Scores: Roanoke College (R)–25
College of William and Mary (WM)–32

November 5 was warm and humid as the Roanoke team warmed up in Williamsburg. The Maroons had been pointing to this meet all year, because their opponent was the College of William and Mary, the defending Southern Conference champions and the only team to defeat Roanoke during the fall of 1957. The Indians were led by Bob DeTombe, the Southern Conference and Big Six title holder. No Roanoke runner had ever beaten him in a cross country race.

In the early stages of the race this afternoon, DeTombe and Roanoke's trio of George Jocher, Howard Meincke, and Dick Goodlake formed a pack of front runners. Finally, DeTombe moved on out in front, crossing the finish line of the 4.0-mile course in an excellent time of 21:46. In second place was Jocher, who ran a 22:09. Then Goodlake and Meincke staged a close battle for the next two spots. In the last moments of the race, Goodlake moved slightly ahead and beat Meincke by just one second.

William and Mary runners claimed the fifth and sixth spots, with Roanoke's Warren Light taking seventh. Eddie Eades became the final scorer for the Maroons when he crossed the finish line in 9th place. Other Roanoke men included Dick Emberger (10th), Wayne Wilson (11th), and Bob Jenkins (12th).

Roanoke won by a score of 25 to 32. The win was Roanoke's 10th in a row over two years, and elevated Roanoke to the position as the number one cross country team in the state and made them overwhelming favorites to take the Little Eight and Mason-Dixon titles.

Little Eight Conference Cross–Country Championships
November 12, 1958
Bridgewater, Virginia
Distance: Approximately 3.25 Miles

Team Scores: 1st–Roanoke College (R)–30
2nd–Norfolk William and Mary College (NWM)–41

3rd–Bridgewater College (B)–78
4th–Lynchburg College (L)–100
5th–Hampden-Sydney College (HS)–127

Reports from Norfolk showed that the Norfolk Division of William and Mary likely was the only team capable of beating Roanoke in the Little Eight Championships at Bridgewater. Norfolk still had an excellent runner in Baxter Berryhill, but another of their athletes, freshman Virgil Meares, had come on strong during the current season. Roanoke was depending on its group of three up-front runners–Howard Meincke, George Jocher, and Dick Goodlake–to each finish in the top five.

Norfolk's Meares ran a terrific race, tying the course record of 16:42.8 set in 1956 by Meincke. Not far behind Meares came Roanoke's runners–Goodlake (2nd, 16:58), –Jocher (3rd, 17:08), and Meincke (4th, 17:15). Norfolk's top four runners placed 1st, 5th (Berryhill), 7th, and 9th in the race. Fortunately for Roanoke, their 5th man placed only 19th. With Dick Emberger in 10th place and Warren Light in 11th, Roanoke won the team title by 11 points. Eddie Eades was 12th and Wayne Wilson 13th.

The final scores were: 1st–Roanoke–30; 2nd–Norfolk Division of William and Mary–41; 3rd–Bridgewater–78; 4th–Lynchburg–100; and 5th–Hampden-Sydney–127. Incidentally, it was the first time in the past four years that Howard Meincke did not win the individual title.

First NCAA College Division Cross Country Championships
November 15, 1958
Wheaton College–Wheaton, Illinois
Distance: 4.0 Miles

Team Scores: 1st–Northern Illinois (NI)–90
2nd–South Dakota State (SDS)–93
3rd–Central Michigan (CM)–107
4th–Wheaton College (W)–131
5th–Southern Illinois University (SI)–134
6th–Wabash College (WC)–140
7th–Kansas State (KS)–148
8th–Slippery Rock (SR)–202
9th–Ohio Wesleyan University (OW)–205
10th–Mankato State (MS)–217
11th–Roanoke College (R)–231
12th–DePauw University (D)–258

13th–Albion College (A)–319

Other Entries:

Buffalo State (BS)
Elmhurst College (E)
Kalamazoo College (K)
Muskingum College (M)
Southwestern at Memphis (S)
Western Illinois University (WI)

Because of Roanoke's undefeated dual-meet record, they were invited to compete in the first annual N. C. A. A. College Division Championships in Wheaton, Illinois. Coach Bast was confident that they would do well. As he said to the *Brackety-Ack* staff, "If the team's mental attitude is up to par then we'll be hard to beat."

It is unclear from the newspapers in Roanoke City and on the campus just how many men made the trip. The *Brackety-Ack* stated that eight men were planning to run. The results of the meet, however, show only six of them actually finishing the race. Roanoke packed runners and a coach into a single station wagon for the long 750-mile trip to Wheaton. Leaving early in the morning, they drove all day and into the night to reach their destination.

Of the 310 institutions in the country that fit the definition of "small college," 20 of them brought either entire teams or individuals to the meet. As the group of athletes warmed up on the Wheaton College campus, the temperature was in the 20s and the course was in good shape. But it continued to rain.

Unfortunately, the Roanoke men fell back early in the race. Here were the splits for the leading runners during the run: half mile–2:28; mile–4:58; mile and a half–7:28; two miles–10:10; two and one half miles–12:49; three miles–15:15; three and one half miles–17:57; and four miles–20:45. The eventual winner of the meet was Kansas State's Paul Whiteley, who was timed in 20:45. Almost a minute and 40 seconds later, George Jocher became Roanoke's first runner to cross the finish line in the 29th place overall. His time was recorded as 22:23. Howard Meincke was 42nd with a time of 22:47. The other Roanoke runners were Dick Goodlake (51st, 23:03), Warren Light (53rd, 23:08), Dick Emberger (80th, 23:58), and Eddie Eades (85th, 24:11).

After the places of runners with incomplete teams were discounted, Roanoke ended up in 11th place among the 13 scoring teams with 231 points. Other teams were Northern Illinois, 1st, 90 points; South Dakota State, 2nd, 93; Central Michigan, 3rd, 107; Wheaton College, 4th, 131; Southern Illinois University, 5th, 134; Wabash College, 6th, 140; Kansas

State, 7th, 148; Slippery Rock, 8th, 202; Ohio Wesleyan University, 9th, 205; Mankato State, 10th, 217; DePauw University, 12th, 258; and Albion College, 13th, 319. In addition, there were six teams who finished the race with less than five men scoring: Buffalo State, Elmhurst, Kalamazoo, Muskingum, Southwestern at Memphis, and Western Illinois.

Simply put, the Roanoke team had not run well. Whether it was the cold weather, the rain, the long trip, the strain they felt from their Little Eight victory, or the national competition that caused them problems, each runner–and their coach–was greatly disappointed. When the team returned to Salem, Coach Bast told a *Brackety-Ack* reporter that "We came, we saw, we were conquered. Our team did not reach its full potential. Every runner was off about a half a minute for the four-mile race."

Mason-Dixon Conference Cross–Country Championships
November 22, 1958
Bridgewater College–Bridgewater, Virginia
Distance: Approximately 3.25 Miles

Team Scores: 1st–Roanoke College (R)–43
2nd–Bridgewater College (B)–92
3rd–Johns Hopkins University (JH)–101
4th–Loyola College (LOY)–103
5th–Catholic University (C)–109
6th–Lynchburg (L)–114
7th–Washington College (W)–187
8th–Hampden-Sydney College (HS)–240
9th–Gallaudet College (G)–242
10th–American University (A)–244
11th–Mount St. Mary's College (MSM)–293
12th–Towson College (T)–329

Riverside Field at Bridgewater College was the site for the 1958 Mason-Dixon Championships. The course was new so there was no course record for it. Most thought that a time of around 15:28 on this shorter course might represent the equivalent of the record of 16:42.9 originally set on the longer course by Howard Meincke in 1956 and tied by Norfolk Division of William and Mary's Virgil Meares in 1958. Meincke was the defending Mason-Dixon cross country champion but had not shown his usual great form this year.

Coach Bast predicted that the final team scores would be close. Loyola was undefeated for the season, and Johns Hopkins, Catholic, Bridgewater, and Lynchburg were all bringing top runners. Mike Halpin of Catholic, the Mason-Dixon outdoor mile champion, had been beaten only once this year. That loss came to his teammate, John Madison. John Hopkins had two top individual runners in Frank Smilovitz and Morris Jones. Loyola's team also had a good runner, Ken Billeb. It might be difficult for Roanoke to pick up its fifth consecutive Mason-Dixon trophy.

Roanoke's performance at the N. C. A. A. meet was not up to par. Would they run well today? As Alvin Stump, writing for the *Brackety-Ack*, said: "It's difficult to predict how they will run. But the test of a good team is their ability to bounce back after defeat."

The race began at 2:00 p.m. As expected, no one runner dominated the 3.25-mile race. In fact, when Catholic's John Madison lunged across the finish line to win in 15:38, the time margin between him and the 15th finisher was a mere 42 seconds–the closest finish in the history of the meet.

Roanoke's George Jocher came within two seconds of beating Madison, and Dick Goodlake was just five seconds back of Jocher for 3rd place. After Mike Halpin of Catholic, Paul Sherman of Loyola, and King Waddill of Hampden-Sydney finished in the 4th, 5th, and 6th places, respectively, Howard Meincke took the 7th spot with a time of 15:56. Dick Emberger was the Maroons' fourth runner, finishing 15th with a time of 16:20, while Warren Light was 16th in 16:29. Others on the Roanoke team included Eddie Eades (27th, 17:02) and Wayne Wilson (33rd, 17:20).

Roanoke won the Mason-Dixon trophy for the fifth consecutive year and for the seventh time in Homer Bast's coaching career. Bridgewater placed second with 92 points, with Johns Hopkins finishing third on 101 points.

The other teams included Loyola College (4th), Catholic University (5th), Lynchburg College (6th), Washington College (7th), Hampden-Sydney College (8th), Gallaudet College (9th), American University (10th), Mount St. Mary's College (11th), and Towson State College (12th).

Coaches, competitors, and officials attended a short reception given by the Women's Athletic Association and the Varsity Club in Blue Ridge Hall following the race. There, the officials announced the team scores and awarded the winner's trophy to Roanoke. Medals were also distributed to the top 15 finishers in the race.

Roanoke had finished the season as Little Eight and Mason-Dixon champions. They also had completed an undefeated dual-meet schedule–something Homer and his teams had accomplished before in 1948, 1949, 1954, and 1956.

Cross country letter winners included the following men: Wayne Wilson, Johnnie Blanton, William Reaves, Don Ballou, Ken Hamaker, Jr., Tom Sitton, Warren Light, Howard Meincke, George Jocher, Bob Jenkins, Dick Emberger, Dick Goodlake, and John Eades.

Chapter Fifteen

THE 1959 CROSS COUNTRY SEASON

Led by Co-Captains Wayne Wilson and Dick Emberger, the 1959 cross country team began their practices on September 21. Gone were the big stars of the past few years, including Howard Meincke, George Jocher, and Dick Goodlake; however, some talented veterans were returning. They included Wayne Wilson, Bob Jenkins, Dick Emberger, Johnnie Blanton, Bill Davis, and Warren Orndorff. And according to the *Brackety-Ack*, there were several newcomers who might help the team–Derek Stryker, Dick Waltz, Joe Rixon, Jerry Willard, Charles Francis, and John Richards. Stryker was expected to be this group's best runner.

Coach Bast expected to begin the season at Wilson, North Carolina, on October 9. The opponents would be Atlantic Christian College and Pembroke State College. Both had been on the 1958 schedule. Just a few days prior to the meet, however, Atlantic Christian called to say that they were unable to field a team that year. By mutual agreement, Roanoke, Atlantic Christian, and Pembroke State decided to cancel their triangular meet altogether.

Roanoke College vs. Norfolk Division of William and Mary
October 15, 1959
Norfolk, Virginia
Distance: 3.0 Miles

Team Scores: Roanoke College (R)–19
Norfolk Division of William and Mary (NWM)–36

Homer had scheduled the second meet, now the first, with Norfolk Division of William and Mary. Knowing that the Roanoke team would be a weaker one this year, he wished the Norfolk Division meet could have been run later in the season.

Without the Interstate roadways, the ride to Norfolk was long–about 300 miles over mostly two-lane roads. On the morning of the three-mile race, the weather was cool and the footing on the course was wet and very muddy.

The race featured the emergence of "the crow," as Roanoke students often called Bob Jenkins, as a team leader and top runner. He seemed much stronger this year and won the race easily in a time of 16:12.5 over second-place finisher Steele McConegel of the Norfolk Division of William and Mary.

Then Roanoke runners took the third through sixth places to finish with just 19 points. Dick Emberger was third, Wayne Wilson fourth, Johnnie Blanton fifth, and freshman Derek Stryker sixth. The other Roanoke team members were Bill Davis, in twelfth place; Warren Orndorff, in thirteenth; and Dick Waltz, in seventeenth.

Most were surprised about the margin of victory over the Norfolk Division. The meets with the Norfolk team had been close ones during the past couple of years.

Roanoke College vs. Mount St. Mary's College
October 19, 1959
Emmetsburg, Maryland
Distance: 3.2 Miles

Team Scores: Roanoke College (R)–18
Mount St. Mary's College (MSM)–38

Jenkins was a winner again in the second meet. It was held at Emmetsburg, Maryland, with Mount St. Mary's College. The course record was 16:05 by Paul Sherman of Loyola.

The weather was cool, but sunny. Roanoke took five of the top six places to easily win the meet, 18 to 38. Jenkins ran a good time of 16:18.0 to capture individual honors, running the first mile in 4:23, according to an estimate by Coach Bast, and his split at mile two was 9:51. Senior Dick Emberger finished second in a time of 16:47.

Wayne Wilson was fourth, Derek Stryker fifth, Johnnie Blanton sixth, Warren Orndorff tenth, Dick Waltz thirteenth, Bill Davis fourteenth, and Joe Rixon fifteenth.

Roanoke College vs. Hampden-Sydney College
October 22, 1959
Salem, Virginia
Distance: 3.1 Miles

Team Scores: Roanoke College (R)–17
Hampden-Sydney College (HS)–43

Three days later, the team hosted Hampden-Sydney College. It wasn't a very pleasant day–with rainy, humid weather and a course that was slippery in spots–but Coach Bast wasn't worried. Reports were that Hampden-Sydney had a weaker-than-usual team this year.

For the third straight meet, Bob Jenkins quickly drew away from the rest of the runners and won in a time of 16:37.9, some 25 seconds ahead of second-place Johnnie Blanton and third-place Derek Stryker. Blanton and Stryker finished side by side and although Blanton was given second, the times for the two runners were identical.

After Phil Miller of Hampden-Sydney took the fourth spot, Dick Emberger finished in fifth place and Wayne Wilson was sixth. The other six Roanoke runners were Warren Orndorff (ninth), Bill Davis (tenth), Dick Waltz (eleventh), Joe Rixon (fourteenth), Jerry Willard (fifteenth), and Charles Francis (sixteenth).

The team scores were 17 for Roanoke and 43 for Hampden-Sydney. At this early stage in the season, the Maroon record was a surprising 3-0.

Roanoke College vs. Lynchburg College
October 28, 1959
Salem, Virginia
Distance: 3.1 Miles

Team Scores: Roanoke College (R)–25
Lynchburg (L)–34

Lynchburg College runners came to Salem on October 28. It was a good day to hold the meet, with cool temperatures and sunshine.

Coach Bast noted right away after the start of the race that the Roanoke team was packed toward the front. Bob Jenkins, as he had done three other times this season, went to the lead and stayed there all the way to the finish line. His winning time over the 3.1-mile course was 16:37.7. Frank Wagner of Lynchburg was less than five seconds behind.

Wayne Wilson placed third, in 16:48.5, and he was followed by Lynchburg's Tom Cutler in fourth and Sid Clark in fifth place. Roanoke won the meet by grouping five runners in the sixth through tenth places. Johnnie Blanton was sixth, Dick Emberger was seventh, Derek Stryker was eighth, Warren Orndorff was ninth, and Dick Waltz finished tenth. Back in the pack, Joe Rixon of Roanoke was fourteenth, Jerry Willard nineteenth, and John Richards twentieth.

The 1959 cross country team members were: Front row L to R)-Coach Homer Bast, Jerry Willard, Derek Stryker, and Manager Scott McKinney. Back row (L to R): Warren Orndorff, Robert Jenkins, Wayne Wilson, Bill Davis, Jack Richards, Joe Rixon, and Richard Waltz. Absent was Dick Emberger, who along with Wilson, served the team as co-captains; and Johnnie Blanton.

The Maroons won the meet, 25 to 34. They now were 4-0 on the season.

Roanoke College vs. College of William and Mary
November 2, 1959
Salem, Virginia
Distance: 3.1 Miles

Team Scores: College of William and Mary (WM)–25
Roanoke College (R)–30

The Roanoke student body was pleased at how the season had turned out thus far. The team's record was 4-0, despite the loss of several top stars from the 1958 squad. Bob Jenkins' four straight victories had helped the cause, but the other members of the team were also running well.

Members of the 1959 cross country team.
Left Photo: Bob Jenkins and Bill Davis.
Right Photo: Freshman Derek Stryker.

There was only one dual meet left on the Roanoke schedule. Always-strong College of William and Mary was coming to town on November 2. During the last two years, the two teams had each won one of the competitions between the schools. In 1957, in Salem, William and Mary won by a score of 27-31. In 1958, in Williamsburg, Roanoke won the meet, 25-32. Coach Bast couldn't predict how the 1959 meet would turn out.

On a very windy but sunny day, the Roanoke harriers finally tasted defeat after running up an impressive 14 straight wins. Bob Jenkins, still running well, won his fifth race of the year. He covered the 3.1-mile course in a good time of 16:08. Unfortunately for the Maroons, William and Mary athletes took the next three places. Tom Quitko was second, Ed Larson third, and Bob Bassett was fourth.

Johnnie Blanton of Roanoke took the fifth spot, with Joe Robinson of William and Mary taking sixth. Wayne Wilson (seventh), Dick Emberger (eighth), and Derek Stryker (ninth) finished strong, but William and Mary's last scoring runner, Ed Quandt, won the meet for his team by placing tenth. For Roanoke, Warren Orndorff placed eleventh, Dick Waltz was thirteenth, and Jerry Willard crossed the line in 15th place.

William and Mary won the meet by a score of 25 to 30. It was a disappointing defeat for the runners and certainly for Coach Bast.

Virginia State Cross Country Championships
November 9, 1959
Lexington, Virginia
Distance: 4.0 Miles

Team Scores: 1st–Virginia Military Institute (VMI)–30
2nd–College of William and Mary (WM)–56
3rd–Bridgewater College (B)–104
4th–Lynchburg College (L)–123
5th–Virginia Polytechnic Institute (VPI)–139
6th–Roanoke College (R)–141
7th–Washington and Lee University (WL)–145

Coach Bast was not at all optimistic about his team's chances in the large State Cross Country Championships, to be held in Lexington on a rough four-mile course. He knew that with the loss of Goodlake, Meincke, and Jocher, his team was not very strong. It would be hard to match the times of College of William and Mary, V. M. I., V. P. I., and even Bridgewater and Lynchburg.

He was right. The Roanoke team finished the meet in sixth place with a score of 141 points. There were only seven teams entered. V. M. I. took home the winner's trophy.

William and Mary finished second, Bridgewater was third, Lynchburg was fourth, V. P. I. was fifth, and Washington and Lee finished with 145 points.

For the first time this year, Bob Jenkins didn't win the individual title in a meet. In fact, he was well down the line in sixteenth place, with a time that was 1:36 slower than that the one recorded by the winner, Castagnola of V. P. I. Roanoke's Wayne Wilson was twenty-seventh, followed by Dick Emberger (35th), Johnnie Blanton (39th), Derek Stryker (40th), and Warren Orndorff (41st).

Little Eight Conference Championships
November 13, 1959
Hampden-Sydney, Virginia
Distance: 3.0 Miles

Team Scores: 1st–Bridgewater College (B)–36
2nd–Roanoke College (R)–67
3rd–Norfolk Division of William and Mary (NWM)–75
4th–Lynchburg College (L)–82
5th–Hampden-Sydney College (HS)–95

After his team's disappointing showing in the State Meet, Coach Bast was beginning to wonder if the individuals he was coaching were trying very hard. The time margins between his first and fifth men had widened during the past couple of weeks. Were they just tired, or was something else going on?

Roanoke, as usual, should have been the favorite team to win the Little Eight meet at Hampden-Sydney. But Bridgewater had beaten them badly in the State Meet, and so had Lynchburg. Was it possible that Roanoke might come through with a great effort and win the championship trophy? After all, they had won this meet in 1953, 1954, 1955, 1956, 1957, and 1958.

The runners were competing on a three-mile course with good footing. It was just a perfect day to hold a meet. Spectators were treated to a very competitive race, especially in the first three places, where there was only one second difference between the first and third runner.

As the three leaders of the race came in sight of the finish line, they were sprinting side-by-side. In the last few strides, Norfolk William and Mary's Steele McGonegal took a slight lead and broke the tape in a time of 16:05. The time clipped a full 40 seconds off the previous mark for the new course, set earlier this year by Sid Clark of Lynchburg.

Bob Jenkins came close to getting second place, but looking at the dead heat between Bob and Sid Clark, the officials gave Clark second and Jenkins third. Both men's times were recorded as 16:06.

Steady and dependable senior Dick Emberger took the 9th position, with Johnnie Blanton (15th), Wayne Wilson (18th), and Warren Orndorff (22nd) finishing the scoring for Roanoke. The Maroons' Derek Stryker finished 27th and Dick Waltz was 30th.

Roanoke failed to win the team title, but it did finish in second place. Bridgewater was first with 36 points. Roanoke was second (67); Norfolk Division of William and Mary third (75); Lynchburg fourth (82); and Hampden-Sydney was last (95).

Mason-Dixon Conference Championships
November 21, 1959
Washington College–Chestertown, Maryland
Distance: Unknown

Team Scores: 1st–Roanoke (R)–2, 5, 14, 18, 24, 32, 5963
2nd–Bridgewater (B)–8, 9, 15, 16, 23, 26, 3471
3rd–Loyola (LOY)–3, 10, 22, 29, 45, 51, 58109
4th–Mount St. Mary's (MSM)–7, 11, 27, 36, 38, 49, 50119
5th–Johns Hopkins (JH)–4, 13, 31, 37, 42, 48, 55127
6th–Catholic (C)–1, 6, 44, 52, 54, 56, 66157
7th–American (A)–12, 30, 33, 39, 46, 69160
8th–Lynchburg (L)–19, 20, 21, 62, 64186
9th–Gallaudet (G)–28, 41, 43, 47, 65, 67, 71224
10th–Washington (W)–25, 35, 53, 57, 68, 70, 72238
11th–Towson State (T)–17, 40, 60, 61, 63241

Non-Scoring–University of Baltimore (UB)

For two straight races–the Virginia State and the Little Eight Championships, the Roanoke team as a whole had not run well. Homer Bast has always attributed the slump to a lack of effort, noting that there was little difference between an average and a good cross country man except for desire. At the very least, seeing this attitude among his team members, he was expecting perhaps a third- or fourth-place finish in the 1959 Mason-Dixon meet held at Washington College. The team also had a depth problem, having lost by graduation some of the best runners in the state from the 1958 season.

Bridgewater seemed to be the team to beat, although some of the northern division teams might be strong. Each of those schools had at least one outstanding runner in the field.

Mike Halpin of Catholic and Wayne Gallatin of Loyola were the front runners in the race, quickly moving into the lead and spreading the gap between them and the third-place runner. The chilling rain made the course slippery. In the last 100 yards of the race, Halpin sprinted ahead to win in a time of 16:14. Gallatin, his team's only entry in the meet, was just a step behind in 16:15.

Then, as Coach Bast peered down the course to see how his men were positioned, over the last rise came Bob Jenkins, who finished third (officially second) in 17:00. Just 20 seconds later, Dick Emberger was driving toward the line and closed fast for 5th place. His time was 17:20. Even more amazing was the time and position of Roanoke's third runner, freshman Derek Stryker. Stryker, running perhaps his best race of the year, finished 14th with a time of 17:50. Three Roanoke athletes had finished in the top 15 places. Favorite Bridgewater had only one of its men in that group, and Catholic and Johns Hopkins had two each. We might just pull this off, Bast thought. And he looked again to see where his fourth and fifth runners were positioned. Then he spotted Wayne Wilson, who closed fast to finish in the 19th spot with a time of 18:00. Now, Bast thought, just one more guy was needed. And there he was. In a wild sprint toward the finish line were Nolen of Bridgewater, Moore of Washington, and Roanoke's Johnnie Blanton. Nolen finished 23rd (18:24) , Blanton 24th (18:25), and Moore 25th (18:26). The sixth and seventh Roanoke men were Warren Orndorff, 32nd in 18:32, and Dick Waltz, 61st in 19:48.

All of the calculations were done by hand in those days, so there was a delay of 10-15 minutes in the announcement of the team scores. Bast had done his own figuring, however, and if he had spotted the positions of runners correctly, his team and Bridgewater's were very close in score.

Finally, the announcement was made. Roanoke had surprised nearly all of the experts, winning the meet with 63 points on official finishes of 2nd, 5th, 14th, 18th, and 24th. Bridgewater was second with 71 points. The other teams, in order, were: Loyola (3rd–109); Mount St. Mary's (4th–119); Johns Hopkins (5th–127); Catholic (6th–157); American (7th–160); Lynchburg (8th–186); Gallaudet (9th–224); Washington (10th–238); and Towson State (11th–241).

I remember . . . "During the fall of 1959, I remember that we called ourselves the Seven Psychos. Bob Jenkins, Derek Stryker, Warren Orndorff, Johnnie Blanton, and me–and a couple that I can't think of right now. We had not done well in the Little Eight meet, which we were supposed to win. We thought it was pretty good to come back and take the Mason-Dixon meet. That was a big shock to everyone. We took a great pleasure in presenting the trophy to Homer. With all of the stars gone from the Roanoke College team that year, I think most Mason-Dixon coaches thought that, finally, it was their turn to win the title. I don't think we ever told Homer, but I don't know that we were taking things seriously. We had been able to loaf through the season and do O. K. in competition with other teams. So after the Little Eight defeat, we just got together and talked about what was going on. We decided that we were a better team than what we showed when Bridgewater beat us in the Little Eight meet. We felt like we had really let Homer down. I don't ever think that I had seen Coach Bast as upset as he was. We knew we weren't putting out the effort we needed to win. And I think that after that meeting, we realized that it was pretty disrespectful to Homer not to try our best. We had really let him down."

Dr. Wayne Wilson

I remember . . . "Let me tell you a story about that meet. We drove up to Chestertown with Homer. I remember that Wayne Wilson and I wore golf hats. Homer called us his two cool cats. We had no pressure on us. Homer didn't put any pressure on us. We were just going up there to run a race and do as well as we could. We definitely weren't expected to win. Because we had been beaten in the Little Eight meet. Homer took me aside just before the race began and gave me a pep talk. So our team went out, not favored to win at all, and won the meet. But we didn't know who had won for some time after the race was over. The confusion, we learned, came from Johnnie Blanton wearing his number upside down. We had to figure out where he came in. Johnnie finished in 25th place, and that place was critical to our winning or not. We are sitting in the locker room, with no idea of what the team scores were, when Homer comes in and says, "Fellows, we might have won this meet. It all depends on where Johnny Blanton finished." After the meet, Homer took a train back because he was preaching somewhere the next day in the Staunton area. And the team celebrated. We went out on the town and ended up at the Sigma Chi house at the University of Maryland. We didn't know anyone there, but we walked in around 3:00 a.m. and everyone there was arm wrestling on the floor for some unknown reason. And I dropped and broke a bottle of blackberry brandy in downtown D. C. and it was just crazy. We had a ball. Let me tell you one more story. It was about what the team did when they arrived back on campus after the Mason-Dixon win – the meet we weren't supposed to win. I told you that Homer left by train to preach in Staunton. The runners had the station wagon. Many of the athletes lived in that area, so we stayed overnight before driving back the next morning. Somebody got the idea to get some fireworks. So we did. We drove into the College and parked around 10:00 p.m. in back of the Sections. We went into the quadrangle and set up the fireworks, then lit them and ran back to the station wagon. There was a bit of lag time before the fireworks went off. So the team got into the station wagon. I think Derek Stryker and I were up on top on the luggage rack. I was carrying the Mason-Dixon trophy. And we drove in the entrance from High Street just as the fireworks were starting to go off. The sky was lit up. It was

Sunday night with lots of people studying in the dorms. Many of the students came flooding out of the dorms to see what was going on. So we drove in and everyone gathered around the station wagon. Some apparently had heard that we had won. I am up on top of the wagon with this trophy and everyone was screaming and yelling around us. It went on and on. Some began yelling at me–speech, speech. So I stood up on the top of the wagon and simply yelled, "We kicked their ass." Just at that point, I looked down into the crowd and Don Sutton is looking up at me. We knew that fireworks were against the law in Salem. But Don let it all go. He thought that was great sport. We created our own celebration, you know. I'll never forget that night."

Dr. Bob Jenkins

Chapter Sixteen

THE 1960 CROSS COUNTRY SEASON

The 1960 cross country team was the last athletic team Homer Bast would coach. Elwood Fox took over the coaching responsibilities the next year.

This year's team had only three returning lettermen–Captain Bob Jenkins, Derek Stryker, and Warren Orndorff. Some of the newcomers who tried out for the team early in the fall were Doug Wickham, Richie Donnelly, Ed Strong, Jim Meyers, Ed Sala, Denny Mahoney, and Bob Stauffer. Other runners would be Mic Hamaker and Howard Beck, veterans of last year's season, and Gene Griffiths and Rich Waltz were expected to provide some depth and experience.

Roanoke College vs. Lynchburg
October 10, 1960
Lynchburg, Virginia
Distance: 3.2 Miles

Team Scores: Lynchburg College (L)–21
Roanoke College (R)–40

The first meet of the season would be a real test for Roanoke. The team traveled to Lynchburg on a clear and warm day to run the Hornets on their 3.2-mile course.

Bob Jenkins was in good early-season form, winning the meet with a time of 17:07.4. But two Lynchburg runners tied for second, and two more tied for the fourth position, before Richard Waltz finished in 6th place. When Lynchburg's Earl Haga finished 7th, being his team's fifth runner, Lynchburg won the meet by a score of 21 to 40. It was the worst Roanoke defeat in a dual cross country meet since Lynchburg beat Roanoke by 24 points on October 12, 1951.

Mickey Hamaker was 10th, Gene Griffiths 11th, and Ed Strong 12th. Then came Warren Orndorff (14th), Richard Donnelly (15th), and Ed Sala (16th) in the field of 24 runners.

Roanoke College vs. Virginia Polytechnic Institute
October 15, 1960
Salem, Virginia
Distance: 3.05 Miles

Team Scores: Virginia Polytechnic Institute (VPI)–23
Roanoke College (R)–32

Three teams–V. P. I., Norfolk Division of William and Mary, and Roanoke–competed on the Salem course on a beautiful October day. For Roanoke, it was two meets in one. The first competition was between the Maroons and V. P. I. The second meet involved Roanoke and the Norfolk Division of William and Mary. A third set of team scores would be determined between V. P. I. and the Norfolk team.

In the V. P. I.-Roanoke meet, Castagnola of V. P. I. won easily with at time of 15:39.3. He was followed by Roanoke's Bob Jenkins (2nd, 16:03) and Doug Wickham (3rd, 16:54). V. P. I. won the team competition, however, when its next four runners finished in the 4th through 7th positions. Then came all eight of the remaining Roanoke runners. Don Ballou was 8th, Mickey Hamaker 9th, Ed Strong 10th, Richard Donnelly 11th, Richard Waltz 12th, Warren Orndorff 13th, Ed Sala 14th, and Derek Stryker 15th.

Roanoke lost the meet by a score of 32 to 23. The second of the simultaneous meets, however, would be more successful.

Roanoke College vs. Norfolk Division of William and Mary
October 15, 1960
Salem, Virginia
Distance: 3.05 Miles

Team Scores: Roanoke College (R)–26
Norfolk William and Mary–29

In the meet with Norfolk Division of William and Mary, Bob Jenkins finished far in front. Doug Wickham took 2nd, Don Ballou was 6th, Mickey Hamaker came in 7th, and Ed Strong secured the Roanoke win by finishing 10th. Others who finished the race for Roanoke included Richard Donnelly (11th); Richard Waltz (13th); Warren Orndorff (15th),

Ed Sala (16th); and Derek Stryker (18th).

Roanoke won the meet by just three points, placing men in the 1st, 2nd, 6th, 7th, and 10th places. The team scores were 26 to 29.

The third competition of the day was won by V. P. I. They beat Norfolk Division of William and Mary, 26 to 29.

Virginia AAU Championships–Senior Division
October 22, 1960
Williamsburg, Virginia
Distance: 4.0 Miles

Team Scores: Virginia Military Institute (VMI)–15
College of William and Mary (WM)–50

Non-Scoring:Fort Lee (FL)
Little C (LC)
Norfolk Division of William and Mary (NWM)
Roanoke College (R)
University of Richmond (UR)

Homer did not send a complete team of five runners to the State A. A. U. meet in Williamsburg. Neither did two other club teams, along with Norfolk Division of William and Mary and the University of Richmond. The only two scoring teams, therefore, were Virginia Military Institute and the College of William and Mary.

Bob Jenkins, the Maroons' only entry in the meet, ran an excellent time of 22:09 to finish in the 3rd position. George Young of Fort Lee was 1st in 20:41.5, with Lew Stieglita of the Little C Club in second. Young was the United States 3000-meter steeple chase champion in track.

The team winner of the meet was V. M. I., who scored a perfect 15. Second was the College of William and Mary, who had 50 points.

Meet organizers also held a three-mile freshman race. Roanoke's Doug Wickham ran very well, finishing second.

Roanoke College vs. College of William and Mary
November 29, 1960
Williamsburg, Virginia
Distance: 4.0 Miles

Team Scores: College of William and Mary (WM)–27
Roanoke College (R)–28

On November 29, 1960, Homer took a small team of just seven runners to Williamsburg to renew the rivalry of the past three years with the College of William and Mary. He really didn't know what to expect concerning the final score. His team was nowhere near as strong as it was just a couple of years ago, although William and Mary had a thin squad as well.

Bob Jenkins continued to run well. On this cloudy, cold, and wet day, he ran in front for most of the race, pulling out to a 30-second lead over his teammate, Doug Wickham, before winning in a time of 22:24. Doug Wickham finished in second place, running 22:58. William and Mary athletes then took the 3rd, 4th, and 5th spots before Bob Eldridge finished in 6th place. William and Mary came across the line in 7th and 8th positions. Then the Maroons' four and fifth runners–Warren Orndorff and Ed Strong–took the 9th and 10th places, respectively. Richard Donnelly (11th) and Dick Waltz (13th) of Roanoke College then finished out the team performance.

William and Mary's men had taken the 3rd, 4th, 5th, 7th and 8th positions for a total of 27 points. Roanoke took the 1st, 2nd, 6th, 9th, and 10th spots for 28 points.

Little Eight Conference Cross Country Championships
November 5, 1960
Bridgewater, Virginia
Distance: 3.0 Miles

Team Scores: 1st–Bridgewater College (B)–36
2nd–Roanoke College (R)–54
2nd–Lynchburg College (L)–54
4th–Norfolk Division of William and Mary (NWM)–76
Randolph-Macon College–Non-Scoring

In the Little Eight meet on November 5, Roanoke College's Bob Jenkins was favored to win the individual title. The odds were in favor of Bridgewater for the team win.

Running on its own course, the Bridgewater Eagles took first place by placing its men in the 2nd, 3rd, 8th, 11th, and 12th positions for 36 points. In an unusual tie, Roanoke and Lynchburg each scored 54 points for second place. The Norfolk Division of William and Mary totaled 76. Randolph-Macon College did not enter enough men to score.

As expected, Bob Jenkins won the race in a time of 15:49.4. Doug Wickham placed 6th in 16:14.0. Other Maroons included Don Ballou (13th, 16:34); Derek Stryker (17th,

16:51); Bob Eldridge (19th, 16:55); Warren Orndorff (25th, 17:39; and Ed Strong (27th, 17:52).

Roanoke College vs. Mount St. Mary's College
November 10, 1960
Salem, Virginia
Distance: 3.1 Miles

Team Scores: Roanoke College (R)–28
Mount St. Mary's College (MSM)–29

Over the last few years under Coach Bast, the Roanoke team had never lost to Mount St. Mary's College. Most believed that the visitors from Emmitsburg, Maryland, would be the favorites this time around.

At meet time, the weather was cool and the skies clear. The Maroons' Bob Jenkins had no trouble moving to the front and separating himself by some 30 seconds from the other runners. The few students and faculty who witnessed the finish saw Jenkins romp to a win in a time of 15:51. Then they cheered when Derek Stryker, who had not run particularly well this year, came onto the track to finish by himself in 3rd place. The Maroons then took the 7th through 11th places–Don Ballou, 7th; Ed Strong, 8th; Richard Donnelly, 9th; Warren Orndorff, 10th; and Bob Eldridge, 11th–to give Roanoke College a one-point win, 28 to 29.

Virginia State Cross Country Championships
November 14, 1960
Hampden-Sydney, Virginia

Freshman Divison–2.8 Miles

1st–College of William and Mary (WM)–25
2nd–Virginia Polytechnic Institute (VPI)–55
3rd–Virginia Military Institute (VMI)–63
4th–University of Richmond (UR)–108
5th–Bridgewater College (B)–136

Varsity Division–3.9 Miles

1st–Virginia Military Institute (VMI)–25

2nd–Virginia Polytechnic Institute (VPI)–61
3rd–College of William and Mary (WM)–90
4th–Bridgewater College (B)–92
5th–Lynchburg College (L)–104
6th–Norfolk Division of William and Mary (NWM)–167
7th–Washington and Lee University (WL)–182
Hampden-Sydney (HS)–Non Scoring
Roanoke College (R)–Non-Scoring

As he did in the A. A. U. Championships earlier in the season, Coach Bast did not enter a full team in the State Cross Country Championships on November 14. The team's only entry was their top runner, Bob Jenkins.

In the Varsity Division, 65 individuals finished the race. Jenkins again ran well, finishing in 4th place behind Castagnola of V. P. I., Carlton of V. M. I., and Braithwait of V. M. I. Jenkins' time was 19:47, only about 30 seconds in back of Castagnola's winning time of 19:16.6.

The College of William and Mary took the freshman division race by scoring 25 points. They were followed by V. P. I (55), V. M. I. (63), the University of Richmond (108), and Bridgewater (136).

V. M. I. dominated the varsity division. Roanoke and Hampden-Sydney did not enter enough men to obtain a score; however, V. M. I. was first with 25 points, beating V. P. I. (2nd, 61); College of William and Mary (3rd, 90); Bridgewater (4th, 92); Lynchburg (5th, 104); Norfolk Division of William and Mary (6th, 167); and Washington and Lee (7th, 182).

Mason-Dixon Cross Country Championships
November 19, 1960
Bridgewater, Virginia
Distance: 3.0 Miles

Team Scores:

1st–Bridgewater College (B)–4, 7, 11, 12, 21, 55
2nd–Lynchburg College (L)–8, 10, 14, 19, 37, 88
3rd–American University (A)–3, 17, 20, 23, 35, 98
4th–Johns Hopkins University (JH)–2, 13, 24, 26, 33, 98
5th–Loyola University (LOY)–1, 9, 16, 31, 48, 105
6th–Roanoke College (R)–5, 18, 29, 40, 42, 134
7th–Gallaudet College (G)–22, 30, 32, 34, 38, 156

8th–Towson State Teacher's College (T)–15, 27, 47, 52, 57, 198
9th–Mount St. Mary's College (MSM)–6, 49, 50, 51, 58, 214
Catholic University (C)–Disqualified from Team Scoring

Coach Bast, in the hospital at the time, was unable to make the trip to Bridgewater for the Mason-Dixon meet. But November 19 was a clear, dry, and warm day to run.

It was a tough day for most of the Roanoke athletes. Bob Jenkins, the team's star, was expected to contend for the individual title. Instead, he finished in 6th place with a time of 16:09. Rick Frampton of Loyola won the race with a new course record of 15:28.5. That beat the old record of 15:38 set by John Madison of Catholic.

The next Roanoke finisher was Don Ballou, who was 19th with a time of 16:45. His teammates were well down the list. Bob Eldridge was 31st; Ed Strong was 42nd; Richard Donally was 44th; Derek Stryker was 46th; and Warren Orndorff finished 49th.

As a team, Roanoke finished in sixth place. In Homer Bast's 14 years of coaching the school's cross country team, only once–in 1951, just after his year with the U. S. Navy in Alaska–had the team finished this low in the standings. In fact, the Maroons had won the Mason-Dixon meet eight times since 1948

Bridgewater won the championship trophy with a score of 55 points. Lynchburg was 2nd with 88 points, followed by American and Johns Hopkins (tied for 3rd, 98), Loyola (5th, 105), Roanoke (6th, 134), Gallaudet (7th, 156), Towson State (8th, 198), and Mount St. Mary's (9th, 214). Catholic participated, but was disqualified and received no points.

Roanoke College vs. Hampden-Sydney College
November 21, 1960
Hampden-Sydney, Virginia
Distance: 3.0 Miles

Team Scores: Roanoke College (R)–19½
Hampden-Sydney College (HS)–47½

Roanoke's final dual meet of the year came on November 21 at Hampden-Sydney. The season thus far had not been very successful for the Maroons. They had lost to Lynchburg and V. P. I. before winning against Norfolk Division of William and Mary and Mount St. Mary's. In the larger meets, Homer had not taken a full team to either the Virginia A. A. U. Championships, nor to the Virginia State Championships. The squad had finished second in the Little Eight meet and sixth in the Mason-Dixon Championships. It would be good if the team could finish strong against Hampden-Sydney.

Bob Jenkins, running one of his best races of the season, had no difficulty winning the meet. In fact, he beat Doug Wickham by about half a minute. Jenkins' time was 15:59.5, which was a new course record. Wickham followed in 16:35. After Bob Eldridge tied with a Hampden-Sydney runner for third, Richard Waltz finished 6th and Ed Strong 7th to complete the team scoring. Don Ballou (8th), Warren Orndorff (9th), Howard Beck (10th), and Richard Donnelly (11th) were the other Roanoke runners.

The team score was Roanoke, 19½, and Hampden-Sydney, 47½. The meet marked the end of a successful coaching career for Homer Bast. Some of the Maroons–Derek Stryker, Bob Eldridge, Richard Donnelly, Ed Strong, and Dick Waltz–did compete a couple of weeks later in the First Annual Christmas Season 10,000-Meter Road Race in Buena Vista, Virginia, but that race was an open event and gave no team scores.

For the next few years, beginning with the 1961 season, Elwood Fox (formerly the soccer coach) took over the coaching of the cross country team. Since 1947, Homer Bast had become–and still is–the most successful coach in Roanoke College history.

Chapter Seventeen

The Teams and Individuals of 1957-58, 1958-59, and 1959-60

Homer Bast retired from track coaching after the 1956-57 season. Elwood Fox, a staff member of the Physical Education Department and the school's soccer coach, took over the leadership of the team. Elwood was a graduate of Roanoke College, and quite a good football player in his day. He had joined the College staff in 1946, the same year as Homer was hired to teach history, and was a personable individual with a good sense of humor; however, he admitted that he knew little about track and field athletics. On the other hand, he inherited a team that still had a lot of talent left over from Homer's final year. It took a few more seasons, in fact, before Fox's teams began to be runners-up in Little Eight or Mason-Dixon competition.

Here, we will use a condensed format to trace the next three teams following Homer Bast's tenure. Please remember that we are writing mostly about the athletes who were with Homer Bast at least one year.

The 1957-58 Indoor Season

January 24, 1958
The Philadelphia Inquirer Games
Philadelphia, Pennsylvania

Roanoke's team of Dick Engel, Bill Davis, freshman George Bopp, and Tom Sitton entered the mile relay, finishing an extremely close second to a team from Rhode Island College from Providence, Rhode Island. The winning time was 3:31.4, with the Roanoke team running 3:31.5. Westchester State and Brown were third and fourth, respectively, in the race. The Roanoke time set a new school record. The old record, set last year, was 3:34.4.

The Inquirer Games was the first of two competitions for the team this weekend. The athletes then went to Washington, D. C. for the next night's Evening Star Games.

January 25, 1958
The Washington Evening Star Games
Washington, D. C.

In the Evening Star Games, Roanoke entered five events. In the Mason-Dixon Sprint Medley Relay, a team (names unknown) finished a narrow second to winner Catholic University. Catholic's time was 3:39.6. Both teams broke Roanoke's year-old record by some two seconds.

Catholic also won the Class "A" mile relay in a time of 3:34.7. Roanoke's Russ Palochko, Scott McKinney, Dick Engel, and Bill Davis finished third. No Roanoke time was given.

The Bast teams, and even some coached by Elwood Fox, often went to the Washington Evening Star Games. On the right is Tom Sitton, one of the best quarter milers that Coach Bast coached.

For the Class "B" and Intercollegiate Mile Relay competition, Roanoke ran Russ Palochko, Scott McKinney, Dick Engel, and Bill Davis. They finished third behind two unspecified teams. Their time was not provided.

Roanoke also entered the Intercollegiate Two-Mile Relay. Howard Light, Wayne Wilson, Tom Sitton, and George Jocher finished in second place behind LaSalle College. LaSalle's time was 8:15.3. Roanoke's time is unknown.

In the A. A. U. One-Mile Handicap Race, Roanoke again placed second. The Maroons' team of Bill Davis, Russ Palochko, an unknown runner, and George Bopp finished close behind the men from the Baltimore Olympic Club. The Roanoke foursome, with a 15-yard handicap for the race, ran an excellent 3:28 with Bopp closing fast to overtake the Baltimore Cross Country Club, which finished third.

February 8, 1958
Virginia Military Institute Winter Relays
Lexington, Virginia

No team scores were given in this large and popular meet. Competing were teams from the University of North Carolina, Duke University, Georgetown University, the Naval Academy, and many other large schools along the east coast.

Roanoke placed third in the Distance Medley Relay behind winner University of Maryland and second-place Naval Academy. Georgetown ran a time of 8:10.0; however, Roanoke's time and names of its runners were not recorded. The *Brackety-Ack*, in an article published prior to the meet, said that Pete Wise, Tom Sitton, Howard Meincke, and George Jocher would be entered in this race.

Although no results were published, the *Brackety-Ack* also said: "George Bopp, Dick Engel, Russ Palochko, and Tom Sitton are probably entrants in the 880-Yard Relay, with Bopp and Sitton coming back later to team up with Bruce Johnston and Howard Meincke to run the Sprint Medley Relay. Meincke, Warren Light, Wayne Wilson, and George Jocher will take the legs in the Four-Mile Relay, and the Shuttle Hurdle Relay will close out the evening with Johnston, Lou Dapas, Dick Emberger, and Vin Ahearn the Maroon entry in this event."

After the meet, a writer for the *Brackety-Ack* also noted the following: "The Maroons did manage to pick up three thirds–in the Distance Medley, the Sprint Medley, and the Shuttle Hurdle Relay. Considering that it took Navy, Georgetown, and Maryland to beat us, each a perennial track power and each with indoor training facilities, the Maroons didn't do too badly at that."

February 15, 1958
Little Eight Championships
Lexington, Virginia

For the Little Eight Championships, Norfolk Division of William and Mary was expected to bring the strongest team that would challenge the powerful Roanoke squad. The school, in fact, had a number of top athletes. Roanoke was the defending champion, however, and most individuals believed that the Maroons would win the title this year.

Roanoke won the battle of first places, taking 7 of the 12 events. Norfolk William and Mary won the other 5.

Newcomer George Bopp finished first in both the 60-yard dash (:06.6) and the 440-yard dash (53.7). Howard Meincke won the mile in a good indoor time of 4:27.7, and then ran 10:12.8 to win the two-mile race. Bruce Johnston also won two events, taking the high hurdles in :09.1 and the lows in :07.7. The only other win for the defending Little Eight champions was provided by the mile relay team. Dick Engle, Howard Light, Pete Wise, and Tom Sitton were timed in 3:35.6. Unofficial splits were :53.4 for Engel, :55.0 for Light, :54.5 for Wise, and :52.8 for Sitton.

Second-place finishers for Roanoke included Wise (880, 2:07.0); Jocher (two-miles, 10:15.0); Jack Dempsey (broad jump, 21'0"); Vin Ahearn and Dick Stauffer (tie, high jump, 5'9¾"); and Frank Vest (tie, pole vault, height unknown). Taking third places were Howard Light (440-yard dash, :54.1); George Jocher (mile run, 4:42.0); and Jim O'Mahony (broad jump, 20'11½"). Fourth places went to Bill Davis (880-yard run, 2:14.0); Warren Light (mile, 4:44.0); Wayne Wilson (two-mile run, 10:50.0); Vin Ahearn (high hurdles, no time given); and Bob Upton (shot, no distance given).

Tom Sitton sat out the meet after his bout with measles. He was the defending champion in the 440-yard dash.

Roanoke placed first in the meet with a total of 64½ points. Norfolk Division of William and Mary easily took second (51½ points), followed by Hampden-Sydney (9) and Randolph-Macon (3).

February 21, 1958
Mason-Dixon Conference Championships
Lexington, Virginia

The Maroons were able to defend their Mason-Dixon Indoor Championship by beating second-place Bridgewater College by 50 points. Roanoke scored 70½ points and Bridgewater 20½. Other teams included Hampden-Sydney (3rd, 20 points); Mount St. Mary's (4th, 18 points), and Lynchburg (5th, 3 points).

Howard Meincke of Roanoke was the night's outstanding performer. He set a new Mason-Dixon and field house record of 1:59.8 in the 880-yard run. In the same race, Pete Wise turned in his team's second-fastest indoor time of the season in pushing Meincke to his record.

Junior George Jocher was the only double winner of the night. He won the mile in 4:37.5 and the two-mile race in 10:29.3.

Speedy George Bopp won the 60 in :06.6 and finished 4th in the 440-yard dash. Tom Sitton won the 440-yard race in :54.0, and ran third in the 60-yard dash. Bruce Johnston did not compete in the meet, allowing Lou Dapas to win the high hurdles in :09.7. Dapas was also third in the shot put, then tied with Frank Vest for first place in the pole vault. They each cleared 11'0".

Dick Stauffer tied for first in the high jump, clearing the bar at 5'10½". The other first place was taken by the Maroon mile relay team of Bill Davis, Dick Engel, George Bopp, and Tom Sitton. Their winning time was 3:36.5. Cliff Shaw picked up a tie for first in the broad jump, with a leap of 21'4¾", with Jim O'Mahony taking second and Jack Dempsey finishing third.

Others who scored for Roanoke included Warren Light (3rd, mile); Wayne Wilson (4th, two-mile run); Vin Ahearn (4th, 70-yard high hurdles, 2nd, low hurdles, and tie for 3rd, high jump).

The 1957-58 Outdoor Season

From this point on, we will look at the scores of the meets and how each of the individuals from the 1956-57 team, Coach Bast's final year of track coaching, managed to perform. We begin with a special trip south.

April 3, 1958
Roanoke College vs. Florida State University
Tallahassee, Florida

Team Scores: Florida State University–79
Roanoke College–43

The streak had to end. Until this day, Roanoke had not lost a dual or triangular meet since Davidson College beat them in the spring of 1953. Recognized as one of the strongest teams in the southeast, Florida State recently won the team title in the Florida Relays in Gainesville. During the early weeks of the 1958 season, they also won the champion's trophy at the Coliseum Relays in Montgomery, Alabama, and defeated Furman University easily in a dual meet.

Here are the more outstanding performances by Roanoke athletes:

Howard Meincke–In the best race of his career, Howard set a new school record in the mile by running the race in 4:24.5, placing second. His time took two-tenths of a second off the second oldest record on the Roanoke books–a 4:24.7 time set by Alvin Smith in 1949.

Mile Relay Team–Three of the four mile relay team members were on the 1956-57 team. Pete Wise, Howard Light, Tom Sitton, and George Bopp (new to the team this year) ran an excellent early-season time of 3:24.5 to win the event.

Dick Emberger–Dick cleared the bar at 6'0" to win the high jump. The sophomore star also placed third in the high hurdles and jumped 11'6" for third in the pole vault.

Bruce Johnston–Bruce won the 120-yard high hurdles in :15.8 and also placed second in the 220-yard low hurdles.

Outdoor track team in 1958.
Sitting (L to R): Vincent Ahearn, Pete Wise, Dick Emberger, Cliff Shaw, Scott McKinney, and Frank Vest.
Kneeling (L to R): Bill Davis, Howard Meincke, Russ Palochko, George Bopp, Tomas Sitton, and Geoge Jocher.
Standing (L to R): Dick Stauffer, Jim O'Mahony, Wayne Wilson, Warren Light, Bob Upton, John Hylton, and Dick Lewis. The Co-Captains of the team were Howard Light (left insert) and Bruce Johnston (right insert). Other trackmen, not pictured, were Johnnie Blanton, Lou Dapas, John Snyder, Dick Engel, Jack Dempsey, and Bill Driscoll.

Other Roanoke efforts included:

Tom Sitton–Tom placed third in the 440-yard dash.

George Jocher–In the two-mile run, George ran one of his best races since coming to Roanoke. His time was 10:09.5, placing him second in that event. His one-mile split was 5:02.0.

Jack Dempsey–Jack's distance in the broad jump was a respectable 21'7", good for second place.

Cliff Shaw–Third place in the broad jump went to Cliff, just two inches in back of Dempsey.

Dick Stauffer–Dick's jump of 5'10" brought him a second place in the high jump.

I remember . . . "I remember that trip to Florida State and Miami very well. When we left Salem, there was snow on the ground. Most of our workouts had been inside because of the weather. We were all bundled up. But when we reached Tallahassee, the weather was much warmer and those kids had been training for the past six months. And it was the first meet that we lost since 1953. Now, we didn't lose by very much. I still blame the loss on the fact that we just weren't prepared and in shape. Florida State had already had several meets and had, I believe, been their conference champion the year before. So they had some good, well-trained athletes. We went on down to Miami after the Florida State meet, and we beat them by a wide margin. It was a good trip."

Bruce Johnston

I remember . . . "Another trip I remember was in 1958. We went to Florida State and Miami on the spring trip. I got up on the morning of the Florida State meet covered with measles. It was so bad that they had to put me in the Florida State infirmary. And they left me there. Whenever I talk with Mary Jane Bast these days, she brings that up. She would say, 'We hated so much leaving you there.' But it didn't turn out so bad. My girlfriend was spending her spring break with her freshman-year roommate in Tampa, where the roommate's family lived. I got out of the hospital and, since I was still on spring break, hitch-hiked to Tampa. And I spent a week with my girlfriend."

Frank Vest

I remember . . . "I didn't get to go on the spring break trip to Florida State and Miami. That was the year when I had the measles. Dr. Smiley was our team and school doctor. He had that old nurse who would paint your throat with mercurochrome. The infirmary was in a little white building. So I had to stay home for that trip."

Wayne Wilson

I remember . . . "I was one of the chauffeurs on the trip we took to Florida. I think they paid us something like five cents per mile."

Warren Light

I remember . . . "We went to Florida State to run in the spring of 1958. I remember that the two teams probably had a total of 20 false starts in the 220 that day. I don't think there was any rule that disqualified you for false starting. Sometimes an athlete would jump and at other times the gun would mis-fire."

Dick Engel

I remember . . . "On the Florida State trip, they gave us liver for our training meal (or perhaps the meal after the meet). Most of the guys didn't like liver and they said they couldn't eat that meat. Even so, they couldn't cut it because the school didn't give them any knives. So that time, I had to reach into my own pocket just to give them something decent to eat. I think I gave each one a dollar and a quarter. Actually, that was a substantial sum of money in those days. We had 15 to 20 kids, at least, with us on the trip. During our later winning years, there were times when we would take five or six cars on a trip. And many times, we didn't have the college station wagons. We often had to take student cars. I would ask if anyone wanted to take their own cars. Surprisingly, a lot of them volunteered. I told them that I would always give them gas and oil. That's all I could do. On those spring meets, they were eager to go. On occasion, a student would want to go home to see a girl friend or family. But in general, they went with us and had a pretty good time. Many had never been away from home except to come to Salem. Howard Light told me that our spring trips were the most distances away from home he had ever been. He and Bruce Johnston were Roanoke boys and had really never been away from Roanoke. So it was an education for the boys. They had an opportunity to see the country and see some other schools and sometimes I would take them by, for example, the University of Georgia campus to let them see what it looked like. And they enjoyed seeing those schools and comparing them to the small Roanoke College campus. And if there was a place we were passing that was of historical significance, we'd stop by to take a look."

Homer Bast

April 5, 1958
Roanoke College vs. the University of Miami
Miami, Florida

Team Scores: Roanoke College–72
University of Miami–45

Left Photo: Six members of the 1957-58 outdoor track team were (L to R) Howard Meincke, George Jocher, Dick Engel, Dick Emberger, Tom Sitton, and Pete Wise.
Right Photo: Tom Sitton (L) and Pete Wise (R) were two excellent 440-yard dash men in 1957-58.

Just two days later, Roanoke met the University of Miami in Miami, Florida. The Maroons, smarting from the rare loss to Florida State, defeated Miami by a score of 72 to 45. In doing so, they won 7 of the 13 events.

Outstanding performances by Roanoke athletes included:

Dick Engel–In the 220-yard dash, Dick placed only third; however, his time was :21.5, only three-tenths of a second in back of first. The time was especially good because it came in just the second meet of the year. It would have been a school record, but George Bopp finished in 1st place, running :21.2, which beat the old record of :21.7 set by George Gearhart.

Pete Wise–In the sunny warmth of Miami, Pete ran a :50.5 440-yard dash. The time was a new school record, beating the old mark of :51.0 set by Howard Light and Dick Lewis.

Howard Meincke–Howard coasted through a 1:58 half mile to win the event. The time was another record, beating Dick Lewis' 1:58.7. Howard also won the mile run in 4:42.0.

Bruce Johnston–Bruce ran :25.1 in the low hurdles to win the event, and also placed second in the 120-yard high hurdles with a time of :15.6. He also showed his speed by running :22.6 in the 220.

Dick Emberger–Dick tied the school high jump record, going 6'1". The record was held by Jay Jackson and Chris Rittman. Emberger also placed second in the pole vault with a height of 12'0", second in the low hurdles (:26.4), and third in the high hurdles (:15.7).

Mile Relay Team–The mile relay team of Dick Engel, Howard Light, George Bopp, and Tom Sitton continued to run well, recording a first-place time of 3:25.7. Splits included: Engel–:51.3; Light–:51.4; Bopp–:52.1; and Sitton–:51.1.

The team also had other notable performers:

Howard Light–Pushing first-place finisher Pete Wise, Howard Light finished his quarter-mile race in an excellent :50.7. His time, like Wise's, was also below the old school record.

Tom Sitton–Tom Sitton, usually a 440-yard dash man, ran the 880-yard run in 2:02.8 to finish second behind Meincke. He also ran a :10.2 100-yard dash.

Cliff Shaw–Cliff's broad jump of 20'9" brought him a second-place finish.

Jack Dempsey–Jack's broad jump was 20'8", good enough for third place.

Dick Stauffer–Second place in the high jump went to Dick Stauffer, who cleared 5'11".

Lou Dapas–Lou's 11'0" in the pole vault brought a third place in the event.

I remember . . . "When we went down to Miami, Ray Brown, Physics professor, drove down to see us run. When we got there, we checked into a motel. And Bruce Johnston–he and I had been friends from high school–walked into our room and there were bed bugs all over the place. Neither one of us had any money, but we said that we weren't going to stay there under those conditions. There were a couple of runners from Miami there, and they asked us to come on over to the fraternity house to stay with them. It was a brand new fraternity house and no one was there on the spring break. So we went over there and stayed. And Ray Brown let us use his car while we were there. And when we had a track meet at Roanoke College, it seemed like half of the faculty was down on the track helping to run it off. They timed and judged for Homer. It was a big affair."

Howard Light

I remember . . . "Well, I loved Coach Fox, who took over track from Homer in the 1957-58 season, when I was a senior. But he really didn't want to coach track. He would have told you that he didn't know much about the sport. My senior year, Bruce Johnston and I were Co-Captains, and Fox gave us a workout for the team to run one day. It was ungodly. He probably just took one of Coach Bast's sheets and not knowing any better, gave us a workout that was one for mid-season athletes."

Howard Light

I remember . . . "When Elwood Fox took over the team my senior year, he didn't know much about track and freely admitted that. He was more of a chaperone for us–there when we needed him. He sort of turned us loose. It was like, 'You know what you are doing. Just go do it.' "

Bruce Johnston

April 12, 1958
Roanoke College vs. Atlantic Christian College
Salem, Virginia

Team Scores: Roanoke College–113
Atlantic Christian College–12

The margin of victory in the win over Atlantic Christian–113 to 12–was one of the largest in the history of outdoor track at the College. The Maroons won 11 of 12 events, 10 of 12 second places, and 11 of the 12 third places. Among the outstanding performances were:

Bruce Johnston–Bruce won both hurdle events in times of :15.5 for the highs and :25.0 for the lows. Homer also tried him in the 100-yard dash and he was timed in a respectable :10.2 for second place. That time would come down to :09.9 by the end of the season.

Howard Meincke–Howard recorded a 4:29.0 to win the mile run.

Tom Sitton–Continuing to run well, Tom won the 440 in :50.6, only a tenth of a second off his school record.

Dick Engel–His time of :22.5 earned him second place in the 220.

Pete Wise–Peter ran 2:02.9 in the 880, winning that event.

Cliff Shaw–Cliff took first place in the broad jump with a distance of 21'7".

Dick Stauffer–His winning jump in the high jump was 5'10½".

Dick Emberger–Dick took first in the pole vault with a jump of 11'6".

There was no mention of the mile relay having been run in this meet; however, George Jocher says that in his personal notes, the team actually ran 3:28 and that he, himself, had a split of :51.7–the fastest 440 he had run at Roanoke College.

Bruce Johnston, Roanoke's outstanding hurdler and 100-yard dash man.

April 19, 1958
Roanoke College vs. Newport News Apprentice College
Salem, Virginia

Team Scores: Roanoke College–91½
Newport News Apprentice College–24½

April 19, 1958, was a sunny and warm day in Salem. There was almost no wind and the track was fast. It was a perfect day for a track meet.

Bruce Johnston–Bruce had an outstanding day. First, he ran the 100-yard dash in a school record-tying :09.9. The only other Roanoke athlete to run that fast was George Gearhart, who graduated in 1957. Bruce then won the 120-yard high hurdles in :15.4 and the 220-yard low hurdles in :24.6. His 15 points led all scorers.

Dick Emberger–Becoming a better athlete day-by-day, Dick was second in the high hurdles with a personal best :15.5 and also finished second in the low hurdles with a time of :25.8. He then tied for first place in the pole vault with Lou Dapas and Frank Vest, jumping 10'6".

Dick Engel–His second-place time in the 220 was :22.4. He also finished third in the 100.

Howard Meincke–Howard's 9:51.1 in the two-mile run was the best thus far among times from the 1958 Little Eight and Mason-Dixon Conferences, and was less than six seconds from his own school record.

Bill Driscoll–In the discus event, Bill won with a throw of 122'0".

Jack Dempsey–Jack won the broad jump with an excellent distance of 22'6½", just 2½" short of the school record held by Jim Nichols.

The mile relay was not counted toward the team score. Roanoke, however, did run an "exhibition" team for a time of 3:28.3. Coach Fox gave the splits as: Dick Lewis–:53.8; George Jocher–:51.8; Dick Engel–:51.5; and Howard Light–:51.2.

Roanoke won the meet easily, with a Maroon finishing first in 11 of the 12 events. The score was 91½ to 24½.

April 21, 1958
Roanoke College vs. Norfolk Division of William and Mary
Norfolk, Virginia

Team Scores: Roanoke College–66
Norfolk Division of William and Mary–56

The Roanoke team drove to Norfolk on April 20 for the next day's track meet with rapidly-improving Norfolk Division of William and Mary. There were several stars on the Norfolk team, including Ken Harmon and Gerald Tiedemann. Harmon was a top dash man with outstanding jumping ability. On this day, in fact, he would win the 100-yard dash in :09.8 and the 220-yard dash in :21.9. He also broad jumped an incredible 24'1½". No one in Virginia had ever jumped that far.

Tiedemann, the state's best shot and discus man, won the shot put with a throw of 52'1½". He also won the discus, although his toss of 119'6⅝" was not one of his best.

For Roanoke, several athletes did well:

Bruce Johnston–Again, Bruce ran :09.9 in the 100-yard dash to match the school record he had tied two days before, although he finished second to Harmon's :09.8. He also won both hurdles races–the highs in :15.0 and the lows in :23.6. The high hurdle time was a new school record, breaking the old mark of :15.1 set by Dave Foltz. The low hurdle time missed Foltz's record by a tenth of a second.

Howard Light–Howard seemed to be rounding into shape for his best event, the 440-yard dash. He placed first in the 440 with a time of :50.6. He would break the 50-second mark by the end of the year.

Dick Lewis–Dick ran 2:00.2 to win the 880. It was the first time in two years that Ronnie Drumwright of Norfolk Division, who finished second, had been beaten in the 880. The last person to beat him had been Roanoke's Peter Wise in Wise's freshman year.

George Jocher–His excellent time of 10:01.2 not only won the two-mile event, but in that race he pushed Howard Meincke to second place. Meincke already had won the mile in 4:29.8.

The team scores were the closest of the year for Roanoke. Roanoke won with 66 points, but Norfolk Division of William and Mary had 56.

I remember . . . "One thing I do remember is the Norfolk William and Mary meet. Actually, I was going to go home for the weekend, but instead came back to the campus with the team. I think we were on spring break. We were riding in the college station wagon. There were about seven or eight of us in the wagon coming back when we had a blowout of one tire. The car ran off the road, up an embankment, and down again. It just demolished the car. But all of us got out of the car unhurt, except for me. I wound up with a black eye. They cleaned up the eye. Some of our fraternity brothers came out and took us back to the campus. The next morning, I woke up in the dorm room and there, sitting in a chair in the room, was Don Sutton. He said, "I want you to get dressed. We are going to the doctor's office." I think the guy in the back seat, probably Jim O'Mahoney, and Bill Davis (one or the other) hit his head on the window on the side we flipped on . . . if he hadn't physically pulled his head away from the glass, I don't know what would have happened. I was in the second seat when we crashed, and the Sitton brothers were on each side of me. I was in the middle. When the roof caved in during the roll, the dome light was what caught me in the eye. I think the car had to be demolished. Either Dick Lewis or Phil Shaw was driving, I think. Maybe Bill Davis was in the car. I remember that just before the car left the road, I was reaching over to grab the wheel because the driver said he couldn't control the car after the tire blew."

Cliff Shaw

April 25, 1958
The Penn Relays
Philadelphia, Pennsylvania

The Penn Relays annually brought together some of the best track athletes in the world. This year, spectators would see a number of national stars: Greg Bell of Indiana, ranked first in the broad jump the previous year; Ron Delaney, senior from Villanova, the 1956 Olympic 1,500-meter champion; Glenn Davis of Ohio State, ranked first the past two years in the 400-meter hurdles and an Olympic team member; Bobby Morrow of Abilene Christian, the Olympic champion in the 100- and 200-meter races; Dave Sime, a senior at Duke, the world-famous sprinter; and many more.

Roanoke had tried several times to win the mile relay in its class at the Relays. The team had come away with two second-place finishes and one third. This year, however, it would be different.

Twelve teams entered the college-class one-mile relay–Cortland State Teachers, U. S. Merchant Marine Academy, Delaware, William and Mary, Connecticut Teachers, Lafayette, Virginia State, Catholic, Mount St. Mary's, Delaware State, Bucknell, and Roanoke. The Roanoke team was composed of Dick Engel, Captain Howard Light, Dick Lewis, and freshman George Bopp.

At approximately 5:33 p.m., the teams were brought to the starting line. Within a few minutes, the starter fired his gun to begin the race. Engel led off and, according to reports, ran a fast :51.5. He handed off to Howard Light, who in turn passed the baton to Dick Lewis. As Lewis came down the front stretch, the team was behind despite the fact that all three runners had recorded good times. Lewis passed off to George Bopp, a young runner of enormous talent. Bopp took off after the front runners and caught them by the start of the backstretch. "It was like he put his legs in overdrive," one person said. A stopwatch for split times caught Bopp's quarter as less than 49 seconds. He broke the tape in front, helping the team win the 12" bronze plaque and the four Maroons their own wreath plaques. The time for the winners was 3:25.1. Virginia State finished second, Connecticut Teachers third, U. S. Merchant Marines fourth, and Delaware fifth.

It is interesting to note that George Bopp, the anchor man, was only at Roanoke College this one year.

I remember . . . "I remember the Penn Relays, which were probably the highlight of my running career at Roanoke. It was in my senior year. We were all scared to death. Here we were, a small college, trying to run against some of the best teams around. They had you so well-organized, with chutes and everything. And finally, we got on the track to run. Dick Engel led us off, and I ran second. Dick Lewis took the third leg, and then there was George Bopp, who really won the race for us. When George took the baton, he was behind the lead runner by several yards. And he just took off. I don't know what his split was on that quarter, but he did a great job and crossed the line well ahead of the second-place team."

Howard Light

April 26, 1958
The Mason-Dixon Conference Relays
Washington, D. C.

With three first places in relay events, and two more in the field events, the Roanoke team dominated the Mason-Dixon relays on April 26.

Roanoke's team of Bill Davis, Johnnie Blanton, Howard Meincke, and George Jocher won the Distance Medley Relay in a time of 10:50.9. The Maroons' 440-yard relay team–Jim O'Mahony, Bruce Johnston, Dick Engel, and George Bopp–posted a new school record of :43.4 to win their event. The third relay won by Roanoke was the Four-Mile Relay. In that race, Wayne Wilson, Warren Light, Johnnie Blanton, and Dick Emberger, crossed the finish line in 19:34.6.

In individual events, Dick Emberger not only won the high jump (6'2"–a new school record) but also placed first in the pole vault (10'6"). Others from Roanoke who placed in the field events included Dick Stauffer, tied for second in the high jump; Jack Dempsey, who placed second in the broad jump; and Frank Vest, tied for second in the pole vault.

Other teams included American, Bridgewater, Catholic, Gallaudet, Hampden-Sydney, Loyola, Lynchburg, Mount St. Mary's, Randolph-Macon, and Washington. Under a conference rule, no official team scores were kept. The conference held that the competition was not a meet, but a relay invitational.

April 29, 1958
Roanoke College vs. Hampden-Sydney College
Hampden-Sydney, Virginia

Team Scores: Roanoke College–$73^5/_6$
Hampden-Sydney College–$48^1/_6$

Roanoke's final dual meet of the year came on April 29, 1958, with a trip to Hampden-Sydney, Virginia. The visitors would have little problem winning the meet. The final score was Roanoke, $73^5/_6$, and Hampden-Sydney, $48^1/_6$.

Although Dick Emberger did not compete, there were a number of impressive performances on this windless, track-heavy day at Death Valley.

Bruce Johnston–Again, Bruce was the star of a meet. He won the 100-yard dash in :10.0, along with the high hurdles (:15.2) and the low hurdles (:24.9).

Howard Light–Howard won the quarter-mile race in :50.5. That time tied the school record set on April 5 by Pete Wise.

Dick Engel–Dick won the 220-yard dash (:22.5) and also was second (:51.3) in the 440.

Howard Meincke–The best middle-distance and distance runner in the Little Eight Conference, Howard again set a new school record, finishing in 1:56.6 in the 880. He broke the old mark of 1:58.0 that he had set on April 5, 1958.

Bill Driscoll–A throw of 119'5½" gave Bill a win in the discus.

Cliff Shaw–Cliff won the broad jump with a leap of 21'1", beating Jim O'Mahony's 20'6".

Dick Stauffer–It was a good day for Dick Stauffer. He cleared 6'0" to gain a tie for first place in the high jump.

Frank Vest–Frank's 10'6" jump in the pole vault won the event.

May 2, 1958
Roanoke College vs. Bridgewater College
Salem, Virginia

On the day before the Bridgewater meet, tornadoes and soaking rains originated in Texas and traveled through the lower Mississippi Valley. The effects, especially flooding, were felt even in Virginia. As Coach Fox surveyed the track on the morning of the meet, he knew that the constant rainfall and a track that was virtually under water all the way around would prevent the Bridgewater meet from being held. The meet was cancelled early in the day.

Roanoke, therefore, had run its last dual meet of 1958. After the loss to powerful Florida State at the first of the season, the Maroons had won five straight meets, took first in the mile relay at the Penn Relays, and were clearly the class team in the Mason-Dixon Relays.

May 9, 1958
Little Eight Conference Championships
Hampden-Sydney, Virginia

There were many people on the Roanoke team who had broken or tied school records during the past season: Bruce Johnston (100 and high hurdles); George Bopp (220); Peter Wise (440); Howard Light (440); Howard Meincke (880 and mile); Dick Emberger (high jump); and the 440-yard relay team of Jim O'Mahony, Bruce Johnston, Dick Engel, and George Bopp. Now it was time to break more records in the Little Eight Conference Championships.

As of the end of the 1957 season, these were the Little Eight meet records. Roanoke this year had run better times in four of the events below (including the 440, 880, mile, and high hurdles):

Event	*Name*	*School*	*Mark*	*Year*
100	Wayne Spangler	Bridgewater	:09.6	1952
220	Wayne Spangler	Bridgewater	:21.5	1953
440	Dick Lewis	Roanoke	:50.7	1957
880	Ronnie Drumwright	Norfolk W&M	1:59.5	1957
Mile	Howard Meincke	Roanoke	4:26.5	1957
Two Miles	Dick Goodlake	Roanoke	9:58.2	1956
120 HH	Bruce Johnston	Roanoke	:15.1	1957
220 LH	Shifty Myers	Bridgewater	:24.3	1952
Mile Relay	Dick Engel, Howard Light, Dick Lewis, and Tom Sitton	Roanoke	3:26.5	1957
Shot	Gerald Tiedemann	Norfolk W&M	50'7¾"	1957
Discus	Jim FraserHampden-	Sydney	150'7"	1957
High Jump	Cenolate	Lynchburg	6'2¼"	1939
Broad Jump	Ken Harmon	Norfolk W&M	23'2¼"	1956
Pole Vault	Ray DeCosta	Roanoke	13'6"	1952

Roanoke was favored to win the meet, although their dual meet with the Monarchs of Norfolk Division of William and Mary had been close and they could surprise. Ken Harmon, Ronnie Drumwright, and Gerald Tiedemann gave them three of the best athletes in the meet.

Bruce Johnston–Dependable Bruce Johnston was almost a sure bet to win two, if not three, of his races. He finished first in the 100 with a time of 10:0, first in the high hurdles (:15.1), and first in the low hurdles (:24.5). The high hurdles time tied the existing meet record.

Howard Light–Howard set a new meet record by running the quarter mile in :50.5. He also participated on the winning mile relay, which set another meet record.

Howard Meincke–Although Howard finished in third place in the 880, he won the mile run in 4:27.9. That time was only 1.4 seconds off the meet record.

George Jocher–George did not win either of his events, but his times were excellent. He placed secon in the mile run, being timed in 4:28.0 and almost beating Meincke. In addition, he placed second in the two-mile run. His time in that event was 10:12.0.

Dick Emberger–Dick finished first in the high jump, clearing 6'0". He also tied for second in the pole vault.

The Mile Relay Team–The four-man team of Dick Engel, Dick Lewis, Howard Light, and George Bopp won the mile relay with a time of 3:24.7. The time was a new meet record. Roanoke men won 8 of the 14 events to take home the team trophy. The scores of the six teams in the meet were:

1st–Roanoke College–84
2nd–Norfolk Division of William and Mary–56
3rd–Bridgewater College–36½
4th–Hampden-Sydney College–17
5th–Randolph-Macon College–11½
6th–Lynchburg College–2

May 16-17, 1958
Mason-Dixon Conference Championships
American University in Washington, D. C.

Some 211 participants from 14 schools entered the Mason-Dixon Championships at American University. According to the local newspaper, the meet drew about 2,500 spectators.

Roanoke would be trying for its fifth straight victory in the meet. If the Maroons won, it would be the only team ever to win that many consecutive championships.

The meet, as usual, was held over a two-day period. Some events required athletes to qualify for Saturday's competition, and those qualifying races and field events were always held on Friday. Generally speaking, the more people your team qualified for the Saturday finals, the better chance the team had of winning the meet.

Here is how the Bast Boys–those who were with Homer Bast during his last year of coaching track–fared in the trials:

Discus	1st–Bill Driscoll–126'3/10"	
Shot	No Qualifiers	
Broad Jump	2nd–Jack Dempsey	
120 HH	First Heat:	1st–Bruce Johnston–:15.2
	Second Heat:	2nd–Dick Emberger
	Third Heat:	No Qualifiers
100	First Heat:	1st–Bruce Johnston–:10.1; 3rd–Dick Engel
	Second Heat:	1st–George Bopp (not on Bast team in 1956-57)

440	First Heat:	2nd–Dick Engel
	Second Heat:	1st–Howard Light–:51.0
	Third Heat	:No Qualifiers
220 LH	First Heat:	1st–Bruce Johnston–:25.0
	Second Heat:	1st–Dick Emberger–:25.6
	Third Heat:	No Qualifiers
220	First Heat:	1st–George Bopp (not on Bast team in 1956-57)
	Second Heat:	2nd–Howard Light
	Third Heat	:2nd–Dick Engel
880	First Heat:	No Qualifiers
	Second Heat:	2nd–George Jocher

On Saturday, Roanoke scored over twice the points as did the second-place team. In the 100-yard dash, Bruce Johnston fought through heavy gusts of wind to win in a slow time of :10.3, with George Bopp just behind in second.

Bopp came back to win the 220-yard dash. His time was :22.6. In fifth place was Dick Engel.

George Matthews of Catholic University, along with Howard Light and Dick Engle, both of Roanoke, put on the show of the day in the 440-yard dash. As the three came down the stretch, it was difficult to tell which one of the three might win. At the last moment, Matthews lunged for the tape and beat Light by inches. Engel was just behind. Mathews' time was :49.5, which beat Mike Favo's meet record time of :49.7, set in 1956. Howard Light's time was :49.9, a new Roanoke College record. Engle's excellent time of :50.2 marked his best quarter time and also broke the old 440 school record of :50.5.

Another great race was the mile run. Again, coming down the stretch, any of three men–Mike Halpin of Catholic, Howard Meincke of Roanoke, and George Jocher of Roanoke–could have won. Halpin was clocked in 4:24.7 to win, with Meincke at 4:24.8 and Jocher in third with 4:24.8.

Even with the winds, Bruce Johnston won both hurdle events. He was timed in :15.2 in the highs and :25.4 in the lows. Bruce became the first triple winner in the meet since the early 1940s.

Left Photo: Jack Dempsey poses for a broad jumping photograph in the handball cage of Alumni Gymnasium.
Right Photo: Co-Captains of the 1958 outdoor track team: Bruce Johnston (L) and Howard Light (R).

Dick Emberger finished fourth in the high hurdles and third in the low hurdles. In addition, he tied for third with Dick Stauffer in the high jump and finished in a tie for first at 11'0" in the pole vault. Frank Vest managed to pick up a tie for third in the pole vault.

Jack Dempsey won the broad jump with a distance of 21'10½", with Cliff Shaw in third place on a jump of 21'3¼.

The Roanoke mile relay team (names unknown) was beaten by Catholic University, who won with a meet record time of 3:21.6. George Jocher remembers being a part of that team, running his leg of the race in :52.6.

Finally, Bill Driscoll placed third in the discus with a good effort of 124'11½".

The final team scores were:

1st–Roanoke College–75½

2nd–Catholic University–35
3rd–Bridgewater College–31
4th–Mount St. Mary's College–11¼
5th–Loyola University–11
6th–Randolph-Macon College–10½
7th–Washington College–9
8th–American University–8½
9th–Johns Hopkins University–8
10th–Hampden-Sydney College–4
11th–Lynchburg College–4
12th–Gallaudet College–2½
13th–Western Maryland College–1¼
14th–Towson State College–1

The *Brackety-Ack* reported that 12 members of the team were awarded letters. They included George Jocher, Howard Meincke, Brendan Cavanagh, Tom Sitton, Joe Sitton, Pete Wise, Bill Davis, Dick Emberger, Jack Dempsey, Tommy Long, Don Ballou, and Dick Goodlake.

I remember . . . "Outstanding. That's how I would describe Howard Light. I think he did a good job in everything he did when he got out of Roanoke. When he was a runner, he would do anything you told him to do. If you told him to go run for an hour, he'd do it. He was a wonderful person to work with, and he had those qualities of leadership that you look for. The boys elected him Captain, along with Bruce Johnston, and he did a good job. They made wonderful Co-Captains."

Homer Bast

I remember . . . "I remember Don Ballou, and have a pretty good story about him. He also lived in Hildreth. We got $20 together one time after dark and bet him that he wouldn't run naked through the snow and touch the girls' dorm next door. He took the bet. What he didn't know, however, was that we called the girls' dorm and told them to look out their windows and turn on the outside lights when they saw Don coming. So there was Don, streaking through the snow with nothing on, and suddenly the lights came on and the girls began to yell."

Wayne Wilson

I remember . . . "I remember Howard Light well. He and I were pitchers on the college fast-pitch softball team. One year we went to the state championships in Richmond in late spring. Howard had a lot of 'stuff' on the ball. At the same time, I had more speed on the ball than he did. But, unlike Howard's ball, mine didn't move very much. At the tournament, we went all the way to the finals. The other team had this guy pitching by the name of Bob Saunders. Now, I have seen a lot of softball pitchers, but I have seen very few as good as he was. The game went into extra innings, and none of us seemed to be able to hit Saunders. Howard had pitched a couple of games and was getting tired, and they were starting to hit him a bit. So they put me in, hoping the change of speed might help. The other team finally beat us, but I think the final score was 1-0. Howard was a fabulous pitcher. He could just move that ball all over the place. That summer, between leaving Roanoke College and going to the Medical College of Virginia, I pitched for Salem Hosiery in a league there in Salem and Roanoke. Salem Hosiery actually created a job for me, such as mowing the grass around the company buildings. And I pitched for several years after that also. Then I displaced a disc in my neck and gave up the game."

Bill Driscoll

The 1958-59 Indoor Season

January 24, 1959
The Washington Evening Star Games
Washington, D. C.

The team's annual trip to the Evening Star Games resulted in two second-place finishes–one in the Mason-Dixon Sprint Medley Relay and the other in the Mile Relay. First, Coach Fox entered Tom Sitton (440), Dick Engel (220), Dick Emberger (220), and Howard Meincke (880) in the Sprint Medley Relay. The team finished second to Catholic University. No time was given.

Sitton, Bill Davis, Engel, and George Jocher also entered the Mile Relay. Montclair State won the race, Roanoke was second, and the College of William and Mary placed third. Again, no time was provided.

In the Distance Medley Relay, the Roanoke team did not place. The only split for this race was provided by George Jocher, who was timed for his 880-yard leg in 2:04.2.

The meet was marked by a superb performance by Bobby Morris, the 1956 Olympic sprint king from Abilene Christian College. Morris swept the 70-, 80-, and 100-yard sprints.

February 7, 1959
The V. M. I. Winter Relays
Lexington, Virginia

The *Brackety-Ack*, on the day before the Winter Relays was held, said that Roanoke would be entering six events:

Event	*Participants*
Sprint Medley Relay	Tom Sitton, Dick Engel, Russ Polochko, and Howard Meincke
Distance Medley Relay	Tom Sitton, Dick Goodlake, and George Jocher
Mile Relay	Bill Davis, Russ Polochko, Dick Engel, and Pete Wise
Two-Mile Relay	Mick Hamaker, Dick Emberger, Bill Davis, and Don Ballou
Shot	Bob Palm
High Jump	Dick Emberger

Very little information about the Maroons' participation in the individual events was available. *The Roanoke Times*, however, did note that Roanoke placed fourth in the Distance Medley Relay. Duke University (Bazemore, McNaker, Nourse, and Weiseger) won the event in 10:39.1 and were followed in order by Navy, Maryland, and Roanoke. The time of 10:39.1 set a new Winter Relays record, beating the old record of 10:50.0 set by the University of North Carolina in 1955 and tied by Roanoke College in 1957.

The only other details we know about the meet come from George Jocher, who has kept a personal diary of his own times over a number of years. He says that in this meet, he ran a mile in 4:42.0 (in the Distance Medley Relay) and an 880 in 2:06.0 (race unknown).

The *Brackety-Ack* also mentions another detail from the Distance Medley Relay. Apparently, Dick Goodlake ran his ¾-mile leg with a bad gash in his foot. He was spiked while reaching to get the baton. Even with the injury, he turned in a respectable 3:23.0 performance.

In an article from the *Roanoke Times*, the Associated Press reported that the University of Maryland's powerful track team won 7 of the 16 events and tied for first in another. The United States Naval Academy also did well, scoring wins in two events and finishing in a first-place tie in another. North Carolina and Duke, teams with two event wins each, were the next-best squads.

Maryland's Bjorn Anderson, who set a record in the pole vault with a leap of 13'9", won the award as the outstanding performer in field events. North Carolina's Wayne Bishop, who finished first in the two-mile race (9:30.1–a record) barely beat out Cary Weiseger of Duke for an award as outstanding runner of the meet.

For the day, seven records were shattered and three others tied.

February 15, 1959
The First Annual State Indoor Championships
Lexington, Virginia

The First Annual State Indoor Championships was held on February 15 at the V. M. I. field house in Lexington. Roanoke finished second in the meet, competing against much larger schools. Here are the final team scores:

1st–Virginia Military Institute–51
2nd–Roanoke College–21$\frac{1}{6}$
3rd–Virginia Polytechnic Institute–16
4th–University of Virginia–13
5th–College of William and Mary–12$\frac{5}{6}$
6th–Norfolk Division of William and Mary–11
7th–Hampden-Sydney College–5
8th–University of Richmond–1
9th–Washington and Lee University–0

V. M. I. was favored to win the meet. They were the reigning Southern Conference indoor track champions and more than doubled the score on Roanoke, the powerhouse team of the Little Eight schools.

The meet's high scorer (9$\frac{1}{3}$ points) was Roanoke's Dick Emberger. He won the high hurdles in :08.9, tied for first in the high jump at 6'3", and tied for third place in the pole vault. In the high jump, he barely missed clearing 6'5" on his final jump.

Jack Dempsey, with 22'5", placed third in the broad jump. First place, with 22'10", was taken by Jim Nichols, who was a Roanoke College track man before transferring to Virginia Tech. George Jocher, who led all the way until the last lap, was second in the mile run. Running a 4:32.1, he was beaten by Larry Williams of V. M. I. And Roanoke's team (names unknown) placed fourth in the mile relay.

Tom Sitton did very well in the 440-yard dash. He ran :51.9 to win the event. The time was a new school indoor record, beating his old mark of :52.7, set in 1957. It was also a new field house and state record.

The 1958-59 Outdoor Season

Before the start of the 1958-59 outdoor season, the College made a few changes on Alumni Field. Both the high jump and broad jump runways received a topping of asphalt. Alumni Field and many other track facilities Roanoke visited over the past few years were still using dirt or other non-asphalt surfaces on their runways and jumping areas. On the trip to Florida in 1958, the team saw the benefits of having solid, smooth surfaces when Dick Emberger cleared 6'2" in the high jump on Florida State's and Miami's asphalt jumping areas.

These three athletes were among the best runners that Homer Bast coached. L to R: Pete Wise, Howard Meincke, and Tom Sitton.

April 4, 1959
Roanoke College vs. Hampden-Sydney College
Hampden-Sydney, Virginia

Team Scores: Roanoke College–71⅔
Hampden-Sydney College–45⅓

The Maroons had little difficulty beating Hampden-Sydney College on April 4 on a sunny, cool day. The meet score, in fact, was 71⅔ to 45⅓.

It was an early-season meet with very few outstanding performances. The more notable efforts were by:

Dick Emberger–Dick Emberger ran a :15.1 to win the high hurdles. That time was just one tenth of a second off the school record. He placed second in the low hurdles, running :25.5, in a dead-heat finish with Chapman of Hampden-Sydney. Emberger also won the high jump with a height of 6'0", threw the discus 110'6" for second place, and tied for a win in the pole vault with 11'0".

Pete Wise–Pete won the 440-yard race in a time of :51.7.

Jack Dempsey–His jump of 20'0" was sub-par for him, but it was enough for him to win the broad jump.

Dick Emberger finished the meet with 18½ points. Roanoke's Howard Meincke, who won both the mile run (4:40.5) and the two-mile race (10:05.9), had 10 points. Dick Goodlake, with seconds in the 880 (2:05.2) and broad jump (19'0"), and thirds in the pole vault (10'0") and high jump (tie) had 7⅓ points.

April 14, 1959
Intrasquad Practice Meet
Salem, Virginia

The Maroons held an intrasquad practice meet on April 14. Here are the results:

Pole Vault	1st–Emberger and Goodlake–11'3"
440-Yard Dash	1st–Sitton–:51.1; 2nd–Davis–:51.5; 3rd–Engel–:52.0
100-Yard Dash	1st–Cavanagh–:10.5; 2nd–McKinney–:10.6; 3rd–Chesley–:10.6
120-Yard HH	1st–Ahearn–:17.4; 2nd–Orndorff; 3rd–Ballou
High Jump	1st–Emberger–6'1½"; 2nd–Clegg–5'9"; 3rd–Ahearn–5'7"

880-Yard Run	1st–Meincke–2:00.6; 2nd–Long–2:02.5; 3rd–Hamaker–2:07.2
220-Yard Dash	1st–Sitton–:22.5; 2nd–Cavanagh–:23.0; 3rd–Davis–:23.8
Two-Mile Run	1st–Meincke–10:14.9; 2nd–Jocher–10:16.1; 3rd–Reeves–11:36.0
180-Yard LH	1st–Ahearn–:21.7; 2nd–Engel–:21.9; 3rd–Ballou–:22.9
Broad Jump	1st–Emberger–21'10"; 2nd–Cavanagh–21'4"; 3rd–Goodlake–18'4"
440-Yard Relay	1st–Engel, Emberger, Cavanagh, Unknown Runner–:45.9

April 18, 1959
Roanoke College vs. Norfolk Division of William and Mary
Salem, Virginia

Team Scores: Roanoke College–86½
Norfolk Division of William and Mary–35½

Roanoke won 12 of the 14 events to beat Norfolk Division of William and Mary by a surprisingly-large margin–86½ to 35½. The Maroons had beaten them only by 10 points last spring.

There were a number of good performances by Roanoke athletes:

Dick Emberger–Dick placed first in six events and third in one. He won the 120-yard high hurdles in :15.0. That time tied Bruce Johnston's school record from1958. In the 220-yard low hurdles, he was first in a time of :25.1. He was a member of the mile relay team (with Dick Goodlake, Pete Wise, and Bill Davis), which finished first with a time of 3:31.8. His other three wins came in the broad jump (20'4¾"), the pole vault (11'6"), and the high jump (6'3¾"). The latter height broke his own school record of 6'2", set in 1958. He topped off the day with a third-place showing in the shot put. The busy afternoon gave him a team- and meet-high total of 27½ points.

Dick Engel–Sprinter Dick Engel won both the 100-yard dash (:10.1) and the 220-yard dash (:22.3), then ran a leg on the winning mile relay team. In the 220-yard dash, Tom Sitton was second in :22.8.

Howard Meincke–Howard again set the school record in the mile run. His time of 4:19.3 broke his own 1958 record of 4:24.5. Meincke also finished third in a fast two-mile run, being timed in 10:04.5.

George Jocher–George crossed the finish line of the two-mile race in 9:46.3 to beat Norfolk's Castagnola, who took second place with an excellent time of 9:53.0. Jocher's mark was close to being a new school record. The old mark was set at 9:44.6 by Howard Meincke at the Hofstra meet in 1957. George also placed third in the mile with a time of 4:45.5.

Pete Wise and Tom Sitton–Pete and Tom tied for first place in the 440-yard dash in a fast time of :50.0.

April 25, 1959
Mason-Dixon Conference Relays
Washington, D. C.

Eleven schools, including Roanoke, entered the Mason-Dixon Conference Relays on April 25 at American University. Although no team scores were awarded in this annual meet, Roanoke men did win or tie for first in 6 of the 13 events. Here are the winning efforts:

440-Yard Relay–The team of Dick Emberger, Brendan Cavanagh, Tom Sitton, and Dick Engel won the event in :44.7. The next three places in order went to Gallaudet College, Bridgewater College, and Catholic University.

880-Yard Relay–Roanoke's team of Cavanagh, Bill Davis, Sitton, and Engel won with a time of 1:31.7, just four tenths of a second off the school record. They were followed across the line by American University (2nd), Gallaudet College (3rd), and Washington College (4th).

Mile Relay–Cavanagh, Sitton, Engel, and Davis teamed for a win in a time of 3:27.6. They beat Bridgewater College (2nd), American University (3rd), and Western Maryland College (4th).

Sprint Medley Relay–Pete Wise, Davis, Sitton, and newcomer Don Long ran 3:40.5, only :00.4 off the old school record. In second was Gallaudet College, with American University finishing 3rd and Hampden-Sydney in 4th.

High Jump–Dick Emberger tied for first place in the high jump with Fred Diehl of Bridgewater. The height was 6'0".

Pole Vault–Again, Emberger tied for first place. He and Bob Cuthrell of Western Maryland cleared 12'0".

Incidentally, Emberger's ties for firsts in the high jump and pole vault were unusual. While each event was still in progress, he cut his chin badly as he came down in the pole vault. He was taken to Georgetown University Hospital for stitches. The officials ruled a tie for first in each event because Emberger could not continue.

May 1, 1959
Roanoke College vs. Bridgewater College
Salem, Virginia

Team Scores: Roanoke College–77
Bridgewater College–45

Roanoke and Bridgewater had not been opponents in a dual meet since May 3, 1957, when Roanoke won by some 35 points. The Maroons also were expected to win this 1959 meet.

Dick Emberger–Emberger was the high scorer for the meet. He set a new school record in the high hurdles by running :14.9. The old record of :15.0 was set by Bruce Johnston in 1958 and tied this year by Emberger. He also won the high jump (6'1"), the pole vault (11'6"), and the broad jump (21'½"). Those four wins gave him 20 points for the afternoon.

Dick Engel–Dick also won more than one event. He ran :10.1 in the 100-yard dash and :22.0 in the 220.

George Jocher–George's two wins came in the 880 and mile. The talented runner's 880 time was 1:59.8, while he recorded a 4:46.0 to tie Dick Goodlake in the mile run.

Pete Wise–It was Pete's last chance at home to get a school record. He was entering the final straightaway when he heard the loud voice of Homer Bast saying "Go, Pete, go. This is your last chance for a record." Pete heard him and immediately picked up the pace, driving through the tape in a new school record of :49.7. He beat the old mark of :49.9 set in 1958 by former teammate Howard Light. Tom Sitton was right behind him, running :50.4 in second place.

Howard Meincke–Howard, who would graduate with three school records (880, mile, and two miles), placed first in the two-mile run. His time was 10:01.0.

The mile relay team–Roanoke's team of Brendan Cavanagh, Pete Wise, Tom Sitton, and Bill Davis ran the mile relay in 3:23.4. The time was almost a school record. The old mark had been set at 3:22.6 by Al Ide, Pete Wise, John Summers, and Dick Lewis. Coach Fox wrote down these splits: Cavanagh–:51.4; Wise–:50.9; Sitton–:50.5; and Davis–:50.7.

The Bridgewater track team, which had been a thorn in Roanoke's side since Homer Bast brought the sport back in 1947, was now no match for the strong Maroon team. The team score was 77 to 45 in Roanoke's favor.

I remember . . . "I saw great possibilities in Pete Wise. I felt that if I could build more speed into him, that we'd have a pretty good quarter miler. And as it turned out, he was one of the two or three best 440 men I ever coached. He set the school record in his senior year by running a :49.7. He also won the Little Eight Conference 440-yard dash that year. While he was at Roanoke, we ran Pete in several events, but I felt that the 440 was his stellar event."

Homer Bast

May 9, 1959
Little Eight Conference Championships
Hampden-Sydney, Virginia

In the Little Eight Championships at Hampden-Sydney, Roanoke's excellent depth and major star power brought the Maroons an easy victory. The team scores were:

1st–Roanoke College–74½
2nd–Norfolk Division of William and Mary–45¼
3rd–Bridgewater College–38½
4th–Hampden-Sydney College–31
5th–Lynchburg College–8
6th–Randolph-Macon College–7½

Unfortunately, Roanoke men set no new school records in the meet:

Pete Wise– Pete ran an easy :50.5 to win the 440-yard dash. He was followed in third by Tom Sitton and in fourth by Bill Davis.

Dick Engel–Dick was second in two races, the 100 and 220. His 100 time is unknown, but the 220 time is recorded as :22.6. He was also a member of the winning mile relay team.

Howard Meincke–Howard won both the 880 and the mile. His 880 time was 2:00.7, and his mile time was an equally-impressive 4:24.2.

George Jocher– George finished second in the mile run with a 4:26.6. He also was second to Castagnola of Norfolk William and Mary in the two mile, running 10:06.9.

Dick Emberger–Surprisingly, Dick failed to win both hurdle races. He did place first in the high hurdles on a time of :15.3, then took third in the 220-yard lows. He also was 4th in the broad jump, 1st in the high jump (6'0"), and 1st in the pole vault (12'0").

Mile Relay–The team of Goodlake, Sitton, Engel, and Davis won the mile relay in 3:30.4.

Pete Wise wins the 440-yard dash in the Little Eight Championship Meet at Hampden Sydney on May 9, 1959. His time was :50.5. Tom Sitton, white shirt, was third. Bill Davis, just behind Sitton, was fourth. Pete's :49.7 in a dual meet late in the season set a track and school record.

Others–Dick Goodlake tied three others for third in the pole vault, with a jump of 11'0". He also placed 5th in the broad jump. Jack Dempsey placed second in the broad jump, going 21'1".

May 15-16, 1959
Mason-Dixon Conference Championships
Baltimore, Maryland

Roanoke had won every Mason-Dixon Championship Meet since 1954. This year, however, in the meet at Johns Hopkins, the team knew that there were a lot of good competitors in the conference and the team scores could be close.

It was not particularly a good meet for Roanoke, even though they qualified the most men for Saturday's finals. In the Friday qualifying, Dick Emberger ran a :14.7 in his high hurdles trials, setting a new meet and school record.

Dick Engel became one of the best three sprinters who ever competed for Coach Bast. On the left, he wins the 220-yard dash against Norfolk Division of William and Mary in 1960, running :22.3, with Tom Sitton (unseen) in second with :22.8. Brendan Cavanaugh (left) was third (:23.0) and Ken Garren trailed in the inside lane.

Here are others who did well for Roanoke:

Dick Engel–Dick failed to win one of the short sprints, but he did finish third in the 100 and third in the 220. He also helped Roanoke set a new record in the mile relay.

Pete Wise–Pete ran :50.6 in the 440, giving him third place.

Mile Relay Team–We are not completely sure about the composition of the Roanoke mile relay team, but we think runners were Dick Goodlake, Tom Sitton, Dick Engel, and Bill Davis. The team set a new Roanoke record by finishing second to Catholic

University and running 3:21.9. The time beat the old mark of 3:22.6, set by Al Ide, Pete Wise, John Summers, and Dick Lewis.

Bob Palm–Bob returned to the team and placed third in the shot put. His throw of 43'2½" was only 1½" short of second place.

Dick Emberger–Besides his school and meet record, set in the trials on Friday, Dick also placed fourth in the broad jump (21'6½"), won the high jump (6'1"), and tied for second place in the pole vault with a leap of 11'6". On the other hand, it still is a mystery why Dick does not show up as a competitor in either hurdle event on Saturday. With his points in the hurdles–likely coming from two first places, or even a first in the high hurdles and a second in the lows–Roanoke would have gotten either 9 or 10 more points.

In a surprising finish, Roanoke lost the meet. Here were the final scores:

1st–Catholic University–41
2nd–Roanoke College–37
3rd–Bridgewater College–32
4th–Hampden-Sydney College–23
5th–Loyola University–13
6th–American University–12
7th–Lynchburg College–11
8th–Washington College–9
9th–Western Maryland College–8,
Gallaudet College–8, and Johns HopkinsUniversity–8
12th–Mount St. Mary's College–6
13th–Randolph-Macon College–2
14th–Towson State College–0

I remember . . . "Let me tell you something about the Mason-Dixon meet. I drew the outside lane and guess what? There were nothing but mole hills for the first 150 yards. It was like running through beach sand. So my time really suffered."

Pete Wise

I remember . . . "Dick Goodlake was an outstanding runner. Just outstanding. He was disappointing his last year (1959), but there was a reason for it. He and several others were kicked out at the end of his third year because of a panty raid prank. So he lost a year. But he did come back. And he had kept himself in fairly good shape. But Dick was a cigarette smoker in college, and just couldn't break the habit. He was a good runner. He really was. He had natural ability. He had the build of a fine runner. And his son went to Tennessee on a scholarship, but before that as a high school athlete, he ran a 9:02 two-mile race. He now works for a major shoe company. His son took after his dad, running with ease."

Homer Bast

I remember . . . "The 1958-59 season brought to an end the college career of one of the best distance runners in the Mason-Dixon or Little Eight Conference–Howard Meincke. He knew how to motivate himself. When he went off by himself before a race, almost in a trance, neither I nor his teammates could approach him. He graduated with three school records–in the 880, the mile, and the two-mile run. The remainder of his life, however, was tragic. He taught for a few years and then moved to Miami and joined the police force there. And he married one of the Roanoke College girls and they were doing great together. Then he came down with a debilitating, fatal illness. You could see him deteriorate rapidly. His legs went bad, along with his arms, and he was forced to use a wheel chair. At about the time when it was a sure thing that he wouldn't live much longer, Howard, his wife, and his two children came to Roanoke College. He wanted to see the trophies he had helped his teammates earn while he was at Roanoke. They were on the second floor–the balcony–of the old gym at that particular point. We carried Howard, in his wheelchair, up the steps. He wanted to be by himself after his wife and kids had seen the trophies. It was the same old Howard. When he was finished, he called to us and we carried him back down the steps. He thanked me for being there in his life and what I had meant to him while he was at Roanoke College. I remember that day well. It was not only hard on Howard and his family, but it was extremely hard on me, seeing Howard in his physical condition. Howard and his family left the campus, and that's the last time I saw him. He died within the next few weeks."

Homer Bast

The 1959-60 Indoor Season

January 23, 1960
Evening Star Games
Washington, DC

The author has been unable to find the results of this meet. What we do know is that the team intended to enter the One-Mile Mason-Dixon Sprint Medley Relay, along with the Class A Mile Relay.

If the Maroons actually did enter the meet, the *Brackety-Ack* stated that the competitors in the sprint medley would be taken from this group: Bill Davis, Richard Waltz, Dick Engel, Ken Garren, Brendan Cavanagh, or Al Kerstitch. The mile relay team of four runners would come from this group: Brendan Cavanagh, Dick Engel, Bill Davis, Richard Waltz, or Al Kerstitch.

The *Brackety-Ack* made one additional comment about the meet. It said that Dick Emberger received a personal invitation to participate in the pole vault; however, the top four or five vaulters in this meet traditionally had gone over 15', so Dick may not have made the trip.

The Associated Press reported that the news of the meet centered on Duke's red-headed sprint star, Dave Sime. Sime, ranked as one of the top sprinters in the world, strained a leg muscle while winning the 70-yard dash in :07.0 and withdrew immediately from the 80- and 100-yard dashes.

February 6, 1960
V. M. I. Winter Relays
Lexington, Virginia

In this ninth annual meet, Maryland–the Atlantic Coast Conference Champions–and V. M. I. captured the most honors. Roanoke entered the 880-yard relay, the mile relay, the four-mile relay, the 60-yard dash, the shot, the 70-yard high hurdles, and the pole vault.

Alex Kerstitch led off the 880-yard relay qualifying race. Ken Garren took the baton for the second leg, and when he handed off to Brendan Cavanagh, the team had a 10-yard lead. Brendan Cavanagh, running the third leg, stretched the lead even farther. Dick Engle anchored the relay. The *Brackety-Ack* noted that he crossed the finish line 40 yards ahead of the pack. The team finished fifth in the finals. Here are the first four teams:

> 1st–University of Maryland (Goldstein, Pitts, Pixton, and Smith)–1:35.8; 2nd–V. M. I.; 3rd–University of Virginia; 4th–Naval Academy

Dick Engel, Dick Lewis, Bill Davis, and Brendan Cavanagh took second in their heat of the mile relay. It does not appear, however, that the team placed. Here are the first four teams in this race:

> 1st–V. M. I. (Nelms, Zimmerman, Crow, and Durrette)–

3:28.8; 2nd–Naval Academy; 3rd–University of Maryland;
4th–University of North Carolina

In the four-mile relay, Roanoke ran the team of Johnnie Blanton, Derek Stryker, Wayne Wilson, and Morris Creggar. Again, the meet results do not show Roanoke finishing in the top four teams:

1st–V. M. I. (Braithwaite, McDougall, Carlton, and Williams)–
18:38.7; 2nd–University of Maryland; 3rd–Naval Academy;
4th–Georgetown University

Dick Engel and Ken Garren entered the 60-yard dash. The *Brackety-Ack* reported that in his qualifying heat Engel ran a close second to the final winner Butch Spiegal of Maryland. The final results were:

1st–Spiegel (University of Maryland)–:06.2; 2nd–Whittaker
(University of Maryland); 3rd–Van Houtten (Naval Academy);
4th–Mankowich (Naval Academy)

Maroon freshman Larry Arrington entered the shot put event, but was no match for the 50-foot throwers:

1st–Tiedemann (Norfolk Division of William and Mary) and
Bartek (Naval Academy)–51'3¼"; 3rd–Kovalakides
(University of Maryland); 4th–Hart (Naval Academy)

Alex Kerstitch was Roanoke's lone entry in the pole vault. He did not place.

1st–Andersen (University of Maryland)–14'7¼"; 2nd–Glass
(University of Maryland); 3rd–Maxon (Naval Academy);
4th–Kleinderfor (Naval Academy) and Tiedman
(University of North Carolina)

Roanoke's best athlete, Dick Emberger, entered two events. In the high jump, he finished in a tie for second:

1st–Hilder (Naval Academy)–6'4¾"; 2nd–Emberger (Roanoke
College) and Estes (University of Maryland); 4th–Marshall (Naval

Academy) and Stevens (Duke University)

Emberger also ran the 70-yard high hurdles. Emberger won his initial qualifying heat and the *Brackety-Ack* noted that in doing so he unofficially set a new Roanoke College indoor record. He was eliminated in the semifinals. Unfortunately, the newspaper did not give his times. In the finals, Bill Johnson of the University of Maryland tied the national indoor 70-yard high hurdles record:

1st–Johnson (University of Maryland)–:08.3; 2nd–Hoddinott (Georgetown University); 3rd–Neal (Naval Academy); 4th–James (Norfolk Division of William and Mary)

The Winter Relays, with the following schools present for the meet, did not give team points:

Duke University
Furman University
Gallaudet College
Georgetown University
Naval Academy
Norfolk Division of William and Mary
Roanoke College
University of Maryland
University of North Carolina
University of Richmond
University of Virginia
Virginia Military Institute
Virginia Polytechnic Institute

February 13, 1960
The Virginia State Indoor Championships
Lexington, Virginia

The final meet of the indoor season–the State Championships–came in Lexington, Virginia, in the V. M. I. field house. Eleven men from Roanoke took part in the meet. Surprisingly, against much larger teams, the Maroons took fourth place.

Bill Davis finished fourth in the 440-yard dash. Crow of V. M. I. won the event in a time of :52.3, but no time was given for Davis.

The mile relay team also placed fourth in the finals of the mile relay. The event was won by V. M. I. in a time of 3:33.2.

But the most outstanding performances of the meet came from Dick Emberger. He scored 16 points and set five new records. First, he broke the old high jump record of 6'¾" with a tremendous leap of 6'5¼". The height was a new state indoor record, a new field house record, and a new school record.

In the 70-yard high hurdles, Emberger went 22'5¾" for second place. That distance was just ¼" behind the winner, Moss of V. M. I.

He also jumped 12'0" for second place in the pole vault. The winner was Henry of William and Mary, who cleared 12'6".

Here were the final team scores:

1st–Virginia Military Institute–58
2nd–College of William and Mary–24
3rd–University of Virginia–19½
4th–Roanoke College–18
5th–Virginia Polytechnic Institute–11
6th–University of Richmond–1½
7th–Hampden-Sydney College–0
7th–Washington and Lee University–0

The 1959-60 Outdoor Season

April 2, 1960
Roanoke College vs. American University
Salem, Virginia

The season began with a home meet on April 2 against American University. The temperature was cool, the skies were overcast, and there was a slight breeze against the runners on the home stretch.

Of the men who had been coached by Homer Bast, these individuals did well:

Dick Emberger–Dick was everywhere, it seemed, winning five separate events and placing third in another for a meet total of 26 points. He took firsts in the pole vault (12'0"), broad jump (22'¼"), high jump (6'2"), 120-yard high hurdles (:15.1), and 220-yard low hurdles (:25.3). He also threw a couple of times in the discus, picking up a third place with 107'5".

Dick Engel–Physically injured for much of his senior year, Dick was second in the

100-yard dash and third in the 220. He was also a member of the winning mile relay team (3:34.0).

Wayne Wilson–Wayne won the two-mile race in a slow 10:42.9.

Derek Stryker–The mile race also was run at a slow pace, with Derek winning the event in a time of 4:46.1.

Johnnie Blanton–Johnnie placed second behind Stryker in the mile run, with a time of 4:48.7.

Bob Palm–Bob, school record holder indoors and outdoors in the shot put, won the shot put against American with a good throw of 44'7¾".

Dick Lewis–Dick ran on the first-place mile relay team.

Bill Davis–Bill anchored the mile relay team, which finished with a time of 3:34.0.

Bob Jenkins–Distance man Bob Jenkins placed third in both the mile and two-mile events.

Other Maroons included:

Brendan Cavanagh–Brendan won the 100-yard dash in a time of :10.3, running into the wind. He also placed second in the 220 with a good time of :22.5 and third in the high jump.

Howard Beck–Howard was known for his easy, smooth stride. He ran a :51.1 quarter but finished third behind two runners from American. He also helped the mile relay team win its event.

Larry Arrington–Larry placed second to Bob Palm in the shot, then came back to win the discus with a throw of 122'½".

Vin Ahearn–Vin took second place in the high jump, clearing 5'10".

Al Kerstitch–Al tied for second in the pole vault with a jump of 11'6"

Mic Hamaker–Mic finished third in the 880-yard run with a time of 2:06.0.

Roanoke had no real trouble winning the meet. The final team scores were Roanoke, 81, and American University, 36.

April 6, 1960
Roanoke College vs. Hampden-Sydney College
Salem, Virginia

April 6 was a cool and windy day; unfortunately, the Alumni Field track was wet. The Maroons enjoyed another easy victory, beating Hampden-Sydney by a score of 92½ to 29½, again riding the back of senior Dick Emberger.

Dick Emberger–Emberger won five events himself, and placed third in another. His total of 26 points was almost more than the total score for Hampden-Sydney. He won the high- and low-hurdle races, although he had good competition from Hampden-Sydney's Chapman in both events. Dick also won the high jump (6'0"), the broad jump (21'2"), and the pole vault (10'10"). And he was third in the discus.

Dick Engel–Dick was second in the 100 with a time of :10.3, and third in the 220.

Wayne Wilson–Wayne's time of 10:39.1 gave him first place in the two-mile race.

Derek Stryker–Derek won the mile run in 4:43.8 and placed third in the two-mile race.

Bill Davis–Running with Morris Creggar, Mic Hamaker, and Howard Beck, Bill helped win the mile relay in a time of 3:32.8.

Bob Palm–Bob continued to throw well, winning the shot put with 44'1" and placing second in the discus (122'7½").

Bob Jenkins–Bob, not in the best of condition yet, placed second in the two-mile run with a time of 10:40.0.

Other Maroon athletes helped build the score:

Brendan Cavanagh–Brendan took second place in the 220 on a time of :23.6. He also placed second in the high jump.

Jim O'Mahony–Jim took second in the broad jump with an effort of 20'5½".

Larry Arrington–Arrington, a day-student freshman, won the discus with a school-record throw of 130'9" after placing second to Bob Palm in the shot put.

Ken Garren–Dash man Ken Garren ran the low hurdles, placing third in :28.1.

Morris Creggar–Morris, a stellar basketball player for Coach Buddy Hackman, placed third in the 880 and ran on the winning mile relay team.

Howard Beck–Howie won the 440 in a good early-season time of :51.0. He also ran with Creggar, Hamaker, and Davis on the mile relay team, which won with a time of 3:32.8.

April 9, 1960
Roanoke College vs. Bridgewater College
Bridgewater, Virginia

The Roanoke team traveled to Bridgewater, knowing that they were likely to win the meet; however, it was a horrible day for track. The weather was cold and raw.

Again, Dick Emberger was the star of the meet, winning three events and placing second in another, as the Roanoke team won its third meet of the year, 83 to 38.

Dick Emberger–As usual, Dick won the 120-yard high hurdles. His time was :15.6. His other wins came in the high jump at 5'10" and the pole vault at 10'0". He did not compete in the low hurdles.

Bill Davis–Bill placed third in the 440 and helped the mile relay team win in a slow 3:44.0.

Dick Engel–In difficult weather, Dick placed second in the 100 but won the 220. Neither time was particularly fast.

Bob Palm–Bob again threw over 44', winning the shot with 44'11". He also placed third in the discus.

Bob Jenkins–Despite the bad weather, Bob won the two-mile race.

Derek Stryker–For the third meet in a row, Derek placed first in the mile run.

Wayne Wilson–Wayne was second in the two-mile run.

Other Maroons who figured in the scoring included:

Brendan Cavanagh–Cavanagh won the 440-yard dash with a time of :52.7 and placed third in the high jump.

Howard Beck–Howard not only anchored the mile relay team to its win, but he was second in the 440.

Kenny Garren–Garren finished second in the low hurdles.

Don Ballou–Don won the 880 in 2:03.0, a fairly good time considering the weather.

Larry Arrington–Arrington tied for first place in the discus with Diehl of Bridgewater. They each threw 123'7½". He also placed third in the shot put.

April 24, 1960
Roanoke College vs. Norfolk Division of William and Mary
Salem, Virginia

On a day with excellent weather, Roanoke won a close meet with Norfolk Division of William and Mary, 67½ to 54½. The Maroons were paced by Dick Emberger's four wins and 23 points; however, most of his teammates also did well.

Bob Jenkins–Bob, running his best time of the year, won the two-mile race in 10:06.0.

Dick Emberger–Dick won the pole vault (12'0"), the high jump (6'2"), the broad jump (20'8⅞"), and the 220-yard low hurdles (:24.7). He failed to win the 120-yard high hurdles for the first time all year, trailing James of Norfolk William and Mary, who ran a spectacular time of :14.3; however, the judges decided that that time was not a record, noting that James won as a result of a false start. The runners could not be recalled because of a jammed starting gun.

Bob Palm–Bob placed second in the shot put behind an excellent Norfolk thrower, and was third in the discus.

Bill Davis–Davis was second in the 440, running a good time of :52.2, and ran a leg on the winning mile relay team. He, Howard Beck, Don Ballou, and Brendan Cavanagh were timed in an excellent 3:26.1.

Derek Stryker–For the first time this year, Derek failed to win the mile, placing second behind Mears of Norfolk William and Mary.

Wayne Wilson–In the two-mile run, Wayne finished third.

Among the others on Roanoke's team, these individuals scored:

Brendan Cavanagh–Brendan tied for second in the 100-yard dash, won the 220 in a good time of :22.5, and anchored the mile relay team.

Larry Arrington–Arrington was second in the discus.

Howard Beck–Howie finished third in the 440, running a :52.8, and led off for the mile relay team.

Mic Hamaker–Mic placed second in the 880 with a time of 2:01.5.

April 30, 1960
High Point Relays
Davidson, North Carolina

Seven teams competed in the annual High Point Relays. For the first time in the 1960 season, however, Roanoke would not win a meet.

Roanoke teams did win two of the five relay events. In the 440-yard relay, Roanoke finished in fourth place (runners unknown). The winner of the event was Davidson, who ran an excellent :43.7. In the 880-yard relay, a team of unknown Roanoke men placed second behind Davidson's 1:31.5. In the sprint medley relay, Roanoke was third. High Point won that race in 3:39.3.

The Maroons did win the mile relay and the distance medley relay. In the mile relay, the team (unknown runners) recorded an excellent time of 3:22.0. Roanoke also won the distance medley relay, crossing the finish line in 10:56.3.

Others from the Roanoke team did well in individual events. Larry Arrington finished second in the shot put and fifth in the discus. Dick Emberger won three events–the broad jump, the high jump, and the hop, step, and jump (later called the triple jump). His broad jump measured 21'6¾". He high jumped 6'1⅜". And he did 43'0" in the hop, step, and jump event. Emberger's lone non-win was in the pole vault, where he finished in a four-way tie for second.

Here are the final team scores for the day:

1st–Davidson College–53
2nd–Roanoke College–44
3rd–Presbyterian College–27
4th–Lenoir Rhyne College–17
5th–High Point College–15
6th–Catawba College–14
7th–Atlantic Christian College–9

May 7, 1960
Virginia State Championships
Lynchburg, Virginia

Roanoke seemed to be improving. In fact, the Maroons finished third in the Virginia State Championships held at Lynchburg on May 7, 1960. The team scores were:

1st–Virginia Military Institute–72⅓
2nd–University of Virginia–42⅔
3rd–Roanoke College–27
4th–College of William and Mary–21⅓
5th–Norfolk Division of William and Mary–19
6th–Virginia Polytechnic Institute–16
7th–Hampden-Sydney College–12
8th–Bridgewater College–9⅓
9th–Washington and Lee University–7
9th–University of Richmond–7
11th–Randolph-Macon College–3⅓
12th–Lynchburg College–3

Howard Beck ran a time of :49.8 in the trials, then finished in fourth place in the finals with a :50.2. The first-place man, Crow of V. M. I. also had a time of :50.2, meaning that the top four men in the finals crossed the line together. Brendan Cavanagh didn't place, but did run an excellent :50.2 in a qualifying heat.

Don Ballou placed second in the 880-yard run. In his best race ever, he was timed in 1:58.5.

Derek Stryker ran a 4:34.5 mile. He finished in fifth place.

Bob Jenkins of Roanoke, getting stronger each meet, was timed in 9:58. That time placed him third in the two-mile race.

Dick Emberger picked up a second place in the high hurdles in a very close finish, won the high jump with a height of 6'0", finished second in the broad jump (22'3½"), and placed second in the hop, step, and jump. He led all scorers with 17 points.

May 13-14, 1960
Mason-Dixon Conference Championships
Washington, D. C.

The annual Mason-Dixon Championships this year were conducted over a two-day period at American University in Washington. Fourteen teams competed in the meet.

Roanoke's Dick Emberger was back in top form. In fact, his 19 points, on three firsts and a second, led all scorers. He won the broad jump with a distance of 22'1¼", the high jump with a height of 6'2¼", and the 120-yard high hurdles with a new conference record of :14.6. The old high hurdles record of :14.7 was set by Emberger in 1959. In the 220-

By his senior year, Dick Emberger had become the best all-around track man in the history of the college.

yard low hurdles, he placed second to Diashyn of Washington College, who ran a time of :24.7.

Bob Palm threw 44'9" for a third place in the shot put. Fellow thrower Larry Arrington placed fifth in the shot and second in the discus.

Howard Beck was fourth in the 220-yard dash. He also finished third in the 440.

Don Ballou ran second in the 880. He was just in back of Hampden-Sydney's Caperton, whose time was 1:59.3.

In the mile run, Roanoke's Derek Stryker finished second, while teammate Bob Jenkins was second in the two-mile run.

Finally, Roanoke runners (names unknown) won the mile relay in 3:22.3.

The final team scores were:

1st–Roanoke College (R)–50
2nd–American University (A)–32
3rd–Tie: Bridgewater College (B) and
Hampden-Sydney College (HS)–22
5th–Tie: Johns Hopkins University (JH) and
Loyola College (LOY) and Lynchburg College (L)–18
8th–Mount St. Mary's College (MSM)–13
9th–Washington College (W)–10
10th–Western Maryland College (WM)–7
11th–University of Baltimore (UB)–5
12th–Gallaudet College (G)–4
13th–Randolph-Macon College (RM)–1
14th–Tie: Towson College (T) and
Catholic University (C)–0

May 21, 1960
Little Eight Conference Championships
Hampden-Sydney, Virginia

The Roanoke team had won the Mason-Dixon Championships. In this, the last year of Dick Emberger's college career, could they win their eighth straight Little Eight meet? The answer was a resounding "yes," and with room to spare.

Emberger, the talented star from Bloomfield, New Jersey, was at his best. He won four separate events to become high scorer for the meet with 20 points. He ran a sensational meet-record time of :14.6 in the high hurdles to win that event. He also ran :24.5 in winning the low hurdles. And then he managed wins in two field events–the broad jump (21'1½") and the high jump (6'3¼"). The high jump mark was another meet record.

Freshman Derek Stryker won the mile run in 4:36.6. Bob Jenkins was second. Jenkins also captured the two-mile title, running 10:18.4.

Howard Beck set a new meet record by running :49.8 to win the 440-yard dash. Not far behind was Brendan Cavanagh in second place. Beck also won the 220-yard dash in a time of :22.3. Cavanagh finished third in the race.

Don Ballou finished second in the 880. He was beaten by Caperton of Hampden-Sydney.

Bob Palm was fourth in the shot put. Larry Arrington did not place in the shot, but did finish second in the discus.

Al Kerstitch finished third in the broad jump, and the team of Don Ballou, Brendan Cavanagh, Bill Davis, and Howard Beck won the mile relay in a time of 3:27.9.

Here are the final team scores:

1st–Roanoke College–78½
2nd–Norfolk Division of William and Mary–48
3rd–Hampden-Sydney College–28
4th–Lynchburg College–22
5th–Randolph-Macon College–15½
6th–Bridgewater College–15

Chapter Eighteen

A Tribute to the Coach

In part, this book is about the many young men who decided to enroll at Roanoke College and then to spend their time and energies in being part of the school's cross-country and track teams. But the remarkable individual in this story is Charles Homer Bast, their coach. At the publication date of this book, Homer is 94 years old. Until recently, he still lived with his wife, the former Mary Jane Lightner, in the same house they built in 1952 in Salem. Unfortunately, Mary Jane passed away quietly and painlessly on June 2, 2008, after a lingering decline in her health.

Homer has lost some mobility, walking with a cane, and has some difficulty with sight and hearing; however, he loves to talk about the days he coached. He still is an articulate, caring, and gentle man who loves the many letters, phone calls, and visits he receives from former athletes. He coached indoor and outdoor track from 1946-47, retiring officially from that position after the 1956-57 season. He continued to coach cross country until the 1960-61 school year.

Homer is a man who is genuinely loved not only by his former athletes, but also by those who once sat in his history classes (where he was an extremely talented and memorable teacher), and the many colleagues with whom he worked for so many years. Since his retirement, the College has awarded him an honorary doctorate, named a new physical education and athletics building in his honor, and dedicated a newly-refurbished track complex to him in a 2006 ceremony. Students today may not know him, but they certainly see his name every time they cross the campus. Perhaps this book will let them know exactly why he still is considered the most successful coach in the history of Roanoke College.

The Early Years

Homer was born in Baltimore, Maryland, on August 7, 1914, the elder son of Charles and Beula Bast, at the home of his grandparents, John and Mollie Bast. The family lived in that house for nine years, in a third-floor apartment rented from his grandparents, then moved to a house just outside of a small town called Easton on the eastern shore of Maryland. Homer entered the fifth grade at Easton Elementary School. The Basts lived on three acres of land in a rural setting. With chickens, a cow, and pigs, there were lots of chores for the 11-year old Homer. He sold eggs and berries to the parents of his new friends and to some of the stores in Easton. With his proceeds, he bought tennis and baseball equipment with one half of the money and saved the other half.

Left Photo: Homer as a small boy with his mother and father in 1920.
Center Photo: Stephen Bast, Mary Jane Bast, and Michael Bast at the gravesite of William Lightner in Bast County.
Right Photo: Homer stands outside Alumni Gymnasium with his son, Michael, in 1972. Michael was an excellent distance runner for the college.

Homer was a good student from the beginning, graduating from the elementary school ranked number one in his class. He went on to attend Easton High School. During those years, he worked in the A&P grocery store on weekends and in the summers, where he earned enough money to join the Talbot County Country Club. At the club, he became the runner-up in the boys' tennis championships. He also enjoyed the summer Saturday night dances.

In June of 1931, Homer graduated from Easton High School as President of his class. During those high school years, he participated in soccer, basketball, baseball, and track. Because of his interest in sports, unfortunately, his grades left much to be desired.

Joining four of his friends from Easton and Oxford, Homer then entered Mercersburg Academy for a year of prep school. While at Mercersburg, he waited on tables, made the honor roll, and earned his letter in soccer. He also was a member of the school's powerful track team and was an alternate on Mercersburg's national championship mile relay team.

His experiences during that year at Mercersburg prepared him for college. Students at the prestigious school were competitive both in the classroom and on the athletic field.

He applied to attend the University of Virginia, and was accepted and given an Alumni Scholarship. Little did he know at the time that he would remain a student at Mr. Jefferson's University for the next eight years.

As a freshman, Homer made the honor roll and was an outstanding 440 man on the frosh track team. At the conclusion of his second year, Homer earned intermediate academic honors.

In his first meet of his sophomore year, he won two races–the 440 and the 880–against V. M. I. The team went to the University of North Carolina the next week. After the publicity he received following the V. M. I. meet, everyone expected him to dominate both races. At the least, he was a dark-horse favorite. Unfortunately, Carolina brought out it stable of quarter-milers, and Homer felt lucky to get third place. The worst part, however, was that in this race he pulled a chest muscle. Even today, he can hear Coach Hahn's voice, saying "Bast. What am I going to do with you? How do you pull a muscle in your chest? I've never heard of such a thing." During his University career, he also suffered from pulled hamstring muscles.

At the time he got hurt, he was running in the low 50s in the quarter, a respectable time in those days. He had stopped running the 880 because of the problem with his chest muscle. Finally, Hahn took Homer to the doctor, who confirmed that, indeed, he had a chest muscle pull and told him that he would be hurting from it for a long time. Hahn then wrote the Southern Conference in an attempt to get Homer an extra year of eligibility. The Conference agreed, allowing Homer to run during his junior and senior years, as well as during a possible post-graduate year at the University.

He did run the quarter mile throughout his junior and senior years–but he did so against the will of his professors in the history department. To the man, they were not in favor of his frittering away his time with track. Some of his history classes were scheduled from 2:00 p.m. until 5:00 p.m. invariably; he would have one of these classes at the same time as a track meet and would need to miss three hours of class time.

Top Photo: Homer (second from the left) as a member of the mile relay team at Easton High School.
Bottom Left Photo: Homer's University of Virginia cross country team.
Bottom right: The University of Virginia's track team.

As for cross country, Homer tried out for the team at the beginning of his junior year. That effort was cut short, however, when he pulled a hamstring muscle. He wasn't the same runner for the rest of the year. Here he was, with half a year gone and he hadn't even rounded into shape. In those days, doctors didn't know what to do for sports injuries, so they simply recommended complete rest. After resting during his junior year in track, he knew that he needed badly to heal the leg muscle and get in shape for his senior year of running.

Homer had a good friend, Charlie Wheeler, who was interested in track and was about to enroll at the University. That summer, just after Homer's junior year, his friend and he went up to property owned by Charlie's parents. They were descendents of a family who had received an original grant of land in Talbot County in 1660. They owned 1,000 acres of land and called the site Canterbury Manor. Homer remembers training that summer on a mile-long, beautiful lane leading to the main house. With steady running and little stress on the legs, Homer's leg muscle began to respond and he gradually got back in shape.

His senior year at the University, he felt good and performed well in track. He picked up second place in the Big Four Championships as a quarter miler, and even ran a number of 880 races and was a member of the mile relay team. In the Big Four meet, his mile relay team won the title with an excellent time of 3:21.

Homer set his site on three goals while he was a student at the University of Virginia–three letters in track, a Phi Beta Kappa key, and the presidency of the student body. The objective of lettering for three years was realized after he ran for the track team during his fifth, or post-graduate year of eligibility. He still remembers running on a talented mile relay team. "We won the Southern Conference relay championship in a time of 3:19" he said, "and it was a record that stood in the state of Virginia for several years. I believe that eventually a high school team ran a faster time. I have forgotten what leg I ran during the race, but I did O. K. We had one pretty good quarter miler who was running in the 48s at the time. And there was another fellow, Billy Hopkins, who was a sprinter (later trying out for the Olympics 100-meter team), who could run a pretty good 440 himself. I think Archie timed me at :49.3 during my leg of the relay." After Homer's postgraduate year, the University awarded him the last of his three letters.

He never realized the dream of getting a Phi Beta Kappa Key while at the University of Virginia; however, many years later, Roanoke awarded Homer and several others the Key after the College finally qualified for its first Phi Beta Kappa chapter. It was an honor that he cherishes even today.

During his senior year, Homer met his third objective. He ran for President of the Student Body at the University, and despite some tough competition, won the position. As President, one of his most important functions was to be a member of the Honor Committee. This group was composed of the Presidents of the various schools. It was a tremendous responsibility. In one 10-day examination period, for example, Homer helped preside over nine separate trials. Those trials began at 7:00 p.m. and would continue, one after the other, until about 4:00 a.m. The worst scenario was that Homer might himself have had an exam the next day.

At the insistence of the diminutive Coach Hahn, Homer ran cross country once again to build up his stamina. Archie and Homer had gotten to be good friends by this time. As Homer put it, "I think he respected me a great deal by this time. And he liked the fact that I was President of the student body." That friendship lasted for many years. Homer was honored that Archie's family asked him to come back to Charlottesville and be one of

Archie's pall bearers at his funeral.

The fact that Homer was President also helped him smooth over the reluctance of his history professors, who had thought his running would hurt his studies. "As President of the student body," Homer said, "I had a different relationship with members of the history department–different from the relationship between them and regular students."

Homer's undergraduate degree was a Bachelor of Science. During his first postgraduate year, he was able to get a prestigious DuPont fellowship. Most thought the DuPont was the best fellowship available. The recipient of this fellowship paid the school no money. In fact, the University paid Homer to go to school. And he got a lot of publicity for being a DuPont fellow. During this year, he had a couple of jobs on campus. At the end of that year, he was able to finish his coursework, thesis, and oral exams for his Master of Arts degree. Instead of picking up the M. A. that year, however, he chose to receive it during the next year. Had he taken the degree in that first graduate year, the school would have required him to take Latin and Greek. By the time he started his second graduate year, however, the administration had eliminated that requirement.

In his second graduate year, the Rural Social Economics Department had a go-getter professor, Wilson Gee, who was a tremendous fund raiser with good contacts throughout the country. Homer had gotten to know him well through several of Homer's fraternity brothers. They had decided that perhaps agricultural economics was a pretty good field to go into. Homer could see that they were being paid lots of money by the University to be a part of this program. So Homer, who could sense a good thing, began to play tennis with Dr. Gee. They would play as doubles partners on afternoons when there were no classes and the two of them were looking for something to do. "He not only got to know me," Homer remembered, "but he also got to know my folks because he visited us one time down on the river on the Eastern Shore. And Dr. Gee decided that he was going to get me, a history major, into agricultural economics. He offered me an instructorship in rural social economics. I had never had a course in that subject in all of my life." He reminded Dr. Gee of that fact, but Gee told him that all Homer needed to know was research. So he ended up taking a short course–in introductory research for agricultural economics–and his main job was preparing economic and social surveys of various Virginia counties that Gee was working on at the time. Homer was also the co-editor of a newsletter that his department published twice a month. At that particular time, it was the year of Franklin Roosevelt's "one third of a nation ill-fed, ill-housed, and ill-clothed" policy to help the South. Homer wrote one article on housing and another on manufacturing, along with several others. All seemed to get good publicity. The contents of these papers even became the subject of the Richmond Times Dispatch editorial page.

The newsletter that Homer co-edited was distributed widely throughout the South. Homer had gotten a good reputation from his work. Dr. Gee then asked Homer to accompany him on a trip through the South. He was to visit Auburn and a lot of "cow towns" and wanted Homer to be with him so he could point out his protégé as being the author of the various articles he had written for the newsletter. Of course, an alternative reason was to get Homer interested in this agricultural program and to become one of his majors. Gee's students would stay in Charlottesville for one year, and then travel to different "cow colleges" for another year to get the experience of what farm life was about. Then he would give them lucrative fellowships. It seemed like a tremendous opportunity; however, Homer finally decided not to participate. He told Dr. Gee, "Your offer is wonderful, but I just love history."

By that time, Homer had finished his coursework for a Ph.D. in history. He even had a dissertation topic: Alexander McGillivray, King of the Cretes. About half the dissertation had been written when, suddenly, a doctoral student from the University of Oklahoma published his own dissertation on the very same topic. Homer was left with no other choice but to select another subject and start over. His new dissertation topic became: Crete Indian Diplomacy: 1775 to 1795. So during that year, he continued to write the dissertation. At the same time, he was teaching one history course for the University, for which the school gave him $2,950. In the middle of the Depression, 1938-39, that was a lot of money. With this stipend, Homer was able to send his younger brother to prep school.

The money also helped him run over to Sweetbriar College about every weekend. He had fallen desperately in love with a Denver girl at Sweetbriar. This was not just puppy love, either. She was an extremely popular girl with filthy-rich parents. She came down to the Bast family home on the Eastern Shore near the end of Homer's second year in graduate school. Homer thought she just wanted to meet and size up his parents. Her mother also drove down from Baltimore, taking a ferry boat ride across the Bay, to see where the Basts lived. "I met Mama," Bast said, "and knew that this was one courtship that would never last." He could tell that the girl's mother was not impressed. During the following year, the relationship cooled off dramatically. He went on with his studies and she, a true debutante, began to date a number of new boyfriends at Yale, Harvard, Brown, the Naval Academy, and other schools. Homer knew that he couldn't compete with those boys, and certainly not with the girl's family. Homer's mother and father didn't have a lot of money. The only reason they had a house on the water was because his dad had made a good deal to buy the property. Homer's father was not dirt poor by any means, because he had owned a hardware and furniture store. Yet, Homer knew instinctively that he just wasn't in her class. The girl finally married a doctor after she graduated from Sweetbriar. Years later, she even served on the school's Board of Trustees. As Homer said, "That's one of the perks of having lots of money." She ended up giving Sweetbriar quite a large monetary gift.

Later in life, after the girl died, Homer asked Sweetbriar to send him an obituary. He discovered that she had three daughters and a son. He wrote the oldest girl, who lived in Cleveland, who told him that she remembered her mother speaking highly of him. For three or four years, the daughter and Homer corresponded regularly.

Meanwhile, Homer continued to work on his doctorate. In 1940, he had finished all of his requirements except for the oral exams. This was his fourth year of graduate school. He had taken a year off because of the one year when he was an instructor for the University. During that time, because of his teaching, he didn't read as much as he should have. He was working frantically to get the dissertation completed. The manuscript was essentially complete, with the oral exam to be scheduled, when the stress caught up with him and he decided to leave the University for a year or so. He had drawn down his savings account to meet expenses, served as a counselor in the resident halls with Mortimer Caplin (later Director of the I. R. S.), and continued to grade papers. By the end of this year, the dissertation, *Creek Indian Policy*, was completed and approved. His doctoral advisor called the document "one of the best ever prepared under my direction." At this point, the time had come to leave the University he loved and complete the dissertation while he started a career.

World War II was fast approaching. Homer didn't have a low draft number, but it wasn't high either. So there was a chance he might be drafted. He had already decided that he didn't want to be a buck private, and he was determined that he wasn't going to go into the Army. So, near the very end of his doctoral program, he decided to join the Air Force. He went down to the Air Force recruiters' table, when they came to the campus, and said "Here I am. Take me." But his mother said, "I'll not hear of it." She seldom put her foot down, but this time she was adamant. He finally convinced her that he very likely was going to be required to go into the service and that the next time he tried to join, it would be with the Navy.

Homer's First Job Outside the University

First, however, he took a one-year teaching and coaching job at Staunton Military Academy in Virginia. They gave him five classes to teach and had him coach the junior varsity football, swimming, and track teams. He had never coached any of the three sports. Homer still remembers how he got the junior varsity football players to accept him. He had played soccer as a high school student, and one day at a fall practice, he took his shoes off and punted the football bare-footed–and for a considerable distance. As Homer says, "The boys stood by in admiration, and I instantly won them over."

During this year, he was also trying to prepare for his oral exam at the University. Unfortunately, with all of the duties of his new job, he didn't have very much time to

read. He knew that preparing for an oral exam was difficult under the best of conditions. But he felt it was almost impossible while working a full-time job.

He also was falling in love. One Sunday, when the Mary Baldwin College girls came down to Staunton Military Academy to watch the Academy's full-dress parade, he met Mary Jane Lightner. She was a junior at Mary Baldwin at the time. Mary Jane was a true southern belle with knockout looks. They dated throughout the year and Homer finally asked her to marry him.

Joining the Navy and Marrying Mary Jane

It was apparent that war was about to break out. Because he didn't want to be a private in the rear ranks, he took the examination to qualify for serving in the Navy. In the summer of 1941, he received a letter from the Navy telling him that he had been selected to participate in the Naval Midshipman program. He was to report for duty in the middle of September, 1941. He resigned his position with Staunton Military Academy and with the stress of time, stood for his Ph.D. oral exams the week before reporting as an apprentice seaman. He was unprepared for the exams and should have postponed them.

The Midshipman program involved training aboard the Prairie State, one of the battleships from Teddy Roosevelt's Great White Fleet. At the time, the Prairie State had been decommissioned, stripped of its guns, and anchored along 137th Street in New York. Homer mostly trained, ate, and studied aboard the ship. His group of trainees began as apprentice seamen, learning first to tie proper rope knots. Some training took place on a long pier extending into the Hudson River. Then they moved on to subjects such as gunnery, navigation, and seamanship. It was a rigorous four-week training program for the crew of college graduates.

On December 7, 1941, while still on the Prairie State, Homer and the other trainees heard the news about the attack of Pearl Harbor. They all knew that war was coming, but never when or where it would begin. Beginning that night, Homer and others were issued ammunition for their guns and they began a 24-hour vigil in rotating patrols. For Homer, it was a night to remember–full of mysterious shadows with imagined figures in the dark. As it turned out, that night and many other nights that followed were uneventful. But so spooked were the trainees that an Ensign who had attended the University of Virginia actually shot himself in the foot with his .45.

Fortunately, no one from Homer's Midshipman program was called to duty, and he was able to complete his program. Ensign Bast was assigned to inshore patrol in Boston and continued his training on a higher level. Part of their work consisted of inshore patrolling of many of the harbors in the area, including those in Boston, New York, Delaware Bay, and Chesapeake Bay. Homer and six other ensigns found quarters in a row house in Boston, which had a room rent of $7 per person per month.

About eight weeks later, Homer was assigned to an anti-submarine school in Miami. Part of his training consisted of going out on submarine chasers, learning how to dock and anchor the ships.

In April, Homer traveled on an overnight train to Staunton to get married, despite the fact that Mary Jane and Homer had talked about the possibility of postponing the wedding until after the war. Mary Jane was the first coed at Mary Baldwin who got married while still a student at the school. To marry Homer, she had to get special permission from the College. Both came back to Miami after the wedding and she stayed there with him for another week. She then returned to Staunton to finish her course work at Mary Baldwin.

In another week, Homer was assigned to a PC, number 571, which was being built in Portland, Oregon. The PC571 was a 170 foot submarine chaser. It had a three-inch gun on the front deck, along with a couple of machine guns. The boat was equipped with sonar, but had no radar equipment. While the crew was waiting for the completion of the PC572, Homer and others were sent to Portland. Homer struck up a friendship with the commanding officer of the PC571, which was closer to being finished than the PC572. The commanding officer took a liking to Homer and soon had him transferred to his boat as an Ensign. The 571 was commissioned soon, assigned a crew, and sailed from Portland down the Columbia River to the Pacific Ocean. Finally, Ensign Bast had some real responsibility on a ship. And it was the first time he had been to sea without an instructor watching his every move.

The 571 proceeded to the Bremerton Navy Yard, where the ship picked up supplies, ammunition, and equipment. The crew's first assignment was to protect the Straits of Juan de-Fuca from Japanese submarines. They patrolled an area around Cape Flattery in two-week shifts, returning to Seattle for R & R after each shift. They had no real encounter with a Japanese sub; however, once they were sent to find a sub that had shelled the Oregon. The sub was long gone when they arrived.

Left Photo: Mary Jane was a beautiful bride. This picture was taken just before her marriage to Homer in April of 1942.
Center Photo: This picture of Mary Jane Bast was taken on April 4, 1942, shortly after her marriage to Homer.
Right Photo: Mary Jane and Homer after their marriage.

The 571 also patrolled Port Townsend, between Cape Flattery and Seattle, which had a narrow entrance. They only had to anchor at the entrance and listen for possible submarines.

They continued this type of duty until the summer of 1942, when they were sent to Alaska. The Japanese had captured Attu and Amchitka, the final two islands in the Aleutian chain. The 571 was one of many vessels ordered to Alaska in anticipation of a major Japanese attack. When the 571 arrived, it picked up another duty–rescuing Navy pilots who had been shot down over the Gulf of Alaska.

Ensign Bast saw little action there. The 571 occasionally would detect a Japanese sub, or what they thought might be a sub, but there was never any fighting involved. Historians noted, however, that the Japanese never used their subs very effectively in this area. Often, weather conditions were so bad that the Americans' sonar was useless. At these times, submarines were almost undetectable. Eventually, the brutal weather took its toll on the 571 and other PCs, and they all had to return to Seattle for major repairs.

After 19 months, Homer was sent back to Miami and later to gunnery school at the Washington Navy Yard. He was slated to become a gunnery officer aboard a destroyer escort. Unfortunately, it was at this time that his mother died. He went immediately to the family home and stayed there as long as his leave allowed. He fell so far behind his training schedule that he was given the choice of starting his gunnery training from the beginning or transferring to the amphibious program in Norfolk. He chose to transfer to the amphibious program but wanted to be the commanding officer of a Landing Ship Tank (LST). The LST program was begun to support amphibious operations by carrying significant numbers of vehicles, cargo, and landing troops directly onto an unimproved shore. The Navy granted his request because of his experience and he was assigned his crew and officers over a period of about six weeks. After training as a unit, they were sent to Pittsburgh to be assigned to a ship under construction. Once the ship was completed, the crew and officers took it down the Mississippi. Now a Lieutenant, Homer was completely in charge of the LST. They arrived in New Orleans and traveled across the Gulf of Mexico to Panama City for more training. From there, they returned to New Orleans to pick up a load of Jeeps, tanks, and other equipment and supplies for delivery to a key island in the war. Then they sailed south, crossed through the Panama Canal, and went on to San Diego. There, they picked up more equipment and set out for Pearl Harbor accompanied by three other ships.

After arriving in Pearl Harbor, Homer was called ashore and told that his ship had been designated to be converted from an LST into a supply ship. Again, Homer was given a choice. He could be assigned to another LST as its commanding officer. Or he could stay with his new supply ship. Homer chose to stay with his current ship, now known as LST(M) 677 and soon to be called the USS Yolo, because he had established good relationships with all of his officers and knew that he had a good crew.

The officers and crew stayed in Pearl Harbor for another three months as the ship was converted. The Navy put refrigerators on the tank deck and two Quonset huts on the main deck. One of these Quonset huts was dedicated to baking projects, able to produce 1,000 loaves of bread a day or 500 pies and cakes. A water evaporation unit also was installed, enabling the crew to make about 100,000 gallons of fresh water every day. That capability was essential to the war effort, for many of the smaller ships did not carry much fresh water. The ship, of course, carried various other supplies to be off-loaded to another American ship.

Once the conversion was complete, Lt. Bast and his supply ship went to Guadalcanal and then on to Ulithi, a circular series of small, low-lying islands that were large enough to get the fleet inside. The next step was to join a large convoy headed for Okinawa. They reached Okinawa on April 1, the exact day of the invasion. Homer's ship wasn't a participant in the invasion because it was no longer a landing ship; however, they anchored about a half mile away from the Japanese airfield. They remained there for almost 90 days and sustained some 260 air attacks.

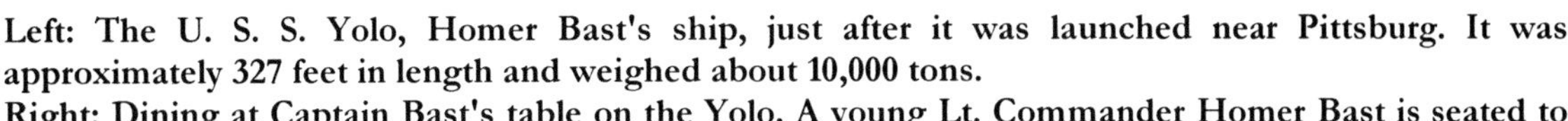

Left: The U. S. S. Yolo, Homer Bast's ship, just after it was launched near Pittsburg. It was approximately 327 feet in length and weighed about 10,000 tons.
Right: Dining at Captain Bast's table on the Yolo. A young Lt. Commander Homer Bast is seated to the right.

On June 29 the ship headed for the Philippines to prepare for the invasion of Honshu, which was one of the Japanese home islands. The term "home islands" was used to define the area of Japan to which its sovereignty and the constitutional rule of the Emperor would be restricted. The invasion was scheduled for October 1, 1945. Homer's ship helped in the days of preparation leading up to the invasion by carrying mail around the Philippines and running selected errands. At this point, no one knew about plans for the United States to drop the atomic bomb. Everyone, almost to a person, thought that soldiers would have to invade Japan and that the invasion would bring with it thousands of deaths on both sides. All of the ships, including the one that Homer commanded, had been given instructions about what to do and where to go during the invasion. So there they were, just waiting for the date to go in. Then the rumors began. Pilots who came aboard Homer's ship, for example, were talking about some secret weapon that would end the war.

The atomic bombs were dropped on Hiroshima and Nagasaki, and the subsequent Japanese surrender put an end to the invasion. Lt. Bast heard the news about the surrender on the American radio frequency. At the same time, Tokyo Rose was putting out propaganda that said Japan had sunk a hundred aircraft carriers and battleships. She even named the ships. Homer laughed at this announcement because he could look out and see many of those ships anchored next to his.

Homer's ship was sent to Japan with one of the first convoys to arrive there on about September 2, 1945. As they sailed into Yokohama, they could see the damage done during the war. The citizens of Yokohama showed no animosity toward the Americans.

So Homer could use some the Japanese as workers. They were paid in food and cigarettes. They didn't want the cigarettes in order to smoke them; instead, they would sell them on the black market. To help feed the Japanese, Homer had his men dump their leftover food on the dock. The citizens of Yokohama also received leftover wooden and cardboard boxes, which they used as housing.

Homer also remembers his officers and crew trying to take care of other needs. "One little boy was an orphan," he said. "His parents had been killed by American bombings and he was pitifully small and almost without clothes. We brought him aboard and gave him some ice cream. His teeth were so bad that he couldn't eat it. Then we got some trousers and a shirt from the smallest sailor aboard our ship. We cut off the legs of the trousers and the arms of the shirt. So we fit that little boy with at least one set of clothes. We also negotiated with a Navy dentist, from a large ship anchored near us, to fix the boy's teeth. Finally, he could enjoy his ice cream."

Orders for Homer to return home came on November 5, 1945, after he had accumulated the necessary points for discharge. He had been in the service since September of 1941–over four years. Finally, the war was over for Homer and many others. He had served on two ships–the PC 571 and the USS Yolo. The Yolo, in particular, had provided him with good memories. Homer wrote in his Captain's Diary, "Yolo has been a joy and I feel that we had a great ship, not just a good one. We have received nothing but praise for the work we have done. I am so excited tonight. I cannot believe that I am going home. Neither can I put down in any sort of thoughtful or meaningful way my feelings of how I have lived, worked, and been through tough times with this great group of boys who have become men."

On November 6, at 1400, the crewmen ran him across the quay to the Calvert. The next day, all lines were let go and the Calvert left for the United States. "We were not only at sea," Homer thought, "but another experience and a great responsibility in my life was over."

When he was discharged from the Navy, in about March of 1946, he discovered that the transition from the commanding officer of the Yolo to civilian life was extremely difficult. Needing a job, he went back to Staunton Military Academy to see about resuming his pre-war position. They didn't want to give him his job back, however, and he had to tell them that he would take them to court. Federal law at the time required employers to take back workers who left their jobs to enter the service. So the Academy buckled and gave him a job, but it was nothing meaningful. He took the title of Assistant Superintendent. There was no teaching involved, although he also helped Lou Honesty coach that year. One of his friends at Staunton Military was Jimmy Baer. Playing for the Randolph-Macon football team in 1939, he was the second-leading scorer in the country. When Homer was taking his physical to enter the Navy, Baer was there also. He told

Homer, "You go in first. I want to know if they make you take off your socks." A small guy, he wanted to know if he would be able to put four silver dollars in his shoes, tucked under his heels, so he could make the height qualifications. The fellow giving the physicals never caught on, and Baer got in the Navy.

Homer's First and Only College Job

After the end of the school year at Staunton Military, Homer decided that he really wanted to teach history. His dreams of a doctorate were long gone, but he knew that teaching was to be his life. In search of that dream, he applied for a job at Roanoke College and was hired at a meager salary to be an Assistant Professor in the College's history department. That first year, his teaching load consisted of four sections of World Civilizations and a class in English History, taught over a six-day week. The selection and number of courses, plus all of the quizzes and papers to be graded (and returned within 48 hours), made for a very busy first year of college teaching.

One of his achievements in that first year of employment at the College, besides keeping a day ahead of students in preparing his lesson plans, was getting Buddy Hackman, the Athletic Director, to approve of his coaching track and then, the next fall, cross country. At the time, Buddy was operating his department with little money, but when Homer promised him that expenses would be minimal, he agreed.

He set out to re-build the College's cinder track, which had been completed during the 1928-29 school year. Just a year later, track as an intercollegiate sport was dropped at Roanoke. So the track had sat there un-tended to from 1930 until 1946. The school did play football inside the oval, but the track surface itself became overrun with weeds and Homer barely could find the inside and outside rails. With the help of the railroad, who donated tons of cinders, and the City of Salem, Homer was able over a period of months to create a new and better track. Providing lots of help were the College's Maintenance Department, headed by Harry Hodges, and many of the boys who were on the first track teams.

Looking toward the spring of 1947, Homer scheduled three meets. None could be run on the Roanoke track, of course. They surprised Bridgewater College by squeaking out a two-point win. Randolph-Macon won the second meet handily, and then Roanoke beat Lynchburg by about 35 points in the third meet of the spring. Homer was fortunate to finish the year with two wins and one loss. He had pulled this team together with a combination of notices on bulletin boards and articles in the *Brackety-Ack* newspaper. He also had a keen eye for outstanding talent on other teams. Big, strong Jim Doran came from the basketball team, as did the talented Jim Ruscick. He recruited Paul McCarty, a fine distance runner, from the baseball team.

During the summer of 1947, Dr. Brown asked Homer to teach three different courses. It would not be an easy task for the young college professor. As Homer said, "Once again, the assignments were tough. Teaching three hours each day, five days a week, for nine weeks, took a great deal of time. The summer was not fun, although Mary Jane and I spent many afternoons at the Senter pool with colleagues and their families. We were always available for chaperoning and Mary Jane presided at the punch bowl during college functions."

Homer could see the advantages of having a cross country team that fall. Almost no small college teams at the time had very many good distance runners, so he began a cross country program in the fall of 1947. His early success in college coaching actually was built around his distance runners. Four of his early runners, Alvin Smith, Bruce Davenport, Paul McCarty, and L. Z. "Red" Crockett, were labeled "the Big Four" and received much publicity across the state. It wasn't uncommon for four or five of Roanoke's teammates–including Frank Aldred and White Rhyne–to be so far out in front at the end of their races that they would wait on each other, joining hands as they crossed the finish line.

In the three fall seasons before Homer was called as a reservist to active duty just before the 1950-51 session, his cross country teams posted a string of 12 wins and no losses. The Little Six Conference had no championship meet in 1947, but in the next two years Roanoke won the Little Six Championships twice. In Homer's first attendance in the Mason-Dixon Championships in 1949, the team placed first. And they won the Virginia AAU Championships in 1949.

In September of 1949, Homer was appointed Associate Professor of History. Noting the time he spent in coaching, the administration reduced his teaching load to four classes. At the same time, his church commitments began to consume more and more of his time. He was elected President of the Men's Club at St. Paul's Episcopal Church, which sat diagonally across from the town's post office, and a vestryman in November of 1949. Some years later, he was named a trustee of the church.

His coaching was respected by the student body. In fact, on May 19, 1949, he was named an honorary member of the Monogram Club, a campus organization open to athletic letter winners from all varsity sports.

Just before the beginning of the 1950-51 session, three significant events occurred. One was the birth of his first son, Michael Keene Bast, on July 16, 1950. Michael would go on to be not only a student at Roanoke College but to become one of the school's all-time best distance runners and a member of the Athletic Hall of Fame.

The second event of importance was his appointment in the spring of 1950 to be Director of Admissions, taking the place of the deceased Stuart Hanks. With his experience in serving on the Admissions and Scholarship and Promotions committees, his transition to an administrative position was made easily.

The third event ended up being one of the most traumatic experiences of Homer's life. While Homer was in the Naval Reserves, serving as commanding officer of the Naval Reserve Surface Division in Roanoke City, he was called to active duty. He managed to coach the first cross country meet that fall–a one-point victory over Hampden-Sydney–before leaving for duty in Washington State and Alaska. During his absence, the team was coached by former top runner, Alvin Smith, who now was ineligible as a student. Alvin's team won three meets and lost another that year. They finished second in the Little Six meet and third in the Conference Championships. Alvin's outdoor track team finished its season with a record of one win and two losses in dual meets, along with a fifth-place finish in the Little Six Championships and a ninth-place finish in the Mason-Dixon Championships.

After Homer's return to the College, his cross country teams had two mediocre seasons. The combined records for the 1951-52 and 1952-53 squads were just three wins and four losses. They failed to win either the Little Six or Mason-Dixon meets. Alvin Smith, an interim coach for the College, wasn't expected to recruit new students for the cross country and track teams. So the distance teams really didn't have many quality runners. It was at this time that Homer decided to write letters–and lots of them–to high school and preparatory school coaches in the New York/New Jersey area, where there were many good athletes. For periods of time, he would force himself to write no fewer than five letters a day. For the next several years, he could see the results of those letters in the quality of his teams.

Once, he even wrote to nationally-ranked Al Oerter when he was in high school. Later in his career, Al Oerter was the only athlete ever to win the same Olympic event–the discus–four times in a row, setting Olympic records each time. Homer and Al corresponded with each other for some time. "Of course," said Homer, "he was such a horse that he wasn't ever going to come to a school like Roanoke College." Actually, Homer seldom wrote to a talented field event man because he felt that most of them would end up playing football in college.

Meanwhile, Mary Jane and Homer bought a lot on Locust Avenue in Salem, not far from the College. On January 1, 1952, construction on their new house–the one they lived in for almost 60 years–was begun. The builders completed the construction of the two-story house in April and the family moved in.

In the spring of 1952, Homer and Bob McLelland–former student and now Sports Editor of the *Roanoke World-News*, conceived of the City-County Track Meet to be held annually on the Roanoke College track. Homer served as the meet's Director for some 10 years. Often, it was held concurrently with one of the College's own meets. The only participants were the all-white schools in the area. Addison High School, with only black students, did not compete. Unfortunately, the meet was cancelled after the 1962 session with smoldering race relations being the major cause. The Cosmopolitan Club of Roanoke began its own long-term sponsorship of the meet several years later.

On March 26, 1953, Mary Jane gave birth to a second son–Stephen Todd Bast. Stephen, like Michael, later attended Roanoke College and competed as a talented middle-distance runner. After Stephen's birth, Mary Jane needed some help raising her two young children. Homer would help after teaching his courses that first summer. And he would always try to assist with the boys after cross country and track practices. On occasion, Mary Jane's mother even came down from Staunton to help. From time to time over the next few years, the Basts asked some of the track and cross country boys to baby sit Michael and Stephen while Homer and Mary Jane socialized with friends.

As the cross country team was building, the 1953 team won three meets and lost two, but was good enough to win the Little Six Championships and to finish third in the Mason-Dixon meet.

In the spring of 1954, Homer was named Registrar of the College. He carried out these duties along with a usual teaching load. To help, the administration lightened his teaching load by assigning him four sections of World Civilizations. Preparation time was lessened, although grading papers for 50-55 students was very time consuming.

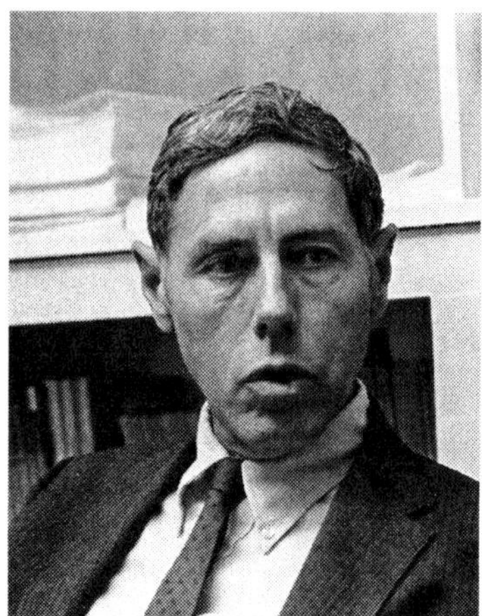

Homer served for many years as the College's Registrar.

Homer's 1954 team showed that distance running at Roanoke was back on track. In this season and in the next four, his teams won every single Little Six, Little Seven, or Little Eight meet. They also won the Mason-Dixon Championships in 1954, 1955, 1956,

1957, 1958, and 1959. The dual and triangular meet records were equally astounding. The 1954 team was 6-0; the 1955 record was 5 wins and 2 losses (both losses by a total of three points); the 1956 team went undefeated at 7-0; the 1957 team won six meets and lost by four points to William and Mary; the 1958 team went 9-0 for a perfect season; the only loss out of five meets in 1959 was also with William and Mary (by five points); and the final Bast team in 1960 finished with a respectable record of three wins and two losses. Along the way, the teams recorded dual- and tri-meet winning streaks of 8, 15, and 14.

For all of the cross country teams Homer coached, from 1947 until 1960, his record was 58 wins and 13 losses. Very few coaches in Virginia, or for that matter in the country, have compiled such a fine record.

The Indoor Track Program

When Homer began the track program, there were few indoor meets that were close enough to Salem so as not to exceed the meager amounts of money set aside by Buddy Hackman for travel. Usually, he was able to take a few of the team members to the Washington Evening Star Games as well as to variously-named indoor meets in Chapel Hill. The Evening Star meet had at least one event designated for Mason-Dixon teams. In the Chapel Hill meets, he generally could enter athletes in the non-Conference division. Both meets had outstanding contestants. Later, beginning with the 1953 season, athletes were able to compete at Virginia Military Institute's newly-converted indoor track facility. It took about an hour to drive from Salem to V. M. I., and the Maroons sometimes used the field house in Lexington for practice. Also, starting in 1953, the V. M. I. field house allowed the team to compete in dual meets with V. M. I., the new indoor Mason-Dixon Conference meet, and the Little Six/Seven/Eight indoor meet. The team also began to participate in the V. M. I. Winter Relays, which brought together superior athletes from colleges and universities throughout the eastern and southern areas of the nation.

From 1953 through 1957, when Homer gave up the head coaching job for indoor and outdoor track, his teams won both the Little Six/Seven/Eight titles each year. Beginning in 1954, the first year for a Mason-Dixon Indoor Championship Meet, the Roanoke team won each Mason-Dixon meet until Homer retired.

The Outdoor Track Program

Homer's outdoor track teams had modest success throughout the first five or so years of his coaching. In fact, the record stood at 10 dual-meet wins and 10 losses through the end of the 1952 season. Beginning with the 1953 season, however, the success of the teams and the magnitude of Homer's reputation, took a major leap forward. At the beginning of the 1953 season, the team took a trip south to Clemson and then Davidson for dual meets. Both meets resulted in losses; however, from that point on through the end of Homer's career, his outdoor teams never lost another dual meet. There were five straight wins in 1953; eight in 1954; eight in 1955; seven in 1956; and eight more in 1957, the final year before his retirement from track coaching. No other coach in the College's history ever ran up a winning streak of 36 meets. During this streak, the average score was 89.57 for Roanoke and 34.12 for opponents.

As the team gained more depth, especially in the 1955-57 years, Roanoke also began to win all of the major meets it entered. It won the Little Six meet in 1953; the Little Seven meet in 1954 and 1955; and the Little Eight Championships in 1956 and 1957. In the Mason-Dixon Conference, they won all of the titles from 1954 through 1957.

Indeed, Homer and his boys were the toasts of the campus. Roanoke College students considered Homer a wonderful teacher, advisor, and friend. The 1955 *Rawenoch*, Roanoke's yearbook, was dedicated to him. The reason for this honor was expressed in the following statement: "Because you have shown such interest in each of us, and have taken our individual problems as your own; because you have taught us of our great American heritage and have prepared us for our future roles as leaders of tomorrow; because you have taken a deep interest in clean sportsmanship and have coached many championship teams; because you have given your best to Roanoke College and have succeeded in making it a better institution of higher learning; because we want you to know that your undivided time have been appreciated by all."

What Makes a Good Coach?

I don't know if I have ever met an individual who didn't like Homer Bast. That alone would make a good epitaph for his life. He is remembered for a lot of wonderful traits. Phil Shaw once said, "Homer became the male mentor of my life. He was just an unbelievable person. You couldn't help falling in love with the guy if you were around him. His whole persona was something to behold. The thing I really admired about Homer more than anything else was that he was not just a track coach. He was a mind builder. He taught me how to build my mind and mental capacity. After I got married, my wife couldn't believe how often I talked about Homer. She had never met him. We went back to the College one time and she finally got a chance to talk with him. She walked away shaking her head and told me she finally knew why I talked about Homer all of the time." As I compiled the information for this book, I asked each person I interviewed why they liked Homer–why he was considered such a good coach. I will summarize a few points that they made.

First, by the time he was hired to teach at Roanoke Colleges, he was a bit more than 30 years of age with leadership skills keenly honed in the Navy. Students soon learned about his experiences aboard the 571 and USS Yolo, and about the fact that he was responsible for the safety of hundreds of crewmen and officers over a five-year period. Students also came to respect him for his record at the University of Virginia. He had been elected President of the Student Body and had barely missed getting his Ph.D. in history. It is human nature to develop great respect for people we consider exemplary. And Homer was truly worthy of their respect.

Students found that Homer had his priorities in order. He taught every student that academics were first and sports were second. They knew that he could teach–and teach very well. To Homer, teaching history was very much like telling a good story. Over the years, few people ever slept through his classes. He was knowledgeable, dedicated to his teaching, and fun to watch. Sometimes, he would lean on that old podium at the front of the class, moving his face toward you as he talked and making eye contact with everyone. When he found that students had limited hearing, as he once did with one of his own athletes, he would move them up front and make sure that, if needed, they could read his lips. At times, he would stop his lecture and talk one-on-one with someone in the class who was having problems. Some remember Homer spinning his tales while hanging onto a fireman-type pole at the front of the room. Earl Johnston says, "I never had a teacher who was so forceful and energetic in his teaching. I still remember him hanging off of that pole in the classroom. He'd hang onto that pole with one arm and spin around it, almost like an exotic dancer, while he was teaching. He really worked that pole."

He not only taught well, but he gave some of the most difficult tests of any professor on campus. It was common for somewhat frightened freshmen–whose major problem in high school was in remembering to study an hour or so for the next day's test–to pull an all-nighter before one of Homer's tests. He was not happy if you did poorly on a test, and was outwardly ecstatic if you got an "A." But whether you were a superior student or someone who just wanted to pass his course and move on, Homer was always courteous and encouraging.

Another of Homer's strengths was that he sincerely wanted his athletes to be successful, both on and off the field. As Warren Light said, "I feel that the main reason he is remembered today is because he cared for every individual." He asked his athletes for the best efforts they could give–nothing more, nothing less. Jim Wallwork, on the occasion of Homer's retirement from track, said: "It is not just your coaching ability that makes you the respected man you are. It is the personal interest you take in each individual. It is men like you, Mr. Bast, that give Roanoke College its good name."

Homer realized, of course, that for an athlete to do his best, he had to be motivated.

Sometimes, this motivation came one-on-one, between coach and athlete. Students often sought him out in his office, and he would take the time to talk to them about topics ranging from training to the individuals they would be competing against that week. Then there were the many visits he paid to dorm rooms, just to say hello and perhaps to leave a "you can do it" thought in someone's mind.

His efforts to motivate his athletes were very effective. "I would tell the boys how interested the school would be, and how we would be personally, in their success," Homer said. "I would tell them that they were champions and that if they tried their best, they couldn't be beaten. I learned a lot from Archie Hahn at the University of Virginia, because he definitely was not a motivator. He never said anything to me about anything. I would tell my team that I wasn't going to kill them in practice. I thought that academics were very important. Sometimes, I would leave them little notes. And I put out these publications with quotes of inspiration in them. And to each individual, I stressed the power of saying, 'You can do it. I believe in you. Just give it your best effort.' "

Often, Homer provided motivation in the form of written words. For example, several times over the years, he sent out versions of this poem by Rudyard Kipling:

If you can keep your head when all about you
Are losing theirs and blaming it on you,
If you can trust yourself when all men doubt you
But make allowance for their doubting too,
If you can wait and not be tired by waiting,
Or being lied about, don't deal in lies,
Or being hated, don't give way to hating,
And yet don't look too good, nor talk too wise:
If you can dream--and not make dreams your master,
If you can think--and not make thoughts your aim;
If you can meet with Triumph and Disaster
And treat those two impostors just the same;
If you can bear to hear the truth you've spoken
Twisted by knaves to make a trap for fools,
Or watch the things you gave your life to, broken,
And stoop and build 'em up with worn-out tools:
If you can make one heap of all your winnings
And risk it all on one turn of pitch-and-toss,
And lose, and start again at your beginnings
And never breath a word about your loss;
If you can force your heart and nerve and sinew

To serve your turn long after they are gone,
And so hold on when there is nothing in you
Except the Will which says to them: "Hold on!"
If you can talk with crowds and keep your virtue,
Or walk with kings--nor lose the common touch,
If neither foes nor loving friends can hurt you;
If all men count with you, but none too much,
If you can fill the unforgiving minute
With sixty seconds' worth of distance run,
Yours is the Earth and everything that's in it,
And--which is more--you'll be a Man, my son!
--Rudyard Kipling

Distance runner Les Noel also remembers in particular a motto that Homer used each and every year: "Life's battles don't always go to the strongest or fastest man, but soon or late, the man who wins is the man who knows he can."

Especially in the latter years of his coaching, Homer would send out track and field newsletters to his boys. Here are some examples of the inspirational words he used:

> *December 07, 1955*– Those of you who are in this track game realize the great importance the "mental" plays in this sport, and every sport for that matter. There are slumps or periods when improvement is slow; in fact, it seems to halt almost altogether. You must realize that improvement in all fields does not occur in a straight line, but by plateaus and valleys, just as Civilizations. These periods of failure to improve occur at two phases in the training season. The first comes at the start of the season (4-6 weeks after beginning) when there is a tendency you crowd in too much work too soon, and when you begin to evaluate yourself in terms of your teammates. A period of physical and mental adjustment must take place, during which time improvement is likely to stand still or even fall away. The second period usually occurs toward the end of the season. At this time, anything that removes the burden of impending failure or that makes fun of what has now become drudgery, should be followed.
>
> You are likely to maintain your enthusiasm as long as your improvement is steady; your goals seem achievable and your fatigue does not carry over from one day to the next.
>
> *December 14, 1955*– The proper mental approach to an event and to

competition is often the difference between success and failure. A fine state of mind from the first day of practice until the last day of competition is typical of the champion athlete. Determination, confidence, and the desire to win are the basic ingredients of success, and without them no athlete can perform up to capacity. Competent coaching, adequate competition, and encouragement are the factors which develop pride and confidence, and the resulting proper mental attitude. Believing that nothing is impossible, and then setting out to prove it, is the result of sound mental preparation. The axiom I followed seems a good one today: speed, stamina, strategy, courage, concentration, and condition. Having those I can only say to each and every one of you, "Hi, champ."

December 21, 1955– A true sense of values is one of the most important lessons taught through track practice and competition. Of course, you receive from your participation just what you put into your training and practice. Champions must work hard to become champs. There is no easy road–and to you of cinder fame the stop watch and tape objectively appraise your every performance. Everything in life has a price.

"The heights which great men gained and kept
Were not attained by sudden flight;
But they while their companions slept
Were toiling upward in the night."

But even with all that, there is friendship. Get to know your teammates, give them a pat on the back. It is wonderful. Try it. Let there be rivalry and competition, but honest, sportsmanship, and friendship will rise above it all. Give yourself and it will be returned to you a hundredfold. Records are merely transitory, but love, faith, friendship, and honesty will remain much longer than the records.

March 28, 1956– I'll just say a word or two along the lines of our gentleman's agreement about practicing over the holidays and then I'll quit.

All track and field men should understand that conditioning is primarily a matter of building resistance to the many effects of fatigue. This is done by gradually increasing, as muscle efficiency improves, the

> amount of work that is done, much as one gives increasing dosages of vaccine in building resistance against certain diseases.
>
> In other words, you need those practice sessions at home. Do not get discouraged, as some of you will, but keep at it and the improvement will come. To some of you, the sleep, the exercise, and the change in food will come as a welcome relief. On the other hand, several of you should get some vitamin pills. From the looks of your eyes, some of you have a low red blood count. All those are important factors. Get checked and come back with some determination to make this year the greatest year you have ever had in track personally and the greatest team Roanoke College ever had.

Homer also was a master motivator on the athletic field. His was a laid-back approach as a coach, interrupted by a few well-placed arm pumps when someone did well. Homer always made sure that his athletes knew the caliber of their competition, but also knew that their coach thought they could win with the right effort. There were many pep talks just before and event began. And occasionally, this usually quiet coach could be seen yelling and rooting an athlete along, motivating him to do his best. Pete Wise, for example, remembers the day on the Roanoke track in the spring of 1959, with Bridgewater as the opponent. Pete was running one of his last three 440s in a long and very successful career at the college. "The gun sounded and we made our way around the first turn. I was with the front group at the 220 mark when I glanced to my left and saw Coach Bast running across the field toward me. 'Go, Pete, go,' he yelled. 'This is your last chance to break the 440 record!' He knew how much I wanted that school record. I had worked hard my senior year to get it. His words gave me an extra shot of adrenalin, and I came across the finish line in first place, running a :49.7." It was, indeed, a new school record. In a letter recently sent to Homer, Pete said, "Well, my friend, coach, and mentor, it was really you who went under 50 seconds that day. Yes, I was only a puppet in your hands and heart. I still look at the :49.7 as one of my finest achievements."

Coach Bast, a compassionate man always willing to help, treated everyone with respect. He listened, he advised, and sometimes served as a father figure. And he communicated well. Les Noel came to Roanoke College from the small town of Buena Vista. He had no running experience, and had grown up on his own, without parental guidance. He later said of Homer, "For a few of us on the team, like me, he knew that we needed help to adjust to college life. In my case, I had grown up alone. He really took me under his wing. He was not only my professor in class, but he was a fatherly figure to me. He really taught me a lot. He taught me how to live my life and do the best I could. Under Homer you not only wanted to win for yourself, but you wanted to win for him and the team. He got the best out of everybody, in fact. He could really work with people. He was a good motivator. We worked hard for him, in the classroom as well as on the track."

Does Homer feel now that as a coach he had any weaknesses–weaknesses he might correct if he could start over? The author asked him that question. Homer replied, "I probably could have devoted more time to the athletes if I had had the time. Coaching was not my major occupation. Teaching history was. And in 1955, right at the crucial time when we were beginning to move into the higher echelons of track and cross country, I became Registrar. And that added a lot of work. Nothing was ever taken away from me. So that was one weakness. Maybe I could have had a more hands-on approach, especially during meets. I noticed that some of the coaches would gather their boys together to outline what they wanted to do. My only thing was to get in there and run as hard as you can. That's the thing we were after. So, I don't know. Maybe I didn't give all of the time necessary for some of these boys. But, as you know, it takes an inordinate amount of time to do a good job coaching. I mean, it's not just going out on that field. You have to keep in contact with these kids. So that's what I tried to do. And there was one more thing. Maybe one of my great failings was that I was hard on my athletes on occasions. I wanted their success, not only as a team but as an individual. Not only in college, but in life. I was teaching the battle of life. I told those kids that every time they ran a quarter of a mile, they were running the battle of life. They would find everything in a quarter of a mile that they would find in life."

Did his athletes see him as a father figure? In some cases, Homer remembers, the answer was "yes." He noted, "During my career as coach, we had a number of athletes who had lost their fathers–George Jocher, Dick Goodlake, Derek Stryker, David Moore, Dave Foltz, Les Noel, Roger Stanton, and others. I tried to be there for them and tried to say the right thing. I may not have been very old, but I had all of that service time behind me. When I was in the Navy, I was often called on to advise younger seamen. Many of these individuals were just kids, maybe 18 years old. And some were just 17 years old, having lied about their age to get in the Navy."

He was always teaching. Sometimes that teaching came in the form of a trip to a dorm room at night. Bruce Fariss remembers these trips well. "Homer used to show up in the dorms around 10:00 p.m. All of a sudden, there would be this knock on the door. And there was Homer. He would close the door and sit talking with you for a few minutes. Occasionally, he would have this polite little conversation with you. You had the feeling that Homer knew everything you were doing–that he had eyeballs focused on you all the time." On other occasions, of course, the talk might be about almost anything. He would ask about the student's life and always see if there was anything he could do to help. Many times, these dorm visits were at random. At other times, because he had good ears around the campus, he came for specific reasons. Pete Wise recalls one of these visits.

His roommate at the time was Howard Meincke, and they lived in Wells Hall. According to Pete, "I can tell you one instance that influenced me. Howard got soused one night when he was a freshman. He drank a little too much and the next day, he had trouble walking around. He definitely was hung over and as a consequence, he missed his workout that day. Homer heard about the situation and instead of flying off the handle or kicking butt, he came up to the dorm room and sat down. He talked to Howard just like he was his father. Because of Homer's understanding approach, Howard never again had another incident like that. Homer was a model for human warmth and kindness."

He always believed that education did not end in the classroom–that he should try to convince students to come by and see him, especially if they had a problem. At the University of Virginia, where he graded papers for Professors, even if students failed a test they would not come in to see him and talk about why they failed. They might just drop the course. At Roanoke, Homer thought, he would try a different tactic. He decided to visit them. He missed a lot, of course, not being with his wife and two children. But he made a decision that he could do the most good visiting students in their dorms. Of course, he also received visits in his office during the day or would talk with his athletes during practices on Alumni Field. Some of the boys were interested in what married life would be all about. Some were not considering marriage at all because they felt they couldn't support a wife and children. To these individuals, Homer pressed the fact that, if they did get married, it was a form of job for them. They had to work at a marriage if they wanted it to succeed.

Often, Homer talked with them about the values and the battles of life. One of his favorite analogies was that if you were out for track, no matter what event you were in, you were running the battle of life. Winning on the field and in life required dedication, personal values, integrity, and much, much more.

Sometimes, these conversations would occur on track or cross country trips. The boys liked to sing and so Homer and they sang for a while, and the singing turned to discussions of life. Often, Homer would stop and shift the athletes around from car to car so they had different people to talk with.

Homer also was a good communicator in many other ways. In the summer time, he not only published a small newsletter for the athletes two or three times in the course of the summer, but he also wrote individual letters to them if he thought they needed them. He would hear "So and so is running this summer." And he would immediately write to that person. All of this type of thing brought them together. He was trying for cohesiveness and a team concept. Each one of the Bast Boys was a different person. And they each had to be handled in a different way.

Homer remembers that the long trips the team took, from traveling to Mason-Dixon Meets in the Washington area to the spring trips north or south, were wonderful because of the bonding that occurred on those long rides. This bonding was between athletes, of course, but it also brought Homer closer to his athletes.

For those athletes who piled in a car with Homer, any topic was fair game. Sometimes, the conversation might turn to girls and romance. These were young men who were thinking of their future, and they would often ask Homer about his thoughts on marriage. Should they get married, what should they look for in a wife, and how could one assure that the marriage would be a success. Homer hadn't been married that long, but he tried to give them the best advice he could. These trips were very relaxed, and occasionally Homer would throw in a risqué but memorable story to illustrate a point. Here is an example. During Homer's experience in the Navy, he had heard this story. He memorized it and, while standing watch he would recite it to those young Navy seamen who were on watch with him. Once, when someone asked about sex, Homer told them this story:

> "I told them that there was only one piece of advice I could give them. And this is pretty important. Before you get married, you go out and get yourself a gallon jar of mayonnaise. Then empty that jar. Also, get yourself a five-pound bag of white beans. Now, after you are married, then what you do (including your wedding night) is to put one bean in that jar for every time you have sexual intercourse. You put that bean in there every time for one year. After that year, then you begin to take those beans out – one for every time you have sexual intercourse. I told the boys, no matter how long you live, you'll never get all of those beans out of that jar."

Not long ago, Homer's wife, Mary Jane, laughed about the boys' reaction to this story. "You know," she said, "well after they graduated, I got phone calls wanting to hear that story one more time. I don't think they ever believed that Homer would tell them such a risqué story."

Indeed, he was reluctant to tell that story because he thought the boys were too young. Eventually, however, he would also recite this short ditty:

> From 20 to 30 if a man lives right,
> It's once in the morning and once at night.
> From 30 to 40, if he still lives right,
> He cuts out the morning or else the night.
> From 40 to 50, it's now and then.
> From 50 to 60, it's gosh knows when.

From 70 to 80 if he's still inclined,
Don't let him kid you; it's all in his mind.

In summary, we know from the compliments Homer has received through the years, that he was an exceptional individual and coach in many ways too numerous to mention. He was someone who led by example. He was enthusiastic about his coaching and teaching. He was committed to his work and especially to his athletes.

What made Homer a good coach? Here are just a few suggestions not mentioned above.

I remember . . . "He was a very even-handed guy. He would talk to you one on one about your possibilities and what you needed to do to improve. He never yelled at anyone. He inspired confidence in you. He made you feel like you should work hard. He was just a very good man, easy to talk to. He was a very moral type of guy, a very decent human being who didn't look down on anyone. He was a very motivational coach."

Jim O'Mahony

I remember . . . "Everybody seemed to like Homer. He was a friend and never had anything bad to say about anything or anybody. He was a very likeable person. He had a very even temperament and was never mad about anything, but was always encouraging. I was surprised that he even took the time to work with me."

Bob Nilson

I remember . . . "From the moment I joined his cross country team, Coach Bast took me under his wing and shepherded me along. I told him up front that I wasn't very talented. But he said that it was unimportant, and he just kept working with me. He knew my family situation and always kept an eye out for me. He was always friendly. I remember one day that he said he wanted to give me something. He handed me a pass to the Colonial Theater, which then was located on West Main Street at about the spot the CVS Pharmacy is sitting today. He gave me and the other members of the cross country team these passes, which you could use any day of the week for as many times as you wished. I think they were good for a year and they didn't have any blackout dates. Homer just had a good relationship with the owner of the theater, who lived near him. That was typical of the kinds of things Homer would do for us. He was always thinking of us. I got to know Mrs. Bast well. They had two children. Mrs. Bast was a knockout–a real beauty. I was pretty shy, but Mrs. Bast was always so gracious to me. She would come over and give me a hug and ask how I was doing. I almost felt like I was part of the Bast family."

David Moore

I remember . . . "Homer was on top of things, but he wasn't excitable. He would give a little hand pump now and then when something good was happening. I just remember him as being very low key. He was a quiet motivator. He wasn't a screamer or yeller. He would never threaten you or do anything like that. Ultimately, however, he always got his way. And being a part of this great team, you felt that you had a responsibility to keep that dynasty going."

Dick Seed

I remember . . . "Homer was my guide, affecting my whole existence. I am proud to have accepted his tutelage."

Pete Wise

I remember . . . "I have always had a lot of respect for Homer Bast. He's a good man. And he was a good coach. He was very encouraging. He was the kind of person that I really admired. Every year, he threw a little get-together at his house for members of his teams. I remember that when I was at the College, he lived right down there near the campus on Market Street."

Ray DeCosta

I remember . . . "It is difficult to sum up our experiences with Homer. In some ways, he is one of the most complete human beings I ever knew. He is a man for all seasons. He is an academic, an athlete, a compassionate, generous person, and he is, for me (and this is a real plus) a deeply religious and devout man. He was a surrogate father for hundreds of people. I lost my father at about the time I was at Roanoke College. And Homer and Don Sutton filled that void for me."

Frank Vest

I remember . . . "Homer simply cared about people. He had the personality of someone you wanted to work hard for. I think he expected a lot of us. Somehow, he just made you want to work hard. He was calm most of the time. But he was also forceful. He could get out of you the best you had. I had a difficult time learning how to study, in particular that first year. Homer would come over to the dorms and help me with my studies. That's so unusual for a college coach to do. He genuinely cared for all of us, seeing that we did well not only in track but in academics. He was a real motivator."

Jim Wallwork

I remember . . . "Homer was a physical presence. He presented himself well. He looked good physically and he talked like he knew what he was talking about. He looked like someone who really cared about you and was worth listening to. I still won't forget his history class. He seemed to be very interested in history. I was impressed by his involvement in World War II, and loved his tales about Midway and other places. I think he was very proud of his military service. And he was very patriotic in that sense. Even before I knew his family, I was impressed that he was an easy-going, southern, folksy person. Yet, you could tell right from the start that he was also someone you didn't want to mess around with. He knew how to handle himself. I thought he had a pretty good hold on life. Guys from the cross country and track teams would often come over to baby-sit for Michael and Steven. He wanted you to finish what you started. And he asked you to do your best. You didn't have to be best in the world, but should at least give it a try and finish what you started. One of his lines was, 'You just run to the next telephone pole.' When you think you can't take another step, just give it one more try. Just run to the next telephone pole."

Dr. Wayne Wilson

I remember . . . "The Indians have an expression: 'In strength there is gentleness, and in gentleness there is strength.' That expression applies to Homer Bast. His caring was not with words. It was with action. Today, I just give Homer A+ across the board."

Pete Wise

I remember . . . "I think so highly of Homer. I think he is just an outstanding person–a man of integrity, compassion, and intelligence. I could never say enough good things about Homer Bast. I will never forget him. As a person and as a track coach, he had a big influence on me. He taught me that I should try to be a better person. He was a good motivator. Now on the field, he had to spread himself thin to cover all of the events. But I think he was good at observing technique, at motivating you and trying to get you to work hard, working on your form, and that kind of thing. He encouraged me to gain some weight. He knew that I was just too darn thin to throw the discus. He was a very low key person. He would never try to force you into an event."

Bill Driscoll

I remember . . . "The thing about Homer was that we all respected him. Even to this day, and especially back then as a student, we would never call him Homer. It was always Coach Bast or just Coach. He had earned that respect. And for a guy like me, just past 17, he was a rather imposing figure. He was relatively thin and in shape. When he coached you, he was very encouraging. And he was a firm individual. He was someone you certainly grew to respect and appreciate."

Bob Upton

I remember . . . "He was great. He gave me an opportunity to participate. Our team of four athletes went up to Washington, D. C., and actually won a relay race. That was a fun way to begin my career at Roanoke. For our indoor seasons, we had to practice on the quadrangle. The cinder track wasn't in any condition to be used during the winter."

Walt Tramposch

I remember . . . "The first time I saw Homer Bast, I had just reported to the college. We were taking those entrance tests that we all took over in the Commons. Coming out of those tests, he was standing at the back of the Administration Building talking to Clarence Caldwell. Someone told me that there was Homer Bast. I was too embarrassed to go over to him. I knew I would see him at the first track practice. And I did. And we got to be good friends. I listened to everything he said. His philosophy about life, people, and what you believed in meant more to me than anything else. Later, when I was a flight officer in the Navy, I used his name time and time again in speeches I gave. I used Homer as an example of what leadership meant and what I thought people in positions of leadership had to have in order to make their lives and the lives of their subordinates mean something. Homer convinced me and others that it was possible to do whatever we wanted to do, as long as you did it right. On track trips, we had the most fun. Everyone liked him. I have never heard anyone say anything negative about him–ever. I don't think anyone on the team would have allowed it. As far as our team was concerned, we didn't want power. We just wanted to be good at what we did. We wanted people to look at us and say, 'There goes that track team,' or 'There are the guys who do the right things all of the time.' We didn't want to get into trouble. We always wanted Coach Bast to be proud of us. If he wasn't, that would hurt our feelings forever. I can remember many a Friday or Saturday night being over to Coach's house looking after Michael and Steven. At the time, I was going with the campus May Queen, Corina Henderson, and we spent a lot of time with them. You got to know the family, and you got to know more about what they thought. It was like a Leave It to Beaver episode. You'd sit there and say, 'isn't that great.' You always felt like you meant something to him–that you were important. Maybe you weren't very important if you considered what you meant to the team, but you were important to him as one of the parts that went into making up the whole. One year, I was running against one of the best runners in the south, at Clemson. I knew that Homer knew how good the guy was, but I don't know if he knew that I knew. I would ask Homer, 'How good is this guy?' Homer would say, 'Don't worry. You can beat him.' He would never let you doubt yourself. So you went out there thinking, 'Coach thinks I can win.' I had two coaches, one in high school and the other in college, who meant so much to me. Although my high school coach approached life differently than did Homer, both were two of the greatest men I have ever known other than my dad. They could do so much for you because they always thought that you had something you could give back."

John Summers

I remember . . . "I liked Homer's coaching style. You just knew that he was interested in you. He got the best out of you. But he never did it by screaming and yelling. He was a con artist. He could con you into doing what he wanted you to do. And you would think it was your own idea. He convinced me that I could be a good hurdler, when I had never hurdled before. Homer was very close to us all. The last time I was at his house, not too long ago, I was sitting on the sofa with him. He took my hand. And he said, 'I love you. You know that, don't you?' Well, I was about to cry. He had that feeling about everybody. You knew it. And because of that, you would do anything for him. But he was very low key. He never raised his voice. Everybody loved him to death. You got an emotional attachment to him, just like you would do with your own father. In fact, he often treated you as if you were his son. And you responded to him as a son would to a father. You always wanted to please him. You wanted to make him proud of you. And that was his method of motivating people. He engendered that love and caring to you, and he looked after you. At one point, when I was making low grades, he never yelled at me nor fussed. He just said, 'Dick, you'd better get busy, now. Let's get these grades up before the end of the semester.' You just didn't want to let him down."

Dick Seed

I remember . . . "Well, I was around Coach Bast some in high school. All of the high schools in the area had to run their track meets at the college. When we could come up here, he was almost our high school coach. He'd see you doing something not right, and he'd take you aside and tell you what you were doing wrong. Do this. Do that. So it wasn't a big surprise to talk with him. But I never, never imagined at that early age that he was as great as he was. I think he was ahead of his time in track–in training methods. I had been to V. M. I. and watched track meets and practices there, and I never saw down there the types of workouts that Coach Bast had us doing. His whole attitude was that if you do the best you can, that's all you can do. I'll be happy, and you'll be happy. And that put pressure on you. Sometimes, you knew that you hadn't done your best. He would see me after French class, and he would say, 'Let's go talk to Professor Lindsey.' So we would. Coach Bast was a second father to me. And to me, that's saying a whole lot, because I had a great dad and a great uncle in my life. But we just loved Mr. Bast. That's all you could say. When you were running, you could hear that big, booming voice yelling things like 'Get up there.' "

Howard Light

I remember . . . "Well, Coach Bast and I meshed well, I guess. He is a fine man. He really is. For one thing, he had leadership abilities. Most of us knew what he had accomplished in his Naval career. And that was no small thing. He had been a very good track man at the University of Virginia. So we knew that he sang the song. He had paid the price. He was intelligent, yet he was tremendously understanding. I don't ever remember him playing favorites."

Jay Jackson

I remember . . . "Writing a letter to Homer is like writing one to Jesus. What can you say? It's like sending a million dollars to a billionaire."

Pete Wise

I remember . . . "He was an honest person with a lot of integrity. You could discuss anything with him. He was just an understanding, totally compassionate man. In him, you could see the love for what he was doing–and the love toward his athletes. Now, he was strict. He instilled in you that you should do the best you could. And you knew that he was always behind you. His compassion and his understanding of people were immense. He was the one person who was instrumental in my staying in school. You know, I often think about going by and seeing him, and sitting down and talking like we did back then–

just one on one. I'd like to tell him how much I appreciate what he did for me."

Cliff Shaw

I remember . . . "I went to a meet indoors and Coach Bast asked me to run in a sprint medley relay. 'You can do it,' he said over and over again. We ended up running it, and I was on the second leg. I was against a boy from Hampden-Sydney. We were about even when we each got our batons. I ended up beating him. Coach Bast came over and patted me on the back and said, 'I told you that you could do it.' "

Jim O'Mahony

I remember . . . "When I talk to friends who have competed in track at Roanoke College in the 50s, the will say something like 'I ran for Mr. Bast.' They don't say, 'I ran for Roanoke College.' That's a reflection on him, of course. He put the personality into the program. He just exuded enthusiasm. He was a quality person and that showed through. He was intensely interested in his athletes, whoever they were and at whatever level they competed. He gave back much more than you gave to the sport. He is my hero. I haven't met many people in life whose image and persona sticks with you like they do for Mr. Bast. He was, and is, very unique and very special. And I think that showed through in his boys. You didn't fail Mr. Bast. You always tried to do your best. Some don't think Mr. Bast was a strong, technical coach. But he had unique leadership abilities. He just had a knack of getting the people around him to get the most out of themselves."

Earl Johnston

I remember . . . "Coach Bast was fond of saying, 'You know, there is something greater than ourselves.' I will never forget that one thing about him. Every day, as I run through the woods here in Oregon, I think of him. His inspiration doesn't disappear beyond the Baccalaureate Degree."

Pete Wise

I remember . . . "I think Coach Bast cared about people. And he had the personality of someone you wanted to work hard for. I think he expected a lot from us. Somehow, he just made you want to work hard. He was very calm most of the time. But he was forceful. He could get out of you the best you had. I had a difficult time learning how to study that first year. Homer would come over to the dorms and help me with my studies.

That's so unusual for a college coach to do. He genuinely cared about all of us, seeing that we did well not only in track but in academics. He was a real motivator."

Jim Wallwork

I remember . . . "He was not only our coach, but also friend and counselor to all the boys on his teams. That meant more to them than he could ever know. I enjoyed running for him more than for anyone else in my athletic career."

Gordon Highfill

I remember . . . Homer was an unbelievable motivator–and a great con artist. He conned me into becoming a hurdler, in fact. I was a high jumper, and my idea of a workout was to lie in the sun for a while, and then do a few stretches, run around the track once or twice, and take a few jumps. Then one day, Homer said to me 'You know, you ought to run the hurdles. Why don't you just jump over some of the hurdles and get the feel for them? In fact, you could use the hurdles as a warm-up for high jumping.' So I humored him, and jumped over a few hurdles, and at the beginning of the next meet I looked at the entry sheet and there I am, in the hurdles."

Dick Seed

I remember . . . "In my freshman year, I had very little confidence in my running ability. When I hung my head after a race, Coach Bast used to say, 'Hold your head up high. Be proud. Let people know you have won.' And there were the times I would be running behind, and the very sound of his voice encouraged me to try harder. Above the noise of the crowd, I could hear him yelling, 'Go boy!' and somehow extra strength seemed to come to me. I just knew that I couldn't let him down. Although we weren't able to overcome all the obstacles, he put us on the road. For as he used to say, 'Life's battles don't always go to the stronger or faster man, but soon or late the man who wins is the man who thinks he can."

George Gearhart

I remember . . . "I am sincerely indebted to Coach Bast, for he has shown me the true meaning of loyalty and sportsmanship, which he displayed so well for his athletic teams."

Dick Emberger

I remember . . . "I have never met a coach who has taken any more interest in his entire team and not in just the top players. While he was coaching, I was completely green as far as the shot put was concerned. Thanks to Coach Bast, however, I gained a general idea of how the event should be executed. I want to thank him for taking time out to help the inexperienced as well as the experienced."

John Hylton

I remember . . . "Homer was perhaps the one person who guided me through the first year of college. During the time I spent with Coach Bast, I gained more respect and admiration for him than for any other person I ever met. As a freshman at the College, he helped me more than he ever knew. I don't know if I could have survived that year without his help and encouragement. It is an important thing that a man believes in himself and knows what he wants from life. I will always think of Coach Bast as one of the finest men I ever met."

Jack Dempsey

I remember . . . "Each time Homer helped one of his boys 'fight life's battle,' I learned something new in how to handle people."

Don D'Agostino

I remember . . . "I suppose Coach Bast's success with his teams was due to one major factor above all others. He knew and understood each of us. He was interested in each of us, first as a person, and second, as a track man. I personally know that he has done much in molding my character and outlook toward life. He always found a minute for a little chat, no matter how busy his day was. Those talks together always gave me a lift. The things he taught us as a coach are easily forgotten. Our days as track men were all too short. We were privileged to know him. He gave us a big start on the road toward becoming men."

Jay Jackson

I remember . . . "Coach Bast's personal, sincere way taught me lessons that carried me through life long after I had forgotten the disappointments and thrills of my track life."

David Moore

I remember . . . "Everybody seemed to like Homer. He was a friend and never had anything to say negatively about anything or anybody. He was a very likeable person. He had a very even temperament and was never mad about anything, but always encouraging. I was surprised that he took the time to work with me."

Bob Nilson

I remember . . . "When I first came to Roanoke, a big, dumb country boy, ignorant of so many things, I found someone who took me under his wing and fathered me for four long, happy years. I found in this person a father, which I had never had, and as a result had unlimited faith to try with determination whatever he suggested. I suppose that one of my greatest pleasures in life was to come back from running a race and to be congratulated by Coach Bast. I look at myself and say, 'What would I have made out of myself if he hadn't done so much and helped the way he did?' "

Dave Foltz

I remember . . . "It is seldom that one meets a person who is willing to give of his time and effort as enthusiastically as Coach Bast has given toward the successful coaching of the Roanoke College track teams."

Red Crockett

I remember . . . "I can't remember going into a meet thinking that we were undefeated and we have to work hard to keep that streak alive. It was just assumed that we were going to win. We had several good athletes in every event. And Homer had the knack of pulling people out of the student body and making them into good athletes. Once he got them on the team, it was just a matter of motivating them to succeed."

Dick Seed

I remember . . . "As one of Coach's non-champions, I send my sincerest thanks for your patient tutelage. I can state with the certainty of personal experience that those of us who never took a single first place profited just as richly from our association with you as the many men whom you guided to the tape."

Joe Baldwin

I remember . . . "I remember Coach Bast mostly from my first two years of running, when he officially was the coach of the track team. He was a person very similar to my high school coach–someone you wanted to run for. He was a person who instilled in you a feeling that you should go out and do your best. If your best wasn't that good, that was O. K., as long as it was the best you could do. And I feel in those first couple of years that I was certainly doing my best. In retrospect, after I finished my college career, perhaps I did feel a bit guilty that I didn't always perform to my capacity. I felt like I let Homer down in my last two years of running. All in all, he was a guy you just loved–a guy you wanted to work hard for. He was definitely a good motivator. He never had to scream at you or use bad language. He was quiet in his demeanor as he talked to you. He knew how to treat each individual. He was a master of psychology. He never played favorites."

Dick Lewis

I remember . . . "I think Mr. Bast's coaching philosophy was simple–do the best you can. Soon, you felt that if you didn't do your best, you had let him down. He wasn't one who would fuss at you, or scream and yell, in a mad way. He was always patting you on the back, saying (no matter what time you ran) 'That was a great job. Now, let's work on this or that.' He was really good to people. I remember that years and years after I graduated from Roanoke and was to retire from the Roanoke City School System, the teachers had a little celebration or party for me. Homer gave up a major event in his own family to come to my event. To me, that's just fantastic."

Howard Light

I remember . . . "He was one of the greatest individuals I have ever known. If it hadn't been for him, I never would have finished college. He just made me hang in there. I got pretty discouraged a couple of times, and he (as only Homer could) had a real talent for getting the best out of you. He was a great motivator. For example, I never in my wildest dreams thought I would run the dashes. In high school, the coach said, 'If you want to be on my team, you're going to be a hurdler.' Before any meet started, Homer knew almost to the point how the meet was going to turn out. He got the best out of everybody who ran for him. He motivated you. If I am in Salem, I will make it a point to visit him."

Bob Fagg

I remember . . . "Homer was extremely important to me. Maybe part of it was the death of my dad, who died of a heart attack. Homer truly cared and you sensed it. You sensed that he was a man of tremendous leadership skills–someone you wanted to emulate. You didn't want to disappoint him. He would never scream or yell at you, but he had a way of looking at you and turning away that you would tell yourself that you never wanted to do that again. He was a man of high energy with boundless enthusiasm. I can still hear him offering encouragement as I ran a race or trained."

Derek Stryker

I remember . . . "I don't know if there was any one thing about him that I admired. I think it was just that he gave you the confidence to compete on the field and in the classroom, and do things well. During my freshman year, when we took the spring trip to South Carolina, he would make the guys take tests while on the road. And he was not just interested in you because you were a track man. He was interested in seeing that every student became a whole person. He kept a close check on everybody. I remember–maybe during my freshman year–that Homer saw some guy on another track team that wasn't doing something right. Homer helped him, telling him what he was doing wrong in terms of form, and the fellow turned around and beat the Roanoke athletes."

George Gearhart

I remember . . . "He was a great mentor. He just took everyone under his wing. He was always concerned about your doing well in school as well as in track. Academics were big with him. He wanted to make sure that we got good grades and graduated on time. Even after he officially retired, after the 1956-57 session, I remember Homer being on the field for practice almost every day. I remember him going on many of the trips we took, such as the spring trip to Florida State and Miami in 1958."

Dick Engel

I remember . . . "You know, Homer connected with everybody. Here is a cute story. One of our best runners went out one night and got himself a six-pack of beer. He was living in the Kappa Alpha house. He snuck the beer up to his room, locked the door, and drank all six cans. The next day, when he arrived at practice, feeling a bit worse for the wear, he walked up to Homer, who was standing on the track with his clipboard. Homer said, 'Well, Schlitz. Let's see what we can do for you today.' Homer never said anything to him about the drinking, but he knew that Homer knew."

Dick Seed

I remember . . . "Coach, I don't think I ever told you how much a comment you made in my freshman year meant to me. I went to your office a little dejected and told you I was dismayed that I was beating everyone on the opposite teams in cross country but was scoring no points. You pulled out some stats and observed that my times were better at that stage than the men on our team who were beating me. Mr. Coach/History Professor, that is called putting things in historical perspective. That is also why you were such a great coach and professor. It is also a partial explanation of why you got so much out of our team and students."

Emory Bogle

I remember . . . "One time Coach Bast and I were talking and he said to me, 'You may not realize it, but I get up for these events just like you do. But you can go run the event. I can't. I'm just as worn out afterwards as you are.' And that opened my eyes. People should tell people things like that."

Boyd Carr

I remember . . . "Homer sometimes had us compete in different event from one meet to another. Not randomly but obviously with a goal to maximize our abilities against a particular team's strengths and weaknesses. He seemed to build his teams around the quarter mile distance and then at times move some individuals down to the sprints and others up to the longer distances. At times he would have a 100 yard dash man run the 440, a miler run the 440, or a quarter-miler run the 100 yard dash or the 880. Of course, we each had our specialty but that didn't mean that was the event we were competing in on any given day. It definitely kept things interesting. What he was doing worked because in reviewing the meet summaries I can't recall us winning any dual meet by less than 30-40 points. I think it was like a game of chess to him and that he spent some time figuring out what combination would gain the most points for the team."

Allen Ide

I remember . . . "I think he is a very special person–one who normally doesn't come along in a lifetime. I am fortunate to have met him and to become his friend. He is an exceptional person. And the reason is that when you ran cross country for him, you always wanted to do your best. You did your best for yourself, of course, but you also did it for him. It was the crazy feeling you had that you couldn't let him down. You don't usually find people like that –people that you want to go all out for. It's great when you can get an athlete to think like that. You always felt that Homer was looking out for you, even though you were just one of many students needing his help. He always knew who you were and would try to help you out. You always felt special when you were around him."

Bill Cerelli

I remember . . . "He was a father figure for all of us. He was just an all-around, wonderful man. He was sincere about what he told you about your running and what you ought to be doing. He was a good motivator. You know, in looking back on my running career, I didn't do as well as I could have. I was studying, and I was in love, and maybe a little mixed up. So Homer never really got me to put out, but it wasn't his fault. It was mine. He was a really inspirational person. I was kind of a natural runner, so that accounted for some of my good times. Homer was a leader. He was President of the Student Body at the University of Virginia. He was an officer in the Navy. He was a doer."

Bruce Davenport

I remember . . . "Homer Bast was my real mentor at Roanoke. He helped me to grow up. He got down on your level, and was very humble. He was sincere, and you knew where you stood when you were with him. He just made you feel like you were a real part of the team."

Dr. Dick Dodd

I remember . . . "He was dedicated as a coach and an historian. He was amazing. He kept track of everything. I still have flyers that he put out every week. And George Jocher kept all of them, too. Homer kept you informed and he kept you fired up. It was his love of history, his love of people in general, that was exceptional. He had this overwhelming desire to build something. He just had this fantastic ability to get you to do your best. He was always there for you, that's for sure. He was just interested in people, trying to help them become better. He would go out of his way to help people, whether in his history class or on the field. I used to baby-sit his boys occasionally. Later in life, he told me that whenever he would ask his sons who they wanted as a babysitter, they would say, 'We want Hamburger.' In terms of his coaching, Mr. Bast couldn't do enough for you. We had an immense respect for the man. When he asked you to do something, you never asked why. You just did it."

Dick Emberger

I remember . . . "Coach Bast made it possible for me to come to Roanoke College in 1955 on a small track grant. I was there only two years before going on to Virginia Tech to finish my engineering degree. Coach Bast is a great person and made a great impression on my life. I'll always remember those days and the two years our track team was undefeated."

Jim Nichols

I remember . . . "I was there at the beginning of Coach Bast's tenure at Roanoke College. Not only did he train athletes, but he taught me, as a reporter covering sports activities for the *Brackety-Ack*, how to shape and mold a report of a sports event. I considered myself privileged to travel with the cross country and track teams of the 1947-50 era and report their successes not on campus but to the Roanoke newspapers as well."

Bryce Flora

I remember . . . "I have always thought of Homer Bast as just a good person. He never showed any favoritism. He would fool around with you, but when we went down to the track to train or have a meet, he was all business. Everyone who ran track knew that. I can't remember anyone goofing off. There was a lot of camaraderie between track members."

Jim Nichols

I remember . . . "You worked for Coach Bast. Not that he demanded that you work, you just did. And he gave you a sense of team also. Now a really tough coach may have gotten into my head and said, 'You can do a lot better.' I could have done two-a-day workouts, but Homer realized that team members were also students who needed time to study and go to labs. We loved him, you know. He was tremendous as Registrar and coach. I thought the track dedication ceremony was wonderful, especially when I heard him say, 'Well, let me tell you how it was.' It was his training techniques that I remembered most when I started running again in 1978. He emphasized quality more than quantity. We never ran the distances that people do now. I knew that I had to incorporate Fartlek, hills, interval training, etc., into my training routine."

Dr. Bob Jenkins

I remember . . . "Well, I already knew Mr. Bast when I got to Roanoke. Our high school team would often go up to the Roanoke track to work out as a team, and Coach often was down there with us. Even after we started our freshman year, he would come down and suggest how to exercise and stretch the right way. And, of course, he would tell me how to get across the top of those hurdles without killing myself. He was always out there encouraging everyone to do the best they could possibly do. That was all he was asking of you. But he always had suggestions. When it got down to competing in meets, he could always tell you about your opponents, their times, etc. I call it a 'poop sheet.' When I got to Roanoke, I wasn't the most academic person on campus. Obviously, he didn't want me to flunk out of school, and he was always there to help me and to encourage me to learn. And he often had to teach me how to learn, a skill you often don't learn in high school. Academics were always important to him. I got a minor in history, and that was one of the things I thoroughly enjoyed at Roanoke. His classes were very interesting. In fact, after all of these years, I still have his books. During his classes, he would always cover the events we were studying in history. He was very organized. He gave hard tests and wouldn't cut you any slack whether you were one of his athletes or not. He expected you to know what he was teaching. That World Civilization class was hard for me in my freshman year. Coming out of high school, I was not prepared to study. When it came time to arrange our schedules for the next year or semester, he was always there to help. He walked me through the classes I would need to take to graduate. Of course, there were a couple of those courses that I wished I had never taken, but that's another story. I had some academic problems through my sophomore year, but after that I sort of caught on to what was expected of me, and had a much easier time."

Bruce Johnston

I remember . . . "Coach Bast had many good traits. One was his ability to relate to people and make them feel comfortable. He was somewhat older than us, but you just found it so comfortable being around him and his wife, Mary Jane. I used to baby-sit Michael and Steven every once in a while. I almost felt as if Homer and Mary Jane were my parents. Homer just had such a tremendous impact on my life. I remember another thing about him. We would come in from track practice, for example, and on the stair risers leading up to our rooms, we would find little inspirational sayings on cards. Things like, '. . . the one who wins is the one who thinks he can.' Also, he loved his athletes as much as we loved him. And we knew it. When we went on trips to away meets, we used to use college station wagons. And some of us–like myself and John Summers - would drive the rest of the team. We'd be sitting there with five to seven people in the car, singing and telling stories. And Homer would be in one car, and perhaps switch to the other from time to time. You know, there would have been no way for me to attend college financially if it weren't for Homer's help. He found me a couple of jobs on campus. One was the dry cleaning pickup and delivery man on campus. Also, he got me a position as the light fixer in the gym. I stayed over in Hildreth at the time, and I became the janitor of that building. Many people on the track team lived in Hildreth and it was my job to clean up after them. Dick Seed, I remember, was my roommate in Hildreth."

Phil Shaw

I remember . . . "Well, it was so different at Roanoke than it was at Carolina. In Chapel Hill, they have all of these runners, and they barely know your name. Homer was more like my high school coach. Now, early in his career he may not have known much about coaching track, but he was a good salesman–a good motivator. And that's how Homer was. As you know, he organized a team from scratch. He just went into the dormitories and pulled some people out and said, 'Let's make a track team.' "

Alvin Smith

I remember . . . "He was an excellent coach and a fine friend. I never go back to Roanoke College without seeing him in person. He knew what he was doing. He had run himself. He was very interested in his boys and had a close bond with each one. Now my high school coach was very different from Homer. He was very distant from his athletes, although he was an excellent coach in terms of fundamentals. But you didn't pal around with Jim McGomery. He was on a different level from where you were. Homer, on the other hand, had that personal relationship with everybody on the squad. I remember trips down the valley after races with Bridgewater. We would stop by Mary Jane's parents' house in Staunton, Virginia, and her mother would have cookies and a drink for us."

White Rhyne

I remember . . . "Homer Bast was a wonderful teacher. I took his World Civilization class when I was a freshman. Now, I didn't agree with a lot that he said. He was a typical academic guy and a bit liberal. At least he was liberal according to what I had been used to. I came from a middle-class, middle-income family that was somewhat conservative in its outlook. And I hadn't been exposed to the real world very much. So I caught myself disagreeing with him. But I think that he would have loved that. Even though his politics and mine were different, he certainly planted questions in my mind. So I argued with him internally. I never would have argued with him in the open. That would have been a sure trap. I would have been eaten alive. I remember that educational experience, and to this day I think that it was a very important part of my education. I can remember riding in the car with Mr. Bast to meets. And Mr. Bast was always teaching. He would talk about a lot of subjects. He was eclectic in his knowledge. And he had an open mind. We would talk about a lot of things. When we were on the track, his enthusiasm showed through. When we were running, you could literally see him at the finish line doing his 'dance,' you know. He put a lot of effort into his coaching. I remember our trips together. Now, he was not 'one of the boys.' I never saw him in that way. I always saw him as an authority figure. But he was close to us–close enough, but not too close. That's often a hard thing for a coach to manage."

Earl Johnston

I remember . . . "One thing that I do remember him for was his enthusiasm while coaching, whether it was just in practice or in a conference meet. There is this one image I guess I will always have of Homer. I can't even recall the location or the time now, but it happened as I was coming off the last turn of the 440, just as I was starting to pass another runner I heard something that caused me to throw a glance over toward the infield. There was Homer about as close to the track as one could be without actually being on it, doubled over in a crouch and pumping his fist in encouragement, yelling at me as loudly as he could. You had to know Homer to appreciate the sight as the man could be extremely expressive when he wanted to be. For whatever reason, that image has remained with me for a half century. He was an outstanding motivator."

Allen Ide

I remember . . . "Many traits made Homer so successful. He was such an admirable person. You couldn't help but to do your best for him. Because of him, we all tried to show up for practice every day. We never wanted to let him down. You just couldn't. His integrity was obvious. He certainly got your best out of you. He was a very humble guy. I know that he commanded a ship in the war before coming to Roanoke, under sometimes dangerous circumstances, but he never told us about that part of his life. He was an excellent motivator. Because of him, I would never fail to do the very best I could. When he said 'jump,' I jumped. And so did the others on the team. He motivated me quite well."

Dick Fraley

I remember . . . "Bast has long been a favorite on the Roanoke College campus, not only for his track teams but for his kind, considerate attitude toward all who work with or under him. The fruits of his work show in the record books which the Roanoke track squads have practically re-written. Although coaching was just a sideline for him, few coaches can boast of a record comparable to Bast's."

Tom Hulvey
Brackety-Ack–September 13, 1957

The Years After Coaching

Homer officially ended his track coaching career after the 1956-57 session. His new position as Registrar of the College was too time-consuming for him to continue to coach. By the next school year, however, he showed up on the field almost every day to help Elwood Fox coach the team. He was even listed in some places as the team advisor.

At the opening convocation of 1957-58, in the old Methodist Church on College Avenue, his former athletes surprised him with a "retirement celebration." He was presented with many gifts, such as a set of luggage, a considerable sum of money donated by friends and students, and many letters from former athletes. President Oberley said to the audience: "I wish to present an individual among us who has not only recognized and accepted the responsibility of his duties as teacher, counselor, and coach, with several generations of students, but who has also exemplified superior qualities of leadership in the manner in which he has discharged these duties."

When Homer gave up the coaching of track, his many friends and former students gave him a book of letters, a thank-you plaque, and numerous gifts.

S. White Rhyne '52, one of the "Bast Boys," then made the presentation of a plaque to Homer. The inscription on the plaque read:

C. Homer Bast

With sincere appreciation
for a decade of coaching
from those to whom
he gave of himself
so willingly and effectively
as coach and friend.

Roanoke College
1947-1957

Homer was especially grateful for the plaque. It has been hanging on a wall in his home since 1957. In a letter to Rhyne in October of 1957, he said that the recognition at the convocation, along with the plaque, was "the most wonderful thing that has ever happened to me. I shall not forget it as long as I live; nor will I forget the part you played in staging the ceremony."

The letters from his former athletes, students, and friends filled a large scrapbook. The campus *Brackety-Ack* noted the following: "That Bast's former athletes chose to send their letters of appreciation is not surprising. He had taken a personal interest in everyone of 'his boys," giving advice, encouragement, and praise, always when needed, always at the proper time.' "

Homer continued to coach the cross country team each fall through 1960-61, after which he gave the coaching duties to Elwood Fox. From that point on, he coached only from his office in the Administration Building. Many of the cross country and track men visited him, some almost daily, to ask for advice ranging from training routines to personal problems.

For the most part, his final four cross country teams were very successful. Here is a summary of those years:

1957	6 Wins, 1 Loss Won the Little Eight Championships Won the Mason-Dixon Championships
1958	9 Wins, 0 Losses

	Won the Little Eight Championships Won the Mason-Dixon Championships
1959	4 Wins, 1 Loss Finished Second in the Little Eight Championships Won the Mason-Dixon Championships
1960	3 Wins, 2 Losses Finished Second in the Little Eight Championships Finished Sixth in the Mason-Dixon Championships

In 1958, Homer was named a full Professor on the College staff, as well as Director of the Summer School Program. He also served as Director of the Evening Program from 1961 through 1963.

At about the end of the 1959-60 session, Homer experienced a major health problem–angina. He had experienced some warning pains before, but never thought to see a doctor about them. Then, on a night in the spring of 1960, he had a 7:00 p.m. speech to give at the Lab Theater on the campus. His speech was a part of the school's Great Books lecture series. He was late in getting away from his house, so he jogged a bit on the way over to the Lab Theater. Then he got his first pain, which lasted all the way to the College. It was one of his first indications that anything was wrong. Even then, he didn't think much of it. He thought he simply was out of shape.

A few days later, he decided that he would cut down a small tree in his yard. After about six swings of the ax, he got the same kind of pain. As he put it, "I thought, 'Whoa, man. What's happening now?' " So he went next door and told his neighbor, Dr. Russell Smiley, what had happened. He looked at Homer and said in his southern drawl, "You've got angina, boy." And he sent Homer to Johns Hopkins in Baltimore right away for tests. Hopkins told him that his blood pressure–about 210 over 110 at the time–was awful.

One of the good parts of the trip to John Hopkins was the fact that Dick Dodd, one of the early track men on Homer's team, was now a doctor doing work at Hopkins. Dodd was very happy to see Homer again, and took the time to escort Homer through all of his testing stations over a 12-hour period.

Homer's angina problems soon were solved with an operation. Since that time, he has had one other similar heart problem, also solved, and another few health setbacks that mostly were the result of age.

During the fall of 1961-62, the College's *Cherobiblos* publication was dedicated to Homer with this remark: "To one who is a constant inspiration and a true friend to those with whom he works, whose own code of living serves as a guide to others and whose abilities as a teacher are manifold."

Mary Jane and Homer were feeling the need for more room in their house. In the spring of 1962, they had a den and bathroom built on the south side of the house.

During these years, the Bast family each summer happily took vacations in Daytona Beach, Florida. Mary Jane was doing much of the work in the household, raising Michael and Stephen, caring for the house, and trying to visit her aging parents in Staunton. Her hobbies were card playing–mainly bridge–and competing for blue ribbons in flower arranging. She also attended the Salem Book Club meetings and, in her church, handled Altar Committee duties. Mary Jane was a devoted mother and daughter–the one who completed much of the household work while Homer was spending much more time with the College and his church.

From late November of 1964 until January of 1965, Mary Jane and Homer lived in Addis Ababa, Ethiopia. Homer had been selected by the Ford Foundation on Delos Myers' recommendation to assist Haile Selassie University reorganize their registration and scheduling procedures. While overseas, the Basts had an opportunity to visit parts of Western Europe as well as eastern Africa.

After the arrival in 1965 of Dean of the College Ed Lautenschlager, the Board of Trustees in 1968 appointed Homer to the new position of Assistant Dean of the College. With that move, Dr. Harry Poindexter became Chairman of the History Department at Homer's urging. President Kendig, Dean Lautenschlager, and Homer all believed that from this point forward, all departmental chairpersons must have their doctorates.

During 1965, Mary Jane's father, Grover Lightner–in failing health–retired from business and he and his wife, Lillie moved to Salem to live with Mary Jane and Homer. To provide them with adequate living space, another wing to the house was constructed in the spring of 1966. Both Grover and Lillie lived in the house until they died–Grover in 1969 and Lillie in 1976. Having both of them in the house gave Michael and Stephen a chance to live with their grandparents around the clock. The experience was good for the entire family.

The College began selections to its Athletic Hall of Fame in 1971. In that first selection of athletes to be honored were Homer and the following members of his cross country or track teams through the years:

Jim Doran '48
Dick Emberger '60
Dave Foltz '56
Howard Meincke '61
Jim Ruscick '48
Alvin Smith '52

In its tribute to Homer, the Hall of Fame selection committee said:

C. Homer Bast
Inducted '71

> "A graduate of the University of Virginia, where he was a star track man. In 1947, he started rebuilding the track and field program at Roanoke. The following year his team won the State Little Eight Championship. From 1954-58, his teams captured cross country and track championships in the Mason-Dixon Conference. The track team compiled over 80 wins in 100 meets, completing five unbeaten seasons, nine Little Eight titles, eight Mason-Dixon Conference Championships, and two state AAU titles."

Although Homer was no longer a coach, he continued to spread the word about Roanoke at club meetings, banquets, and schools throughout Virginia. In addition, Homer delivered the 1971 summer school commencement address in which he talked about excellence, hard work, and commitment as goals to guide the graduating students. He gave the same speech at the commencement exercises in the fall of 1971.

During the second half of the 1972-73 session, the College gave Homer a partial sabbatical. For two weeks, he and Mary Jane and another couple toured Mexico.

Michael Bast graduated from Roanoke in 1972. His had been an exceptional four years, with many athletic and academic awards. He entered the Naval Flight Program at Pensacola in the summer of 1972, receiving his wings and qualifying for multi-engine planes. In the summer of 1975, he and Winkie Waters–a college girl friend–were married.

Stephen entered Roanoke in 1971, graduating in 1975. Like his brother, he also won many honors and awards. Following family tradition, he was one of his team's premier runners, concentrating on the middle distances in outdoor track. After his days at the College, he entered the Navy in their Officers' Training Program. He married Rebecca Krebs, a graduate of Roanoke, in October of 1977.

Michael Bast, Homer' son, on the day of Michael's graduation from Roanoke College.

In the spring of 1977, at the Duke University Medical Center, Homer went through a by-pass operation which eased his 20-year battle with angina. His recovery from the operation was difficult, but by June he was back on his job and preparing for the 1977-78 session.

In 1978, the College recognized Homer for his many outstanding accomplishments by naming him an "honorary alumnus." His framed award stated, "Homer Bast, Associate Dean and Registrar of the College, was named an honorary alumnus by the Alumni Association at the annual Alumni Banquet on May 6, 1978. Bast served the College for more than thirty years as coach, professor, and administrator. We honor him for the outstanding contribution he made to Roanoke College and for his loyalty and unfaltering interest in alumni everywhere." The resolution presented to him encouraged him to maintain an active voice in College affairs so that Roanoke would not lose the unique qualities which he had brought to the campus community.

Also in 1978, Homer was surprised to receive another honor. Walt Cormack was a respected coach for many years at Virginia Military Institute. V. M. I. had begun to give a special award to state college and university coaches whose coaching of track or cross country was considered exemplary. Homer and Dr. Harry Jopson, a good friend of Homer's and one who had coached very successful cross country and track teams at Bridgewater, attended one of the large indoor track meets in Richmond. Neither knew that he was there for an award. They both were called to the center of the arena to be presented plaques honoring their work in athletics. A statement on each of the Walt Cormack Track and Field Award plaques stated:

> "Awarded Annually To A Coach In Virginia Who Has Made Outstanding Contributions In The Promotion Of Track And Field And Who Emulates the Qualities Coach Walter B. Cormack Has Demonstrated In His Years As V. M. I. Track And Cross Country Coach"

Homer still prizes that award. He keeps it on a bookcase in his house.

In 1979 Homer finally retired from Roanoke College. Upon that retirement, the school awarded him the honorary degree of Doctor of Humane Letters. The following decree was read to faculty, staff, and friends of the College on that occasion:

> You are a native of the Eastern Shore of Maryland–a habitat you share with the blue crab, the oyster, and the skipjack.
>
> You are a graduate of Mercersburg Academy and Mr. Jefferson's University in Charlottesville. You have been an outstanding student at both the undergraduate and graduate level. You are an athlete of

> tremendous courage and skill. As commanding officer on perilous duty, you helped the United States Navy win not one, but two, wars with courage and devotion.
>
> In your chosen dry land profession, you have served with distinction as professor of history, director of admissions, director of the evening program and of the summer school, and as registrar–and last and surely not least, as one of the truly great track coaches of our time. You are indeed, sir, a renaissance man and a Virginia gentleman sans peur et sans reproche.
>
> For all these things and many others, your colleagues and your college hold you in the highest esteem.
>
> Mr. President, I have the honor to present to you Charles Homer Bast, upon whom is to be conferred the honorary degree of Doctor of Humane Letters.

In the next decade after Homer retired, he and Mary Jane traveled extensively. Sometimes they visited their sons. At other times, they took several Caribbean cruises and a yearly trip to the beach.

In 1981, the *Rawenoch* again dedicated its yearbook to Homer. The reason for the honor was given as follows: "[Homer Bast] . . . is one who has devoted himself to the growth and development of Roanoke College . . . [and his] . . . dynamic personality and warm friendship have produced students who are mentally, physically, and spiritually qualified to take their places in society."

A remarkable contribution by John and Nancy Mulheren made possible in 1983 the building of a new sports and physical education building adjacent to the old Alumni Gymnasium. John graduated from Roanoke in 1971. His wife, Nancy, graduated a year later. The building was named the Bast Physical Education and Recreation Center in honor of Homer's outstanding work as a coach from 1946 through 1960.

When John took the Alumni Banquet podium on October 23 to make his surprising announcement, he told the gathering of alumni, students, faculty, parents, and friends that there had been two special individuals at Roanoke College when he was an "attendee." He refrained from calling himself a "student," saying that to do so would be "insulting a number of people in this room."

One of the special individuals singled out in Mulheren's talk was, he noted, a person who had taken upon himself to see to it that "I got out of college," and the other had made it his business to see to it that I didn't get thrown out." The former was Bast, whose classes in Western Civilization he had attended more regularly than any others. The latter was former Dean of Students Donald Sutton, for whom the Mulherens donated a sizeable amount of money to dedicate the new student center in his honor. At the time, Sutton was serving as Director of Alumni Relations.

The surprise dedication of both buildings, which the Board had approved just the day before, was made possible by a gift of more than one million dollars from John and his wife, Nancy Baird Mulheren. Those who knew John Mulheren had seen him grow from a rascal of a college student–notorious for his pranks–to a major stock broker in New York City.

In the Bast Center today there is a special bas relief plaque surrounded by trophy cases. The plaque reads:

C. HOMER BAST

PROFESSOR, COACH,
ADMINISTRATOR AND COUNSELOR,
FOR HIS 33 YEARS OF DEDICATED SERVICE
TO ROANOKE COLLEGE
C. HOMER BAST CENTER
FOR PHYSICAL EDUCATION AND RECREATION

MADE POSSIBLE BY
NANCY AND JOHN MULHEREN '72 '71

Bas Relief artwork created and
donated by Dr. Emory Bogle '60

To the Bast building the College later added the 5,000 square foot Belk Fitness Center, outfitted with many new pieces of exercise equipment. The facility was funded by a $750,000 gift from the Belk Foundation of Charlotte, North Carolina. Mary Claudia Belk '96 represented her family's foundation at the news conference and center dedication.

This bas relief was created and donated by Dr. Emory Bogle '60. It can be found on the wall near the display cases on the second floor of the C. Homer Bast Center for Physical Education and Recreation.

Rebecca and Stephen Bast became parents to Christopher Todd Bast in February of 1982 and another son, John Matthew Bast, was born in February of 1987. Homer and Mary Jane were the usual doting, caring grandparents, watching the two boys grow and mature.

In 1985 Homer was diagnosed with colon cancer; however, Dr. Tom Henretta's operation saved Homer from having a permanent colostomy. After a long recovery period, with much love and assistance from Mary Jane, Homer was back to normal.

Within a short time after retirement, Homer's consuming hobby became a search to find his roots. Using genealogy research, he tried to construct the background of every family member. Some of his research took him as far back as the 17th century.

His other interests centered on analyzing the action reports and war diaries of each ship which, like Homer's Yolo, was stationed off Okinawa during the 89 days he was there. It was a prodigious project, taking him to many locations around the country.

Life after retirement was good, with Caribbean cruises and sailings. With advancing age, however, there were some health problems. In 1990, while doing research at the Maryland Historical Center, Homer suffered a severe nose bleed. The next year, he was forced to undergo a second by-pass operation, performed in Roanoke. Again, recovery was slow. In October of 1988, Homer slipped and fell, breaking his left elbow. His arm was in a cast for three months. Although the injury mostly healed, he was left with nerve damage.

Over the years, Mary Jane also had health problems. A bad hip caused pain. Her eye sight began to fail. And she began to lose her balance on occasions.

During Alumni Weekend of 2000, Homer received another surprise. The College honored the individual distance runners who, in the late 1940s, were known as the Big Four. At 5:00 p.m. on April 14, a short special recognition ceremony was held in the Joseph "Buddy" Hackman Hall of Fame Room to honor Alvin Smith '52, Bruce Davenport '51, Lawrence "Red" Crockett '50, and Paul McCarty '50, members of the original Big Four. Dr. Frank Aldred, whose improvement in running was so significant that he was considered the fifth member of the Big Four unit, also attended. Homer Bast was present, although he was told of the ceremony only in time to make sure he attended.

In the summer of 2003, Homer received yet another honor. Dr. Emory C. Bogle '60 presented his mentor and former professor with a beautiful bas relief sculpted in Homer's honor. This likeness of Coach Bast today is on the wall of the trophy room on the second floor of the C. Homer Bast Recreation Center.

When Homer was 90, he was among a host of people honored as Roanoke College installed its chapter of Phi Beta Kappa, the nation's oldest and one of its most prestigious undergraduate honors organization. Roanoke College's chapter, Nu of Virginia, was the 13th chapter in the state and the 267th in the country.

On April 9, 1988, during Alumni Weekend activities, the "Big Four Plus One" came together. L to R: Bruce Davenport, Alvin Smith, White Rhyne, Red Crockett, and Paul McCarty.

"The day has finally arrived," said David Gring, college President, during the installation ceremony in Olin Hall. "This day represents a dream come true. It's the culmination of a five-decade journey."

The College's quest to install a Phi Beta Kappa chapter began in 1952 with Bast and the late President Perry Kendig. Homer, an associate dean and registrar emeritus, had led Roanoke's efforts to obtain a chapter of the country's oldest and most respected academic honor society. Gring, who was just a few months from retiring after 15 years with the College, had continued working with others on campus to make the dream a reality.

Homer, Associate Dean and Registrar Emeritus at Roanoke, was one of five foundation members inducted into the society as part of Friday's ceremony. He turned in the first application for Phi Beta Kappa membership in the 1950s. The others were:

For years, Homer and others on the campus tried to petition for a Phi Beta Kappa chapter. The day finally arrived with this ceremony.

Norman Fintel, President Emeritus; John Turbyfill, class of 1953 and retired Roanoke College Trustee; Dr. Charles Fisher, class of 1928; and adjunct research professor of chemistry; and Dr. Carol Swain, class of 1983.

Foundation members were chosen because they were instrumental in the formation of the chapter.

Also inducted were 28 faculty and administration members who already had a Phi Beta Kappa key from chapters at their alma maters. During a later April ceremony, 18 undergraduate students would be inducted.

It was a moment more than 50 years in the making. Following the ceremony, President David Gring threw his arms around Homer and exclaimed, “Homer. We did it!”

In September of 2006, Homer was honored in a ceremony near the College’s refurbished track. The new facility was named “the C. Homer Bast Track” that day. The dedication was made possible by a generous donation from Roger Sandt of Lancaster, Pennsylvania, who graduated from Roanoke in 1964 and was taught and coached by Homer. The former coach attended the event along with his wife of 64 years, Mary Jane, and their sons, Steve and Mike. Roanoke College alumni, including former athletes, students, and colleagues, also traveled from across the country to attend the dedication. Onlookers included many of Homer’s athletes, from Olympian Dick Emberger ’60 to Alvin Smith ’52.

Top Left: Homer Bast rides in the college golf cart to the presentation ceremony.
Top Center: Homer's wife, Mary Jane, waits in the front row for Homer to speak. Mary Jane, Homer's wife of 66 years, later passed away on June 2, 2008.
Top Right: Homer tells it "like it was," describing how his track and cross country teams did so well.
Bottom Left: Alumnus Roger Sandt '64, who donated the money for the new track, speaks to the large crowd.
Bottom Center: Dr. Sabine U. O'Jara, then President of Roanoke College, makes her comments on behalf of Roanoke College.
Bottom Right: Dr. Finn Pincus, current track and cross country coach, waits his turn to congratulate Homer.

Top Left: Homer looks at the engraved batons he was given. In the middle is Dr. Sabine U. O'Jara, and to the right is Roger Sandt.
Top Center: George Jocher, one of Coach Bast's two best distance runners, talks with former Roanoke College Professor Guy Ritter.
Top Right: The new field dedication plaque stands at the entrance to the new track.
Bottom Left: Members of the men's and women's track team were part of the celebration.
Bottom Center: Alumnus and former coach Paul Dotson with Jean Beamer (L) and Fran Ramser (R), long-time teachers and coaches at Roanoke.
Bottom Right: Many members of the Bast family attended the dedication ceremony.

During the ceremony, Dr. Sabine U. O'Hara, then President of the College, gave the opening remarks. She was followed by a short talk by Roger Sandt. Sandt recognized his former coach as "an exceptional mentor and positive influence on his personal philosophy." Rev. Guy "Tex" Ritter '48 then spoke, followed by a short talk by Homer himself.

As this book was being written, Homer and Mary Jane lived in the same house on Locust Street that they built in 1952. He turned 94 years old of age in August of 2008, and Mary Jane was about six years younger. Mary Jane began to have physical problems in 2006, and in June of 2008, she passed away quietly and without pain at home.

Today, Homer uses a cane, but gets around fairly well. Until recently, he still drove his car. His eyesight is diminishing and he finds it necessary to wear a hearing aid. On the other hand, he is still the articulate, alert, story-telling person we all remember. Almost no day goes by that he doesn't answer the phone to talk to a former athlete or personal friend. Many of his boys from Roanoke College stop by to see him when they are in town.

Charles Homer Bast, we salute you and thank you for everything you have done for us over the years. As Henry Eyring once said, "Let us consider the nature of true greatness in men. The people who can catch hold of men's minds and feelings and inspire them to do things bigger than themselves are the people who are remembered in history . . . . those who stir feelings and imagination and make men struggle toward perfection." You, sir, are a great man. We will remember you always.

The author, at the end of some 20 interviews with Homer Bast, asked him one final question: If today you had in one room with you all of the boys you coached during your tenure at Roanoke, what would you say to them? In summary, here is what he replied:

> "It has been wonderful to know you all for these many years. I still remember all of the good times we had together. Good luck and God bless you. It is my privilege to have spent time with all of you boys. You were all great. I never had one moment of trouble with any single person I coached. Thank you for all of your letters, and good wishes over the course of the years. You have meant so much to me in my life."

Homer relaxes for a moment before the start of commencement exercises.

Chapter Nineteen

The Bast Boys

Dear Reader:

This book has focused on Coach Homer Bast for good reason. He is admired for the person he is and was, and for his devotion to students throughout a long and distinguished career at Roanoke College. But the book is also about the athletes who competed on Homer's cross country and track teams. These men were known by the student body as the Bast Boys. In this chapter, you will find short biographies of many of these athletes. The biographies were taken from interviews with each individual. Sometimes, I was able to visit them in their homes, or they came to see me. On other occasions, they allowed me to call them on the telephone and record our conversations. For me, these interviews have been the highlight of writing the book. These are good people, and worth writing about.

There were many more students on Homer's teams than just the ones mentioned here. You may wonder how these particular individuals were chosen. Knowing that time constraints would prevent me from interviewing everyone, I decided that the athlete must have been an active member of Coach Bast's track teams at some time from the spring of 1947 through the spring of 1957, or must have been on at least one of his cross country teams from 1947 until 1960. Secondly, the person received one point for each time he appeared in one of these categories.

The athlete was:

One of the top-five all-time performers in his indoor event(s);
One of the top-five all-time performers in his outdoor event(s);
One of the top-five all-time record holders in his indoor event(s);
One of the top-five all-time record holders in his outdoor event(s);

A top-10 finisher in a Little 6/7/8 championship meet in cross country;
A top-15 finisher in a Mason-Dixon championship meet in cross country;
A winner of an event in a Little 6/7/8 championship meet indoors;
A winner of an event in a Mason-Dixon championship meet indoors.
A winner of an event in a Little 6/7/8 championship meet outdoors.
A winner of an event in a Mason-Dixon championship meet outdoors.

If an individual totaled a minimal number of points, and also was coached by Homer Bast for at least one year, I made an effort to contact that person to get an interview. Some who qualified, of course, were deceased. In a few other cases, College personnel did not know where someone lived. For these last persons, I did try *many* times to reach them without success. If you are one of these athletes, I apologize. I would not have been searching for you if you weren't a superior athlete at Roanoke. Your experiences at Roanoke, and especially your career after leaving, would have made interesting reading.

Larry W. Arrington, Ed.D.

Aldred, Dr. Frank

Frank spent his high school years at Virginia Episcopal School, a college preparatory school in Lynchburg, Virginia. At V. E. S., he lettered in track although he says he wasn't very good in the sport. His primary event was the quarter mile, but he did run some 220 races for the team. He also played football.

At the end of his three years at V. E. S., he enrolled at Davidson College in North Carolina. After two years at Davidson, however, he realized that he wasn't very happy there. His father was a construction engineer working for American Electric Power, and the family was forced to move around frequently. He was going to have a job in Roanoke for about a year and, since he and Frank had not seen very much of each other for some time, Frank decided to move back to Roanoke and enroll at Roanoke College. It was a choice that he never regretted.

Frank Aldred

He was at Roanoke College for only two years–1948-49 and 1949-50. During the first of those two years, he lived off-campus. At the beginning of the second year, he moved into the Sections dormitories (the part closest to the Commons). His roommate was John Byerly, Jr., who later became a minister and served for some time on the College's Board of Trustees. It was a very enjoyable year for Frank. He hadn't enjoyed living off-campus in 1948-49, when he was located about a mile away from the school in the direction of Roanoke. He had to walk to and from the campus each day, a routine that got old fast.

Frank was both a cross country and track runner at Roanoke. In his first year as a cross country athlete, newspapers were already lauding the talents of the Big Four–Alvin Smith, Paul McCarty, Bruce Davenport, and Red Crockett–who often were so far ahead of the other team that they would join hands and jog across the finish line. Frank found himself in about sixth place on the team, just in back of freshman White Rhyne. By the second year, with some additional training on his own, he had become better than at least one of the Big Four–and a significant contributor to the team.

In track, the race he most often ran was the 440. "Maybe," he said with a smile, "that was because the team didn't have anyone else who wanted to run the quarter." Although he never considered himself to be much better than an average runner, he did run a :52.6, and a :53.0 before completing his career.

He still remembers how Homer Bast set up his training schedule. "One of the most interesting things he was doing at the time," he said, "was to use sprints for the distance runners. I don't think many other coaches were doing that. We got very tired of running 60s and 300s, but I think it made us better. Homer was always so supportive and always patted you on the back whether you came in first or not."

Frank's degree from Roanoke was in History. His interest in the subject grew as he took classes from Homer during his two years at the College.

Frank's career objectives involved teaching History and coaching. He interviewed in the summer of 1950 with several schools, primarily in Tennessee, and received three offers. The best of the offers was from Virginia Episcopal School, however, and that was the job he accepted. He taught history for V. E. S. that year, but the school had no cross country team. He was prepared to become an assistant coach for track that spring; however, he was called to active duty by the military in 1951. His decision was to join the Navy. During most of the 4½ years he was in the service, he was stationed mostly in East Asia. He became an officer after attending an Officer Candidate School (OCS). He took the flight physical twice, but because he couldn't pass the eye exam, he ended up in Intelligence. He was assigned to a fighter squadron stationed on the west coast. During the subsequent years of his service obligation, he went to Korea and came back to the United States for nine months before going back out, literally around the world.

In 1955 Frank married Phoebe King. They had three daughters. The oldest was Amy, who later received a Ph.D. from the University of Virginia and now lives in Charlottesville. She works for the State of Virginia and has two children. His second daughter was Leslie; unfortunately, she died of a brain aneurism in 1980 at the age of 22.

Leslie had attended Randolph-Macon College. Phoebe and Frank's third daughter, Mary, lives in Milton, West Virginia and is a social worker.

When released by the Navy, Frank stayed in the Inactive Reserves and went back to teaching at Virginia Episcopal School. At first, he taught all History courses and served as Assistant Coach in track. When he left that job after the 1963-64 session, he was Head Coach of track and taught all math. One of the things he is proud of today is starting a cross country program at V. E. S. in 1959. He was able to put together some very good teams. The terrain in Lynchburg allowed running on hills and through forested areas. During that period of time, he kept in touch with Coach Bast, asking for his opinions on coaching. He appreciated Homer's input.

Frank had decided to pursue a doctorate in history. During the latter years of his teaching at V. E. S., he had gotten his Master's Degree in history at Marshall University. He enrolled in the History doctoral program at the University of Virginia. During the program, he served as a Graduate Assistant in the department–attending all of the lectures of the classes for which he was grading exams. His dissertation topic concerned a conference that was held in 1938 in Brussels after the Japanese had declared war on China.

After receiving his doctorate from the University of Virginia, he began a successful, 25-year teaching career in History at Marshall University. In 1980, he married for the second time. His wife was a Charleston, West Virginia, resident named Pamela Givens. Today the two are about to celebrate their 27th anniversary. After meeting, they moved into a house she was building in Charleston. Pamela, her father, and Frank helped finish it. They lived in that house until about two years ago, when they moved nearby to Hurricane.

Carr, Boyd

Boyd grew up in Roanoke City, the son of parents who were separated. His high school days were spent at Fork Union Military School near historic Charlottesville. At a weight of only 136 pounds, he played junior varsity football, although to his dismay he was used sparingly. He became a cheerleader and, when a junior, served as head cheerleader. He also went out for baseball, a sport he enjoyed but also one he never mastered. Then, trying out again for the J. V. team in football his senior year, he was surprised when the coaches elevated him to the varsity. Boyd was only a scrub, but did get into a lot of the games. His team lost only one game that year.

Because of his immaturity, he stayed for a postgraduate year at Fork Union. He was an offensive end and a defensive player in varsity football. His team won the state championship for the second straight year.

Boyd Carr

Boyd also participated in track. In his first year in the sport, he decided to try the hurdles. Fork Union had a good hurdler the previous year, and Boyd thought the event was impressive. Eventually, he became Captain of the track team, until he violated school rules and encouraged friends to bring a bottle of gin back to the campus. He and the other boys almost were expelled from the school. This discipline was not imposed; however, they were busted to lower ranks and were made to do extra duties. Boyd wanted to go down to the University of Richmond to try out for their football team, but the administration refused to allow him to leave the campus. All of the school's track meets, except for one, were away meets–preventing Boyd from competing in them. For the single home meet, he persuaded the Commandant to allow him to run. Track coach Gus Lacey really didn't want to let him compete, but finally permitted him to run the 100 for the first time. He would have won the event had he not slowed his speed near the finish line. Then they put him in the low hurdles race. The school had only enough hurdles to run two athletes at a time. And they had only 120 yards for the race. Boyd ended up placing second.

By the time he finished his fifth year at Fork Union, he was over six feet tall and a fairly good athlete. No one in his family had ever gone to college. His father, who would be paying his way through college, wanted Boyd to go somewhere that had a strong program in medicine, law, or engineering. But he didn't want his son to play football. At the time, Boyd's father owned an optical supply business.

Someone told Boyd that he should look into attending Wofford College the next year. Wofford had a good football team, and replied to Boyd's letter. He told the Wofford coach that he would hitchhike down for an interview. After the interview, Wofford gave him a four-year scholarship. After his graduation from Fork Union, Boyd went to the Wofford campus to participate in two-a-day drills. He even went to class for a day. Then his dad said that if he played football in college, Boyd would have to pay his own way. Football players in those days did not have a very good reputation.

So after a day of classes, Boyd had to face the reality of trying to survive at Wofford with no spending money. Boyd decided to leave, and his father came to pick him up. His dad now tried to persuade him that he should enroll at Virginia Tech, where he could join the Corps of Cadets and get some military experience. Then Boyd heard from his father's partner that Roanoke College had a preliminary course of study that allowed students to transfer to Virginia Tech after two years. He went to the College and talked with an administrator who was also serving as the school's soccer coach. Although the 1951-52 classes already had begun, Roanoke admitted him. Of course, it helped that the coach needed a soccer goalie and there was Boyd, an athlete who was in shape. Although he had never played soccer, he picked up a few pointers and within a short period of time, became the number one goalie for the team.

Boyd played soccer during his entire freshman season, but really didn't like the game. The next year, when the team picked up some better players, he dropped the sport altogether.

Boyd skipped the ratline that fall although he was just a freshman. For years, the ratline at Roanoke consisted of an indoctrination to college life of freshman by sophomores, juniors, and seniors. Freshmen wore beanies, assembled in the quad on command, memorized the school song, obeyed the commands of any upperclassman, and more. Whenever upperclassmen asked him why he wasn't in the ratline, he fibbed and told them that he was transferring in from Wofford. The word got out in the spring that he was, indeed, a freshman and some were not pleased.

As a freshman, he wanted to go out for track; however, being a day student, he heard nothing about an indoor season and did not participate until spring. His major events were the high and low hurdles, although he occasionally participated in the broad jump. In his first meet on April 5, 1952, he won the 100-yard dash in a slow time of :10.6, then placed third in the 120-yard high hurdles. He and Paul Barker had been on a double date until 2:30 a.m. and when he reached the campus that morning, his good friend Don Fleming put him to bed in the fraternity house. The house was quiet because everyone was in class, so Boyd got a few good hours of sleep. He got up just in time for the meet to begin. After the 100 and high hurdles, he was sitting in the stands because Coach Bast hadn't told him what events he would be in that day. Bast then motioned to Boyd and said, "Why don't you go for the low hurdles record today?" So he ran the event and ended up winning in a school-record time of :26.6. Looking on was Rud Rosebro, who had set the former record (:27.0) in 1948. "From that point on," Boyd said, "I was finally someone on campus. Everyone knew my name."

Indeed, Boyd was the team's premier hurdler and one of the best in the Little Six and Mason-Dixon Conferences. In the third meet that year, he lowered the low hurdle record to :26.3. At the end of April, he set a new Alumni Field and school record by running :15.7 in the high hurdles against Davis and Elkins College. He placed second in the low hurdles in the Little Six meet and fourth in the high hurdles at the Mason-Dixon meet. In the final meet of the 1952 season, he set yet another low hurdle school record by running :26.3.

In the 1952-53 indoor season, he continued to improve. He finished second in both the low and high hurdle events against V. M. I., running against the Keydets' now-famous Johnny Mapp. He also helped Roanoke win the team title in the Little Six meet by finishing second in the high hurdles and winning the low hurdles in a time of :08.2. The low hurdle mark set a new meet and school record.

Outdoors that year, the team made a spring-break trip to Clemson and Davidson. In the Clemson meet, Boyd finished second in both hurdles races against excellent competition. During the Davidson meet, he won the high hurdles and broke his own school record by running a time of :15.6. The loss to Davidson, incidentally, was the last dual or triangular meet loss until Coach Bast gave up the team after the 1956-57 season. Later in the meet, he won the low hurdles in :25.6, breaking the school record by :07 second. Against Hampden-Sydney, running on the Salem track, he set yet another low hurdle record by running :25.5.

In the Little Six Championships that spring, held in Lynchburg, Boyd was second in the high hurdles and first in the low hurdles. His low hurdles time of :24.9 again was a new Roanoke College record. The peak of his fine season came a week later at the Mason-Dixon Championships at Catholic University. He tied the school record of :15.6 while winning the high hurdles. In the low hurdles, he won with a time of :25.0, a new meet and stadium record.

At the end of his sophomore year, Boyd was faced with a decision. Should he stay at Roanoke or transfer to another school? He thought about becoming a Mathematics major, but his father would have none of it. He told Boyd, "I can hire a math major any time I want to." Coach Bast even offered him a bigger scholarship if he would stay. Instead, Boyd applied to and was accepted at Georgia Tech. During the summer of 1952, he asked his father for $25 to reserve a room. But his dad had just come back from the University of Virginia, and decided that Boyd should attend that school. He thought that his son might benefit from the University's small, successful engineering school. Boyd wrote the University and got an application, which he completed and sent in. When Coach Bast found out that he actually was transferring, he was mystified. He had a long talk with Boyd and then with his father. Boyd remembers the meeting one night that Bast had with his father–a meeting that Boyd sat in on. "I felt like somebody's property that night," Boyd said. "I sympathize with celebrities who have agents, and who are handled. Sometimes they talked about me as if I weren't there." But nothing Bast could say changed either Boyd's or his father's mind. Boyd was headed to Charlottesville.

At the University of Virginia, Boyd was a two-year member of the track team. He was never a star athlete for the Cavaliers, but did run well.

When he graduated, he received the school's first aeronautical degree, although he never used the degree in any of the jobs he had after that point.

At about this time, he married "a nice girl" named Joan, who was a nurse. The marriage resulted in three children. One, a boy, died of a bacterial infection. The other two are in Roanoke today, living together. Joan and Boyd finally got a divorce in 1978 after being married for some 18 years.

He had been in the R. O. T. C. while in Charlottesville, and after graduating, went into the Air Force. He wanted to be a fighter pilot, but soon gave up that dream when the Air Force told him that he would have to stay in the service a minimum of five years, instead of three, so they could get their money's worth out of him. So he changed his career path with the Air Force and got out after just two years.

When he left the Air Force, he had a wife and a family and no money. He badly needed a job. He had thoughts of moving his family to a farm in Dinwiddie County and going to New York to make his fortune as an artist. Friends, however, told him to go home and make amends with his father and ask for a job. He did, and spent the next 19 years working in his father's business. At first, he took over the sales position for Blue Ridge Optical Company on Day Avenue in Roanoke. Eventually, he moved to Charleston, West Virginia, and took over the business there.

After many years in that position, the company's optical business in Charlottesville was sold, and the one in Charleston wasn't doing well financially. Then, Boyd's two sisters came to Charleston and fired him. But the loss of that job wasn't devastating. "It saved my life," Boyd now says. "That was when I got married again, this time to Gloria, who was a nurse." She got a job with a local church and the two of them built a house on a hillside in South Charleston. Gloria encouraged him to try his hand at art again, at least for a year or so. Art has been Boyd's hobby ever since, although he has made very little money from painting.

Presently, Gloria has macular degeneration and it takes her longer to do most things. Driving is a problem for her, in particular at night. Boyd has had some physical problems during the past few years. He had a triple by-pass operation in 2006, and it took him some time to get over the surgery.

When he first became self-employed, he thought seriously about going into the wholesale art business, even making his own art work. Unfortunately, those plans didn't work out. But he had inherited some money, and had other money in various investments, so he and Gloria have lived a frugal, but comfortable life.

Today, the couple lives just outside of Bedford, Virginia, in a house they built. They made the move to be closer to the family. Boyd is a professional story-teller and is especially talented as a caricature artist. He has also written several books. One, *My.th*, is sold online by http://www.amazon.com, and is a monograph. According to Boyd, it "purports to develop the universal myth in the literate culture. It is a story of a story line that runs through Math–The Blood Flow Cycle and Time–using squares, circles, triangles, and stick figures, tracing the connecting links between us and those heavenly objects which we can observe. We become story tellers because we know our life span is finite and we aim for the stars and the infinite." The Roanoke College library also keeps a copy of *My.th.*

Another of his books is *the first won hundred poems*, which contains an interesting poem written about one of his athletic experiences. It deals with a Roanoke College track meet with Hampden-Sydney, when Boyd came from fourth place in the 220 to finish second to George Gearhart. This book also is in the library archives at Roanoke.

A third book is about to be published. It will be entitled *My Lane to Run In*, or perhaps *Hi Hurdler*. It is an autobiographic sketch, with a series of essays taken from his memory.

Boyd's poems and illustrations have appeared in numerous publications, including the *Appalachian Journal*. According to the Appalachian Journal home page, the magazine is a "peer-reviewed quarterly featuring field research, interviews, and other scholarly studies of history, politics, economics, culture, folklore, literature, music, ecology, and a variety of other topics, as well as poetry and reviews of books, films, and recordings dealing with the region of the Appalachian mountains." As Boyd puts it, his illustrations for the "Signs of the Time" section of the Appalachian Journal is his paying job these days. He doesn't do the covers, but has contributed many illustrations inside. He usually does about four illustrations per issue.

Incidentally, former athletes of Coach Bast may remember the large, brightly colored painting of a runner that was framed and hung in Bast's office for many years. It was a real conversation piece. Boyd is the individual who created that painting, donating it to his coach in the mid-1950s. Homer said that his sons, Michael and Steven, always thought the painting was of a runner who had hit the top bar of his hurdle and broke it into many pieces. Homer once told him that when he turned to view the painting, he could see all of the boys who had run for him through the years. Boyd has always said that the interpretation of the painting was in the mind of the viewer.

After leaving Roanoke, former track star Boyd Carr created this colorful painting for Homer. Homer framed the painting and hung it in his office for several years.

Cerelli, Bill

The son of William and Frances Cerelli, Bill was raised in West New York, New Jersey. Also in the household were an older brother, Frank, and a younger sister, Joan.

Bill attended Memorial High School in West New York and played tennis. He had never run competitively before attending Roanoke College.

Gail and Bill Cerelli

One of his relatives had a son who had gone to Roanoke and that fact, simple as it was, convinced Bill to enroll there himself in 1954. In his first few days on the campus, he found that the school at the time had no tennis program. Wanting to participate in athletics, he decided to try cross country and track. In his sophomore year, he and several other students convinced Dr. Frank Snow to coach tennis. From that time until he graduated, he ran cross country in the fall and played tennis in the spring.

The reason he chose cross country that first year was that he had Coach Bast as a World Civilization teacher. Bill liked Homer and, knowing that he was the cross country coach, decided to try out for the team.

He turned out to be a fairly good cross country athlete. He was never going to be a number-one runner, but he contributed considerably to the team successes. He ran during the heyday of the cross country program. Over the four years he competed, the team won 24 dual meets and lost only 3. In 1954 and 1956, the team had perfect records. The four teams also won the Little Seven or Little Eight meets as well as the Mason-Dixon Championships in each of the years Bill was running.

He remembers his days with Homer Bast well. "I think it was in a Randolph-Macon meet during my sophomore year," he says, "when I was running with a buddy and we came to the end of the race. As we headed toward the tape, there was the finish line ribbon still stretched across the track. We knew something wasn't right, because several of our teammates were far better than us and should have already finished. After breaking the tape, we found out that the front runners for Roanoke had gotten lost during the race. But the team was so strong that Roanoke beat the other team anyway." In another meet during the 1955 season, with Virginia Polytechnic Institute," he remembers, "if I had beaten the guy who was a second ahead of me, we would have beaten them. V. P. I. won the meet by one point." And he also remembers the Mason-Dixon Championships his sophomore year, when the Maroons placed seven runners in the top 15 places. Bill himself was 13th.

He admits that his best distance running came during his sophomore year. "Then, for whatever reason," he said, "I got out of shape and never did as well in my last couple of years as I had done in that sophomore season."

Bill graduated from Roanoke at the end of the 1957-58 session, with a major in biology. His first job was as a teacher of biology at PS-1 and 3 in West New York. He taught there for three years, and then moved to Memorial High School, the school from which he had graduated. There he taught for another three years before moving to a high school in the locality where he lives now–in the Franklin Lakes area.

In 1961, Bill married Margaret, his first wife. They were together for about three years. Soon after the breakup, he married his second wife, Gail. They have three children. William is the oldest, Amy is the middle child, and Kerry is the youngest. Today, William works for Equitable, selling to brokers. He has three children, all boys. Amy runs a fly fishing shop in Virginia. Kerry is in Colorado. She has a Master's Degree in Psychology and works in that field. Neither Amie nor Kerry is married.

Bill continued to teach during almost his entire career, retiring in 2001. During this time, he taught mostly biology, although he did teach some chemistry and life science. During his educational career, he coached boys' and girls' tennis for 20 years and football for 5.

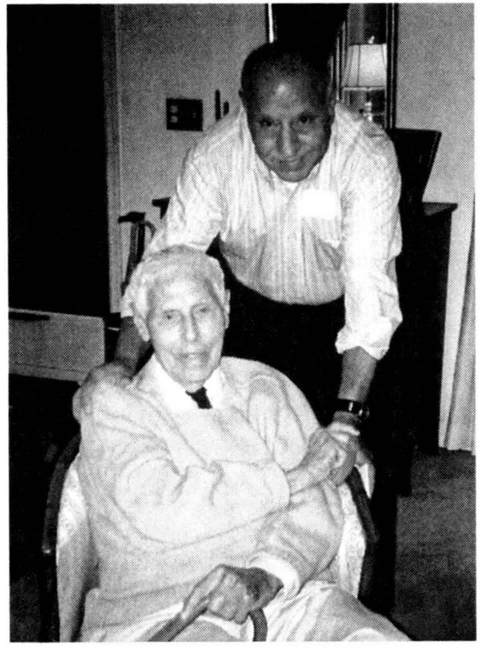

Today, he has had no major health problems, and tries to play a lot of tennis. He still keeps in contact with Homer Bast, and they have become close friends over the years. "I think Homer is and was a very special person," he says. "He is the type of person who seldom comes along in a lifetime. I am fortunate to have met him and to become his friend. He is an exceptional person. All of us on his team wanted to do our best. You did your best for yourself, of course, but you also did it for him. We all had the crazy feeling that you couldn't let him down. You don't usually find people like that–people that you want to go all out for. It's great when a coach can get an athlete to

Former runner Bill Cerelli visits Homer Bast on the day the track was dedicated to Homer in late 2006.

think like that. You always felt that Homer was looking out for you, even though you realized that you were just one of many students needing his help. He always knew who you were and tried to help you out. You always felt special when you were around him."

Davenport, Bruce

Bruce was born and raised in Roanoke City. His father had been a runner at V. P. I. before 1920 and was a very good miler, with a time just over 4:20.0. He was about Bruce's size–5'6" and 130 pounds.

Bruce attended Jefferson High School, but when Bruce was a student there, the school had no track team. Nevertheless, he enjoyed recreational running.

He had two brothers, an older one and a younger one who also went to Roanoke College and graduated just a year after Bruce. For a year, he served as the Manager for the track team. Neither of Bruce's parents is alive today. His father died in 1960 and his mother in 1975.

Left to right: Bruce Davenport, Elsa Wieboldt, Nan Davenport, Ali Wieboldt, and Pring Davenport. Kit, the third daughter, took the picture.

Bruce went directly from Jefferson into the Army in 1945. He tried to join another branch of the military, such as the Navy, but didn't qualify. At the time, the Army was discharging lots of soldiers, mostly coming from Europe. Bruce went to the separation center at Fort Meade in Maryland and pushed papers as a clerk for nine months before going on to his basic training. That training occurred at Fort McClelland in Alabama. Then he was headed for Japan but instead ended up in California and then Fort Knox. He was discharged after just 14 months, and he entered Roanoke College in the fall of 1947. He commuted to the campus from his home during his first two years of college, and then lived in the dorms during his third and fourth years.

His college running began with the cross country team of 1947. That was the year before the first season of the famous Big Four–Alvin Smith, Bruce, Red Crockett, and Paul McCarty–all of whom frequently jogged across the finish line in first place, hand-in-hand. Bruce and Alvin Smith were the best of the four. Alvin, who transferred to Roanoke from the University of North Carolina at the beginning of the second semester, ran a 4:24 mile. Bruce was the first Bast runner to run a time below 10 minutes in the two-mile race, recording a 9:58. Both times were school records for several years.

Bruce remembers his running days well. "It was satisfying to be in front most of the time. And I remember the trips we took. The overnight trips in particular were lots of fun. I remember almost everyone who was on the track and cross country teams in those days. Many of us were from the same fraternity–Kappa Alpha–who had a house on High Street."

Over a four-year period, Bruce was an outstanding cross country runner in the Little Six and Mason-Dixon Conferences. In his freshman year, he won the Little Six Championships and also placed first in the two dual meets in which he ran.

In his sophomore year, at the height of the Big Four group of runners, Bruce either won or tied for the win in six straight meets, including the Little Six. He also was third in the Mason-Dixon Conference meet.

As a junior, he won or tied for the win in four consecutive dual and triangular meets, capping the season with a second in the Little Six meet, a third in the Virginia A. A. U. Championships, and a first place in the Mason-Dixon meet.

His senior year performance wasn't quite as sparkling–although in fairness, runners such as Merle Crouse of Bridgewater were becoming much more competitive–as Bruce finished third in the Little Six and second in the Mason-Dixon.

Over this four-year period in cross-country, Bruce's team won 14 meets and lost only 2. They won the Little Six Championships in three of the four years and the Mason-Dixon Championships in two of three years. The team was also first in the Virginia AAU Championships in Bruce's junior year.

During his outdoor track career at Roanoke, Bruce ran mostly the two-mile race, although he also ran the mile and participated in some relay events. In 1947-48, the second year of track's revival, he and Alvin Smith dominated the mile and two-mile races. Bruce was second in the Mason-Dixon Conference two-mile race and won the event in the Little Six meet. He also tied with Smith for first in the Little Six mile run.

In his sophomore year, Bruce ran the best two-mile race of his career On May 2, he was timed in 9:59.8 in a dual meet with Randolph-Macon. At the time, sub-10:00 miles were rare for track teams from small colleges. In the Little Six meet that year, he tied with two teammates for first place in both the mile and two-mile races. He also won the two-mile events in the Mason-Dixon and Virginia A. A. U. meets to finish the year.

In 1949-50, his junior year, Bruce won the Little Six two-mile run. He also placed second in the same race in the Mason-Dixon Championships.

Bruce graduated from Roanoke with a B. S. degree in Physics. His first job was with

Bendix in Baltimore, where he worked in research and development.

Meanwhile, in September after his graduation, he married Nancy Pringle–who liked to be called "Pring." She had graduated from Roanoke a year before Bruce. While they were in school, the relationship between the two began to grow. "We had a track meet in Baltimore," Bruce recalls, "and I was there for a couple of days. While there, I went to see her family. Her mother and I fell for each other. And from then on, Nancy and I were closer."

Bruce stayed with Bendix for a few years, and then joined Sperry Rand Corporation. There, he worked mostly in radar design and production. Except for a short period when he was laid off, he stayed with Sperry until he retired in 1986 as a Senior Engineer. In that job, Bruce traveled quite a lot, which "was a good experience" for him.

Along the way, Pring gave birth to three daughters. Nan Ashby Davenport now lives in Oakland, California, where she is a freelance artist on the Internet. Katherine "Kit" Davenport lives in Arcata, California. She is a ceramist and teaches classes at College of the Redwoods and Humboldt State. Daughter Alison Bruce lives in Newport News, Virginia, where she has a studio and makes jewelry. She and her husband, Tom, have one daughter. Elsa was born in 1993.

At retirement, Bruce and Pring were living in the country outside of Charlottesville, Virginia. Their home was an old farm house on six acres. When they left the house in about 2006, after about 46 years, they moved to a retirement community in Charlottesville. Today, they live in a comfortable cottage and enjoy being near all of the town conveniences, along with having someone else take care of the upkeep.

When Bruce retired, the Davenports continued some of their interests. For years, they had helped band birds for the Fish and Wildlife Service. Because of this hobby, the two of them traveled to many good birding spots. They used to enjoy vegetable gardening, but are not able to continue this hobby at the senior community. On the other hand, Bruce has kept up his interest in identifying plants and dabbling in other nature activities. He has also done some water-color painting.

DeCosta, Raymond

Ray was born in 1928 in New York City, the son of an unwed mother. When he was about four years old, his mother took him and his sister, Irene, to the local police station and gave up custody of her children. When the authorities found that she had no visible means of support–no husband or other provider–they deported her to Portugal.

Both Ray and Irene were turned over to the state, being placed in foster homes on Long Island. Their names were changed from DaCosta to DeCosta so that the new name sounded Italian. They thought Italians were a more accepted group. When she was older,

Ray DeCosta and Partner, Jean.

Ray's sister actually changed her name back to DaCosta.

At age 10, Ray was transferred to a Leake Watts Children's Home in Yonkers, which is where he lived until he finished college. Even during his breaks while at Roanoke College, he returned to the Home.

He went to high school in Yonkers at Saunders Trades School. There, he was active in sports, playing halfback in football and pole vaulting during track season. He found that he had some natural talent for vaulting, once clearing 11'6" to set a record not broken until around 1997.

Fortunately for Ray, the Edwin Gould Foundation financed a college education for him and others at Leake Watts. As he finished his senior year in high school, and after he spent a year at Halston Prep School in Yonkers, he had little idea about which college he should attend. But one day someone who was a graduate of Roanoke College approached him and told Ray that he should consider going down to Salem for his college education. He said that the school had a good track program and was a friendly place to live.

Sight unseen, he showed up at Roanoke in the fall of 1948. He was pleased at what he found and thought the campus atmosphere was wonderful. During the first year or two, he lived in the Sections. Later, he moved to Hildreth Hall, rooming for his last two years with basketball star Tony Proietti, from West New York, New York.

Before track season began during his first year, he was jogging around the track to keep in shape, when Homer saw him. He asked Ray what he did in track and invited him to try out for the team. It was the start of one of the most successful athletic careers in Roanoke's history.

Homer Bast was primarily a runner's coach at the time, but helped Ray with his form as much as possible. For the most part, however, Ray was self-taught.

His pole vaulting teammate in those early days was Bill Williams. Both of them at first used bamboo poles. As time went by, Ray graduated to a Swedish steel pole and then during his final year, a fiberglass pole made in California. The Swedish pole was thick in the middle and tapered toward the ends. He was vaulting about 2½' over his grip. Ray constantly studied the previously great stars of pole vaulting, including Rev. Bob Richards, the Olympic pole vaulting champion who had begun his jumping at Bridgewater College before transferring schools. Ray was thrilled once when he got to meet him. Richards came down to Roanoke College to speak at one of the assemblies. Later, as Ray's skills improved, he competed against Richards in Madison Square Garden.

While at Roanoke College, his achievements in vaulting were significant. In summary, Ray was the Little Six and Mason-Dixon champion in the pole vault in each of his four years at the College. He won the event in 19 of 20 outdoor track dual meets, never failing to win in dual meet competition after his freshman year. He jumped 13'3" indoors and 13'6" outdoors, the best heights of any small college vaulter in the south. The best pole vaulters in the nation, in both colleges and universities, were seldom jumping more than 14' at that time. In fact, 14'1" was the approximate height that won the 1948 Olympics. His school record in indoor track has never been exceeded by a Roanoke athlete. His outdoor record held up for 52 years, until it was beaten by three inches in 2004.

According to Coach Bast and Ray's teammates, Ray was a hard worker, practicing his skills every day. He was always cooperative and well-liked by his teammates.

All of the achievements came during a time when facilities and equipment for vaulting were not very good. Pole vaulters landed in a foot or two of sawdust. Athletes had to tend to their own pits, making sure on occasion that the sawdust was dug up and turned over to give a softer feel. Runways were often just dirt paths in Ray's day. "I would have loved to have a paved runway," he says, "where I could use sneakers. We used the old field event shoes, with spikes on the ball of the shoe. Bill Williams and I both cut our legs open on those spikes as we came down."

Ray majored in Education and Psychology at Roanoke. But after graduation in 1952, not being sure what he wanted to do in life, he decided to go directly into the Army where he spent the next two years. Successful at most of the things he tried, he was named "outstanding soldier of the cycle" at the Army's Transportation Replacement Training Center in Fort Eustis, Virginia. The award was given to the outstanding member of a training company in recognition of superior performance of duties.

Incidentally, it was at Fort Eustis that he found himself bunk mates with the famous Giants outfielder Willie Mays. Mays was serving temporarily as a physical education instructor, waiting for his release from the Army pending the approval of his application for a dependency discharge as sole support of his mother and nine brothers and sisters.

The Army sent Ray to Japan instead of Korea, where many soldiers were serving. They assigned him to a steam fitter position on ships. Finally, he did get to Korea, but shortly after the transfer, he was released from military service.

During those first few years after Roanoke College, Ray continued to vault in the New York area. Performing for the New York Athletic Club, he entered meets throughout the northeast–including some indoors at Madison Square Garden. For a time, he had a home business–the American Athletic Equipment Company–and turned out unbreakable fiberglass cross bars. He received lots of orders for these bars, but couldn't keep up with the demand. He made the molds himself and ran the entire process. Early on, he made a large batch of bars and sold them all almost immediately. There was no one at the time making a similar bar.

Ray also dabbled with producing vaulting poles out of fiberglass. His problem, however, was in not having the means to form a cylinder and keep it hollow. His pole had to have a core, but that wasn't the answer. He had no way to get a big company to finance his project, so finally he just let the entire business go.

His first job after his military service was working for the City of New York, in the east side of Manhattan, taking charge of youngsters who were remanded until their court trials. He was assigned one floor for a 48-hour period of time. He stayed with that job for about six months.

He had decided not to teach, although he had a teaching degree from Roanoke. Then he realized that his talents were artistic in nature. He looked around and saw a typesetting machine. He was able to get hold of two of those machines, financed by a friend. So he turned to typesetting for printing companies. He would subcontract some of their work, printing their forms. He did well in this business for a couple of years, but then began to see the advantages of getting into printing itself. So he went to work for a local printer in a job that lasted for some 25-30 years. Ray took care of customers, did camera work and layouts, made plates, oversaw the press work, and more.

He eventually left the company when the owner decided that he could farm out his work cheaper than having it done on his premises. For some three years, he spent his time in Pennsylvania, building a house on 40 acres of land. He intended to live in the house, but decided to return to the printing company after about three years. He worked for the owner for another couple of years.

Meanwhile, he met Jean, whose husband–a police officer–had just died. The two decided that they would make a life together and bought a house in an area north of New York City on the Jersey side and close to the Hudson River.

There, Ray set up his own printing company. The company began to show some promise after a year or so, and Jean decided to come on board as a partner. Together, Ray and Jean ran that company in Nanuet, New York, for about 10 years.

When Ray was 65, he retired from the business. He wanted to move down to Florida, where he and Jean had owned a getaway condominium. But Jean, who was 14 years younger, wasn't ready to retire. So she stayed on with the new owner as a 50-50 partner for another three years, and Ray temporarily retired to the Nanuet house.

When Jean finally decided to retire, the two of them moved to Florida. Their condo was in Melbourne Beach, on the east coast of the state, and they lived in the condominium for a few months while they built a new house in the same general area. That's the house they live in today. They enjoy the community where they live and the people around them.

Since moving to Florida, Ray occasionally plays the guitar, an instrument he has enjoyed for some 40 years. He has also written a number of songs, most of which have been published. In fact, Ray gave the author several CDs of his music. One featured Ray Stark, singing about 13 songs written by Ray. Another CD, entitled "Glad Tidings," contained one of his Christmas songs called "A Christmas Wish." Along the way, Ray also wrote a number of country songs.

Dodd, Dick

One of the best short-distance runners that Homer Bast coached in the late 1940s, Dr. Richard Wine Dodd grew up in southwest Roanoke. He ran track at Jefferson High School, competing in the 100, 220, and on relay teams. The Jefferson team was fairly accomplished, with meets versus schools such as Andrew Lewis High School in Salem, William Fleming High School in Roanoke, William Byrd High School in Vinton, and always-strong E. C. Glass High School in Lynchburg. These were the days, however, when the number of meets per year was low–perhaps three or four in all.

This picture of the Dodd family was taken in February of 2008. From left to right: Dr. Richard Dodd, age 44, Savannah, Georgia - Anesthesiologist; Whitney Goodwin, age 51, Atlanta, Georgia - Nurse at Emory Hospital; Sally Pellarin, age 48, Charlotte, North Carolina - Advertising, with Subway; Ann Dodd; and Dr. Dick Dodd.

Dick's father, Harold, was an accountant at the Appalachian Power Company. Ula Wine Dodd, his mother, was a homemaker. He had one sister, Dorothy, who was eight years older. She married a man who graduated from Roanoke College.

As a senior at Jefferson, he narrowed his choices of college to Roanoke and Virginia Military Institute in Lexington; however, after a visit to Lexington to look at the V. M. I. campus, he "got chicken" about going there. Besides, he knew that if one went to Roanoke and majored in chemistry, a good academic record would get you into medical school. Dr. Robey in the Chemistry Department apparently had some kind of inside road to the Medical College of Virginia. Dick had heard from many people that if you took Dr. Robey's four years of chemistry, you automatically were on your way to medical school. And he knew when he was in high school that he wanted to be a doctor.

He entered Roanoke College in 1947. Because he was a day student, living at home, he has always felt that he lost a lot of the camaraderie and spirit of college that one might get living on campus. He and a high school friend, also a student at Roanoke College, were able to purchase on old Desoto to get to the campus and back.

That first year, he ran track but wasn't particularly active on the team. He was heavily weighted down with labs and didn't want to endanger his academic progress. He did join the Pi Kappa Phi fraternity, and during one of his undergraduate years was Business Manager of the college yearbook. Beginning with his sophomore year, he figured more prominently in the success of the team.

To this day, he remembers Homer Bast well. "During our practice times," he encouraged us constantly to do as much as we could. He wanted us to keep in shape, meaning that we had to do our calisthenics and running exercises. He tried to get me to run the 440, but now I believe I was just too lazy to train for that. Running the shorter races was enough for me. Homer always had a soft spot in his heart for quarter milers, since the 440 was his major event at the University of Virginia. But there was no doubt that Homer was my real mentor. He helped me to grow up while at Roanoke. He was a humble man, who could get down on your level. You always knew where he stood on an issue. And he made you feel like you were a real part of the team."

Dick probably did better in the 220 at Roanoke than in the 100, although he ran good times in both. In the 100, he ran two races in :10.3. But he did run a :22.6 in the 220 at Lynchburg in 1950 and a :22.8 in the Little Six meet in Lynchburg in the same season. He also ran on several successful relay teams during his college career.

During his 1950-51 senior year, he was accepted at the Medical College of Virginia. He stayed at M. C. V. for four years, after which he received his doctorate. Then he interned in Richmond on a rotating internship before getting drafted to serve during the Korean War. Many of his friends also were drafted at that time. The Army sent him to serve as a routine medical officer–a family doctor treating retirees, their children, etc. For this work, he was stationed at Vint Hill Farm Station, an Army security post that did the early listening for the Cold War. "We had a couple of thousand troops," Dick said, "and they stayed in these small barracks, mostly underground. I spent two years in that job. After leaving the Army, I then spent four years at Johns Hopkins in Baltimore, arriving there in 1958."

While at Johns Hopkins, he was walking across the campus near the hospital when he spotted Homer Bast. Homer had hitched a ride to Baltimore with Derek Stryker, a young track athlete at Roanoke, who was headed north to his own home. Homer was at Johns Hopkins to undergo a series of tests for his angina problems. Knowing that Homer had never been to the huge hospital complex, Dick was kind enough to escort Homer to the various testing sites. "My wife and I tried to get together with Homer one night while he was at Hopkins for a meal at our apartment, which was very near the University," Dick said. "Apparently, we thought the other would be at a different door of the hospital." At any rate, Dick's kindness toward his old college coach would be long remembered by Homer.

Dick had been married since his first year in medical school. His new wife was a Roanoke girl, Ann, who had gone to Mary Baldwin. She and Dick are together today, after some 55 years. They have three children and seven grandchildren. The oldest of the three children is Whitney, now in her 50s. She and her husband have two boys, Will and Graham. Her husband, Scott, works for a drug company. The second-oldest child was Sally, about four years younger than Whitney. She married a classmate at Davidson College. Daniel and Sally have one boy and one girl. The third child for Dick and Ann was Richard. He and his wife, Leanne, have three girls.

Dick practiced medicine in Richmond until he retired in 1991, concentrating his efforts in the fields of ear, nose, and throat. His career spanned about 30 years.

He has played golf for several years, belonging to the prestigious Country Club of Virginia in Richmond. Unfortunately, he says, Ann is not a golfer herself. He and Ann do a bit of traveling–both overseas and in the United States. A few years ago, they bought a mini-farm of about 75 acres just for hobby activities. He rents out the pasture on his property for hay.

Driscoll, Bill

Bill Driscoll was one of Homer Bast's best discus throwers. During his three years at Roanoke College, he consistently threw the discus between 120' and 130', coming close to getting the school record.

He was born in Bedford, Virginia, growing up on a farm. His mother and father were Sammie and Irving Driscoll. They got a divorce when Bill was four, and he lived with his mother on her family farm. His dad got married again, and he and his new wife had more children–giving Bill two step sisters and a step brother. His father went on to become the Superintendent of School in Buckingham County, Virginia.

Bill Driscoll and his wife, Patricia.

While Bill was attending Bedford High School, he participated in basketball and outdoor track. In the track program, he threw the shot and discus, ran the high and low hurdles, high jumped, and was a member of the 440 relay team. His best event, even in high school, was the discus.

When it came time to choose a college, he knew that he wanted to be a dentist and he needed to attend a school with a good pre-med program. He wanted to get into dental school after just three years of undergraduate work. Roanoke had a good reputation for sending many of its students into medical doctorate programs. He was a bit scared at taking Dr. Robey's course in chemistry, however, so he went to the University of Virginia one summer and took and passed organic chemistry, transferring the credits back to Roanoke.

When he got to the College in 1955-56, he thought about competing in the hurdle events as well as in the discus. But because Roanoke already had a lot of good hurdlers, including Dave Foltz and Bruce Johnston, he decided to concentrate on the discus.

Bill was active in campus life, becoming a member of the Kappa Alpha fraternity and joining the Monogram Club. During his first year in Salem, he lived in a white house just across High Street from the Sections. He then moved into the Sections for the remaining time in Salem. Win Niles was his roommate in 1956-57. Win, of course, was an outstanding pole vaulter for Roanoke during his short time at the College.

After just three years at Roanoke, without an undergraduate degree, he left Roanoke and went to the Medical College of Virginia for dentistry. He soon found that M. C. V. was a difficult academic school. His freshman and sophomore years in Richmond were the hardest. Having taken Dr. Holloway's histology course at Roanoke, however, he did find that he had a great background for M. C. V.'s histology course. All in all, he enjoyed his stay in Richmond. M. C. V. was a good school with a good reputation.

During his first year at M. C. V., he finished second in his class. After four years, he was still in the top 10 of his class.

Bill finished his work in dentistry in 1962. Afterwards, he worked for the U. S. Public Health Service. He and Nancy were married during his senior year at M. C. V., in 1961, but had no children together during the early years of their marriage. Nancy was a nursing student at M. C. V. Later, in 1969, Michael was born. Nancy and Bill are now divorced as of about 1975 after about 14 years together.

During the early years after M. C. V., Bill and Nancy lived in Seattle as he completed his dental internship. The two then moved to an Indian reservation near the Grand Coolie Dam. The work was demanding.

After the divorce, Bill married his second wife, Patricia, in about 1983. She was working at the time at N. I. H. (National Institute of Health) and she and Bill have been together for the past 25 years.

After he left Seattle and the Indian Reservation job, Bill made a career with the Public Health Service in their Commission Corps. They provided medical and dental services. In 1965, Bill got out of clinical dentistry and pursued dental research when the opportunity came. To make the change, he moved back to Bethesda and began to do clinical studies in such areas as preventing tooth decay. After a year in Bethesda, he and Nancy were transferred to San Francisco. In 1967, he went to Johns Hopkins to get a Master's Degree in Public Health. That course work continued through June of 1968. He then went to San Francisco again, from 1968 to 1971, doing the same types of clinical trials–preventing tooth decay and more. In 1971 that program was discontinued in San Francisco and he was transferred to the National Institute of Dental Research–a part of N. I. H.–in Bethesda. He stayed in that job until he retired in August of 1992. He had been employed with the Public Health Service for 30 years.

Since his retirement, he has done nothing in the way of dentistry. One of his passionate hobbies, however, had been the driving of automobiles. He drove a race car with the Sports Car Club of America, in national competition, for about 10 years–from 1976 through 1984. Since then, he has spent time pursuing performance driving. He has two sports cars–a Pantera Alium sports car that he has owned for 36 years and a 2007 Z-0 6 Corvette. He has taken them both on road racing courses just to keep his hand in performance driving. He has raced on tracks up and down the east coast, from Watkins Glen to West Palm Beach.

There are some dangers in driving, of course. In 2000 at West Palm Beach, he was driving a friend's car, lost control of it, and hit a barrier on the inside of the track. The wreck banged Bill up a bit, giving him a broken vertebrate, all kinds of torn ligaments, and more. Those types of cars are not protected as well as NASCAR vehicles, but the wreck certainly didn't' spoil his interest in high performance driving.

His health in recent years has been fairly good. He did have a bout with colon cancer in 1995, but the cancer was taken care of by surgery and chemo–and there has been no recurrence.

Emberger, Dick

Dick Emberger may have been the finest all-around track athlete in the history of

Roanoke College. Perhaps this statement is arguable, but no athlete has ever been so skilled in so many events. No athlete has dominated both the state and conference championships. And no athlete before or after him has ever gone on after college to represent the United States on its Olympic team and, by his performances on that team, make the College and its alumni so proud.

Dick Emberger and his wife, Rosemary, at Peggy's Cove in Nova Scotia.

He had a humble beginning, born on July 3, 1938, in New York City to Helen and John Emberger. Dick had one sister who today is married. She and her husband had two children. One was born with mental deficiencies and passed away. The other child, playing on farm equipment, had his spinal cord cut and he has spent his life in a wheelchair. The family moved to live with Dick's aunt in New Jersey when he was about three years old. His dad was a tool and die maker and his mother was a homemaker.

Dick attended Bloomfield High School. There, he participated in cross country and indoor and outdoor track, and even served as manager of the school's basketball team. He was able to run :16.4 in the high hurdles and in the high jump cleared 6'1½" once at Madison Square Garden and 6'1" during the outdoor season.

As he entered the final years of his high school career, his intentions were to join the Navy after leaving Bloomfield and to see the world. His grades were just average and his parents did not have much money to send their son to college. One day, however, he had a talk with his coach, Peter Wilson, who told Dick that he should get his act together and, because he was already showing above-average athletic ability, he should try to get a college scholarship. He didn't point Dick toward any particular college at the time. But not long afterwards, Sam Good came to the high school one day and Dick talked with him about Roanoke College. Roanoke ended up offering Dick some small amount of financial aid–at least the cost of books and room and board. As they say, the rest is history. He enrolled at Roanoke College in the fall of 1956.

Dick had never met Homer Bast before arriving on campus. But he did have Homer for a freshman history course. His track career to this point was not outstanding. In high school, he began as a 4' high jumper during his freshman year. He had tried to learn the pole vault, but–in his words–"I almost killed myself." While a junior at Bloomfield, he did set the school record in the high jump, but this record was the only thing that might have been a predictor of later success.

At Roanoke College, the school gave him a room to live in which was in the basement of Alumni Gymnasium. He lived there during all four years of his stay at Roanoke. His roommate the first year was Don D'Agostino, who was a senior. For the next three years, he roomed with Larry Johnson.

According to Coach Bast, he went down to the track one morning and there was this freshman high jumping at one end of the athletic field. Homer and Dick struck up a conversation and soon Dick was on the cross country and indoor and outdoor track teams. He wasn't a strong cross country runner, but he had participated in the sport in high school and knew how valuable distance running could be for a track man. He was never to be as good a runner as Howard Meincke, Dick Goodlake, or George Jocher, but Dick from the beginning had that competitive spirit which often brought him across the finish line as one of the top four or five runners. But he had enjoyed his earlier running, although he had a strict coach. His high school cross country coach was nicknamed "the whip" because he was a stickler for putting in the mileage and training well. If he caught a runner loafing, he would make him carry a brick. Like Homer, he was a history teacher.

After an inauspicious freshman year in cross country, Dick matured into a fine cross country runner. Note these accomplishments in the team's larger meets:

Year	*Meet*	*Results*
1957	Little Eight Conference Championships	7th Place
	Mason-Dixon Conference Championships	15th Place
1958	Virginia A. A. U. Championships	15th Place
	Little Eight Conference Championships	10th Place
	N. C. A. A. National Championships	80th Place
	Mason-Dixon Conference Championships	15th Place
1959	Virginia State Championships	35th Place
	Little Eight Conference Championships	9th Place
	Mason-Dixon Conference Championships	6th Place

In the winter months, Dick competed in both swimming and indoor track. In the swimming program, he was a diver. He had never dived for a team before, but living in the gym he often went into the pool and even played around by doing cannonballs off the diving board. He didn't know it at the time, but Frances Ramser, the swimming coach, was looking for a diver. One day, she walked through the double doors leading to the pool and saw Dick doing summersaults. She then asked him to join her team. In subsequent weeks, she taught him how to dive and he ended up winning the Little Eight and Mason-Dixon Championships for a couple of years. He also got talked into swimming the 100-yard freestyle event occasionally, but the exertion almost did him in.

His indoor and outdoor track abilities were legend by the time he was a senior. In both sports, however, he began his career as an important member of the team–but not someone that the team depended upon to win.

The 1958-59 and 1959-60 indoor seasons were his best. In the 70-yard high hurdles, he set a new school record of :08.9 in 1959 during the Virginia State Championships. In the same meet a year later, he broke the record again by running :08.7. He broad jumped 22'5¾" in 1960 and during the same year pole vaulted 12'0". His high jumping continued to improve to the point where he was considered the best jumper in Virginia. At the State Indoor Championships in 1959, he tied for first in the high jump by clearing the bar at 6'3", a new school record. He almost cleared 6'5" that afternoon; however, on his final jump, he barely displaced the bar. During his senior season, in 1960, also in the Virginia State Championships at Lexington, he set a new state indoor record, a field house record, and a school record by jumping 6'5¼".

In outdoor track, he began to show his decathlon talents as he progressed from a sophomore to a junior to a senior. In the 120-yard high hurdles, he broke the :15.0 barrier three times and was consistently good in the other races:

Date	*Time*	*Location*	*Meet*
04/21/58	:15.0	Norfolk, VA	Norfolk William and Mary
04/04/59	:15.1	Hampden-Sydney, VA	Hampden-Sydney
04/18/59	:15.0	Salem, VA	Norfolk William and Mary
05/01/59	:14.9	Salem, VA	Bridgewater
05/15-16/59	:14.7	Baltimore, MD	Mason-Dixon Championships
04/02/60	:15.1	Salem, VA	American
04/06/60	:15.1	Salem, VA	Hampden-Sydney
05/13-14/60	:14.6	Washington, DC	Mason-Dixon Championships

In the low hurdles during these years, he ran :24.7, :25.0, :25.1, :25.3, and :25.5 on separate occasions. The shot and discus events were a bit weaker for Dick, although he did throw occasionally in meets and had bests of 33'5" in the shot and 112'3" in the discus. He long jumped at least 22' several times, and pole vaulted a height of 12'0" on five occasions. And his high jumping was excellent. During his last three years at Roanoke, he held the top 15 high jumps for the Maroons:

Date	*Height*	*Location*	*Meet*
04/05/58	6'1"	Miami, FL	Miami
04/26/58	6'2"	Washington, DC	Mason-Dixon Championships
05/09/58	6'0"	Hampden-Sydney, VA	Little Eight Championships
04/04/59	6'0"	Hampden-Sydney, VA	Hampden-Sydney
04/18/59	6'3¾"	Salem, VA	Norfolk William and Mary
04/25/59	6'0"	Washington, DC	Mason-Dixon Relays
05/01/59	6'1"	Salem, VAB	ridgewater
05/09/59	6'0"	Hampden-Sydney, VA	Little Eight Championships
05/15-16/59	6'1"	Baltimore, MD	Mason-Dixon Championships
04/02/60	6'2"	Salem, VA	American
04/06/60	6'0"	Salem, VA	Hampden-Sydney
04/22/60	6'2"	Salem, VA	Norfolk William and Mary
04/30/60	6'1⅜"	Davidson, NC	High Point Relays
05/13-14/60	6'2¼"	Washington, DC	Mason-Dixon Championships
Unknown	6'0"	Unknown	Virginia State Meet

Even more impressive is how he handled himself in the big meets, such as the Virginia State, Little Eight, and Mason-Dixon Championships, as well as meets featuring much larger and more talented schools:

Year	*Meet*	*Place*	*Event*	*Mark*
1957	Little Eight	First (Tie)	High Jump	5'11"
1958	Little Eight	First	High Jump	6'0"
	Mason-Dixon Relays	First	High Jump	6'2"
	Florida State	First	High Jump	6'0"
	Miami	First	High Jump	6'1"
1959	Little Eight	First	High Hurdles	:15.3
		First	Pole Vault	12'0"
	Mason-Dixon Relays	First (Tie)	High Jump	6'0"
		First (Tie)	Pole Vault	12'0"
	Mason-Dixon	First	High Jump	6'1"

		No Place	High Hurdles	-----
		No Place	Low Hurdles	-----
1960	Virginia State	First	High Jump	6'0"
	High Point Relays	First	Broad Jump	21'6¾"
		First	High Jump	6'1⅜"
		First	Triple Jump	43'0"
	Mason-Dixon	First	Broad Jump	22'1¼"
		First	High Jump	6'2¼"
		First	High Hurdles	:14.6

By competing in cross country, swimming, indoor track, and outdoor track, Dick ended up winning 11 varsity letters before graduating from Roanoke. He would have had 12, but he came down with measles one winter and failed to get enough points to receive his letter.

Dick always has appreciated the work that Homer Bast and Elwood Fox did to help him become a better athlete. "I take my hat off to coaches who work hard and are so dedicated to helping their athletes," he says. "Homer may not have had the best of athletes, but he made his teams what they were–just like my high school coach. Homer was enthusiastic, always challenging you to do your best. That trait carried over from the History classroom to the track. He was just an amazing guy."

In outdoor track, Dick closed out his career in spectacular form. After the Little Eight Championships during his senior year, he held several school records. In 1960, he scored 166¼ points during the outdoor track season, the most ever accumulated by a Roanoke athlete. He had scored the most points in a Little Eight Meet (20 in 1959). He had also scored the most points (20½ points in 1960) of any athlete in a Mason-Dixon Conference Championship meet. He had scored the most points (17 in 1960) in the Virginia State Meet. His 4 first places in the 1960 Little Eight Championships was a record, as was his three first places (a tie with Bruce Johnson in 1958) in a Mason-Dixon Championship meet.

Graduation for Dick came in 1960. He really didn't know what he was going to do after college, but one day as a sophomore he was on the track when a military recruiter came to see him. He told Dick that Coach Bast had said that Dick might like to be a Marine. Soon after that day, he decided to join the Marines.

Initially, he went into the Platoon Leaders' Course (PLC) program during his junior and senior years at Roanoke. When he graduated, he received his commission. Basic training for Dick was at Quantico, Virginia.

Just after finishing his basic training, he and Rosemary Lotuso (a sophomore at the College) were married. Her home was in Syosset, New York. Then he received orders to report to Camp Pendleton, which is located 38 miles north of downtown San Diego. He and Rosemary honeymooned their way across the country, and the couple ended up staying at that location for about 4½ years. Dick was assigned to an artillery unit, with former College track man Dick Seed as the Commanding Officer. He went from there to an artillery battery.

In 1962, recognizing Dick's special talents in track and field athletics, the Marines transferred him with special orders to the track team. His training with the Marine team was interrupted in 1962, when during the Cuban crisis, he was sent with his group to the Canal. They spent about 30 days floating around the Jamaican and Haitian waters as a show of strength. And, of course, their presence was required in case there was a landing at Guantanamo.

In 1963, Dick made the U. S. team that traveled to the Soviet Union. In order for an individual to make the Olympic Team, he had to be one of the top six collegians or one of the top six individuals from the A. A. U., or a top athlete in a pre-Olympics meet. The top six from that competition then went on to the Olympic Trials. From that meet, the top three became members of the U. S. A. Olympics Team.

Incidentally, Dick was a newcomer to the decathlon, having competed in the event for the first time in 1962 at a meet held at Mount San Antonia College. Also competing in that meet was C. K. Yang, the 1960 Olympic decathlon silver medalist for Taiwan and a U. C. L. A. track star. He set a new world record for the decathlon that day.

In 1963, as a potential Olympic decathlete, Dick entered a decathlon at an A. A. U. meet in Corvolas, Oregon. He placed second there with a score of 7,331. That second-place finish put him on the U. S. team that went to Moscow to compete. In Moscow, Dick totaled 7,113 points to finish in fourth place.

He then moved on to the AAU Championships in Walnut, California and finished in the top six. Here are the top finishers in the meet:

Place	*Name*	*Points*
1st	C. K. Yang (Taiwan)	8,641
2nd	Paul Herman (U. S.)	7794
3rd	Don Jeisy (U. S.)	7,768
4th	Russ Hodge (U. S.)	7,729
5th	Bill Toomey (U. S.)	7,620
6th	Dick Emberger (U. S.)	7,502
7th	J. D. Martin (U. S.)	7,343
8th	Don Shy (U. S.)	5,911

Dick then moved on to a semi-final Olympic trial at Randall's Island in New York. From the top six finishers in this meet, the first two made the Olympic team and the third person would be picked in the final competition at the Coliseum in Los Angeles. Dick finished in the top six at this event, with Paul Herman and Don Jeisy placing first and second, respectively, making the Olympic team. Now there was only one spot open, to be decided at the Olympic Trials meet at the Coliseum.

The Olympic Trials decathlon competition on September 13, 1064, resulted in the closest contested decathlon of all time. On day two, Russ Hodge and Dick were in a virtual tie as they entered the final event of the day, the 1,500-meter run. Here is the account of that final race as given by a reporter from *Track and Field News*:

> Starting the 1,500 meters, the muscular Hodge led Emberger by six points. Hodge needed to finish within about four yards of Emberger to protect his lead and win the one remaining spot on the team. But Emberger ran at a . . . [fast] . . . pace and led Hodge by as much as 25 yards. With half a lap to go, Hodge started his drive from 20 yards back. With 50 yards to go, he was only three yards behind and appeared to be the winner. But then he tied up, and lost inch by agonizing inch as he approached the finish. He finished about 4½ yards behind. After a long wait, the official times were announced–4:11.9 and 4:12.7. Emberger had gained six points. It was Hodge's second tie in two consecutive decathlons, and for the second time he lost because his opponent had beaten him in more than five events. Jeisy fell in the hurdles, costing him a possible victory. Points were scored from a new scoring table, unlike the system used to choose Herman and Jeisy for the team. It seemed unfair, and Hodge lodged a fruitless protest. Herman lost this decathlon in the shot put when he dropped three feet under his Mt. San Antonio mark. Jeisy, in addition to falling in the hurdles race, lost three tenths in the 100 and 18 feet in the javelin. Emberger showed great improvement in the broad jump, pole vault, and javelin.

As Dick told the *Roanoke World-News*, "I knew I had to win the 1,500 by a decent margin if I hoped to tie or beat him. I ran the first half like a scared rabbit. Toward the end of the race, I looked over my shoulder to see where Hodge was. There he was, breathing right down my neck. I lowered my head and gave it all I had." Amazingly, the difference in time between the two decathletes in the 1,500-meter run brought them into a tie, each with 7,728 points. The tie was broken by comparing the head-to-head competition between Emberger and Hodge. The judges chose Emberger to take the final place on the Olympic decathlon team. "If I had run a tenth of a second slower in the 1,500 meters," Dick said recently, "Russ would have gone to the Olympics and I would have been left off the 1964 team."

Here is the order of the top six decathletes at the Trials:

Place	Athlete	Score
1st	Dick Emberger	7,728
2nd	Russ Hodge	7,728
3rd	Paul Herman	7,701
4th	Bill Toomey	7,615
5th	Don Jeisy	7,426
6th	Don Shy	5,911

Hodge, days later, also made the team. He replaced the injured Don Jeisy.

So here he was, this almost-unknown decathlete whom *Track and Field News* in January of 1964 had ranked as the 20th-best decathlon man in the world and the only the 7th-best in the United States. Here he was, the product of a small college in Virginia which most people in the United States had never heard of, going to the Olympics in Tokyo.

Emberger, however, had worked hard to get to this point. All of his times, heights, and distances in the ten decathlon events had improved. The Coliseum Olympic Trials victory showed what an outstanding athlete he had become. For example, he pole vaulted 13'9", broad jumped 23'9" (more than a foot better than his previous-best jump), and threw the javelin over 191' (up from his best throw of 170'). He high jumped 6'4½" and ran the high hurdles in :14.9. His total of 7,728 points was 526 points better than any score he had compiled before.

Now it was time to prepare for Tokyo. In one letter he wrote from the Olympic Village, Dick said, "It has been a long, hard grind, but we finally made the big jump. I only hope I can make this one a really big one. I am going to be a little more daring and go for all the marbles this time. In the past, I feel I have taken far too many jumps in the high jump and lost my spring for the higher ones. I feel I have tried to relax and throw and jump the first one easy just to get a mark. I have the confidence now to go all out from the start. I am also going to bare down on my first tries in the broad jump, shot, and discus."

Dick's wife, Rosemary, was with him in Tokyo. He was pleased that she would get to see him compete. He was also pleased with the Olympic Village; in fact, all he could complain about was how much weight he was gaining from eating such good food.

Former coaches, administrators, and friends sent him encouraging letters and telegrams. After word that Dick was headed to the Olympics reached Roanoke College, for example, President Perry Kendig wrote him a letter. In that letter, Kendig said:

Dick Emberger practices the javelin while in the Marines and before the Olympics of 1964.

> "I offer you hearty congratulations on being the first Roanoke College alumnus to win a place on the U. S. Olympic team. This is a great achievement and a great honor for you. Your Alma Mater rejoices with you and basks in reflected glory."

After the formalities of a typical Olympics, including the opening ceremony in the track stadium, the decathlon was ready to begin. A nervous group of decathletes warmed up that first day. The first five events were slated to be the 100-meter dash, broad jump, shot put, high jump, and 400-meter dash. Unfortunately, it was rainy and misty throughout the day. And it got no better the second day.

In his section of the 100-meter race, Dick ran :11.2, which was not as fast as his best time of :10.9 in this event. C. K. Yang and some of the others were faster, but were expected to place ahead of Dick. The :11.2 mark wasn't that slow, he thought, because his typical 100 had been in the :11.0 to :11.1 range. Willi Holdorf of the Unified Team of Germany, along with Hector Thomas, tied for first with 879 points based on times of :10.7. Dick tied for 12th with three others, gaining 756 points.

In the second event, the long jump, Dick recorded a jump of 22'¾". Unfortunately, the distances of many people were poor because they were jumping off a clay surface, and that surface in the rain was very slippery. In California, where Dick lived and where the Olympic Trials were held, most of the runways were hard-surfaced–usually rubberized asphalt. Dick had problems getting his steps down. The overall winners of the long jump were Rein Aun of the Soviet Union and his teammate, Mikhail Storozhenko. Both received 865 points on jumps of 7.22 meters (23'8¼"). Emberger finished in 13th place with 761 points, just in front of Russ Hodge. Paul Herman took 8th in the event.

The shot put and discus throws were not Emberger strengths. In the shot on this first day, he threw 38'8½". Mikhail Storozhenko of the Soviet Union placed first with a throw of 16.37 meters (53'8½"). Dick was 18th, Hodge was 3rd, and Paul Herman was 8th.

In the high jump, he cleared the bar at 6'2¾". It was an acceptable jump, but he had gone higher. In the Trials, for example, he had cleared 6'4" and previously had gone about 6'6". Again, the slick, clay run-up surface hindered all jumpers. Hans-Joachim Walde of Germany jumped 1.96 meters (6'5"), picking up 822 points. Dick finished in a tie for 4th, receiving another 769 points. Paul Herman tied for 6th place and Russ Hodge took 13th in a tie with two others.

The 400-meter race was the fifth and final event of the first day. Dick's time was :49.1. The best he had done in this race before the Olympics was :48.9, so he was satisfied with his effort. Willi Holdorf of Germany ran :48.2 to win the event. Dick finished in 4th place, in front of Paul Herman (tie for 5th) and Russ Hodge (9th).

At the end of the first day, here were the decathletes' scores:

Place	*Athlete*	*Country*	*Points*
1st	Willi Holdorf	Germany	4,090
2nd	Hans-Joachim Walde	Germany	4,074
3rd	Rein Aun	Soviet Union	4,067
4th	Horst Beyer	Germany	3,910
5th	Mikhail Storozhenko	Soviet Union	3,908
6th	Paul Irvin Herman	United States	3,876
7th	Werner Duttweiler	Switzerland	3,837
8th	Russell Arden Hodge	United States	3,813
9th	Yang Chuan Kwang	China	3,803
10th	Vasily Kuznetsov	Soviet Union	3,793
11th	Richard John Emberger	United States	3,719
12th	Hector Thomas	Venezuela	3,704
13th	Valbjoern Thorlaksson	Iceland	3,640
14th	Alois Buchel	Liechtenstein	3,631
15th	Bill Gairdner	Canada	3,568
16th	Eef Kamerbeek	Netherlands	3,522
17th	Franco Sar	Italy	3,454
18th	Suzuki Shosuke	Japan	3,415
19th	Koech Kiprop	Kenya	3,288
20th	Dramane Sereme	Mali	3,277
21st	Guerrino Moro	Canada	3,261
22nd	Wu Ar Min	China	WD
23rd	Samir Ambrose Vincent	Iraq	WD

The misty rain continued on day two. In the first event, the 110-meter hurdles, Emberger crossed the line in :14.9. "That was pretty slow for me," he said. "My best in a decathlon had been :14.4 and I had run :14.0 in an open highs. Don't forget, however, that we spent eight hours on the track during each of the two days. That alone takes a lot out of you." Yang Chuan Kwang of China ran :14.7 to win the event. Dick finished in a tie for 3rd with Vasily Kuznetsov of the Soviet Union. Paul Herman was 8th and Russ Hodge was 15th.

In the discus throw, Dick's distance was 115'10½". Again, it was not his best event, and he had spent little time after getting to Tokyo working on either the discus or shot events. Franco Sar of Italy won the event with a throw of 47.46 meters. Hodge was 4th, Herman was 6th, and Emberger was 16th.

His height in the pole vault was 12'1½", but he thought he should have gone higher. Because of the damp, chilly weather, all of the decathletes had blankets. Near the first part of the event, Dick put a blanket around him and then sprayed his hands to get a better grip on the pole. Inadvertently, he grabbed the blanket and the residue from it stuck to his hands. He was slipping all over the pole on subsequent jumps. He could have asked to go into the locker room to wash his hands, but an Olympic official would have had to accompany him. So he decided to continue even with the residue on his hands. Two athletes tied for the top mark, at 4.6 meters. Yang Chuan Kwang of China and Guerrino Moro of Canada each scored 957 points. Herman finished in a tie for 7th, with Emberger and Hodge in a tie for 15th.

The next-to-last event was the javelin throw. At Roanoke College, Dick had almost never thrown the javelin. The event was not a part of either the Little Eight or Mason-Dixon Conference schedule of events. When he did get a chance to throw at Roanoke, his distances were around 140' to 150'. Today, however, he managed to throw 188'9¼". His coach at Camp Pendleton, Tommy Thompson, had been at the Naval Academy and was retired. His son was living on the west coast, so Thompson came to Camp Pendleton to help coach. He was an Olympic gold medalist in the high hurdles. Under his guidance, Dick had thrown the javelin almost 190'. The event was won by Yang Chuan Kwang of China, who picked up 858 points on a throw of 68.15 meters (223'7"). Herman was 3rd in the competition, Emberger finished 9th, and Hodge was 15th.

Now the group of decathletes was running in the final event, the 1,500-meters race. Dick ran a winning time of 4:19.3, just slightly off the 4:11.9 he had recorded at the Olympic Trials. It was also, however, one of the best times run in this event for many years. As Dick told a friend, "All those college cross country days definitely helped." Emberger picked up 665 points for the win. Hodge crossed the line in 5th place, while Paul Herman was 6th.

To Coach Bast,
USA
Many thanks for all your guidance and help in Track.
Dick Emberger

For many exhausted athletes, their competition in the Olympics of 1964 was finished. The United States had placed all three of their athletes in the top 10. Here were the final standings:

Place	*Athlete*	*Country*	*Points*
1st	Willi Holdorf	Germany	7,887
2nd	Rien Aun	Soviet Union	7,842
3rd	Hans-Joachim Walde	Germany	7,809
4th	Paul Irvin Herman	United States	7,787
5th	Yang Chuan Kwang	China	7,650
6th	Horst Beyer	Germany	7,647
7th	Vasily Kuznetsov	Soviet Union	7,569
8th	Mikhail Storozhenko	Soviet Union	7,464
9th	Russell Arden Hodge	United States	7,325
10th	Richard John Emberger	United States	7,292
11th	Bill Gairdner	Canada	7,147
12th	Valbjoern Thorlaksson	Iceland	7,135
13th	Franco Sar	Italy	7,054
14th	Alois Buchel	Liechtenstein	6,849
15th	Suzuki Shosuke	Japan	6,838
16th	Guerrimo Moro	Canada	6,716
17th	Koech Kiprop	Kenya	6,707
18th	Dramane Serame	Mali	5,917
	Werner Duttweiler	Switzerland	DNF
	Hector Thomas	Venezuela	DNF
	Eef Kamerbeek	Netherlands	DNF
	Wu Ar Min	China	DNF
	Samir Ambrose Vincent	Iraq	DNS

After the Olympics, with just eight months to go until he could leave the service, he got his orders to report to Okinawa and then to Danang, Vietnam. He spent about six months in Danang, working on the division staff, handling R & R and U. S. O. shows. During this time, he was promoted to Captain.

After finishing his work in Danang, Dick left the service. But he continued to compete. Darrell Horn, a long jumper from Oregon State, was going to start a club in the Oakland area. So Dick went to Oregon and got a job with the Berkley Recreation Department while training. He then ran for the Athens Track Club for a couple of years before making it back to the Olympic Trials. During part of this time, he had been training with Sam Bell, who came down from Oregon State. Bell had come to take over the head coaching position at the University of California. He ended up training a bunch of pretty good athletes there.

Unfortunately, Dick was not selected as a decathlete on the 1968 Olympic team. The decathlon that year was won by Bill Toomey of the United States. Dick did place 3rd in the A. A. U. meet, but couldn't place high enough to make the final team. "I was happy to get as far as I did," he said later, "but in truth, I was starting to go downhill. I was about 30 years old and had injured my knee a number of years before. The knee always bothered me."

After failing to qualify for the Olympic team going to Mexico, he and his wife moved back to the San Diego area and he enrolled at San Diego State University to get his teaching credentials. Rosemary was working in Probation, while Dick took a job in a junior high school. He taught junior high physical education for the next seven years and then switched to teach at a high school. There, he taught physical education for a couple of years and then language arts for another 22 years. He finally retired in 1999. During his teaching career, he also coached; however, none of his head coaching responsibilities were in track. He helped coach swimming and water poly for a couple of years. And he was Assistant Track Coach for a couple of years.

In recent years, he has played a lot of golf, hiked, read books and publications, and gardened on his and Rosemary's 2½ acres. In December of 2007, he had surgery on his right knee. Previously, he had been forced to have cortisone shots for his knee pain.

Congratulations to Dick Emberger–the only Roanoke athlete ever to make an Olympic team.

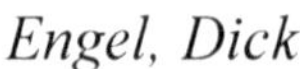
Engel, Dick

The son of Hans and Margaret Engle, Dick was born in Philadelphia and attended Lincoln High School. He had one sister, two years younger than he. His dad was a foreman in a manufacturing plant where they built rail cars. His mother was a homemaker.

At Lincoln, Dick was a multi-sport athlete. Not only did he run cross country and track, but he was a swimmer and a soccer player.

Dick Engel and his wife, Jimmy.

He enrolled at Roanoke College, beginning with the second semester of 1956-57, primarily on the recommendations of friends–such as Don Kerr and Harry Clegg–along with his track coach's son, all of whom attended Roanoke. When he arrived in Salem, he was a long way from home–more than 400 miles. His new surroundings, however, didn't seem to present any big adjustments for him. After all, he had gone to summer camp many times, and was a camp counselor.

At Roanoke, he played soccer for three years. But he also became one of the premiere outdoor track sprinters in the Little Eight and Mason-Dixon Conferences.

He hadn't met Homer Bast before arriving at Roanoke, although he knew of him through the people who had encouraged him to come. Even today, Dick has a warm place in his heart for Homer, who took Dick and others under his wing and promoted the idea that academics were just as important as sports. Like others before him, Dick often babysat with Homer's two sons at the Bast house. He still appreciates that his coach, although retiring officially from track coaching after the 1956-57 season, still came down to the track almost daily and helped whenever he could during Dick's last three years of running. He also remembers Homer going on some of the trips the team took after 1956-57, and in particular the spring trip in 1958 where the squad met Florida State and Miami.

Dick's sprint times improved over the four years he was on the outdoor track team. During his junior year, he recorded two :10.1 races in the 100-yard dash. He also ran a :10.2 in his sophomore year, and had an identical time in his junior year.

His best races, however, came in the 220-yard dash. In the 1958 season, he ran :21.5, :22.3, :22.4, :22.5, and :22.5. The next year, he ran :21.9, :22.0, :22.3, and :22.6.

In 1959, Dick placed third in the 100-yard dash at the Little Eight Championships, and was second in the 220 at the Mason-Dixon meet. At the end of the 1959 season, he was third in the 100 at the Little Eight meet and third in the 220 at the Mason-Dixon meet.

During his senior year at Roanoke, he pulled a hamstring muscle. He was never the same quality sprinter that year that he was in 1958 and 1959.

Dick graduated in the summer of 1960 with an Education and Psychology degree. His first job was at Fork Union Military Academy, teaching General Science in their middle school program. He also coached track.

He stayed at Fork Union only one year, coming back to Roanoke City to teach at Lee Junior High School for the next two years. While at Lee, he helped coach junior varsity and freshman football at nearby Jefferson High School. At the same time, he assisted with the track team.

He then went back to Fork Union in a teaching and coaching position. He started a new soccer program for the school, and served as an Assistant Track Coach on a state champion track and field team.

After seven years at Fork Union, he took a job as teacher and coach at Buford Junior High School. There, he taught health and physical education and coached both football and track. Again, he organized the school's first soccer team. The remainder of his educational career–totaling some 28 years–was spent at Buford. He retired in 1998 when he turned 60. He continued to live in Charlottesville after his retirement.

Dick married for the first time in 1962. He and Jane had one daughter, who today is a special education teacher at a school for the blind. The two were divorced, and Dick re-married in Princeton, West Virginia, in 1968. He met his new wife, Jimmy, in Charlottesville, although she grew up in West Virginia.

Dick's hobbies include gardening, golf, and traveling. He and his wife love to go on cruises. He has had a few health problems over the years, as you would expect from someone his age. He had open heart surgery a few years ago and a heart by-pass operation. Not too long ago, he picked up a stint. He has diabetes and the resulting neuropathy, asthma (under control), and a touch of high blood pressure. Despite these problems, he continues to officiate soccer–mostly for Division III colleges–throughout central Virginia. He also has been an official basketball scorer at the University of Virginia for several years, and has even worked the Atlantic Coast Conference finals. In addition to his soccer duties today, he also officiates college football and just gave up lacrosse officiating last year.

Even today, he remembers fondly the days he spent at Roanoke. "I give Roanoke credit," he says, "for everything good that happened to me after I graduated. I really enjoyed going to college there. It's a great school and I would recommend it to anyone. It is just a fine liberal arts school, small in number of students, and with a good atmosphere. I enjoyed my college career, as an athlete and student. Being away from home, I built a lot of lasting friendships. To this day, I greatly appreciate the coaching of Homer, Elwood Fox, and Frances Ramser. If I could re-live my college career, I suppose I might try to be a better student. Maybe it was too many Pi Kap weekend parties, or perhaps it was those visits to the Brook Club."

Fagg, Bob

Bob was born in Baltimore, and after his family moved to Roanoke, he attended Jefferson High School. His family consisted of his mother and father, Mary and Robert, Jr., and one brother, Jack. Jack, who was younger than Bob, is not living today. He drowned while coming back from his service in Korea.

In high school, Bob was a member of the track team for two years. At that time, he was a hurdler.

When he graduated, he chose to attend the University of North Carolina. His last day in high school was June 12, 1942, and he started his work at U. N. C. the next day. His coach at Jefferson had recommended him for a scholarship at U. N. C.; unfortunately, his stay at Carolina didn't work out. After two quarters at the school, and partly because of the amount of money it would cost him as an out-of-state student, he transferred to Roanoke College just in time to enroll for the second semester of the 1942-43 session. Soon, the Army drafted him and he served as an infantryman for the next 33 months in places such as Africa and Italy.

Bob Fagg

After leaving the Army, he returned to Roanoke College in January of 1946–before Coach Bast joined the Roanoke staff in the fall of 1946. There was no track program at the College at the time, so he wasn't involved in running until the spring of 1947, when Bast began the new cross country and track programs.

Coach Bast wanted to start the school's new track program in his first year at Roanoke; unfortunately, there were few students on the campus who had any track experience. Bob, fortunately, had not only run in high school, but also in the service. He had run hurdles races for his regimental track team, the division team, and finally in the fifth army track meet in Milan, Italy. Some of his teammates in the service were well known and talented, like Harrison Dillard.

So Bob was one of the first students that Coach Bast turned to as he began a track program. Actually, says Bob, "Homer thought I was just a playboy until I showed up for the first of his track practices that spring."

"We began by re-building the old track around Alumni Field," he said. "Some of the cinders for the track came from the College's furnace room. We took cinderblocks by their ends and pounded the cinders into dust so we could put them on the track. I think we ended up with a pretty decent track for those days."

It was a small, rag-tag group that made the drive to the first meet that spring at Bridgewater College. Coach Bast drove one car and Warren Snead, a sophomore, drove the other one. "I remember that meet," Bob says. "We had a boy on the team by the name of Thanning Anderson. He had hearing problems and when the gun went off, you almost had to punch him to get him to start his race. Some of my other teammates included Jim

Doran and Jim Ruscick, both known primarily for their basketball talents. Doran was big and strong, and he was able to throw the shot, discus, and javelin, and could even broad jump and high jump. He was about 6'3" in height. Ruscick was like a cat, with more spring than anyone I had ever seen. Ruscick was a forward on the basketball team, and Doran was the center. They both transferred from Muhlenberg College at mid-year. Frankly, they both knew more about basketball than Coach Hackman. They played a real Yankee-style ball. We also had runners like Paul McCarty and Red Crockett, as well as Bill Williams, who was lucky to be alive. Once, he was vaulting with a bamboo pole and it broke, and he fell on the end of it."

Bob also remembers the Lynchburg College meet that first year. He still thinks that the track at Lynchburg was eight feet lower at one end than it was at the other end. "I ran a :10.0 100-yard dash at the meet," he laughs, "and Homer had me at :09.9."

The Lynchburg track also had a 220-yard straightaway. In Bob's second year at the College, the Mason-Dixon Championships were held at Lynchburg. He was running on that straightaway in a qualifying heat, feeling good and cruising toward the finish line about 20 yards ahead of his nearest competitor. Someone in the infield yelled, "Slow down. You're killing yourself." So he slowed down and still won easily. "If I hadn't cut back on my speed," Bob said, "I would have set a new meet record."

Bob also remembers the outdoor Randolph-Macon meet that was held on the Roanoke track during his second year. "You'll notice," he says, "that on the meet results sheet, there is no mention of a mile relay. There is a story behind that omission. Before the meet, Homer had told me that Roanoke could win the meet if the team didn't have to run the mile relay. The team just didn't have enough runners. So he omitted the mile relay from the schedule, and when the Randolph-Macon coach got his copy of the schedule, he didn't notice that the race was not listed. He didn't realize the fact until he got to the point where the mile relay should have been run. He was getting his men together for the race and had, in fact, pulled one of his best quarter milers out of his regular race to save him for the mile relay. When he realized that the relay wouldn't be run, he raised some kind of hell. He even appealed the loss of the meet to conference officials."

One person Bob remembers well is Alvin Smith, one of the best distance runners in the South. Smith transferred to Roanoke in the middle of the 1947-48 session. In Bob's words, "Alvin and I had run together in high school. They said that if Alvin had worn all of his medals that he had won over the years, he would look like the American flag. In one race at Roanoke, his shoe was stepped on and he ran in his sock feet to win the race. He had a great sense of timing. If we wanted to run a series of 60-second quarters, he could maintain his pace within a tenth of a second per quarter over a training session of ten quarters."

Bob completed his college education at Roanoke at mid-year, in February of 1949, with a degree in General Science. His first job was as a trainee in Indianapolis for the Grain Dealers National Mutual Fire Insurance Company. He worked for the company for one year in Indianapolis before they transferred him to Richmond. He left the organization in February of 1957, when he took a new position as State Agent for the Northern Insurance Company of New York. He was then transferred to Baltimore as a Division Manager in charge of the home owner's department and their multi-peril department.

In 1967 Bob received his certification as a property and casualty underwriter. He finished his career with the Maryland Casualty Company, working for them for 30 years to a day, retiring on February 1, 1987.

Bob was married on January 7, 1950, not long after leaving Roanoke College. His new wife was a Salem girl, Charlotte Goodwin. Subsequently, Bob and Charlotte had two children. Susan was born on January 7, 1951, and Robert was born on January 7, 1953. Both of his children are still living. Susan works for Pizza Hut in Wilmington, North Carolina. Robbie is a Vice President in the loan department of the DuPont Fiber Credit Union, based in Richmond. Unfortunately, Charlotte died in 1977, and Bob was re-married to his current wife, Fay, in 1981.

Since his retirement, Bob has led an active life. He worked as a Marshall and Starter for the famous Country Club of Virginia for a couple of years and enjoyed his work. Until a couple of years ago, he often played golf himself. In fact, he has shot his age four times–twice at 78, once when he was 80, and again when he was 81. He had a back operation two years ago, however, and hasn't been able to play golf since that time.

Today, he is active in his church–All Saints Episcopal–where he is in charge of the church committee that does the mailings. He has also served on the church's search committee for a new minister.

Fariss, Dr. Bruce

Bruce was a self-described "poor country boy" who had hardly seen anything before coming to Roanoke College besides cow pastures and country roads. He was born in the same small town where he lives today–Allisonia, Virginia. Allisonia is about 50 miles southeast of Salem. He went to Draper High School, a small school which graduated 25 students and Bruce. It wasn't uncommon for students to drop out of school to work on their parents' farms. And some of them even went to work at local furniture factories. The only ones who stayed at Draper, it seemed, were the ones who were interested in getting an education.

Dr. Bruce Fariss and family. L to R: Carolina, Sarah (2004), Adam (2007), Bruce (1957), Cheryl, and Henry (2005).

Draper High School had basketball and baseball teams, but Bruce remembers that he wasn't very good in either sport. There was no such thing as track or cross country. In fact, he had never seen a running track before getting to Salem.

In his family were parents Alven and Hetty Fariss, along with Bruce and two brothers and two sisters. Bruce was the oldest child. The next sibling in age was Don, followed in order by Patsy, Rachael, and Michael. All are living today.

Remarkably, Bruce decided at about age four that he wanted to be a doctor. After that point, everything he did in school was pointed toward medical school. His mother finished high school and his father dropped out of school when he was in his third year of high school. But they always preached to their children that education was important. This lesson apparently was taken to heart. Not only did Bruce attend Roanoke College, but all of his brothers and sisters followed him to college-level courses of study.

Bruce picked Roanoke for three reasons. First, it was a small school. Second, it was far enough away from home, yet allowed him to come home when he wished. And third, and perhaps the most important, it had an 85% acceptance rate into medical schools. If you were a pre-medical student at Roanoke, and especially if you could get a recommendation from Dr. Robey in Organic Chemistry, you were on your way to medical school.

Roanoke College and Bruce were a good fit. The school gave Bruce a good education; in fact, he says, when he went to medical school, the academic work there was easy compared to Roanoke's.

At Roanoke, Bruce majored in Biology, with a minor in Chemistry. Like a small kid in a candy store, he was fascinated by all of the activities he could participate in on campus. Part of his plan for getting into medical school was to have more on his plate than just good grades. He joined the Kappa Alpha fraternity–but almost didn't. He had no discretionary money. Before attending Roanoke, he had worked at Radford, Virginia, for 14 months, saving every penny he earned in order to attend college. When he got to Roanoke, he looked at the K. A.s and liked the fraternity because many of their members were track and cross country athletes. But he had to tell them that although he would like to join the fraternity, he just didn't have the money. Someone–and to this day he doesn't know who did it–actually paid his initiation fee and dues for him. That individual also paid for his fraternity membership for all four years.

Bruce was also involved in many other activities. He was a member of Blue Key National Honor Society, the Monogram Club, the Language Club, and other campus organizations.

He was a major contributor to the teams that Homer Bast coached. When he got to Roanoke, he became a member of the cross country and indoor track teams. But his athletic career almost was cut short. At an indoor meet that year, he became stuffed up. Coach Bast told him that he needed to see a doctor. Reluctantly, he went to see Dr. Smiley, the College's physician. Smiley examined Bruce and told him that he had a heart murmur. He also found that Bruce's blood pressure was elevated. He told Bruce that he was officially off the track team. So Bruce went back to Homer and plead his case, saying "Look. There's nothing wrong with me. I have been active my whole life and I've never had any problems." But Mr. Bast told him that there was nothing he could do. Not knowing what to do, Bruce finally checked into a hospital to have a work-up done. At the end of his tests, the doctors told him that what Dr. Smiley had heard was what the medical profession calls a split-second sound. It sounded like a murmur, but wasn't. So after skipping all of his freshman outdoor season, he came back to the College for his second and third years, and was able to participate in cross country as well as indoor and outdoor track. During his senior year, he did not run outdoor track because of his class load. He went to Homer to explain why. "I like you," he said, "and I like running for you, but going to medical school is the most important thing to me." Organic Chemistry at Roanoke was unbelievably difficult, but students knew that the course was a rite of passage that led you to medical school.

"Dr. Robey was an interesting person," Bruce laughed. "He would write with one hand and erase with the other. That's not just a story. He would really do that. And I never had another exam that was like the ones he gave. Very few members of his classes made an "A." Almost nobody. If you walked out of his class with a B, you felt really, really good."

One of Bruce's courses at Roanoke was World Civilizations, taught by Homer Bast. Bruce remembers that Homer never gave you any breaks. He thought at first that, being an athlete, he would have an easy time in history. "No way," Bruce says. "One thing he did that made a lasting impression on me was that he was never critical. When you ran for him, or if you were simply in his class, he never said anything but 'Well, I think you can do better next time.' That was as critical as he would ever get."

After he graduated from Roanoke, Bruce went to the University of Virginia, staying there in medical school for four years. He finished his work at the University in 1961.

From there, he did his internship at the University of Virginia in internal medicine. While in medical school, he received his notice to report for induction into the military. He told the Dean, and the Dean took care of the problem–at least for the moment. The Army simply said that he could stay in medical school, but they would take him as soon as he finished his degree.

When he finished the medical degree, after another year, Dr. Fariss was inducted into the Army. People with medical doctorates didn't have to go through the regular basic training. Instead, the Army sent Bruce to Fort Sam Houston for a couple of months. As Bruce puts it, "They teach you how to put on your uniform, how to salute, and what end of the gun a bullet comes out from."

So he did his residency at Fort Sam Houston, Texas and was there for three years. Then he went to the University of California, where he did a fellowship in endocrinology. He was in California for some two years before the Army decided that they wanted him to run a research unit at Fort Lewis, Washington. He stayed in that job until 1979. Most of his work dealt with diabetes. He also became part of a program that trained other doctors to be endocrinologists.

The Army sent Bruce to be the Consultant in Medicine for the U. S. Army in Europe for three years. From there, he went back to Fort Lewis to the medical center, finally leaving the Army in August of 1984. He had spent 22 years in the service.

Bruce came back to his old home town and set up a medical practice. He sees a lot of people who have diabetes.

He plans to continue his practice. "I don't see any future in retirement," he notes. "I watch all of these people around me retire, and they get up in the morning and are not sure what they will do today. On the other hand, I know what I am going to do every day. I think a man, even more than a woman, needs an identity–and the identity is what they do. It can be writing a book or it can be that you are a plumber. Whatever. But men just need an identity."

In his spare time, Bruce remodels old houses. He does the electrical work and the plumbing. He builds his own cabinets for the kitchens. To this date, he and his two sons have remodeled a total of six houses. His sons don't help with the work anymore, but each will take possession of one of the houses.

Bruce has been married twice and has a total of eight children. His first marriage took place in the second year of his medical school work. His wife was Ruth. Ruth and Bruce had four children, two of whom were twins. The oldest children, the twins, were Bruce, Jr., and Melissa. Then came Margaret and Susan. Bruce Jr. is an Urologist today in Knoxville, Tennessee. Melissa is the manager of a restaurant in Wisconsin. Margaret is the office manager for an insurance company. And Susan is in Washington, D. C., working for the U. S. Government.

Ruth and Bruce stayed together from about 1958 until 1975, when they divorced. Bruce then married Cheryl in 1976. At the time, he was stationed at Fort Lewis, Washington. Cheryl worked at the hospital. Cheryl and Bruce are still married and together had a son, Henry, twin girls (Sara Jane and Caroline), and another son, Adam.

Fraley, Dick

Dick Fraley was born in Roanoke to parents Howard and Louise. Besides Dick, there was one brother and two sisters. The oldest was a sister, Betty, who graduated from Roanoke College. Dick was the second oldest child. Then came Randal and Judith. Dick's father worked for Norfolk and Western Railroad, and later for the U. S. Post Office. His mother stayed at home until the children were grown, after which she went to work.

Dick Fraley and his wife, Betty.

Dick went to Jefferson High School, but never participated in athletics there. He always assumed that he would go to college, especially after Betty had enrolled at Roanoke. He also liked Roanoke because he could commute to the campus and live at home. There were others in his life who influenced his interest in Roanoke. For example, he had two uncles–later doctors–who attended the Salem school, and another uncle who attended Roanoke and became a chemical engineer.

Today, Dick thinks that Roanoke was a good choice. He was involved in a fraternity (Kappa Alpha) and had a "great social life." When he was a senior, he was elected the Kappa Alpha's #1, and lived at the K. A. house. Doug Frith, also a track athlete, was his roommate.

He also met his future wife while at Roanoke. When he was a senior, she was a freshman. He participated in a number of class activities and was President of his senior class.

Dick never knew Homer Bast before getting to college, but Homer was his history professor that first year. Through Bast, he became interested in running. He knew that by comparison with his friends, he considered himself to be fairly fast.

The sprint events in those days were run under primitive conditions. The team had no starting blocks, so the sprinters simply dug holes in which to brace their feet. In addition, the track had just been re-built after last being used in 1930, and the surface was rough. Any number of large cinder "clinkers" could be (and were) found each day. In other events, conditions were equally primitive. Pole vaulters used bamboo poles, ran toward the bar on an uneven dirt path, and landed in sawdust. Shot and discus men threw out of dirt circles. The high jumpers took off from dirt. And the hurdles men had to wait on the Maintenance Department to build enough hurdles to have a race.

The teammates Dick remembers most are Bruce Davenport, White Rhyne (not fast, but good in the longer distances), John Turbyfill (a pretty good track man), Bob Fagg, Dick Dodd, Alvin Smith (our best miler), and Ray DeCosta (a tough little kid who wasn't tall but very strong). He also remembers Paul McCarty well. Paul had died by the time this book was written, but according to Dick, "He was a fine person and a Kappa Alpha brother."

Dick's major was Business Administration and Economics. His actual degree, a B. A., was in Economics. He knew that he would be going into the Army as soon as he graduated from Roanoke and thought that after his service days, he likely would go into some kind of business endeavor.

True enough, he graduated in 1951 and immediately went into the Army. He eventually ended up in Hawaii for his basic training. The Army then sent him to Korea for the next 15 months. In Korea, he was in a headquarters outfit. He could hear the shells exploding in the distance, but his group never took any direct fire. He ran a military history section for the Army, keeping track of what was going on and forwarding that information to the War Department. His degree from Roanoke helped him get that job and kept him off the front lines. He was in the service for about 23 months before he was released in 1953, eager to get back to normal life.

During September of 1953, he married Betty Gardner, the student that he had known as a senior while at the College. By the time of the wedding, she had left Roanoke. Dick and Betty became the parents of three children over the next few years. The oldest was Neil, the next oldest was Philip, and the youngest was Susan. All are married today. Dick and Betty have five grandchildren and four great grandchildren.

His first job was as a clerk for a jewelry store, Hitch Jewelers, located on Campbell Avenue in downtown Roanoke. He worked for Hitch for about a year. Then he took a teaching job at Jackson Junior High School in Roanoke. He had attended that school when he was young, and was teaching alongside many who had taught him. His job was to teach seventh graders–which meant that he taught them all of the seventh grade subjects, from English to Math to Science. He had no teaching degree, however, and the state required that he take education courses if he were to continue after his second year.

Instead, he left his teaching job in 1955 and joined General Electric in Roanoke/Salem. The company paid him far more money than we would have earned as a teacher. Dick worked for General Electric in marketing and sales. Later, still employed by G. E., he moved to Clearwater, Florida, working out of the Tampa sales office for more than 20 years. In all, he worked for G. E. for some 33 years, finally retiring in 1988. At the time of his retirement, he lived in Clearwater.

He and Betty sold their house in Clearwater in 1992 and moved to Dunedin, Florida. Dunedin, also near the ocean, was just above Tampa and not very far away from Clearwater. "We love it here," Dick says. "It's a great place to live."

Since he retired, Dick reads constantly. He also enjoys riding his bicycle and walking. His daughter owns the house and Dick and Betty live in an adjacent apartment. The arrangement gives Dick an excuse to get some additional exercise by taking care of his daughter's yard.

"This is a great place to ride your bicycle," Dick says. "Not only is it flat around here, but the weather all year long is very nice. And we have a great riding trail near our house. The trail is along an old railroad track. They took up the track, smoothed out the surface, and now we can ride on the surface all the way from Tarpon Springs to St. Petersburg."

Gearhart, George

George, one of the school's top sprinters in the 1950s, attended Andrew Lewis High School in Salem, which was located just a stone's throw from the Roanoke College campus. The school didn't field a track team until George's junior year. His coach at Lewis was Herb Copenhager, who made it clear to George that he would definitely be going out for track. Copenhager didn't know much about track, however, so George was largely self-taught. As George put it, "I just practiced my high jumping every day and almost never practiced my running."

He remembers his first meet well. It was in his senior year, and Lewis was competing with William Byrd High School from Vinton, Virginia. "I had never been on a track before, and didn't even know how to start," he said. "We took off in the 100-yard dash, and as I was trying to catch up with the guy ahead of me, I was leaning so much that I fell and slid face down. I didn't even finish the race. And then I had to run the 220 after that. If I were lucky, I might have been able to run a :24.0 or :25.0 in those days. We didn't know much about training or starting or things like that."

George's team often traveled to Municipal Field in Salem to practice. At other times, they went to the Roanoke College track. He remembers that the takeoff area for the high jump at Roanoke was made of packed clay. If it rained before or during a meet, jumping was difficult. "I remember planting my left foot," he says, "raising my right, and sliding right under the bar because of the slippery footing."

George Gearhart

Homer Bast had done a good job in making the track better. Even with his work, however, one often found large rocks mixed with the cinders. George recalls running on the track one day while he was a high school senior, hitting one of those chunks and breaking two or three spikes off his shoe.

In 1950-51, George and his Andrew Lewis classmates were trying to decide what to do with their lives after graduation. George himself had never thought about going to college. In 1951, as he worked out at the College's track, George was noticed by Homer Bast. That day, and over the next few weeks, he began to talk with George and a teammate about coming to Roanoke College the next year. George says that he listened to Homer politely, but in the back of his mind he knew that he would never go to college. His family didn't have the money to send him, and he had never taken the academic courses that most colleges required. Homer persisted. He finally called George at his home one day and asked him to meet on Alumni Field. George showed up, wondering what the meeting was all about, and Homer handed him an old used pair of flats to run in. The shoes were quite a gift for George, because he and his teammates normally ran in tennis shoes. For several minutes, Homer talked to George about coming to Roanoke and running track the next year. He said that he would talk to the administration at Roanoke, and perhaps get George a scholarship.

Still, George didn't think much about going to college. Quite a few of his friends at Lewis were planning to join the military–and George was ready to follow. It was getting close to graduation day, and still he had made no choice.

George was working part-time at the Salem Kroger store. His manager was from

Wytheville, Virginia, and had run the half mile in high school. He became interested in George and his plans. When George mentioned that he was going to join the military, he suggested that George should make them come and get him. Over a number of days, the Manager encouraged George to go to Roanoke College the next year. Finally, he said to George, "If you will go to college next year, I will give you a full-time job here at Kroger's." George gave in, agreed to the full-time job, and began to save every penny he could. He still hadn't applied to Roanoke because he thought his high school background would make it very difficult to get in.

Then, in August of 1951, a friend of George's told him that he was going to Roanoke College. The school was letting him in on probation. George suddenly realized that he was a better student than his friend, and that maybe Roanoke would take a chance on him also. So he walked up to the campus and applied for a place in the fall's freshman class. And he asked the College for financial aid.

He took the financial aid form home for his dad to sign. But his father saw that he would have to divulge his income to get the financial aide and he tossed the paper back at George. "You're not filling out this form," he said. "I'm not going to tell anyone that I can't take care of my own kids." By this time, George really did want to attend Roanoke, so he told the administration that he wanted to attend even if he couldn't get a scholarship. His store manager promised to give him all of the part-time work that George could handle to help him pay the way. In September, George was a Maroon.

The first year of college was tough. "I'd never worked so hard in my life," George said, "trying to work part-time, go to classes, and participate in sports." Homer had returned from his year in the Navy, and worked hard to help George become a better runner. In track that year, he had some fairly good times. Homer taught him how to start a race but did have difficulty teaching him how to relax. George had a tendency to try so hard during a race that he would clinch his fists and run with a lot of tension in the upper body.

Boyd Carr was also a freshman that year. Boyd was a good sprinter, hurdler, and broad jumper. He had more experience in track than George, and could always beat George on the start–a fact that aggravated George.

After his freshman year, George enrolled in summer school. In August of 1952, however, just before summer school was finished, he went home one day and found a letter from Uncle Sam. It was his draft notice. George went to break the news to Homer. Because George had only a couple of weeks left before summer school let out, and not wanting him to lose the money what he had spent on tuition, Homer and the administration petitioned the draft board and got George's reporting date postponed until the latter part of August.

The Army sent George to Fort Meade, Maryland, for induction. Then he was transferred to Camp Rucker, Alabama. In all, George served in the Army for 21 months. With many others, he was let out because of the end of the Korean War.

George was discharged, having made Sergeant in 17 months. He decided to return to Roanoke College. While he was in the service, he saved a lot of his money so he wouldn't have to work while attending classes and running track. He was looking forward to his return. During his days in the Army, he had worked hard at running–perfecting the way he came out of the blocks, swinging his arms, and more. He still remembered that he couldn't always beat Boyd Carr, although he thought he was faster, and he wanted another shot. "Wouldn't you know it," he discovered, "when I got back to Roanoke, Boyd had transferred to the University of Virginia."

With the G. I. Bill and a significant amount of savings, the second phase of George's education at Roanoke was better. He still didn't get any money from the College, but Homer occasionally would help out. For example, once he asked George to come up and help register freshmen for their classes. And the school would pay him some small amount for his work. The College also hired students to grade papers for certain professors. As a Business Administration major, George was able to make some money by grading papers for accounting teachers.

His sophomore, junior, and senior years in indoor and outdoor track were outstanding in terms of performance. The team around him was gaining strength, adding more and more top athletes. State small college and Mason-Dixon Conference championships were routine. And as George matured, so did his own marks improve.

And he was good both in indoor and outdoor track. Before graduating in 1957, he set the school record in the indoor 60-yard dash at :06.3. He also was a member of the school record-setting mile relay, 880-yard relay, and sprint medley relay teams indoors.

In outdoor track, he finished his career as the school record holder in the 100 and 220, as well as in the 440- and 880-yard relays. He ran one :09.9 and five :10.0 100-yard races. In the 220-yard dash, he ran two :21.7 races, two :22.0 races, and three :22.1 races. He also helped his team run a :43.9 440-yard relay and a 1:31.3 880-yard relay.

George graduated following the 1956-57 session. He was torn as to whether he should teach or go into business. He finally got a job with an accounting firm–the Alexander Grant Company in Roanoke. He stayed with that company for two years. Then Ray Buzzard, track coach at Andrew Lewis High School, began to ask him to come over and work with his sprinters. So George accepted the offer and helped as much as he could after work. Ray, realizing how much George meant to his sprinters, told George that he ought to be in teaching. He said if George were a teacher, he'd be pleased to have him help coach his team.

Finally, in 1959, George applied for a teaching job in Roanoke County. His plans were to help Buzzard coach the Lewis track team, of course. He would have done so, gladly, without pay. So he got the teaching job, but Buzzard left for another job.

George started his education career as a teacher, with no coaching responsibilities, at South Salem School. He was there about a week with the equivalent of two classrooms of seventh graders before the administration moved him to the Andrew Lewis Annex. He finished the year there. The next year, he applied to go to the new Northside High School in Roanoke County. They were supposed to open the school in September of 1960; however, they didn't finish the construction on time. Instead of moving to Northside, George was sent to Mountain View School, teaching eighth graders physical education, science, and social studies.

In January, he did make the move to Northside and finished the year there. Ralph Isabel was coaching at the high school and asked George to come out and help with track. George agreed initially to come out and help a day or two each week. But it ended up that he was helping about six days every week.

George wasn't being paid for his coaching, but the Superintendent finally decided to give him $100 for helping that year. At the end of the year, another teacher asked George if he were coming back the following year. George told him that he was. The teacher said, "Well, I heard that you are going to be a Principal next year. At least, that's what all the kids are saying." George had no idea what she was talking about. But the rumor was true. That summer, George was working for the county's summer maintenance crew and happened to be in the School Board Office building one day. Dr. Horne, the Superintendent of Schools, stopped him in the hallway and asked him to go to Clearbrook School as Principal. George had taught for only two years at that point. He told Dr. Horne that he didn't have a Master's Degree and that he didn't think he was ready to be a Principal. Horne said that lack of experience wasn't important. He gave George one week to make up his mind.

George didn't know what to do and asked others for their advice. The Northside Principal told him that he had to think of his family, and that he really needed to take the principalship. So he took Dr. Horne's offer and became the leader of Clearbrook School. He didn't know much about being an administrator, but to this day thinks that his military experience probably helped.

He stayed on as Principal of Clearbrook for six years, until about 1967. Apparently, the school system was impressed with his work. Once or twice, another system offered George a job, but people like Arthur Trout, Chairman of the School Board, encouraged him to stay.

The next year, he moved over to Conehurst School, where he remained as Principal for another 15½ years. At the end of that period, Salem City was thinking of opening its own school system–with its schools no longer a part of the Roanoke County School System. George got a call from a School Board member in Salem, offering him a position in their central office. But he told the gentleman that he wanted to stay with the county. He remained at Conehurst until the school was closed, when he transferred to Burlington Elementary School. He retired from Burlington as Principal in 1989.

Today, George lives with his wife, Rebecca, in west Salem. George and Rebecca have been married since 1960. Their only offspring, Keith, was born in May of 1961.

George doesn't have many hobbies now, but he used to belong to an investment club and occasionally enjoys refinishing antique furniture. In general, his health is good. Some 30 years ago, he went through a spell with prostate cancer, but surgery seemed to leave him cancer free. Rebecca also has had some problems with cancer in years gone by.

George lives only a short distance from Homer Bast. He checks up on his former coach frequently, often talking over old times and taking the Basts small gifts such as tomatoes from their summer garden.

Goodlake, Dick

Dick was born in Nashville, Tennessee, in 1936. His father, Richard, was a store manager for S. H. Kress & Co., a chain of "five and dime" retail department stores in the United States. Richard, his wife Frances, and their two sons (Dick and a younger brother) were destined to live in many parts of the country over the next few years. During his younger years, Dick lived in Tennessee, Texas, Louisiana, New York, and California. His first two years of high school were spent at South Pascedena High School in South Pascedena, California. The family then moved to New York and Dick finished his last two years of pre-college work at Garden City High School on Long Island.

Richard Goodlake and his wife, Beth.

In sports, Dick competed in track. At Pascedena High, he primarily was a decathlete. He pole vaulted, long jumped, high jumped, as well as competing in the 10-event decathlon. When he transferred to Garden City High School, he became a distance runner. He went out for cross country and track and discovered that he was very good in those sports. His specialty was the mile run, an event in which he was timed once in 4:44. At the same time, he high jumped between 5'10" and 6'0". He also long jumped about 20'.

Track athletics was a very competitive sport among high schoolers on Long Island. Two athletes who came from those Long Island programs, for example, were Tom Courtney, United States 1956 Olympic gold medalist, and Al Oerter, a four-time Olympic discus champion.

Dick selected Roanoke because he was recruited by Homer Bast. Throughout almost his entire senior year at Garden City, he was sure that he was headed for Indiana University. In fact, he had already been accepted to attend Indiana when Homer came by his school on one of his treks to east coast schools. Whatever he said to Dick must have worked, because he convinced Dick that he would be better off going to a small school like Roanoke. "I thought Homer was a very charismatic guy," said Dick recently.

Financially, Dick's upper middle class family could have sent him to even the most expensive school. They lived in a fairly affluent area in California and New York, so Dick could apply to any school without asking for financial aide.

During his first year at Roanoke, Dick lived in Hildreth Hall. Phil Shaw was his roommate, and Howard Meincke and Pete Wise lived on the second floor. Other students and track men in Hildreth included Tom Sitton and his brother, Jose.

Dick joined the Kappa Alpha fraternity, but he says that he was so involved with cross country and track that he never tried to become an officer of the group. In cross country, he became one of Roanoke's premiere runners. His main competition came from his own teammates. First, there was Les Noel, followed by Howard Meincke and George Jocher. This threesome, along with Dick, dominated the distance running scene in Virginia's small-colleges for a number of years. Sometimes, Dick would win a meet. At other times, he was just steps behind the first Roanoke man.

During his indoor track career, he won the mile event in the Little Eight and Mason-Dixon Championships in 1956. He also won the Mason-Dixon mile run in 1957, and during his college years ran on the Roanoke relay teams.

He ran the mile and the two-mile races during outdoor track. He was the mile champion in the 1955 Mason-Dixon meet and won the Mason-Dixon and Little Eight two-mile events in 1956. In 1957, he won the Little Eight two-mile race

Here are his best mile and two mile times while at Roanoke:

Mile

4:25.5	Norfolk, VA	Norfolk William and Mary	04/01/57

Two Miles

09:57.2	Salem, VA	Washington and Lee	04/24/56
09:58.2	Hampden-Sydney, VA	Little Eight Meet	05/16/56
10:02.8	Johnson City, TN	East Tennessee State	04/12/57
10:04.7	Baltimore, MD	Mason-Dixon Meet	05/11-12/56
10:05.0	Salem, VA	Newport News Apprentice	04/14/56
10:05.4	Hampden-Sydney, VA	Little Eight Meet	05/10/57

His mile time ranked him third among all athletes coached by Homer Bast. Only Alvin Smith (4:24.4) and Howard Meincke (4:19.3) ran faster times. In the two-mile race, Howard Meincke was the only Maroon to run a better time (09:44.6), but Dick ended with the second, third, sixth, ninth, and tenth best times under Bast.

After college, Dick left the Roanoke area. He first worked a year as a manager-trainee for the J. C. Penny Company in Levittown, New York. Then, he decided that he wanted to be a Marine officer. He enlisted with the Marines in 1960 and attended Officer Candidates School at Quantico, Virginia. In September of 1960, he was commissioned as a Second Lieutenant.

From that point, he went on to serve 23 years in the Marine Corps in locations such as California, Okinawa, North Carolina, and Hawaii. He also put in time in Vietnam during the Vietnam War in 1969-70. The Marines awarded him the bronze star while he was in Vietnam, essentially for meritorious service in a combat area.

Arriving back in the states, he served in the 1970s in Denver, Colorado, training Marine reserves. He then went back to Camp Pendleton, California, where he was placed as second in command of research development and test facilities for the Marine Corps. He was promoted to Captain and Major in Hawaii in the period from 1965 to 1967. He again was promoted, to Lt. Colonel, in 1977. In 1981, he retired. He had been with the Marines on active duty for 21 years, and he also had two years of reserve duty. At the time of his retirement, he was ready to leave the Marines. He just didn't want his family to move around anymore.

In terms of his family, Dick was married in 1961 to Beth, who was a senior at Mary Washington College. He met Beth while he was stationed at Quantico. Beth gave birth to two sons–Richard in 1962 and Ted in 1966. As this book was being written, Richard was still single. Ted was married with three children of his own, including a seven-year-old son adopted from a family in Vladivostok, Russia. Ted attended the University of Tennessee and ran for Stan Huntsman, a well-known track coach who went on to coach at Texas. Ted was a San Diego C. I. S. cross country champion and a two-mile champion while in high school. At Tennessee his senior year, he was the Southeastern Conference

10,000-meter champion. Dick thinks he may have run about 30:00 for the 10,000 while at Tennessee and may still hold the national junior record at 10,000 meters (about 32:00), recorded when he was just 16. He went on to become the running shoe coordinator for PUMA U. S. A. His boss was Jay Piccola, the former outstanding basketball player for Roanoke College in the 1970s. Piccola had risen to the position of President of PUMA U. S. A.

Retiring from the Marines gave the Goodlake family more stability. They were able to buy a home, living in that house for more than 20 years. Dick also went to work for Hughes Aircraft as a Senior Systems Engineer not long after his retirement. He stayed with Hughes until 2001, although he continued to consult for them for a couple of more years. Then he took a job with C. A. C. I., a medium-sized aerospace company. "I'll probably work until I fall over," Dick says, "simply because I enjoy working."

In retirement, Dick works out a lot, running and lifting weights. He has also run in a 5,000-meter race (the Carlsbad 5,000 in California), along with some 5,000 and 10,000 runs locally. He believes his running helps him keep an active mind.

Ide, Allen

Growing up in Arlington, Virginia, Allen lived with his parents–Robert and Virginia–and a brother and sister, Henry and Anne. Henry was three years younger than Allen and was a good basketball player. He played basketball for Washington-Lee High School and later for the U. S. Navy basketball team. Anne was the youngest of the three children.

Allen went to Washington-Lee High School in Arlington. As there were no other high schools in Arlington at the time, his school was much larger than the average high school in Virginia. In fact, there were about 580 students in his senior class. Football and basketball were the sports that commanded the most attention at Washington and Lee, but Allen participated in track. He hurt his ankle just before the state meet in his senior year. Despite the injury, Homer Bast contacted him and asked him if he wanted to come to Roanoke. His specialties were the 100, 220, 440, and broad jump.

Allen Ide and his wife, Frida.

Instead, Allen enrolled at Washington and Lee University in Lexington,

Virginia. He soon found, however, that W & L was not particularly a good sports school. He wanted to participate in track, but W & L just didn't have the caliber of team that he wanted. So he transferred to Roanoke College after a year and a half, entering the school halfway through the 1953-54 session. Indoor track for the year was already finished, but he was able to run outdoor track in 1954 and then indoor and outdoor track in 1955 and 1956.

At Roanoke, he was Vice President of the Monogram Club, but otherwise participated in few extracurricular activities besides track. He lived in Hildreth Hall, where many of the track men were located over the years, and Chris Rittman was his roommate for at least part of the time he was there. "It was a great place to party," he jokes. He was a good student and if he were interested in a particular subject, he worked hard in that class.

After graduating from Roanoke with a degree in economics, his first job was with I. B. M. He stayed with that company for several years, but left them when he decided to move into sales and marketing. For the last couple of years of his career, he was working for himself–selling computers and computer software to various industries. He retired in 1996.

Allen married Frida (Maier), also a student at Roanoke College, in 1956. They have three children–Sharon, Steven, and Stacey–and seven grandchildren, ages 16 to 22.

Since he retired, Allen has done a lot of writing. Most of his writing is political in nature. He finds it takes up much of his time, especially the research connected with the articles.

He has had a few medical issues over the years, although these days he is in good health.

Jackson, Jay

Jay grew up in Roanoke, graduating from Jefferson High School in 1951. He was a lanky, skinny kid–too light for football. He also didn't have the skills for basketball, and there was no track team at the school.

After leaving Jefferson, he enrolled at Hampden-Sydney College, choosing the school because he heard that it had a good reputation. It also didn't hurt that several of his friends were also headed for Hampden-Sydney.

He wanted to participate in college athletics and his first choice was track, although the school didn't have much of a track team in those days. Jim Hickey, the football coach, was the track coach. He didn't know much about track, but Jay and several others were interested in competing and joined the team.

Jay decided that he would become a broad jumper and a high jumper. Of course, he had never jumped before and pretty much had to learn the events on his own.

His experiences at Hampden-Sydney were good ones. He had a lot of friends, did fairly well in track, and was a pre-dental student. At that time at Hampden-Sydney, a student didn't major in a particular subject. Instead, he aimed toward a B. A. or a B. S. degree and then took the necessary hours to qualify for one or the other.

Jay Jackson and wife Carole.

After spending his freshman and sophomore years at Hampden-Sydney, and after some gentle persuasions from Homer Bast, Jay transferred to Roanoke College. "Coach Bast was starting to get a reputation as a good teacher, coach, and man," Jay noted. "I had met him at some of the meets between Roanoke and Hampden-Sydney. For an interesting but unknown reason, three schools in the Little Six Conference–Roanoke, Hampden-Sydney, and Bridgewater–were very friendly toward each other. We felt a kinship."

When he discussed the transfer to Roanoke with Homer during the spring of 1953, Homer told him that he would welcome him as a member of the team. But he also warned him that in some of the meets, he might be ineligible. Jay said he understood. "It wasn't like I was a football player," Jay later said, "looking to go into the N. F. L. Track was very much a hobby with me."

He did well in track during his first year at Roanoke, although he was a better athlete outdoors than indoors. He admits that he was never comfortable with indoor track. Maybe it was the feel of the floor, the surroundings, or a number of other problems.

He found that it was difficult getting in the needed practice time. He had so many biology labs that year, but had taken no biology courses before going to Roanoke. Until his senior year, he still planned on becoming a dentist. During his final year, however, he contracted pneumonia and had a tough time recovering from his illness. He could attend no classes for about two weeks. During this period, he did some thinking. He suddenly realized that he didn't have the personality to spend a career within 18" of someone's face all day long. So he dropped dentistry as a possible career. "I said to myself, here you are with an almost completed major in biology and a minor in chemistry. What are you going to do now?" He didn't feel that there many jobs in those days for a biochemist. And he didn't want to teach. Out of this confusion, finally, came a thought. What about law? So he took a course in constitutional law at Roanoke with Julius Prufer. Getting into the University of Virginia Law School was a lot easier in those days than it became later. He applied to the University and, surprising even himself, he was accepted. With a law degree, he thought, he could do a number of things in life.

In outdoor track, Jay became one of Homer's stars. In the broad jump, for example, his best efforts in the 1954 and 1955 seasons were 21'8½", 21'4¾", 21'3¾" (twice), and 21'2¼". There were many more jumps that were close to the 21' mark. In 1954, he even high jumped 6'1" in a dual meet versus the Norfolk Division of William and Mary.

When he came to Roanoke, he knew that Homer had been a college runner himself and might not be able to coach him well in the jumping events. "He was frank with me," Jay said. "He said before I transferred that his ability to coach the high jump and broad jump was a bit limited. But he did recommend a book for me to read. The book, which I bought, talked about your form. Now Homer was conversant enough that he could help you with your form, particularly in the high jump. Our form on those days and the form used today are very different. We used the roll, where you took off on one leg. The leg goes up and you stomach roll over the bar. He knew that form. Now there weren't a lot of secrets to broad jumping. You either had the runway speed, or you didn't. In my case, I wasn't tremendously fast. Homer never ran me in the 100. Most of my accomplishments in the broad jump came not from speed but from good lift."

His campus activities were not extensive, because his Biology major took so much of his time. He was a member of the Kappa Alpha fraternity, as were many of the men on the track and cross country teams. He had been a Kappa Alpha at Hampden-Sydney also.

After graduating from Roanoke in 1955, he went to the Law School at the University of Virginia. Getting a law degree required a three-year course of study, and he graduated there in 1958. Uncle Sam was breathing down his neck at the time. He took the bar exam and wasn't able to pass it the first time. At the end of July, he was drafted. The Army sent him to Fort Jackson, South Carolina, where he stayed for two weeks. During the physical examinations, they noted that Jay was blind in one eye. About all he could do was to count fingers from about three feet. That problem was enough for the military to reject him and he came back home and devoted the fall to studying for his bar exam once again. He took the exam for the second time in the winter of the 1957-58 session and passed.

Now it was time to look for a job. He talked to some law firms and businesses, and settled on a job offer from State Farm Insurance. The position he took required a law degree because he was to handle personal injury claims. Beginning in May of 1959, he worked in Staunton, Virginia, for three or four months. Then the same type of job came open in Roanoke, and he applied for a transfer. The company moved him to their

Roanoke offices. He lived with his parents during this period of time.

In about December of 1964, State Farm told Jay that they thought he could make a successful career with the company, and offered him a promotion to Claims Superintendent. For that job, he had to move to Charlottesville.

Jay and Carole Weeks had begun to date while they each were in high school. Both had grown up in northwest Roanoke. They had dated off and on over the years, and then went their separate ways. In 1965, they finally married. They had one son, Jeff, who was born in 1967. Today, he lives at home with his parents, having his own apartment of about 1,000 square feet in one part of the house.

The Jacksons lived in Charlottesville until about 1969. At that time, some problems were occurring for State Farm in Raleigh and they suggested that Jay make a lateral transfer down there. Jay and Carole lived in Raleigh for about 18 months until the company gave Jay a promotion to the position of Divisional Claims Superintendent. For that job, they moved back to Charlottesville, where they spent the next three years.

State Farm began to expand its number of claims offices and sent Jay to Roanoke. He and Carole thought it was a good move. Jay was about 40 at the time and had an excellent chance of being promoted to a lucrative job as Vice President with the company. In Roanoke, they would be able to stay close to their widowed parents.

Jay and his wife stayed in Roanoke until 1995, when he finally retired. He had spent some 36 years with State Farm.

They were able to buy some 35 acres of country land in Botetourt County when Jay retired. The only buildings on the land were an old barn and a machine shed. The gentlemen who owned the property had planned to put a riding stable on the property. Unfortunately, they overextended their finances with the project and went bankrupt. After the title was cleared, Jay and Carole built their new home on the land.

Over the past few years, Jay has had a few health problems. Rheumatoid arthritis was his first major problem as he grew older, coming on in the middle or late 1980s. The condition is pretty much under control today, with advances in medication. At the worst stages of the disease, he had a lot of stiffness attacking him in the shoulders and hands.

Another problem has been with prostate cancer, which came along three or four years ago. It was discovered through a prostate specific antigen (PSA) test. The PSA was elevated and the doctor elected to wait to see what would happen. Jay waited three to six months and then took the PSA test again. At that point, they did a biopsy. The biopsy report–and a follow-up report from Johns Hopkins–found that the doctors needed to take some action quickly. One doctor said that at 70 years of age, Jay was too old for surgery. But he did give Jay some books to read about prostate cancer and told him to come back to talk again. The next time the doctor, Jay, and Carole talked, it was if they had never had the previous conversation. So Jay decided to change urologists. In consultation with the new doctor, they decided to go the route of external radiation. Jay took those radiation treatments five days a week for 42 weeks at Lewis-Gale Hospital. Then it was a matter of waiting to see what happened. That waiting period was about 18 months, with Jay having a PSA test every six months. To this point, it seems like Jay is doing well.

His blood pressure today is good and so is his heart, according to doctors. He has never had diabetes, a common malady for those over 70. He does have a touch of genetic neuropathy, which affects him from the knees down. And he has had restless leg syndrome in the legs, for which he takes medicine.

Even today, Jay remembers his athletic experiences at Hampden-Sydney and Roanoke as being good parts of his life. If he had it to do over, would he have transferred? "Probably not," he says. "Hampden-Sydney is a super school, and so is Roanoke. I never had the chance to live on campus at Roanoke, however. So it is difficult to compare the two schools. But I do remember that Hampden-Sydney had a whale of a nice campus life. So I just don't know. I have asked myself that question many times. Did I make the right decision when I changed schools? In fact, did I make the right decision to change professions?"

Jenkins, Dr. Bob

Bob went to East Rockaway High School on Long Island. It was the smallest high school in his county, having about 65 seniors when he graduated.

Bob Jenkins, right, visits Homer Bast at Homer's house on Locust Avenue. On the left is former track man George Jocher.

He was the son of Mabel and Ellis Jenkins. Mabel was a homemaker, but worked outside the home as well. Ellis was in quality inspection for companies such as Grumman. Bob had one sister, Peggy, who was younger than he.

Despite his outstanding cross country and track career at Roanoke and as an age-group runner later on, Bob never ran on a team at his high school. He applied to two colleges, and was accepted at both. One was St. Lawrence University in northern New York. The other was Roanoke. He chose

Roanoke because the school was located in a warmer clime and also because the College was less expensive to attend. In addition, the mother of a Roanoke College basketball player, Tom Maxwell, recommended strongly that he attend Roanoke. Tom, a senior, became Bob's big brother in the Sigma Chi fraternity during his freshman year.

Bob's first year in college was 1957, but he didn't begin to run with the Roanoke team until the following year. His Sigma Chi brothers saw him run up and down the basketball court and suggested that he run in the annual intramural cross country race in the fall of 1958. Because he seemed to have some running ability, the fraternity put him at the front of their group at the starting line. "Just before the race," Bob noted, "I talked with my roommate, Pete Vanderwater. He told me that distance running was difficult and gave me a shot of bourbon to help me make it through the race. So we came to the line and I realized that I had to take off quickly or else I would get trampled. The gun sounded and I sprinted to the front. Halfway through the race, we were running on the Hawthorn hills, and I was still in front. Then, two red-shirted Kappa Alphas caught up with me. One was Scott McKinney and the other was Luther Mauney. Well, Kappa Alpha was the Sigs' chief competitor, and suddenly I just took off. And I ended up breaking the school record for the intramural meet. Coach Bast was there at the finish line and, like Uncle Sam, he said 'We need you.' To heck they did. They had a national-class college cross country team that year, including Howard Meincke, George Jocher, Warren Light, Dick Goodlake, Dick Emberger, Wayne Wilson, and others. I told the Coach that there was no way I would join the cross country team. I said that his team ran twice the distance of the intramural race, and right now, I am throwing up after crossing the finish line. Maybe it was the effort to beat the K. A.s; maybe it was the bourbon."

During the following week, Bob recovered and felt much better. He went to his Saturday morning Spanish class. Joe Sitton, the cross country team manager, came up to him and handed him a uniform and a pair of flats. He said, "Be warmed up for the cross country race. We're running at halftime of the soccer game this afternoon." Against his better judgment, Bob showed up on the field and joined the runners in their race. He didn't run with any particular pace in mind. After the start, the team ran diagonally across the soccer field and Bob was keeping up with Howard Meincke. Many of the major runners on the team were taking the day off because they had just been in a tough race against William and Mary at home, which they won. Surprising himself, Bob finished the race in second place, beating established runners such as Dick Emberger and Wayne Wilson. As he was nearing the finish line, running across the soccer field, Chuck Stagliano ran along with him yelling "You're an athlete, Bob. You're an athlete."

Early the next week, Coach Bast asked Bob to join him on the town golf course so he could see what he might be able to do as a runner. Bast stood at the top of a hill with his stop watch and Bob ran around the course and "climbed that freaking hill"–in Bob's words–several times. As a result, he was on Bast's team and did some pretty good running that year. He was young and inexperienced as a runner, so was not included in the group which went to the national championships that year.

Interestingly enough, Bob was not a member of the spring track team during his sophomore year. His summer job was in the Catskills in New York, but before he left Roanoke, he told Coach Bast that he would run cross country the following fall. He trained during the summer and came back ready to go. He almost felt a responsibility to run well for the team. As Bob put it, "I really felt that I was part of the team. Our first meet was at the Norfolk Division of William and Mary. I won the meet and came within about 10 seconds of breaking Howard Meincke's course record. The second meet that fall was at Mount St. Mary's College. I won that race and I think I broke the course record. We had a downhill, flying start. So I was now a major player on the team. I went on to win several other meets that fall. William and Mary came to Salem, and I won that race. I was cranking. As a team, however, we lost by about five points. In the Virginia State Cross Country Championships, I ended up in the 16th place. I may have been sick or injured; otherwise, I think I would have finished better."

In the Little Eight Championships in 1959, the Roanoke team finished second while Bob was in third place. Amazingly, however, Bob was only one second away from winning the race.

To everyone's surprise that year, Roanoke came back to win the Mason-Dixon meet. "Let me tell you a story about that meet," said Bob recently. "We drove up to Chestertown with Coach Bast. I remember that Wayne Wilson and I wore golf hats and Homer called us his two cool cats. We had no pressure on us. And Homer didn't put any pressure on us either. We were just going up there to run a race and do as well as we could. We definitely weren't expected to win, primarily because we had been beaten in the Little Eight meet. Coach took me aside just before the race began and gave me a pep talk. So our team left the start line, not favored to win by anyone, and we ended up winning the meet. But we didn't know the final team scores for quite a while after the race was completed. The confusion, we learned, came from Johnnie Blanton wearing his number upside down. Finally, we realized that Johnnie finished 25th, which was critical to our winning. We were sitting in the locker room with no idea as to what the team scores were when Homer came in and said, 'Fellows, we might have won this meet. It all depends on where Johnnie Blanton finished.' So we were all elated."

After the meet, Coach Bast took a train back because he was preaching the next day in the Staunton area. And the team celebrated by going out on the town in the College station wagon and ending up in the Sigma Chi house at the University of Maryland. They didn't know anyone who lived at the house, but walked in around 3:00 a.m. and had a good time. Later, they drove through D. C., where Bob says he dropped and broke a bottle of blackberry brandy. To a man, the team was crazy with excitement.

On Sunday night, the guys reached the Salem campus. Someone got an idea on the way to pick up some fireworks. They arrived at the school around 10:00 p.m. and parked the station wagon in back of the Sections. Then they went around the buildings to the quadrangle and set up the fireworks. They lit the fuses and ran back to the car, driving quickly through the High Street gate onto the quad to watch the explosions begin. Bob and freshman Derek Stryker stood on the top of the station wagon, with Bob holding the Mason-Dixon trophy over his head. Many of the students were studying in their dorms, but hearing the fireworks, they came out to the quad to see what was going on. Everyone gathered around the station wagon. Some already had heard that the team was the winner of the Mason-Dixon meet. The sky was lit up and the crowd was screaming. Some began yelling at Bob, saying "Speech. Speech." So he stood up on the top of the wagon and said loudly, "We kicked their ass." Just at that point, Bob looked down into the crowd and saw Don Sutton, the Dean of Men, looking back at him. The members of team knew that fireworks were illegal in Salem and Bob thought for sure that all of them would be put on probation or even tossed out of school. But Sutton let the infraction slide, knowing how much the Mason-Dixon win had meant to the team.

All in all, Bob had a very successful running career at Roanoke. During the 1959-60 cross country season, he won all five of the team's dual meets. He also finished 16th in the Virginia State Championships, and 3rd in both the Little Eight and Mason-Dixon Championships. The team finished with a 4-1 record.

During his senior year in cross country, he won four of the six dual meets, finishing 3rd in the State A. A. U. meet, 1st in the Little Eight meet, and 6th in the Mason-Dixon Championships. The team record was 3-2.

In outdoor track, Bob was an excellent distance runner. He ran a 9:58.0 two-mile race in the Virginia State Championships in 1960.

As good as he was at distance running in college, Bob thinks that he could have been better. "In those days, I was running just to run. I was good in the sense that I had the physiology and structure for running. But I wasn't out to improve as much as I could. I was a Biology major and had a lot of labs. I also had a chemistry minor. Now, I did what Homer asked, but I could have pushed myself so much harder. But I didn't. And I didn't get too disappointed when I didn't win. I just had a lot of pushes and pulls on my time and energy–with biology and chemistry courses and a fraternity life. So Homer, realizing this, never really pushed me to reach my potential. We knew he was there and we did what he asked. I had the talent, but never the attitude of a Howard Meincke. And track was a disaster for me, of course. I came out late and never got into good shape. I never ran winter track."

At the end of the 1960-61 session, Bob graduated from Roanoke with a degree in biology. He then attended Virginia Tech for the next two years, taking courses in the University's Master's program in biology, although he didn't get an advanced degree from that school. Instead, he worked for a year at the Smithsonian in Washington. There, he was an aide to an ichthyologist and wrote the major part of his thesis.

He attended Cornell for four more years, from 1964 through 1968. There, he finished most of his work toward a doctorate. He came back to Roanoke College to become a member of the biology faculty in 1968, receiving his doctorate from Cornell in 1970. He taught at Roanoke until 1977, when he took a full-time teaching and research job at Virginia Commonwealth University. He left Roanoke primarily because he wanted to work at a school with a graduate program–and somewhat less teaching time. After a couple of months at V. C. U., however, he was second-guessing the move. Following two years at V. C. U., he jumped at the opportunity to return to Roanoke College. The individual who had taken his place at Roanoke two years before left to go back to Oklahoma University.

In 1967, Bob and Diane Jordan were married. He had met Diane when she was a secretary to his major professor at Cornell. The two had two children–Glenn and Katherine. Today, Glenn and Katey both live in the area of Vail, Colorado. Katey is a jewelry designer, while Glenn is a "varied worker." Neither is married.

The marriage to Diane lasted 20 years, after which they obtained a divorce. Bob never remarried.

Bob stayed at Roanoke College for the remainder of his career in teaching and research, finally retiring as an Associate Professor of Biology in August of 2007. His professional vita for these years is outstanding. In terms of honors, he won the Thomas Jefferson Medal for Outstanding Contributions in Natural Science. He was one of Roanoke College's Sesquicentennial Distinguished Alumnus in 1992. Roanoke also awarded Bob the Professional Achievement Award in 1992, and he was inducted into the College's Athletic Hall of Fame in 1980 primarily because of his international-class distance running during his post-undergraduate days.

The co-writer of two highly-acclaimed books on freshwater fishes in Virginia and North America, Bob also has authored or co-authored 36 different journal publications and has presented papers at almost 60 conferences across the country. As a researcher, he has been the recipient of more than 50 grants and contracts. He holds memberships in societies ranging from the American Society of Ichthyologists and Herpetologists to the Virginia Academy of Science.

Other activities include: a reviewer and referee for primary scientific journals; a director of numerous student research projects at Roanoke College; the delivery of nine oral presentations on the Roanoke campus; community service projects throughout Virginia; curatorial work with the Roanoke College Fish Collection; provider of technical assistance to students, colleagues, institutions, and agencies in the United States; and thousands of hours of committee service to the College and community.

After graduating from Roanoke and beginning his long career in teaching and research, Bob was–as he said–a total dropout from running. But at one of the local high school track meets in 1977, he saw that they were offering a Master's Mile event. He decided to enter the event, thinking that he could win easily even though he knew he wasn't in shape. He couldn't. The race, however, did convince him that he might be able to compete in road races if he trained well. In Richmond, while he was at V. C. U., he met a bunch of guys who were training for the Richmond Marathon. He began to train with them–although running only 35 miles a week–and competed in the Richmond Marathon in 1978. His time was 2:53, a time that surprised him and which qualified him for the Boston Marathon.

By 1979, Bob was running 50 miles a week and that distance climbed to 60 in 1980, 70 in 1981, and 80 or more in 1982. Some weeks during this period of road racing and marathons, he ran over 100 miles. His best time in the marathons were going down in 1981-82 at the rate of about two minutes per race.

In October of 1982, at the New York City Marathon, he ran 2:24.08. There was a headwind that day; otherwise, he thinks, the time could have been at least 2:22. With his time, he became the first American in the Masters, 40 or older, division. Only a Mexican Olympian and a runner from England were able to beat him in his age group.

Bob's old friend, Chuck Stagliano, picked him up with about a quarter mile to go. He said, "2:23, Jenks, 2:23." Then Bob got a glimpse of the finish line as he came to a straightaway. The larger timer said 2:22.52, and he said to himself, "Damn, there is no way I can get to the finish line in eight seconds."

One thing he regrets about that race is that it was held on a Sunday. The day before, the new Bast Center on the Roanoke campus was dedicated to Homer Bast. Bob wanted badly to be there for the ceremony, but couldn't. During his age-group running career, Homer had been an advisor to Bob–someone to turn to for training tips and encouragement.

During his last two years of distance running, he was competing for Adidas. As he said recently, he was "their token Master's runner." He walked into the Adidas suite the day before the Boston Marathon and told one of the representatives that he was interested in representing Adidas. He already wore their shoes and liked them. Some of the other Masters runners at the time were being supported by Nike. The representative asked Bob who he was and what times he had recorded. Bob told him that two weeks before, he had broken the national record for his age group in a ten-mile race. The fellow told Bob that he would watch the results of the next day's marathon and then decide about whether to provide support. Unfortunately, the race went badly and Bob had to call up the Adidas representative a couple of days later to tell him that he had run a poor race. Still, he had recorded a 2:33 time. He thought that Adidas would drop him fast; however, the clothing, shoes, and travel money began to come in during the coming weeks. Running had become his second career. His wife, Diane, became his trainer. She had read some of the running magazines and knew who Bob's chief competitors were around the country.

He continued to run for a while, with the money coming in almost every month. "I must tell you," he said, "that I was in my prime at age 42. If it hadn't been for the book I was writing at the time, I think I could have been one of the best distance runners around. After the New York Marathon, I opened my mail and there was a check for $500 from a bank that sponsored the Marathon. Adidas also provided me with incentives. If I broke a personal record, they would send me $1,000, for example. And I was getting travel money just to show up for races–either from Adidas or the race sponsors."

Bob's age-group running finally came to an end in about 1982. At that time, he was beginning to work on a book which turned out to be some 1,100 pages in length. His training distances went down and down. So he left running for a second time and returned to his other career at Roanoke College.

Today, after his recent retirement from Roanoke, Bob is recognized by his many friends and colleagues as an outstanding scholar and one of the finest athletes in the history of the school. Throughout his life, he has been a true champion–one fired by a desire, a dream, and a vision to be the best he can be.

Jocher, George

George grew up near New York City. His father was the Vice President for a bank in the area and taught courses at the American Institute for Banking. He was very capable in terms of making and saving money, as are George and his siblings today. His mother, after getting all of the kids out of the house, was a business manager in the Berkshires.

George had two sisters. He was the oldest child. Three years younger was Phyllis, who became a registered nurse. George remembers her as being a smart, capable person who spent 10 years out on Long Island running a Critical Care Department–dealing with traumatic events such as drug overdoses and car crashes. "Phyllis was a very cool customer when it came to disasters," George says. "And she is still that way."

His youngest sister still lives in the Berkshires. She has three children of her own and her husband–a General Dynamics Vice President–spent practically his entire career with Navy Ballistic Missile subs. "My sister was on the National Security Council with Reagan, George Bush the first, and George Bush the second," George says, "until she finally retired. She came out of Harvard with a doctorate and, as a nuclear specialist, spent a lot of time in Russia with Dr. Perry when he was Secretary of Defense."

Early in his high school career, George attended Sewanaka High School on Long Island, one of the largest schools in the area. He remembers running a 2:14 half mile as a sophomore, in junior varsity competition, before he transferred to Mercersburg Academy for his junior and senior years. Mercersburg Academy had been the school Homer Bast and his brother attended earlier.

Former distance runner George Jocher (right) poses in front of the bas relief plaque in the Bast Center. With him are two of Bast's excellent athletes, Dick Goodlake (left) and Phil Shaw.

At Mercersburg, George received a working scholarship. He made spending money by waiting on tables.

He also participated in sports. In the fall, he ran cross country for Coach Jimmy Curran who, over the years, worked with a number of Olympians. Curran had been a professional runner in Scotland, competing for money. He remains the coach at Mercersburg today.

George was a good cross country and track man at Mercersburg; although he admits that his times were good but not great. After graduating from Mercersburg, he decided to enroll at Hofstra University, mostly because of money. His parents had supported him while he was on the working scholarship at Mercersburg.

Unfortunately, George never really enjoyed his time at Hofstra. The school, he thought, had no spirit. Everyone simply got into their cars after classes and went home. Living at home himself, he was on the cross country team and did well in some of the meets around the area. He wrestled in the winter (a requirement of his coach) and ran track in the spring. But the workouts weren't very intense.

One day, he was reading the sports section of the Long Island Daily Press. An article on Roanoke College caught his attention. The writer noted that Roanoke was going to come up to Long Island in the spring of 1957 to run against some of the teams from that area. The article caught his attention, and he soon contacted Roanoke about transferring after the year was over. He was intrigued to read about the track team and its capabilities. He even drove down to Salem in February of 1956 with a couple of friends. One of the friends was Suzie Vail, whose brother, Chip, was already a student at Roanoke. The Sigma Chi fraternity put George up for the weekend. The group looked around at the campus and talked to a lot of students. And he talked with Homer Bast. It was a nice visit, George remembers, and he was impressed. "The Blue Ridge Mountains," he says, "were a magnetic attraction." He headed home with the distinct impression that Roanoke was a very nice school with a lot of good people. "People actually knew each other on a first-name basis," George remembers. "And I wanted to get out of being at home on Long Island. I wanted to do my own thing."

George's first year at Roanoke was 1956-57. He was ineligible to run in most of the cross country and track meets because of his transfer, although he often did unofficially with the permission of the coaches. He got himself a job waiting on tables in the Commons. At the time, the waiters all wore white coats. During his second year, the College changed over to cafeteria style serving. He also inherited the campus laundry route from Phil Shaw, a fellow Kappa Alpha brother. "Phil really took me under his wing," said George. "He would go through all of the dormitories and pick up students' dirty laundry on Mondays and then take back clean laundry, and collect, on Thursdays. I trained with him and, the next year, he turned the laundry route over to me because he was graduating."

His Commons and laundry jobs only lasted his first two years. But he decided not to work his senior year. As he put it, "I had been working my tail off. I was involved with just about everything going on at Roanoke. I graduated as class president. I was on the Honor Council and was the Associate Yearbook Editor. I was in Who's Who in American Colleges and Universities. I enjoyed all of that stuff. It was always fun. But when it came to my senior year, I said to myself that I didn't want to be working so hard that year. I had been working on Long Island golf courses in the summers. We'd get out there at 7:30 a.m. and be finished by 4:00 p.m. Before my senior year at Roanoke, I was not only working at the golf course during the day, but was running a driving range from 7:00 p.m. until midnight. I was wiped out by the end of the week, and would just sleep practically all weekend. But I pulled in a double load of earnings that summer, and in that way I didn't have to work during my senior year."

George very much enjoyed his three years at Roanoke. The school was small, had probably more men than women, and there were excellent parties. Everyone seemed to be on a first-name basis. The academics were good. The physical plant was in good shape. The scenery around the campus was excellent. And fraternity life was the best.

In 1956-57, he was a transfer student and ineligible to run officially in many of the cross country and track meets. In the 1957 and 1958 seasons, he ran on Homer Bast's cross country teams. In 1958 and 1959, he ran the 880, mile, and two-mile races on the track team. He was elected Co-Captain of the cross country team in 1958 and served as Co-Captain of the track team in 1959.

His top two-mile times–about 9:45 and 9:46–were sensational for a small-college runner. He was named to the "All State College and University Track Team" in 1959, and was designated as the top two-miler in Virginia. George also received the College's "Athlete of the Year" trophy for the 1958-59 session.

George ran on some talented Roanoke teams. He remembers Pete Wise, Dick Goodlake, Dick Emberger, and others like he was running only yesterday. He particularly remembers his competitions with distance running star Howard Meincke. Meincke had been an excellent New Jersey runner before he came to Roanoke. During the first two years that George was at Roanoke, Meincke normally would beat George in the races in which they faced off. During his senior year, the tables were reversed. George became the number one distance man on the team.

Before he graduated, George had become one of the best distance runners in the state. Here are just a few of his accomplishments:

> He was the Mason-Dixon Conference champion in the two-mile race in 1959, running 9:45.8.
>
> In the fall of his senior year, George won six cross country meets.
>
> In his senior year, he placed second in the Mason-Dixon Cross Country Championships.
>
> He placed 26th in the nation in 1958 in the N. C. A. A. Cross Country Championships in Wheaton, Illinois.
>
> George helped his cross country team in 1958 to win the Little Eight Conference, the Mason-Dixon Conference, and the Virginia A. A. U. Championships titles.
>
> In the fall of 1958, his cross country team beat William and Mary, the champions of the Big Six and Southern Conferences.
>
> During the 1957-58 indoor season, he won the Mason-Dixon Conference mile and two-mile races in the championship meet.

> George won three cross country meets in 1957 and was second in the Little Eight meet and third in the Mason-Dixon Championships. His team won the Little Eight and Mason-Dixon titles.
>
> During the 1956-57 outdoor season, he won the mile in three meets while ineligible because of his transfer from Hofstra University. He set the Roanoke College track record in one of these meets.

During his college career, George ran a 4:24.8 and a 4:26.6 mile. Howard Meincke was the only teammate who did better. George's two-mile times were even more spectacular. By the end of the 1958-59 season, he held the school's two second-best times–9:45.8 and 9:46.4–trailing only Meincke's 9:44.6, which was a time set in 1957.

After George's graduation from Roanoke, he joined the Navy and went through the Navy Officer Candidate School at Newport. He had wanted to join the Marines, but knew that his eyes were not good enough. He was commissioned at Newport, finishing about 50th in a large class of 1,100 people. "We had people from Harvard and Yale flunking out," George says. "A lot of it had to do with stamina. We were studying every night until 11:30 p.m. or so for pop quizzes. And they woke us up at 5:30 a.m. So everyone was constantly beat. We were doing physical drills, gunnery, navigation, operations, and trying to absorb lots of esoteric content. Our progress was based in large part on the pop quizzes. I finally was appointed as sectional leader for 45 guys, probably because I was able to hang in there academically and could run those 45 guys in formation. After that point, the Navy put me through about a year of nothing but training–combat air control, combat air control supervisor, and assignment to a fighter squad down at Key West when Cuba was a hot situation."

While at Key West, he married Nancy Humphries in May of 1960. She was a fellow classmate at Roanoke and a Kappa Alpha Sweetheart. There wasn't much of a honeymoon. They were only in Key West for a month, but George and the men were doing combat air control maneuvers at night and had their days off. One of the perks he still remembers is that the Navy had fighter squadron boats and would take individuals like George out fishing off the keys or in the channel between Cuba and Key West.

During his time in the Navy, he was on a missile cruiser at one point. On the ship were an Admiral and some of his staff of about eight officers and perhaps 40 enlisted men. They were losing a lieutenant and needed someone with all of the certifications which George had just picked up. So the Admiral grabbed George for the job. He became one of eight officers reporting to the two-star Admiral. He became a junior grade lieutenant, and then worked his way up to be a lieutenant and spent time on three missile cruisers, three aircraft carriers, on three Mediterranean deployments. When he came back from the Mediterranean, he had many of the experiences needed for top jobs. Over a period of time, he reported to three different Admirals and picked up numerous certifications. It was almost funny. In the middle of the night, he might well be the guy giving the orders to 12 ships. And he was only 23 to 24 years old.

He left the Navy in December of 1962, but stayed in the Navy Reserves. Under the G. I. Bill, he earned a Masters in Business Administration, and then, with top-secret classification, he was hired by I. B. M. The company put him through a six-month program of classes involving all types of operating systems and computer languages, and they sent him to a night vision laboratory at Fort Belvoir during the run-up to the Vietnam War. He spent about two to three years working with the night vision lab.

Then he worked with a top-secret team that was involved with retrieving seismic data between Montana, Norway, and Alaska. These sites had listening gear that was in bedrock, and they had about 220 seismometers in a 200-mile circle. When the Russians or Chinese set off their nuclear tests, the resulting shocks would travel down to the core of the earth and then back up some 6,000 miles, where the team could read the data. This data was sent to Wisconsin Avenue in Washington, D. C., where scientists and military officials in a simple brick building could perform their analyses.

George stayed with I. B. M. for about 29 years. He was in the Far East for a period of time, and then was sent to Spain in a job involving anti-submarine helicopters. He was in Spain with his family from 1981 until 1985, after which he came back to Washington, still working for I. B. M. Soon, I. B. M. sent George to Germany, where he spent five more years in Intelligence. It was a busy, important job, but he admits that he had a chance to travel around the country and to enjoy the scenery.

In 1977, he and Nancy, his first wife, got a divorce. During their marriage, two sons were born. The oldest was Steven, who graduated from Roanoke College in 1986. Today, Steven has three degrees and works as a chemical engineer and also a safety engineer. George says that he is a very sharp individual who has done well in his short career. In fact, Southern Maine University–one of the schools from which he received a degree–recently selected him as their Alumnus of the Year. Steven and his wife have two daughters.

George's younger son from that marriage is a talented handyman, who does a lot of work on houses, etc. He never went to college, although he did receive an Associate's Degree from Northern Virginia Community College. He is not married.

In 1978, George was married for the second time. His new wife, Isabel, was an airline stewardess, an individual George met while on one of his trips around the world. Together, they had one son, Glenn. George says that Glenn is a sharp guy who works for B. A. E. Systems in San Jose. Just out of high school, he went to the Naval Academy. But he stayed there only two years, transferring to Perdue University, where he received an aeronautical engineer's degree. Joining B. A. E. Systems, he was sent to San Jose to run a simulation team. He is not married.

Isabel and George divorced in about 1999. He then married Carmen De Perignat, whom he met while hiking on the Appalachian Trail. She is an American citizen, but grew up in Spain. A very talented legal officer, she is about 15 years younger than George.

George does have a fourth son, Gary, who was born in Madrid. He graduated from Roanoke College in 2007, with a degree in finance and business.

At the time of this interview, George was working for Northrop Grumman and had been with them for the past 11-12 years. He was the program manager for a 65-million-dollar Army electronic classroom program. Northrop Grumman places and maintains training centers on 15 Army training bases. These centers are very sophisticated units dealing with the simulation of war games.

George has been very loyal to Roanoke College over the years. In fact, he has donated to the school for each of the past 25 years or so. "Roanoke gave me a wonderful education," he says, "and this is just my way of paying them back."

Over the past few years, George and his wife have led a number of hikes. He has been the President and Vice President of his hiking club. The club members tend to hike in all kinds of weather, even when there is snow on the ground. They also enjoy canoe trips.

George has also spent much time with local Cub Scouts. He was a Cub Scoutmaster for his oldest sons and helped in the same way with his younger sons in Germany and in the United States. He also has been an Assistant Scoutmaster for the Boy Scouts of America. He and several dads even took a group of boys out to Philmont Scout Ranch for two weeks of solid, tough backpacking. Philmont is the Boy Scouts of America's premier high-adventure base, which challenges Scouts and Venturers with more than 200 square miles of rugged New Mexico wilderness.

George, himself, has also backpacked more than a third of the Appalachian Trail in sections. That's about 650-700 miles of hiking.

Johnston, Bruce

Bruce, one of the best hurdlers and sprinters in the history of Roanoke College, was born in 1935 in LeNoir, North Carolina. The family consisted of his parents, Bruce Sr. and Marjorie, and two sisters. Bruce Jr. had two sisters, both living in Roanoke today. One was Vicki and the other was Peggy.

Bruce went to Woodrow Wilson Junior High School and then to Jefferson High School in Roanoke. At Jefferson, he played football as a linebacker and field goal kicker. He also ran track. None of the high schools in the Roanoke Valley, including Jefferson,

Bruce Johnston with his wife, Barbara.

had track facilities in those days. Often, Coach Rudy Rohrdance would load the team on a school bus and take them to Roanoke College for practices. And sometimes, they would have a meet versus local or district teams on the College track.

Bruce always wanted to go to college. At one point, he had set his sites on North Carolina State University; however, financially that was out of the question. He then narrowed his choices to Roanoke and V. P. I., just up the road in Blacksburg. When he and his team used the track, Coach Bast would often talk with him about coming to Roanoke. According to Bruce, "Homer was so congenial that you couldn't help but to enjoy talking with him." In the spring of his final high school year, he decided to come to Roanoke. The V. P. I. coach came down to the high school, trying to convince Bruce and others to come to Virginia Tech, but Bruce really didn't want to be in the Corps. Homer was excited to hear that Bruce, who was a young 17, and fellow track star Howard Light, would be enrolling at Roanoke that fall. Bruce received a small amount of financial aid from the College–around $100–for that first year. The money helped buy Bruce's textbooks.

Because his lived at home during his college career, Bruce didn't get involved in many campus activities. His family was not wealthy by any means, and he just couldn't afford to live on campus.

But he became one of the best track men in Virginia. He began his career at Roanoke in competition with super star Dave Foltz, who ran the hurdles, sometimes the sprints, and competed in several field events. His sprint competition at Roanoke was George Gearhart, who twice ran :09.9 in the 100 and two :21.7 times in the 220. By the time Bruce reached his senior year, however, he was the premiere performer in the Little Eight Conference as well as the Mason-Dixon Conference in the 100, 220, high hurdles, and low hurdles. He ran two :09.9 races in the 100, along with two which were recorded at :10.0. In the 220, he ran :22.6 at Miami in 1958. He ran :15.0 in the high hurdles and :23.6 in the lows.

He was a superb competitor, particularly in big meets. During his junior year, he won both the high and low hurdles at the Little Eight meet. He also won both events at the

Mason-Dixon Championships.

As a senior, in 1958, he was equally as talented. He won the 100, high hurdles, and low hurdles at the Little Eight meet and did the same at the Mason-Dixon meet.

During his junior year in indoor tack, he won the low hurdles in the Little Eight meet and was first in both the highs and lows in the Mason-Dixon meet. During his senior year, he won the high hurdles and the low hurdles in the Little Eight meet.

Bruce had one physical disability that most people noticed. He had no use of his left hand. He was born with the problem. Apparently, his mother carried him in a position before he was born that stopped the proper development of his hand. Fortunately, Bruce turned out to be right-handed, so the problem wasn't that serious for him. In fact, he even learned how to play a guitar. He just turned it around backwards.

When Bruce graduated from Roanoke in 1958, he had a B. A. degree in Economics and Business Administration. His first job was difficult to find. He finally took a job with American Bakeries Company in their offices, but he stayed with the company only four months.

Around this time, Bruce and his girlfriend, Barbara McDaniel, were married. She had been working with the local telephone company. Both of them had graduated from Jefferson High School. Barbara and Bruce had two boys. The oldest, Kenneth, passed away when he was in his earl 30s. The youngest, Keith, is now in his early 40s and has taken over the company that his father founded.

After working for American Bakeries Company, Bruce went to work for Harleyville Insurance Company as a Claims Adjustor. He stayed with that company for about 20 years–sometimes working out of Roanoke, sometimes out of Raleigh, and occasionally out of Greenville, North Carolina. At some point, however, he realized that a job in insurance wasn't going to pay the greatest income while he was trying to raise two children. He ended up running a business that his father had started–Sterling Bruce, Inc. Sterling Bruce produced laminate veneer parts for upholstered furniture frames. His company glued veneer together to create the frames. As it turned out, it was a very successful business, so he stayed with the venture until 1992, when he struck out on his own with Bruex, Inc, the same type of operation. He stayed with Bruex until he retired, as owner and C. E. O. of the business, about five years ago. At the time, he was about 66 years of age. Bruce's son wanted to take over the business and is doing a great job with it.

Barbara and Bruce have several grandchildren. All have been spoiled rotten by Bruce and his wife. They live in Hickory, North Carolina.

Since retiring, Bruce has had colon surgery. Later, when he was living in LeNoir, he owned some horses. One day, one of the horses kicked Bruce in the knee. After several years, he had to have that knee replaced. While in the hospital, he had a stroke. He had a hole in his heart and never knew it. Today, his speech and recall, along with his vision, are all affected. Because of the stroke, he had to stay at the Baptist Hospital in Winston-Salem for about a month. It took about two years to bring him to the point where he felt he was progressing. Just after the stroke, his speech was slurred and his vision was bad. He couldn't even read. He is much better today, but still has some problems that can be traced to the stroke.

Recently, Bruce and Barbara moved to the eastern part of North Carolina. Bruce loves to fish and they have a boat.

Johnston, Earl

Earl was a local boy who attended Andrew Lewis High School in Salem. Until his senior year at Lewis, he didn't compete in track. But in his final year before coming to Roanoke, he did high jump a few times, using the old Eastern roll, and ran the high and low hurdles. He doesn't remember scoring a single point for the team; however, the competition did whet his appetite for more participation in track.

Earl Johnston and wife Margaret Ann.

Earl was the only child in the family. For a number of years, his father managed Brown Hardware in downtown Salem, working for the Brown family. Earl grew up working in the hardware store, a job he now calls "my exposure to the real world."

Early on, Earl never thought about going to college. Around the middle of his senior year in high school, he considered briefly enrolling at Virginia Military Institute. To this day, he doesn't know why V. M. I. was a favorite. Then, he talked with Happy Mann. Mann was Clarence Caldwell's predecessor in the finance department at Roanoke College. Today, he thinks he chose Roanoke more because of Happy Mann than anyone else. He has never regretted his choice. "My stay at Roanoke was a wonderful experience," he says. "I wasn't a strong student, and many people at Roanoke helped me to graduate. I definitely benefited from being in a small school. I needed that support and attention. Even Coach Bast looked after me, getting me out of bed one morning at the Kappa Alpha house so I wouldn't be late (again) for my morning class."

Earl enjoyed a fine track career at Roanoke. He and Dave Foltz ran the high hurdles together, although he didn't feel that he was very successful in the lows because he never really liked the race. Occasionally, he ran the 440, but "not in a particularly good time."

Earl's form in the high hurdles improved over his first three years. But his major competitor on the team, Foltz, was one of the best hurdlers in the state. "He was just too strong for me," Earl admits. "One time I got to about the seventh hurdle in an outdoor high hurdles race and I had the lead on him. It was really a nice lead. It was one of those days when everything was working well for me. I was flowing–just cruising. Then I nipped the next hurdle and that took me out of the race. Dave flew by me to win."

During his track career, Earl primarily considered himself to be a hurdler. He often high jumped for the team, and even broad jumped a few times, but the hurdles were his first love. He thinks that many of his times in the high hurdles were good. In fact, although his time generally wasn't recorded when he didn't finish first, he believes those second-place times may have set either school or field records. In addition, he notes, there were seldom more than three timers and, unlike today, timing was done by hand. Individual times often were suspect.

Earl was on the Homer Bast track teams which were beginning to get stronger each year. After an early-season defeat by Davidson College in 1953, for example, they went 36 straight dual and triangular meets without a loss. He particularly remembers two of the athletes who contributed to the teams' success. Dave Foltz was one. "Lots of people thought Dave was arrogant, self-centered, and not a team person," Earl said. "But there was no doubt that he was a tremendous athlete with the build of a football player. With his physical attributes, he would have been good in any sport. Personally, I believe he could have been a tremendous decathlete–just like Dick Emberger was after leaving Roanoke following the 1959-60 season."

Another person Earl remembers well is Boyd Carr. "You know," he said, "there is one person who doesn't get the credit he deserves. That's Boyd Carr. He was one of my favorite track men. And he was an interesting person. If he had stayed at Roanoke instead of transferring to the University of Virginia after his sophomore year, he would have been remembered as one of the all-time great Roanoke stars. I remember that when he was at Roanoke, Boyd would draw cartoons and caricatures. I remember that on one of our track trips, he used the back of a pizza box to draw a caricature of each person in the car. He could do quality work. He was a big, likeable person–just a good guy."

In indoor and outdoor track, Earl was never the top athlete on the team, but was always a contributor to the team's success. During his indoor seasons, he ran :09.4 in the high hurdles and :08.4 in the lows. Outdoors, his best recorded high hurdles time was :16.2 (although he likely ran under :16.0 seconds on some occasions but finished out of first place and had no time recorded). His best time in the low hurdles is listed at :26.9.

Besides participating in track, Earl was a member of the Kappa Alpha fraternity and was elected their number two official. Mac Minnick, the fraternity's number one at the time, was a good friend and the two had grown up together in Salem.

Earl lived at home his first two years, because it was less expensive for him to go to college, and then moved to the campus and into the Kappa Alpha house. The house was located on High Street at the time. During the first part of his senior year, he began to have some eye problems. In fact, he lost part of the vision in his right eye, probably due to an infection. The condition bothered him so much that, just before the outdoor season in the 1954-55 session, he was forced to drop out of school altogether. He finally did return to Roanoke and graduated in 1956.

One day, while he was in the V. M. I. field house, he met his future wife–Margaret Ann Smith. She had come down from Madison College (later renamed James Madison University) with a group of girls. "I asked another girl for a date," Earl notes, "but she turned me down. So Margaret Ann became my substitute date. And the rest was history. I guess you could say that I owe my marriage to the track program at V. M. I. We got married in 1958, although we had met for the first time around 1953."

After graduating from Roanoke with an economics degree, Earl began what was to be a very successful career. He got into banking in 1957 after working with his dad for a couple of years. Eventually, he became President of a bank in Tappahannock, Virginia, during the last 15 years before he retired. His experiences in banking were varied, and he did a lot of civic work along the way–concentrating his energies in the hospital and health care areas.

The marriage to Margaret Ann brought three children, all boys. Tragically, he and his wife had a fire in their home in March of 1973 and lost the two younger boys in that fire. They were just 9 and 11 at the time. "I will never forget the compassion shown to us by Homer Bast," Earl says. "My wife and I were just coming away from the graveside service in Salem when we looked up and saw Homer. There he stood with his arms open. And he gave me a big hug. I'll never forget that memory."

More tragedy came a few years later. The oldest of their three boys had gone on to graduate from the University of Virginia; however, in 1991, at the young age of 31, he also died.

Today, with his home in Culpeper, Virginia, Earl is enjoying his retirement. He participates in a senior golf group, which gives him and his wife an excuse for a bit of traveling. They went to Panama in February of 2007, saw the Canal, and played some golf. They have also been on golfing trips in Costa Rica, the Dominican Republic, and Prince Edward Island, among other places. Once, Earl even got a chance to play St. Andrews in Scotland and some of the other famous courses in that part of the world. "I'd love to go back to St. Andrews," he says, "but they don't allow any carts to be used. Unfortunately, at my age, I couldn't walk those courses anymore."

Lewis, Dick

Dick Lewis and wife, Margie.

Dick Lewis was one of the best athletes Homer Bast coached during the 1950s. He was born in Changewater, New Jersey, which is in the western part of the state. He was about nine years old when his family moved to Cranford, New Jersey, where he later went to Cranford High School.

His mother, Frances, worked in the Cranford School System as a secretary. Floyd, Dick's father, was a maintenance supervisor and foreman for Redline. Dick had two brothers and one sister. The oldest was Russell, who is six years older than Dick. He now lives in California. The next oldest was a sister, Elaine, who lives near Philadelphia today. The youngest sibling by six years, Don, went to Rensselaer. He finally owned his own business and is retired.

In high school Dick played football and ran track. His athletic strengths, however, were in track. He was always fast. Beginning with the second half of the ninth grade, his coach had him running 440s occasionally, but he was a better 880 man. He had just won the 880 in the New Jersey state meet, and he was beginning to be known as a rising star. His coach, Seth Weekly, in fact told him that he would like to see Dick in the Olympics one day.

From the first, he wanted to go to a small school, and Roanoke was on his list. He applied to Roanoke and was given a partial scholarship. Homer Bast also contacted him, inviting him to come down and look at the College. So he paid the campus a visit and fell in love with the area. He had never been to Virginia before. And he also liked the small-school atmosphere. He chose Roanoke.

The first weeks at the Salem school were interesting. He had cross country to keep him busy, but found his academic work to be a problem. He missed his home and his girl friend in New Jersey.

Dick didn't join a lot of campus activities, but he did become a Kappa Alpha brother and was a member of the Monogram Club. His life was filled with running and an ongoing battle to keep his head above water in his academic work.

He became good friends with Bob Palm, who would break all shot put records in indoor and outdoor track. Dick and Bob talked about leaving Roanoke after two years and transferring to an engineering school. Right at the end of his sophomore year, however, Bob, Dick, and others became involved in a panty raid in a girls' dormitory on campus. Bob and Dick had already been accepted to transfer to V. P. I.'s Department of Engineering the following fall. It was the night of the last exams. Their group came back from a Kappa Alpha party, headed for Hildreth Hall. On the way, they cut in behind the girls' dorm. Dick remembers that the dorm may have housed girls on one side and boys on the other. Each had its own entrance. The girls' dorm was under curfew when the group got there, and some of the girls were at open windows, yelling out to the people below, hanging their bras out the windows, and more. Dick, Bob, and others ended up getting in the dorm and partying. Nothing serious really happened, but Dick recalls that it was just the challenge of entering the girls' dorm after midnight that made them do it. By the next morning, someone had reported the boys to Dean Sutton's office.

Surprisingly, getting into this type of trouble didn't really bother Dick and Bob. They already had been accepted to Virginia Tech. What could Roanoke do to them? There were actually four guys involved that night, but Dick and Bob took the blame for the incident. So Don Sutton suspended the two for one semester. Still, they thought they were going to Virginia Tech, and weren't really bothered at Sutton's decision.

Then V. P. I. got word of the suspension. They rescinded their offer of admittance. And Bob and Dick saw that there was nothing to do but to stay out of school until the spring semester of the next year. Sutton forced them to write letters to the College, apologizing for their actions. And the Roanoke administration let them back in at mid-year. Soon, Dick and Bob forgot about their pursuit of an engineering degree. Dick changed to economics with a math minor. Later, he would go into the Marine Corps and never really used the degree.

To summarize Dick's college career, he entered in 1955 and was there for two years before the girls' dormitory event occurred. He then was out of school for a semester, coming back for the second semester of 1958. He changed degrees–meaning that he was required to take additional courses–and then stayed to graduate in 1960. Actually, he didn't get his degree until the end of the summer of 1960. He stayed around for one course, religion, taught by Guy Ritter. Religion in those days was a requirement for graduation.

The classmate who influenced Dick the most was Phil Shaw. Dick looked up to Phil, who was a couple of years ahead in school. They were competitors in track and cross country. When Phil graduated, he went into the Marine Corps. Then, when Dick left Roanoke, Phil talked him into joining him in the Marines just after finishing that last college course.

Dick went to Quantico as a "90-day wonder." In those days, the Marines were looking for pilots, and after taking a test he was picked for the program. Unfortunately, however, he never got his wings. He was in the flight school for 18 months and was in the final stages of helicopter training when the Marines told him that he took too many chances. They told him that he needed to clean up his act or leave the program. But Dick thought he was a good candidate and was a bit cocky. He was washed out of the helicopter program and went back to Quantico in Officer Candidates School to become an infantry officer. He quickly got into the amphibious side of training and over the next few years became an amphibious expert.

He got on the first ship that was designated for amphibious work–the U. S. S. Mount Whitney. Then he spent a little more than a year in Vietnam (all of 1968 and the first half of 1969), and by that time he was a Captain. He picked up a bad case of malaria after about four months in the field and by the time he got out of the hospital in Guam, someone else had taken command of his ship. The Marines tried to keep him at Okinawa; instead, he was placed back aboard a ship as the Intelligence Officer. By that time, he was also an aerial observer. In that job, you call in naval gunfire. The Antietam was out there at the time. It was a ship that had 16" guns. In 1968, Dick was one of the observers who brought that ship in and directed its guns to fire into the Cason area.

Most of his career in the Marines after 1968 was spent in the Norfolk area. Sometimes he was on a ship and sometimes not. His position varied from being Senior Operations Officer to serving as an instructor for amphibious operations.

As far as Dick's family life was concerned, he married a girl from the Roanoke area, Sandra, who had attended Jefferson High School. The wedding took place in 1961. Their first child, Steven, was born soon after their marriage. Steven began to have grand mal seizures at five months of age. Today, he still has an average of four seizures a month. Being mentally retarded and epileptic, Steven eventually was placed in a special school in New Jersey. He had been there in a developmental center ever since. According to Dick, "Steven is a beautiful kid today."

The second child was Mark, who was born about a year and a half after Steven. He later graduated from Old Dominion University. Living in Denver, Colorado, he is an environmentalist. He started his own handyman business several years ago.

Dick and his wife Sandra were divorced in 1985. A year later, Dick met Margie–from Tarboro, North Carolina–and the two were married in December of 1986. They are together today after some 21 years of marriage.

In all, Dick stayed in the Marine Corps for 26 years, finally retiring in 1986. He was given the rank of Major early in his career, and when he was in Vietnam, became a Senior Captain. Later, before his retirement, he became a Colonel. Because he wanted to be near his son, Steven, he passed up a couple of opportunities for command.

After retiring from the Marine Corps, he realized that he had always wanted to be a Civil Engineer. In addition, he loved the outdoors. So he decided to take a job working for a small construction outfit, beginning as a project supervisor and ramrod. He worked in that job for almost 15 years and really enjoyed his work.

Finally, on September 15, 2001, he retired officially. For a while, he played golf and ran. Today, however, his back and knees won't allow him to run anymore. Now he substitutes cycling for running. He also enjoys hunting and fishing, and so does his wife.

In 1997, Dick and Margie bought some property near Farmville, Virginia, as their getaway and hunting property. They go to the property often for deer, turkey, and squirrel hunting. "Actually," Dick laughs, "we look at deer more than shooting them." Margie actually is a better hunter than Dick, recently getting a nice eight pointer for their wall.

They also have a number of relatives who enjoy visiting them at their getaway. They spend a lot of time with Margie's family, entertaining her son, his wife, and the family dog.

In 2007, the Lewis' bought an RV. It is a Phoenix Cruiser with two slide outs and a 450 diesel engine. Sometimes, they take the RV down to the Eastern Shore area with Margie's family. They tow a four-wheel drive with behind the RV. The four-wheel vehicle allows them to get out on the beach and do some surf fishing.

They used to own a time share in Nassau, but eventually traded it for one in Williamsburg, Virginia. The Williamsburg facility was more convenient for the family.

Today, Dick enjoys talking about the old days at Roanoke, and about the students and faculty members that he grew to know so well. When he got to Salem, he ran cross country that fall–but he really didn't want to. Homer Bast, however, convinced him that cross country would build up his stamina. "Actually," he says now, "I never did as well in the 880 in college as I did in high school. In high school, when I won the state championship, I ran a time of 1:56.8."

Actually, Dick turned out to be a good cross country runner. During his freshman year, the team lost a couple of meets by just a few points; otherwise, they did well. They won the Little Eight and Mason-Dixon Conference meets. In outdoor track, the mile relay team went to the Penn Relays and finished third. In 1958, during the year he came back to school from his suspension, his mile relay team actually won the event in the Penn Relays.

Dick ran cross country during his freshman and sophomore years, and ran indoor and outdoor track all four years he was eligible at Roanoke. He even won the 880 indoors early in his career. He notes, however, that he probably never reached his potential. "I don't think I came close to running to my ability. In some ways, I disappointed myself, probably Homer, and my high school coach, Seth Weekly. Part of my problem, of course, is that when I got to Roanoke College, I became heavily involved in fraternity life. Somewhere in my college career, I just lost that competitive drive–the drive to excel."

Before entering Roanoke, Dick had gone with one girl for four straight years. They considered themselves to be soul mates. Unfortunately, she got killed in a car wreck right after she graduated from college, during the same summer Dick graduated from Roanoke. "When we were in high school," he says, "a lot of what I did in running, I did for her. I excelled just to impress her. I didn't want to let her or my coach down. At one point, she and I had planned to get married some day. After I got to college, I just lost a lot of that drive."

Dick has seldom been back to the College campus since he left in 1960. But he does remember and appreciate the work that Homer Bast did in those days as coach. "He was someone very similar to my high school coach," Dick said. "He was a person you wanted to do well for. You always wanted to do your best when he was around. After my first two years, I think I felt a bit guilty at letting him down. He was such a good motivator and, in addition, a guy you just loved. He never screamed at any member of the team. He never cursed. He never played favorites. I thought he was a master of psychology."

Dick still remembers many of his teammates. George Gearhart, for example, was a great sprinter for Roanoke. "Of course," Dick says, "he was susceptible to being hypnotized. Once there was a show featuring a hypnotist that came to town. Many of us went down to the old Salem Theater to see it. The fellow ended up hypnotizing George, and it took him days to get over it."

Dick also remembers the talented Dave Foltz. "We called him a pretty boy," Dick said. "He even bleached his hair. He was a little cocky at times, coming across like a spoiled movie star. But he was one of the most talented athletes I ever saw."

And then there was Pete Wise. "He was also one of the pretty boys of the team," said Dick. "We were good friends, but had a lot of head-to-head races. We both liked to work out with weights. We believed in being strong runners. To this day, I think that cross country just tears you down."

Others he remembers well are Bruce Johnston, Howard Light, Bob Palm, and Jim O'Mahony. Dick, Bob, and Jim were particularly good friends.

Light, Howard

Howard Light, one of Roanoke's best quarter milers during the Bast tenure as coach, was also an excellent athlete in high school. He attended Roanoke City's Jefferson High School. His main sport was football, and he was quite a talented quarterback for the Magicians even though his playing weight was only about 155 pounds. He also played halfback, fullback, and even linebacker at times.

There was no track program when he first arrived at Jefferson. Coach Rudy Rohrdance, the football coach, told the boys that the school was going to field either a baseball team or a track team that Spring. He let the boys vote on which sport they wanted. No one ever saw the results of that vote, but Rohrdance was a former track man,

Howard Light and his wife, Shirley.

so the track program was begun.

Rohrdance took the new track team over to Highland Park one day and announced that the team needed some quarter milers. Howard asked what a quarter miler did. Rohrdance told him that it was just once around the track. Howard thought this race would be a snap, so he volunteered. Several days later, the team went to Roanoke College to practice. It was the first time that Howard or any of his teammates had ever run a quarter. "I thought I was going to die," Howard said. "I was so sick after that practice that I couldn't see straight."

As his senior year progressed, he began to get offers from Virginia colleges to play football. In fact, he had offers to play at Virginia, V. M. I., and Washington and Lee. Washington and Lee probably would have been his choice.

He was working at Burlington MillS in Vinton and came home one day to find Bob McLelland, locally-famous sports writer for the *Roanoke World-News,* sitting in his front yard talking to Howard's father. Bob said, "Get dressed. We're going to see Coach Bast at Roanoke College." Howard explained to Bob that he didn't have any money to pay his way at Roanoke. Bob said, "No one said anything about money." So the two of them drove over to Salem to see Coach Bast. Howard and Bast knew each other well because the Jefferson team had used the Roanoke track so much for meets and practices. Homer said, "Howard, why don't you come up to the college and be a part of our track team?" Howard said, "Coach, I just don't have any money." And Coach Bast said, "We never said anything about money. You let me work on that for you."

So Howard Light made the decision to attend Roanoke College. In hindsight, Howard said recently, it was one of the best decisions he ever made.

Homer and the College did, indeed, take care of Howard's financial needs. Most of his tuition, books, and fees were paid for by the College. For the four years he was at Roanoke, he lived at home. To help with incidental expenses, Howard occasionally worked at the Optimist Club.

Unfortunately, Howard struggled a bit academically during his freshman year in 1954-55. He wasn't prepared to go to college. He had taken trade school courses all through high school. But Coach Bast helped in small ways. For example, he created Howard's first schedules of classes. Howard remembers him saying, "We don't want to take too much the first year, now." And he put Howard in his history class so he could watch and guide his progress.

Not many people know this fact, but when Howard first got to Roanoke, he almost dropped out of school. He went home and told his mother that he wasn't going back. She said, "Howard, you've gone this far, and you're the only one of five brothers who has gone to college. You're going back." So he did, and never regretted the decision. "Coach Bast really helped me get through some of the hard times," Howard remembers. "If it hadn't been for him, I never would have stayed in school. I would have been working at some mill in the area."

Howard went on to become one of Homer Bast's finest athletes during his career from 1954-55 through 1957-58. In the spring of 1957-58, he became the first College quarter-miler to dip below :50.0 (:49.9) in a race. That record held for one more year until Pete Wise ran a :49.7. Howard also ran at least eight more races with times ranging from :50.0 to :51.0.

Perhaps the performance he remembers best today is the mile relay at the Penn Relays during his senior year. "We were all scared to death," he said. "Here we were, a small college, trying to run against some of the best teams in the country. I had never seen such a meet. They had you so well organized with chutes and everything to keep you where they wanted you before you came on the track. Finally, we got on the track for the race. Dick Engle led us off, and I ran second. Dick Lewis took the third leg, and our anchor man was freshman George Bopp. When George took the baton, he was behind the lead runner by several yards. And he took off. I don't know what his splits were for the quarter, but he did a great job and crossed the line well ahead of the second place team. We were stunned. We had won the mile relay at the great Penn Relays."

One of Howard's best friends was teammate Bruce Johnston. They had been terrific athletes together at Jefferson High School, and both enrolled at Roanoke in 1954-55. Bruce early on concentrated on the high and low hurdles, but by his senior year was also running excellent 100 and 220 times. The two were Co-Captains of the track team during their senior year at Roanoke. And the friendship continued for years after college. Bruce, for example, was the best man at Howard's wedding.

Howard and Shirley Blackstock met in high school, and were married during Howard's last year in college. "My marriage to Shirley was another one of the best things that ever happened to me," Howard admits. Shirley and Howard had three children–two daughters and one son. One of the daughters lives in Roanoke, while the other is in Charlottesville. One is an attorney and the other is a Vice President for Shenandoah Life. His son is in construction. Howard laughs when he admits that all three are making more money that he ever did.

After Howard left Roanoke College, he went down to the University of North

Carolina in Chapel Hill to work toward his Master's Degree. He spent a year there, and then received a Master's Degree in Physical Education. At that point, he accepted a teaching job in the Roanoke City Public School System. He initially was scheduled to go to Monroe Junior High to teach; however, the wrestling coach at Jefferson High School left his job suddenly. So the administration asked Howard if he would come to Jefferson to teach and coach. They also told him that one of the sports he had to coach was wrestling–an activity he knew nothing about. But he muddled through the year, coaching track, football, and wrestling.

Howard stayed at Jefferson until a new city high school, Patrick Henry, opened in 1961. He stayed at Patrick Henry through 1966, when he went to Jackson Junior High School as Assistant Principal for a little more than a year.

The administration then moved him to the central office, which is where he remained until his retirement. At first, he was Supervisor of Boys' Athletics and Health and Physical Education and Driver Education. Finally, he took over both the boys' and girls' programs, after which he retired in 2000 from the Roanoke City Public School System.

Light, Warren

The son of Stephen and Helene Light, Warren and his brother, Larry, were reared in Baldwin, New York. Warren attended Baldwin High School, participating in cross country, basketball, and track.

When it came time for Warren to choose a college, he heard of Roanoke. It was a small school and he liked the fact that Roanoke was affiliated with the Lutheran Church. He and his family were Lutherans. In addition, he wanted to participate in sports while in college and he felt that Roanoke had the type of athletic program that wouldn't overwhelm him.

Warren Light and his wife, Judith, on their 2007 trip to Hawaii.

Homer Bast, seeing from Warren's application that he was enrolling at Roanoke, and knowing that he had been involved with cross country and track, wrote a letter encouraging Warren to get into shape for the coming fall season, and welcomed him to the distance team.

So in 1955, Warren came to Roanoke. He found the campus, the students, and his teachers to be just what he was looking for. He did have some physical problems, however, during that first season of cross country. He was plagued by side stitches. He and Coach Bast looked at all kinds of possible solutions–from changes in diet to new breathing techniques. Nothing seemed to work. "Every now and then," Warren remembers, "I would be in the middle of a race and doing very well, and this problem would hit and practically double me over. Later in life, when I was coaching high school runners, I even heard of another solution–pinching your upper lip. Another technique was to belly breathe. But for me, in my freshman year, no solution seemed to work. As a result, I was happy with most of my results that fall, but I always felt that I could have been better."

There was definitely one good thing about his experiences in cross country and track. He had joined teams that were getting better and better. He was able to run with terrific runners such as Howard Meincke, Dick Goodlake, George Jocher, Dick Lewis, and many others who were the best in the Little Eight and Mason-Dixon Conferences. "And you can't believe," said Warren, "how much of a close-knit group we were. There was such camaraderie that it was unbelievable. And we were very good as a team. There were times in cross country, for example, when we were strong enough so that Coach Bast actually could split the team, holding two meets simultaneously."

In cross country, Warren typically placed in the top five on his own team and often wasn't far behind the leaders. He finished 10th in the large Mason-Dixon Championships his freshman year, third in the Little Eight meet his sophomore year, and that same year was 10th in the Mason-Dixon meet. In 1956, he finished 39th in the first NAIA Cross-Country Championships in Omaha, Nebraska, on a bitterly cold day. In his junior year of cross country, he was eighth in the Little Eight meet and 12th in the Mason-Dixon meet.

All of these accomplishments came with physical problems. During his sophomore and junior years, he picked up some bad shin splints. They were so bad that even the sheets on his bed would hurt him.

In outdoor track, Warren had his best year in 1957. He ran a 4:31.6 and a 4:34.5 in the mile that year, and also had times of 10:04.6 and 10:07.2 in two-mile races.

In campus activities, Warren was a member of Kappa Alpha. In fact, he was their #9 at one point. One year, he was President of the Monogram Club. He also worked for spending money. He was the "milk man" in the Commons, taking care of the milk machines, and also washed team uniforms.

His major was Biology. As he said recently, "I just loved the subject. I had had great biology teachers in high school." When he graduated in 1959, therefore, he took a job teaching biology at the high school level in Babylon, New York. It was a small school and because of its size, Warren got a chance to teach everything from Life Science for seventh graders all the way up to Advanced Placement biology for seniors. It was a job in which he spent 33 years of his teaching career, all at the same school.

In addition to his teaching responsibilities, Warren also coached cross country and track. He was Head Cross Country Coach for 28 years. He was also an assistant track coach. In basketball, he served as a junior varsity and junior high school coach.

In 1965, Warren and Judith Fiedler were married. He met Judith on the first day of teacher's meetings in 1964. He had been teaching at Babylon since 1960. A year later, they held their wedding. From the marriage came one daughter, Christina, who began her work career as a teacher. After beginning her own family, however, she dropped teaching and became a stay-at-home mom. Later, Christina resumed work in education as a first-grade teacher.

Judith also gave birth to another daughter, Catherine. Unfortunately, Catherine died at age five from leukemia. It was a very traumatic time for both Judith and Warren.

Today, the Lights have two grandchildren–both boys–including Justin, age six, and Nelson, three. They live only about 10 miles away from Warren and Judith, "and my wife and I," Warren notes, "have spoiled them to death.

Judith retired about two years ago, while Warren retired some 15 years ago. For hobbies, Warren tries to play a lot of golf and tennis. "Tell Homer," he said, "that I have tried to live my life the way he taught us to. I am still running. In fact, I am in a 5K race tomorrow morning. I'm hoping to win my age group. Thankfully, I have been fairly successful in age-group running."

Moore, David

David Moore was born in Salem. His dad owned the Moore Milling Company, the largest private employer in town. The company produced flour, seed, livestock foods, and corn meal. It was located in the western part of Salem and employed about 150 workers.

He grew up with his mother and father, Bernice and Munsey, along with four additional boys. Drew was the oldest, followed by Tony, David, John Paul, and Munsey.

David attended Andrew Lewis High School through his eighth grade year. Tragically, during the year when he became an eighth grader, his father's business burned down. There was about $100,000 in insurance to cover the building, but it would have taken $1,000,000 to replace it. In despair, David's father killed himself about seven or eight months after the fire. Not long after his death, David's mother also committed suicide.

The three oldest boys, including David, then went to live with their grandfather, Drewry Moore, in Salem. John Paul went to live with a cousin in Salem, and Muncey went to Chase City, Virginia, being adopted by an aunt and uncle.

After a half year at Andrew Lewis, David and his two older brothers transferred to

Randolph-Macon Academy in 1949 at the suggestion of the family's new pastor at the First Methodist Church in Salem. At R. M. A., a Methodist boarding school, David spent four and a half years. He played varsity basketball, but didn't participate in track even though the school had a good track program. He didn't think he was good enough to make the team.

David Moore and wife, Betty, in 2008.

Fortunately, David had the economic resources to go to college. His parents left the children in good financial shape when they died. He always wanted to go to college, and was accepted at V. P. I. in Blacksburg. But in the summer of 1953, before the college year began, his brother, John Paul, decided to come live with David's grandfather. His grandfather was in his 90s at the time. So David made the decision to stay near home and to attend Roanoke College.

He contacted Al Bowman, a banker in Salem, and told him that he wanted to attend Roanoke. David knew that Roanoke might not accept him because it was very close to the start of the fall classes. So Bowman called the Admissions Office at Roanoke and argued David's case. The next day, Bowman told him that he was accepted. What David didn't realize was that Mr. Bowman was on the Board of Trustees at the College.

David entered the 1953-54 freshman class at Roanoke, graduating four years later in 1957. He ran cross country during that first year, but knew that he didn't have much talent for distance running. He did realize, however, that the team had some good runners. "We had some interesting people on that team," he said. "Les Noel, for example, wasn't a big guy, but he was a tremendous runner. Les was always number one or two in our meets–and maybe the best in all of the Virginia small colleges. And there was Bennie Irvine, a day student from Roanoke. He was also a good runner." David ran that year at the invitation of Homer Bast. "He was just such a great guy, and he took a personal interest in me," David remembers. "But he trained us with the Fartlek system, which got us into very good shape. I still use the training system today in my bicycling program." Although he didn't run cross country during the next three years, David did want to do something in athletics, although he never imagined that he would ever earn a letter in any college sport.

So he joined Homer Bast's track team, and decided to try pole vaulting. In those days, you could win points for the team if you could vault 10'6" or more. With effort, he managed to get to the point where he could clear 11' and sometimes went higher. "I really wasn't a very talented guy in sports," David points out. "Homer taught me from ground zero how to pole vault. I didn't know a thing about the event. At the time, we had these bamboo poles, although a lot of the teams we competed against were using the newer Swedish steel poles. Homer kept promising us that he would buy us a Swedish pole, and I think in my second year of vaulting, he finally was able to get us one of the poles. Homer told me to hang a rope from a tree limb at home so I could swing up on it and pull myself up, similar to what I would do on a pole. So I fixed me up a rope at my grandfather's house."

David had told Homer up front that he wasn't very talented in sports. But Homer responded that being talented wasn't that important. He just kept working with David, building up his strength and skill in the pole vault.

Homer, of course, knew about David's home situation primarily through an uncle and aunt who lived near Homer in west Salem. Because Homer knew what David had endured, David thinks that may have been why his coach always kept an eye out for him. He took his freshman history course from Homer. "He certainly made you study," David said, "but he was also a great lecturer."

During the summers, David worked to keep his car going. In the summer before he entered the College, he worked for the Town of Salem, helping to lay sidewalks. In fact, his crew of workers laid the sidewalks on College Avenue near the town entrance to the campus. Homer would come by occasionally on his way to town. One day, David approached him and introduced himself as someone who would be coming to Roanoke in September. Homer reciprocated by inviting him to come out for cross country and track. After that day, Homer would always speak to David as he walked by on the way to town.

David continued to work during each of the summer breaks. Between his freshman and sophomore years, he again was employed by the Town of Salem. During his junior and senior years, he took on what almost amounted to a full-time job, and the work schedule ended his athletic career following the sophomore year.

Throughout his stay at Roanoke, most of David's teammates were members of the Kappa Alpha fraternity. David chose to be a member of Sigma Chi, so he feels even today that he didn't become very close friends with many on the team. He says that the reason he initially chose the Sigma Chi fraternity was because of fellow student and teammate Wylie Barrow. Wylie had attended Randolph-Macon Academy. Wylie's father was a Sig at Roanoke, and it was understood that Wylie would be a Sig when he got there. So soon after his freshman year, David was "dragged along" to the Sig house by Wilie. Wylie stayed at Roanoke for two years. He then transferred to Virginia Tech for their engineering program.

David and Betty Moore, a graduate in 1953 from Jefferson High School, were married at the beginning of his senior year. They rented a small apartment on the corner of Main and Academy Streets. Their oldest child, born in 1958, was David. The next oldest was Lewis, born in 1961. The third and final child, also a boy, was Bryan (1965). All three of the boys are still living. David graduated from James Madison University and is a banker. He is married with one child. Lewis went to Elon College, although he never graduated. Today, he is in business for himself as a constructor of homes and home additions. Bryan graduated from Radford University and is in public relations. Today, he is with the Newport News Shipbuilding and Drydock as their special events coordinator.

David graduated from Roanoke in 1957 with a degree in Economics and Business Administration, going directly into the Navy. He had encountered some problems with his blood pressure, however, and didn't know if the Navy would take him. Finally, after a trip to Richmond to the Regional Recruiting Center for evaluation by a Navy Commander doctor on Broad Street, David was accepted into the service. In 1957 the Navy sent him to New London, Connecticut, to serve on a submarine rescue ship. At the time, Betty taught school at South Salem Elementary School.

Aboard the ship, he was a Supply Officer, a Communications Officer, and also held several other jobs as an ensign. As it turned out, he went on to spend 20 years with the Navy, rising to the rank of Commander when he left the Navy in 1977 to go into business. He bought a bicycle shop and sporting goods business in Virginia Beach and enjoyed the work. While in the Navy, he had gotten a Master's Degree in International Relations through George Washington University.

One day, a man walked into his shop. He had been in the Navy with David. He asked why in the world David was in this particular business, especially after he had gotten a Master's in International Relations. David, who enjoyed the irony, joked that he was working on Japanese bicycles.

David owned the shop for about seven years and sold out in 1984 when someone offered a good price. He then went to work for Randolph-Macon Academy in fund raising for a few years. He ran the Academy's Capital Campaign, helping them raise several million dollars for a new building.

He came back to Virginia Beach in 1987 and became a manufacturer's representative for a medical company until about 1993. The job dealt with all kinds of handicapped equipment with Electric Mobility in New Jersey. He demonstrated the equipment in homes and business, and to doctors.

At that point, in 1995, David bought some real estate, going into partnership with his banker son. They bought some rental property, fixing up those properties and renting them out. In 2007, he and his son split their properties and David gave his properties in Virginia Beach to Randolph-Macon Academy in a charitable trust. R. M. A. then sold them and took the money. It was at that point that David finally retired.

During the past few years, David has had atrial defibrillation, although he still feels good. After his wife joined a local health club, David also joined. In December of 2007, he was working out on a step machine. His heart rate went from 68 to 150. The guy in charge of the exercise facility, a physiologist, warned him that his heart rate shouldn't be that high. So he gave David a total of three EKG exams right there in the health club. He told David that he probably had atrial defibrillation, and sent him immediately to the emergency room. The emergency room doctors agreed with the diagnosis and gave him some medicine to get his heart back into sync. Today, he is on a low-fat, low-cholesterol, no-salt-added diet. And he eats plenty of fruits and vegetables. Fortunately, he never smoked during his life, and seldom had any alcohol except for an occasional glass of wine.

One of his major projects today is helping to run a bicycle ministry at his church, the Virginia Beach United Methodist Church. It was a program initiated by his pastor. The project ministers to those who do not have adequate transportation, and the church gives out about 300 bicycles a year. There is a bicycle workshop at the church.

David is an avid bird watcher, and often rides his bicycle. He goes down to Emporia each year to attend the Great Peanut Ride with some 1,500 other riders. They ride all through the countryside near Emporia.

He also is an interdenominational Stephen Minister. Stephen Ministers supplement the work of the minister in churches, visiting people in the hospital or after they have returned home. A Stephen Minister is a lay person who meets with surviving spouses once a week, or there may be other calls for his service. Churches give Stephen Ministers the names of people to visit. To be a part of this ministry, one goes through some 50 hours of intensive training. At this point, David himself is qualified to conduct this training. At his church, there are some 30 Stephen Ministers, some of whom being used to help those, on a one-on-one basis, to cope with a recent divorce.

David also keeps busy with his Rotary Club. He has been a Rotarian for some 17 years. Within the organization, David has held many offices, including President. He is also the group's fund raiser, having recently secured some $25,000 for their projects.

He also serves these days as a Trustee for R. M. A. That Board meets three or four times a year.

Nichols, Jim

At Jefferson High School in Roanoke, Jim participated in football and track. The coach for both sports was the highly successful Rudy Rohrdance. In track, Jim ran the sprints, broad jumped, and was a member of the relay teams. In the 220-yard dash in the large City-County Meet during his senior year, he pulled an upset by winning the 220 and the broad jump, and placing third in the 100.

Jim Nichols

At Roanoke, for the two years he competed, his main event was the long jump. He jumped 22'9", 21'6⅞", 21'4½", and 21'4" (twice), and went more than 21' two more times.

In 1953, during his junior year in high school, Jim's father was killed in a railroad accident. Throughout that year and most of the next, he had no plans to go to college. At the time, he had four sisters and two brothers. One day, his older sisters and brother sat him down and told him, "You're going to be the first from our family to go to college." Their mother had received a lump sum of money from the railroad for a settlement, and that's what the kids in the family used for college expenses.

When he reported to Roanoke for his freshman year, Coach Bast was able to get him a $250 Land Grant scholarship. But because he didn't have the math background to enter college, he had to go to summer school first. He took an entire year of geometry in six weeks, attending classes mornings and afternoons.

Jim's younger brother also attended Roanoke, and went on to Virginia Tech like Jim. He was two and one-half years in back of Jim.

Jim loved Roanoke College. It wasn't a big school, so everyone seemed to know everybody. Students were a diverse group. Most were from outside the Roanoke Valley.

He also had good experiences in track. "I remember a lot of the guys who were on the team when I was," he says. "My favorite was probably Dave Foltz. He took me under his wing when I got there. I think he was a senior when I was a freshman. He kept me straight. I remember that he lived in the basement of the gymnasium. Don D'Agostino was one of the people who roomed with him there. Dave taught me things like how to get out of the starting blocks quickly. He always gave track events his best effort. I think that when he went into the Marines, he set a Marine record for carrying a 50-pound backpack for 440 yards. He was a strong guy."

While at Roanoke, Jim wasn't involved in many campus activities outside of track except for the Monogram Club. But day students–living at home–often weren't.

Jim had many friends on the track team. He particularly remembers Jack Dempsey, another good broad jumper, and Dick Goodlake and Howard Meincke, both excellent middle-distance and distance runners. "Dick was a small guy," Jim says, "but he could run very well. And Meincke was great. I remember running down at V. M. I. in the mile relay. Howard was the anchor. One of the runners behind him stepped on his ankle, ripping his shoe off. He ran with that shoe off his foot for the rest of the event."

After two years at Roanoke, in a pre-engineering course, Jim transferred to Virginia Tech. He spent three years there, getting a degree in electrical engineering. Although he did very well in track during those years–participating in the 100, 220, broad jump, the hop-step-jump event, and some relays–he made a promise to himself that he would never stay up past 12:00 midnight studying. He thought that after midnight, studying was a waste of time. You were tired and needed the sleep. The track coach was Don Divers, the individual who took the job when Homer Bast turned it down.

"One meet at Tech that I remember well happened during my senior year," Jim said. "We were down at the Southern Conference meet at, I think, the Citadel. I hadn't done very well in the 100 and 220, so I was putting all of my efforts into the long jump. I jumped 22'8" and some kid from the Citadel came up and jumped 22'10½". I had one more jump. I got off a good jump, going 23'2½", and won the event. That wasn't the best jump of my career, however. My best jump was at the University of Virginia, where I jumped 24'0", but they called me on a foul. My coach said that I didn't scratch, but the official said I did. I ran :09.7 in the 100, and my best 220 time was :21.5. I got beat running that :09.7, however. The other team had a foreign student who ran the 100 in :09.5."

While at Virginia Tech, Jim married Nancy Garst. She subsequently gave birth to three boys, and the Nichols adopted a girl. The youngest boy is Berkley, a Major in the Air Force, who is scheduled to become a Lt. Colonel soon. He is an instructor pilot, and he and his wife have two children. The middle son is Timothy, who works in computers. He has three children. The oldest son is James, Jr., who works as a broker.

After leaving Virginia Tech, Jim went to work for the Boeing Company and moved from Roanoke to Seattle. He had interviewed with the company while at Tech. In Seattle, he worked on projects such as missile systems.

He left Seattle and went to Nebraska, where he helped put in 200 Minute Men missiles in Nebraska, Colorado, and Wyoming. Then he worked on the Apollo Space Program, which he thought was a great job. He worked there until 1973.

When the space program took a nose dive after America went to the moon, he moved to a job with the U. S. Postal Service in Memphis. He worked in design and construction, at first designing and building post offices. Then he became a contracting officer and did all the contracting for that.

He has been retired for seven to eight years and lives in Germantown, just east of

Memphis in Tennessee. He tries to play as much golf as possible these days and belongs to one of the local country clubs. He did have by-pass surgery not long ago and because he was in the hospital for six days, his play certainly slowed a bit. On the other hand, outside of minor bouts with arthritis, he has been fairly healthy.

Nilson, Bob

Bob and Doris Nilson

Bob was born in Washington, D. C., and lived in Alexandria, Virginia, for the first six years of his life. His family then relocated to Richmond, Virginia. His father, Ralph Nilson, worked for the Patent Office and because the government thought that Washington might be damaged during the war, it was decided to move certain technical jobs out of Washington to various places around the country. At the end of the war, the family moved back to Maryland.

Bob lived with his father, Ralph, and mother, Agnes, along with a brother. His brother, six years older than Bob, is deceased.

Living in Bethesda, Maryland, Bob attended Bethesda Chevy Chase High School. It was a fairly large school with a graduating class of more than 300. He never played sports at the school, although he was a swimmer during the summer at the local Y. M. C. A.

Bob admits to not being a strong student academically, but it was always assumed that he would attend college. His College Advisor at Bethesda Chevy Chase suggested that he apply to a small school. So the family selected six possible colleges for Bob to consider. He applied to each one and was accepted by five of the six, including Roanoke. Clarence Caldwell, Business Manager for Roanoke, also helped recruit students on occasion. Clarence showed up in Bethesda one weekend in the spring of 1953. His visit was a surprise to Bob. He called Bob's father and asked if he could come over. Mr. Nilson agreed to talk with him. Bob thinks today that they may have gotten together at the A & P grocery store where Bob had a part-time job. Everything went well during the meeting. Almost on the spot, Bob decided to attend Roanoke, even though he had previously thought he would go to Virginia Military Institute in Lexington. His father agreed that Roanoke would be a good choice.

Bob, without good high school grades, felt fortunate to be going to college at all. He thought, "This is my last chance."

He showed up at Roanoke site-unseen. As he said, "I was just a kid and didn't know what to expect. I was pretty immature at that time."

He enjoyed his two years in Salem. He made good grades–especially in his pre-engineering courses–and had no problem transferring to Virginia Tech. Ray Brown, head of the College's Pre-Engineering program, even awarded Bob the school's first award for the outstanding engineering student. When he transferred, as schools often did in those days, all of his good course grades automatically became Cs at Tech. That disappointed Bob, because all of his grades at Roanoke were As and Bs. Things turned out well at Virginia Tech, however, because all of his junior and senior grades were Bs or above.

While at Roanoke, Bob joined the Sigma Chi fraternity. During his freshman year, he lived in Hildreth hall near the gymnasium, rooming with Wylie Barrow. In that year, he didn't participate in track.

He lived in the Sigma Chi house his second year, rooming with three others, including Barrow. The house was located on Market Street at that time, down a bit from the track toward the middle of town, and housed a total of about 11 or 12 guys and a house mother. During this year, he and Barrow threw the shot and discus on Homer Bast's track team.

Bob stood about 6'1" tall and weighed about 195 pounds. Although he had no experience in outdoor track and field athletics, Bob was a strong athlete, throwing the shot 41'10¼" and 40'11½" his sophomore year. He also recorded the fourth-best discus throw while Homer Bast was coaching the track team. The distance, 126'1¼", barely missed the school record of 129'3" set in 1947.

Bob was scheduled to graduate with an Engineering Degree from Tech in June of 1957; however, because he needed one more course in order to graduate, he went to summer school and took a course in statistics. Because of the extension, his diploma actually is dated as 1958.

His first and only job during his long career was with the United States Patent Office. Although he also got offers from several companies, the Patent Office offered him a draft deferment. He was married at the time, so he thought the deferment would be a good deal. The job they were offering him was considered crucial to the national security. He became a Patent Examiner, a job that required an engineering or science degree.

He was married in December of 1956, just six or seven months before graduating at Tech. His new wife's name was Doris and he had met her on a blind date in Washington, D. C. At the time, he was still pals with Wylie Barrow, and they often ran around together. Wylie and Bob were home for the holidays when Wylie, who had a date, suggested that Bob go along with one of his date's girl friends, Doris. She was going to American University at the time, although she graduated later from another school.

Doris and Bob had two children. The oldest was Karin, born in 1959. The youngest, who was born in 1961, was Kathleen. Today, Karin lives in Frederick, Maryland, and has four children of her own–triplets and one more. Kathleen has three children herself and lives in Maryland near Baltimore.

During his years with the Patent Office, Bob began as a Patent Examiner. As he became more experienced, he ended up as a Primary Patent Examiner. During all of this time, he and Doris lived in Potomac, Maryland, and Rockville, Maryland. His specialty was in the area of fluid handling–any patents having to do with hydrolic, pneumatic servo systems, etc. He also handled certain medical devices having to do with control fluids.

Bob retired in January of 1996. Today, he enjoys playing golf and has a handicap of about 19. Doris just began playing the game this past year. Since 2005, their residence has been in The Villages, a retirement community in north central Florida. They live in a brick designer home with three bedrooms, a two-car garage, and even a golf cart garage. The community contains a number of golf courses and many swimming pools. There are a variety of activities that are planned each week for residents. Doris enjoys painting and volunteers in many local activities. She has sold some of her art work over the years, and enters many art shows.

Noel, Lessely

Lessely's son, Chris, his wife, Sherry, granddaughter Kay and grandson Tristan, JoAnn (Les's wife), Les Noel, and son Michael (white shirt).

When Les was just six months old, his father died. He grew up, as he puts it, "way back in the country." When he was 12 years old, he set out on his own, moving by himself to the little town of Buena Vista, Virginia. Buena Vista was about 60 miles from Salem, near Lexington, Virginia.

In Buena Vista, Les lived by himself in a single room, worked odd jobs, and attended school. He was a four-year athlete at Buena Vista High School, playing football, basketball, and baseball. The school had no track program. Most people considered him to be a good athlete despite the fact that he wasn't very big, weighing about 140-148 pounds at the time.

His high school Principal, a graduate of Roanoke College, suggested that Les attend Roanoke. Roanoke gave Les a small amount of scholarship money, but not much. To pay his way, he maintained three jobs on campus. He worked in the dining room all four years, he picked up the dry cleaning from students, and he worked for Professor Masters three nights a week. Masters had a small chemical plant in which he made soap for Roanoke businesses.

Les thoroughly enjoyed his early days at Roanoke. Instead of living by himself, he was surrounded by new friends.

Coach Bast had no idea that Les would become such a talented distance runner. In fact, it was when Les won the annual intramural cross country race that his running potential first showed. Coach Bast congratulated him at the end of the race and invited Les to come out for cross country and track and field athletics. He joined the cross country team right away.

His freshman year in cross country wasn't a spectacular one in terms of achievement, although he did manage a 20th place finish in the Mason-Dixon Meet. White Rhyne, then a senior, was the star of the team. He and Les ran fairly close together, at least at the first of the year. Of course, White had been a distance runner for several years and it was all new for Les.

During his sophomore, junior, and senior years, however, Les became one of the best cross country runners in Virginia. As a sophomore, he won three of three dual meets and finished 4th in the State A. A. U. meet, 1st in the Little Six Championships, and 11th in the Mason-Dixon meet. While a junior, he won four of the four dual- and tri-meet events he ran, finished second in the A. A. U. meet, won the Little Six Championships, and was 1st in the Mason-Dixon meet. Finally, as a senior, he won five dual meets and was second in another. He also became the Little Seven champion and finished 2nd in the Mason-Dixon race.

Indoors, he ran a 4:30.5 mile and a 10:22.0 two-mile. He also ran on Roanoke's sprint medley, distance medley, and two-mile relay teams.

Les admits today that he really liked outdoor track more than indoor track. "Our problem," he said, "was with practice facilities. In the coldest of weather, we were practicing outdoors. It was pretty tough."

After a fairly uneventful freshman year outdoors, Les became one of the conference's premier runners. In his sophomore season, he won both the mile and two-mile races in the Little Seven meet. As a junior, he took first place in the two-mile run at the Little Seven and Mason-Dixon meets. And as a senior, he was first in the Little Seven mile run.

His best times over his career at Roanoke were: 2:02.5 for the 880, 4:30.6 for the mile run, and 10:08.9 for the two-mile run. All were good times for the early 1950s.

In 1955, Les graduated from Roanoke College and joined the Marine Corps. That gave him a chance to improve his skills in running. In the service, he began to run with some high-power athletes. In fact, he made the Marine Corps track team, one of the best track teams in the country. He was able to run with the United States' best miler, Wes Santee, and Les learned a lot from him about distance running. Sometimes, Les would pace Wes as he tried to break the four-minute mile.

Les brought Santee to Roanoke College one time and Dick Goodlake, Santee, and Noel ran with him in a mile exhibition. Noel paced him for three quarters. He was so tired at that point that he dropped out of the race, but Santee just kept going.

At Quantico, Santee and Noel practiced together many times, especially in cross country. The Quantico Marines had the best team in the country. In track, Noel's team even beat Villanova by a point at a time when Villanova was considered the best track team in the United States.

Les stayed in the Marine Corps for almost four years. When he left the Marines, he held the rank of Captain. Later, while in the Marine Reserves, he became a Major. He stayed in the Reserves for some 14 years, getting out only because he was living in Maryland and his meetings were in Washington once a week. His personal life was also fairly busy at the time as he and his wife were starting their family.

Les married Jo Ann Deke in 1960. They are still married today. Jo Ann and Les had two children, both boys. Chris now lives in Greenville, South Carolina, and works as a dental specialist in root canal surgery. The other son works for a company in Gainesville, Georgia.

After leaving the Marines, Les went to work for Traveler's Insurance Corporation in management. Today, the business is called CitiGroup. He stayed with that company for 34 years, mostly as a Financial Services Manager. Jo Ann and Les have lived in Miami, Baltimore, and Atlanta over the years. He retired in 1991.

Les and his wife are avid golfers. She has been the club champion 16 of the past 21 years. Les, himself, has won the championship 15 times. Occasionally, they play tennis as well.

In golf, Les actually qualified in 1973 for the National Amateur Championships, which was being held in Toledo, Ohio. Unfortunately, he had to play a Ryder Cup player in the first round of match play. "He beat the heck out of me," says Les. "He was really good."

Today, he and Jo Ann live just east of Atlanta. It's a part of the country they really enjoy.

O'Mahony, Jim

Both of Jim's parents–William and Nora–were born and raised in Ireland and came to America in their mid-20s. They then became naturalized citizens.

L to R: Eric (Grandson), Sarah (Granddaughter), Elizabeth O'Mahony, Ethan (Grandson), and Jim O'Mahony.

Jim had two older sisters, Noreen and Pat. Today, Noreen is married with six boys. Pat had two sons and three daughters. After Jim came a brother, Toby, who lives in a group home. The last of the five O'Mahony children was a sister, Eileen.

Jim was raised in Nyack, New York, about 18 miles north of New York City, and went to Nyack High School. There, he played soccer and ran track. He was Co-Captain of the soccer team and played left halfback. When he got to Roanoke, he played several positions–but mostly right wing opposite Cliff Shaw.

In high school track competition, he competed mostly in the long jump. He had above-average speed, jumping 20' or more.

Jim didn't intend to go to college. No one in his family had ever gone past high school. One day, however, he got a letter from the Roanoke soccer coach, Elwood Fox, and then one from the University of North Carolina. Comparing the two, he decided to go to Roanoke. It helped that the College came up with a small scholarship.

His soccer coach encouraged him to go to Roanoke, mostly because other members of his team had enrolled at Roanoke to play soccer. The coach had graduated as an All American soccer player from Carolina.

In 1955, therefore, Jim began his college career at Roanoke. He joined the Kappa Alpha fraternity, as did many on the track team. He played soccer all four years. In his senior year, he and Don Kerr were Co-Captains. They had a good team and played many larger schools, such as North Carolina, Duke, N. C. State, and the University of Baltimore. On these teams were a number of All American players.

Jim also competed in track for Coach Bast and Coach Fox for the first three years, then elected to play golf his senior year. He broad jumped over 21', although he had some good competition on his own team with Cliff Shaw, Jack Dempsey, and Jimmy Nichols. Coach Bast even persuaded him to run the low hurdles a couple of times. He usually got just enough points during the season to get his letter.

Besides being a member of Kappa Alpha, he didn't participate in many other campus activities. He roomed with Don D'Agostino his freshman year. Don also grew up in

Nyack. During his second year, he lived in the K. A. house with Dick Goodlake and one other student. His junior year, he and several friends–Bob Palm, Dick Lewis, and Warren Light–rented a house several blocks north of the campus. In his senior year, Jim moved to the new fraternity house on High Street. The new house sat diagonally across the street from the Pi Kappa Phi house.

His major at Roanoke was Education and Psychology. Although he was supposed to graduate in 1959, he stayed until 1960 because of changes he had made in the choice of majors

Jim's first job was with the U. S. Army. He volunteered just to get his military obligation over with. He went into the Army in the fall of 1960, stayed two years, and then was back to civilian life in 1962. His basic training took place at Fort Dix, where he ran into Warren Light. At the time, Jim was a Personnel Psychology Specialist. Everyone who went into the armed forces had to go through the recruiting main station where they had their physical and mental exams. When you finished those tests successfully, the Army sent you off to boot camp. Jim was responsible for administering two different tests–the Armed Forces Qualification Test and the Army Qualification Test, a battery of different tests to give an idea of what kind of job you should have.

After leaving the Army in 1962, Jim first got a job with the Insurance Company of North America (I. N. A.). He was a liaison between the independent insurance agents and the company. The agents generally had 10-12 companies with whom they could write policies. His job would be to show the agents his company's policies and explain how his company might be their best choice. He stayed with I. N. A. for about two years and then transferred to loss control engineering for them. He would go out to where they were going to write a piece of business and check out the machinery, etc., to see if the company was up to standards. He worked his way up to a Senior Loss Control Representative and then to the position as Manager of the Loss Control Department. He was promoted again, becoming the Regional Director.

In all, he stayed with I. N. A. for 29 years. He finally left them after they had merged with another company into SIGNA in 1992. For the next five years, he worked for another company, Maryland Casualty. With Maryland Casualty, he went from a local manager for their largest office to become Regional Director for Pennsylvania, New Jersey, and the New York City areas. He finally became Vice President for the entire country. He retired in about 1998.

Jim has been married twice. His first marriage, to June, came in 1965. June and Jim had three boys. The oldest was James, Jr. The second was Bill, and the third oldest was Seth. Bill was the only one to marry and today he has three children. June and Jim divorced in 1980.

In 1982, Jim married for the second time. He and his new wife, Elizabeth, met each other at a meeting for separated and divorced people. She brought two of her own children to the marriage. The oldest was Mark and the youngest was Beth. Mark is married without children, while Beth has three children.

Jim really hasn't picked up any new hobbies after retirement. He has always been an avid fisherman, however, and has helped develop a number of Trout Unlimited chapters in the New England area. He was the National Director for New Hampshire for several years, and became the National Membership Chairman for another couple of years. All of these activities came before he retired. He still does a lot of fishing with buddies, and some hunting as well. His family goes to Lake Champlain for a vacation each year.

Rader, Richard

Dick Rader was born in 1934 in the small community of Trinity, Virginia, which lies between Daleville and Fincastle. His parents lived on a farm very near where Dick lives today. His mother was Ruth Snyder, a registered nurse who worked for a local doctor. His dad was a farmer most of his life. Dick also had a younger sister–Pat Rader Smith–who graduated from Roanoke College and was the school's May Queen one year. She married Richard Smith, who was a dentist in Troutville. Unfortunately, Pat died of cancer within the past few years.

Dick attended Troutville High School, where he played football and basketball, and also ran track. He was an excellent athlete.

In his senior year in track, his school went to the state meet where Dick won the 100 and 440, and took a second place in the high jump (an event in which he used the old-style scissors kick). He even received a nice write-up by sports writer Bob McLelland in the *Roanoke World-News*.

Top: Richard Rader and his wife, Harriet. Bottom: Richard poses with three daughters. Left to right, they are Sherri Rader, Susan Snow, and Sarah McClure

Apparently, Homer Bast had heard about Dick's talents in track. One day, he and Clarence Caldwell showed up at the Rader farm for a visit. Dick and his father were working out in a field. Dick, his dad, Homer, and Clarence gathered at the fence for a talk. Whatever Homer and Clarence said, it was enough to convince Dick that he should go to Roanoke. He already had made up his mind that he was going to Bridgewater College because his family went to a Church of the Brethren and Bridgewater was affiliated with the Brethren Church.

When he got to Roanoke, Homer talked him into coming out for cross country. Dick was never very good at distance running, however. He was a good enough athlete, of course, that he could finish in the top five on his team. He finished 19th in the Little Six meet and 40th in the Mason-Dixon Championships that freshman year.

In 1953-54, during outdoor track, Dick ran mostly the sprint and relay events. His best 440 time was :52.4, and he participated on a number of mile relay teams. In fact, he was on the team with Don Moore, Chris Rittman, and John Summers that won the Little Six mile relay event.

At the end of his initial year at Roanoke, Dick felt like he didn't know how to study. So after just one year of College, he dropped out of school and went to work. He was employed for Norfolk and Western Railroad for about two years. Then his Pastor talked him into going back to school. He entered Bridgewater and joined the football and track teams. His track coach was the legendary Dr. Harry Jopson, who in temperament was very much like Roanoke's Homer Bast.

At Bridgewater, Dick majored in Physical Education. He took his student teaching course his senior year, but never thought he would ever be a school teacher. But he did go into education and enjoyed the work.

His first job was in a four-room school near the cement plant in Botetourt County. In essence, he was the custodian, the physical education teacher, and did any other job that was asked of him. Teaching at the school were three ladies and Dick. He remembers it as a very enjoyable year. Even today, he will see kids who were at the school at the time. There were only about 13 of them. The other three teachers had first and second, third and fourth, and fifth and sixth grades. Dick had the seventh.

The next year, he worked at Breckinridge Junior High School on Williamson Road in Roanoke. There, he taught Physical Education and coached baseball, basketball, and assisted with football. At the end of that year, he married a senior at Bridgewater, Harriet Flora. She had grown up in Franklin County. He met her just before she began her stay at Bridgewater. Dick had gone to a family reunion and Harriet was with a youth group going up on the Blue Ridge Parkway for a picnic. A girl from Roanoke whom Dick knew introduced him to Harriet and he ended up going with her and the group to the Parkway. The next day, she was a freshman at Bridgewater and Dick was a senior. They dated that one year, and after that Dick left the college and began his teaching career.

After Harriet and Dick married in August of 1962, he taught in the Rockingham area near Bridgewater. His job was at Bridgewater Elementary School, teaching seventh grade students. He and his wife's two oldest daughters were born in Harrisonburg during this time. The older of the two was Sarah, now Sarah Elaine Rader McClure, born in 1963. Today, she and her husband, Dave, have a little girl named Keli. Sarah works for a C. P. A., while Dave works in sales in the Roanoke area.

Their next oldest child was Susan, born in 1964. She is married to Greg Snow and the couple has two children, Tyler and Allie. Greg is in the stocks and bonds business. Susan is a financial secretary at a large church in northern Virginia.

After Sarah and Susan, the Raders in 1971 had one more child, a girl named Sherri. She lives in Charlotte, North Carolina, working for a large construction firm in their offices.

All three children went to college. Sarah graduated from Bridgewater, Susan became a graduate of the University of Virginia, and Sherri graduated from Virginia Tech.

Dick stayed at Bridgewater Elementary School for three years. Then he and Harriet moved back to Roanoke and he began teaching at the old Melrose Elementary School. He stayed at Melrose for several years, until it closed down. He moved to the old Monroe Junior High School at that point. The school had been re-named as Northwest Elementary School. He stayed at Northwest for the last 25 years of his teaching career, retiring in 1990. His wife, also a teacher, retired the next year.

After his retirement, he went to work that first summer at Hollins Hardware. He worked for the company, stocking and selling, for 11 years until they closed down.

Even today, he hasn't fully retired. He has been working for a surveyor since about the time the hardware closed. He helps survey farms and other properties, ranging in location from Roanoke to Smith Mountain Lake. He works for them almost daily, sometimes about eight hours per day.

As far as hobbies go, Dick enjoys gardening. He and Harriet sold their farm about three years ago, which has freed up more of his time. He enjoys watching sports on TV.

Rhyne, White

S. White Rhyne, called "Whitey" during his time at Roanoke (1948-52), lettered all four years in cross-country. In track he lettered all but his freshman year, when he was hampered in the spring by illness. He was best known as the usual fifth-place finisher in cross-country his first two years, behind the "Big Four" ("Red" Crockett, Bruce Davenport, Paul McCarty and Alvin Smith) who won most meets crossing the finish line four-abreast.

White and Rosemarie Rhyne

He attended the academically-elite Central High School in Philadelphia, where he ran for three years on the track and cross-country teams, including a city championship cross-country team his senior year. Looking back on his first cross-country practice at Roanoke, though, he said he knew by the end of the practice that "there were only four aces in this deck."

White came from a family of athletes. His father, S. White Rhyne '18, is in the College's Athletic Hall of Fame (www.roanoke.edu/athletics/hof/swrhyne.htm) for football, basketball and tennis. His younger brother, Charles, who graduated from Wittenberg College and did graduate work at the University of Chicago, was a nationally ranked half-miler. He ran in Olympic trials and was a member of a Chicago Track Club cross-country team that won a National A. A. U. Championship.

Except for an unsuccessful application for a full scholarship at Swarthmore, in which he finished second in statewide competition, White never considered any college but Roanoke. That was because of his father's loyalty to the school from which he graduated and later received an honorary degree. He also knew of the achievements of the "Big Four" because his father, a former Business Manager of the *Brackety-Ack*, received a courtesy copy of each issue in the mail. When White was accepted at Roanoke, Stuart Hanks, then the Director of Admissions, let Coach Bast know to look for him.

From virtually the beginning of the 1948 cross-country season, White fell into the role of fifth-place finisher behind the Big Four, sometimes sharing that honor with Frank Aldred. He recalls, though, one meet where he and Frank were both ahead of the entire other team. The Big Four slowed down about 100 yards from the finish line to let them catch up, so there was a six-abreast Roanoke finish. That race ended on the quadrangle (now the "back quad") and was witnessed by large numbers of students and faculty who gathered to watch the team turn from High Street onto the quad and cheer it on to the finish. For that season and the next, cross-country at Roanoke became a "spectator sport."

Sometimes the home course for meets ended with a lap of the track on the athletic field, located on Market Street. White remembers: "We went up High Street and then took a left turn onto Hawthorne, which had a stretch that contained two killer hills. We then turned right and headed uphill to the Baptist Orphanage. After circling the

Orphanage we came back down to Market Street and ended with a lap on the track. Or sometimes we continued back over those Hawthorne hills to High Street where we turned onto a final lap of the quad. In either case, we were usually met by a cheer from the waiting crowd, 'Here they come!' as the Big Four came into sight with sometimes a lead runner or so from the other team on their heels."

In White's first cross country season at Roanoke, the team finished the season undefeated in dual and triangular meets. They also won the Little Six and Mason-Dixon championships. In his sophomore year, 1949-50, the team again was undefeated and won the two conference championships. That year, they also won the large Virginia A. A. U. meet– one in which there were many seasoned and successful runners from throughout the state.

During the following season most of Roanoke's stars, including Alvin Smith, were gone. Also, Homer Bast had been called up by the Navy Reserve for a year of service in Alaska. "Smittie," who had used up his eligibility as a runner, took over the team that year as coach. Bruce Davenport and White became the top runners on the cross-country team. Although it had some early success, they finished second in the Little Six meet and third in the Mason-Dixon Championship.

Runners on other teams were beginning to improve. Merle Crouse of Bridgewater, for example, became a dominant distance runner during his junior and senior years. After graduation from Bridgewater, he attended a theological seminary in Chicago and ran with White's brother Charles on the Chicago Track Club team that won the National A. A. U. Championship.

When Homer returned for the 1951-52 season, the cross country team was not very strong. "Yes," White says, "I was the best runner on the team. I think we finished with about an even record of wins and losses during the regular season. On the other hand, that was the year Les Noel, a freshman, first ran for Roanoke. He started out as an average runner that year but by the time he was a senior he was almost the best distance runner in either conference."

White never was a top runner during track seasons at Roanoke, though he contributed much to the teams in terms of leadership. But his times on the track were not outstanding. He was best in the longer distances afforded by cross-country. He finished his track career with a 2:20.3 in the half mile, a 4:52 mile, and a 10:25.0 two-mile race.

He was also involved in many campus activities at Roanoke. He became Editor-In-Chief of the *Brackety-Ack* and also wrote a sports column for the paper. In writing that column he succeeded Bob McLelland, who after graduation became a top sports writer and even Sports Editor for the *Roanoke Times and World-News*. McLelland's column in the *Brackety-Ack* was called the "Sports Korner." White renamed it "MaroonNotes." He found it fun to write, reporting not only on what current teams in the various sports were doing but also chronicling what had been done by outstanding Roanoke College teams of the past.

He was a member of the Honor Council and was named to Phi Society, a local substitute for Phi Beta Kappa which Roanoke did not have at the time. He was also a member of Blue Key National Honor Society. Those and other activities earned him recognition in *Who's Who Among Students in American Universities and Colleges*.

White lived in Hildreth Hall during his first year. That building, which no longer stands, housed only freshmen. During his sophomore year, he roomed with Ted Blackwelder in Wells Hall. Ted's and White's fathers had been friends when both were students at Roanoke, and they were later roommates at the Lutheran Southern Theological Seminary.

Ted and White became members of the Kappa Alpha fraternity. At the time, the KA House was just south of the main gate to the College as one approached from College Avenue. The school later moved the gate down toward the town, placing the KA house inside the gate. The building was a small frame house with no central heat. Occupants led a rough life during winter months.

Just before White's junior year, the fraternity finally acquired another house, on High Street, with much more space and central heat. The old house was torn down. White and Ted moved to the High Street house where they continued as roommates. They, now also with their wives, have remained close friends ever since graduation.

In those days, and even through the end of the 1950s, many track and cross country men were members of the KA fraternity. Three of the four members of the Big Four were KA's. Only Alvin Smith, who never joined a fraternity, was not.

After graduating from Roanoke, White received a scholarship to the University of Virginia Law School and planned to room there with classmate Jack Shannon. However, the scholarship paid only in-state tuition which was much less than tuition for an out-of-state resident such as him. Then the University of Pennsylvania Law School offered him a full tuition scholarship. Since his home was in Philadelphia, he could live there inexpensively and commute to the Law School. That would remove the burden of tuition, room and board from his parents, who had borne that expense for four years while he was at Roanoke and by then had another son in college. So he made an economic decision to go to Penn, where he graduated near the top of his class and was an Editor of the *Law Review*.

He says he never regretted his choice of law school. Meanwhile, however, Jack Shannon enrolled at the University of Virginia Law School where he distinguished himself academically, finishing first in his class and being elected Editor-in-Chief of the Law Review.

In the mid-1950's, all able-bodied males were subject the military draft. They could be deferred to complete their schooling, and in the case of law students to take the bar exam after graduation. But three days after White took the bar exam he was drafted into the Army and was on a train for Fort Jackson, South Carolina. After completing basic training at Fort Jackson, he was sent to Fort Monmouth, New Jersey, where he completed coursework at the U.S. Army Signal School.

He says he had hoped while in the Army to "see the world," and upon completing the Signal School he had his choice by class rank of thirty assignments. He chose Germany, and was permitted a last weekend to visit his parents in Philadelphia before shipping out to Europe from Maguire Air Force Base on Monday.

But when he returned to Fort Monmouth he found that the Army had sent down a requisition for an instructor and his orders had been changed to keep him at Monmouth, where he spent the rest of his active duty with the Army as an instructor in the Signal School working about 100 miles from where he grew up. While initially crestfallen, he says it became for him a lesson in life, that "you never know what's good for you." It was while at Monmouth that he met his future wife, Rosemarie. "That," he says "made up for everything."

White had always assumed he would practice law in Philadelphia, but shortly before discharge from active duty in the Army he received a request for an interview with a law firm in Washington, DC, headed by a cousin whom he had never met but with whom he had corresponded while in law school in connection with an article he was working on for the Law Review. It was a good fit. He took the job offer, became an associate in the firm and began an exciting legal career in Washington that lasted 48 years until his retirement in 2005.

He and Rosemarie were married in 1959. Shortly afterward he was offered a Fellowship by Georgetown University to participate in a flagship graduate program in trial advocacy at its Law School, leading after a year to an LL.M degree. He later taught part-time at Georgetown Law. Upon completing the clinical practice program, he joined two other young lawyers in a new firm that later grew to eleven lawyers. He served as Managing Attorney at that firm for 25 years.

The practice of the firm, and his own practice, was largely in the area of communications law. He became active in the 3,000 member Federal Communications Bar Association and in 1994 was elected its President. He also served for more than ten years on the Board of Directors of the Bar Association of the District of Columbia, was a frequent member of the House of Delegates of the American Bar Association, and is now a Life Fellow of the American Bar Foundation.

White also had a career-long association with the Legal Aid Society of the District of Columbia, providing pro bono services to some of its indigent clients, serving on its Board of Trustees, and for two years as the Society's President. He retired from active law practice in 2005, but when in 2007 the Legal Aid Society celebrated its 75th Anniversary he was honored as one of two recipients of its "Servant of Justice Award."

Since 2002, White has been listed in Marquis *Who's Who in American Law, Who's Who in America*, and *Who's Who in the World.*

Rosemarie and White Rhyne have had three children, and now have five grandchildren. The oldest of their children is Patricia Ruth Rhyne, now Patricia Rhyne Kirsch, who with her husband Peter has three children. She and Rosemarie are partners in residential real estate sales. Patty lives in Kensington, Maryland, which is a suburb of Washington. Rosemarie's and White's older son is Kendall S. Rhyne, who is an architectural draftsman working and living near Baltimore with his wife Tracy and two children. Their younger son is Randall "Randy" Rhyne, who is unmarried and teaches biology at a high school near Richmond, where he also coaches soccer. In past years Rosemarie and White have also, at various times, included 25 foster children in their home.

Rosebro, Rud

Rud grew up in Roanoke, the son of Henry and Evie-Hume. He had two older sisters and a younger brother.

He went to Jefferson High School, but in his third year there, his academic average was so poor that his parents sent him to Augusta Military Academy.

Rud was deferred from military service until June of 1944, when he would finish his final year at Augusta Military. He was scheduled to report in June, but broke his arm and got a deferment extension until August. He finally went into the service in August of 1944, spending 22 months in the service as an infantryman in Germany. He joined his outfit during the Battle of the Bulge. At the end of the 22 months, he left the Army with a rank of Staff Sergeant.

He chose to go to Roanoke College because it was near his home. He really wanted to go to the University of Virginia, but knew that he didn't have the grades to be admitted there. Actually, Roanoke also thought his grades were too low, but allowed him to go to summer school in the summer of 1946. They told him that if he got a C average, they would let him enroll in the fall. He did get the C average and reported for his first classes at the beginning of the 1946-47 session. It was the same year that Homer Bast joined the College staff.

At Roanoke, Rud was a day student, living at home and riding to and from the College each day with Larry Stephens, a friend, who lived near him in Roanoke. Rud joined the Sigma Chi fraternity and still remembers their house mother, Ma Mason, who was "a doll." He enjoyed his fraternity life. "They didn't have the raunchiness that came along in later years," Rud remembers. "Ma really kept her eyes open for things that shouldn't be happening."

Rud was never an outstanding athlete at Roanoke, but he did contribute a lot to the team. In cross country, he generally finished in the top five of his own team and was 15th in the Little Six Championships in 1947.

In the spring of 1946-47, Bob Fagg and some of the veterans who had run track in high school decided that they wanted a track team at the College. The school hadn't had a track program since about 1929. They got with Homer Bast, who had run at the University of Virginia, and the new program was underway.

During his brief track career at Roanoke, Rud competed in a number of different events. He ran a :27.2 and a :27.0 low-hurdle time–a school record–and also competed in the high hurdles (:16.6), the broad jump, the distance medley relay, and the 480-yard shuttle hurdle relay. He remembers running the high hurdles in a time below :16.0 in one of his qualifying races. His distance medley team–Bob Fagg, Paul McCarty, Alvin Smith, and Rud–won the Milligan Relays' distance medley event in 1948.

The team as a whole enjoyed having Homer Bast as their coach. Rud says, "We loved him. He was great. He was so personable–so hands-on in his coaching. And he was helpful. When he and I first talked, I told him that I had never run track before. And I asked him the secret to running the 440. He said, 'Well, you run as fast as you can for 400 yards, then you run faster than you ever ran before for the final 40.' In one of the meets, my parents came to see me run. When we got through, my father said, 'Look. Your face is too red entirely too long after your race.' That comment led to a trip to our family doctor, who told me that I had a slight heart murmur. He told me not to run longer distances–anything 440 yards and over–and I would be O.K. So I told Homer that I had to quit running the quarter mile. I told him that I wanted to try the hurdles. From that point on, I ran the high and low hurdles. The biggest thing about running the low hurdles was to get your steps down between the hurdles so you don't break stride. You also had to learn to step over the hurdles rather than jumping them. The first high hurdles I ran included only four hurdles. That's all we had. In terms of Homer teaching me to hurdle, I do remember him telling me on the high hurdles to reach forward with both hands and pull my torso down. I tried that technique and found that I was more comfortable doing it a bit differently. I led with my left foot and thrust my right hand forward and my left hand back. I was pretty limber in those days. I really didn't have any problems with clearing the hurdles. I was about 6'1" tall and weighed perhaps 187 pounds. After transferring to Virginia, I really didn't get any help from the coach, Archie Hahn."

Unfortunately, Rud stayed at Roanoke only two years, transferring to the University of Virginia. He sent the University his grades from the first two years, including a grade of D in Physics, in order to be admitted. The people at the University of Virginia actually gave Rud a quality credit for that D because they thought that Roanoke had such a superior Physics Department.

Rud stayed at Virginia for his final two years, graduating in 1950. While there, he competed in track, becoming the team's fourth man in the high hurdles.

He then went to work for his father, who had a business called Roanoke Wholesalers. They were wholesale distributors of home appliances. Later, the family sold the business and Rud went to work for a company in Richmond called Reliance Equipment. He stayed with Reliance from 1963 until 1970.

After his college career, in 1955, he married Shiela Crabtree. Shiela and Rud had three boys–Robert, Cortland, and William. Today, Rud has three grandchildren. The marriage lasted until 1970, when they were divorced. Rud never re-married.

He moved to Raleigh, North Carolina, as a distributor for Safeguard Business Systems and stayed with that company until about 1981. Eventually, he formed his own company and worked until his retirement in 1991.

He plays a lot of golf these days. "I used to be pretty good at golf," he says, "but now I am not ready to go to Augusta." He also does voluntary carpentry for Habitat for Humanity. He has been blessed with good health over the years. A few years ago, he did have both of his knees replaced and recently he had minor heart problems. Other than these issues, he has had no health problems of significance.

Seed, Dick

Born in Philadelphia, Dick was the grandson of a good baseball pitcher and the son of a terrific soccer player who seemed headed for the Olympics. Unfortunately, Dick's brother backed a car into him and broke his leg.

Dick's dad never graduated from high school. His mother had a high school education, but didn't go on to college. Financially, times were tough in the Seed family, which is one reason that Dick ended up at Roanoke College.

Dick had made a name for himself as a high school soccer star. The soccer coach at Roanoke at the time was Richard Stine. Stine was able to get Dick a small scholarship to play soccer and run track at Roanoke. It wasn't much–perhaps $300 per year, later boosted to $400–but with Roanoke's low tuition and fees, the school seemed like the place for Dick. He showed up at Roanoke in the fall of 1953 without having laid eyes on the campus. He played soccer that fall and, over the next four years, became one of the best in the conference.

He was equally skilled in track, where he concentrated on the high jump and hurdles. He was only 5'9" in high school and college, but jumped over 6'0" numerous times at Roanoke. He was also a very good hurdler.

Dick and Barbara Seed in 2007

In the high jump, he won the Little Eight meet his freshman year. That year he also won the high jump in the Mason-Dixon Championships. In his sophomore, junior, and senior years, he again won the Mason-Dixon title–one of just a few to win four straight conference meets in a single event.

He was also a very good hurdler while at Roanoke. In the high hurdles, he ran a :15.5 and five times ran a :15.7. In the 220-yard low hurdles, his best time was :25.0 and he ran several other races under :26.0. His real competition in the hurdles came from teammates, such as Dave Foltz and Bruce Johnston.

Dick never really got to know Homer Bast until after the soccer season that first year. As Dick puts it, "He let me play soccer before he latched onto me." During his freshman year, he participated in soccer along with indoor and outdoor track. Between his freshman and sophomore years, he remembers spending the summer doing construction work. He gained weight up to about 160 pounds. When he arrived back on campus to begin his sophomore year, Homer took one look at him and said, "Oh, my God. Thank goodness for soccer." Within two or three weeks of beginning soccer practice, Dick remember, he had taken off the extra weight. His playing weight in those days was between 130 and 140. Amazingly, that's the weight he has maintained throughout his life.

Dick enjoyed his days at Roanoke. He thought nothing of playing three sports, one right after the other. In fact, athletics gave him a group of people who became his best friends. He joined the Kappa Alpha fraternity. At that time, most track men seemed to be K. A. men, basketball players mostly joined Sigma Chi, and soccer players were pretty much divided as to the fraternities they chose.

In soccer, Dick played halfback all four years. He was left-handed and predominantly left footed. His coaches, first Richard Stine and for the last two years, Elwood Fox, positioned him on the left side of the field. In reality, however, he could kick well with either foot and was a good scorer for the team.

In track, he was Co-Captain his senior year along with sprinter George Gearhart. The College still maintains a picture of Seed, Gearhart, and Coach Fox in its main trophy cases near the Athletic Hall of Fame room.

Dick was a member of the outdoor track team during the years when it was undefeated in dual- and tri-meet competition, and when it annually won the Little Seven/Eight and Mason-Dixon championships. He attributes most of this success to Coach Bast, who was a superb motivator. And the teams he was a part of had great depth–often several stars in each event.

Many of Dick's close friends, such as Phil Shaw, came from the track team. He and Phil met for the first time on the train taking them to Roanoke College to begin their freshman year. Dick got on the train in Philadelphia, and Phil had boarded in New York. They ended up living on the same floor of Wells Dormitory. Phil ran track and cross country, and they both became K. A.s. Even after graduation, they stayed close. Each joined the Marine Corps, although neither knew the other had done so. When they went to Quantico, both were in the O. C. S. program, in the same platoon. Phil stayed in the Marines for 30 years, while Dick stayed for 22 years.

Others he remembers well include Dick Goodlake, Bruce Johnston, and Dave Foltz. "Dave was a very brash guy," Dick says. "He was a real braggart. He would say, 'I'm better than anyone else," and he was generally right. He was a super, outgoing kind of guy. He looked and acted like a Greek God."

As mentioned before, Dick joined the Marines just after graduation from Roanoke. Several of his friends had joined, such as Les Noel and Dave Foltz. And it seemed like at the time it was a good thing to do for his country. Dick Goodlake, Phil Shaw, and Seed all made a career out of the Marines.

Dick's occupational field was artillery. He intended to marry his wife, Barbara Healy, in 1959. He had met Barbara in a Spanish class at Roanoke. They dated, but she was about two years behind him in school. At the time, he had orders to go to Okinawa. So they put off the marriage for a while. Then, the Marine Corps decided to create a group of track athletes at Quantico, trying to assemble a good team for the 1960 Olympics. The Marines cancelled Dick's orders for Okinawa and sent him to Quantico. That allowed Barbara and Dick to get married in October of 1959, and they lived at Quantico.

While part of the Marine Corp track team, Dick ran the hurdles and high jumped. He soon realized that he would be better in the hurdle events. While in the Marines, he won the Marine Corps championships. His time was about :15.4 in the high hurdles. He had many good teammates, one of whom was the famous javelin thrower and world record holder, Al Cantello. He watched Dick hurdling one day and offered some suggestions on how to improve. At that time, Dick was floating over the hurdles, losing overall time. Cantello marked where his foot was coming down and then where the trail leg was hitting the ground. There was only about two feet between the two marks. So Dick began to extend that trail leg, getting it out in front of him instead of letting it float over the hurdle. As Dick said, "I had to whip it through and get it out in front of me in order to increase my speed."

Other world-class stars at Quantico included pole vaulters Bob Gutowski, John Ulesyss, and Dave Tork. Dick's team at Quantico put four people on the 1960 Olympic team.

Barbara and Dick had three children. Richard IV is in his mid 40s today. Jeffrey is about two years younger, and Jennifer is the youngest by about two more years. Jennifer, before she stopped working, taught elementary school children, getting her Master's Degree in Social Work from the University of Georgia. Then she moved into a job which tried to bring spiritual and ethical considerations into education.

Jeffrey went to Roanoke College for a year. After his freshman year, during which he had a wonderful time–so Dick says–he took a year off. But he never went back. He tried landscaping, but eventually went back to college at Drexel and got a degree in accounting. He now has his own business. His company serves as pension consultants for companies with less than 1,500 employees.

Dick's oldest son, Richard IV, attended Virginia Tech but never graduated. Today, he is very successful, owning his own construction company. The company specializes in building custom homes. One recent such home has about 14,400 square feet of space. He lives only about 20 minutes from his parents.

Dick had two tours in Vietnam. In his first tour, he was a Battery Commander and part of the first group of the First Marine Division to go to Vietnam. Then he came home for three years, serving at a Marine Corps training center. "That was an experience," Dick says. "Part of my job was to notify families of servicemen who had been wounded or killed while on duty. So for three years, I was the Casualty Officer for part of Los Angeles and parts of the surrounding areas. I had 63 Killed in Action (KIA) notifications during that time. We also notified families of those who were wounded. The Marine Corps started the notification program, and then the other services picked it up themselves. I was the guy who knocked on the door. And in those days, you didn't take anybody with you. You'd think that the families would remember you only as the one who came and told them the bad news. You'd think they wouldn't like you at all. But they had this big hole in their lives, and you were standing there, and they would suck you right in. Eventually, we had a lot of close friends. They would invite Barbara and me over to their houses. One fellow invited me to lunch, and it turned out that he had an airplane. So he flew me over to Catalina for lunch. What the Marine Corps started was absolutely spectacular. Sometimes, I'd just go home and sit there and watch the clock. At 6:00 p.m. I would say 'Let's have a drink.' I knew that they would never call me about a notification after 6:00 p.m. The job was a real eye-opener. Then I gave up that job and the Marines sent me back to Vietnam."

Dick was a Captain during his first tour of Vietnam, and a Major for the second tour. On that second trip to Vietnam, he was the Executive Officer of an Artillery Battalion. He had the opportunity in 1969-70 to become the Senior Aide to a three-star general, who was in charge of all of the Marines in Vietnam.

As part of another position he held, at about age 39, he had to go to jump school. He was in good shape physically, but on Thursday of the first week they were training to parachute, he was so sore that he could hardly move. The soreness came from the pounding of training jumps off of platforms to learn how to fall. The men would do it, and then do it again and again.

The Marines were very good at training jumpers. Dick remembers his first jump. "A psychological trick they use on you when you are about to make your first jump is that they have you there at 4:30 a.m. They get you completely suited up, including the parachute. And then, by 8:00 a.m., they put you on an airplane. And you go up. By this time, you would do anything to get out of that damn parachute–including jumping out of an airplane. Because of my rank, they insisted that I be the first person out the door. So there I was at the open door. The light came on, and I jumped. The only thing that surprised me was how hard you hit. I always thought you kind of floated down, landed softly, and just walked away. But no. It's like jumping out of a second-story window. That's how hard you hit the ground."

Then Dick got to the point when he began to think about leaving the Marines. He didn't want to go back to Okinawa, and just didn't see a future for himself in the Marine Corps. He was a Lieutenant Colonel when he retired, and may have made Colonel the very year he retired. But even if he made Colonel, he thought, what then? It was at that time that he decided to retire. His final job in the Marine Corps was as a briefer for the Chairman of the Joint Chiefs of Staff. He briefed a group each day, including the Chairman, and the Secretary of Defense on Wednesdays. He had to show up to work at 2:00 a.m., pick up what everyone had collected, write the script, have the graphics and video displays prepared for him, and then he would brief the higher-ups. He had three screens, and during his talk he would bring everyone up to date on what was going on. He stayed in that job for a year. Then he asked himself where he was going from that point on in his military career. There he was, talking with the Secretary of Defense and the Chairman of the Joint Chiefs of Staff each and every week. What could be the next challenge in his life? After 22 years in the Marines, he finally retired in 1979. He separated completely, not remaining in the Reserves.

While he was in the Marines, he had gotten a Master's Degree in Psychology. So he took a job with a "beltway bandit." The company needed someone with military experience who also had a degree in Psychology. But he never really liked the job. Barbara had already started teaching in Stafford County, Virginia. One day, at a social function at Barbara's school, Dick was talking to her Principal. Right on the spot, he offered Dick a job. Dick was intrigued. So he quit his job and began teaching. He ended up teaching high schoolers and middle schoolers for some 15 years. Then he and Barbara moved to where they live now, in Northern Neck, and Dick took another teaching position in a high school down there. He taught high school students for another ten years.

In this latter teaching position, Dick taught a low-level math course which ended up in the second year being a low-level Algebra I. He never told the students that they were learning Algebra, because if they knew that, "they would freak out on you." The students were not rocket scientists, and would never be taking Calculus or any other advanced math course. But Dick enjoyed what he was doing, and so did his kids. They used a lot of hands-on materials. He did similar things in a biology course he taught.

During his high school teaching career, he became the coach of the girls' volleyball team. He had played a lot of volleyball earlier in his life, but the school didn't have a volleyball team. When the Principal learned of his interest in the sport, it didn't take long for him to whip up a coaching contract for Dick. He forced the girls to play the game correctly. His first year, the team didn't win a single match. But during the second year, his team was district champion and came in second in the regionals. His insistence on playing the game correctly paid off.

"Volleyball is a great game," Dick says. "Now, I was a fraud in teaching marine biology. I would stay one chapter ahead of the kids. But I wasn't a fraud in volleyball. I played intramural volleyball at Roanoke and, being a high jumper, had some skills in getting up over the net. Even at 5'9", I was a hitter for the team. And I played on a volleyball team in the Marine Corps that was in the All-Marines Championships."

He finally gave up teaching in 1997. Both Barbara and he have been "really retired" since that point. They moved down to the Northern Neck before retirement, close to the Potomac. Their house sits on the water, and their sailboat is anchored just a few feet from the house. Their hobbies now center around the boat–a 42-foot Grand Banks Trawler. "The boat is very comfortable," Dick notes. "We live on it from the end of October until the middle of April. Generally, we winter in the Bahamas. We've done that now for eight years. We take the boat from home and go down the Intercoastal Waterway to the Bahamas. We rent a car down there. And then, at the end of our season, we wend our way home. We really love it down there."

Not long ago, they had just left to come back home when the boat's engine overheated. So he and Barbara turned around and went back. When they couldn't get the boat repaired right away, however, they stayed over several days. On the third day back in port, Dick had a stroke. As fate had it, if he had not had engine trouble, he and Barbara would have been in the ocean near St. Augustine, Florida, and in the middle of nowhere, when the stroke might have occurred."

As they go down to the Bahamas, they have a chance to stop and visit with friends along the way. They even stopped to see Cliff Shaw and his wife. Cliff was a former Roanoke athlete who lived in Vero Beach, Florida, before his recent death. Their first visit turned out so well that they continued to see the Shaws every year–once going down and once coming back. Cliff was a year behind Dick, but they were on the same track team, both played soccer, and each was a K. A.

As a result of his stroke, Dick was left with some minor speech problems, but nothing more. He has no real balance problems or any trouble with his coordination. The only thing that's really different in his life these days, he laughs, is the number of pills he takes each morning.

Shaw, Cliff

Cliff and Frances Shaw

Cliff Shaw was primarily a broad jumper on the Bast teams. As a young jumper in 1955, he showed promise, usually recording jumps in the 19' to 20'+ range. He had his best outdoor seasons in 1957 and 1958, however. In 1957 his jumps were 21'0", 21'1", 21'4", 21'5", and 21'6". The last jump, 21'6" brought him the Mason-Dixon Conference champion's medal in 1957 at Hampden-Sydney, VA. He also was third that year in the broad jump at the Little Eight meet. During his final outdoor season, 1958, his jumping was equally consistent: 21'7", 21'5", 21'3½", 21'3¼", 21'1", 20'11½", 20'11", and 20'9".

Cliff was born in Newark, New Jersey, and raised in Irvington, New Jersey. In the family were Clifford and Marion, his mother and father, and one sister, Ida, who was seven years older than Cliff.

Irvington High School was Cliff's second home in those days. There, he played soccer and participated in track during his senior year. Soccer, which he began to play when he was six or seven years old, was his favorite sport. But he grew to like track that senior year, which he still thinks encouraged him to join Coach Bast's team at Roanoke.

Cliff always wanted to go to college. He was influenced to choose Roanoke by a student at Roanoke who had gone to Irvington High. He encouraged Cliff to apply. There was no trip down to see the College, and Cliff simply showed up in the fall to enroll.

While he was at Roanoke, he was active in campus activities. For example, he worked for the *Brackety-Ack*, served as President of Blue Key, and was a member of Kappa Alpha fraternity. Many people on the track team were K. A.s in those days. But he has never thought that membership in a particular fraternity meant much to the athletes. "We were a close group all four years," he remembers.

The only real hitch in Cliff's career at Roanoke came as a result of his freshman year. "I enjoyed myself," he said. "I moved up to the fraternity house and spent a lot of time with the juniors and seniors. And I had a good old time with them. Unfortunately, my grades went down and down during the year." When he got back to the campus the next fall, he discovered that he was on probation and was prevented from participating in any sports during the year until his grades came up to an acceptable level. The news was devastating. For the next day or so, Cliff was really down–even thinking of dropping out of school. Then his whole attitude changed. In a chance meeting with Homer Bast near the Administration Building, the two of them had a talk while walking toward town. Here's is how Cliff remembers the conversation: "He said to me, 'You know, why don't you stop comparing yourself to everyone else–worrying about grades and this and that? Think about yourself and do your studying like you should. And give it some time.' It was really some kind of conversation. And I decided right then and there, 'I think I will do that.' "

After that semester, Cliff was hanging around the Administration Building to learn what his grades were. Homer was the first person out of the building and, as Cliff remembers, ". . . came up to me with that big grin and said, 'Do you know what you did? You made the honor roll.' Just by talking with him that day in the early fall, he kept me from dropping out of school. He just had that way about him."

Cliff's major at Roanoke was Education and Psychology. After his graduation, he intended to go into the Marines at Quantico. Then his father became very ill, with Lou Gehrig's disease, and subsequently he passed away. The Shaws had a small family business–a foundry–so Cliff joined the Air National Guard in the New Jersey area and worked in the business for a couple of years.

Cliff got married in 1959, when his new wife, Frances, graduated from Roanoke. Their youngest child, Karen, was born on their first wedding anniversary. Their next child was Craig, followed by Mari. Frances today works as a charge nurse in a labor and delivery hospital. Craig is a fireman in North Carolina. And Mark is a paramedic police and fireman in the same town where Cliff and Frances live.

He then took a job with Colgate Palmolive in New York, working as a Systems Analyst in the very early years of computers in the workplace. That job lasted only a couple of years, however. He simply didn't like sitting indoors all day. So he became involved with another family business. His wife's father owned his own business and asked Cliff if he wanted to work for him. He had a large farm with thousands of chickens. They also raised research animals for laboratories. The company supplied embryos for flu vaccines. Cliff did join the business and stayed with the job until about 1973-74. He then went into real estate sales, and was involved in that field for many years.

Since he unofficially retired about six or seven years ago, Cliff enjoyed gardening and helping his kids with their homes. He was a good handyman, having learned a lot of construction skills while working on the farm.

He had some ailments during the last few years, including C. O. P. D., which limited him to what he could do physically.

Note to the Reader: Cliff Shaw died in May of 2008 prior to the publication of this book. We send our condolences to his wife, Frances, and to the Shaw family.

Shaw, Phil

Phil grew up in Irvington, New York, a small town on the Hudson River some 20 miles north of the Bronx. He went to Irving High School for four years. It was a small school with only 120 students. There, Phil was always involved with sports. He participated in football, basketball, and baseball. He joined the track team in his junior year. In track Phil primarily was a half miler, although he occasionally ran the mile. In terms of his running talent, he was a bit better than most athletes in the area, but was not outstanding.

Jeanette and Phil Shaw

His mother and father–Meta and Will–were very supportive of their son as he played sports. Phil also had an older brother and a younger sister. His sister has since passed away, but his brother lives in New York today.

About mid-way through his senior year of high school, he had almost made up his mind that he would attend New York University, Boston University, or another school in the area. Then Homer Bast showed up at his home. After meeting Homer, and talking with him at length, Phil and his parents were swayed. Homer described the school in such a way that the Shaws thought Roanoke would be a perfect fit for Phil.

And it was. He boarded the train for the ride down to Salem and at the Philadelphia stop, future teammate Dick Seed boarded. They became best friends. When he got to the campus, Phil was ecstatic that he had made such a good choice. It was a comfortable setting, small enough to allow Phil to know many people and fit in easily.

At Roanoke, Phil majored in Education and Psychology, planning on a teaching career. He was so influenced by Homer Bast and his influence on others that Phil wanted to follow in his footsteps.

His first roommate at Roanoke in the fall of 1953 was Les Noel, who already had become one of the best distance men in the area. They lived together in the Sections.

With Homer Bast's help, Phil worked at a few jobs on campus. One was the dry cleaning pickup and delivery service for laundry. He laughs today as he says, "I liked that job. I was the only guy on the campus to have access to the ladies' dormitories. I would open the door and yell, 'Man on the floor,' and just walk right in." Phil also was hired as the "light fixer" in the gym. He would replace the burned-out bulbs, especially over the basketball court. And during the time he was rooming in Hildreth Hall, it was his job to clean up the building. At the time, he was living in Hildreth with Dick Seed.

Phil was fairly active on campus. He was a member of the Kappa Alpha fraternity, for example, and served as President one year of the Monogram Club.

Phil was never an outstanding cross country runner, but most of the time he was in the top five finishers on his own team. He even served as the team's Co-Captain, with Bruce Fariss, during the 1955 season. He finished 9th in the Little Eight meet in 1955 and again in 1956, and placed 4th in the Mason-Dixon Championships in 1955.

In outdoor track competition, Phil did well. He was one of only five Roanoke athletes coached by Homer Bast to run under 2:00.0 in the 880. His time of 1:59.7 was recorded during his senior year in the Little Eight meet. He also ran several 880s in times that were barely over two minutes.

When Phil graduated, he knew that the military draft was looming ahead. Instead of going into teaching, therefore, he decided to join the Marine Corps. Not only did a number of Homer's track athletes choose the Marines–such as Dick Seed, Jack Dempsey, and Dick Emberger–but Phil had met a recruiter from the Marines on campus a couple of time. "He impressed the daylights out of me," said Phil.

Still, Phil had no intention of making a career with the Marines. After meeting the recruiter in 1956-57, he had joined the Marine Reserves as a junior. After he graduated from Roanoke in 1957, he went into the Marine's O. C. S. program. After O. C. S., he was a second Lieutenant and ended up going to the Basics School. At that point, he was what the Marines called a "grunt." He worked often with younger marines–who may have been 17, 18, or 19 year old kids–who needed additional help. It was almost like having a teaching career.

Phil's career with the Marines flourished and he stayed with the position for some 32 years. He retired from the Marines as a Bird Colonel in October of 1988. During his time in the Marines, he was a Platoon Commander, Company Commander, Battalion Commander, and more. He also held staff jobs as Operations Officer, Executive Officer, Second in Command, and similar positions.

He also had a couple of tours of duty. One took him to Thailand for a year. It was a situation he enjoyed. He worked with the Joint Casualty Resolution Center, where they dealt with those countries the United States was fighting to recover the bodies of soldiers who had died during the fighting. At another time, he was an Inspector/Instructor for the entire western section of the United States with the Reserve Marine units

Today, Phil has no regrets about spending so much time in the Marines. "There were a few moments early on," he says, "when I wondered at my sanity in choosing the Marines as a career, but the experience overall was outstanding."

After retiring from the Marines, Phil immediately went into teaching at the high school level. He ended up leading a Navy Junior R. O. T. C. program and teaching Government. In the R. O. T. C. program, he believes he had a tremendous influence on his students. Even today, he hears from some of them and has even gone to a few of their weddings. Some of the kids went into the military after finishing high school. Phil stayed with the R. O. T. C. job for about eight years, retiring in 1996.

At that point, Phil became immersed with volunteer work. He volunteered for Hospice, with the Armed Services Y. M. C. A. unit working with military families who had loved ones deployed, his own Lutheran Church, and much, much more.

He enjoys playing golf, and he and his wife love to travel. Among other places, they have traveled recently to Denmark, Sweden, and Finland. And they took an enjoyable trip to Hawaii in late 2007.

He and Jeanette married in 1962, first meeting at a party when she was working for an officer in Supreme Allied Command Atlantic Headquarters. She is an American citizen today, but originally came from Denmark. Jeanette and Phil have two children. The oldest is Annette, who was born in 1966 and is unmarried. The youngest child was Anthony, or Tony, and he is married with two young boys.

Smith, Alvin

Alvin grew up in Roanoke, Virginia, attending Jefferson High School and running very successfully for the Magicians' track team. He wanted to go to college, but his

Alvin and Betty Smith standing near the entrance to the newly-refurbished track. The plaque dedicating the track to Homer Bast is at the right.

parents had little money. He decided to stay in high school for an extra year, and then for a second year. He was hoping that he could get good enough to attract some attention from college coaches. His parents certainly couldn't pay for him to get a college degree. As Alvin said recently, "My parents couldn't help me even with five dollars."

After six years at Jefferson, he finally received an offer of a scholarship from Seton Hall. His best high school mile time was 4:34.6. The state record for Virginia high schools at the time was 4:33.3. One of his high school teammates and future runner at Roanoke College, Gordon Highfill, finished a year ahead of Alvin and enrolled at Seton Hall. The school provided a combination of a prep school and college. Gordon spent a year in their prep school. During Alvin's senior year at Jefferson, his coach sent him to run in the nationals. He finished in fifth place and caught the attention of the coach at Seton Hall. So he enrolled there with a scholarship.

Seton Hall's major emphasis in those days was on indoor track. Unfortunately, Alvin could see what might happen soon. The beginning of World War II might just cancel the entire track program at the school. Alvin also knew that he had a good chance of getting drafted into the Army.

At mid-term, therefore, he dropped out of Seton Hall and came back to Roanoke in 1942 to work. Still, he had run well in high school and continued to receive interest from several coaches. Soon, he decided to get financial aid at another college. So he went down to Duke to see if that school was a good fit for him. He had been a runner in some of Duke's invitational meets, and the coach asked him to enroll at Duke during the following semester. The school accepted him as a student and he was all set to attend the school in the fall of 1942.

At the beginning of the 1942-43 session, he showed up on the Duke campus to attend a freshman orientation program for two or three days. He came home again, ready to return and start his classes. Before the classes began, however, he got his draft notice. He had to call the Duke coach and tell him that after all he had gone through to get him a job on campus along with a place to stay, he couldn't come.

Instead of entering the Army, he decided to join the Navy. He went through a year of military training, working for a short time at the Health Department in Pensacola, Florida. The Navy trained him as a Lab Technician. When it came time for the Navy to move him to a permanent job, he was assigned to the U. S. Navy pre-flight school at the University of Georgia. A perk was that he would have the full use of the University's facilities, including its running track. There were a number of coaches at the school. Most seemed to be from the Southwest Conference. One of the coaches, Chuck Sportsman, had coached at North Texas State. He was nationally known, partially because he had coached two sets of twins. One set ran distances and the other two runners were quarter milers. Sportsman saw Alvin working out on the track one day and said, "Do you think we could get a team together here?" Alvin told him that he thought the idea was a good one. So Sportsman brought a team together and Alvin ended up running in some of the bigger meets. As he put it, "Many of the big-shot runners were off fighting the war, so I got my chance to win a few events at some of the important meets." Sportsman also formed a cross country team for the fall. The team ended up winning the Southwest A. A. U. Championships.

When Alvin finally was assigned to sea duty, the Navy put him aboard a small aircraft carrier. This placement gave him a place to run. When the planes weren't flying, he could run on the deck, sometimes covering several miles in one session.

Alvin finally got out of the service and entered the University of North Carolina in the fall of 1946. He had thought about majoring in public health, but finally decided to switch over to chemistry. U. N. C. had about 3,500 students at the time; however, they picked up a lot of additional students as the war ended, growing to a size of 6,600 students. The school grew so fast that graduate students and even undergraduate seniors were teaching classes.

At that time, he had an old car that he could use to run back and forth from Chapel Hill to Roanoke. It was an old 1937 Chevrolet. On the way back to Chapel Hill one day, the car broke down near Gretna, Virginia. As a result, he missed a chemistry quiz and lab. He soon found out that the misses were going to make him fail that chemistry course. He went in to appeal the grading, making an appointment with the Dean of the Chemistry Department. All he said to Alvin was, "You boys don't have any business running home on weekends." Alvin thought to himself, "You rascal, you. I have been out there in a war for four years and you tell me I don't have any business going home on a weekend."

Other problems appeared also. There seemed to be some discrimination by the

University toward some of the athletes as to which individual was getting what money. Although Alvin did have a place to stay, some of the boys who had come to the school before the war had been getting paid for meals and books. Others, like Alvin, weren't.

So Alvin ended up staying at U. N. C. for five quarters–about a year and a half. Gordon Highfill, his old friend and a pretty good hurdler, had enrolled at Duke University. But he told Alvin that he didn't like it there. So the two of them decided to attend Roanoke College. As Alvin tells it, "I went on up to Roanoke College, and I could kick myself for not doing it sooner. The team was just getting started, and I was the top dog there." He was also impressed by the people at Roanoke. "A few days after getting to the campus," Alvin said, "Dr. Charlie Smith spoke to me by my first name. Here was the President of a college asking me how I liked life on the campus. He was an excellent speaker and could preach a sermon without using a single note card."

The Roanoke campus was entirely different from the one at Carolina, he thought. In Chapel Hill, the campus was so big that a student seldom knew anyone outside the small group he or she associated with each day. At Roanoke, everyone seemed to know everyone else. Of course, there were only a few hundred students there as compared to U. N. C.

Alvin was a day student, living in Roanoke, but he probably spent more time on the campus than many others from the Roanoke area. He had lost some credits by transferring from U. N. C., of course, and pretty much started over in his academic work.

His relationship with his new coach was excellent. Homer was delighted that he decided to transfer, knowing the excellent times that Alvin had recorded during the past few years. In turn, Alvin appreciated Homer for his enthusiasm in building a good distance running program. Homer was much different from any of the coaches at U. N. C. In Chapel Hill, coaches had so many talented runners that the staff barely knew their names. But Alvin found Homer to be very much like his high school coach. He could see that Homer was a good motivator, willing to do what it took to develop good teams, and related well to his athletes.

In this environment, Alvin thrived as a runner. He became part of a celebrated group of cross country runners commonly known around the campus and Commonwealth as the "Big Four." That team at first consisted of Alvin, Paul McCarty, Bruce Davenport, and Red Crockett. People were amazed that they were so far ahead of the competition in some races that they crossed the finish line together, sometimes holding teammates' hands high in the air. By the beginning of the 1949-1950 fall season, the Big Four had added a bit of talent, such as Frank Aldred and White Rhyne, and in a sense the group became the Big Six.

During Alvin's first year of running cross country at the College, the team won all five meets and won both the Little Six and Mason-Dixon Championships. In his second year, they again went undefeated over four meets and won the Little Six, Virginia State A. A. U., and Mason-Dixon Championships.

At times, such as in the larger meets, Alvin would move out in front in order to try for a win. At other times, Homer would send Bruce Davenport ahead and ask Alvin to pick up and mentally support the runners behind him.

In the 1948 Little Six meet, he finished in a tie for first with a teammate. In the Mason-Dixon Championships that year, he was second.

During the 1949 season, Alvin won the Little Six Championships, tied for third with two teammates in the state A. A. U. meet, and finished third in the Mason-Dixon competition.

In track, he proved himself to be an excellent runner. Homer used him in the two-mile, mile, 880, and even the 440 on occasion. His Roanoke team had two wins and two losses during the 1948 outdoor season, losing to V. M. I. and Bridgewater. The team did well, however, in the big meets at the end of the season, winning both the Little Six and Mason-Dixon Championships. At the end of his first semester at Roanoke, members of the Monogram Club voted Alvin the school's "Athlete of the Year."

He also competed on the 1949 spring team, which finished with two wins and three losses. The team ended the season with a second-place performance in the Little Six meet, as well as a fourth-place showing in the Mason-Dixon Championships. In addition, they were fifth overall in the state A. A. U. competition.

His best times in spring track meets were: 2:00.3 in the 880, 4:24.4 in the mile (a state A. A. U. record), and 10:27.4 in the two-mile race. The mile time was the school record for ten years. Howard Meincke finally broke the record twice in 1959.

In the 1947-48 season, when he first ran for Roanoke, Alvin tied with a teammate for first place in the mile, and also won the 880 race, in the Little Six Championships. In the Mason-Dixon meet, he won the mile run.

He won the 880 in the 1949 Little Six meet, but also won the mile run (in a tie with two other Roanoke runners) and finished first in the two-mile run, also crossing the line with two teammates.

His performance in the Mason-Dixon Championships that year was also excellent. He won the mile run.

An interesting fact about Alvin is that today, despite his many accomplishments in running at Roanoke, he thinks that he was really past his prime when he enrolled at the College. He says that his best days for running came while he was at the University of Georgia. He ran better times then, and faster quarters.

During his academic work at Roanoke, he also switched majors. Professor Robey wanted every Chemistry major to take German. Alvin had taken French in high school, and wasn't about to tackle German, a more difficult language to master. So he switched his major to Biology. He tried to take 10 hours of lab work a week, but soon he got behind on his quality points. After running on the Maroon teams for four semesters, he found himself academically ineligible for competition at the beginning of the second semester in 1949-50. It wasn't long before he heard that Homer had been called for service by the Navy and would miss the 1950-51 seasons altogether. As Alvin put it, "The College had 'suggested' that I should leave school and take some time off. If I hadn't done so, the administration was going to put me out of school themselves."

Buddy Hackman asked him if he would consider coaching the cross country and track teams while Homer was away. He quickly said that he would, knowing that Homer had assembled fairly-talented teams. In addition, of course, he knew everyone he would be coaching except for any incoming freshmen. Homer had set up the schedules before he left for the service, so Alvin's main job was to keep the boys together, line the track before each meet, and round up the equipment and supplies needed for the cross country and track seasons. As he began the fall cross country season, he quickly found that he needed to watch the meager amount of money that Buddy Hackman allotted for various teams. Buddy, of course, spent little money on any of the College teams, even his own basketball squad. Some remember that if Hackman's basketball players didn't win a particular game, he wouldn't feed them at all on their way home–no matter how long the trip.

The 1950 cross country team that Alvin coached finished with three wins and one loss. The loss was by a mere three points to Virginia Military Institute. His team finished second in the Little Six meet and third in the Mason-Dixon Championships. His 1951 outdoor track team had only three dual meets, and finished with one win and two losses. Roanoke was fifth in the Little Six, ninth in the Mason-Dixon, and seventh in the state A. A. U.

Finally, after the 1951-52 session, Alvin graduated from Roanoke College at 31 years of age with a degree in Education. He thought he'd like to be a teacher and coach. He did his practice teaching at his old high school, Jefferson, under the direction of M. G. White. White was Assistant Principal and also taught chemistry. The chemistry class that Alvin took over was made up of hand-picked students–all sons or daughters of doctors and lawyers, it seemed. Alvin found, however, that he probably shouldn't have done his practice teaching with such a well-behaved and motivated bunch of students.

Roanoke City Schools hired Alvin the next fall, giving him a teaching position at Woodrow Wilson Junior High School. In Alvin's words, "That was the worst school in Roanoke to be a teacher. I had a bunch of hellions. I lasted from September until February. Then an administrator came around and asked me if I wanted to get out of my contract, and I said 'yes'." For the rest of the year, he did some part-time teaching at Jefferson High School, and considered getting out of teaching altogether.

Needing a job, he relied on one of his hobbies. He had worked some with radios, so a friend managed to get him a job at the WROV radio station in Roanoke. The station was using a rock and roll format at the time and Alvin was a Technician at the station. He was responsible for a lot of recording projects. For example, he would record a program off the network and play it back later over the air. He also recorded local commercials.

Unfortunately, he wasn't making much money and was barely getting by. So after a couple of years with WROV, he began to look around for another job. He was offered a chance to go to Richmond and teach at St. Christopher Prep School, but he turned it down even though the job would have involved coaching in addition to teaching. He also had a chance to return to teaching locally, at Monroe Junior High School in Roanoke City, but decided against that move. He continued for some time to submit applications to companies in the area. He ended up taking a job with Piedmont Airlines in Lynchburg, Virginia–a job he thought might be his career. He hadn't married yet, although he had dated his future wife almost from the time he got out of college.

Then, General Electric came to Salem, and Alvin sent them an application. For some time in 1955, he tried to get a job with them, but couldn't. In 1956, however, General Electric finally hired him. He was to become a Technician in their Engineering Department. A short time before reporting for the job, the company sent him to get a physical examination. Following the exam, he was told that he would need to have surgery on his chest. They had found a sizeable tumor there, which Alvin had never known existed. As a result, he just knew that he wasn't going to get hired. But his employer was considerate and held the job for him until he was able to recover from the surgery.

He started his new career with General Electric and everything was going well. He wanted to get married, but suddenly the company laid off many of its employees, including Alvin. So the marriage was postponed. He took a temporary part-time job with WROV just to pay his bills. It wasn't until a year after the layoff that Pete Peterson in the General Electric Personnel Department called him back to work. He was just four days shy of losing all of his seniority with the company. Alvin had laid the groundwork for his return by checking in with Peterson often to let him know that he was ready to get back to work. During his layoff, Alvin needed money so badly that he considered taking another teaching job in the Roanoke City Schools. They had signed him for a teaching position, in fact. Then he went up to the General Electric offices one day to speak to Peterson. He said to Alvin, "Let me call up to the department where you were working. Maybe they can use you. I'll get back to you this afternoon with an answer." Fortunately, the Engineering Department had just gotten a contract with the Navy, which would bring in a lot of money and more staff. So Alvin told the school system that he wouldn't be with them the coming year, and went back to his old job with General Electric the following Monday morning.

In July of 1960, Alvin and Betty McDowall finally got married. She later told Alvin that she didn't know until the marriage whether or not she'd ever get him. And he admitted that he didn't know if he would get her. Just before the marriage, they managed to buy a small house on Fleming Avenue in Roanoke City. It was just a starter house, but the type of house they were looking for. The house had been owned by Duke Mayberry and his wife. He was well-known in the area because he had been a sandlot referee for many years. The Mayberrys were building another house and needed to sell the one in which they were living at the time. The couple moved to their new house just in time for Alvin and Betty to move in just after their marriage. One of the first things the Smiths had to do was to re-paint most of the interior walls. As Alvin said, "Some of the rooms were painted in two colors. Two walls might be painted white and the other two were orange. It looked just like Howard Johnson's. So we painted over those walls pretty quickly with a light green paint. Then we got married and moved in."

Alvin's job with General Electric continued for many years, with different responsibilities, until he retired in 1984. At that time, he had been with the company for about 27 years, not counting the year he was laid off.

At the time he went with General Electric, he was out of competitive running. The last A. A. U. race he entered, in fact, was in 1954. Occasionally, he ran in light workouts, trying to stay in shape. Then, the Vinton Dogwood Festival was started. A friend of Alvin's, one of his co-workers, encouraged him to work out a bit and compete in the Festival's 5K run. Despite some reservations, he began to lengthen his practice runs and entered the race. There were few people as old as Alvin in the competition. He won the 50-and-older division of the race. He didn't run again until the Dogwood Festival the next year. Soon, he was running 35 to 40 races each year, training for them on the streets in the Williamson Road area in Roanoke.

After that first Dogwood Festival race in 1977, for example, he ran eight races. His records today show that he ran 37 races in 17 towns in 1982. There was one weekend in which he ran three times–competing in a master's race at the University of Virginia on Saturday, in Greensboro on Sunday in a 5K during a twilight meet, and then finished up the next day in Covington, Virginia, at another race.

His running continued for several years:

1983–38 races in 20 towns
1984–35 races
1985–28 races in 15 towns
1986–31 races in 17 towns
1987–24 races in 6 towns
1988–27 races in 15 towns

1989–31 races in 21 towns
1990–27 races in 18 towns

After 1990, his total number of races each year declined. Most of his competition was in road races, although occasionally he would try a master's run indoors. By 1993, he was competing in 18 races, while in 1993 he entered only 12. In 1996, he had cut his races to 12 and in the next year, to 9. The totals then were 9 races in 1997, 4 in 1998, 3 in 1999, and just a couple of races in 2000.

In 2002, he finally had to stop his training and racing. That year, he lost one of his kidneys because of a malignant tumor and his doctor told him to stop taking his arthritis medicine because the kidneys wouldn't process it very well. So he dropped the medicine, but found that he was beginning to lose his balance and fall. Instead of continuing to run and risk a fall resulting in a bone break, he decided to stop running altogether.

For many years after finishing his running days, Alvin and his wife have been major Roanoke College fans. In fact, they try to attend as many cross country and track meets as possible each year. Alvin brings along his camera and donates many of the resulting photographs to Coach Finn Pincus and his team members. In 2001, they even traveled to the Nationals to see Roanoke's Casey Smith run.

At one point, Alvin became concerned that many of the trophies from the early days of cross country and track at Roanoke College were stored unceremoniously in a small room under the steps in the old Alumni Gymnasium. Many of these trophies had been on display for years in a case outside Buddy Hackman's office. Now, they needed a new home. He asked Coach Pincus just what it would take to move those trophies to a prominent place in the C. Homer Bast Physical Education Center. Finn checked with the administration and found that, with a donation of money, the school could build and install two new cases on the runway above the basketball court. So Alvin worked out a deal. He would donate part of the money for the cases, with matching funds being provided by General Electric. Then Alvin dug out the old trophies, many in disrepair, and took them home to work on them. He repaired the broken trophies and polished them all. They can be seen today by visitors to the Bast Center.

Stryker, Derek

Derek was a fine distance runner who competed for Roanoke for four years in cross country and track. During his first year at Roanoke, 1959-60, he was fortunate to have Homer Bast as his cross country coach–the next-to-last season Bast coached any sport at the College.

Derek and Betsey Stryker in 2007

Born in Detroit, Derek lived there until 1953. Unfortunately, his mother, Beth, died in 1947 and Derek lived with Clyde, his father, after that point. He had a sister, Helene, who was 16 years his senior.

Derek attended Massapequa High School. His football and rifle coach at the school was Alec Baldwin, the father of the famous movie star of the same name. He played football in the eighth grade and also competed in cross country, track, and rifle. In cross country and track, he didn't win consistently, but always seemed to finish in the top two or three on his team.

He chose Roanoke College because it was a small school, affordable, with a good reputation in track athletics. A friend, Vinnie Ahearn, entered Roanoke a couple of years before Derek, and recommended the school to Derek. In addition, Derek's high school guidance counselor knew that Derek was looking for a college that the family could afford, a school that had a good pre-engineering reputation and one that was small and in the south. The counselor pointed to Roanoke as being something which might interest Derek.

So in June after his senior year at Massapequa, Derek and a friend drove down to Roanoke to look over the campus. He had yet to apply to the school for admittance in the fall. He was impressed by the Shenandoah Valley and the Salem area's beauty. As soon as he got to Roanoke, he met Homer Bast for the first time–although for just 15 minutes. Apparently, that meeting provided the spark that got Derek to apply to Roanoke. According to Derek, "I met Homer and fell in love with the man. I thought he was the most fabulous person I had ever met. He was wonderful. My talk with Homer, plus the fact that the school just felt comfortable for me, led me to apply. I could see from the visit that the small size of the campus would allow me to know people better. Everything just clicked."

When he began his four years at Roanoke, like many other students, he really didn't know what he wanted to do in life. He thought for a while that he might want to go into the service when he got out of college. He did know, however, that early on he wasn't a particularly serious student. He finally chose economics as a major because he thought that type of major made the most sense for his career after Roanoke.

Derek was involved in lots of campus activities. He was in the Kappa Alpha fraternity (#3 at one point) and a member of the Rat Council, track and cross country teams,

Monogram Club, Commons Committee, and more. He became Vice President of the Student Body and during his last year was selected for *Who's Who in American Colleges and Universities.*

He also held down campus jobs. A friend and student Larry Johnson got him a three-times-a-week job picking up and delivering women's laundry. For his work, he received some needed spending money and was introduced to lots of other students.

During the early days of Derek's freshman year, he and his dad shared an apartment on High Street. That arrangement lasted until his father decided that with Derek in school all day, it was just too lonely living in the apartment. So he went back to Long Island after Thanksgiving and unexpectedly died of a heart attack the following February. Derek moved into Section Four of the dormitories. Charlie Tempkin was his roommate. Then, Derek was placed in Hildreth Hall and stayed there for about a year and a half. Most of the residents of Hildreth were athletes. Warren Orndorff and Ken Hamaker were two of the guys who lived in the building. Bill Davis was there for a while. Wayne Wilson was Derek's roommate during the first semester and then Derek lived with Bob Stauffer for the next year. For his junior and senior years at Roanoke, Derek moved into the fraternity house. Fred Fishel, David Chalfant, and Am Freund–"the three coolest guys on campus," laughs Derek–were his roommates.

His plans after graduation became clear as he approached graduation day. He decided to go into the Navy, although not as a career. He and Elizabeth "Betsy" Baily '64 were married just as soon as she graduated from Roanoke. The wedding was in Alexandria, Virginia, her home. The marriage brought three children. The oldest was Bryan, followed by Jeffrey and then Sally. Today, Derek and Betsy have six grandchildren.

Meanwhile, Derek entered the Navy, went to Officer Candidates School, and then on to school in New Mexico. After that assignment, he was moved to the Naval Weapons Station in Yorktown, where he served until he was released from his Navy obligations. During the time he was in the service, he went to graduate school at night. He knew that in order to get the job he wanted, he not only wanted to have at least a year in the Navy, but also a graduate degree. Finally, he left the Navy as a Lieutenant.

With his Master's Degree in Business–technically in personnel and labor– Derek took a job with Avon and stayed with the company for the next 10 years. He worked for them in operations, marketing, and sales. He and Betsy lived in Connecticut and he worked in Rye, New York. His final position with Avon was as a Division Sales Manager.

At this point, he switched jobs, being hired by Shaklee and working out of Pennsylvania, although the company's main offices were in San Francisco. Shaklee, of course, was a giant nutrition-based company. For Shaklee, Derek was a Regional Sales Manager before becoming their Regional Sales Manager and then their National Sales Director for the entire United States. He was with Shaklee for about seven years, and when he left the company he and Betsy were living in San Francisco.

Then he was recruited by Sara Lee, which owned a company named Fuller Brush. Fuller Brush at the time was not a profitable company, however, and Sara Lee's instructions to Derek were to make it profitable so they could sell it. In those times, Sara Lee controlled many companies. Although Fuller Brush was worth some $70,000,000 on paper, it wasn't very profitable. Derek over the next five years was able to turn the company around and Sara Lee sold it.

In reality, Derek earned enough money during his stay with Sara Lee that he was able to consider retirement. But at just 50 years of age, he took another job instead. He became Executive Vice President for the United States and Canada for a Japanese skin care company called Noevir. It was a large company, but most of their business was conducted in Japan and Korea. He stayed with Noevir for two years, and then bought his own company. The company name was Finelle and Derek became President and Co-Owner. A manufacturer and distributor of skin care cosmetics in the United States and Canada, Finelle was based outside Boston near Andover, Massachusetts.

Derek retired from Finelle after selling the business. For about seven or eight years afterwards, he was a consultant. After retirement, he and Betsy moved to the Lake Norman area near Statesville, North Carolina. They stayed in that area for about nine years, partly because they liked North Carolina and partly because they had a son and grandchildren there. Their house was right on the water.

About a year or so before this book was completed, the Strykers sold their house and moved a short distance away–to Sun City Carolina Lakes, a Dell Webb community consisting of 1,230 acres of rolling woodlands punctuated by 10 lakes. That's about 10 miles south of Charlotte, North Carolina, in the northern portion of South Carolina. They live near the Catawba River.

These days, Derek still works about half a day each week for a friend. He also spends his time in a woodworking group. Woodworking has been one of his hobbies over the past few years. He especially likes to turn bowls. He and Betsy have a son and grandchildren near them and family takes up some of their time.

Derek has taken up Yoga and, on occasion, has been involved with local politics. Betsy and he also travel, sometimes just to visit their family; however, not long ago, they did spend about two months in France. They enjoyed the country and wanted to spend some time there without having to move around very much. They rented a small house in southern France, just outside a moderate-sized town, and were only about an hour and a half trip from the Mediterranean. During the time they were in France, they took numerous day trips with the other two people who accompanied them. At one point, their children came over and another time, Derek's older sister stayed with them.

Homer Bast always has been one of Derek's favorite people. During his first year at

Roanoke, Derek was not a very good student and didn't know how to study. After his father died in February, he said:

> "Homer could not have been more gracious and helped me sort out my feelings. And I was glad to help Homer when he had his own heart problems, taking him to Johns Hopkins on my way home. In my sophomore year, I was on academic probation. To add to my problems, I was placed on social probation as well. That was because of the 'kill Harry Ballou' prank. Wayne Wilson was my roommate. He had taken a starter's gun away from a girl because he didn't want her to get into trouble. It was a starter's gun that was designed to shoot blanks. The barrel wasn't plugged. One day, Wayne and I decided to take soap and put it in a shell in place of the lead. Harry Ballou, a fellow track man, lived over us. We were told that Harry was a bit antsy about the gun being in Hildreth and as a result Wayne and I decided to play a trick on him. Both Harry and I had been dating Nancy Ballentine. I had stopped dating her at the time of the prank, but Harry had been dating her for a while. So Wayne and I started to make some noise over the next hour or so. We let it be known to Harry that I was really angry with him because of Nancy. Then I got some beer cans and staged a scuffle outside of Harry's door. We even threw the cans down the stairs and said loudly, 'O. K., Harry. I'm leaving, but when I come back I'm going to get you.' So I left the building. Then Wayne and another resident began to talk up the prank. Wayne and I then communicated by phone and finally it was time for the trick to be played. I came back into the building, yelling loudly that I was coming to get Harry. Wayne pretended to struggle with me. I said, 'I'm tired of Harry.' And I shot the starter's gun. Wayne yelled out, 'Help. I've been shot.' And then both of us ran up the steps to tell Harry that it had all been a joke. We opened his door and the room was empty. Apparently, Harry had been able to get out through one of the screened-in windows, panicking that I was coming to shoot him. It must have been about 10 feet from the window to the ground. We cleaned up everything and made like we were serious students. About 20 to 30 minutes later, we looked outside and there were two, maybe three cop cars surrounding the building. And there was Harry in one of the cars. A cop comes in and asks us what was going on. We said, 'Nothing, sir." He told us that that was bull, because he had a guy in the car who was scared to death. So we broke down and told him the story, and that we had hidden the gun down next to the maintenance

> building near Hildreth. Harry, of course, was furious with us for quite a while after that. The next day, a Monday, Dean Sutton called us in. We ended up getting put on social probation. I told Mr. Sutton that it was all my idea. I was just a freshman, but Wayne was on his way to medical school. In fact, he already had been accepted. And he was getting married soon. Still, the Dean put us on social probation for the rest of the semester."

After this incident, Derek remembers Homer taking him under his wing. Here he was, on academic and social probation, and he realized at that point that he had let Homer–and himself–down. It was perhaps the turning point in Derek's college career. He began to understand that he needed to buckle down and study. He did, and then got back into good graces with Dean Sutton and the administration. During this period of maturation, Homer would often touch bases with him–even though he was no longer Derek's coach. When mid-term grades came out the next year, Derek remembers the excitement that was on Homer's face because Derek had finally gotten his 2.0 average.

During Derek's long and successful business career, he often had to write to his staff. A number of times, he would tell them some of the stories Homer had told his team while he was at Roanoke. For example, when they were being challenged by tough economic times, he might give them a favorite saying from Homer. "In a long race, don't give up. You only have to run to the next telephone pole."

Summers, John

When John was in high school, his family was poor. It looked like there would never be a chance for him to attend college. One of five siblings, who all were brought up in the Catholic Church, John became interested in the spiritual reason for being what you are. So he began to attend St. Stephen's Church, a beautiful Catholic church in his home town of Kearney, New Jersey. He got in the habit of going there in the afternoons after school. He would sit in that church and pray that there would be some way that he could go to college.

One day, he went to his high school gym class on a day when the students were doing pull ups, push ups, a rope climb, etc. Then the class went outside and ran the 100-yard dash. Coach Harold Jardene, an outstanding coach in New Jersey with state championship track and cross country teams each year, saw him in the hallway after all of the scores had been tabulated. He said, "I was just looking at your times. You can run. You need to come out for the track team. Come on down this afternoon and I will get you your uniform and sweats. We'll put you on the track team and see how things go." So

John joined the team. He discovered that his coach wanted to build an interscholastic champion mile relay team. John was just a freshman at the time.

The team already had the state champion in the quarter, who was running about :48. He may have been one of the two best in the nation, in fact. The team also had Jimmy Norton, who played football and could run like a deer, and another fellow who was the state sprint champion in the100-yard dash. John, of course, was the youngest and slowest of the four. But with this group as a mile relay team, John could run about a :51 quarter.

He began to go to church more often, and stayed there longer each time. Maybe, he thought to himself, this track thing is my key to college. John had a talk with Coach Jardene, telling him how much he wanted to go to college, and Jardene took a liking to him. He said, "Don't worry. We'll get you into college."

In his senior year of high school, John actually had a chance to attend Pennsylvania State. Coach Chick Warner there was building a mile relay team, but John soon realized that the school could have its pick of any of dozens of great runners. He knew that he might not measure up enough to get a decent scholarship. It was at that time that he came home one day from school and there on the table was a letter from Homer Bast at Roanoke. It was just after his team had won the New Jersey state championship. "It was such a nice letter," says John, "and he talked about Roanoke College and how I would like it there. I thought that Roanoke must be a great place to go. So I wrote him a return letter. And then I took my College Boards. Unfortunately, my scores weren't very good. Coach Bast wrote me another letter, saying that he was very sorry, but that Roanoke couldn't accept me based on the scores." Not to be deterred, John sent Homer another letter, telling in detail what his dreams were. Homer was touched and got the Admissions Committee to change their decision. His next letter to John said that the College really did want John to be able to come to Roanoke. "Well, I just died," John said. "I went back to the church and thanked the Lord, because I knew that through Homer Bast, all of my prayers had been answered."

Several months ago, long after his college days were finished, John was at the church again. He spotted a priest coming out of the church and stopped him to ask if he could talk to him for a moment. The priest agreed, and John said that he just wanted to tell him what happened to him in life. He told him that he was a retired Admiral n the U. S. Navy, and related the story above. The priest said, "Are you going to be here on Sunday?" John told him that he was headed back home. So the priest asked if he could use the story John had just told him in one of the Sunday services. John said he didn't mind and, in fact, was very pleased.

Just out of Kearny, John showed up on the Roanoke campus with barely a cent in his pockets. Homer had gotten him a scholarship, which paid for his tuition. The school also hired him to work in the Commons, where he waited tables. That job paid for his room and board. And his family was able to send him $7 each week. Most of that $7, John remembers, was donated to Our Lady of Perpetual Help.

College was a moving experience for John. At Roanoke, the things he learned were the important things in his future life. He was always glad that he went to a small college like Roanoke. He knew the community. He made life-long friends both from his experiences in cross country and track and through his membership in the Kappa Alpha fraternity. The fraternity house was on High Street at the time. Where it sat is now a vacant lot. John never lived in the fraternity house while he was in college, except for a half semester, because he had a scholarship and couldn't pay the fraternity for his room and board.

Homer Bast persuaded John to run cross country, although he had never done so before. Bast wanted everyone possible to run cross country in order to help them build stamina and endurance. John hated running distance races, and especially the training it took, but he turned out to be a decent cross country man. He used to ask Les Noel, "How can you be laughing while you are doing this? Nobody laughs and runs this far."

The track team John was on was the one that started the long streak of 36 dual and tri-meet wins. "Personally," John says, "we always knew where we were during the streak. None of us wanted to see it end. Every time we won another meet, Coach Bast was just beside himself. I don't think he used the streak to put pressure on the athletes, but he knew at all times where the team was on that streak."

In track, John had an excellent college career. He had good speed, witnessed by the fact that he ran :23.0 and :23.2 in the 220-yard dash. In the quarter mile, he held several school records. He ran two :51.5 times and many other races below :52.0. On rare occasions, Homer would use him in the 880, where he ran 2:03.2 and 2:03.6. He was particularly successful as a member of some very good mile relay teams. He, Al Ide, Pete Wise, and Dick Lewis, in fact, set a new school record in 1956 during the Mason-Dixon Championships by running a time of 3:22.6, a spectacular time for that era. In the Little Eight Championships, he won the 440-yard dash in both 1953 and 1954, while in 1953, 1954, and 1956, he ran on the teams which won the Little Eight mile relay medals.

Indoors, John ran a :53.6 and competed on several Roanoke mile relay, sprint medley, and distance medley teams. Twice, he even ran on two-mile relays for Roanoke.

After college, John went on active duty with the Navy. When he came back after active duty, he joined John Hancock Insurance in 1960. He believes now that he chose insurance as a career because at the time there were very few jobs available and the economy was bad. Actually, he almost ended up with the Navy as his career. He had already signed up to go back in, in Naval Intelligence, and was going to become an Air Attaché. Then the General Agent for John Hancock called him. Not knowing exactly what to do, John went to talk with the gentleman about joining the John Hancock team.

He could see that the fellow had a good career, so he ended up joining the company. He worked as an Insurance Agent, an Agency Supervisor, and then an Assistant General Agent and a General Agent. He ran that agency, his own business, from 1974 until 1991 or 1992. He really enjoyed what he was doing.

He had stayed on in the Naval Reserve during all of this time. He was in a squadron in Norfolk and the company was good to him. There was a lot of active duty and John probably spent close to six months a year on Navy business.

At one point, he was promoted to Captain and the Navy gave him a good job working for the Secretary of the Navy and the Secretary of Defense in Washington. His job was to work on specific projects for them. He eventually earned his rank as Admiral, getting one star in 1983. In 1984, he became Chief of Staff for Logistics and Readiness in London, working for the Commander In Chief of U. S. Naval Forces Europe. He spent nine years in that job.

During this period of time, he would be overseas for a couple of weeks, and then would come back to Roanoke, where his insurance agency was located. Once, he went to the John Hancock people and asked them if they wanted to replace him. But the President of the company said he wanted John to remain an agent. John Hancock, John says, was very good to him.

The Navy then gave John a readiness command in Washington and he was responsible for 20,000 military personnel in Washington, Maryland, and Pennsylvania. That meant that he had the job in London, the one in Washington, and at the same time he was running his insurance business in Roanoke.

He finally retired from John Hancock when he was about 59 years old. He began receiving his Navy pension at the age of 60, and received his company pension beginning the year he retired.

John is proud of all he did. His insurance business was very successful. "The insurance business," he says, "is especially difficult for a beginner. Lots of people–perhaps as many as 97%–drop out. In fact, I had a son, Tim, who went into insurance, but he didn't stay in the business. He could have, but didn't like rejection. He went into teaching, and loved it. He teaches over at Oak Grove in the second grade. He not only likes what he is doing, but he is a very good teacher. He also has a Celtic band and they play all over the place. He is a wonderful acoustic guitar player. The name of their group is "The Beggar's Circus."

John had two children, Tim and Ann; unfortunately, Ann committed suicide as a result of severe depression. "It was an awful time in my life," John says. "and it was something I thought I would never get over. No one knew about her depression. When she died, she was 28 and was teaching."

Today, Tim's daughters are very talented. One is an accomplished ballerina.

Although she still is in high school, she has starred in the Nutcracker Suite, is in the marching band, and is a talented musician. His other daughter plays a trumpet and is in her marching band.

Tramposch, Walt

Walter Tramposch, generally called Walt by his friends, was born in Brooklyn, New York, and raised in Queens. His parents were Ralph and Alice Tramposch. Walt had two brothers. One was Ralph, who also attended Roanoke College. The younger one was Bob.

Walt and Pat Tramposch pose with members of their family.

Walt attended Newtown High School, which had an excellent track coach by the name of Ira Terwiliger. The coach gave a number of students tryouts, watching them run, and asked Walt if he wanted to be on the team. He said, "Sure," because the track team was a good one and usually won the Queens Championships without any trouble. And they did well in the City Championships.

Coach Terwiliger put him in the quarter mile and also had him run in the 1200-yard relay race. In the latter race, each boy ran 300 yards–a distance that Walt really liked. Terwiliger was a tough coach and was different from Roanoke's Homer Bast in that he would have the guys compete against each other every day.

During his senior year, Walt began to think about college. He took the New York University examination for engineering and passed it. But his brother, Ralph, failed it. Their mother was not happy. So she had the boys look around for other schools to attend. At the time, Walt's father was a Superintendent for Conn Edison. One of the guys who worked for him had attended Roanoke College, and he recommended the school.

Walt arrived on the Roanoke campus in the fall of 1949. He had never spoken with Homer Bast before the first few days, when the freshmen were getting their gym gear. Homer was helping hand them out. Homer spoke to Walt and it was obvious that he knew that Walt was an athlete.

Walt did not run cross country for Homer; instead he played soccer every fall. The soccer team during that time wasn't really very good. Before one of the games, Coach Elwood Fox became so frustrated that he told the team that he would pay them $5 for every goal a person scored during the season. After Walt had scored five goals himself, Fox walked up to him and handed him $25, which was a lot of money in those days. "Fox was a good guy," Tramposch says. "I liked him. He didn't know a great deal about soccer, of course. He would often yell at us from the sidelines during a game, saying 'Use your elbows.' That was Foxie's approach."

In outdoor track, Coach Bast used Walt in the 220, the 440, and on relay teams. He teamed with Dick Dodd, Frank Aldred, and Paul McCarty to win the Little Six mile relay trophy in 1950.

Walt stayed at Roanoke for only two years, leaving after the 1949-50 session to transfer to Hofstra College. There, he tried to participate in sports; however, when they told him that he would have to sit out a year because of the transfer, he became discouraged and never competed. He graduated after being at Hofstra for three years, completing one year of study in night school. His degree in 1953 was in Physics.

During that last year at Hofstra, when he took all night classes, he also worked as a technician at Hazeltine Corporation. The company focused on military electronics. Once he got his degree from Hofstra, he began a job at Hazeline as an Engineer. At the same time, he went to New York University to get a Master's Degree in Physics. After receiving that degree, he stayed at Hazeltine and advanced through the ranks. Eventually, he would become their Director of Engineering.

While he was doing his night school work, Walt married Patricia Ellis. That marriage lasted for some 58 years. In 2000, Walt and Patricia held their 50th wedding anniversary celebration.

About a year after their marriage, their first child was born. Her name was Lynn. After Lynn came two more girls. One was Gail, who attended Roanoke College, and the second one was Janet. Janet never wanted to go to college. The final child was a son, Walter, who was born in 1962. He also went to Roanoke for a couple of years and was a basketball player.

Walt remained an employee of Hazeltine for 27 years, leaving for two years for another job, and then returning to Hazeltine for another five years. He then left them one more time, but again came back. During the latter period, he got to spend about a year in Turkey, a few months in England, and some time in Egypt. He was serving as a consultant.

He retired from Hazeltine in 2000. His main hobby in retirement was playing the piano. He had excellent training on the piano when he was younger. He especially enjoyed jazz music.

In addition, he and his wife were very heavily involved in sailing. At one time, they had a 50-foot yacht down in the Caribbean. One of their sons was its Captain and he was making a living on it. Today, he is the Manager of two marinas out on the end of the island.

Note to the reader: Sadly, Walt passed away in June of 2008, prior to the publication of this book. We send our condolences to his wife, Patricia, and all of the members of his family.

Upton, Bob

Bob and Sally Upton are in the center of the picture, holding the two babies. They are surrounded by their four children, their spouses, and grand children.

The only child of Donald and Violet Upton, Bob was born in Brooklyn, New York. He grew up in Garden City, N.Y. and attended Garden City High School. He was a member of the cross-country team and a sprinter on both the indoor and outdoor track teams. He was also Captain of the track team in his senior year. Bob was a competitive high school sprinter, running official times of :10.1 in the 100 yards and :22.6 in the 220 yards. He had a :10.0 in the 100 yards, running against a college student. That's not too bad for the early 1950's.

His high school track coach, Warren King, had been an alternate on the 440-yard relay team, with Jesse Owens, for the 1936 United States Olympic Track Team. Coach King was also an All American Football Player at Dartmouth. He was most anxious for Bob to attend St. John's University in New York City. In fact he pretty much assured Bob that he would get a full track scholarship. However, Bob had no desire to attend a city university and thus he began the search for another school.

During the early summer of 1954, just after graduating at age 17 from high school, he and his parents visited Roanoke College to see the campus. On the trip they were fortunate enough to meet Coach Homer Bast. Bob and his parents were most impressed by Coach Bast's enthusiasm, personality and dedication to track athletes. He could not wait for September to roll around so he could get down to Roanoke College and Coach Bast's track team. Bob had great aspirations of having a wonderful track career at Roanoke College.

Well, the best laid plans of mice and men can certainly take a weird turn and it did for Bob. At the conclusion of his summer job in 1954, he and a friend traveled to Vermont to do some camping and mountain climbing prior to the start of college. Bob capped off the "Vermont Vacation" by falling from a 65-foot cliff. Needless to say he suffered some significant injuries, like breaking his left ankle in four places, fracturing his pinky finger and removing significant amount of skin from his hand and fingers that required 70 stitches.

A few weeks later, Bob boarded an airplane and flew to Salem, arriving at the College with casts on both his left leg and his right hand. When all was healed some 3-4 months later, he had the nasty and difficult experience of learning that he simply lost all of his "natural speed." His days as a collegiate sprinter were over.

Well, that would not have been a total catastrophe if he had not been honest and forthright when people asked him what his high school times were in the sprints. Bob went from a very competitive high school sprinter to a pretty good collegiate intramural sprinter. Couple the aforementioned with some freshman academic challenges and his freshman year in college was a disaster.

However, his sophomore, junior and senior years were fantastic. Bob started doing some weight lifting and joined Coach Bast's team in the shot put and discus. Coach Bast was always the encourager and motivator.

While on the team, he ended up throwing the shot almost 40 feet and the discus a respectable 125 feet. He finished fourth in the discus at the Little Eight Championships in one of his track years, which earned him a varsity letter. As Bob stated, "I may have lettered in track and field with the fewest number of points in the history of Roanoke College Athletics and was *not* inducted into the Roanoke College Hall of Fame."

While at Roanoke, Bob was a member of the Kappa Alpha Fraternity. He was Assistant Treasure his junior year and Treasure his senior year. He graduated with dual majors in Business Administration and Sociology. Upon graduation Bob entered Virginia Tech in Blacksburg, VA with the intent of securing an MBA. However, it never came to fruition, as he and his college sweetheart Sally Randolph, who graduated in 1960 from Roanoke College, were married that August.

After a few business ventures Bob joined Texaco Inc. in October of 1962, which was the beginning of a long and successful career. He held a wide variety of management positions in marketing along with numerous special assignments during that period of time. Bob retired from Texaco Inc. on January 1, 1993, after 31+ years of service.

Also, a most rewarding experience for Bob occurred just prior to his retirement when he was advised that he was a recipient of the Roanoke College Sesquicentennial Distinguished Alumni Recognition Award in 1992.

The past fifteen (15) + years of retirement for Bob & Sally has included extensive volunteer work with The Salvation Army, Fairfax Area Christian Emergency & Transitional Services Inc. (FACETS), geared to working with the homeless, Court Appointed Special Advocate (CASA), for abused children, Wolf Trap National Park for the Performing Arts, Pakistan American University Group (PAU), establishing an American University in Gujaranwala, Pakistan, Meals on Wheels, Campus Crusade for Christ and numerous responsibilities with First Baptist Church of Springfield, Virginia their home church.

Bob and Sally have four children, one son and three daughters, all of whom are married. Two of their daughters graduated from Roanoke College–Kimberly Upton McAleer in 1989 and Heather Upton Singley in 1992. Heather worked for Roanoke College upon graduation for a number of years. She was the Assistant Director of Admissions and Director of International Recruitment. They currently have six grandchildren with twins expected in June of 2008 and another grandchild due in December 2008.

Today, Bob and Sally live in an apartment in McLean, VA and delight in no longer having the responsibilities of a single family home. They both love their current living accommodations, which is centrally located and very close to all family members.

Vest, Frank

Frank Vest, Jr., was born in Salem and raised in both Salem and Roanoke County. His father, Frank, Sr., had gone to Roanoke College in the 1920s and was a member of the Pi Kappa Phi fraternity. Sometimes called "Red" because of the color of his hair, the elder Frank was a good football player and on the same team as legendary players Hunk Hurt, Ted Webber, and others. The younger Frank's mother was Viola, who usually was called Jackie.

Frank's father never graduated from Roanoke. The Depression hit and he dropped out of Roanoke to go to work. During his career, he was a business executive for Old Virginia Brick for a while. He also worked for a cinderblock company in Roanoke. Jackie was a teacher. Before she married Frank, Sr., she taught at Salem High School, the precursor to Andrew Lewis High School. Later, she taught at William Byrd High School in Vinton and even later at Bedford High School.

There was one younger brother in the family–Jim Vest–who went to V. M. I. He ended up as the President and C. E. O. of a company named Piedmont Labels.

At Jefferson High School, Frank ran the quarter mile in track, and he also played football. He was at Jefferson for two years. In his senior year, the family moved to Blacksburg and Frank played for Blacksburg High School. He always considered football to be his best sport.

Roanoke was his first choice of colleges, primarily because his father went there. During the first part of his freshman year, he had no intention of participating in any sport. He just didn't think he was a very good athlete–and especially not a good runner. Of course, Roanoke had dropped football in the 1940, so he couldn't be a part of his favorite sport.

Frank Vest, Jr.

One day, he was fooling around in the old college swimming pool, doing some casual diving. Coach Bast just happened to walk through the double doors and watched him dive. He came over and asked Frank, "Have you ever pole vaulted?" Frank told him that he didn't think he would be much of a vaulter, but Homer said, "Well, I can teach you how." Frank quickly figured out that if you were on an athletic team, you could drop your physical education course. His gym class had been scheduled for Tuesday-Thursday-Saturday at 8:00 a.m., so he immediately decided to become a pole vaulter.

Frank was never a great vaulter, but could definitely get the team some points in most meets. He cleared 11'6" some five separate times, in fact, which was a pretty good height in those days.

Track, of course, made up only a portion of his extracurricular activities. He served as student body President and was on the Honor Council for three years. He was President of his class during each of his first three years, and didn't run for the office his senior year. George Jocher, fellow athlete, fraternity brother, and close friend, took over as President of the Class instead. Frank also served his fraternity well. He was the K. A. #1, #2, and #9 during his stay at Roanoke. He was nominated to be #1 again during his senior year, but he declined. It was a time-consuming job and he felt that it was someone else's time to take over.

Frank was chosen the outstanding K. A. in Virginia. The faculty nominated him for a Rhodes Scholarship, and one of his later regrets was that he didn't follow up on that award. At the time, he was in love with Ann Booth Jarvis and didn't want to go away from home. Incidentally, Ann and Frank were eventually married in 1961 and lived together as husband and wife for more than 47 years prior to his death in 2008. Ann was a student at Randolph-Macon Women's College, and she and Frank dated all four years he was at Roanoke.

Frank's major at Roanoke, thanks to Homer Bast, was History. He went to Roanoke with the idea of majoring in English; however, Homer got him so excited about History in his World Civilization course that Frank ended up majoring in the subject. He also had thought about going into engineering, but decided that he should at least look into going into the seminary and an engineering degree was probably not the best background for entering the seminary.

Frank had been very active in the church as a child and young person. While at the College, he was the only person at the K. A. house who went to church each week. He remembers that when he got to be #1 in the fraternity, he would occasionally turn on the fire alarm when he left the house to go to church on Sunday mornings.

Frank became Valedictorian of his class. Betty Sue Siler–a brilliant woman, Frank remember–was the Salutatorian. She turned out to be an excellent scientist, going to Duke for her Ph.D. Today, she is one of Roanoke's most distinguished alumni.

When Frank graduated from Roanoke, he went directly to the Virginia Theological Seminary in Alexander, remaining there for three years. He was graduated and ordained by one of his heroes, Bishop William H. Marmion, who at the time was Bishop of the Diocese of Southwestern Virginia.

His first position was with St. John's Church in Roanoke as Assistant Pastor. He was there for two years before transferring to Radford as the Rector of Grace Church. He was at Grace for another four years.

Then he came back to Roanoke, serving for five years at the Rector of Christ Church on Franklin Road. Moving to Charlotte, North Carolina, he became Rector of Christ Church for some 12 years. At that point, he was elected Bishop Suffragan of the Dioces of North Carolina and was headquartered in Raleigh. In that position, he was responsible for visiting all of the congregations, exercising oversight over the clergy, being the chief pastor for the clergy, and more. At the time, he was about 49 years old. Four years later, he was elected as the Diocesan Bishop of Southwestern Virginia. He stayed in that job for nine years, retiring in 1998.

Frank and Ann had a happy marriage. After their wedding in 1961, they eventually had three children. The oldest was Nina, now in her mid-forties. She is a professor of English at Lynchburg College and runs the writing centers at V. M. I. and Washington and Lee. A busy person, she has three teenage sons.

The second child is Frank III, generally called "Hank." He works in the real estate business in Nashville. Frank III and his wife have three sons.

The third child is Rob. He is in Charlotte as an investment banker. He and his wife have a daughter and twin sons. In all, Frank and Ann have eight grandsons and one granddaughter.

After his retirement, Frank expanded on his favorite hobbies–reading, golf, and tennis, along with fly fishing.

Note to the reader: The author's interview with Frank Vest took place on November 5, 2007. On that day, he was articulate, very happy to talk about his experiences at Roanoke, and added much to this book. He never once talked about his health. Unfortunately, in April of 2008, Frank died of C. O. P. D.-related health problems. He was a special person, and will be missed greatly.

Wallwork, Jim

Jim Wallwork, Jr., was born in Dumont, New Jersey, the son of Jim, Sr., and Marian. He had one sister, Deborah, who was two years older than he. His father was an engineer with Westinghouse in New York City. His mother ran a private school for students from pre-school to sixth grade.

Jim went to Tenafly High School in Tenafly, New Jersey. He participated on a very good track team. In fact, they were state champions during the four years he was there.

He always intended to go to college, but it was his high school track coach who recommended Roanoke to him. Jim was never quite sure whether the coach had some connection with the College, or whether he even knew Homer Bast. At any rate, Jim was the only student from his high school to come to Roanoke that fall.

In track at Roanoke, Jim mostly ran the quarter mile. He was especially valuable to the team as a relay man. Sometimes, he even ran the hurdles. As he puts it, "I had never run the hurdles before getting to Roanoke College. I think Homer Bast taught me how to hurdle because he was trying to figure out where to put me. I remember that in my first meet, he had me running the 60, the 440, and the relays."

Jim has fond memories today of the some of the athletes on his indoor and outdoor track teams. He says, "I remember Les Noel, who was a hard-working guy. In the Commons, he used to wait tables. He was a really dedicated guy. I also remember Bruce Fariss. He came and visited me in New Jersey one time, and he and I took a trip over to

Kay (white top) and Jim (golf shirt) poses for a group picture in 2007 with their three children, their spouses, six grandchildren, and a fiance of their oldest grandson.

New York City. I also remember Jack Summers. He and I had run together, on separate teams, in high school. During one high school meet, someone's foot knocked the baton out of my hand. At the time, I didn't know who did it. Once in college, however, we figured out that it had to be Summers. He was a good 440 man in college. Another person I remember is Bill Lund. I believe he was a sophomore when I got to Roanoke. He had lost the use of one of his eyes. He and I were roommates at one point. I also lived with Phil Shaw."

Although Jim was at Roanoke for three years, he ran track only two of those years. After three years, he transferred to Fairly Dickinson University, going to night school to catch up on his studies. He transferred not because he didn't like Roanoke. It was just what he expected it to be. Today, he calls it "a great school." But Roanoke just didn't have the courses he needed. He graduated in about two and one-half years from Fairly Dickinson, with a degree in business.

After his graduation in 1957, he worked for Amoco as a salesman in New Jersey. Two years later, he was promoted to a job with the company in New York City. He stayed with Amoco for about 10 years.

Meanwhile, about a year after leaving Roanoke and while he was taking night school courses, he married Charlotte. She had been in the same class with Jim at Tenafly High School. Together, they had three children. The oldest was Peter, followed by Liza and Charis. His son today is a Captain in Fire and Rescue in South Florida. Liza teaches school in North Carolina, near Charlotte. Chris does promotional work for Saks Fifth Avenue, although he lives near Raleigh, North Carolina. Peter has two boys, James and Tyler. Lisa's children are Nick and Katherine. Chris' children are Kyle and Katlyn.

After leaving Amoco, Jim took a job with Monroe Auto Equipment Company.

Beginning in sales, he became Sales Manager for them in New York and then a District Manager in Chicago. Jim and Charlotte actually moved to Chicago during that period. The job lasted 12 years, after which Jim worked for a company called Steego Corporation. Steego is a holding corporation, dealing in auto parts, in West Palm Beach, Florida. That job necessitated another move for the family to Florida. Jim became their General Manager for Merchandising in the automotive division. Steego had warehouses and public stores all over the United States and Canada. The company finally disbanded and broke up, selling off the company into smaller pieces. That's when Jim left.

He then re-married in 1991 to a lady named Kay. She had worked for the State of Illinois before changing to a job in Florida, where they met. Jim was about 65 when he retired some five or six years ago. He and Kay have an RV and travel, mostly in the RV, all over the United States. In fact, they travel an average of about four to five months out of each year. They also have been to Hawaii, which Jim says "is a paradise if you get off the main island."

Today, Kay and Jim live in Springfield, Illinois. One of his hobbies is re-building old houses.

Williams, Bill

Bill was born in Palmerton, Pennsylvania, the son of Anna and Henry Williams, Sr. He had four siblings, three boys and two girls. The boys in order from youngest to oldest were Richard, Bill, Robert, and Henry III. Bill's youngest sister is Bertha. The other sister was a year older than Bertha. Today, Bertha is the only one of the five still living.

Bill attended Palmerton High School, where he participated in basketball and track. In track, as it was in college, his specialty was the pole vault, although he did some high jumping as well. His best vault was about 10'6". He wasn't able to compete in track during his senior year, however, because of World War II.

Just after graduating from Palmerton in 1943, he decided to join the Navy. Unfortunately, after a year in the Navy, he really wanted to leave the service altogether. The Navy had put him in a school, but he flunked out at mid-term. They even wrote a letter to Bill's father, saying that he had flunked out on purpose. So they sent him to boot camp and he stayed in the Navy for about three years.

In 1946, he enrolled at Roanoke College. He chose the school because of the recommendations of a friend and fellow high school basketball player. "At Roanoke," he remembers today, "I found that the book work was too damn hard."

Even though basketball was his real passion, Bill chose track. "In reality," Bill says, "if I had made Hackman's team, I would have flunked out of school. And I knew it." During one winter season, he was a member of the swimming team.

Bill had brought some credits with him from other schools, so he stayed at Roanoke for about three years. He competed in track for all three years. In his first and second years, he was Homer's main pole vaulter, consistently clearing between 10 and 11 feet. In his third and final season, during the 1948-49 session, he was joined by Ray DeCosta. DeCosta, shorter than Bill, was stronger in the upper body. DeCosta eventually jumped 13'6" during his career at Roanoke. In 1949, Bill's last year at Roanoke, he jumped 11'8" at the Milligan Relays in Johnson City, Tennessee.

He was jumping at a time when athletes mostly used bamboo poles and the pit and runway conditions were not good. At best, he landed in a foot or two of sawdust. And the dirt runways were often not in good condition. He thinks that his high school facilities may have been better than those at Roanoke. At Roanoke, the jumpers had to dig up the sawdust themselves.

While he was in high school, he first practiced vaulting on a hanging rope. As he looks back today, he thinks that although he was determined to be a good pole vaulter, he really never was strong enough. And he didn't have good speed. At Roanoke, Bill was about 5'9" tall and weighed only 155.

When he joined the team at Roanoke, no one was using a metal pole. At least, he never saw one. His first pole was one made from bamboo. It was kept from day to day in the old Quonset hut near the track. But in that facility, the pole picked up moisture. Bill still remembers one incident when the Maroons were competing against V. M. I. His pole, being damp, had begun to bend too much. But it sprung back quickly. A V. M. I. vaulter saw Bill jumping and asked him if he could try using the pole. So Bill agreed that he could. It turned out, however, that the V. M. I. athlete was much heavier than Bill and although the pole bent under his weight, it failed to spring back.

A short time later, Bill began to have nervous thoughts about the pole. Finally, during a practice session, he thought to himself, "I think I will give it all I have." He sprinted down the runway, planted the pole, and as he rose upward toward the bar, the pole snapped into two sections. The break threw him into the pit. He landed awkwardly and sprained his ankle. He never came close to being impaled on the pole, although that was a story later told by some teammates, but some vaulters in his day did have bamboo poles break and they were hurt by the splinters that resulted. The sprained ankle kept him out of competition for a while. At the beginning of the next season, Homer Bast told him that he would have a new pole made of metal. The pole, as Bill remembers, was actually just a big aluminum pipe and he thought it was totally worthless. He even had problems jumping 10' with the pole.

Bill remembers that Coach Bast never bought any shoes for him. He was forced to use a pair of his own running shoes, which didn't have spikes on the heel as did regular field event shoes. In his last meet in 1949, and on his last jump, those shoes were a problem. As he landed, his spikes ripped his leg open. He still thinks that he should have competed in flat-soled shoes instead of the spiked shoes.

He graduated from Roanoke in 1949 with a degree in philosophy. His first job was as a teacher in Halifax, Virginia, but that job lasted just a year. In the middle of that year, he married Ann Braucher. "Then," he asked himself, "what in the world am I doing getting married. I can't afford a wife." When Ann and Bill met, he didn't know who she was. It turned out that her father was a famous Pennsylvania high school basketball coach.

The two had three children. The oldest was Dan, the next oldest was Ben, and the youngest was Janet. All three still are living today.

At the end of his first year of teaching in Halifax, the Principal asked Bill if he were coming back the next fall. He told his boss that he wouldn't mind coming back, but didn't want to coach again. Besides his math teaching, the school used him as a coach of basketball and baseball. But the Principal told him that Bill couldn't just teach. He needed him as a coach and besides, if he did nothing more than teach, they would have to decrease his salary.

Bill, therefore, decided not to go back to the school. Instead, he went to a college that summer, while his wife worked, to get a teaching certificate. Unfortunately, he found that his G. I. bill wouldn't pay for the courses he needed. Instead of completing the coursework, Bill took a job as a stock clerk at a local hospital in Allentown. Soon he took another position at Bethlehem Steel; however, he never told his employer that he had a college degree. He was hoping to move into a position in production where he could earn higher wages. He was with Bethlehem Steel for one year before he applied for a job with Weston Electrical. To get that job, he had to pass a test. Unfortunately, he failed the test. The company told him that he could take the test again if he wished, so he spent the summer studying for the test and when he took it again, he passed.

He worked for Weston Electrical for the next three years as an Electronic Maintenance Worker. Then he heard that a friend was trying to pass a test so he could work for I. B. M. Bill decided that he would also take the test. He passed it and went to work for I. B. M.

His company sent him to school, but Bill found that the courses were very difficult. As a result, he changed jobs again, moving to DuPont to become a Lab Technician. This time, in his seventh job in seven years, he stayed with the company for the next 23 years. He says that he really enjoyed the DuPont job, but decided to retire from that position in 1982 at age 57–thanks to the generosity of his wife. The two were bringing in good salaries, so he suggested to her that she might want to retire. Absolutely not, she replied. She enjoyed working. Then she told Bill that he should retire instead, and he agreed with one condition. Ann would need to work another five years at least in order to make up for lost retirement income. She agreed.

Today, Ann and Bill are still married. They each enjoy their retirement years. Bill, now 82, enjoys playing the piano, although he says that he gets satisfaction from the piano well out of proportion to how well he plays. Until he turned 80, he occasionally played some pick-up basketball in the community to get some exercise; however, at his current age, he has dropped this type of activity. At his current age, he feels fortunate that thus far he has had no major illnesses.

Wilson, Dr. Wayne

Dr. Wayne Wilson and his family. L to R: Wayne, Andrea (daughter), Jo (wife), Sara (grand daughter), Jamie (daughter in law), Wilson (grandson), Brad (son), Lisa (a Roanoke College graduate), and Coy (Lisa's husband).

Wayne was born in Washington, D. C. His father died when he was about a year old and the family sent Wayne to Iowa to live with his aunt and uncle on a farm for some five or six years. During this time, his mother was still living, but would have had great difficulties supporting Wayne.

He lived with the aunt and uncle until his mother re-married. Then Wayne moved back to Alexandria, Virginia, at about six or seven years old.

Living on a farm had a big influence on Wayne. Even after moving to Virginia, he went back to Iowa in the summers to help on the farm.

After his mother re-married, she and her new husband had one child together. Billy Ramey was about eight years younger than Wayne and today is a Psychiatrist in Rochester, New York.

Wayne attended Wakefield High School, which opened in 1956. His tenth grade class was really the senior class that year and became the first class to graduate from Wakefield. His coach was Buddy Stein, an inspirational person very much like Roanoke's Homer Bast. He had attended George Washington College in Washington, D. C., and was a sprinter on their track team. Stein was very enthusiastic about his coaching and was a true role model for the students.

Wayne, himself, did not do particularly well in distance running in high school, although the school did win the state championship his senior year. For many years afterwards, that was the only state championship that the school had won.

At times during high school, Wayne thought about becoming a farmer and not going to college. His mother was horrified. Then one day, he noticed the lifestyle of his pediatrician, who practiced out of his home and seemed to be in control of his own life. Wayne saw that he seemed to help a lot of people. Wayne was impressed and began to look at future careers that might be interesting and provide a fairly stable lifestyle. Maybe, he thought, a career in medicine would be the appropriate choice. But he didn't know if he could go into a field which required extensive, costly course work.

He explored the possibility of attending a college in Iowa, so he could be closer to his extended family. He also looked at some of the bigger colleges and universities in the East. He had been raised as a Lutheran, however, and knew that Roanoke College was affiliated with the Lutheran Church. Luther Mauney's father was high up in the Lutheran monarch, so Wayne and his high school friend, Scott McKinney (a sprinter), came down together to look over the Roanoke campus. One of the first people at Roanoke who impressed Wayne and Scott was Homer Bast. They visited him in his office and thought he was pretty laid back. Dick Goodlake was in the office when they arrived, and Dick and Homer were joking with each other. Dick was telling Homer that he had just aced his test. A couple of other track guys were also hanging around. For some reason, Homer just reminded Wayne of his high school coach. Homer was relaxed, but very interested in what you were doing. And he was interested in students not only because they were runners, but also he wanted to know about their character.

Wayne began his college career at Roanoke in the fall of 1956. It would be Homer's last year as the head track coach, although Wayne would be coached by him in cross country until he graduated.

Wayne participated in many campus activities. For example, he was on the Honor Council, President of the Junior Class, and served one year as the Kappa Alpha fraternity's #1. In fact, in the K. A. position, he followed on the heels of Frank Vest. He even won a swimming letter one year. During his freshman year, he lived in Hildreth Hall with a lot of the other track guys. Then, the K. A.s bought the brick house up on High Street near the Pi Kappa Phi house. For his final two years, he lived in the fraternity house.

During his first fall of running cross country, it looked as if he would have a bright future in distance running. The team started its season at Mount St. Mary's College. Wayne roomed with Homer Bast that night and went on to finish third in the meet. George Jocher finished second, but wasn't eligible because he had just transferred from Hofstra. Howard Meincke, as usual, won the race. Then, in the meet with Washington and Lee, Wayne hurt his foot and was forced to drop out of the race. Eventually, the foot healed, but the injury took him out of competition for just about the remainder of the cross country season.

In his sophomore year, the team went to the Mason-Dixon Championships at Gallaudet. Coach Bast took the entire team over to Wayne's house for dinner. Even Wayne's high school coach, Buddy Stein was there. In the meet the next day, Wayne finished 11th and he still remembers it as being one of his best races. Today, he continues to show off his medals on one of the walls of his office. Another medal came in the Little Eight meet his sophomore year, when he finished fourth.

As he thinks back on the four years he competed in cross country and track, he says that he is proudest of the year after Meincke, Jocher, and the other great distance runners had gone. Wayne and his teammates put together a hodge-podge team that they called "The Seven Psychos" and went on to surprise everyone by winning the Mason-Dixon Championship.

"And I remember Dick Emberger," says Wayne. "One time he was trying to press a weight over his head and fell backward with the bar on top of him. He lay there with the bar across his neck until we came down and took it off him. Emberger was a kid from New York who came down to Roanoke as a high jumper. He had a pretty mediocre first year. Then we just watched him grow. He got into swimming and became a very talented diver. He weight trained a bit. And by his last year, 1959-60, he was so good in track that he would score almost more points than the other team." Emberger and Larry Johnson lived downstairs in the gym for several years. Larry worked for Buddy Hackman as Assistant Director of the Elks Boys' Camp, where Buddy was Director during the summer months.

"I also remember Howard Meincke very well," Wayne says. "He was an Elvis Presley fan. Elvis was his idol. He would get very serious before a race. I remember that he always wanted to beat a guy named DeTombe from William and Mary. DeTombe had these long legs. DeTombe beat Howard, but Meincke gave it all he had. When they barely beat Roanoke in a 1957 cross country race, Howard was in the shower up in Hildreth after the race. He just sat there for a long, long time, with just the hot water running over him. He could barely breathe. I think that both he and DeTombe that day recorded times that were under the old course record."

At Roanoke, Wayne majored in Biology. After graduation, he enrolled at the Medical College of Virginia in Richmond. He had looked at the University of Virginia, Duke University, and other medical programs. But when he visited M. C. V., he found that students got more practical experience there. He was thinking at that point about going into general practice, perhaps in an area such as Wytheville, Virginia. Although Virginia and Duke both offered Wayne admittance to their programs, he accepted the first offer he received, from M. C. V.

He began his four-year program in Richmond in the fall. When he finished, he had his doctorate. He then interned at Mercy Hospital in Springfield, Ohio. At Mercy, he became interested in surgery. General practice was changing a bit at that point and he decided to pursue a surgeon's career. He ended up going to Dr. Zollinger at Ohio State University in Columbus, Ohio, for his surgeon's training. Dr. R. M. Zollinger had a syndrome named after him. The Zollinger-Ellison syndrome is a condition in which one or more tumors form in the pancreas or in the upper part of the small intestine. This condition causes excessive production of acid by the patient's stomach, leading to peptic ulcers.

"Dr. Zollinger could scare the crap out of you," Wayne says. "There were legends about him all through the surgical world."

Wayne stayed for four years at Ohio State, from 1965 through 1969, to complete his General Surgery Program.

While in medical school, in 1961, Wayne and Mabel Jo Umberger were married. Mabel Jo also went to Roanoke College and the two dated some while they were undergraduate students. They have three children. The oldest is Lisa Lynn, born in 1962. The second oldest is Andrea Dawn, who was born in 1965. The youngest is Bradley Duane, who came along in 1969. Today, there are two grandchildren, ages 14 and 12, whose mother is Lisa. All are living near Mabel Jo and Wayne. Wayne and his wife own five acres of land, and Lisa also lives on a nearby five acres. Their son lives just up the street.

In 1969, during the Vietnam War, Wayne had signed up for something called the Berry Plan. It allowed him to finish his specialty training before going into the military. At that time, it was almost a sure thing that you were going to be drafted and sent overseas. So Wayne went to a general hospital in Japan after his training as a surgeon. He and others would treat the Vietnam casualties and Wayne was put in charge of the far eastern burn unit. They would bring the majority of the burn patients from the war to his treatment center. Wayne helped stabilize the injured and most of them would then go back to San Antonio, Texas, where there was a burn unit at Fort Sam Houston.

As Wayne was in Japan, he began to think about an academic career. His boss in Japan ended up going to Walter Reed. Soon, after Wayne had been in Japan for some two years, he called for Wayne to join him. Wayne became the Assistant Chief of Surgery at Walter Reed for the next five years.

After getting out of the service in 1977, Wayne took a position with the Veterans Administration Hospital in Salem. The hospital has an affiliation with the University of Virginia, which means that they have their residents and their medical students rotating down through the hospital's surgical rotation. During the past 30 years or so, Wayne has been working with the residents and students from Charlottesville. Serving the veterans' population has been interesting, he says. "They are just a great bunch of guys."

Wayne still works today at the V. A. Hospital in Salem. He was the Chief of Surgery there until some two years ago, when he stepped down. Now he is a staff surgeon and is thinking of retiring. He is also a Professor of Surgery in Charlottesville and he goes up there about twice a year. During those trips, he examines the medical students to make sure they are making good progress. In Salem, there are five of the University of Virginia residents at any one time. And they host six medical students at a time. Those students rotate through for six-week periods. During that time, Wayne gives them some eight or ten lectures.

Wayne's wife, Mabel Jo, has a special interest in dyslexia. Two of their children were dyslectic. She received extensive training in that field and today is recognized as an expert in dyslexia and has worked with many adults.

When Wayne does retire, he'll likely remain in the Roanoke area. "Southwest Virginia is God's country," he says. Most of his family is rooted in the area. His daughter is a veterinarian and has her own practice. His son works at Roanoke Memorial Hospital in the cardiology lab. One of his daughters-in-law just graduated from nurse practitioner school. Right now, he says, he is trying to think of something that will keep him active and stimulated once he does retire.

As far as hobbies go, he has his tractors and enjoys gardening and yard work. He looks forward to having more time for those activities. He also is interested in history and looks forward to doing some research in that field. He may even do some work on the history of medicine.

Wise, Rev. Peter

Pete, one of the best quarter milers and 880 runners in Roanoke's history, was born in August of 1936 in Atlantic City, New Jersey. He lived with his father, Leo, and his mother, Esther, along with a younger brother, Nicholas. Nicholas today is a retired seaman, working for Exxon Mobile. He has one child.

Pete attended Pleasantville High School in Pleasantville, New Jersey, which is seven miles across the bay from Atlantic City. The school had no track facilities; however, Pete did participate in outdoor track his senior year. He ran six 880 races, and broke six records. His academic average wasn't high, not more than a low C, but Coach Bast was able to get him admitted to Roanoke.

Coach Bast knew about the records he had been setting and sent Pete a letter. He was able to get Pete a small grant-in-aid and Pete arrived on campus in the fall of 1955, never having seen the school. Although Pete was not a distance runner, Coach Bast encouraged him to run cross country to build up his stamina.

Peter Wise poses at his house in Oregon.

Fortunately, Pete's roommate was Howard Meincke, one of the school's all time greats in distance running. They drove down to Roanoke together in an old Plymouth to begin their college careers. The two were good for each other, keeping in contact during summer breaks, and encouraging one another to run better. Recently, Pete talked about Howard: "Howard Meincke was truly incredible. I lived with him in the same dorm room for three years. We were in Hildreth Hall up until my senior year. Howard would play Elvis Presley music while we ran around in our workouts. Meincke was an orphan, raised by a foster family in New Jersey. He had a hard time with his studies in his first three years. He overcompensated and became a member of Blue Key National Honor Society. Howard and I never missed a workout, come rain, snow, hail, or sleet. In the winter time, he suggested that the two of us buy long johns and dye them some bizarre colors. We did that and worked out in the coldest of weather. We would go around the track even if there were eight inches of snow on the ground, brushing the snow aside with our feet. He was totally dedicated to his sport. I owe a lot of my own running skills and prowess to Howard, along with Homer Bast. While Howard was thoroughly focused before a meet, I was scared to death."

Pete remembers well many of the other athletes he competed with in the 1950s. "Dick Goodlake was always cheerful," he says, "and I think that cross country was his best sport. He was always nice to me. Recently, he has called me a couple of times, and that made me feel really good. He was not only a wonderful runner, but a wonderful human being. Probably Meincke, Goodlake, and I were the most dedicated runners at the College."

During his freshman year in outdoor track, Pete ran :52.4 and :52.5 quarters, along with a 2:00.6 in the 880. He also ran on the school record mile relay team in the Mason-Dixon meet that year. The foursome of Al Ide, Pete, John Summers, and Dick Lewis recorded an excellent time of 3:22.6.

As a sophomore, in 1957, Pete ran :52.4 in the quarter mile and times of 2:01.3 and 2:02.0 in the half mile. He also helped the team of Dick Engel, Wise, Howard Light, and Dick Lewis run a 3:26.4 mile relay.

During Pete's junior year at Roanoke, he ran injured. One day early in the 1958 season, Coach Bast called him into his office and told him that he had been nominated for the All-State team. At that point, Pete had the fastest 440 time in the state. The next day, running in the cold and rain, he pulled his hamstring muscle. With that injury, he didn't make the progress he thought he should. On the other hand, he did run a :50.5 quarter that season, along with a 2:02.9 and a 2:03.0 half mile. He also ran on the mile relay team of Wise, Howard Light, Tom Sitton, and George Bopp which recorded a time of 3:24.5.

Pete's senior year was a memorable one. Not only did he run several times of just barely more than 50 seconds, but against Bridgewater at Salem he smashed the school and Alumni Field record with an outstanding time of :49.7. That was the same year that he joined with Brendan Cavanagh, Tom Sitton, and Phil Davis to run a 3:23.4 mile relay.

After graduating from Roanoke College, Pete became the Athletic Director on the S. S. New Amsterdam, a cruise line out of Hoboken, New Jersey. That job lasted six months before he returned home and found a letter of induction from the U. S. Army.

So he left for Fort Benning, Georgia, in the dead of winter. After his stay at Fort Benning, he was sent to Fort Collins, South Carolina, as a radio operator. He stayed in the Army for the required time (which was extended 79 days because the Berlin Wall was built).

After getting out of the Army, Pete spent a year with the General Motors Corporation. He then entered a theological seminary in Chester, Pennsylvania. It was the same seminary that graduated Martin Luther King, Jr. There, Pete received a Master of Divinity degree.

After getting that degree, he went to work for Lippincott Publishing Company. He did some traveling to colleges, involving indirect sales. And he did some editing, which he enjoyed. He stayed with Lippincott for three years.

In 1966, Pete happened to pick up a couple of hitchhikers. They took him off the beaten path "up to the woods" in Oregon where Pete now lives. He has been there for some 40 years. During this time, he has earned a couple of other Master's Degrees and has done more than 50 hours of advanced study at the University of Oregon in an attempt to get a doctorate.

At one point, Pete's father was not doing well. So Pete got him an apartment nearby in Medford, Oregon, and looked after him until his death.

In all, Pete now has a Bachelor's Degree from Roanoke, a Master of Arts degree from Southern Oregon University, a Master of Science degree from Southern Oregon University, a Bachelor of Divinity Degree, and a Master of Divinity from Colgate

Rochester. "These days," he says, "I just hang out in the woods."

During the 40 years that he has lived in the wilds of Oregon, he has paid his bills by relying on a long list of odd jobs. Although he doesn't preach, he does function as a minister in the sense that he serves those around him at no cost. Many of them simply need counseling. Also, and at no cost, he performs an occasional wedding.

He is also a landlord. He is in the process of restoring, cleaning up, and selling properties near him. One of the things he misses is living near a running track, where he could get in good shape again. With a tinge of nostalgia, he says, "I would love to get in such good shape that I could go out there and run those 30-second 220s again. And I'd like to run in age-group meets, too."

Most mornings, he rises and takes care of his birds–his pigeons, chickens, and ducks–feeding and caring for them. He also takes care of various chores. The closest town to his log home, which he built himself, is Medford, about 25 miles away. The closest town "with a reputation" is Ashland, the home of Southern Oregon University. Ashland is about an hour away.

Much of his efforts are centered on his own community–160 acres of land which he owns. Some people lease property long-term from him. Some rent for a short period of time. He deals with a diverse group of people, most of whom he enjoys living around. But he has had to work hard to get rid of those with problems such as drug addiction and theft. Two of his seven houses have burned down, leaving him with five that he can rent.

During all of the years after Roanoke College, Pete never married; however, he does have a beautiful daughter named Melissa. She works for Health and Human Services, graduating Summa Cum Laude from Southern Oregon University. Her husband teaches high school math.

Pete has no plans to move from his current location. His daughter has been after him to "simplify and consolidate," however. If he did move, he says, it would probably be to the beautiful Olympic Peninsula.

Athletes Not Located

Clegg, Harry
Dempsey, Jack
Hylton, John
McLaren, John
Niles, Win
Palm, Bob
Rittman, Chris
Schreiner, Bill

Sitton, Tom
Stauffer, Dick

Deceased Athletes

Anderson, Willis
Crockett, L. Z. "Red"
Doran, Jim
Foltz, Dave
Hal Dunbar
Irvin, Bennie
Lawson, Peter
Lund, Bill
McCarty, Paul
Meincke, Howard
Moore, Don
Ruscick, Jim
Walsh, Robert

Notes

When I finished writing this book, the main text totaled over 600 pages. In addition, the Appendix was almost 400 pages in length.

My publisher would not allow me to submit a manuscript that contained more than 800 pages; therefore, I have placed the Appendix on a web page where it can be downloaded by the reader. In this section of the book, you will find at least the following information, most of which is not presented in the main text itself:

Cross Country Meet Results from 1948 Through 1960
Summary of Wins and Losses: Cross Country–1947 Through 1960
Indoor Track Meet Results from 1948 Through 1960
Summary of Wins and Losses: Indoor Track–1948 Through 1957
Outdoor Track Meet Results from 1947 Through 1960
Summary of Wins and Losses: Outdoor Track–1947 Through 1960
Indoor Track Records: 1948-1960
Outdoor Track Records: 1947-1960
Alumni Field Records: 1947-1960
Top Twenty-Five Ranked Performances in Indoor Track: 1948-1960
Top Twenty-Five Ranked Performances in Outdoor Track: 1947-1960
Winning Little Six/Seven/Eight Conference Outdoor Track and Field Marks: 1948-1957
Winning Mason-Dixon Conference Outdoor Track and Field Marks: 1948-1957
Conference Cross Country Champions Coached By Homer Bast: 1947-1960
Conference Outdoor Track Champions Coached By Homer Bast: 1947-1960

You may download all of the Appendices at once, or specify which parts of the information you want to retrieve. The download is free to you and any others who wish to see how the Bast Boys did during the heyday of cross country and track athletics at Roanoke College.

For your own downloads, please go to:

http://www.arringtonbooks.com

Larry W. Arrington, Ed.D., Author

Bibliography

Books

Miller, Mark F. *Dear Old Roanoke: A Sesquicentennial Portrait, 2842-1992.* Macon, Georgia: Mercer University Press, 1992.

Keller, George. *Prologue to Prominence*: *A Half Century at Roanoke College*. Minneapolis, Minnesota: Lutheran University Press, 2005.

Yearbooks

The Rawenoch, Roanoke College Yearbook, 1947-1961.

Periodicals

The *Collegian*, March, 1946–May, 1958.

Photographs

Most of the photographs are the property of Roanoke College. Any individual photographs of athletes or athletes and families were sent to the author with explicit intent that those images would be used in the book. Some photographs were supplied by C. Homer Bast from his own collection and from selected athletes, with their permission to publish them.

Newspapers

The Brackety-Ack, Roanoke College Student Newspaper, 1946-47 through 1960-61.

The Norfolk Ledger-Star, 1948-1958.

The Roanoke Times and World News, 1946-1960.

The Washington Star, 1948-1958.

Special Documents

Personal notes and papers supplied by C. Homer Bast.

Notes and papers from the Roanoke College Archives.

Personal Interviews

Aldred, Dr. Frank–February 14, 2007.
Bast, Dr. Homer–February 12, 2007, February 13, 2007, June 8, 2007, July 27, 2007, July 28, 2007, July 30, 2007, July 31, 2007, August 1, 2007, August 3, 2007, August 6, 2007, October 5, 2007, October 10, 2007, October 12, 2007, October 16, 2007, November 6, 2007, November 8, 2007, November 9, 2007, and Unknown Date, 2007.
Carr, Boyd–February 8, 2007.
Cerelli, Bill–November 26, 2007.
DeCosta, Ray–February 4, 2008.
Driscoll, Dr. Bill–February 3, 2008.
Davenport, Bruce–February 9, 2007.
Dodd, Dr. Richard–October 15, 2007.
Emberger, Richard–November 18, 2007.
Engel, Richard–October 9, 2007.
Fagg, Bob–October 18, 2007.
Fariss, Dr. Bruce–October 29, 2007.
Fraley, Richard–March 25, 2008.
Gearhart, George–January 29, 2007 and February 12, 2007.
Goodlake, Richard–November 20, 2007.

Ide, Allen–March 6, 2008.
Jackson, Jay–October 9, 2007.
Jenkins, Dr. Bob–December 10, 2007.
Jocher, George–April 2, 2007.
Johnston, Earl–April 27, 2007.
Johnston, Bruce–October 22, 2007.
Lewis, Richard–November 17, 2007.
Light, Howard–February 6, 2007.
Light, Warren–October 12, 2007.
Moore, David–January 2, 2008.
Nichols, Jim–October 9, 2007.
Nilson, Bob–March 5, 2008.
Noel, Lessely–April 23, 2007.
O'Mahony, Jim–January 2, 2008.
Rosebro, Rud–October 29, 2007.
Rader, Richard–November 27, 2007.
Rhyne, White–April 25, 2007.
Seed, Richard–April 24, 2007.
Shaw, Cliff–November 5, 2007.
Shaw, Phil–October 11, 2007.
Smith, Alvin–January 26, 2007 and June 8, 2007.
Stryker, Derek–February 5, 2008.
Summers, John–February 7, 2007.
Tramposch, Walter–October 26, 2007.
Upton, Bob–November 28, 2007.
Vest, Frank–November 5, 2007.
Wallwork, Jim–December 4, 2007.
Williams, Bill–October 25, 2007.
Wilson, Dr. Wayne–November 28, 2007.
Wise, Rev. Pete–October 15, 2007.

Printed in the United States
130656LV00007B/7/P

9 781432 722050